Cinema in Service of the State

Film Europa: German Cinema in an International Context
Series Editors: **Hans-Michael Bock** (CineGraph Hamburg); **Tim Bergfelder** (University of Southampton); **Sabine Hake** (University of Texas, Austin)

German cinema is normally seen as a distinct form, but this series emphasizes connections, influences, and exchanges of German cinema across national borders, as well as its links with other media and art forms. Individual titles present traditional historical research (archival work, industry studies) as well as new critical approaches in film and media studies (theories of the transnational), with a special emphasis on the continuities associated with popular traditions and local perspectives.

The Concise Cinegraph: An Encyclopedia of German Cinema
General Editor: Hans-Michael Bock
Associate Editor: Tim Bergfelder

International Adventures: German Popular Cinema and European Co-Productions in the 1960s
Tim Bergfelder

Between Two Worlds: The Jewish Presence in German and Austrian Film, 1910–1933
S.S. Prawer

Framing the Fifties: Cinema in a Divided Germany
Edited by John Davidson and Sabine Hake

A Foreign Affair: Billy Wilder's American Films
Gerd Gemünden

Destination London: German-speaking Emigrés and British Cinema, 1925–1950
Edited by Tim Bergfelder and Christian Cargnelli

Michael Haneke's Cinema: The Ethic of the Image
Catherine Wheatley

Willing Seduction: *The Blue Angel*, Marlene Dietrich, and Mass Culture
Barbara Kosta

Dismantling the Dream Factory: Gender, German Cinema, and the Postwar Quest for a New Film Language
Hester Baer

Belá Balázs: Early Film Theory. *Visible Man* and *The Spirit of Film*
Bela Balazs, edited by Erica Carter, translated by Rodney Livingstone

Screening the East: Heimat, Memory and Nostalgia in German Film since 1989
Nick Hodgin

Peter Lorre: Face Maker. Constructing Stardom and Performance in Hollywood and Europe
Sarah Thomas

Turkish German Cinema in the New Millennium: Sites, Sounds, and Screens
Edited by Sabine Hake and Barbara Mennel

Postwall German Cinema: History, Film History and Cinephilia
Mattias Frey

Homemade Men in Postwar Austrian Cinema: Nationhood, Genre and Masculinity
Maria Fritsche

The Emergence of Film Culture: Knowledge Production, Institution Building and the Fate of the Avant-Garde in Europe, 1919–1945
Edited by Malte Hagener

Imperial Projections: Screening the German Colonies
Wolfgang Fuhrmann

Cinema in Service of the State: Perspectives on Film Culture in the GDR and Czechoslovakia, 1945–1960
Edited by Lars Karl and Pavel Skopal

German Television: Historical and Theoretical Perspectives
Edited by Larson Powell and Robert R. Shandley

CINEMA IN SERVICE OF THE STATE

Perspectives on Film Culture in the GDR and Czechoslovakia, 1945–1960

Edited by Lars Karl and Pavel Skopal

berghahn
NEW YORK • OXFORD
www.berghahnbooks.com

First published in 2015 by
Berghahn Books
www.BerghahnBooks.com

© 2015, 2017 Lars Karl and Pavel Skopal
First paperback edition published in 2017

All rights reserved. Except for the quotation of short passages for the purposes of criticism and review, no part of this book may be reproduced in any form or by any means, electronic or mechanical, including photocopying, recording, or any information storage and retrieval system now known or to be invented, without written permission of the publisher.

Library of Congress Cataloging-in-Publication Data

Cinema in service of the state : perspectives on film culture in the GDR and Czechoslovakia, 1945–1960 / edited by Lars Karl and Pavel Skopal.
    p. cm. -- (Film Europa: German cinema in an international context)
    Includes bibliographical references and index.
    Includes filmography.
    ISBN 978-1-78238-996-5 (hardback: alk. paper) — ISBN 978-1-78533-738-3 (paperback) — ISBN 978-1-78238-997-2 (ebook)
    1. Motion pictures--Political aspects--Germany (East) 2. Motion picture industry--Germany (East)--History--20th century. 3. Motion pictures--Political aspects--Czechoslovakia. 4. Motion picture industry--Czechoslovakia--History--20th century. I. Karl, Lars, 1973- editor. II. Skopal, Pavel, editor.
    PN1993.5.G33C57 2015
    791.430943--dc23

2015014048

British Library Cataloguing in Publication Data
A catalogue record for this book is available
from the British Library.

ISBN: 978-1-78238-996-5 (hardback)
ISBN: 978-1-78533-738-3 (paperback)
ISBN: 978-1-78238-997-2 (ebook)

Contents

Acknowledgements vii

List of Figures and Tables viii

List of Abbreviaions ix

Introduction 1

PART I. Cultural Policy and Cinema

Chapter 1. From Soviet Zone to *Volksdemokratie*: The Politics of Film Culture in the GDR, 1945–1960   15
David Bathrick

Chapter 2. Czechoslovak Culture and Cinema, 1945–1960   39
Jiří Knapík

PART II. Production and Co-production

Chapter 3. 'Veterans' and 'Dilettantes': Film Production Culture vis-à-vis Top-Down Political Changes, 1945–1962   71
Petr Szczepanik

Chapter 4. Barrandov's Co-productions: The Clumsy Way to Ideological Control, International Competitiveness and Technological Improvement   89
Pavel Skopal

Chapter 5. Co-productions (Un)Wanted: 1950s East/West German Film Collaborations and the Impact of Sovietization on DEFA's Prestige Agenda   107
Mariana Ivanova

Chapter 6. No TV without Film: Production Relations between the DEFA Studios and Deutscher Fernsehfunk   125
Thomas Beutelschmidt

PART III. Nonfictional Cinema

Chapter 7. Military Film Studios before 1970: Between Cinematic Avant-Garde and Films on Command   145
Václav Šmidrkal

Chapter 8. Socialism for Sale: Czechoslovakia's Krátký film, Custom-Made Film Production, and the Promotion of Consumer Culture in the 1950s   166
Lucie Česálková

PART IV. Children's Cinema

Chapter 9. Between Magic and Education: The First Fairy Tale Films in the GDR   189
Christin Niemeyer

Chapter 10. Children's Films: Between Education, Art and Industry   205
Lukáš Skupa

PART V. Film Festivals

Chapter 11. Decreed Open-Mindedness: The Leipzig Documentary and Short Film Festival in the 1960s as an Example of the Self-Representation of the East German State   229
Andreas Kötzing

Chapter 12. National, Socialist, Global: The Changing Roles of the Karlovy Vary Film Festival, 1946–1956   245
Jindřiška Bláhová

PART VI. Distribution and Reception

Chapter 13. Cinema Cultures of Integration: Film Distribution and Exhibition in the GDR and Czechoslovakia from the Perspective of Two Local Cases, 1945–1960   275
Kyrill Kunakhovich and Pavel Skopal

Chapter 14. A Decade between Resistance and Adaptation: The Leipzig University Film Club (1956–1966)   315
Fernando Ramos Arenas

Chapter 15. Screening the Occupier as Liberator: Soviet War Films in the SBZ and the GDR, 1945–1965   341
Lars Karl

Filmography   381

Index   391

Acknowledgements

It is important to acknowledge the contributions that friends and colleagues have made to this project. Kevin B. Johnson provided excellent proofreading of various drafts of the entire manuscript, translated two chapters (one from German and one from Czech), and provided valuable comments. Individual chapters benefited from observations by Alice Lovejoy and Jenny Alwart. Editorial suggestions by Stephan Troebst came at an important juncture. The whole project is obliged to the Humboldt Foundation, which provided research funding for Pavel Skopal, as well as to the Leipzig Centre for the History and Culture of East Central Europe (GWZO) which supported Lars Karl during his work within the project 'Post-Panslavism', and to the Faculty of Arts, Masaryk University, which financially supported the publishing of this volume. Additional came from funding has also been provided by the German Research Foundation (DFG). Five of the book's chapters are updated versions of essays originally published in the book *Naplánovaná kinematografie. Český filmový průmysl 1945 až 1960*, edited by Pavel Skopal (Prague: Academia, 2012).

Figures

Illustrations

Figure 7.1	Yearly production volumes of the AFS (footage in metres, 35 mm film)	148
Figure 7.2	Yearly production volumes of the ČAF (footage in metres, 35 mm film)	148
Figure 7.3	Shooting for the training film *Seskok padákem* (Parachute Jump)	149
Figure 12.1	Global peace as the main star	260
Figure 13.1	The number of Soviet movies distributed in the GDR and the Czech Lands	288
Figure 13.2	The number of West European and American movies distributed in the GDR and the Czech Lands	289
Figure 13.3	The number of screenings in Czech cinemas	296

Tables

Table 10.1	Czech animated production in the period 1945-1955	213
Table 10.2	The number of Czech children's feature films in the period 1945-1955	215

List of Abbreviations

AFS - Army Film Studio (Armeefilmstudio)

KVP - Barracked People's Police (Kasernierte Volkspolizei)

ÚD - Central Dramaturgy (Ústřední dramaturgie)

HV Film - Central Film Administration (Hauptverwaltung Film)

KSČ - Communist Party of Czechoslovakia
 (Komunistická strana Československa)

KPSS - Communist Party of the Soviet Union
 (Kommunisticheskaya Partiya Sovetskogo Soyuza)

ČAF - Czechoslovak Army Film (Československý armádní film)

ČSFÚ - Czechoslovak Film Institute
 (Československý filmový ústav)

ČSF - Czechoslovak State Film (Československý státní film)

DEFA - Deutsche Film-Aktien Gesellschaft

DFF - Deutscher Fernsehfunk

FRG - Federal Republic of Germany

FIUS - Film Artistic Board (Filmový umělecký sbor)

RFK - Film Chamber of the Reich (Reichsfilmkammer)

FR - Film Council (Filmová rada)

FAMU - Film faculty of the Academy of Performing Arts
 (Filmová fakulta Akademie múzických umění)

FDJ - Free German Youth (Freie Deutsche Jugend)

KPD - German Communist Party
 (Kommunistische Partei Deutschlands)

GDR - German Democratic Republic

FIAPF - International Federation of Film Producers Associations
 (Fédération Internationale des Associations de Producteurs de Films)

MFF KV - Karlovy Vary International Film Festival
 (Mezinárodní filmový festival Karlovy Vary)

ÚV KSČ - KSČ Central Committee of the Communist Party of Czechoslovakia

LUF - Leipzig University Film Club (Leipziger Universitätsfilmklub)

MPAA - Motion Picture Association of America

NVA - National People's Army (Nationale Volksarmee)

VEB - people-owned enterprise (Volkseigener Betrieb, VEBpeople-owned enterprise)

KF - Short Film (Krátký film)

SED - Socialist Unity Party of Germany (Sozialistische Einheitspartei Deutschlands)

GDSF - Society for German-Soviet Friendship (Gesellschaft für Deutsch-Sowjetische Freundschaft)

SEF - Sovexportfilm

SMAD - Soviet Military Administration in Germany (Sowjetische Militäradministration in Deutschland)

SBZ - Soviet Zone of Occupation Zone (Sowjetische Besatzungszone)

TOBIS - Ton-Bild-Syndikat AG

UFA - Universum Film AG

Introduction

Pavel Skopal and Lars Karl

Historical studies of the Soviet influence in Eastern Europe after World War II have undergone a radical transformation as a consequence of the fall of communism. This is due in part to the ability of historians from the region itself to ask fresh questions and offer new judgements on their own past, free from the strictures of Marxist-Leninist historical orthodoxy, party control, and the strict injunctions of state-sponsored censorship. Even more important is the loosening of state control over archival collections that document the Soviet role in the establishment of communist states during the period 1945–1965. This volume strives to benefit from both of these stimulants for original historical research.

This volume focuses on the first two decades of the postwar period. While individual essays regularly and inevitably begin their stories in the 1940s and follow them into the 1960s, the primary focus is on the 1950s, a period of rapid and rather abrupt changes in international relations, cultural policy, the economy and indeed, the film industry within the Soviet Bloc in general and the German Democratic Republic (GDR) and Czechoslovakia in particular. In the GDR, the decade was strongly influenced by the relationship with its Western alter ego, the Federal Republic of Germany (FRG). As the editor of a recent volume addressing the cinema culture of the GDR's Western counterpart phrased it, 'the long 1950s' marks the period 'between the founding of the two German states in 1949 and the building of the Berlin Wall in 1961'.[1] At the same time, it was a decade of ideological alignment between the

GDR and Czechoslovakia, squeezed between decades of tension, animosity and war atrocities at one end,[2] and the subsequent ideological estrangement of the 1960s at the other. Only two of the essays in this volume are explicitly comparative, whereas others address transnational phenomena like film festivals or international co-productions. Most of the essays are grouped into parallel pairs or thematic clusters offering perspectives on the two film cultures and industries at the centre of this volume. The first two essays, by David Bathrick and Jiří Knapík, aim to provide an overview of the rich historical context and orient the reader within the sphere of cultural policy, addressed by all the individual essays. In effect, and despite the fact that most of the essays are not comparative in their methods, the thoroughly researched topics collected here give readers a clear 'stereoscopic' overview and deep understanding of phenomena that so far have been analysed only within national frameworks, if at all. The perspectives in this volume, although situated outside the national context, thus offer insight into the two national industries, their indigenous specificities and respective relationships, and above all their position with regard to the USSR, which provided inspiration, influence and direction.[3] The essential advantage of this approach is that it rids 'national' histories of their nonreflexive conceptions of 'specificity' or 'special paths', thereby revealing structural similarities. Ultimately, though, specificity lingers in the re-evaluation of the individual national cultural traditions, political practices and economic and social structures enabled by this stereoscopic approach.

The GDR and Czechoslovakia

Although relations between the GDR and Czechoslovakia were not fully harmonious in the sphere of cinema in the 1950s, they were certainly very intimate and motivated by a number of mostly pragmatic interests that allowed the uneasy alliance to survive the era of Khrushchev's Thaw. While East German officials occasionally envied Czechoslovak production (they admired Czech comedies and fairy tales, which were popular with audiences too, particularly the fairy tales),[4] party officials and film industry leaders in both countries were alarmed by the pace of the 'October' reforms in their shared neighbour, Poland.[5] At the same time, the practitioners and leaders of both leading national film studios, Barrandov and DEFA (formally the Deutsche

Filmaktien Gesellschaft), gazed ambitiously towards the West. Within this mode of ideological distraction, the Czechoslovak and East German film industries often promoted their mutual cooperation and cultural exchange in the 1950s as proof that they were sufficiently active, loyal members of the Eastern Bloc.

At the same time, the relationship between the two countries was influenced by their specific geopolitical position as members of the so-called Northern Triangle, together with their rebellious Polish neighbour. The USSR understood Czechoslovakia, the GDR and Poland as a defensive bloc on the border of the FRG.[6] The unique position that the GDR and Czechoslovakia occupied in the eyes of the Soviets confirms that the political and social links between the two states in the postwar order did not arise from their geographical proximity alone but were also fostered by the Cold War strategy of Soviet hegemony.

Any functional implementation of a geopolitical bloc, though, encounters fundamental barriers and contradictions. In the GDR and Czechoslovakia, these were rooted in the historical memory of the states and their citizens, as well as in the attitudes of party leaders in each state. The Czechoslovak population's resentful attitudes towards Germans and the resulting strain on political relations and cultural contacts with the East German state were not as strong as those in Poland,[7] but memories of the Protectorate of Bohemia and Moravia as well as the postwar expulsion of Germans from Czechoslovakia still caused tensions and mistrust between these two allies.[8] Like their Polish neighbours, Czechs and Slovaks did not entirely buy into the imagined division between 'good' Germans in the socialist state (constructed on the myth of antifascism) and 'bad' Germans in the FRG, the alleged inheritor of the Nazi empire.[9]

The coalition had its own internal motivations and driving forces: in addition to sharing certain economic interests, the partners were unified in their resistance to the militarization of the FRG at the end of 1954. Unfortunately, another major point of convergence between the East German and Czechoslovakian socialist programmes was a negative one – a shared scepticism of the Polish 'October' and Władysław Gomułka's attempt to restore relations with Western nations. This pragmatic rapprochement – which survived until the mid-1960s, when the East German leadership grew to distrust the process of Czechoslovak liberalization – influenced the sphere of cinema culture via a bilateral exchange of movies (in both directions) and film practitioners (mostly from Barrandov to DEFA).[10]

A Closely Watched Alliance – the Sovietization of the Cultural Sphere

Along with analysis of the dynamics of the bilateral relationship between the GDR and Czechoslovakia, a proper evaluation of the cultural-political dimension of the region's transnational cinema culture in the 1950s necessarily demands consideration of a third entity, namely the USSR and its implied influence, typically labelled Sovietization.

With regard to its influence on the cultural sphere, Sovietization could be defined[11] as a process of export from the USSR of organizational principles, norms and values, which were implemented through orders and administrative measures, or by cultural policy and film production practitioners in the satellite nations. Sovietization has been investigated from various perspectives in the last two decades, notably in a thoroughly researched comparative study of the Sovietization of higher education.[12] Nevertheless, historical research on the film industries in the Soviet Bloc has not yet focused on the question of how far Soviet cultural functionaries or film industry leaders attempted, successfully or not, to implement their own standards and norms within the cinema culture of the socialist countries. Many of the essays in this volume point to obvious traces of such efforts, but they clearly were not part of a systematic endeavour, and their efficacy was strongly influenced by local functionaries' activities. Besides, Sovietization tendencies took widely varying courses in different countries due to specific local traditions in film cultures and industries as well as variable degrees of distrust towards Soviets. While Russophobia was strong and deep-rooted in postwar Germany, acceptance of Soviet culture was significantly greater in Czechoslovakia, where a strong sense of Germanophobia prevailed.[13]

Some scholars criticize the use of the term 'Sovietization', claiming it oversimplifies the complex processes of give and take between the Soviet Union and its East European subordinates.[14] They instead promote the concept of 'self-Sovietization', which shifts the emphasis to the many East European functionaries who willingly adopted and used Soviet models themselves without direct instructions or pressure. The concept of 'self-Sovietization' is used to describe the activities of people and organizations with a degree of structural independence from the regime and a seemingly obsessive interest in introducing Soviet methods and practices. John Connelly has fruitfully applied this conception (originally coined in the context of standard 'political' discussion of Sovietization in the GDR) in his study on the Sovietization of universities in Central European communist countries.[15] However, he uses the term in a relatively narrow sense to describe the efforts of the 'compulsive Sovietizers' among communist functionaries. In the case of film industry and culture, this term can also describe (communist or noncommunist) activists who were fascinated by communist values and technology as well as by the communist emphasis on 'planning'.

As the detailed research contained in this volume implies, there was no systematic, successful Sovietization of film industry or cinema culture, even though discussions about the Soviet lead were intensive and the demand to follow the organizational principles was occasionally strong, as various industry reorganizations according to the Soviet model in the early 1950s demonstrate. The Soviets never invested sufficient resources to consistently implement a transfer of organizational principles, and in effect the most radical and active initiatives indeed came from ambitious promoters of 'self-Sovietization' – 'Learning from the Soviet Union means learning to win,' went the famous East German mantra. A representative example of this phenomenon would be the director of the 'creative unit for Soviet-Czechoslovak co-operation' who, in 1950, developed a proposal for reorganizing feature film production according to the Soviet model.[16] But as Petr Szczepanik's essay demonstrates, many features of the traditional production culture that had taken shape in the 1920s and 1930s and been consolidated during World War II survived into the 1950s. Both the Soviet film industry and the Soviet Ministry of Culture attempted to maintain influence on production and distribution throughout the Soviet Bloc countries, but the implementation of their interests and wishes was significantly dependent on the 'sensitivity' of the respective state functionaries. Their tendency to fulfil all the Soviets' demands and follow their signals was much weaker in cases when it contradicted their own local interests. This was especially obvious in the sphere of film distribution and exhibition, as the essays by Lars Karl and by Kyril Kunakhovich and Pavel Skopal illustrate with relevant examples.

Though the concept of Sovietization might seem worn and actual intentional Soviet influence was often lacking or ineffective, the current moment is a propitious one to revisit the many dimensions of the imposition of Soviet-style institutions, culture, politics and 'life itself' in the East European film industries that fell under Moscow's sway after World War II. This volume's contributors focus on topics suited to the task. International film festivals could serve Soviet global ambitions and ideological interests, as Jindřiška Bláhová shows in her research on the festival in Karlovy Vary. Meanwhile, other festivals (or even the same one, a few years later) were instead shaped by the political and representative interests of their host country, as Andreas Kötzing's research on the Leipzig Documentary and Short Film Festival reveals. The essays by Mariana Ivanova and Pavel Skopal show that while some co-productions were made under compulsion from Soviet representatives demanding cooperation between the socialist countries, others were shot with partners from capitalist countries in projects undertaken by film studios ambitious to gain access to better technical equipment, skilled practitioners, higher profits or international prestige. Yet at the same time, Mariana Ivanova's story of DEFA's 'undercover' co-productions with a West German film producer vividly illustrates the specificity of the East German film industry in comparison to Czechoslovakia – a specificity based on DEFA's shared past with, yet present political distance from, West German filmmakers.

Two Film Industries – Comparison and Transfer

The process of Sovietization is not analysed here (or elsewhere) within the conceptual framework of cultural transfer, for an obvious reason: transfer studies emphasize cultural exchange between two entities that are relatively equivalent and commensurable, which was not the case with the Soviet Union and its satellite countries. Nevertheless, the application of the notion of transfer to the supposedly one-way process of cultural flow from a centre of power to peripheries can reveal the possible simplifications entailed by the model of Sovietization – as well as that of Americanization.[17]

A history of cultural transfer follows a relationship between two entities (e.g. nations, regions, cities, institutions) and focuses on phenomena that cross the borders (technology, sport, a model of a social state, etc.), highlighting the role of various mediators, such as booksellers, publishers and universities[18] – and in this case we could add filmmakers, cultural functionaries and movies. These processes come into being through migration as well as through personal meetings or the study of texts originating in the other culture.[19] No such history of cultural transfer between the GDR and Czechoslovakia in the sphere of cinema has yet been written,[20] and it would be beyond the scope of the current volume. Such an approach would inevitably demand a significantly different perspective from that adopted here. Rather than focusing on mutual influences, this volume attempts to highlight structural and functional similarities between the respective film industries and the cultural policies related to their respective position within the Soviet Bloc. But the existence of obvious conceptual differences between the approach of transfer studies on the one hand and comparative studies on the other does not mean that they are entirely incompatible. Indeed, they can be quite complementary:

> Without explicit comparison, historical studies of transfers and of entanglements are in danger of becoming airy and thin. On the other hand, comparative studies are not damaged, but improved by considering connections between the units of comparison wherever and whenever they exist.... Such connections – i.e., mutual perceptions and influences, transfers and travels, migrations and trade, interaction, relations of imitation and avoidance, shared dependence from one and the same constellation or common origin – may contribute to explaining similarities and differences, convergences and divergences between the cases compared.[21]

The present volume aims to take a step in this direction, that is, towards a better understanding of the Soviet bloc film industries from a transnational perspective, hopefully providing a foundation for future research on cultural transfer.

The essays collected here illustrate how the regimes used cinema culture for self-presentation in two directions: externally to the West, and Internally to their own citizens. The intensity of the centrifugal or centripetal tendencies of the regimes shifted constantly, as indicated by the essays dealing with the prestige co-productions of DEFA; Barrandov's pragmatic co-production alliances; the international film festivals in Karlovy Vary and Leipzig; and the exhibition of movies from the other side of the Iron Curtain, whether as part of the regular distribution network or presented in film clubs, some of which arose as an alternative distribution sphere organized 'from below', as Fernando Ramos Arenas illustrates in his study on the Leipzig University Film Club. The essays in this volume provide insight into the role of institutional networks and cinema infrastructure and their influence on the intended construction of a specific socialist film culture. Christin Niemeyer and Lukáš Skupa each present a story of children's cinema as a kind of production that the government and party authorities promoted as ideologically significant, although production efficiency was influenced by the varying degrees of institutionalization in this branch of moviemaking. Thomas Beutelschmidt reveals the contradictions inherent in the relationship between the two institutions that represented the two mass media most highly valued by top GDR functionaries: the DEFA film studio and state television broadcaster

Deutscher Fernsehfunk. Václav Šmidrkal's comparison of the military film studios in the GDR and Czechoslovakia vividly depicts significant differences in both the use of the studios' film facilities and the artistic ambitions of the personnel in accordance with the attitude and goals of the army leadership. While the case of military film production is obviously a paramount example of a 'cinema in service of the state', all the essays inevitably deal with the influence of state demands, intentions and ideological programmes. Equally inevitably, however, these essays based on meticulous archival research reveal tensions and contradictions rooted not only in the varying intentions of the individual participants, but also in the different temporalities of various processes and structures. Lucie Česálková's essay on so-called "custom made film production" offers an illustrative example: while this production was obviously and quite directly intended to 'serve the state' and its planning, the contrasting temporalities of moviemaking and the production of consumer goods created situations whereby movies promoted items that were not in fact available on the market. Consequently, this type of film production was often, in effect, rather a disservice to the state.

This volume offers generalizations as well as a better understanding of specificities. The East German and Czechoslovak film industries are well suited for this purpose because they were among the most prolific in the Soviet Bloc and followed two different yet related traditions. What is distinctly, and fully intentionally, missing from the book is an aesthetic history of textual objects and their interrelations. Some of the essays deal with textual features of individual movies, but they do not place aesthetic concerns at the centre of their research and always locate the 'text' within a wider nexus of research questions concerning institutions, political discourses, film industry strategies or cinematic reception. A good number of books in English focus on individual, mostly 'representative' DEFA movies, on the history of the DEFA studio in the 1950s, or on the distribution of Western movies in the GDR, and at least a word or two has been published on Czechoslovak production of the relevant period.[22] We intend to follow a rather different research programme, however. From our point of view, the history of East German and Czechoslovak cinema is not a history of ideologically charged regime prestige projects, works of creative talent marred by 'them', or a few 'hidden gems' to be revealed and newly interpreted. We see it rather as part of a broader history of institutional structures, international diplomacy, state economies, personal networks, education, marketing strategies and consumption. This volume aspires to contribute one small grain to the mills of cinema history.

Notes

1. Sabine Hake, 'Introduction', in John Davidson and Sabine Hake (eds), *Framing the Fifties: Cinema in a Divided Germany* (New York and Oxford: Berghahn Books, 2007), p. 2.
2. For excellent books in English that deal with Czech-German relationships from the viewpoint of national policy, national self-determinacy or national behaviour, see Tara Zahra, *Kidnapped Souls: National Indifference and the Battle for Children in the Bohemian Lands, 1900–1948* (Ithaca and London: Cornell University Press, 2008), Nancy Wingfield, *Flag Wars and Stone Saints: How the Bohemian Lands Became Czech* (Harvard: Harvard University Press, 2007), and Chad Bryant, *Prague in Black: Nazi Rule and Czech Nationalism* (Harvard: Harvard University Press, 2009).
3. Two recent volumes, though focused solely on the East German studio, put DEFA into a transnational perspective; see Michael Wedel, Barton Byg, Andy Räder, Skyler Arndt-Briggs and Evan Torner (eds), *DEFA International: Grenzüberschreitende Filmbeziehungen vor und nach dem Mauerbau* (Wiesbaden: Springer, 2013) and Marc Silberman and Henning Wrage (eds), *DEFA at the Crossroads of East German and International Film Culture* (Berlin and Boston: De Gruyter, 2014).
4. See Volker Zimmermann, 'Medzi kooperáciou a konfrontáciou. Kultúrnopolitické vzťahy medzi NDR a Československom v 50. a 60. rokoch 20. Storočia', in Dušan Kováč, Michaela Marek, Jiří Pešek and Roman Prahl (eds), *Kultura jako nositel a oponent politických záměrů. Německo-české a německo-slovenské kulturní styky od poloviny 19. století do současnosti* (Ústí nad Labem: Albis, 2009), pp. 321–348.
5. 'October' refers to the Polish 'thaw', a period of political reform between October 1956 and early 1958 initiated by the appointment of Władysław Gomułka as First Secretary of the Party after he had been expelled from the Polish United Worker's Party and imprisoned.
6. See Beate Ihme-Tuchel, *Das „nördliche Dreieck": Die Beziehungen zwischen der DDR, der Tschechoslowakei und Polen in den Jahren 1954 bis 1962* (Cologne: Wissenschaft und Politik, 1994).
7. Sheldon Anderson, *A Cold War in the Soviet Bloc: Polish-East German Relations: 1945–1962* (Boulder: Westview Press, 2000), pp. 5–6.
8. See e.g. Volker Zimmerman, 'Proměnlivá spojenectví. NDR a její vztahy k Československu a Polsku v padesátých a šedesátých letech 20. století', in Christoph Buchheim, Edita Ivaničková, Kristina Kaiserová and Volker Zimmermann (eds), *Československo a dva německé státy* (Prague: Kristina Kaiserová and Albis International, 2011), p. 86.
9. See e.g. Ihme-Tuchel, *Das „nördliche Dreieck"*, p. 48.
10. See Pavel Skopal, 'Reisende in Sachen Genre – von Barrandov nach Babelsberg und zurück. Zur Bedeutung von tschechischen Regisseuren für die Genrefilmproduktion der DEFA in den 1960er und 1970er Jahren', in Michael Wedel, Barton Byg, Andy Räder, Skyler Arndt-Bryggs and Evan Torner (eds), *DEFA international: Grenzüberschreitende Filmbeziehungen vor und nach dem Mauerbau* (Wiesbaden: Springer VS, 2013), pp. 249–266.
11. We use 'Sovetization' as an analytical term. Nevertheless, it has its own long history: used by Soviet leaders as early as the 1920s to describe the consolidation of Soviet power over the non-Russian republics, it was then more widely applied by critics of the Soviet regime in the 1950s. See Konrad H. Jarausch and Hannes Siegrist, 'Amerikanisierung und Sowjetisierung. Eine vergleichende Fragestellung zur deutsch-deutschen Nachkriegsgeschichte', in Jarausch and Siegrist (eds),

Amerikanisierung und Sowjetisierung in Deutschland 1945–1970 (Frankfurt and New York: Campus Verlag, 1997), pp. 20–21; E. A. Rees, 'The Sovietization of Eastern Europe', in Balázs Apor, Péter Apor and E. A. Rees (eds), *The Sovietization of Eastern Europe: New Perspectives on the Postwar Period* (Washington DC: New Academia Publishing, 2008), pp. 1–3.

12. See John Connelly, *Captive University: The Sovietization of East German, Czech, and Polish Higher Education, 1945–1956* (Chapel Hill: University of North Carolina Press, 2000); Michael David-Fox and György Péteri (eds), *Academia in Upheaval: Origins, Transfers, and Transformations of the Communist Academic Regime in Russia and East Central Europe* (Westport, CT: Bergin & Garvey, 2000).
13. Muriel Blaive, *Promarněná příležitost. Československo a rok 1956* (Prague: Prostor, 2001), pp. 280–282.
14. For a brief account of the debate, see Norman Naimark, 'The Sovietization of Eastern Europe, 1944–1953', in Melvyn P. Leffler and Odd Arne Westad (eds), *The Cambridge History of the Cold War*, vol. 1: *Origins* (Cambridge: Cambridge University Press, 2010), pp. 195–197.
15. It is important to note that in the standard political debate on Sovietization as the establishment of communist regimes, this notion has met strong criticism for implying that the USSR's role was not vital to the result. Indeed, 'self-Sovietization' must be understood as just one, and definitely not the most important, mode of the whole Sovietization process. Connelly, *Captive University*, pp. 45–46.
16. Národní filmový archiv, Prague, f. Filmová rada, k. R9-SI-4P-9K, 1950–1953.
17. See e.g. Russell A. Berman, 'Anti-Americanism and Americanization', in Alexander Stephan (ed.), *Americanization and Anti-Americanism: The German Encounter with American Culture after 1945* (New York: Berghahn Books, 2007), pp. 11–24.
18. Philipp Ther, 'Comparisons, Cultural Transfers, and the Study of Networks: Toward a Transnational History of Europe', in Heinz-Gerhard Haupt and Jürgen Kocka (eds), *Comparative and Transnational History: Central European Approaches and New Perspectives* (New York and Oxford: Berghahn Books, 2009), pp. 204–225.
19. See Hartmut Kaelble, 'Between Comparison and Transfers – and What Now? A French-German Debate', in Haupt and Kocka, *Comparative and Transnational History*, pp. 33–34.
20. However, small steps have been taken in this direction; see Skopal, 'Reisende in Sachen Genre – von Barrandov nach Babelsberg und zurück'.
21. Heinz-Gerhard Haupt and Jürgen Kocka, 'Comparison and Beyond', in Haupt and Kocka, *Comparative and Transnational History*, pp. 20–21.
22. Daniela Berghahn, *Hollywood Behind the Wall: The Cinema of East Germany* (Manchester: Manchester University Press, 2005); Joshua Feinstein, *The Triumph of the Ordinary: Depictions of Daily Life in the East German Cinema, 1949–1989* (Chapel Hill: University of North Carolina Press, 2001); Seán Allan and John Sandford (eds), *DEFA: East German Cinema 1946–1992* (Oxford: Berghahn, 1999); Sebastian Heiduschke, *East German Cinema: DEFA and Film History* (New York: Palgrave Macmillan, 2013); Rosemary Stott, *Crossing the Wall: The Western Feature Film Import in East Germany* (Bern: Peter Lang, 2012); Anke Pinkert, *Film and Memory in East Germany* (Bloomington: Indiana University Press, 2008). Two volumes address Czechoslovak cinema of the 1950s to a significant degree: Mira Liehm and Antonín Liehm, *The Most Important Art: Soviet and Eastern European Film After 1945* (Berkeley: University of California Press, 1980) and Peter Hames, *Czech and Slovak Cinema: Theme and Tradition* (Edinburgh: Edinburgh University Press, 2010).

Select Bibliography

Anderson, Sheldon. *A Cold War in the Soviet Bloc: Polish-East German Relations: 1945-1962*. Boulder: Westview Press, 2000.

Apor, Balázs, Péter Apor and E. A. Rees (eds). *The Sovietization of Eastern Europe: New Perspectives on the Postwar Period*. Washington DC: New Academia Publishing, 2008.

Berghahn, Daniela. *Hollywood Behind the Wall: The Cinema of East Germany*. Manchester: Manchester University Press, 2005.

Bryant, Chad. *Prague in Black: Nazi Rule and Czech Nationalism*. Harvard: Harvard University Press, 2009.

Connelly, John. *Captive University: The Sovietization of East German, Czech, and Polish Higher Education, 1945-1956*. Chapel Hill: University of North Carolina Press, 2000.

Davidson, John, and Sabine Hake (eds). *Framing the Fifties: Cinema in a Divided Germany*. New York and Oxford: Berghahn Books 2007.

Hames, Peter: *Czech and Slovak Cinema: Theme and Tradition*. Edinburgh: Edinburgh University Press, 2010.

Heiduschke, Sebastian. *East German Cinema: DEFA and Film History*. New York: Palgrave Macmillan, 2013.

Liehm, Mira, and Antonín Liehm, *The Most Important Art: Soviet and Eastern European Film After 1945*. Berkeley: University of California Press, 1980.

Silberman, Marc, and Henning Wrage (eds). *DEFA at the Crossroads of East German and International Film Culture*. Berlin and Boston: De Gruyter, 2014.

Wingfield, Nancy. *Flag Wars and Stone Saints: How the Bohemian Lands Became Czech*. Harvard: Harvard University Press, 2007.

Zahra, Tara. *Kidnapped Souls: National Indifference and the Battle for Children in the Bohemian Lands, 1900–1948*. Ithaca and London: Cornell University Press, 2008.

PART I

Cultural Policy and Cinema

Chapter 1

FROM SOVIET ZONE TO VOLKSDEMOKRATIE

The Politics of Film Culture in the GDR, 1945–1960

David Bathrick

From UFA to DEFA: 1945–1948

The planning for film production in the Soviet Occupation Zone (Sowjetische Besatzungszone, SBZ) was already underway a scant four months after Nazi Germany's total capitulation in May of 1945. The call for a gathering of those committed to working on such a project resulted in a now famous meeting at the Hotel Adlon on 22 November 1945. Here Soviet occupation officers and political leaders of the German Communist Party (Kommunistische Partei Deutschlands, KPD) met with German film and literary artists, some coming from Soviet exile, others from so-called 'inner emigration' or from the Nazi Film industry. The president of the newly formed Central Administration for Education, Paul Wandel, opened the proceedings with a call for renewal that was to be repeated often in the succeeding years: 'Let us make films which breathe a new spirit, films with humanist, antifascist, and democratic content, films that had nothing in common with UFA'.[1]

Making films that had nothing in common with UFA? That task, it turned out, would be far easier said than done. The two-day meeting of the Central Administration was devoted to laying the ideological and organizational groundwork for what would emerge one year later as the Deutsche Film-Aktiengesellschaft, known as DEFA. The personages assembled also quite literally prefigured some of the confluences of old and new that were fated to make any absolute renewal a difficult, protracted affair.

Let us begin with ideology. Certainly all present in the Hotel Adlon saw the struggle against the 'Ungeist der UFA-Traumwelt' (the pernicious ideology of the UFA dream world) as the central cultural and political task in the rebuilding of mass forms of media communication with the potential to have an impact upon millions within a beleaguered population. 'Everyone was united in their loathing of racial hatred and genocide, the cult of the Führer and war mongering'.[2] Less clear, and indeed, increasingly contested already in the late 1940s, were precisely the inherent meanings of signifiers such as humanist, antifascist and even democratic. Initially serving within the cultural policies of the SBZ as the lowest common denominators for political reconciliation around a once imagined 'united front', they gradually transmogrified into the ideological binaries of a growing Cold War culture. The term humanism soon generated its pejorative Other in the fight against modernist aesthetic variants of so-called 'formalism', 'avantgardism', and 'degenerate art'. Antifascism connoted a legacy of genuine artistic attempts to come to terms with the Nazi past that later became re-encoded within the cultural discourse of an emerging authoritarian Stalinist infrastructure. And democracy – a linguistic representative for the once hopefully shared notions of liberation and egalitarianism – was soon folded into the metanarrative of 'dialectical materialism's' claim for legitimate power by the chosen representative of proletarian good will, the Socialist Unity Party of Germany (Sozialistische Einheitspartei Deutschlands, SED). All modes of political discourse – culture generally, and film more specifically – were to find their expression within these cultural and political frameworks, and we shall return to that expression in a discussion of filmmaking and its development throughout the 1950s.

But what of the resources at hand – in this case experienced artists and technicians as well as capital and equipment? Another look at the 1945 conference, this time focusing on the immediate histories of the writers and filmmakers assembled, is revealing.[3] With the exception of the left-wing writers Friedrich Wolf and Günter Weisenborn, all others present had been active participants in the Nazi public sphere. Of the nine filmmakers named in the programme, seven had worked in the studios of UFA and Ton-Bild-Syndikat AG (Tobis), another important film production and distribution company in Germany. Most prominent among them were Wolfgang Staudte, Gerhard Lamprecht and Hans Deppe. Staudte, director of the first postwar German film, *Die*

Mörder sind unter uns (The Murderers are Among Us, 1946) for DEFA, had played small roles in a number of films, including two of the most notorious Nazi feature films – Veit Harlan's *Jud Süss* (Jew Süss, 1940) and Arthur Maria Rabenalt's *...reitet für Deutschland* (Ride for Germany, 1941) – in addition to directing one of the premiere comedies of the period, *Akrobat schö-ö-ön* (1943). Lamprecht and Deppe, both prolific directors of light entertainment films, went on to make films for DEFA in the immediate postwar period. Lamprecht's *Irgendwo in Berlin* (Somewhere in Berlin, 1946) became the classic rubble youth film of the period. Deppe's considerably more forgettable *Kein Platz für Liebe* (No Room for Love, 1947) and *Die Kuckucks* (The Cuckoo Family, 1949) were soon to be overshadowed by his now classic Heimat films, *Schwarzwaldmädel* (Black Forest Girl, 1950) and *Grün ist die Heide* (Green is the Heath, 1951), which he made in the Federal Republic.

One survey states that between 1949 and 1952, 62 per cent of all DEFA directors, 73 per cent of its camera people, and 60 per cent of its producers had once worked for UFA or Terra.[4] This high percentage of former Third Reich filmmakers working for and affiliated with DEFA was emblematic of a dependency on the remnants of the Nazi film industry in all the allied zones that would last well into the 1950s. In their discussions in Moscow during the spring of 1944, the KPD cultural émigrés and their Soviet colleagues were already stressing the importance of postwar political rehabilitation for film and electronic media, given that 'still too many people who would not be reading newspapers not to mention the books, will be going to the movies'.[5] Certainly this emphasis upon the powers of 'controlled policies' (*gesteuerte Politik*) carried over into the early decision to build a powerful centralized cinema industry, and as such marked out clear differences between the Soviet and the other three zones in postwar Germany. Unlike in the SBZ, decision makers in the western zones, particularly the Americans, initially remained suspicious of the potential misuse of the manipulative powers of the cinema, embracing instead print media as primary for 'denazification' and relegating cinema to the realm of entertainment, which in their minds could be covered by Hollywood.

Thus, whereas Western allies were initially concerned with breaking up any German cinematic monopolies that might form, the SBZ devoted itself to building a concentration of large-scale production and distribution in the areas of documentary and feature films.[6] Such a project, of course, entailed a large outlay of material resources at every level of production – a considerable challenge, considering that the technical capacities of the once all-powerful UFA and Tobis concerns lay in ruins. The bombing attacks on Berlin in the last two war years and on Potsdam in April of 1945 had destroyed 90 per cent of the (then) largest film industry in Europe, and the reparation policies implemented by the Soviet Union made accruing capital to rebuild studios and individual cinemas, and produce technical equipment and film stock – difficult in and of itself – even more so.

Even more off-putting was the lack of experience and personnel in the form of artistic and technical know-how. Whereas a significant number of leading German literary writers had returned to the SBZ from western and eastern exile (Johannes R. Becher, Bertolt Brecht, Friedrich Wolf, Anna Seghers, Bodo Uhse, etc.), the same cannot be said for those émigrés working in the cinema. From the mass exodus of over one thousand top directors, actors, screenwriters, producers and technicians who had left Germany after 1932 because of racial policies and political oppression, only a small number returned to Germany in 1945, and far fewer of them to the SBZ. One exception was Slatan Dudow, the director of *Kuhle Wampe oder Wem gehört die Welt?* (Kuhle Wampe or to Whom Does the World Belong? Germany, 1932), who did go on to make DEFA films.

Soviet cultural authorities' initial efforts to meet viewing needs resulted in two major policy developments that were to have far-reaching impact upon the media public sphere in the Soviet Zone. The first was their effort to provide cinema entertainment as soon as possible, which in turn led them to release their own films for distribution. One month after the German capitulation, the Soviet Military Administration in Germany (*Sowjetische Militäradministration in Deutschland*, SMAD) commissioned German technicians to refit a synchronization studio in Berlin for the purpose of dubbing Soviet films for German audiences. Here the main emphasis was upon the 'Soviet Classics' of the 1930s and 1940s, together with musicals and light entertainment, as a means of countering anti-Sovietism among the German populace and 'making them acquainted with the achievements of Soviet art'.[7] It should also come as no surprise that for both cultural and political reasons, the Soviet revolutionary avant-garde cinema of the 1920s – films by Eisenstein, Pudovkin, and Vertov – were for the most part withheld from distribution. Eisenstein's *Bronenosets Potyomkin* (Battleship Potemkin, 1925) was not screened until 1949, and *Stachka* (Strike, 1925) and *Oktyabr': Desyat' dney kotorye potryasli mir* (October: Ten Days that Shook the World, 1927) were not shown at all during this period.[8]

A second source of immediate programming came from UFA films of the 1930s and 1940s, for the most part 'harmless light comedies and musicals' that had been inspected to determine whether they 'contained subliminal [*unterschwellig*] traces of fascism, racism or militarism'.[9] By 1948, the Allies had cleared for distribution 454 of the approximately 1,300 feature films and full-length documentaries made in Germany between 1933 and 1945. Once again, entertainment value for legitimation purposes was of prime importance,[10] as Vladimir Gall, a cultural officer for the SMAD during this period, reminds us: 'For the most part these films were "*kitschig*", sometimes even ridiculous [*albern*] and in no way did they contribute to the re-education of the German population ... but they also weren't dangerous and they did provide people with diversion [*Abwechslung*]'.[11] Finally, the population of the SBZ was eventually also permitted to view films from the United States, Great Britain and France.

The Soviets' second commitment during this period was their complete support for the immediate production of German films and the building of a domestic film industry. The first documentary shorts, cultural films and newsreels made by DEFA, beginning with Kurt Maetzig's newsreel series called *Der Augenzeuge* (The Eyewitness), appeared as early as the spring of 1946 at the same time that initial shooting began for Wolfgang Staudte's *Die Mörder sind unter uns*. This was followed by the officially celebrated licencing of DEFA on 17 May. The main speaker at the ceremony was the highest-ranking authority on matters of cultural policy in the SBZ between 1945 and 1949, Colonel (later General) Sergei Tiul'panov of the Information Bureau of SMAD, who stated that:

> DEFA faces a number of important tasks. Of these, the most important is the eradication of all traces of Nazism and militarism from the conscience of every German; the struggle for the reeducation of the German people – especially the young – towards a true understanding of genuine democracy and humanism; and in so doing, to promote a sense of respect for other people and other nations.[12]

Significantly, Tiul'panov's carefully worded statement lacks any obviously ideological implications. Its notion of re-education is devoid even of phrases like 'antifascism', not to speak of references hinting at a socialist future. This is not to suggest that there was a dearth of censorship or control – as the only officially sanctioned film corporation in the SBZ, DEFA soon became a 'German-Soviet Corporation' dominated by members of the SED and under the tutelage of SMAD, with a monopoly on supervisory powers over every single film made on that territory for the next forty-one years. Nonetheless, the Soviets under Tiul'panov also realized from the very outset that the building of a financially viable 'education and entertainment' film industry entailed making compromises with a number of competing constituencies.

The first area of concern emerged at the level of film production. As mentioned above, virtually all the available major artists (directors, actors, screenwriters, technical engineers) had previously worked in the Third Reich, so the cultural-political frameworks of the initial projects were necessarily kept at the rather vague level of phrases such as 'the struggle for a new beginning'. In fact, the Soviets – as opposed to their more partisan brethren in the SED – felt comfortable with a very general notion of antifascism: neither explicitly anticapitalist nor narrowly ideological or didactic, nor by any means encouraging self-initiated terrorist action. Of the first eighteen feature films produced by DEFA between 1946 and 1948, only three suggest any sort of proselytizing for the socialization of the status quo: Milo Harbig's *Freies Land* (Free Land, 1946) attempts to popularize the notion of land reform; Walter Schleif's and Erich Freund's *Grube Morgenrot* (Coal Mine of the Dawn, 1948) agitates in favour of the postwar socialization of key industries; and Arthur Maria Rabenalt's *Chemie und Liebe* (Chemistry and Love, 1948) draws the connection between capitalist greed and war production. The majority of the other films feature individuals struggling with postwar distress and renewal in the broadest sense: returning soldiers and war prisoners, refugees, resettlers, single women, parentless children and homeless youth on the move through the cities, still bearing the marks of their National Socialist upbringing.

Certainly Wolfgang Staudte's *Die Mörder sind unter uns* appropriately serves as a cultural political paradigm for many of the films that followed over the next two years.[13] The narrative of the returning soldier Dr Hans Mertens, who hunts down and seeks to murder his former senior officer, who once issued orders to kill a group of helpless Polish partisans – orders that Mertens himself did not refuse to carry out – is not, in any literal sense, Staudte's own story. Yet, like the works of many of his cinematic colleagues who came from UFA to DEFA, this film did serve as a way to work through his wartime complicity and its aftermath – in this case, the desire for revenge served as an act of atonement for one's own guilt. Staudte's two fold revision of the film's ending represents a compulsive re-enactment of the psychic/collective crime. In the original ending, the filmmaker has the wanton hero Mertens trap his helpless former officer Brückner, now a successful capitalist and family man, and murder him on the spot. Told by the Soviet cultural officer Alexander Dymshits that this kind of vigilante justice would not be appropriate, given the potential mayhem it might encourage among the postwar German population, Staudte settled on an ending in which Mertens simply attempts to assassinate Brückner, only to be prevented from doing so by his faithful woman, the concentration camp survivor Susanne Wallner, who throughout the film has stood by her suffering man as a nurturing source of succour and now quite literally enables his abrupt reversal and rehabilitation. Viewed from the perspective of postwar realities, the final words of this ultimate version of the screenplay stand indeed as a clear example of the humanist *Neuanfang* (new beginning) sanctioned most explicitly by the officers of Soviet Military Administration of Germany in the early days of DEFA.[14]

> Susanne: Hans! We do not have the right to judge!
>
> Mertens: No Susanne, but we do have the duty to bring an indictment, to demand atonement in the name of the millions of innocently murdered people.[15]

The main significance of the ending and indeed message of this first DEFA film was that it 'did not delve into the political background of fascist atrocities, but rather argued from a subjectively moral position (*innermoralisch*), and in so doing, put more emphasis on the inner remorse of the fellow traveller rather than the punishment of the perpetrator – a move that was absolutely in line with official allied policy'.[16]

Already in this first post-UFA feature, we encounter a number of the ingredients that marked the interface of ruptures and continuities, pasts and presents, represented here aesthetically in the suggestive combination of expressionist, classical (Third Reich) UFA, Italian neorealist, and film noir styles peculiar to early DEFA productions as a whole.[17] During this period individual directors wrote their own screenplays, without intense Soviet or SED supervision, and in so doing projected onto the screen their ongoing struggles to work through and subsequently reach resolution, replete with blockage, distortion and revelation, and expressed a continued fascination with and confusion about a past that haunted the present as a chosen means of producing the new through occasional re-enactments of the old.

What is also of importance, beyond its non-tendentious narrative message, is the extent to which *Die Mörder sind unter uns* articulates its contradictions at the aesthetic level. It has often been mentioned that the mise-en-scène of the film strongly suggests a reprise of German expressionist cinema.[18] For instance, the camera work of Friedl Behn-Grund draws on his pre-1930s work, with its focus on differing dimensions of German silent film's suggestive 'dramaturgy of shadow and light' as well as its extraordinary use of camera angle for distortion and highlighting.[19] Displaying inspiration from early expressionist film, *Die Mörder sind unter uns* engages in a painterly transformation of landscape and human figure, whether by demonizing the ruins of Berlin into haunting metaphors of a lost moonscape world or by highlighting physiognomy, particularly in the close-ups of the suffering Mertens, shot at a low angle and casting shadows for the haunting effects of a tortured soul.

Yet as much as Behn-Grund draws on Weimar cinematic expressionism in his enhancement of outdoor space, it is surely his use of light and dark contrasts emanating from a very different system that made him an occasional lighting designer for UFA and Tobis during the Third Reich. If we look more carefully at the camera work, particularly in relationship to its enhancement of facial close-ups, then we see that the counterpoint to the lurking, shadowy, melancholic 'expressionist' Mertens is precisely the paradigm of goodness, virtue and above all patience embodied in the character Susanne Wallner, played by Hildegard Knef. Not accidentally, Susanne's face, whether in close-up or a long shot, is consistently bathed in bright light from the very beginning and in almost every subsequent take. In the words of Ralf Schenk, 'Hildegard Knef hovers ever present as a figure of light (*Lichtgestalt*) throughout the film: with white make-up, her smooth, even face highlighted mostly in bright hues as it rises up out of the darkness of its surroundings – she is indeed a principle of hope. "UFA-Stil" we would say today, in a somewhat abbreviated and inexact way'.[20]

The success of the DEFA studio during the first three years following the war is in no small degree attributable to the Soviet authorities' willingness to provide a policy of industrial support and political leeway for a kind of film production that was surprisingly free of ideological and aesthetic constraint, in terms of both the issues it addressed and the heterogeneity of its modes of artistic expression. There was little effort to invoke a policy of Socialist Realism, although some members of the SED were pushing in this direction. That a majority of the DEFA filmmakers and film technicians were commuting from West Berlin is but further indication of the extent to which this highly eclectic and successful endeavour itself 'arose from the rubble'.

From Soviet Zone to Volksdemokratie: 1948–1955

In the fall of 1947, an eventual unification of Germany 'was still the guiding principle for formulating cultural policy in the SBZ'.[21] Unlike in the other Eastern Bloc countries, which under the mantle of Soviet hegemony would be evolving into so-called 'Peoples' Democracies', the SMAD in the SBZ continued to adhere to a policy that emanated originally from the 'united front' and defined itself officially as the 'antifascist democratic renewal'. But this would all begin to change rather precipitously in the months to follow. The collapse of the London Conference of Foreign Ministers in December of 1947 was followed by increasing economic and political confrontations between East and West globally, culminating in Germany with the Berlin blockade in June of 1948 and the intensification of the Marshall Plan in the three western zones in that same year.

The gradual evolution into 'two Germanys' confronted cultural policymakers in the SED with a complicated situation. On one level, it soon became clear that a policy based simply on a concept of 'antifascist-democratic renewal' would no longer prove adequate within the rapidly increasing intensity of Cold War politics. Just as obvious, however, was that the geopolitical limitations of postwar zonal Germany made this an inopportune time to launch a campaign for a 'People's Democracy' with a fully developed 'socialist cultural policy'. In September of 1948, it was none other than Walter Ulbricht who, in light of the soon to be implemented two-year plan in the SBZ, chose to remind the party's 'culture producers' of their past misdemeanours and expected responsibilities in the rapidly evolving global bi-polarization:

> I am going to begin with the following critique because it can no longer be tolerated that those of you who produce culture feel free to reject the new tasks at hand and simply act as though others will complete these tasks for you. I simply want to state openly what the situation is that we find ourselves in now. We will not be able to complete the two-year plan successfully, if the cultural level (*Niveau*) of the population is not raised at a rapid pace, as well as the ideological level; if the struggle on the cultural front is not carried through with total energy and determination. That is not what is happening today.[22]

The cultural-political implications of an accelerating Stalinization would soon be felt at every level of cultural life in the SBZ. In December of 1948 Alexander Dymshits, the heretofore 'liberal' head of the SMAD information bureau, published a polemic against 'formalistic directions in German painting' in the daily East Berlin newspaper *Tägliche Rundschau* – a clear warning that SMAD might no longer be in a position to support deviations from 'official policy', as once was the case.[23]

In January of 1949, the first SED Party Conference announced the opening of the 'struggle against signs of decadence and the formalistic and naturalistic distortion of art'.[24] What the artists and even some party intellectuals in the SBZ did not always understand is that the language and the cultural politics of the so-called formalism or modernism debate had their genesis in 1946 with the policies of the then Central Committee Secretary and Stalin appointee for cultural policy Andrei Zhdanov. The main principle of the Zhdanov doctrine was often summarized in one phrase: 'The only conflict possible in Soviet culture is the conflict between good and best.'[25] Although initially aimed at the arts, particularly the "bourgeois" music of Dmitri Shostakovich, Sergei Prokofiev and Aram Khachaturian, it soon became clear that the underlying strategy of Zhdanovism was to divide the world into two camps by defining the enemies and the cultural values at the heart of the Cold War itself.

The most important German Democratic Republic (GDR) document to deal with modernism was a declaration of the Central Committee of the SED on 17 March 1951 entitled 'The Struggle against Formalism in Art and Literature for a Progressive German Culture', which was the product of a similarly named conference. The categories it employs reflect its historical origins: formalism or 'cosmopolitanism', we are told, is a form of 'American cultural barbarism' that, when practiced in the new society, 'leads to a rupture with art itself, a destruction of national consciousness and indirect support of the war policies of world imperialism'.[26] Important here is not the content but rather the structure of the political relationship. The rhetoric and posturing with such terms as 'cultural barbarism' and 'cosmopolitanism' were an obvious part of the then prevailing Cold War climate that was later to abate somewhat with de-Stalinization and a greater focus on political conflicts within the social order.[27] But what would not disappear was this re-establishment, within GDR socialism, of the classical antagonism between the institution of affirmative culture, on the one hand, and its potential subversion at the hands of various forms of modernism on the other – an antagonism now transferred into the legitimacy struggles of 'a state that was not supposed to be'.[28]

The politicization of culture is always a double-edged sword. Though Anton Ackermann's demand to wed 'nationalist form to socialist content' did indeed serve nationalist identity claims of the new order – in contrast to the 'cosmopolitanism' of the newly founded Federal Republic – it also meant that any iconoclastic alternative to that form was, perforce, a challenge to the larger political order. Nobody understood this dialectics of legitimation better than Bertolt Brecht,[29] who, when summoned by the highest ministers of the state to discuss the formalist and ideological deviations of his and Paul Dessau's controversial opera *Das Verhör des Lukullus* (The Trial of Lucullus), asked with characteristic double entendre: 'Where else in the world can you find a government that shows such interest in and pays such attention to its artists?'[30]

The shift in political orientation at the upper reaches of the SED towards rigid versions of Zhdanovian *Kulturpolitik* was soon accompanied by administrative reorganization within the party apparatus as well as personnel changes within DEFA itself. Film, along with radio and the press, was relocated from the Department of Culture (*Kulturabteilung*) of the SED to the Department of Agitation. In February of 1950 the Film Commission of the SED became the DEFA Commission, which in turn was resituated within the Politburo. This newly configured DEFA Commission amalgamated leading party functionaries with the top information and political power in both the party and the state. Being accountable only to the Politburo and the Central Committee meant in practice that the newly founded DEFA Commission henceforth became directly responsible for the solicitation of screenplays along with the production, censorship, approval and distribution of every film made in the GDR.

This folding of DEFA into high-level party and state structures would soon affect the daily functions of filmmaking as well as artistic personnel. Those filmmakers not in the party, or for that matter not living in the East, were under increased pressure to toe the line when it came to the choice of subject matter for their films and their aesthetic realization of such themes. Whereas earlier screenplays had often been initiated by individual authors or even directors, now the initiation process increasingly came directly out of the Central Committee itself, in an effort to coordinate the production of cinema in the newly founded German Democratic Republic with the cultural political needs of this or that two-year plan. Here it must be noted that during this first period, this top-down cultural politicization produced somewhat of a double bind within the party itself because it was the experienced 'bourgeois' cinema artists who tended to make the films that, by doing well at the box office, enabled DEFA to compete with German-made films in the other three zones. In 1948, five of seven DEFA films were made by directors who had worked for German companies prior to 1945 and now lived in the West. In 1949, it was six of twelve, in 1950 five of eleven, and in 1951 five of eleven.[31]

Nevertheless, 1949 was also the year when DEFA produced three feature films by pre-eminent communist filmmakers that the SED enthusiastically endorsed as outstanding examples of socialist realism: Slatan Dudow's *Unser täglich Brot* (Our Daily Bread), Gustav von Wangenheim's *Der Auftrag Höglers* (Hoegler's Mission) and Kurt Maetzig's *Rat der Götter* (The Council of the Gods). As an articulation of Cold War tensions, the latter film argues that the same economic and political structures that led to the rise of fascism persist in the Federal Republic of Germany and the United States: 'While IG Farben in the West continues (after Auschwitz) to produce lethal gas and explosives, Germans in the East are taking to the streets in Berlin in an anti-war march on May 1, 1950.'[32]

With *Rat der Götter*, Kurt Maetzig unwittingly provides a poignant testimony to the shifts that occurred in the meanings attached to the notion of an antifascist cultural politics between 1945 and 1950, from both his own perspective and that of the SED. In 1947 Maetzig wrote and directed the film *Ehe im Schatten* (Marriage in the Shadows), which tells the true story of the popular theatre and film actor Joachim Gottschalk who, together with his Jewish wife and son, committed suicide in November 1941 when it became clear that his family would be deported to Theresienstadt. This film shines the spotlight on the persecution of Jews by the German population at home: crimes of omission at the level of the everyday, quotidian acts of cowardice, be they denunciations, a lack of civil courage, or simply a failure of will to do what one knew was right. Twelve million people in the GDR and in West Berlin saw that film, which was so popular in part because its powerful emotional cadences offered Germans a rare opportunity to identify with Jewish victims.[33] In *Rat der Götter*, Maetzig, himself a Jew whose mother had not survived the camps, no longer worked in the way he once had. In the resulting expression of antifascism, the enemy is now American and West German 'imperialism', which he sees as in the process of restaging the Holocaust.

Rat der Götter, though one the first films held up as a model for socialist realism, was by no means the worst product of what Thomas Heimann has described as the 'fatal cultural political narrowness at the beginning of the fifties in which to an extreme degree artistic expression had been totally subordinated to Party doctrine'.[34] In point of fact, the party's acclaimed goal to move ideologically from *Volkserziehung* (people's education) to *Volksdemokratie* (people's democracy), and from critical realism to socialist realism, had in very fundamental ways brought about a crisis of serious proportions with regard to production schedules in the film industry. After setting a production goal of twenty films per year in 1949, by the end of 1952 the party had to face the reality that the annual average for those four years was only ten films, considerably less than the eighteen-film average for 1947 and 1948, the two years prior to the establishment of the GDR. The paucity of films from 1949 to 1952 clearly must be attributed to the increasing interventionist activities of the DEFA Commission, including pre- and post-censoring of manuscripts and films in combination with exertion of constant pressure on filmmakers to adhere to the norms, disallowing what some ideologues might happen to glimpse as an indulgence in the realm of formalism or cosmopolitanism.

The presence of Soviet 'advisers' during the early 1950s was another factor compounding the already excessive monitoring process. As indicated earlier, up through 1948 Soviet advisers most often were liberal artistic professionals coming from the Control Commission and the Soviet Ministry for Cinematography. Between 1950 and 1952, though, the Soviet presence was assuredly more politically oriented to working with the SED leadership at a time of crisis in the Cold War.

In 1953, DEFA officially became a people-owned enterprise (Volkseigener Betrieb, VEB – the GDR's legal form of publicly owned industrial enterprises), which in turn led to the company being split up into 'three constituent studios, each specializing in the production of feature films, educational films and documentary features respectively'.[35] With this structural reorganization in the interest of greater artistic autonomy for individual filmmakers came discussions at the highest level about the need for greater freedom in film production and programming. Speaking at a special meeting between Otto Grotewohl and 'leading personalities of art and culture' in October of 1953, the director of the DEFA film studio Hans Rodenberg made it absolutely clear that fundamental changes in the quality of GDR cinema would only be achieved 'with the help of a powerful advocate with passionate interest in the momentous problems of DEFA'.[36] As things indeed began to open up, Kurt Maetzig felt empowered enough to state publicly: 'It is essential to have free and unrestricted debates about artistic matters. Such debates are valuable if they lead to more and better films. They are pointless when they are exploited so as to put a potential film project out of existence.'[37]

In comparison to the period 1949–1952, the years following Stalin's death and the uprising of 17 June 1953 were a relatively productive period for DEFA in terms of the quantity of films made. This improvement was most probably partly attributable to the so-called *Neuer Kurs* (New Course), a Soviet economic policy introduced in the GDR on 9 July 1953 that aimed to improve the standard of living, increase the availability of consumer goods and relax ideological standards. Whereas the New Course indeed contributed to greater output in the short run, the same cannot be said about the reception of the films by the population at large or their aesthetic quality. Kurt Maetzig's two-part biopic about the life of the Communist leader Ernst Thälmann, with a script by Willi Bredel (*Ernst Thälmann: Sohn seiner Klasse* [Ernst Thälmann: Son of the Working Class, 1954] and *Ernst Thälmann: Führer seiner Klasse* [Ernst Thählmann: Leader of the Working Class, 1955]), was successful at the box office but is most memorable for being an exemplary incarnation of a socialist-realist blockbuster.

From De-Stalinization to Re-Stalinization: SED Cultural Policy 1956–1960

In a speech 'On the Personality Cult and Its Consequences', delivered to a closed session of the Twentieth Party Congress of the Communist Party of the Soviet Union (Kommunisticheskaya Partiya Sovetskogo Soyuza, KPSS) on 25 February 1956, Nikita Khrushchev shocked his listeners and eventually the world by denouncing Stalin's dictatorial rule and the crimes committed by the associates of Lavrentiy Beria. The impact of this policy change on the cultural politics of the Peoples' Democracies initially caused confusion, followed in turn by crisis. On the one hand, it offered hope for much-desired reform and liberalization of a system that had not undergone fundamental structural change since the 1930s. On the other hand, it soon became clear that any departure from the Stalinist era would be accomplished only by the existing ruling parties in the various Peoples' Democracies, and consequently in a manner that would not seriously question the absolute omnipotence of the KPSS itself.

The issue of total control was particularly central and complicated when it came to the cultural organs of the SED. In this case, proximity to the Western 'enemy' was not only politically problematic due to the form of Germany's geopolitically sundered national identities, but also existentially threatening because of the dominant presence of West

German media (film, radio, newspapers and subsequently television) in the everyday life of the GDR. The SED's initial strategy regarding de-Stalinization was to withhold information. The Politburo went out of its way to assure that only mid-level party members – the district party leaders – were permitted to receive written reports about the controversial proceedings. 'A public discussion of the various decisions and reports of the 20th Party Congress was simply not permitted',[38] nor was the SED tolerant of those artists and intellectuals whom they viewed as taking advantage of this perceived 'thaw' on the cultural-political front.

How, then, did cultural intellectuals in the DDR react to the party's crackdown? Perhaps the most unexpected initial response was that of Willi Bredel, revered author of proletarian novels from the 1920s and current member of the Central Committee, who used his status as socialist icon to call for a critique of Stalin within the SED. In so doing, he demanded self-critical behaviour from the party leadership, which in his eyes had 'permitted the political education of the SED to be reduced to forms of deranged collective chanting'.[39] He went on to assert that such dogmatism is the result of a 'sacrosanct cult of personality' whose damaging and impeding effects are synonymous with 'narrow minded notions of art on the part of cultural functionaries and subservient behaviours on the part of writers and artists'.[40]

Bredel was not alone. Not only did such public intellectuals as Professor Hans Mayer turn against the 'pan-politicization' of the authorities, bemoaning as well the lack of 'opulence' in the literature of the land, but established writers such as Anna Seghers, Eduard Claudius, Stefan Heym and Bodo Uhse also voiced misgivings about the 'emptiness' (Claudius) and 'wooden primitivism' (Heym) of the entire cultural scene.[41] In addition, even a select few from the younger generation – artists such as Heinz Kahlau, Manfred Bieler, Jens Gerlach, Manfred Streubel or Gerhard Zwerenz – dared to question the party's claims of omnipotence and its increasing efforts at manipulation. Film scriptwriter Kahlau, inspired by the Polish writer Jan Kott, dared, for instance, to draw a connection between a basically 'anti-Marxist Party mythology' and the 'inquisitional repression of troublesome, yet committed literary works lying in the drawers of writers waiting in vain for their readers'.[42]

But Kahlau and the like were to remain a distinct minority who themselves suffered severely from renewed retaliations by the SED leadership. In this regard, it was none other than Johannes R. Becher, chairman of the newly formed Ministry of Culture, who chose to confront a rebellious group of university students calling for public discussion of their officially forbidden studio films with the following punitive rebuke: 'Here we find a symptomatic attempt being made to reverse everything that has been rightfully disallowed by employing the notion of "academic necessity" as a cover for forcing a public explanation. At that rate it won't be long before the demand will be made that we publish the works of Leon Trotsky, so that individuals can make their own assessments of them'.[43] The fears driving the SED at this historical moment are clear. Given the events occurring elsewhere in the Eastern Bloc in the fall of 1956 – the installation of Gomułka in Poland and the workers' strikes and revolutionary uprising in Hungary (which were supported by Georg Lukács!) – there could not and would not be room for tolerance at the level of cultural policy in the GDR.

At the outset of 1957, the SED officially opened a 'new phase' in the area of cultural politics, initiating efforts to bring intellectuals and artists into line at all levels of cultural life. Special conferences were organized to critique 'ideological revisionism' or the younger generation's demands for more 'self-governance', more 'theories of spontaneity' and more 'discussion about the death of the state'.[44] At a meeting of the 32nd Plenum of the Central Committee, the conformist writer Kuba (Kurt Barthel) delivered a rousing address in which he asserted that GDR writers and artists had theretofore done far too little in defence of the leadership of the SED, 'especially our comrade Ulbricht', against 'enemy attacks'.[45] He then went on to accuse them all of opportunism as regards the question of socialist realism:

> It is now the place and the time to ask the writers and artists why so many of them have so easily put aside their earlier resolutions; and how they deal with the question of honesty; and why some comrades have such a silly grin on their face when they utter the word socialist realism. Ergo the struggle must begin anew. Ergo the Marxists among the writers must fire one across the bow of those liberals shooting out of every buttonhole.[46]

Kuba's allegation was in fact quite valid in respect of a substantial segment of the cultural intelligentsia, and as such stands ironically as a verification of the significant failure of the SED's overly doctrinaire cultural policy.

All these points force the question of whether we can indeed speak about a 'period of thaw' when it comes to the production of films in the latter half of the 1950s in the GDR. Certainly one film subgenre that has often been referenced within the framework of cinematic reform during this period was that of the so-called 'Berlin Films': films set in contemporary Berlin of the mid-1950s that focused on the personal experiences of working-class youth under the age of twenty-five in the divided city.⁴⁷ As Horst Claus argues, 'these films are generally regarded as authentic of a generation which was expected to realize the dream of a fair and equal German society in the East. They also bear witness to their creators' insistence on remaining critical voices within the context of the GDR's changing political and cultural policies'.⁴⁸

The 'critical' aspects of the Berlin Films did not emanate from a rejection of socialist values but rather from a determined desire to realize, and at the same time rub against the grain of, a normative socialist realism. Instead of moralistic recrimination and ideological platitudes, the authors of these films, often with considerable success at the box office, sought to provide something like 'analytical starting points' for understanding the motivations of urban youth: the broken relations within East Berlin postwar families as well as the larger generational and societal conflicts outside the home, to which party youth organizations such as the Freie Deutsche Jugend (FDJ, Free German Youth) and even the *Volkspolizei* (people's police) were failing to provide adequate answers.⁴⁹

Unquestionably, a classic example of the Berlin Films was Gerhard Klein and Wolfgang Kohlhaase's *Berlin – Ecke Schönhauser*, which I intend to read as a dialogue with, rather than a repudiation of, the reigning cultural political policies of the 1950s in the area of cinema. This film tells the story of four teenagers between the ages of sixteen and nineteen who belong to a group of youths whose regular meeting place is underneath the elevated train tracks at the corner of Schönhauser Allee and Dimitroffstraße. They provoke passers-by with rock and roll dancing and aggressive reactions to complaints about their appearance and behaviour. Angela, a seamstress, is the daughter of a single mother whose husband was killed in the war. Dieter (played by Bertolt Brecht's son-in-law Ekkehard Schall), a building worker, has lost both his parents and lives together with his brother, a law enforcement officer with the *Volkspolizei*. Kohle is unemployed and lives in a small flat with his widowed mother and her drunken lover. Karl Heinz, the son of a tax consultant, has dropped out of school. All four end up in trouble with various authorities (parental, legal, political, etc.) in East and West Berlin that leads ultimately to Kohle's accidental suicide and a ten-year prison sentence for Karl Heinz for homicide (in an unrelated incident). Blame for the fates of the four teens is meted out to all the parties involved, as summed up succinctly by a sensitive *Volkspolizist* in an exchange with Dieter at the film's conclusion: 'So it's my fault and it's your fault. Where we are not, there are our enemies.'

Various stylistic components that contributed to the complexity and success of *Berlin – Ecke Schönhauser* are indigenous to other Berlin Films as well. First and perhaps most important, we note a subtlety of individual character development that is resolutely not to be reduced to single valances: these figures rebel, take risks and make mistakes, some of which are seemingly obvious as such, some considerably less so. In many instances, judgements as to 'right or wrong' appear to be left up to the viewer to decide. Here we find a paucity of clear-cut positive heroes – or, for that matter, clear-cut villains. Certainly this indeterminacy regarding the allocation of value (political correctness) became a source of critical displeasure for critics in the party who were dedicated to the principles of socialist realism.

A second component of the film, one that proved equally difficult to decipher in terms of orientation and meaning, arises from its mise-en-scène: the divided city of Berlin. The initial scenes clearly mark their turf as that of East Berlin, but the fast-moving plot has three of the four protagonists circulating back and forth within all four sectors of the city in ways that reflect not only complexity but also a sense of ambivalence on their part concerning borders and boundaries, be they geographical, political, philosophical or even aesthetic.

In a subsequent interview, Wolfgang Kohlhaase stressed the highly pronounced influence of Italian neorealism on DEFA filmmakers during the mid-1950s. Although it had emerged at a decidedly earlier period in a very different (Western) context, Kohlhaase found that neorealism brought 'a reality to the screen that strongly resembled the everyday that we are ourselves were experiencing'.[50] The most influential examples of the neorealist aesthetic were the 'critical realist' films by directors like Vittorio de Sica and Roberto Rosselini. In 1948 the latter made his own 'Berlin Film', *Germania Anno Zero*, which also features a young protagonist. Italian critical realism has been described an 'an aesthetic which identifies controversial issues, opens them up for critical debate, and allows formal experiments which enhance and deepen the understanding of reality'.[51]

To sum up the various stylistic components in Klein and Kohlhaase's *Berlin – Ecke Schönhauser* as an exemplar of the Berlin Films, what we find is a film genre that only barely stayed within the framework of acceptable but not officially desired forms of realism, but nevertheless managed to incorporate styles from beyond its own more narrowly constructed cultural-political boundaries. As for outside sources of impact on the film's thematic focus, one need only list contemporaneous movies in the West that also depicted rebellious youth and adolescent dropouts such as *The Wild One* (Laslo Benedek, 1953), *Blackboard Jungle* (Richard Brooks, 1955), *Die Halbstarken* (Wolf Pack, Georg Tressler, 1956), or *Rebel without a Cause* (Nicholas Ray, 1956), featuring actors who become icons of rebellion, such as Marlon Brando, James Dean and Horst Buchholz.

Berlin – Ecke Schönhauser was a hit at the box office and rapidly became a cult film among a segment of the younger generation. Not long thereafter, however, high-ranking party members began to distance themselves from both the Berlin Films and the entire body of film production they considered to be associated with it. At a meeting between the Cultural Department of the Central Committee and members of DEFA in May 1957, leading cultural functionaries condemned tout court the absolute failure of recent films to 'focus for their content on the important processes of the development of our socialist reality'. What they showed instead, they asserted, was 'the image of youth that has not been brought up in the spirit of socialism in high schools and in factories, on sport teams and in the People's Army, but rather a youth culture that finds its home in reform schools, refugee barracks [in West Berlin] or other places of ill breeding'.[52]

The end of the so-called thaw following the Twentieth Party Congress would indeed have an impact on the area of film production over the following years, as articulated at the annual cultural conference of the SED in October 1957: 'The commitment to making films must first and foremost be based on cultural-political considerations in which issues of financial success should also play a role'.[53] In other words, regarding GDR socialist film in the coming seasons, cultural-political and ideological considerations would once again have absolute priority over financial ones.

Thus, it was no surprise that in March 1958 – in anticipation of the upcoming Spielfilmkonferenz des ZK (Central Committee Conference on Feature Films) in July of that year – Anton Ackermann, director of the Film Office in the Ministry of Culture, called for a 'no holds barred open Party discussion in a manner that would not be possible at a public conference'. As an introduction to the first such *Parteiaktivtagung* (party action conference), Ackermann delivered a fifty-page address summing up his critique of film production in recent years under the title 'Fighting Words Aimed at Revisionist Tendencies in the DEFA Studio'. Ackermann's definition of 'revisionism' and the examples provided thereof make clear the extent to which the New Course being advanced by the SED and the Central Committee represented an effort to turn the clock back to the cultural policies that prevailed prior to

1953. He repudiated the 'petit bourgeois' productions of recent years, such as Konrad Wolf's controversial film *Sonnensucher* (Sun Seekers, 1958) and the Berlin Films; spoke against the indifference among DEFA artists about the growing 'Western' orientation evidenced by certain films; and expressed concern about 'the regression from Gorky's realism to the naturalism of Zola'.[54]

At the much-awaited Film Conference of the Ministry of Culture on 3–5 July 1958, Alexander Abusch gave a speech in which he publicly reiterated many of Ackermann's earlier stated grievances and concluded with his own view as to what the appropriate aesthetic should *not* be for analysing individual alienation in a noncapitalist society: 'It must be clear to filmmakers in the GDR that the aesthetics of the Italian neorealists – intended as they are to expose the irresolvable antagonisms of capitalist society and encourage that society to rebel against it – are not appropriate for films set in a Workers' and Peasants' State.... The use of "critical realism" cannot but leave us with a pseudo-representation of the new reality in which we live'.[55]

It is appropriate that we end our discussion of the cultural politics of GDR film in the late 1950s with this recollection of a group of GDR filmmakers struggling for the right to invoke the use of a deviant aesthetic style. What it once again suggests about the importance of a politics of culture (as opposed a cultural policy) concerns precisely the power of artistic articulation as potential bearer of a message that cannot be reduced to unilateral signification. Socialist realism is dogmatic precisely because it already has the answer before the question is asked. Critical realism, as so eloquently practised in some of the Berlin Films, begins its task creatively with a search for 'analytical starting points'. Given the rigour with which the SED reinforced the rigidity of its system in 1958, things would not start to change until the beginning of the 1960s.

David Bathrick is the Jacob Gould Schurman Emeritus Professor of Theatre, Film & Dance and Professor of German and Jewish Studies at Cornell University. Publications include *The Dialectic and the Early Brecht* (1976), *Modernity and the Text* (1989), *The Powers of Speech: The Politics of Culture in the GDR* (1995, awarded the 1996 DAAD/GSA Book of the Year Prize), *Visualizing the Holocaust* (2008), *Literature and Intermediality* (2011) and numerous articles on modern drama, twentieth-century German literature, critical theory, Weimar culture, the cultural politics of East Germany, European film, Holocaust studies, and Nazi cinema. He is also a cofounder and coeditor of *New German Critique*.

Notes

1. *Auf neuen Wegen* (Berlin: Filmverlag, 1951), p. 10, quoted in Christiane Mückenberger and Günter Jordan, *'Sie sehen selbst, Sie hören selbst...': Eine Geschichte der Defa von ihren Anfängen bis 1949* (Marburg: Hitzeroth, 1994), p. 25. Universum Film AG, better known as UFA or Ufa, was the principal film studio in Germany from the 1920s to the end of the Third Reich in 1945. Under the tutelage of Joseph Goebbels it became a powerful instrument of propaganda.
2. Mückenberger and Jordan, *'Sie sehen selbst, Sie hören selbst...'*, p. 14.
3. See ibid., p. 25 for a list of the entire group assembled that day.
4. 'Richard Groschopp in Conversation with Ralf Schenk', *Beiträge zur Film- und Fernsehwissenschaft* 28(3) (1987), 27. Founded in 1922, Terra Film – the second largest film studio in Nazi Germany – was also known for producing effective propaganda films, in particular the anti-Semitic film *Jud Süss* (Veit Harlan, 1940).
5. Thomas Heimann, *Defa, Künstler und SED-Kulturpolitik: Zum Verhältnis von Kulturpolitik und Filmproduktion in der SBZ/DDR 1945 bis 1959* (Berlin: Vistas, 1994), p. 26.
6. See Heide Fehrenbach, *Cinema in Democratizing Germany: Reconstructing National Identity after Hitler* (Chapel Hill and London: University of North Carolina Press, 1995), pp. 51–91 for a discussion of 'American occupation and the politics of film, 1945–1949'.
7. Heimann, *Defa, Künstler und SED-Kulturpolitik*, p. 64.
8. Ibid., p. 83.
9. Vladimir Gall, *Mein Weg nach Halle* (Berlin: Militärverlag, 1988), p. 131.
10. See Brewster S. Chamberlin (ed.), *Kultur auf Trümmern: Berliner Berichte der amerikanischen Information Control Section Juli-Dezember 1945* (Stuttgart: Deutsche Verlagsanstalt, 1979).
11. Gall, *Mein Weg nach Halle*, p. 131.
12. *Tägliche Rundschau*, 18 May 1946. Cited in Seán Allan and John Sandford (eds), *DEFA: East German Cinema 1946–1962* (New York and Oxford: Berghahn Books, 1999), p. 2.
13. The main works of secondary literature that discuss the importance of *Die Mörder sind unter uns* as an antifascist film include Mückenberger and Jordan, *'Sie sehen selbst, Sie hören selbst...'*, pp. 41–52; Horst Knietzsch, *Wolfgang Staudte* (Berlin: Henschelverlag, 1966), pp. 10–14; Eric Rentschler, 'Germany: The Past that Would Not Go Away', in William Luhr (ed.), *World Cinema since 1945* (New York: Ungar, 1987), pp. 210–213; Wolf-Dietrich Schnurre, *Deutsche Filmrundschau*, 11 November 1946; Peter Pleyer, *Deutscher Nachkriegsfilm 1946–1948* (Münster: Verlag C. J. Fahle, 1965), pp. 173–192; Egon Netenjakob, 'Ein Leben gegen die Zeit: Versuch über WS', in *Staudte* (Berlin: Wissenschaftsverlag Volker Spiess, 1991), pp. 22–28; Heinz Kersten, 'Ankläger der Mörder und Untertanen', in Eva Orbanz (ed.), *Wolfgang Staudte* (Berlin: Verlag Volker Spiess, 1977), pp. 14–18; Ellen Blauert (ed.), *Die Mörder sind unter uns/ Ehe im Schatten/Die Buntkarierten/Rotation: Vier Filmerzählungen nach den Bekannten Defa-Filmen* (Berlin, 1969), pp. 9–73.
14. Heimann, *Defa, Künstler und SED-Kulturpolitik*, p. 60.
15. For Staudte's own discussion of the endings see *Vier Filmerzählungen*.
16. Thomas Brandlmaier, 'Von Hitler zu Adenauer: Deutsche Trümmerfilme', in Hilmar Hoffmann and Walter Schobert (eds), *Zwischen Gestern und Morgen: Nachkriegsfilm 1946–1962* (Frankfurt am Main: Schriftenreihe des deutschen Filmmuseums, 1989), p. 39.
17. See here Barton Byg, 'Defa and Traditions of International Cinema', in Allan and Sandford, *DEFA: East German Cinema 1946–1962*, pp. 26–35.

18. Rentschler, in 'Germany: The Past that Would Not Go Away', mentions *Das Cabinet des Dr. Caligari* (The Cabinet of Dr. Caligari, Robert Wiene, 1919) in regards to this film (p. 211); Mückenberg and Jordan mention both *Das Cabinet des Dr. Caligari* and *Der letzte Mann* (The Last Laugh, Friedrich Wilhelm Murnau, 1924) in *'Sie sehen selbst, Sie hören selbst...'*, pp. 45–46).
19. See Hans-Michael Bock and Tim Bergfelder, *The Concise Cinegraph: The Encyclopedia of German Cinema* (New York and Oxford: Berghahn Books, 2009), p. 32. Here Friedl Behn-Grund is described as 'renowned for his atmospheric lighting, sublime close-ups and ability to adapt to the requirements of individual directors'.
20. Ralf Schenk, 'Auferstanden aus Ruinen', in *Das Ufa-Buch: Kunst und Krisen, Stars und Regisseure, Wirtschaft und Politik* (Frankfurt am Main: Zweitausenundeins, 1992) makes the following qualification concerning the role of German expressionism in Staudte's first film: '"It has been said a hundred times: in 1945 it was normal that German film would pick up again with Expressionism. That proves simply the sterilizing impact of the Hitler period and the fact that one had to start somewhere", wrote the French critic Chris Marker in 1954 in order to excuse postwar German film. Wolfgang Staudte's *Die Mörder sind unter uns* shows one important variation on this theme: with small, unimportant people, who are plagued by big problems, placed into real rubble settings, which appear to be constructed, Staudte gives a sketch of the spiritual condition of the German people. Real victims of the Hitler period are not to be found' (p. 477).
21. Seàn Allan, 'DEFA: An Historical Overview', in Allan and Sandford, *DEFA: East German Cinema 1946–1992*, p. 5.
22. Protokoll der Arbeitstagung der Abteilungen Parteischulung, Kultur und Erziehung der Länderorganisationen der SED vom 7-9.9.1948. Cited in Heimann, *Defa, Künstler und SED-Kulturpolitik*, p. 91.
23. Alexander Dymshits, 'Uber die formalistische Richtung in der deutschen Malerei', *Tägliche Rundschau*, 19 November 1948.
24. Heimann, *Defa, Künstler und SED-Kulturpolitik*, p. 93.
25. Joshua J. First, 'Scenes of Belonging: Cinema and the Nationality Question in Soviet Ukraine during the Long 1960s' (PhD Dissertation, University of Michigan, 2011), p. 25.
26. 'Der Kampf gegen den Formalismus in Kunst und Literatur, Entschließung', *Einheit* 6 (8/9) (1951), 583–591.
27. For a more extensive treatment of the formalism debate in the GDR, see David Bathrick, *The Powers of Speech: The Politics of Culture in the GDR* (Lincoln and London: University of Nebraska Press, 1995), pp. 87–107.
28. Subtitle of an early widely read book on the GDR by the West German scholar Ernst Riechert, *Das Zweite Deutschland – ein Staat, der nicht sein darf* (Frankfurt am Main: S. Fischer Taschenbuch, 1967).
29. See David Bathrick, 'The Dialectics of Legitimation: Brecht in the GDR', *New German Critique* 2(Spring) (1974), 90–103.
30. Quoted in Jürgen Rühle, *Das gefesselte Theater* (Cologne: Kiepenheuer & Witsch, 1957), p. 243.
31. Heimann, *Defa, Künstler und SED-Kulturpolitik*, p. 113.
32. Daniela Berghahn, *Hollywood behind the Wall: The Cinema of East Germany* (Manchester and New York: Manchester University Press, 2005), p. 73.
33. See David Bathrick, 'From UFA to DEFA: Past as Present in Early GDR Films', in Jost Hermand and Marc Silberman (eds), *Contentious Memories: Looking Back at the GDR* (New York: Peter Lang, 1998), pp. 169–188.

34. Heimann, *Defa, Künstler und SED-Kulturpolitik*, p. 138.
35. Allan, 'DEFA: An Historical Overview', p. 8.
36. Heimann, *Defa, Künstler und SED-Kulturpolitik*, p. 172.
37. Günter Agde (ed.), *Kurt Maetzig – Filmarbeit: Gespräche, Reden, Schriften* (Berlin: Henschelvertrag, 1987), p. 249.
38. Carsten Gansel (ed.), *Der gespaltene Dichter Johannes R. Becher: Gedichte, Briefe, Dokumente 1945–1958* (Berlin: Aufbau-Taschenbuch-Verlag, 1991), pp. 139–151.
39. Willi Bredel's remarks at the Third Party Conference of the SED, 1956. Cited in Heimann, *Defa, Künstler und SED-Kulturpolitik*, p. 257.
40. Ibid.
41. See Wolfgang Emmerich, *Kleine Literaturgeschichte der DDR* (Berlin: Aufbau Taschenbuch, 2007), pp. 18–131.
42. Heinz Kahlau, *Forum* 12 (1956). p. 63.
43. Becher's remarks in discussion at the 28th Central Committee meeting on 29 July 1956, quoted in Gansel, *Der gespaltene Dichter Johannes R. Becher*, p. 161.
44. Heimann, *Defa, Künstler und SED-Kulturpolitik*, p. 260.
45. Stenographic recording of the proceedings of the 32nd Central Committee Plenum of the SED, 10–12 July 1957. Cited in Heimann, *Defa, Künstler und SED-Kulturpolitik*, p. 261.
46. Ibid.
47. Here one could mention in particular Heiner Carow's *Sheriff Teddy* (1957), Kurt Maetzig's *Vergeßt mir meine Traudel nicht* (Don't Forget my Little Traudel, 1957) and Joachim Kunert's *Tatort Berlin* (Place of Crime: Berlin, 1957), plus *Eine Berliner Romanze* (A Berlin Romance, 1956) and *Berlin – Ecke Schönhauser* (Berlin, Schoenhauser Corner, 1957), both made by Gerhard Klein and Wolfgang Kohlhaase.
48. Horst Claus, 'Rebels with a Cause: The Development of the "Berlin Filme" by Gerhard Klein and Wolfgang Kohlhaase', in Allan and Sandford, *DEFA: East German Cinema 1946–1992*, pp. 95.
49. Reinhard Wagner, *Vom Ringen um sozialistische Positionen. Über den Beitrag des DEFA Spielfilms mit ernster problemorientierter Gegenwartsthematik zur Schaffung von geistigen Grundlagen des Sozialismus (1950 bis 1962). Akademie der Gesellschaftswissenschaften beim ZK der SED* (Berlin: Dietz Verlag, 1985), p. 179.
50. 'Apropos Kino: Wolfgang Kohlhaase im Gespräch mit Klaus Wischnewski', *Film und Fernsehen* 16(1) (1998), 10–15.
51. Horst Claus, 'Rebels with a Cause', p. 95.
52. Heimann, *Defa, Künstler und SED-Kulturpolitik*, p. 302.
53. 'Für eine sozialistische Kultur – Die Entwicklung der sozialistischen Kultur in der Zeit des zweiten Fünfjahrplanes. Thesen der Kulturkonerenz der SED 23./24 . 10. 1957', *Neues Deutschland*, 7 December 1957.
54. Protokoll der Parteiaktivtagung vom 6.3.1958. Cited in Heimann, *Defa, Künstler und SED-Kulturpolitik*, pp. 306–307.
55. Alexander Abusch, 'Aktuelle Probleme und Aufgaben unserer sozialistischen Filmkunst: Referat der Konferenz des VEB DEFA Studio für Spielfilme und des Ministeriums für Kultur der DDR', *Deutsche Filmkunst* 6(9) (1958), 267.

Select Bibliography

Allan, Seán, and John Sandford (eds). *DEFA: East German Cinema 1946–1962.* New York and Oxford: Berghahn Books, 1999.

Berghahn, Daniela. *Hollywood behind the Wall: The Cinema of East Germany.* Manchester and New York: Manchester University Press, 2005.

Chamberlin, Brewster S. (ed.). *Kultur auf Trümmern: Berliner Berichte der amerikanischen Information Control Section Juli-Dezember 1945.* Stuttgart: Deutsche Verlagsanstalt, 1979.

Fehrenbach, Heide. *Cinema in Democratizing Germany: Reconstructing National Identity after Hitler.* Chapel Hill and London: University of North Carolina Press, 1995.

Gansel, Carsten (ed.). *Der gespaltene Dichter Johannes R. Becher: Gedichte, Briefe, Dokumente 1945–1958.* Berlin: Aufbau-Taschenbuch-Verlag, 1991.

Heimann, Thomas. *Defa, Künstler und SED-Kulturpolitik: Zum Verhältnis von Kulturpolitik und Filmproduktion in der SBZ/DDR 1945 bis 1959.* Berlin: Vistas, 1994.

Hoffmann, Hilmar, and Walter Schobert (eds). *Zwischen Gestern und Morgen: Nachkriegsfilm 1946–1962.* Frankfurt am Main: Schriftenreihe des deutschen Filmmuseums, 1989.

Mückenberger, Christine, and Günter Jordan. *'Sie sehen selbst, Sie hören selbst...': Eine Geschichte der Defa von ihren Anfängen bis 1949.* Marburg: Hitzeroth, 1994.

Pleyer, Peter. *Deutscher Nachkriegsfilm 1946–1948.* Münster: Verlag C. J. Fahle, 1965.

Schenk, Ralf. 'Auferstanden aus Ruinen', in *Das Ufa-Buch: Kunst und Krisen, Stars und Regisseure, Wirtschaft und Politik.* Frankfurt am Main: Zweitausenundeins, 1992.

Chapter 2

Czechoslovak Culture and Cinema, 1945–1960

Jiří Knapík

Culture under the Rule of the National Front (1945–1948)

The basic conditions of public life in Czechoslovakia after World War II differed fundamentally from what the society had known during the so-called First Republic (1918–1938). Even though a significant portion of the public and their political representatives endorsed a democratic system in the tradition of 'Masarykian democracy', in 1945 it was already apparent that the conditions of the so-called Third Republic (1945–1948) would be quite distinct from those that had preceded the war. Free political competition was fundamentally limited because the traditional right-wing parties could not be revived. In addition, the sizeable German minority population was expelled from Czechoslovakia and extensive transfers of property were initiated. At the same time, the Communist Party of Czechoslovakia (Komunistická strana Československa, KSČ) began to exert itself forcefully. Already in these early years, the party was beginning to fundamentally undermine the basic principles of the democratic rule of law by using the state security forces and other armed units to achieve its goals.

These social changes naturally had an effect on cultural activities in the country as well. During the first months of peace, the society was (at least in its external appearance) marked by a sense of euphoria inspired by the renewal of the Czechoslovak state, the end of the cultural and social restrictions that had been in force during the last phase of the war, and the prospect of 'building a new republic'. Czechoslovak cultural life was able to renew active contact with the culture of Western Europe. At the same time, however, the state also began promoting the import of Soviet art – a process vividly evident in the area of film production. After years of censorship during the war, Czechoslovak film received new creative inspiration from Western cinema by way of the world-renowned masterpieces being screened in the country, as well as from the input of the many Czechoslovak artists now returning to the country after having emigrated to escape Nazism. In addition to Western films, Czechoslovak cinemas also played important Soviet works. Italian neorealism became an important model for exploring social themes in film.

The basic political impulse guiding the modifications in cultural life after 1945 was a concept known as 'democratization of culture', which had its roots in the Košický vládní program (Košice Government Programme) as a point of agreement that united the interests of all political parties affiliated with the National Front (Národní fronta).[1] In addition to outlining this idea, the programme also spoke of 'ideological revision', understood as the targeted reinforcement of a 'Slavic', and primarily pro-Soviet, orientation in cultural politics combined with a disavowal of any German cultural heritage in the Czech lands.[2] The Košice Government Plan understood the democratization of culture as 'providing the broadest segments of the population with access to schools and other sources of education and culture' and pursuing the ideological goal of 'popularizing this system of education and cultural appreciation, not to serve a narrow segment of the population, but to serve the people and the nation'.[3] Initially, these formulations were kept sufficiently open and nonspecific to retain the approval of all parties in the National Front, yet their propagation under the attractive motto 'culture for the people' resulted in strict regulation of the book market, expropriation of private theatres, and nationalization of the National Gallery (Národní galerie) and Czech Philharmonic Orchestra (Česká filharmonie).[4] The KSČ became the leading architect and propagator of policy associated with the 'democratization of culture'. The party's primary goals in the realm of culture were to strengthen the state's role in the broadest spectrum of cultural institutions while at the same time gradually limiting private persons' ability to function and operate. The degree to which the private sector should be preserved in the field of culture became an important matter of debate between the KSČ and the other, democratic parties, who rightly saw the further strengthening of state power as a danger that would increase the Communists' influence.

In the first years after the war, cinema industry underwent the process of a 'cleansing'. Indeed, the Košice Government Programme demanded such measures from the culture as a whole as a means of dealing with those who had actively collaborated with Nazism. In reality, though, the process was highly politicized, and in the realm of cinema this 'cleansing' occurred in a very complicated way that ushered in an atmosphere of distrust and chaos, settling of personal accounts and the like. Political pressure from the KSČ also determined the specific course of things. *Tvorba* (Creation), a weekly communist magazine on culture and politics, published a characteristic line of argument, according to which 'it is not only a matter of excluding from Czechoslovak filmmaking those against whom we can use the letter of the law, but also everyone who has offended the national honour in the broad sense of the word'.[5] The original disciplinary committee had found only a small number of offenders, an unsatisfactory result that prompted the communists to call for a review of the results of the audits – which also identified only a fairly small number of evident collaborators. Only a fraction of the approximately 300 investigated cases found their way to the popular court. By contrast, exemplary punishment was meted out to actors and film entrepreneurs who had had high exposure during the occupation. These figures (Vlasta Burian, Lída Baarová, Adina Mandlová, Miloš Havel, etc.) also embodied a strong link with the prewar Czechoslovak film culture and its artistic qualities.[6] A number of others secured their impeccability by acquiring a KSČ membership card.

The most crucial intervention in the development of Czechoslovak cinema was the nationalization of the film industry, which we can understand as one of the primary manifestations of the policy of so-called democratization of the culture.[7] Somewhat paradoxically, the idea of nationalization itself had originated in the thinking of responsible filmmaking functionaries as early as the second half of the 1930s and was subsequently reflected in the concentration of film management in the hands of the state during the Nazi occupation. Thus, the postwar developments did not constitute a major discontinuity in the development of Czechoslovak film. Furthermore, during the war the Czechoslovak resistance had also taken up the idea of nationalizing the film industry and worked on it at various levels. Along with the National Revolutionary Intelligence Committee (Národně revoluční výbor inteligence, headed by Vladislav Vančura), such personalities of film culture as František Papoušek, Jindřich Elbl, František Pilát, Lubomír Linhart and Elmar Klos, among others, participated in preparations for the nationalization. The basic concept (as of the year 1944) was also introduced to Czechoslovak political representatives in exile in London and Moscow. The premise was that the process of centralization that had occurred during the occupation made it impossible to return to the prewar state of things. It was assumed that the inclusion of film in the state-controlled economy would give filmmakers independence from the commercial interests of private producers and subsequently raise the artistic standards of the cinema.[8] Another assumption was that a nationalized cinema would be self-sufficient, in other words profitable, mainly due to revenue from the cinema theatres.[9]

By May 1945, the expropriation of cinemas had begun with those owned by Germans, and the administration of all film studios was taken over by so-called factory councils. The Ministry of Information, a KSČ stronghold, was entrusted with managing cinema affairs. This new state of things was eventually codified in law by the decree 50/1945 Sb., which was signed by President Edvard Beneš on 11 August 1945 and became legally effective on 28 August.[10] This decree became the key standard for cinema throughout the postwar period. It should be added that the cinema was the first branch of the Czechoslovak economy to be nationalized. The decree granted the state the exclusive authority 'to maintain film studios, to manufacture exposed cinematographic films ... to process films in a laboratory, to rent films, and to publicly screen them', and further 'to import and export films for the whole territory of the Czechoslovak Republic'.[11] Existing companies and entrepreneurs were obliged to surrender to the state all operating equipment and resources, including film prints and film stock as well as all business premises, whether owned or rented. According to the decree, former owners had the right to compensation for the nationalized property; however, many entitled claimants never received it. The nationalization of the extensive network of cinemas belonging to important Czech associations and clubs (Sokol, Orel and Dělnická tělovýchovná jednota, among others) became a very sensitive political topic, particularly in the case of Sokol, which was closely linked to the Czech national emancipation at the end of the nineteenth century.[12]

As mentioned above, the KSČ gained considerable influence in the sphere of culture in 1945. It should be remembered that between the wars, Czechoslovak culture had been significantly enriched by a number of modern avant-garde artists with leftist and partially pro-communist orientations.[13] By contrast, Czechoslovak culture had no experience of a phenomenon like the institutionally anchored influence represented by the political leadership of the KSČ with Klement Gottwald at its head. It must be said that the KSČ enjoyed the support of a significant segment of Czechoslovak society, especially in the first year after liberation. Besides the society's general leaning towards leftist parties after World War II, a phenomenon observed throughout Europe, the KSČ specifically profited from a well-formulated political programme free of ideological excesses, which it managed to express in a nationalistically oriented tone that resonated with the majority of Czech society. For a significant number of citizens, the party became a natural guarantor of social progress and 'the Czech path to socialism' that constituted one of the apexes of the entire political process.

The KSČ also gained the support of a significant part of Czech society's intellectual elite and deliberately utilized this support in its campaign prior to the parliamentary elections in May 1946, in which it scored a marked victory.[14] Symbolic evidence of this support can be seen in the so-called *Májové poselství kulturních pracovníků českému lidu* (May Message from the Workers in Culture to the Czech people), signed by nearly one thousand cultural representatives, and not only by organized members of the KSČ.[15] At the same time, it should be stressed, the support of the cultural intelligentsia was based on a carefully constructed 'two-facedness': outwardly, the party promoted a cultural agenda (introduced at the Eighth Congress of the KSČ) that was ideologically oriented towards socialism; yet at the same time it did not enforce any specific art forms to realize this agenda. In this way, the KSČ sought to create the impression that it was not bound by the paradigms of Soviet art that had been formulated in the Stalinist cultural policy of the 1930s. In so doing, the KSČ involved itself in the ideological contest between various artistic and aesthetic concepts that had entered the field of Czechoslovak culture in 1945 and played out against each other in a series of cultural-political polemics in the press and in various cultural forums.

'The tolerant face' of the communist cultural policy was in fact only a carefully constructed strategy to assert the party's influence in the area of culture. In reality, a group of cultural politicians was formed within the core apparatus of the KSČ.[16] Carefully navigating between Marxist orthodoxy and moderate practical politics, this group intervened when necessary among the (pro)communist cultural intelligentsia, or even resorted to administrative measures.[17] The real positions and intentions of the KSČ were partly revealed by the supportive stance its cultural strategists assumed with regard to the Soviet intervention against literary magazines in Leningrad in the summer of 1946. This stance declared the enduring validity of the criteria of the Stalinist cultural policy, as formulated by the Soviet head ideologist Andrei Zhdanov.[18] Evidently, the KSČ's influence among the cultural intelligentsia began to stagnate in autumn 1946, and all public activities of the Communist Party until February 1948 served to polarize the cultural sphere. The KSČ was able to strengthen its influence only through behind-the-scenes machinations. Cultural politics was starting to become a proper weapon in the political struggle.

The aforementioned Ministry of Information, with the prominent communist politician Václav Kopecký at its head, became the foundation of the Communist Party's political and ideological influence on Czechoslovak culture.[19] For a limited time, until the summer of 1946, the communists also had control of the Ministry of Education and Enlightenment, led by historian and musicologist Zdeněk Nejedlý.[20] The KSČ heavily asserted its influence in the broad cultural activities of the Revolutionary Trade Union Movement (Revoluční odborové hnutí), the only trade union allowed after 1945.[21]

Minister of Information Kopecký surrounded himself at the ministry with a number of prominent communist artists. The core of the ministry was composed of five departments: a publishing department, led by prominent Czech poet František Halas; the radio department under the writer Ivan Olbracht; the foreign affairs department, headed by the visual artist Adolf Hoffmeister; the cultural department with its highly substantial role; and, starting in May 1945, a film department directed by the poet Vítězslav Nezval. This latter department supervised the planning, production and distribution of all types of films, handled import and export film contracts, and managed contacts with foreign institutions. It also instituted the legal norms of economic plans in the area of film and directed the operation and building of cinemas as well as their transfer to state ownership. Minister Kopecký also appointed deputies for individual sectors of the film industry, nine of which were operating in film after May 1945: studios and laboratories, production of feature films, rental, management of state-owned cinemas, film import and export, the Czechoslovak film chronicle, the Czechoslovak state Centre for Cinemafication, the Czechoslovak Film Institute and, finally, economic and financial matters. As representatives of the state, the deputies provisionally exercised the exclusive right of the state within the film industry. The Czechoslovak Film Society, with the communist film critic Lubomír Linhart at its head, undertook to administer the nationalized film sector beginning in

February 1946.[22] Paradoxically, prior to 1948 the film society and the film department of the ministry argued heatedly as to their jurisdiction and influence over cinema matters.

At the same time, the film department of the Ministry of Information was in charge of maintaining state dramaturgical supervision of artistic production. To this end an agency named State Dramaturgy was founded to (among other things) guide artists towards specific subject matter. In September 1946, a significant reorganization in the production of art films (including animated films as well as feature-length narrative films) entailed the establishment of an important new authority, the Film Artistic Board (Filmový umělecký sbor, FIUS), which would have influence over the particular look of individual films: An advisory agency of the Minister of Information, the board operated within State Dramaturgy. The board further deepened the state's (not to mention the KSČ's) influence on film production. Minister Kopecký entrusted the chairmanship of FIUS to the writer Jiří Mařánek, hitherto head of the dramaturgy section of the ministry's film department. Important (and predominantly communist) literati such as Marie Majerová, Marie Pujmanová, Václav Řezáč and Jan Drda, as well as leading directors including Otakar Vávra and Martin Frič, became members. Above all else, FIUS assessed the form and quality of particular film scripts and returned them to the authors with comments from its members for binding corrections.

Film art production within the nationalized cinema relied on experienced directors from the prewar era, the majority of whom were in some way loyal to the communists, and a number of young, new directors who either were members of the KSČ or supporters of the Social Democratic Party (which unified with the KSČ after February 1948), or were nonpartisan. The KSČ sought to strengthen its influence over this creative core of the nationalized cinema even before February 1948. The party had made similar efforts (as other parties of the National Front had done with lesser success) between 1945 and 1948 with several professional cultural organizations, which together with state-controlled structures created a marginal space for cultural self-governance that was autonomous, at least from the outside. In the case of cinema, the Syndicate of Czechoslovak Film Artists and Technicians (Syndikát československých filmových umělců a techniků, founded in August 1946) became such a representative organization.[23]

The most notable event in the development of postwar Czechoslovak cinema – the transfer of all elements of the film industry to state ownership – was accepted by most functionaries and artists as a logical and essentially correct step that would lead to optimal use of the state's entire artistic potential. At the same time, though, nationalization enabled the KSČ to take control of cinema more rapidly and to a far greater extent than it could in other areas of Czech culture and art. Before the KSČ seized full state power in February 1948, the nationalized cinema had been able to take pride in a number of outstanding successes seen as confirming the correctness of the path that had been marked out. Karel Steklý's social drama *Siréna* (The Strike, 1947), an adaptation of a novel by Marie Majerová, received the main prize of the Golden Lion at the 1947 Venice International Film Festival. That same year saw the production of the first Czech colour film, Vladimír Borský's historical drama *Jan Roháč z Dubé* (Warriors of Faith, 1947). The nationalization of the cinema gave animated film a major boost, seen particularly in the works of Hermína Týrlová and Jiří Trnka, which achieved worldwide recognition. The process of nationalization also professionalized the film craft: in addition to the founding of the Czechoslovak Film Institute, this period also saw the creation of the Film faculty of the Academy of Performing Arts (Filmová fakulta Akademie múzických umění, FAMU), established by state decree No. 127/1945 Sb. of 27 October 1945.[24]

Culture in Stalin's Shadow (1948–1953)

The period from 1948 to 1953 marks an essential watershed in modern Czech history. During its first three years, the communist regime established the foundations of the new social order, whereby the party, as the country's key postwar political force, was able to take advantage of the trends that had started in 1945 or even earlier. This was also the case in the sphere of culture – by about 1950 the regime had managed to politically and ideologically subjugate the realm of culture and art, and the system that was created at this time managed to persist with only partial modifications (most distinctly after 1956) until the collapse of the communist regime in 1989.[25]

The management of cultural life in the broader sense of the word and the steering of artistic expression relied on the collaboration of two key power structures: on one hand the party and the state apparatus, specifically the Culture and Publicity Department of the Central Committee of the Communist Party of Czechoslovakia (Kulturní a propagační oddělení Ústředního výboru Komunistické strany Československa),[26] and on the other the Ministry of Culture, Ministry of

Information and Enlightenment, and Ministry of Education, Science, and Art. The importance of the party structures in the management of culture steadily increased after 1948 (in accordance with general trends); the exponents of 'kultprop' within the KSČ Central Committee began to operate in the departments formally subordinate to the secretaries in order to push through the party's directives, or more precisely to ensure smooth coordination between the party centre and the state political structures.[27] Such practices were very effective in the early stages of building the system but also harboured certain risks, resulting in tension and competition between the state and party divisions responsible for managing cultural politics in the years 1949–1951.

The state and party organizations maintained control over a colourful palette of cultural groups and institutions, which the communist representatives themselves called the 'transmission levers' (*převodové páky*) for managing culture. Selective groups founded on ideological principles, called 'creative unions' (of writers, plastic artists, composers, etc.), played an important role in the realm of art, as well as educational institutions, cultural facilities and mass communal organizations like the Revolutionary Trade Union Movement, the Czechoslovak Youth Union (Československý svaz mládeže, after 1950) and the Union of Czechoslovak-Soviet Friendship (Svaz československo-sovětského přátelství), which administered specific cultural programmes aimed at different levels of society.

The communist regime always regarded the cinema as an exceptionally important part of the cultural sphere that possessed great potential to influence society and introduce ideas about the nature of the socialist art – hence the KSČ's interventions in film management prior to February 1948. The 'post-takeover' arrangements only continued with these interventions or further expanded on them as necessary.[28] The national enterprise Czechoslovak State Film (Československý státní film, ČSF) had been founded in March 1948 in accordance with government ordinance No. 72/1948 Sb. The Ministry of Information instituted personnel changes to establish a strong central directorate at and also removed Oldřich Macháček from the post of central director, where he had served since summer 1948. In addition, the cinema was also hit by a wave of post-February purges that befell all areas of culture and art and primarily disbarred politically 'inconvenient' personalities from cultural life. These purges played out slightly differently in the film sphere, targeting mainly technical professions as opposed to the artistic elite, who by this time were no longer a concern because the Communist Party had secured control over this sphere prior to February 1948. Besides the nonartistic professions, the purges particularly targeted the workers at Short Film (Krátký film), News Film (Zpravodajský film), the Film Institute (Filmový ústav), the Central Administration of Cinemas (Ústřední správa kin), State Film Rental (Státní půjčovna filmů) and the managers of Prague cinemas, among others.

In autumn 1948, the Committee for Culture of the KSČ carried out a major reorganization that affected the entire process of artistic filmmaking, of feature narrative films in particular.[29] The pre-existing FIUS and the system of pre-February creative production groups were not keeping up with post-February needs. FIUS was therefore disbanded in November 1948 and replaced by two new approval boards: the Film Council (Filmová rada, FR) and Central Dramaturgy (Ústřední dramaturgie, ÚD), which were intended to guarantee rapid turnaround in filming the 'new topics', to ensure consistency in film production planning and to maintain strict ideological supervision. The Film Council, a tool of political surveillance, functioned as an advisory body to the Minister of Information. Its task was to prepare a plan of film production topics according to political and ideological specifications. Basically, its purpose was similar that of the Czech National Edition Council (Národní ediční rada česká), established to control the publishing of books and other nonperiodic publications, or the Theatre and Dramaturgy Council (Divadelní a dramaturgická rada), which the Ministry of Education commissioned to reform the theatre network and its entire repertoire. The other tool for controlling film production, Central Dramaturgy, was run by the director of ČSF and was supposed to ensure uninterrupted production of films. It acquired scripts and processed them with attention to artistic qualities. It also founded creative collective teams modelled on the earlier creative production groups and supplemented by a number of young pro-regime artists (see also Petr Szczepanik's essay in this volume). These teams, meant to serve as a sort of new workshop for daily film activity, were to take the initiative on developing subject matter in the spirit of the 'new topics'.

The effort to rigorously plan and politically control film production in the years 1948–1951 led to the creation of a bureaucratically demanding process of approval that caused an abrupt decline in both artistic and formal standards of films and directly contributed to a disproportional increase in the time needed to make a film because 'fundamental' ideological suggestions could potentially turn up in every phase of the approval process.[30] Film's political importance became evident in the process of systematic 'cinefication', which soon put Czechoslovakia in the ranks of European countries with the densest networks of cinemas. This was yet another sign of the efforts to 'democratize' culture, a goal to be realized through the territorial distribution of cultural estates. With regard to cinema, these efforts also led to the creation, during the first half of the 1950s, of a tradition of workers' film festivals and a specific initiative referred to as 'Film Spring in the Village'.[31]

The ideological demands on artistic production were not applied with consistent pressure in the years after the inception of the regime. Until autumn 1948, we can speak about a certain 'transitional' period when the Communist party allowed certain alternative approaches to linger. The representatives of cultural politics tried to redress this at the Congress of National Culture in April 1948, but later developments show this to have been merely a tactical manoeuvre on their part.[32] In summer and especially autumn of 1948 in the sphere of culture, there emerged new impulses dedicated to promoting Stalin's thesis of 'intensifying the class struggle' during the period of building socialism and later to announcing the politics of 'strict direction'. Consequently the realm of cultural politics was burdened with the programmatic task of quickly building a new 'socialist culture' with the aid of political pressure and administrative interventions. A programme of socialist realism for new art production was laid out, founded on theories of Soviet ideologist Andrei Zhdanov and other representatives of Soviet cultural politics. The national cultural heritage began to be comprehensively revised, and hitherto prevailing values of Czech culture were reinterpreted with the aim of suppressing democratic traditions and Western influences. Thus Czech culture was systematically isolated from the Western world, especially after 1949. The politicians were initially under the impression that this process would be carried out fairly quickly, but these initial conceptions were far from realistic.[33] In particular, the process of 'searching for socialist culture' – the constructive determination of new artistic values – introduced unavoidable pitfalls. A whole series of ideological campaigns, together with a search for diverse cultural 'aberrations', took place within its framework.

The events in the realm of cinema also played an active part in the formulation of new standards for Czechoslovak fine art. The establishment of 'class criteria' for art production in general involved the introduction of panels composed of select blue-collar workers that were intended to serve as a guarantee of 'correct' evaluation of individual works and their contribution to socialist art. These panels were established at the first Workers' Film Festival in Zlín in summer 1948, and their assessments were purposefully compared with the results of the

International Film Festival in Marienbad (moved to Karlsbad in 1950), where a jury of expert film critics still had the first word. Owing to the radicalization of cultural politics in this period, the panels of blue-collar workers gained the power to ban particular artworks and prohibit their authors' further artistic activity. The aforementioned panels at the Zlín festival instigated the ostracization of film director František Čáp, which prompted him to emigrate in 1949.[34] The pressure the blue-collar workers exerted in their role as cultural officers also contributed to the distribution ban on the film *Dvaasedmdesátka* (The Number Seventy-Two, 1948) by director Jiří Slavíček in autumn 1948. They labelled the psychologically oriented film 'ideologically vapid and formalistic junk' and even asked the ČSF management to guarantee that such works would no longer be produced.[35] In addition, the so-called Blue-Collar Workers' Creative Collective became active in the film studios as of spring 1949, although its results would later be contested.

In April 1950 the presidium of the Central Committee of the KSČ passed a resolution titled 'On behalf of high ideological and artistic standards for Czechoslovak film', which proclaimed itself the main cultural-political directive for cinema and went on to have a fundamental impact on film artistic production.[36] The publication of this document, later known as the 'Resolution on Film' (its wording was in fact prepared by the Cultural Council of the Central Committee of the KSČ), became an integral part of the process of comprehensively applying the standards of socialist realism to Czech art, which the Communist leadership had initiated in 1950. This was not a matter of chance but rather the culmination of a three-year process to formulate the elemental principles of totalitarian social governance and the basic framework for party-state cultural management, which was seen as the prime guarantor of the unification of cultural events and artistic expression.

Although the leadership of the KSČ could claim some successes in the realm of film production – among post-February works, they cited in particular Vávra's *Němá barikáda* (Silent Barricade, 1949) and Mach's *Vzbouření na vsi* (The Village Revolt, 1951) – in general the Resolution on Film pointed out 'serious shortcomings' in the process, specifically an 'ideologically vapid routine', an apolitical approach, remnants of formalism and a tendency towards a schematic approach when aiming for engaged production. The resolution addressed in detail two main areas of demands: ideological and artistic standards. In the first case, it primarily advocated greater orientation towards 'engaged topics' – that is, the 'new topics' – in film production. The resolution listed a number of political and economical topics that were to be artistically interpreted; these interpretations were also supposed to present a balanced depiction of socio-historic connections and how they are reflected in specific individuals. This approach shifted the focus of creative work to the dramaturge and scriptwriter, a situation analogous to that in the theatrical arts: the film director was seen as a mere implementer of the work's 'idea'. As for the subject matter aspect of film production, its composition was supposed to ensure the dominance of the current theme of 'building socialism' (with special attention to the process of collectivization).

At the same time, other themes and genres were also supposed to specifically reflect this priority. Particular attention was given to historic films, which were supposed to contribute to the legitimization of communist power ('they must not be an attempt to escape from the current issues'),[37] and comedies ('they must not become only entertaining, apolitical spectacle').[38] Beyond feature films, these viewpoints were intended as a directive also for popular scientific (*vědecko populární*) and documentary pictures, as well as children's films. With regard to artistic interpretation, which it understood as an equally important ideological demand, the resolution stressed the importance of the socialist realist method but also added the caveat that 'film production must refrain from all pitfalls of the naturalist and static description of reality and vulgarization'. With its straightforward simplicity, the Resolution on Film is the pinnacle example of schematism in the realm of art production at the beginning of the 1950s.

The cultural climate from 1949 to 1951 was strongly influenced by power struggles and ideological disputes between the party and state apparatuses, which can be understood as a specificity of the regime's so-called founding period. In terms of cultural politics (as well as the cinema), these conflicts were reflected in the antagonism between the Central Committee's head ideologist, Gustav Bareš, and Minister of Information Václav Kopecký. Particularly when evaluating the development of the cultural politics in the sphere of art, researchers often attempt to interpret this antagonism as a confrontation between more rigid and more liberal directions. Here state officials, represented by Václav Kopecký and to a great extent the prominent communist poet and functionary Vítězslav Nezval, are perceived as exponents of the latter trend, which is characterized by greater respect for the legacy of the interwar avant-garde and other national-cultural traditions.[39] However, this common interpretation is not sufficiently convincing. The root of this whole conflict should not be conceived as an antagonism in the fundamental ideological starting points, but rather as a basic struggle for power.

The years 1951 and 1952 were a very difficult period for cultural politics and artistic life. At this time crises connected with the new system of culture management began to develop. Further exacerbating the situation were the political show trials that crippled the state and particularly the party structures at that time, a development that climaxed in the arrest and subsequent execution of General Secretary of the Communist Party Rudolf Slánský as an alleged head of the 'anti-state conspiracy central'.[40] The crisis combined with militarization to also affect the cultural sphere, that is, cultural politics. The ideological injection that the cultural strategists had imagined would guarantee and speed up 'the building of socialist society' after February 1948 began to have a counterproductive effect. Fatigue from the never-ending series of massive ideological campaigns, frustration with the all-penetrating bureaucracy and even doubts or disillusionment about the correctness of post-February developments began to spread among cultural workers and artists as well as the whole society. In fact, a noteworthy paradox developed. The post-February system had managed quite efficiently and quickly to eliminate all inconvenient personalities and ideas from cultural life, drastically reducing contacts between Czechoslovak culture and the Western world and also trying to change cultural stereotypes. However, this system could not come to terms with the fact that the artificially constructed community of 'industrial workers, peasantry, and working intelligentsia' did not find the 'progressive socialist culture' offered by the state very appealing – in fact, they demanded quite average entertainment and a form of cultural self-realization that differed only moderately from 'bourgeois' culture.

Obvious glitches in the management of cultural operations began to emerge in 1951. A typical example was the unprecedented crisis in film production: only seven feature films were made in 1951 (one of which was a feature documentary),[41] the fewest in Czech cinema's recent history, even counting the period of the Nazi occupation. By contrast, the Resolution on Film had demanded an increase in film production and anticipated the making of twenty-two films. There were also palpable limitations in the distribution of art: despite the massive promotion and organized enrolment of organizations created for this purpose, the system was unable to fulfil the demand for various cultural events. For instance, even Czechoslovak cinemas began to experience a decline in audience numbers – in 1950 attendance hit the lowest levels since 1945.[42] In the years 1950–1952, a massive effort to promote Soviet films (and films from the other 'people's republics') was accompanied by a steep decrease in the import of Western films. It became evident that the total ideologization of cultural events and art was a serious impediment to fulfilling the tasks of the 'cultural front' in 'educating the people' and 'satisfying their cultural needs'.[43]

This was also a period of significant turbulence caused by the power struggle between the Ministry of Information and the central party apparatus. Mutual accusations of incompetence in practical cultural management and incorrect ideological starting points for understanding socialist culture were 'solved' by recalling Rudolf Slánský from the leadership of the party secretariat and gradually removing cultural and ideological workers from their party functions. Personnel changes also occurred in the leadership of creative unions and other culture institutions, including ČSF. On the ideological level, these changes were accompanied by a massive campaign against so-called Slanskyism in 1952. The reorganizations in the power configuration of cultural politics also resulted in certain changes to the ideological criteria and criteria for artistic activity, which made only mild accommodations for more generally acceptable forms of socialist art. However, these changes had no effect on the attitude of leading functionaries, who strictly rejected the noncommunist, democratic aspects of Czechoslovak culture.[44]

Culture during the 'Thaw' (1953–1956)

In 1953, Czechoslovak culture inconspicuously entered a new phase in which it did away with its harshest dogmas. Although the deaths of Stalin and later the head of the Czechoslovak Communist party Klement Gottwald in March 1953 were important stimuli for the turnaround in social conditions, certain ideological shifts in cultural politics had already started in 1952 in connection with the campaigns against so-called Slanskyism. Not until 1953, though, were real, practical measures taken with the intention of repairing the dismal state of cultural affairs and reinstating some of culture's original functions.

The formulation and subsequent announcement of the policy of the 'New Course' in autumn 1953 amplified this trend.[45] Looking at the impact of the New Course on the cultural sphere, we encounter among other things another wave of criticism against dogmatism, demands for a greater variety of genres in art production (particularly for comedies and satire) and support for various forms of popular entertainment. We can also observe a gradual decrease in the share of feature films based on the 'new topics'. Minister of Culture Václav Kopecký most clearly formulated these incentives in his speech against 'killjoys' (*sucha*ř*i*), presented at the meeting of the party's Central Committee in December 1953. Among other things, he reproached the *Literární noviny* (Literary Newspaper) for its 'killjoy' (*sucharské*) appraisal of the tremendously popular film comedy *And*ě*l na horách* (Angel in the Mountains, Bořivoj Zeman, 1955).[46]

Nevertheless, the efforts to liberalize the cultural climate met with political and even social limitations. Disregarding the palpable consequences of the recent monetary reform on people whose daily problems at that time did not include ensuring quality cultural production, these constraints resulted above all from the communist leadership's reluctance to institute any sort of large-scale liberalization, which was clearly demonstrated at the Tenth KSČ Congress in June 1954.

Cultural politics was also affected by vast reorganizations in state management, that is, in cultural ministries and the communist party apparatus in 1953. In January of that year, the communist leadership decided to dismantle the Ministry of Information and Enlightenment and reorganize the Ministry of Education, Sciences and Art, whose agenda (except for education) was divided between the new central offices: the State Board for Matters of Art (Státní výbor pro věci umění), the Board for Foreign Cultural Exchange (Výbor pro kulturní styky se zahraničím), and the Office of the Prime Minister (Úřad předsednictva vlády). The former ministers, Václav Kopecký and Zdeněk Nejedlý, were transferred to the Office of the Prime Minister as undersecretaries to the prime minister in January 1953. In his new position, Kopecký was directly subordinated to the Main Administration for Cinematography (Hlavní správa kinematografie). Ultimately, though, these changes amounted to nothing, for in September 1953 cultural management (including that of cinema) was again unified within a single ministry, namely the Ministry of Culture under the leadership of Václav Kopecký.

After the turbulence of the previous years, cultural politics at this time experienced a period of stabilization, whereby it was able to form new management strategies and sustain a very gradual process of loosening the ideological demands. In fact, this new direction in culture basically confirmed the victory of Kopecký's interpretation of cultural politics, augmented and enriched by elements that by 1953 had become necessary. The regime's art intelligentsia elites remained very loyal. The aforementioned Tenth Congress of the Communist Party of Czechoslovakia provided the basic orientation of the party's demands, outlining the need for a 'fight against schematism' and at the same time warning against 'leaning towards liberalism'. Václav Kopecký stated at the congress that 'no one has a patent on socialist realism. Socialist realism is a creative method', and this fact therefore 'not only does not exclude but demands individual differences in creation'.[47] At the same time, the regime displayed a more accommodating face to some art personalities who had been rejected and persecuted until then. It also tolerated critiques of abuses in cultural affairs, of the state bureaucracy, of the mishandling of finances, and so forth. This was also the case with ČSF. In the summer of 1955, *Literární noviny* organized a three-month discussion in connection with the tenth anniversary of the nationalization of cinema, which was dominated by calls for de-bureaucratization of film work and simplification of the approval system.[48]

The recall of the ČSF central director, Oldřich Macháček, in the spring of 1954 became an emblem of change in the system. He had been denounced for suppressing criticism and for bad management (and was later expelled from the KSČ). The writer Jiří Marek replaced him as head manager of cinema. In November 1955, the Minister of Culture also proclaimed a new Film Council to oversee all types of art production, which was, however, soon replaced by a another new advisory group called the Artistic Council. When the Ministry of Education and Culture was founded in June 1956, the new Central Film Council (Ústřední filmová rada ČSF) took over the role of the Film Council as an advisory body to the central director of Czechoslovak Film.

The gradual process of liberalization was supported by the emergence of new cultural magazines that began to publish tame literary discussions. Together with a more positive view of Czechoslovak cultural heritage, these broadened the hitherto rigid conception of socialist culture. In 1954 the new monthly film publication *Film a doba* (Film and Time) appeared; it was soon recognized as a prestigious scholarly film periodical and gradually became a highly influential force in shaping the cultural climate in Czechoslovakia.[49] In addition, a new generation of filmmakers entered the scene in the mid-1950s (mirroring a similar development in literature and the plastic arts), bringing new creative impulses to cinema art.

One of the most important expressions of the New Course in culture was the invigoration of cultural ties with foreign countries. Making it possible for artists to travel with their cultural programme to foreign countries, especially those that until recently had been regarded as 'enemy' countries in the West, contributed considerably to the new stimuli's gradual revitalization of domestic culture. The increased intensity of cultural exchange had an equally beneficial effect on the general public. Furthermore, the import of 'Western' films increased moderately after 1953, a trend that became especially apparent in 1955, when only 43 out of 111 imported films were from other socialist People's Republics.[50] By 1956, the import volume had increased enough to substantively approach the numbers of the pre-February period.[51]

The appeal of film programmes at this time is evidenced by increased attendance in Czechoslovak cinemas. In 1955 attendance numbers reached approximately the levels seen in 1948, and the period from 1956 to 1957 recorded the highest rates since 1945. This trend peaked in 1957, after which rates dropped slightly.[52] Also in this period, the new medium of television began to have increasing influence on visual culture. The first test transmissions in Czechoslovakia took place in May 1953, and regular television broadcasting began the following year.[53]

In 1956, the consequences of the Twentieth Congress of the Communist Party of the Soviet Union began to affect first the KSČ and then the entire society. The critique of the personality cult around Joseph Stalin voiced at the Congress began to expose the criminal face of the Soviet system. The Czechoslovak cultural intelligentsia in particular reacted very sensitively to this. Initial public doubts in the system were expressed over the course of the first spring months of 1956, whereby the practices of the post-February cultural politics were subjected to the most scathing criticism to date, as were some 'truths' that had been indisputable up to this point. The aforementioned reflections, augmented by the stirred-up atmosphere surrounding the discussions about the Twentieth Congress of The Communist Party of Soviet Union and building on the already existing tolerance towards criticism, enabled the airing of many frustrations that had simmered behind the scene in cultural organizations, editorial boards, publishing houses, and other such entities. Although the artistic and cultural intelligentsia as a whole did not demand changes to the entire system of cultural politics, it clearly spoke in favour of changing the form it had hitherto taken. Despite some fragmentary efforts to do so, the intelligentsia did not publicly deny the role of socialist realism in art production; however, it did voice serious doubts about its current attributes. The importance of socialist realism as a viable aesthetic norm was gradually fading away. Ultimately, despite harsh criticism of previous administrative interventions, censorship practices and other party actions, no voices were raised in opposition to the KSČ's function as manager of cultural politics. These standpoints were formulated most clearly at the Second Congress of the Union of Czechoslovak Writers at the end of April 1956. In general, the year 1956 can be said to represent an important psychological turning point in the relationship between the cultural intelligentsia and the regime. Cultural workers and artists became more critical of the politics of the communist party and began to express doubts about its continuing 'infallibility'. This has been referred to as a 'crisis of ideology' that later prompted some segments of the intelligentsia to try to reform the system from which it was gradually becoming alienated.[54]

In response to the wave of criticism from the creative intelligentsia, the communist leadership made certain changes in the way it interacted with them. In place of restrictions, it adopted a more prudent and long-term approach consisting of an effort to renew the authority of the party workers. It is important to emphasize that Václav Kopecký's position of power, and consequently his direct influence on the management of Czechoslovak culture, declined after 1956, in part because of the generational turnover that was occurring in the leadership.

In connection with the changes in 1956, extensive decentralizing measures became an important and ultimately useful intervention in management of the culture life in the broader sense. The managing bodies had already realized the need of such measures in 1954 and 1955 and had thus partly prepared for them. The decentralization relieved part of the cultural sphere from the stricter supervision of official institutions and offered them the possibility of developing in more pleasant and sheltered conditions in outlying districts. These measures applied primarily to theatre and entertainment culture but also had limited ramifications for film life.

The changes of 1956 further advanced the decentralization of cinema, which had begun with the steps taken in 1954–1955 in reaction to the economic situation of ČSF. As of 1 January 1956, ČSF was divided into six basic, economically independent organizations (in addition to the central directorate): the Narrative Film Studio (Studio hraných filmů), Short Film (Krátký film), distribution, laboratories, Film Industry (Filmový průmysl) and the Film Project (Filmoprojekt). Then, on 1 January 1957, ČSF was dissolved by a government decree and replaced by two new cinema organizations: the Central Administration of Czechoslovak Film (Hlavní správa Československého filmu), headed by Jiří Marek, and the Central Administration of Slovak Film (Hlavní správa Slovenského filmu) together with regional film companies. The Central Administration of Czechoslovak Film managed, coordinated and controlled the following agencies: the Central Directory

(Ústřední ředitelství), Barrandov Film Studios (Filmové studio Barrandov), Short Film (Krátký film), Film Laboratories (Filmové laboratoře), Film Industry (Filmový průmysl), Filmexport and Central Film Rental (Ústřední půjčovnu filmů). The transfer of management and directing responsibilities for cinemas from the former ČSF to (regional and municipal) people's committees on 1 April 1957 signalled a particularly important development in the decentralization process. Regional film companies managed by district people's committees were founded to replace the now defunct district administrations of ČSF. These district people's committees played an important part in film distribution because, among other things, they cooperated directly with Central Film Rental and had the authority to decide about film programming.[55]

Culture during the Storm of Purges and Liberation (1957–1960)

In the second half of the 1950s, a number of contradictory processes were taking place in both the society and the sphere of culture. The common denominator in these developments was the intensification of the KSČ's efforts to build a new type of society, which often included mentions of 'the consummation of the cultural revolution' and the struggle against the remnants of the petit bourgeoisie. These renewed efforts were the Czechoslovak regime's reaction to 'Khrushchevian politics' and to the self-confident appeal for peaceful competition with Western states in terms of living standards. To a certain extent, the new slogan 'catch up with and surpass' represented an effort to accept certain consumerist trends from the Western states and further prove that 'the society moving towards socialism' was even better equipped to satisfy consumer demands awakened by these trends. At this time, the first clear signs of the emergence of socialist consumer society became apparent.

The very successful Czechoslovak pavilion at the World's Fair Expo 1958 in Brussels came to symbolize the pinnacle of modernist trends. It served as proof of Czechoslovakia's competitiveness on an international level and also as a continuation of important cultural traditions from the First Republic and earlier.[56] Modernist trends were a dominant force in the intense campaigns against kitsch that primarily targeted antiquated forms and pseudo-folk products. The crusade against kitsch was also linked with the building of a new lifestyle.

However, Czechoslovak culture was going through a very complicated process at the end of the 1950s. The changes and innovations in the management of cultural affairs took place under the banner of realizing the promises of decentralization, or at least allotting increased autonomy to certain elements, which cannot be automatically associated with an ideological liberalization of the cultural sphere. A number of new laws adopted in this context merely replaced initial post-February measures that were out of touch with the new sociopolitical situation. Take, for example, the new Theatre Law of October 1957 and two laws from December 1957. Passed in reaction to the dissolution of the Musical and Circus Performers' Central (Hudební a artistická ústředna) as the state monopoly mediating agency, the new laws reformed the regulation of musical activities, variety productions, circus shows and public entertainment. These changes were followed by a revision of the norms regulating the cultural sphere and social life, specifically the 'triumvirate' of laws from July 1959: the Enlightenment Law, the Library Law and the Law on Museums and Galleries.

On the one hand, the processes of decentralization in the cultural sphere gradually enabled a partial realization of regional ideas and demands. On the other hand, the initial development of an increasingly marked diversification of the culture scene was observable, specifically in a strengthening of the entertainment and 'consumerist' aspects of cultural life in the mass media (such as the increased popularity of variety shows, pop music, etc.). By contrast, the authentic artistic creation that the communist regime tried to present as the 'mainstream' of the vital national culture oriented towards the general public, began to focus on a narrower audience of intellectually more demanding readers, spectators, listeners and so on. The regime occasionally attempted to exploit the friction between these two tendencies. As a consequence of this diversification in the cultural scene, for example, the social status of the artistic unions that had been regarded as the top representatives of Czechoslovak culture after 1945 began to deteriorate. Only the Union of Czechoslovak Writers was able to maintain its connection with the broader public and thereby its social influence during the ensuing period.[57]

The newly founded 'clubs of friends of art' assumed an interesting function during this process of diversification of cultural life at the end of the 1950s. They served as a sort of bridge between mass consumer culture on one side and 'high art' on the other. At the same time, these formations attracted primarily the younger generation. The legal arrangements at that time did not allow these clubs to acquire legal status, so social organizations, unions and local cultural divisions of the people's committees played an important part in founding and developing these clubs by providing organizational support for the clubs' activities. This was, for example, the case of the Turntable Club (Gramofonový klub), which was founded by the national company Turntable Factory (Gramofonové závody) in 1957. The clubs quickly became more specialized, particularly in larger towns. For example, galleries founded clubs of 'friends of plastic art', clubs of 'poetry friends' were established, and cineastes began to gather in clubs of 'friends of film art'. Due to their popularity, the film clubs achieved a privileged status, and in 1964 they unified as the Czech Federation of Film Clubs (Československá federace filmových klubů) with the initial organizational support of the Czechoslovak Society for Spreading Political and Scientific Knowledge (Československá společnost pro šíření politických a vědeckých znalostí). Film clubs were allowed to exhibit important works of world cinema outside of the main distribution circuit, and after closing an agreement with ČSF they became crucial agents for maintaining contact with modern art around the world.[58]

The contradictory tendencies and efforts to transform the culture in the context of the new conditions of socialist society also provide a good illustration of the unfavourable shifts in the sphere of art, particularly at the very end of the 1950s.[59] These were linked to efforts by the communist leadership to reinforce ideological control over the society in the aftermath of the turbulence of 1956 while at the same time trying to substantially transform society. The overarching impetus for these developments was a broad campaign against the so-called revisionism that fully erupted in 1957 and marked cultural and social events until 1960. In the context of this campaign, we can observe among other things an increase in pressure to liquidate the remains of private companies and private medical offices, together with a wave of labour-political audits at the central offices, the Czechoslovak Academy of Sciences, some universities, Czechoslovak Television and other places. In addition, a new wave of collectivization began in the realm of agriculture.

In the cultural sphere, the campaign against 'revisionism' manifested itself through a number of administrative interventions aimed at slowing down the gradual liberalization of conditions seen for example in the establishment of artistic groups outside of the official structures. Publication of the progressive literary magazine *Květen* (May) – the most important fruit of the cultural 'thaw' of the mid-1950s – was halted in 1959. Shortly prior to this (at the end of 1958), Josef Škvorecký's novel *Zbabělci* (The Cowards) was exemplarily banished.[60] There were personnel changes in editorial staffs of cultural magazines, and at the same time ideological conferences were organized in all the artistic unions. In addition, 1958 saw labour-political audits at several culture workplaces, such as Czech Television. Some creative personalities had to leave television at least for a while.

The Congress of Socialist Culture in June 1959 marked a demonstrative culmination of efforts to tighten the conditions of cultural and artistic life.[61] The name alone announces the political leadership's focused effort to declare the impending achievement of the main parameters of socialist society. Yet the aims declared for practical culture were not successfully realized in the subsequent years. This pointed to the limits of politicians' efforts to create a new official socialist culture and regulate the sphere of artistic culture with the help of activist communist artists and ideological surveyors, especially censors.

Regardless, the very end of this period, namely the year 1960, was imbued with a spirit of great optimism fuelled in part by the grandiose celebrations of the fifteenth anniversary of Czechoslovakia's liberation. The most distinctive expression of this new mood was the ratification of a new constitution that declared Czechoslovak society to be socialist. A quite broad act of amnesty also contributed to the general euphoria, though of course this amnesty certainly did not mean any real departure from the repressive political methods that had been in operation since the beginning of the communist regime.

The political leadership prepared a major ideological intervention in film art for the period at the end of 1958 and start of 1959 and presented it at the First Festival of Czechoslovak Film in Banská Bystrica in February 1959.[62] The festival was originally intended to present a balanced selection of Czech and Slovak film work. By contrast, the opening speech of the Minister of Education and Culture František Kahuda imprinted the festival with the stamp of ideological intervention. The Minister exemplarily criticized the satirical comedy *Tři přání* (Three Wishes) by Elmar Klos and Ján Kadár, the psychological drama *Zde jsou lvi* (Scars of the Past) by Václav Krška, and the musical comedy *Hvězda jede na jih* (A Star Goes South) by Oldřich Lipský. The screening of these films was forbidden – or rather, the films were withdrawn from distribution – and Klos and Kadár were even banned from any artistic activity for two years. In contrast to these films, the official speakers highlighted a number of engaged pictures from the years 1949–1952 as exemplary works: *Nad námi svítá* (The Sun Is Rising above Us, Jiří Krejčík, 1952), *Pan Novák* (Mr Novak, Bořivoj Zeman, 1949), *Pětistovka* (Motorbike, Martin Frič, 1949) and *Karhanova parta* (Karhan's Team, Václav Wasserman and

Zdeněk Hofbauer, 1950). The management of ČSF was hit with sudden personnel purges as a result of these proceedings. Most importantly, the director of the Central Administration of Czechoslovak Film, Jiří Marek, was recalled and replaced by Alois Poledňák, a functionary of the Youth Union. The director of Barrandov Film Studios was also replaced, and the ideological supervision of film dramaturgy was intensified. The Artistic Council (Umělecká rada) was replaced with the so-called Ideological Artistic Council (Ideově umělecká rada), which was filled with reliable party workers. The Ministry of Education and Culture once again strengthened its role in the process of approving new films, restoring the political leadership to the position it had occupied at the end of the 1940s and start of the 1950s.

The political intervention in Banská Bystrica sent a shock wave through Czechoslovak filmmakers. These administrative precautions could only intimidate them temporarily, though, for the society was headed towards another period of liberalization.

Translation: Kevin Bradley Johnson (Appleton, Wisconsin, USA)

Acknowledgement

This essay was made possible through the financial support of the European Social Fund (ESF) and the state budget of the Czech Republic as part of project CZ.1.07/2.3.00/20.0031, 'The Historization of Central Europe'.

Jiří Knapík is the head of the Institute of Historical Sciences at Silesian University, Opava. The focus of his research is cultural politics in Czechoslovakia after 1945, about which he has published the biography *Kdo spoutal naši kulturu: Portrét stalinisty Gustava Bareše* (2000), the directory *Kdo byl kdo v naší kulturní politice 1948–1953* (2002) and two monographs, *Únor a kultura: Sovětizace české kultury 1948–1950* (2004) and *V zajetí moci: Kulturní politika, její systém a aktéři 1948–1956* (2004). He deals with the problems of leisure and lifestyle in Czechoslovakia in the 1950s and 1960s. Together with Martin Franc, he published the two-volume *Průvodce kulturním děním a životním stylem v českých zemích 1948–1967* (Prague, 2011) and the monograph *Volný čas v českých zemích 1957–1967* (2013). He has also published a volume on Czech Silesia, *Slezský studijní ústav v Opavě 1945–1948* (2004), and, with Jaromíra Knapíková, *"Slezský konzulát" v Praze: Od Slezanu ke Slezskému kulturnímu ústavu 1906–1945* (2010).

Notes

1. *Program Národní fronty Čechů a Slováků* (Brno: Rovnost, 1945), p. 19.
2. I understand the term 'cultural politics' specifically as an array of political interventions that were influenced by cultural and artistic activities during the period under consideration. I have in mind primarily the system of regulations for all traditional areas of culture (literature, theatre, visual arts, film, etc.) and public life that established the conditions for artistic creation and enforced various ideological and aesthetic criteria. For more on this issue see Jiří Knapík, 'Jak zpracovávat historii kulturní politiky 50. let?' *Kuděj* 7(1–2) (2005), 180–187.
3. *Program Národní fronty Čechů a Slováků*, pp. 20–21.
4. Jaroslav Kladiva has provided a general overview of the relationship between culture and politics from 1945 to 1948, albeit with ideological overtones. See Jaroslav Kladiva, *Kultura a politika (1945–1948)* (Prague: Svoboda, 1968). See also Alexej Kusák, *Kultura a politika v Československu 1945–1956* (Prague: Torst, 1998).
5. J. Pilař, 'Fraška z očisty českého filmu', *Tvorba* 15(6) (1945), 95–96.
6. See e.g. the memoir of the leading Czech actress Adina Mandlová: *Dneska už se tomu směju* (Brno: Knihkupectví Michala Ženíška, 1993); also see Krystyna Wanatowiczová, *Miloš Havel – český filmový magnát* (Prague: Knihovna Václava Havla, 2013).
7. Šimon Eismann has provided a comprehensive analysis of film politics in the period from 1945 to 1948. See *Film a kulturní politika 1945–1952* (Prague, 1999, manuscript located in the library of FAMU in Prague).
8. The testimonies of several important film figures (F. Piláta, E. Klose, L. Linharta, O. Vávry, E. Sirotka, K. Feixe, V. Kabelka) were published in a series of four articles titled 'Jak byl znárodněn film. (Svědectví a dokumenty)', *Film a doba* 11(2) (1965), 69–74; (3), 125–132; (4) 180–184; (5) 242–243.
9. It should be noted that Czech cinema attendance rose by 60 per cent during the Nazi occupation.
10. Úplné znění dekretu č. 50/1945, *Sbírka zákonů a nařízení republiky Československé* (1945).
11. Ibid. Only film production under the auspices of the Ministry of National Defence (Ministerstvo národní obrany) and amateur filmmaking were exempted from the terms of the decree.
12. For more details, see Šimon Eismann, 'Osudy spolkových biografů v poválečném Československu', *Iluminace* 11(4) (1999), 53–86.
13. See e.g. Kusák, *Kultura a politika v Československu 1945–1956*.
14. Jacques Rupnik, 'Intelektuálové a moc v Československu', *Soudobé dějiny* 1(4–5) (1994), 541.
15. 'Májové poselství kulturních pracovníků českému lidu', *Tvorba* 15(20) (1946), 308, 327. Among the film industry workers signing the message were the directors O. Vávra, J. Weiss, V. Wassermann and M. Jareš; actors J. Plachta, L. Pešek, J. Průcha, F. Filipovský, M. Nedbal, V. Vydra Sr., V. Vydra Jr. and B. Záhorský; dramaturgs J. Kopecký and V. Borský; and poets V. Nezval and L. Linhart.
16. On the structural development of the KSČ in the realm of cultural politics during this period see Jiří Knapík, *Kdo spoutal naši kulturu (Portrét stalinisty Gustava Bareše)* (Přerov: Nakladatelství Šárka, 2000).
17. A typical example is the party's intervention in the affairs of the literary journal *Generace* (Generations), which was published by the nonpartisan *Svaz české mládeže*

(Czech Youth Union). Centred around this publication was an association of young communist intellectuals who were not under the full control of the party. In fall 1946, members of the Central Committee (ÚV) of the KSČ compelled *Generace* to replace its entire editorial board, which resulted in the cultural journal's overall decline and eventual demise in spring 1947.

18. See Alexej Kusák, *Kultura a politika v Československu 1945–1956*, pp. 209–226.
19. Jana Pávová has written a biography of V. Kopecký; however, she only briefly addresses his activities in the cultural sphere. Jana Pávová, *Demagog ve službách strany. Portrét komunistického politika a ideologa Václava Kopeckého* (Prague: Ústav pro studium totalitních režimů, 2008).
20. Jiří Křesťan has long devoted himself to researching the figure of Z. Nejedlý. See e.g. Jiří Křesťan, *Zdeněk Nejedlý. Politik a vědec v osamění* (Prague-Litomyšl: Paseka, 2012).
21. For more background, see Jiří Pokorný. 'Kulturní komise Ústřední rady odborů', in Blanka Zilynská and Petr Svobodný (eds), *Věda v Československu 1945–1953* (Prague: Nakladatelství Karolinum, 1999), pp. 225–232.
22. The Slovak Film Society administered cinema in Slovakia.
23. Jiří Pokorný, 'Odbory a znárodněný film', in Ivan Klimeš (ed.), *Filmový sborník historický 3* (Prague: Český filmový ústav, 1992), pp. 180–215.
24. Dramaturgy, directing and cinematography were taught at FAMU starting in 1947.
25. On the management of Czech culture and the fundamental problems of cultural politics in this period see Jiří Knapík, *V zajetí moci. Kulturní politika, její systém a aktéři 1948–1956* (Prague: Nakladatelství Libri, 2004).
26. After 1951, the structure and name of this department changed several times; however, it came to be predominantly known as the 'department of ideology'.
27. One of the more noteworthy organizations taking part in developing the new system of management in the cultural sphere before 1951 was the Cultural Council of the Central Committee of the Communist Party of Czechoslovakia (Kulturní rada Ústředního výboru Komunistické strany Československa), which was established by the party Central Committee in September 1948. The Cultural Council was intended to mediate between key state and party representatives involved in cultural management. Also under its auspices were the directors of state film and state radio as well as the editor-in-chief of party newspapers and other leading figures.
28. For an overview of developments in cinema and film politics see Eismann, *Film a kulturní politika 1945–1952* and Ivan Klimeš, 'Stav čs. kinematografie po únoru 1948', *Iluminace* 15(3) (2003), 97–104.
29. For an overview of this reorganization see Ivan Klimeš, 'Za vizí centrálního řízení filmové tvorby (Úvod k edici)', *Iluminace* 12(4) (2000), 135–139; see also Jiří Knapík, *Únor a kultura (Sovětizace české kultury 1948–1950)* (Prague: Nakladatelství Libri, 2004), pp. 182–189.
30. As a rule, the political organizations always had the last word. The origin of a film was its story, whose treatment was derived either from the thematic plan or through the individual initiative of a creative collective. The story was then examined by Central Dramaturgy (ÚD) and the Film Council (FR). The ÚD issued 'rulings' while the FR issued 'evaluations' – both judgements being binding on the creative collectives, although those of the FR carried greater weight. A collective then transformed the approved story into a 'literary screenplay', which once again came under the scrutiny of both boards. The Minister of Information, however, had the final word in approving a screenplay. After final approval came the preparations for filming: searching for an appropriate director (approved by the Secretary of the

Central Committee of the KSČ), seeking out places for location shooting, designing the sets, auditioning actors, drafting a budget, etc. Meanwhile, the creative collective (still under the observation of the FR and ÚD) drafted a technical screenplay from the 'literary screenplay'. Once the technical screenplay was approved by the general director of ČSF and the Minister of Information, the director was permitted to begin shooting a 'probationary film'. Both the creative collective and the ÚD were required to monitor the filming. The 'probationary film' was screened for the members of both groups as well as senior party functionaries and occasionally even the entire Cultural Council of the Central Committee of the KSČ. At this point, these groups often made further suggestions that the filmmakers were required to take into account for the final film.

31. See Luděk Havel, '"O nového člověka, o dokonalejší lidstvo, o nový festival". Filmový festival pracujících, 1948 až 1959', in Pavel Skopal (ed.), *Naplánovaná kinematografie. Český filmový průmysl 1945 až 1960* (Prague: Academia 2012), pp. 312–358; and Hana Květová, 'Filmové jaro na vesnici 1951 až 1956. Historie kulturně osvětové akce na českém venkově v 50. letech dvacátého století', ibid., pp. 391–426. The Film Spring in the Village initiative also took place in 1951.
32. The attitudes of the cultural politicians are documented in the collection *Sjezd národní kultury (Sbírka dokumentů)*, Miroslav Kouřil (ed.) (Prague: Orbis, 1948).
33. For more on this problem see Jiří Knapík, '"Do půl roku budeme míti úplně jinou literaturu" (Literární život let 1948 – 1949 v iluzích kulturních politiků)', *Acta historica Universitatis Silesianae Opaviensis* 2(2) (2009), 117–124.
34. Jiří Knapík, 'Dělnický soud nad Františkem Čápem', *Iluminace* 14(3) (2002), 63–81.
35. Jiří Knapík, 'Dělníci proti Dvaasedmdesátce. (Osudy filmového zpracování hry Františka Langera)', in Milena Vojtková and Vladimír Justl (eds), *František Langer na prahu nového tisíciletí* (Prague: Akcent, 2000), pp. 153–162.
36. 'Za vysokou ideovou a uměleckou úroveň československého filmu', *Rudé právo*, 19. April 1950, pp. 1 and 3.
37. Ibid.
38. Ibid.
39. Kusák, *Kultura a politika v Československu 1945–1956*, pp. 290–305. For more on the problem of interpretation see Knapík, *V zajetí moci*, pp. 60–66.
40. Karel Kaplan, *Zpráva o zavraždění generálního tajemníka* (Prague: Mladá fronta, 1992).
41. These films were *Akce B* (Operation B, Josef Mach, 1951), *Císařův pekař* (The Emperor's Baker, Martin Frič, 1951), *Mikoláš Aleš* (Václav Krška, 1951), *Milujeme* (We Love, Václav Kubásek and Jaroslav Novotný, 1951), *Štika v rybníce* (The Pike in a Fish Pond, Vladimír Čech, 1951), *Usměvavá zem* (The Smiling Country, Václav Gajer, 1951) and *Jeden ze štafety* (The One of the Relay, Jaroslav Mach, 1951).
42. Ladislav Pištora, 'Filmoví návštěvníci a kina na území ČR,' *Iluminace* 9(2) (1997), 65–66.
43. For more on ČSF's distribution problems, see Pavel Skopal, 'Za "vysokou ideovou úroveň" a/nebo za vyšší tržby? Filmová distribuce v českých zemích z hlediska konfliktu ideologických a hospodářských cílů (1945–1968)', *Soudobé dějiny* 17(4) (2010), 639–666.
44. See Jiří Knapík, *V zajetí moci*, pp. 109–198. The fundamental attitudes of the leaders of cultural politics during this period are documented in Ladislav Štoll and Jiří Taufer, 'Proti sektářství a liberalismu – za rozkvět našeho umění', *Nový život* 7 (1952), 1053–1069.
45. For more information see Jiří Knapík, *V zajetí moci*, pp. 212–234.

46. See L. Veselý, 'Více pozornosti veselohrám', *Literární noviny* 18 (1953), 6.
47. The text of Kopecký's speech is in *Protokol X. řádného sjezdu KSČ*, Prague 1954, pp. 248–261.
48. See for example Jiří Krejčík, Elmar Klos and Jiří Weiss, 'Před desetiletím státního filmu', *Literární noviny* 4(27) (1955), 5.
49. In fact, the magazine had existed since 1952, but only as an internal publication for the employees of ČSF.
50. Jiří Havelka, *Československé filmové hospodářství 1951–1955* (Prague: Československý filmový ústav, 1972), p. 279.
51. A similar development can be observed in the screening of "Western" and nonsocialist films at the International Film Festival in Karlovy Vary after 1953.
52. Ladislav Pištora, 'Filmoví návštěvníci a kina na území ČR', *Iluminace* 9(2) (1997), 68–69.
53. For the most recent work on the phenomenon of Czechoslovak television see Martin Štoll, *1. 5. 1953. Zahájení televizního vysílání. Zrození televizního národa* (Prague: Havran, 2011); see also Jarmila Cysařová, 'Československá televize a politická moc 1953–1989', *Soudobé dějiny* 9(3–4) (2002), 521–537.
54. Karel Kaplan, *Československo v letech 1953–1966* (Prague: SPN, 1992), p. 64; see also Jiří Pernes, 'Československý rok 1956', *Soudobé dějiny* 6(4) (1999), 595–599.
55. Jiří Havelka, *Čs. filmové hospodářství 1956–1960* (Prague: Československý filmový ústav, 1973), pp. 6, 12.
56. On the importance of the Czechoslovak contribution to the Brussels World's Fair see Emilie Benešová and Karolina Šimůnková, *Expo '58. Příběh československé účasti na Světové výstavě v Bruselu* *Prague: Národní archiv, 2008); and Daniela Kramerová and Vanda Skálová (eds), *Bruselský sen. Československá účast na světové výstavě Expo 58 v Bruselu a životní styl 1. poloviny 60. let* (Prague: Arbor Vitae, 2008).
57. For the most recent work on this topic see Jan Mervart, *Naděje a iluze. Čeští a slovenští spisovatelé v reformním hnutí šedesátých let* (Brno: Host, 2010).
58. Jiří Havelka, *Československé filmové hospodářství 1966–1970* (Prague: Československý filmový ústav, 1975); 'Kluby přátel filmového umění', *Osvětová práce* 18(12) (1964), 209–211.
59. See, for example, Kateřina Bláhová, 'Mezi literaturou a politikou. Souvislosti českého literárního života 1958–1969', *Soudobé dějiny* 9(3–4) (2002), 495–520.
60. See Michal Bauer, *Souvislosti labyrintu. Kodifikace ideologicko-estetické normy v české literatuře 50. let 20. století* (Prague: Nakladatelství Akropolis, 2009), pp. 313–344; and Alessandro Catalano, *Rudá záře nad literaturou. Česká literatura mezi socialismem a undergroundem (1945–1959)* (Brno: Host, 2008), pp. 117–129.
61. The positions of the official functionaries are documented in *Sjezd socialistické kultury. Sborník dokumentů* (Prague: Orbis, 1959).
62. Ivan Klimeš, 'Filmaři a komunistická moc v Československu. Vzrušený rok 1959', *Iluminace* 16(4) (2004), 129–138. This study also includes the documentary appendix 'Bystrica 1959. Dokumenty ke kontextům I. festivalu československého filmu', ibid., 139–222.

Select Bibliography

Bauer, Michal. *Souvislosti labyrintu. Kodifikace ideologicko-estetické normy v české literatuře 50. let 20. století*. Prague: Nakladatelství Akropolis, 2009.

Benešová, Emilie, and Karolina Šimůnková. *Expo '58. Příběh československé účasti na Světové výstavě v Bruselu*. Prague: Národní archiv, 2008.

Bláhová, Kateřina. 'Mezi literaturou a politikou. Souvislosti českého literárního života 1958–1969'. *Soudobé dějiny* 9(3–4) (2002), 495–520.

Catalano, Alessandro. *Rudá záře nad literaturou. Česká literatura mezi socialismem a undergroundem (1945–1959)*. Brno: Host, 2008.

Cysařová, Jarmila. 'Československá televize a politická moc 1953–1989'. *Soudobé dějiny* 9(3–4) (2002), 521–537.

Eismann, Šimon. 'Film a kulturní politika 1945–1952'. Prague 1999. Manuscript (located in the library of FAMU in Prague.)

Eismann, Šimon. 'Osudy spolkových biografů v poválečném Československu'. *Iluminace* 11(4) (1999), 53–86.

Havel, Luděk. '"O nového člověka, o dokonalejší lidstvo, o nový festival". Filmový festival pracujících, 1948 až 1959'. In Pavel Skopal (ed.), *Naplánovaná kinematografie. Český filmový průmysl 1945 až 1960*. Prague: Academia, 2012.

Havelka, Jiří. *Československé filmové hospodářství 1951–1955*. Prague: Československý filmový ústav, 1972.

Havelka, Jiří. *Čs. filmové hospodářství 1956–1960*. Prague: Československý filmový ústav, 1973.

Havelka, Jiří. *Československé filmové hospodářství 1966–1970*. Prague: Československý filmový ústav, 1975.

Kaplan, Karel. *Československo v letech 1953–1966*. Prague: SPN, 1992.

Kaplan, Karel. *Zpráva o zavraždění generálního tajemníka*. Prague: Mladá fronta, 1992.

Kladiva, Jaroslav. *Kultura a politika (1945–1948)*. Prague: Svoboda, 1968.

Klimeš, Ivan. 'Za vizí centrálního řízení filmové tvorby (Úvod k edici)'. *Iluminace* 12(4) (2000), 135–139.

Klimeš, Ivan. 'Stav čs. kinematografie po únoru 1948'. *Iluminace* 15(3) (2003), 97–104.

Klimeš, Ivan. 'Filmaři a komunistická moc v Československu. Vzrušený rok 1959'. *Iluminace* 16(4) (2004), 129–138.

Knapík, Jiří. 'Dělníci proti Dvaasedmdesátce (Osudy filmového zpracování hry Františka Langera)'. In Milena Vojtková and Vladimír Justl (eds), *František Langer na prahu nového tisíciletí*. Prague: Akcent, 2000.

Knapík, Jiří. *Kdo spoutal naši kulturu (Portrét stalinisty Gustava Bareše)*. Přerov: Nakladatelství Šárka, 2000.

Knapík, Jiří. 'Dělnický soud nad Františkem Čápem'. *Iluminace* 14(3) (2002), 63–81.

Knapík, Jiří. *Únor a kultura (Sovětizace české kultury 1948–1950)*. Prague: Nakladatelství Libri, 2004.

Knapík, Jiří. *V zajetí moci. Kulturní politika, její systém a aktéři 1948–1956*. Prague: Nakladatelství Libri, 2004.

Knapík, Jiří. 'Jak zpracovávat historii kulturní politiky 50. let?' *Kuděj* 7(1–2) (2005), 180–187.

Knapík, Jiří. '"Do půl roku budeme míti úplně jinou literaturu" (Literární život let 1948–1949 v iluzích kulturních politiků)'. *Acta historica Universitatis Silesianae Opaviensis* 2(2) (2009), 117–124.
Kramerová, Daniela, and Vanda Skálová (eds). *Bruselský sen. Československá účast na světové výstavě Expo 58 v Bruselu a životní styl 1. poloviny 60. let.* Prague: Arbor Vitae, 2008.
Křesťan, Jiří. *Zdeněk Nejedlý. Politik a vědec v osamění.* Prague-Litomyšl: Paseka, 2012.
Kusák, Alexej. *Kultura a politika v Československu 1945–1956.* Prague: Torst, 1998.
Květová, Hana. 'Filmové jaro na vesnici 1951 až 1956. Historie kulturně osvětové akce na českém venkově v 50. letech dvacátého století'. In Pavel Skopal (ed.), *Naplánovaná kinematografie. Český filmový průmysl 1945 až 1960.* Prague: Academia, 2012.
Mandlová, Adina. *Dneska už se tomu směju.* Prague: Knihkupectví Michala Ženíška, 1993.
Mervart, Jan. *Naděje a iluze. Čeští a slovenští spisovatelé v reformním hnutí šedesátých let.* Brno: Host, 2010.
Pávová, Jana. *Demagog ve službách strany. Portrét komunistického politika a ideologa Václava Kopeckého.* Prague: Ústav pro studium totalitních režimů, 2008.
Pernes, Jiří. 'Československý rok 1956'. *Soudobé dějiny* 6(4) (1999), 595–599.
Pištora, Ladislav. 'Filmoví návštěvníci a kina na území ČR'. *Iluminace* 9(2) (1997), 65–66.
Pokorný, Jiří. 'Kulturní komise Ústřední rady odborů'. In Blanka Zilynská and Petr Svobodný (eds), *Věda v Československu 1945–1953.* Prague: Nakladatelství Karolinum, 1999.
Pokorný, Jiří. 'Odbory a znárodněný film'. In Ivan Klimeš (ed.), *Filmový sborník historický 3.* Prague: Český filmový ústav, 1992.
Rupnik Jacques. 'Intelektuálové a moc v Československu'. *Soudobé dějiny* 1(4–5) (1994), 540–550.
Skopal, Pavel. 'Za "vysokou ideovou úroveň" a/nebo za vyšší tržby? Filmová distribuce v českých zemích z hlediska konfliktu ideologických a hospodářských cílů (1945–1968)'. *Soudobé dějiny* 17(4) (2010), 639–666.
Štoll, Martin. *1. 5. 1953. Zahájení televizního vysílání. Zrození televizního národa.* Prague: Havran, 2011.
Wanatowiczová, Krystyna. *Miloš Havel - český filmový magnát.* Prague: Knihovna Václava Havla, 2013.

PART II

PRODUCTION AND CO-PRODUCTION

Chapter 3

'Veterans' and 'Dilettantes'

Film Production Culture vis-à-vis Top-Down Political Changes, 1945–1962

Petr Szczepanik

This chapter examines the historical development of the basic production teams of the Czech film industry after World War II and between 1948 and 1962, the toughest period of communist rule. The basic production teams were of two kinds: the production, creative or dramaturgical 'units' that coordinated collaboration between writers and directors; and the crews. Focusing on the former category, this chapter looks at how top-down political, organizational and ideological reforms encountered resistance within existing production routines and hierarchies of local production communities. Marginally, it will also consider how often these reforms fell under the category of so-called Sovietization, how much they were hybridized by local or even German traditions, and why they did not succeed in completely changing either the system or the culture of film production. Two examples of failed top-down reorganizations that affected daily production routines will be used as symptomatic cases, one 'spatial' and the other 'temporal': first, an experiment that attempted to change the Barrandov studios into an industrial factory integrating all production personnel in one place; and second, a project to forge a new generation of communist or 'proletarian' filmmakers to replace older 'veterans' who were supposedly corrupted by the bourgeois ideology of the immoral film world.

Methodologically, the chapter builds on empirical historical research using archival documents (from ministerial, party and film studio–related files), top-down directives and official manuals to reconstruct what I would call 'the state-socialist mode of film production', an approach inspired by Janet Staiger's analysis of the Hollywood mode of production.[1] This industrial perspective is combined with a critical cultural analysis, inspired by anthropologically based studies of film 'production cultures' and communities,[2] that utilizes diverse informal sources, such as oral history and (auto)biographies. The resulting confrontation between the top-down and the bottom-up processes allows for an against-the-grain reading of the official documents.

The communist ideologues' primary means of reforming the Czechoslovak production system and its output, termed 'dramaturgy', was organized in a complex hierarchy of dramaturgical institutions with state or central dramaturgy at the top and creative or dramaturgical units at the bottom. In the state-controlled system of production, the 'dramaturge', or the artistic unit head who supervised a group of dramaturges, was basically the equivalent of a producer, though without the usual financial and marketing responsibilities (which were held by the state or the party and its representatives). Dramaturgy was considered the most efficient way for the official ideology to execute control over production processes. Dramaturges and their units oversaw script development, the selection of cast and crews, in some cases the actual shooting as well as post-production, and occasionally even distribution. They acted as cultural intermediaries, or interfaces of the production culture: they mediated between writers and directors, as well as between studios, the political establishment and broader cultural trends. For today's historians, dramaturgy and the units stand as a key feature of the 'the state-socialist mode of film production', distinguishing the socialist production systems from Hollywood and West European cinemas at the level of middle management.

Other Soviet Bloc countries of East Central Europe implemented similar kinds of 'units' or 'groups' (functioning as middle managers, ideological supervisors and cultural mediators), especially after the late 1950s, but dramaturgy was a key concept only in Czechoslovakia and the German Democratic Republic (GDR).[3] The reason for this was likely historical: in both countries, dramaturgy had a long tradition in legitimate theatre,[4] and the respective nationalist cultural policies of the 1930s and 1940s had been quick to adapt it to the needs of film production. To 'improve' the artistic and ideological qualities of films, the two national states implemented special measures to regulate film production not only retroactively through censorship but also early on, in the process of script development (Goebbels' idea of *Vorzensur* was institutionalized in 1934; Czech attempts to institutionalize dramaturgy dated from 1935). In the Czech lands, the mature form of film dramaturgy took shape during World War II, when Prague became an important production centre for the German film industry and an administrative body analogous to the Reichsfilmkammer was established to centralize and standardize the domestic industry. In both countries, dramaturgy represented a striking continuity in the development of their production systems before and after World War II, despite the political differences between the Nazi and the state-socialist regimes.[5]

This middle management structure in the Czech industry, as represented by so-called units, went through numerous reorganizations. In 1948, the 'production units' – which until then had partly functioned as hidden successors of the two private production companies that dominated the domestic industry during World War II – were dissolved and replaced by 'creative teams' staffed with dozens of inexperienced, young communist writers and journalists. Until 1953, these units were progressively centralized, disempowered and isolated from the actual production processes and communities. After 1954, however, a gradual process of de-centralization and liberalization opened a space for increasingly critical and aesthetically innovative films produced by units that functioned as semi-independent producers. In 1970, a year and a half after the Soviet invasion, the units were again disempowered and deprived of executive competences. The following chronology sums up the whole development of the production system, beginning with the nationalization of the film industry and ending with the collapse of the socialist regime:

– 1945–1948: 2–6 production units
– 1948–1951: 8–11 creative teams
– 1951–1954: a central collective board
– 1954–1970: 4–6 creative units
– 1970–1982: 6–7 dramaturgical units
– 1982–1990: 6 dramaturgical-production units
– 1990: plans for 6 creative units (mostly directors as heads, not fully realized)[6]

The existing research on state-socialist cinemas of East Central Europe is characterized by certain pitfalls of its subject. The study of film production in totalitarian or authoritarian states often led either to overemphasis of powerful figures in the state or party hierarchies who dictated and censored production from outside, or to the foregrounding of defiant filmmakers as heroic figures. The latter were usually directors who took advantage of any hint of liberalization and managed, against all odds, to sneak modernist aesthetics or provocative topics through to production. However, such analyses do not explain how the production systems worked or how the communities of filmmakers lived their professional lives.[7] This chapter will take only preliminary steps towards answering these questions, focusing on the units and leaving other aspects of the state-socialist production systems and cultures aside.

Film 'Proletariat' and the State-Socialist Geography of Creative Labour

Before 1948, the traditional geographical centre of the Czech film industry was situated on and around Wenceslas Square, the most upscale business and cultural district in downtown Prague. This square and the surrounding neighbourhoods were home to first-run theatres, distribution and production companies' offices, and cafés and clubs where filmmakers socialized, discussed new projects and proposed them to prospective financiers. As Elmar Klos – a prominent dramaturge and manager who earned his reputation in the 1930s producing industrial documentaries for the Bata shoe company, and who became famous later in the 1950s and 1960s for his collaboration with Ján Kadár – explained, these cafés functioned as 'markets of ideas and proposals', or as 'a real seedbed where the early Czech dramaturgy took shape'.[8] Until 1948 the same applied for so-called production units, which included production management and script development personnel and were closely linked with film crews. Two production units (joined by another four in 1947) constituted the production division of the nationalized film industry. These were separate from the film studios located in Barrandov on the outskirts of Prague, approximately ten kilometres from the city centre. In 1948, after the communist putsch, the production sector was unified with the studios, and the creative teams and their crews had to temporarily move to Barrandov, envisioned as a new 'film town' where all facilities, functions and personnel of film production should be concentrated.

There were several reasons why the new director general, Oldřich Macháček, decided to move the units and crews to the studios. Apart from solving the problem of office space, introducing supposed financial savings and increasing rationalization, the centralization was intended to strengthen the new, largely communist top management's executive power and political control over the various groups of creative workers. Dramaturges, production managers and crew members were relocated to what was now defined as a film 'factory', where they were supposed to merge with the film 'proletariat', integrate with the workers' union and communist cells, and adapt to the industrial operation of the 'plant'. According to the new central dramaturge, Zdeněk Míka, dispersing filmmakers among the support personnel was meant to make them 'identify with the working class.'[9] Politically unpredictable middle managers, writers and filmmakers, often former employees of private production companies or freelancers (the personnel of permanent production units and crews numbered about 170 individuals), were expected to become disciplined and reformed by joining the workers at the studios. Such workers numbered about one thousand, and 80 per cent of them were manual labourers (the rest being technicians and white-collar workers) who had typically sympathized with the Communist Party since the early postwar period (i.e. even before the 1948 putsch).[10]

This unprecedented move towards centralization and control over creative labour was supported from below by the works council representing studio employees, and probably also bolstered by a general sentiment of class rivalry and jealousy. Retrospectively, a satiric article published in a studio journal reflected workers' views after it was clear that the whole 'factory' experiment had gone wrong: 'Who then wanted to see with his own eyes how filmmakers marked their time cards at 7 am … whether writers write from 7 am to 4 pm … to bring intellectuals closer to the workers?'[11] We can only guess what role class hatred might have played here, provoked not only by official politics but also by the workers' envy of the creative personnel's high living standard.

Meanwhile, members of the creative teams and crews perceived their displacement in a very different, negative way. They cited time and financial losses due to complicated transportation and to other practical difficulties, but the underlying ideological argument was that creative labour could not be subjected to an industrial system of production, especially one modelled on heavy industry. As they saw it, filmmakers and writers needed to work irregular hours, often in the evenings; had to be in permanent and lively contact with other arts and artists (especially freelance writers and actors, who were mostly employed in theatres); had to attend film and theatre premieres, and so on.[12] These energetic protests from the filmmaking community resonate with recent findings by economic geographers studying clusters of cultural industries, such as in Hollywood, where the spatial concentration of production companies and creative labour extends social networks and increases the flow of information, learning effects and innovative potential.[13]

The relocation of units and crews to Barrandov was not as smooth as the proponents of the new 'film town' had expected. It shared the destiny of numerous other reorganizations that were typical of the late 1940s and early 1950s, which similarly did not respect informal routines or the traditions and hierarchies of production practices and cultures. As protocols from weekly meetings of so-called creative teams (i.e. units) show, only some dramaturges and writers really moved to their new offices in Barrandov; others preferred to work in cafés or even team member's private apartments.

The cultural conflict between the top-down reorganization and everyday practice can be illustrated by the case of the famous interwar actor and playwright Jan Werich (1905–1980), who was appointed head of one of the eleven creative teams. According to his colleague, director Jiří Kejčík, Werich produced the following ironic daily work report: 'I came to the studio in the morning... Then I marked my time card. I sat in my office and started thinking... I got no idea... After lunch, I finally got an idea and started to write... In the evening it appeared stupid to me. So I cut it out. I marked my time card again and went home.'[14] Across all artistic disciplines at that time, creative work was 'increasingly compared to manual labour with all its period attributes (so-called socialist commitments and planning)'.[15] Filmmakers were understandably afraid that politically empowered workers and functionaries at the studios would interfere with their work and social status.

The new top management that was introduced or promoted after the communist putsch was recruited from among party functionaries and loyal state officials, whereas many experienced practitioners, often former private producers and managers, were either fired and had to leave the film industry altogether, or transferred to less influential positions. The new leadership aimed to achieve two goals: ideological reform, by introducing the rigid aesthetics of socialist realism; and organizational reform, by building a centralized film factory that would follow planning directives like those in heavy industry and adopt so-called production norms slavishly translated from Soviet manuals – without acknowledgement that the Soviets themselves had, since the 1930s, been directly imitating the major Hollywood studios.[16]

The contrast between the industrial factory model and the practice of creative work was emphasized by experienced film practitioners, who criticized the bureaucratic approval procedures and extreme centralization that isolated artists from each other and deprived them of most decision-making competences, access to information and possibilities for collective action. Because they were compelled to defend the status of creative work as nonregulated, unplannable, individualized and embedded in the sociocultural centre of Prague,[17] their protests provided elite filmmakers with a unique and rare opportunity to explicitly articulate the material, cultural, geographic and temporal specificities of creative work at the time. On the one hand, filmmakers under the Stalinist regime were integrated into the centralized corporation of the national cinema, which was subject to the same kinds of strict norms and quantitative goals that other industries had to meet under the first Five-Year Plan. But on the other hand, the creative nature of filmmaking resisted the quantification and standardization introduced by the centralization of production and the unification of working conditions.

However, the final decision to abandon the model of the industrial factory staffed with a new film proletariat did not result from these protests alone. An even more important reason was that industrial planning procedures proved difficult to apply to film production, with its highly specialized (i.e. hard to replace) creative workers, irregular and nonserial production, and unpredictable results (both political and economic), not to mention the many projects halted by the approval committees. Long-term script development and preproduction processes simply could not be planned and measured by the quantitative standards used in heavy industry and serial production.[18] The attempts to apply Soviet-style production norms had only extended production times and increased costs. These norms, passively adopted from Soviet manuals issued in 1947, prescribed standards and quotas for all possible aspects of production, from film stock or shooting days to the exact division of labour.[19] On the whole, the factory style of management combined with rigid ideological control and harsh political purges nearly caused a collapse of production, reducing the yearly number of finished Czech feature films from 24 in 1950 to 7 in 1951.

Only gradually, and in several stages, did the political authorities come to acknowledge film production as creative work that cannot be planned, measured and paid for according to the number of products and working hours. From the failed attempt to implement the Soviet factory-style model in 1950, they went through interministerial discussions of whether film should be defined as industrial production or a cultural-political service (1951–1952),[20] and then through the gradual decentralization of the organizational structure in 1954–1958, until finally, in January 1963, the Central Committee commissioned the director of Czechoslovak Film to liberate film production from all remaining 'inappropriate and outdated indicators for measuring industrial production'.[21] This last move reveals not only that the Central Committee tried to loosen the repressive measures introduced after the notorious Banská Bystrica conference in 1959 and to adapt its rhetoric to the new liberalization processes that anticipated the Czech New Wave, but also that it recognized the commercial potential of Czech cinema. Functionaries readily sacrificed quantitative norms like budget and salary averages or limits on overtime work, as well as lengthy and centralized approval procedures, to allow for more flexible practices that they expected would contribute to further festival awards. These would in turn result in distribution and broadcast deals with 'capitalist' countries as well as more commissions from Western producers, who would rediscover Barrandov and its cheap labour pool and bring much-needed dollars into the country.[22] By that time, though, dramaturges and writers were already back in their clubs and cafés in central Prague.

The Film 'Jungle' and Intergenerational Politics

The filmmaking community's reputation among communist officials (and partly also among the wider public) was not very good. The prejudice against filmmakers was often expressed by the catchphrase 'cinema jungle,' known since the 1930s, which referred to the unscrupulousness, greed, parasitism, adventurousness, untrustworthiness and other negative features of the Prague Hollywood. After 1945, the phrase was used to criticize the social milieu of the old 'bourgeois' filmmaking community. To quote the eager communist film critic (who later turned into an equally eager proponent of the Czech New Wave) Antonín J. Liehm: 'The film jungle, which was often discussed in the past, did not disappear overnight after the nationalization of the film industry.'[23] The way the phrase was used to discredit experienced but politically unreliable professionals is illustrated by the words of director Vladimír Borský in a 1946 report commissioned by the Film Commission of the Central Committee (a body designed to secretly infiltrate the film industry before the communist putsch in 1948):

> Due to difficult living conditions, an insecure future and scarce working opportunities, the film workers were permanently engaged in a struggle

to survive, in jealousy, slander, and demeaning behaviour while searching for jobs; this was a necessary betrayal of moral values, which resulted in a constant sense of inferiority and absolute loss of artistic and human self-confidence. These were the factors that corrupted film artists.[24]

Whereas Borský, as an insider, blamed external conditions, the new communist establishment ascribed supposed low moral qualities to filmmakers themselves, particularly veteran practitioners, colloquially referred to as 'stagers' or 'bacons',[25] and to their class background. However, these politically suspicious veterans – be they directors (like Otakar Vávra and Martin Frič), screenwriters and dramaturges (like Josef Neuberg and Karel Smrž), former producers (like Karel Feix and Zdeněk Reimann), crew members (like director of photography Jan Stallich or editor Antonín Zelenka) or technicians – were the only ones who could provide the practical knowledge, skills, proven routines and standards of professionalism necessary to maintain production and train novices after the nationalization in 1945 and the communist putsch in 1948. Between 1945 and 1948, veteran 'capitalist' managers like Lavoslav Reichl, Vladimír Kabelík and Ladislav Kolda were appointed as high executives, and it was only thanks to their organizational skills that the newborn nationalized cinema did not go bankrupt in 1946.

After the political purges following the putsch in February 1948, veteran top executives were mostly dismissed or demoted, though middle managers and crew members were allowed to stay on. Meanwhile, the new management and their political supervisors at the Central Committee started a unique campaign to recruit a vast new pool of politically reliable and necessarily young, inexperienced creative workers. They employed a variety of methods, but all of them failed spectacularly: for example, a special one-year school was established for accelerated training of new, working-class filmmakers (e.g. a former car factory worker was allegedly trained as screenwriter). Unsurprisingly, all thirty-two students graduated successfully and were sent to Barrandov in 1951, yet most of them became bitterly disillusioned when they could not successfully integrate into the production community.[26]

However, the campaign's most visible and controversial move was the hiring of approximately a hundred mostly young communist writers and journalists in 1948–1949 to replace the existing production units and ideologically reform the process of 'dramaturgy', i.e. the selection of the 'right' subjects and their development into ideologically 'correct' screenplays. Among the new 'dramaturges' were radical proponents of the Zhdanovian aesthetics of socialist realism who were well connected to certain members of the Central Committee, including the head of the Cultural and Propaganda Division, Gustav Bareš. The newly appointed chiefs of creative teams Jiří Hájek, Miroslav Galuška and Jan Kloboučník were soon engaged in a confrontation with a group of Barrandov veterans represented by Otakar Vávra, Elmar Klos, Jiří Weiss and other filmmakers with interwar and wartime experience, who considered the novices mere dilettantes and had their own political connections to a rival group in the Central Committee, led by Minister of Information Václav Kopecký. The conflict between these two generational and political cliques – behind which was another, more high-profile conflict in the Central Committee between 'state power' and 'party power' – culminated in 1949 and 1950 with the relative victory of the veterans, resulting in the dissolution of all eleven creative teams in 1951 and the dismissal of their members.[27] A special report that the Barrandov communist organization compiled on the crisis – referred to as a fight against the 'second centre' (i.e. the power centre created by the 'leftist' radicals associated with Bareš) – stated:

> There were attempts to create conflicts between the young, inexperienced workers, screenwriters and directors, and the experienced masters of art. The apparatus of the Central Committee installed its people in Barrandov ... who were instructed to 'save' Czechoslovak film from the old bourgeois stagers as our prominent filmmakers were often called.[28]

However, the fight between the two power centres did not simply result in the victory of the 'good', authentic filmmakers and the defeat of the political radicals. The parallel political struggle, waged at the highest levels of the establishment that eventually arbitrated the conflict at Barrandov, resulted in political trials, including that of General Secretary Rudolf Slánský, who was charged with high treason and executed in late 1952. The director Otakar Vávra, the loudest of the veterans, used Slánský's case as a political weapon to identify his enemies among the young clique:

> Those henchmen of the conspiratorial centre, sent to Barrandov by the traitor Slánský to overtake power, assembled more than a hundred so-called screenwriters and writers with whom they wanted to expel and replace outstanding Czech writers and filmmakers. Those were mostly untalented but noisy people.... They used leftist rhetoric to vulgarize methods of socialist realism, promoted schematism ... to weaken the authority of the masters.[29]

Vávra's later moves suggest that his goal was not to engage in political struggle with the 'second centre' but to build a strong position in the studio and defend traditional standards of professionalism that were impossible to learn from the state-planned crash courses. In his view, these standards primarily demanded a quality screenplay with classical dramatic structure, meticulous preproduction planning and high production values (large sets and carefully choreographed mass scenes). In no way did these norms of professionalism exclude communist propaganda or attempts to adopt the rigid aesthetics of socialist realism.[30] Rather than higher artistic values, professionalism represented a 'long duration'[31] of production culture subject to top-down reorganizations but still resistant to direct interference into everyday practices and habits, informal hierarchies and implicit values.

The same norms of professionalism that helped the veterans defend their community against 'dilettantes' in the early 1950s served to block generational change in the upcoming years. Another political attack from the top levels of the Communist Party came in 1959 at the conference in Banská Bystrica, which was designed as a crackdown on the liberalization of the post-Stalinist period (1956–1958). The Central Committee criticized the veterans for restriction of the younger generation's work opportunities, for bourgeois individualism and for their alleged desire for wealth.[32] Paradoxically, the new generation that party functionaries promoted as creators of a truly socialist cinema purged of any bourgeois throwbacks was in fact the future Czech New Wave.[33]

Even more interestingly, the new, young generation did not compete with the old one but chose instead to look up to figures such as Vávra or Frič as teachers and truly 'classic' filmmakers who guaranteed continuity of the film craft.[34] The Film faculty of the Academy of Performing Arts (Filmová fakulta Akademie múzických umění, FAMU) played a key role as an intergenerational platform where strong relationships between teachers and students determined the latter's careers. Similarly, the country's sole professional organization of filmmakers, which was first renewed as a part of a theatre artists' guild in 1959 and went on to become an independent film and TV workers' association called FITES (Svaz filmových a televizních umělců) in 1965 (in 1948, the last remaining organization of this kind had been dissolved immediately following the communist putsch), integrated all generational groups and mediated between them. Beyond the differences between the traditionalist approach of the 1950s and the modernist aesthetics of the New Wave, generational conflicts seemed to be overcome:

young filmmakers rediscovered how important it was for their professional culture to share traditions that were embodied and protected by 'classic' filmmakers and teachers.[35]

Conclusion

This essay can only partially address the complex subject of socialist production cultures. My analysis has focused on a group of professional roles whose place might tentatively be thought of as corresponding to the American term 'above the line' – that is, the roles were held by creative decision-makers responsible for the whole conception of a film project, not just its execution. These included artistic and production chiefs, dramaturges, directors and screenwriters, mostly organized within and around so-called units in a typical organizational structure that allowed the state-socialist system to solve the problem of missing producers and middle management.[36] This chapter has shown how hectic, top-down changes met passive resistance from below during the first seventeen years of the units ('production units' and later 'creative units'). Beneath the turbulent reorganizations implemented roughly every two years in a strikingly chaotic manner (in the form of changes to top management, Soviet-style planning, 'working rules' and 'production norms', new organizational structures and jurisdictions, strategies of political control and ideological approval, etc.), the traditional production culture that had taken shape in the 1920s and 1930s and solidified during World War II survived. This culture's everyday habits, working routines and rhythms, informal hierarchies and learning processes, spaces, rituals and shared values formed the cultural environment where innovative creative ideas and new, efficient collaborative networks could take shape.

The top-down political changes happened much faster than the transformation of this local culture, which was embedded in the broader cultural and social milieu of downtown Prague, hidden from the film industrial base at Barrandov. It resisted simple changes that would, for example, transform script development into commission-based 'thematic planning' and film production into a centralized industrial factory, or replace experienced creative talent with new, 'proletarian' intellectuals. The communist rulers had to learn that they could not increase the quality and quantity of films without respecting this production culture and providing the professional community with the necessary level of autonomy and independence (in the form of units).

All of the structural reorganizations rearticulated the links between the new power centre and traditional teams of artists and support personnel, as well as between different sectors of the production community. After 1945, the nationalized film production incorporated the two main private production companies and maintained their modes of operation. Between 1948 and 1953, the period of the most intensive top-down centralization and political repression, these traditional production teams were dissolved and creative talent was pushed to merge with technicians and manual labourers in the Barrandov studios located ten kilometres outside Prague. Script development, supervised by so-called dramaturges, was disconnected from actual production to allow for stricter ideological control. Dozens of politically loyal writers were recruited to replace the experienced production and artistic chiefs. As a result, the production community became deeply frustrated, fractured and immobilized – and production nearly collapsed in the early 1950s.

The death of Stalin in 1953 ushered in a gradual decentralization of the organizational structure, a revival of semi-independent units, the reintegration of dramaturgy into the production process, and the liberalization of ideological control. Writers, directors and dramaturges started to once again build informal but efficient, semipermanent teams, and creative units began to operate as cultural mediators exposing film to new trends in literature and theatre and as defenders against ignorant, unpredictable pre-censorship interference from above. Revitalized informal learning processes in the studios, together with a renewed sense of intergenerational solidarity – supported by strong links between teachers and students at the flourishing FAMU and by the re-established professional association of film artists – helped the production community to redefine its shared value systems (i.e. standards of quality, innovation and collaborative work, etc.), build new alliances (mainly with writers and film critics) and consolidate its negotiating power vis-à-vis the political rulers. After an intermezzo in the wake of the political backlash following the Banská Bystrica conference in February 1959, the process of decentralization and liberalization resumed with still more vigour after 1962, and creative units gained even greater intellectual and organizational autonomy once they were allowed to establish their own 'ideological-artistic boards' (with many revisionist writers among their members) to replace the central approval body. This development marked the beginning of the so-called Czech

New Wave, which lasted until 1970, when the creative units were dissolved and replaced with 'dramaturgical units' that, much as they had done in 1948, diluted the autonomy of creative talent and separated them from production.

In this essay, I have shown how the state-socialist mode of production failed to fully replace the traditional middle management (i.e. former producers) with a new, factory-like organizational model and new 'cadres'. Consequently, it had to reinstall semi-independent 'units' to supervise actual script development and production processes – units that fell back on many practices of former 'capitalist' managers and freelance filmmakers. The top-down reorganizations failed not only because the new strategic management (i.e. the state, the party and their representatives in the studios) did not understand the technical, artistic and economic principles of film production, but also because the filmmaking community and its professional culture mounted passive resistance. This resistance was illustrated by two cases: first, the filmmakers' and dramaturges' protests against their relocation from the centre of Prague to the Barrandov 'factory'; and second, the generational clash between the 'veterans' and the 'second centre' supposedly formed by the young communists and their allies on the Central Committee. Both conflicts pushed members of the community to explicitly articulate their tacit professional knowledge and values in order to differentiate themselves from the young radicals and 'dilettantes'.

Although these values of professionalism and creative labour (e.g. the so-called filmic qualities and dramatic structure of the script versus the dogmatic directives of socialist realism) did not reveal any new or surprising concepts of creativity (from today's perspective), their significance comes to the fore when they are considered within the specific historical context. They mark the cultural limits of the state-socialist mode of production and help us to understand its paradoxical logic: the units, by continuing the practices of independent producers and building informal collaborative networks, saved the system from total collapse and made production efficient and culturally successful; yet they also enabled critical films to flourish and subvert the dominant ideology. The units operated as a battlefield where the top-down interventions interacted with the production community and its everyday working habits while dramaturgy mediated and negotiated between the political establishment (i.e. the actual strategic management) and the production community. The concept of units as middle managers and dramaturgy as a cultural interface became so ingrained in the local film industry that various shortcomings in Czech cinema were blamed on the units' sudden disappearance, even long after the units were dissolved in 1990.[37] The state's role as strategic manager of cultural production was partly overtaken by public service television, which became the main producer and co-producer of local films. Unsurprisingly, however, the heritage of 'units' and of dramaturgy has survived in public television's organizational structure until today.[38]

Acknowledgement

Financial support for this study was provided by the Czech Science Foundation, grant number P409/10/1361.

Petr Szczepanik is an associate professor at Masaryk University, Brno; a researcher at the National Film Archive, Prague; and editor of *Iluminace* (www.iluminace.cz). He is the author of *Canned Words: The Coming of Sound Film and Czech Media Culture of the 1930s* (in Czech, 2009). He has also edited or coedited several books on the history of film thought, including *Cinema All the Time: An Anthology of Czech Film Theory and Criticism, 1908–1939* (2008). His current research focuses on the Czech (post)socialist production system. Some of its findings are published in *Behind the Screen: Inside European Production Culture* (Palgrave, coedited with Patrick Vonderau, 2013). He was the principal coordinator of an EU-funded FIND project, which uses student internships at production companies to combine job shadowing with ethnographic research of production cultures.

Notes

1. David Bordwell, Janet Staiger and Kristin Thompson, *The Classical Hollywood Cinema: Film Style & Mode of Production to 1960* (New York: Columbia University Press, 1985). I have already introduced the concept of the state-socialist mode of film production in P. Szczepanik, 'The State-Socialist Mode of Production and the Political History of Production Culture', in P. Szczepanik and Patrick Vonderau (eds), *Behind the Screen: Inside European Production Cultures* (New York: Palgrave Macmillan, 2013), pp. 113–134.
2. John T. Caldwell, *Production Culture: Industrial Reflexivity and Critical Practice in Film and Television* (Durham, NC: Duke University Press, 2008).
3. In the other Eastern Bloc countries, units were headed mostly by directors, and dramaturges were not recognized as specific and important professionals. For a basic comparison of units in the GDR, Poland, Hungary and the USSR, see

P. Szczepanik, 'The State-Socialist Mode of Production and the Political History of Production Culture'.
4. On the concept of dramaturgy in the history of European and American theatre, see Mary Luckhurst, *Dramaturgy: A Revolution in Theatre* (Cambridge and New York: Cambridge University Press, 2006).
5. Tereza Cz. Dvořáková, 'Idea filmové komory. Českomoravské filmové ústředí a kontinuita centralizačních tendencí ve filmovém oboru 30. a 40. let' (Ph.D. dissertation, Charles University, 2011); David Welch, *Propaganda and the German Cinema 1933–1945* (London and New York: I.B. Tauris 2001), p. 14.
6. For a more detailed historical account of units in the Czech film industry see P. Szczepanik, 'Between Units and Producers: Organization of Creative Work in Czechoslovak State Cinema 1945–1990', in Marcin Adamczak, Piotr Marecki and Marcin Malatyński (eds), *Restart zespołów filmowych / Film Units: Restart* (Cracow: Ha!art, 2012), pp. 271–312.
7. A crucial exception is the excellent recent work on the Soviet filmmaking community of the Stalinist era, focused mostly on the status of screenwriters and directors; see Maria Belodubrovskaya, 'Politically Incorrect: Filmmaking under Stalin and the Failure of Power' (Ph.D. dissertation, University of Wisconsin-Madison, 2011).
8. Elmar Klos, *Dramaturgie je když... Filmový průvodce pro začátečníky i pokročilé* (Prague: SPN, 1990), p. 20.
9. Národní archiv (NA), Prague, ÚV KSČ, fond (f.) 19/7 – Ústřední kulturně propagační komise a kulturně propagační oddělení ÚV KSČ 1945–1955, archivní jednotka (a. j.) 664, složka (sl.) Návrhy pro org. sekretariát, Zdeněk Míka, Dne 1. března 1949 nastoupil jsem do Čs. st. filmu ve funkci ústředního dramaturga... [1949].
10. Národní filmový archiv (NFA), Prague, f. Čefis, karton (k.) R5/B1/2P/5K, Zápis z 1. schůze Prozatímního správního výboru Čefis, 1946.
11. Miloš Cympa, 'Šachový turnaj "par excellence"!', *Záběr* 6(February) (1954), 6–7.
12. NFA, f. Frič Martin, k. 11, inventární číslo 443, Stanovisko uměleckých šéfů k důsledkům, vyplývajícím z reorganisace Československé filmové společnosti, 1947.
13. Allen J. Scott, *On Hollywood: The Place, the Industry* (Princeton: Princeton University Press, 2000).
14. See Jan Kolář, 'Vidět zjitřeně. O to jde! Velký rozhovor s Jiřím Krejčíkem', *Divadelní noviny* 13(22) (2004), supplement 2. This anecdote was recalled by several other contemporaries, as documented in oral history interviews stored in the National Film Archive.
15. Jiří Knapík, *Únor a kultura. Sovětizace české kultury 1948–1950* (Prague: Libri, 2004), p. 110.
16. See Jamie Miller, 'Soviet Cinema, 1929–41: The Development of Industry and Infrastructure', *Europe-Asia Studies* 58(1) (2006), 103–124.
17. NA, f. 07/2 Gustav Bareš, svazek (sv.) 2, a. j. 11, Záznam o poradě, konané 28. října 1949 na Barrandově, p. 6–7.
18. Even the State Planning Office acknowledged this in 1951 by declaring film a unique product and a 'cultural service', and freeing it from the planning and controlling regulations applicable to industrial production. See 'Příprava nového plánu. Jednotný plán kulturní služby', *Věstník Československého státního filmu* 5(6) (1951), 31.
19. The Czech translation of the Soviet norms was published as *Instrukce* (Prague: ČSF, 1953; originally published in Moscow, 1947); the Czech derivative, literally adopting large parts of the Soviet model, was *Jednotné ustanovení o výrobních štábech ve výrobě uměleckých filmů a o právech a povinnostech členů výrobních štábů* (Prague: ČSF, 1951).

20. NA, f. Ministerstvo informací – dodatky, k. 127, Připomínky k návrhu ministerstva financí na přeměnu ČSF na národní podnik, July 1952.
21. NA, ÚV KSČ, f. 02/1 – Předsednictvo ÚV KSČ 1962–1966, sv. 6, a. j. 6/5, Usnesení k bodu Zpráva o současné situaci ve filmové tvorbě, 25 January 1963.
22. NA, ÚV KSČ, f. 05/3 – Ideologické oddělení 1951–1961, sv. 11, a. j. 69, Zpráva o řešení některých ekonomických otázek financování a plánování filmové tvorby, 16. 7. 1963.
23. Antonín J. Liehm, 'Problémy filmové dramaturgie', in *Filmová okénka* 1, no. 4 (2005), p. 25.
24. NA, ÚV KSČ, f. 19/7, a. j. 652/3, Vladimír Borský, Otázky tvůrčích pracovníků a dorostu v českém filmu [1946].
25. E. Klos, *Dramaturgie je když*, p. 53.
26. See Stanislav Šteindler, 'Ústřední dělnická škola Čs. státního filmu', *Kino* 6(20) (1951), 466; NFA, f. ČSF, k. R4/A1/1P/7K, sl. 9.
27. Jiří Knapík, 'Kulturní politika KSČ v oblasti filmové tvorby v letech 1948–1952' (MA thesis, Silesian University, 1998); idem, 'Filmová aféra L. P. 1949', *Iluminace* 12(4) (2000), 97–119.
28. Archiv hlavního města Prahy, Prague, f. 02/1, fasc. 93, i. č. 456, Zpráva o činnosti závodní organisace KSČ Barrandov, 26 January 1953.
29. Otakar Vávra, 'Za ideově uměleckou kvalitu čs. kinematografie a za hospodárné splnění plánu', *Kino* 8(5) (1953), 68.
30. Otakar Vávra, *Podivný život režiséra. Obrazy vzpomínek* (Prague: Prostor, 1996).
31. Fernand Braudel, 'History and the Social Sciences: The *Longue Durée*', in *On History* (Chicago: The University of Chicago Press, 1982), pp. 25–54.
32. See 'Zpráva pro ideologickou komisi ÚV KSČ o současné situaci v hraném filmu, předložená Zdeňkem Urbanem 12. 11. 1959', *Iluminace* 16(4) (2004), 202–203.
33. Ivan Klimeš, 'Filmaři a komunistická moc v Československu. Vzrušený rok 1959', *Iluminace* 16(4) (2004), pp. 136–137.
34. See e.g. Antonín J. Liehm, *Closely Watched Films: The Czechoslovak Experience* (White Plains, NY: International Arts and Sciences Press, 1974).
35. *Konference Svazu čs. filmových a televizních umělců* (Prague: [FITES], 1968), pp. 25–26.
36. Hypothetically, lead actors might also be included, but the term 'above the line' is not applicable to them in this context, since actors in the Czechoslovak production system could not attain the economic status of 'stars'. In addition, they had no major say in the conception of film projects and were not powerful financial partners. They received standardized salaries and honorariums (divided into several levels according to their category) determined by a special evaluating committee, much like all other creative talent did. Although there were several attempts to establish a purely cinematic pool of actors, the vast majority of them were full-time employees of Prague's legitimate theatres whose schedules were prebooked with theatrical commitments, making any film casting an unpredictable adventure.
37. See e.g. the interviews in Štěpán Hulík, *Kinematografie zapomnění. Počátky normalizace ve Filmovém studiu Barrandov (1968–1973)* (Prague: Academia, 2011).
38. The functioning of Czech public television's dramaturgical units, which draw explicitly on their older film models, has been thoroughly described in Pavel Krumpár, 'Česká televize jako filmový producent v letech 1992–2002' (Part 1), *Iluminace* 22(4) (2010), 21–70; and idem, 'Česká televize jako filmový producent v letech 1992–2002' (Part 2), *Iluminace* 23(1) (2011), 21–62. The tradition of units is also very vital in today's Polish film industry; see Edward Zajiček, *Poza ekranem. Polska kinematografia w latach 1896–2005*, 2nd ed. (Warsaw: Stowarzyszenie Filmowców Polskich and Studio Filmowe Montevideo, 2009).

Select Bibliography

Belodubrovskaya, Maria. 'Politically Incorrect: Filmmaking under Stalin and the Failure of Power'. Ph.D. dissertation, University of Wisconsin-Madison, 2011.

Bordwell, David, Janet Staiger and Kristin Thompson. *The Classical Hollywood Cinema: Film Style and Mode of Production to 1960*. New York: Columbia University Press, 1985.

Braudel, Fernand. 'History and the Social Sciences: The Longue Durée'. In *On History*. Chicago: University of Chicago Press, 1980.

Caldwell, John T. *Production Culture: Industrial Reflexivity and Critical Practice in Film and Television*. Durham, NC: Duke University Press, 2008.

Dvořáková, Tereza Cz. 'Idea filmové komory. Českomoravské filmové ústředí a kontinuita centralizačních tendencí ve filmovém oboru 30. a 40. let'. Ph.D. dissertation, Charles University, 2011.

Hulík, Štěpán. *Kinematografie zapomnění. Počátky normalizace ve Filmovém studiu Barrandov (1968–1973)*. Prague: Academia, 2011.

Klimeš, Ivan. 'Filmaři a komunistická moc v Československu. Vzrušený rok 1959'. *Iluminace* 16(4) (2004), 129–137.

Knapík, Jiří. 'Kulturní politika KSČ v oblasti filmové tvorby v letech 1948–1952'. MA thesis, Silesian University, 1998.

Knapík, Jiří. 'Filmová aféra L. P. 1949'. *Iluminace* 12(4) (2000), 97–119.

Knapík, Jiří. *Únor a kultura. Sovětizace české kultury 1948–1950*. Prague: Libri, 2004.

Konference Svazu čs. filmových a televizních umělců. Prague: [FITES] 1968.

Krumpár, Pavel. 'Česká televize jako filmový producent v letech 1992–2002' (Part 1). *Iluminace* 22(4) (2010), 21–70.

Krumpár, Pavel. 'Česká televize jako filmový producent v letech 1992–2002' (Part 2). *Iluminace* 23(1) (2011), 21–62.

Liehm, Antonín J. *Closely Watched Films: The Czechoslovak Experience*. White Plains, NY: International Arts and Sciences Press, 1974.

Luckhurst, Mary. *Dramaturgy: A Revolution in Theatre*. Cambridge and New York: Cambridge University Press, 2006.

Miller, Jamie. 'Soviet Cinema, 1929–41: The Development of Industry and Infrastructure'. *Europe-Asia Studies* 58(1) (2006), 103–124.

Scott, Allen J. *On Hollywood: The Place, the Industry*. Princeton: Princeton University Press, 2000.

Szczepanik, Petr. 'Between Units and Producers: Organization of Creative Work in Czechoslovak State Cinema 1945–1990'. In Marcin Adamczak, Piotr Marecki and Marcin Malatyński (eds), *Restart zespołów filmowych / Film Units: Restart*. Cracow: Ha!art, 2012.

Szczepanik, Petr. 'The State-Socialist Mode of Production and the Political History of Production Culture'. In Petr Szczepanik and Patrick Vonderau (eds), *Behind the Screen: Inside European Production Cultures*. New York: Palgrave Macmillan, 2013.

Vávra, Otakar. *Podivný život režiséra. Obrazy vzpomínek*. Prague: Prostor, 1996.

Welch, David. *Propaganda and the German Cinema 1933–1945*. London and New York: I.B. Tauris, 2001.

Zajiček, Edward. *Poza ekranem. Polska kinematografia w latach 1896–2005*. 2nd ed. Warsaw: Stowarzyszenie Filmowców Polskich and Studio Filmowe Montevideo, 2009.

Chapter 4

BARRANDOV'S CO-PRODUCTIONS

The Clumsy Way to Ideological Control, International Competitiveness and Technological Improvement

Pavel Skopal

As early as the 1920s, film industry representatives in West European countries had made co-production and distribution deals with the intention of maintaining competitiveness with – and protection against – imports from Hollywood.[1] The practice of co-productions also boomed in postwar Europe, particularly after 1946, when a French-Italian co-production agreement was signed. The reasons for such engagements were very similar to those from before the war: to increase competitiveness vis-à-vis the outside threat of Hollywood production. In Western Europe, the co-production model was at its peak from the end of the 1950s to the beginning of the 1960s. In France, a total of sixty-three movies were made in 1957 together with a co-production partner.[2]

The history of Soviet Bloc co-productions offers a very different story indeed in terms of scale, motivation and the dynamic of international cooperation. At the same time, however, we can recognize certain parallels concerning the historical moment when interest in this mode of production emerged, although initial plans to shoot many more movies under co-production treaties in 1948 and in the late 1950s quickly became more restrained. The impetus behind the short-term inclination towards co-productions in the late 1940s was the Soviet Union's geopolitical plotting and its colonizing approach to facilities in Czechoslovakia and the Soviet Occupation Zone/German Democratic Republic (GDR). Very few co-productions had been implemented prior to the mid-1950s, but the period of liberalization following the

Twentieth Congress of the Communist Party of the Soviet Union (CPSU) had the side effect of intensified interest in both intra- and trans-Bloc co-productions, which coincided with the apex of co-production practice in Western Europe. This chapter aims to explain the role co-productions played in the plans and production practices of the Czech studio Barrandov and its partners, and how these productions were influenced by the strategic goals of Soviet cultural policy. Analysis of the abrupt shifts in the Soviet Bloc countries' attitudes towards co-productions raises questions about what possible role Soviet cultural officials had in coordinating the behaviour of the film industries, particularly in proportion to the role of local political and cultural functionaries. I specifically focus on how the dissemination of cultural, technical and technological values influenced the process of co-producing films. More generally, I also consider the various functions that co-productions performed with regard to both film industry goals and cultural policy plans.

Planning to the Rhythm of a Political Campaign: A Postwar Market for Soviet Cinema

While the first postwar co-production treaties between West European countries were based on shared cultural values and meant to help the respective national film industries compete against Hollywood imports, the Soviet Ministry of Cinematography's initial intentions for co-productions were expansive, rather than protective. The first steps in the postwar Soviet model of co-production were driven by plans to become the leader of the European film market, and consequently of the market of ideas.[3] By July 1945, the Council of People's Commissars had instructed the Soviet Ministry of Cinematography to send cameramen to Czechoslovakia, Yugoslavia, Bulgaria, Romania, Austria and Germany. Two years later, Minister of the Film Industry Ivan G. Bolshakov praised the results of these activities, which had established many points of contact in addition to producing shots for use in newsreels.

In January 1948 Mikhail Kalatozov, the deputy of the Minister of the Film Industry, moved beyond this stage of 'networking' towards a more precise vision of co-productions as a tool for ideological expansion and improvement of film industry productivity:

For the fight against Anglo-American expansion in the states of new democracy, for the improvement of exhibition conditions for Soviet movies, and for a deepening of our ideological-political influence in these states, it could be effective to increase the stock of our movies by co-producing with film companies in the new democracies and elsewhere. It is realistic to shoot such co-productions in the film studios of Prague and Vienna and to a certain extent in our country. The project of the Ministry of Cinematography related to this vision was presented at the Central Committee of All-Union Communist Party Bolsheviks... Its implementation would increase our film supply (beyond the production of our own studios) by 10–15 films in the period 1948–1949 and by 20–25 films in subsequent years.

Because co-productions demand the involvement of a wide circle of authors, actors, directors and other strata of the intelligentsia in the states of new democracy, this step would result in a significant strengthening of our ideological-political influence in these countries.[4]

Initially the intent was to develop the extensive co-production plans within the organizational structure of the Ministry of Cinematography by establishing a specific department for foreign production. The plan was to shoot in studios in Prague, Budapest, Vienna and Berlin, with the Soviet Ministry of Cinematography assuming a 55 per cent share and the 'right to control the ideological-political orientation of the movies'.[5]

These plans for co-productions were part of Bolshakov's ambitious goals to produce 80 to 100 movies per year and make Mosfilm one of the biggest film studios in Europe. However, all these visions were destroyed by a decision of the Council of Ministers in June 1948, which argued that the Ministry of Cinematography was overly attentive to quantity at the expense of quality. In the future, every film should be a 'masterpiece' capable of instilling communist consciousness in the masses.[6] The continuation of Zhdanov's campaign against the influence of 'bourgeois culture' and the policy of cultural isolation terminated the yet-to-be-launched model of extensive co-producing as a means to expand into Europe. Bolshakov's and Kalatozov's plans were now limited to the distribution treaties.

The First Soviet Bloc Co-Productions and Their Motivations

Less than a year later, in April 1949, Minister Bolshakov sent a report to Georgy Malenkov, the secretary of the All-Union Communist Party Bolsheviks, about the aid provided to the 'new democracies' for the development of their cinema industries.⁷ This process, however, was not true aid but in fact a tool of Sovietization that spread Soviet aesthetic and production values; moreover, in certain cases it offered the opportunity to survey and become familiar with the technical equipment of these countries. Czechoslovakia was involved in an 'aid' plan, even though the Czech facilities boasted experienced personnel as well as advanced technical equipment and in 1948 the Barrandov studio had produced more movies (19) than all the Soviet studios combined.

The motivation behind the alleged aid to Albania was completely different from technological exploitation. As part of this aid effort, the Soviets promoted the co-production of a movie about the Albanian national hero, *Skanderbeg* (Sergei Yutkevich, 1953). The movie was not completed until 1953, but the Soviet Ministry of Cinematography had sent the prominent scriptwriter Mikhail Papava to Albania as early as 1949. The cooperation resulted in a spectacular colour movie that fit well with Stalin's plans. The project had been launched shortly after Stalin's intervention against Josip Broz Tito's plans to unite Yugoslavia with Albania and establish a Balkan confederation together with Romania and Bulgaria.⁸ It is hardly a coincidence that the second Soviet co-production – *Geroi Shipki/Geroite na Shipka* (The Heroes of Shipka, Sergei Vasilyev, 1954), produced with Bulgaria – was launched in the troubling Balkan region as well. The movie focuses on Russia's Balkan campaign of 1877–1878, emphasizing Russia's messianic role for the Balkan nations in the fight against the Turks and their British allies.⁹ Here, one of the Soviets' motivations was to provide a proper allegorical representation of the line between friends and enemies and to stress the difference between good (Soviet) and bad (British and Turkish) alliances for the Balkan countries, in both the past and the present.

The next co-productions involving the Soviet Bloc countries were launched in the GDR in 1954 and 1955, shortly after Stalin's death, as the result of an unusual partnership between the East German industry and a West German producer disguised as a Swedish company.¹⁰ Later, between 1956 and 1960, the East German studio DEFA (Deutsche Film-Aktiengesellschaft) undertook four rather expensive and prestigious co-productions with France.¹¹ These rather problematic, fragile partnerships provided an unexpected impetus for the first co-production between DEFA and Barrandov. For explicitly identified strategic reasons, in May 1955 the head of the East German Central Film Administration (Hauptverwaltung Film) Anton Ackermann proposed a co-production project to representatives of Czechoslovak State Film (Československý státní film, ČSF). According to Ackermann, although cooperation with capitalist partners was approved, the Socialist Unity Party of Germany (Sozialistische Einheitspartei Deutschlands, SED) supported only co-productions with socialist countries. A first co-production with the Soviets was not within easy reach, and 'the situation when DEFA makes co-productions with capitalist partners but none with the friendly socialist countries as Czechoslovakia or Poland is no longer acceptable'.[12] Ackermann succeeded in closing an agreement with the ČSF representatives to both initiate and finish the first DEFA-Barrandov co-production during 1956, and the Czechoslovak Ministry of Foreign Affairs urged ČSF to comply with Ackermann's terms.[13] However, the first film, *Ročník 21/Jahrgang 21* (Those Born in 1921, Václav Gajer, 1957), was in fact completed with a delay of one year. Based on a novel by a Czech writer Karel Ptáčník, the movie presents the love story of a Czech musician doing forced labour in Germany and a German nurse. Despite reports of East German audiences' generally reserved reception, allegedly stemming from the film's depiction of German Nazis and destroyed German cities, GDR functionaries, including First Secretary of the SED Walter Ulbricht, praised the movie.[14]

Co-productions with Western partners became possible in the post-Stalinist era. They were motivated, as I argue below, by the possibility of exchange of knowledge and technical equipment. Yet at the same time, functionaries in both the GDR and Czechoslovakia felt obliged to demonstrate improved cooperation within the Soviet Bloc. The first DEFA-Barrandov co-production used antifascist discourse as a tool for overcoming the obvious resentments between the former war enemies, now destined to be comrades in socialism. Nevertheless, the primary impetus for realizing the project did not derive from an official demand to cultivate this discourse. Instead, the movie served to excuse the two studios' developing relations with partners beyond the Iron Curtain.[15]

Technological Import, Ideological Export: Co-productions with Western Partners

The official bodies' changing attitudes towards co-productions with Western partners closely mirrored the shifts between offensive isolationism and defensive integrationism in foreign policy.[16] The main ideological justification for co-productions was founded on the argument that they provided a chance for ideological expansion into Western markets. However, the unspoken yet more powerful motivation rested elsewhere, in the technological innovation desired by the film industry and instigated by the party and governmental bodies.

The 1948 Communist putsch in Czechoslovakia brought an end to ČSF's preliminary postwar plans to shoot movies in cooperation with American producers.[17] Five years later, however, the process of liberalization introduced by the New Course[18] resulted in a changed attitude towards collaboration with French filmmakers, and in 1955 a government resolution called upon the Ministry of Culture to strengthen cultural relations with France. The ministry received an assignment to prepare a co-production project with France, and ČSF leaders asked director Alfréd Radok to cast French actors in his movie *Dědeček automobil* (Vintage Car, 1956). Thus the movie featured French actors, including Raymond Bussières, whose 'progressiveness' had been proved by the fact of his participation in a theatrical group's tour of the USSR in 1934.[19]

Both *Dědeček automobil* and the animated feature *Stvoření světa* (The Creation of the World, Eduard Hofman, 1957) were nonetheless indigenous productions. The first co-production with a French company (Le Trident), the movie *V proudech/La Liberté surveillée* (Twisting Currents, Vladimír Vlček, 1957), was realized and distributed under rapidly changing conditions. The movie's fate offers a compelling illustration of both the incentives for co-production and the penetrative impact of the rapidly changing political atmosphere on this mode of production. This movie project was highly important and desired because of its status as the first domestic movie shot in widescreen format – originally there was no intention to shoot it with a foreign partner. But when the filmmakers encountered problems with their freshly bought French Debrie cameras, the director Vlček utilized his contacts in France to draw in the new partner. Despite fundamental changes to the script and the involvement of the French star couple Marina Vlady and Robert Hossein, the project was still officially endorsed, as demonstrated by the presence of then-president Antonín Zápotocký at the shooting. Meanwhile, plans for further co-productions with the West – adaptations of Karel Čapek and Franz Kafka, intended to be shot in Cinemascope – were unanimously supported by representatives of Western governments as well.[20] West European agencies rather properly interpreted the Soviet Bloc countries' activity in this field as the product of a cultural offensive and an attempt to gain access to technical equipment and skills.[21]

By the time the movie *V proudech* reached screens in May 1958, however, the political atmosphere was rapidly changing (in the wake of the autumn 1956 events in Hungary and the Eleventh Congress of the Czechoslovak Communist Party in June 1958). This film in particular and co-productions with Western partners in general were harshly attacked in the press as introducing the danger of cultural colonization, purveying exploitative exoticism in terms of the Western view of Czechoslovak society, and so on.[22] As outlined below, the Soviets shared and supported this shift in attitude towards co-productions.[23] The Soviet film industry did complete the Mosfilm-Alkan co-production *Normandie-Niémen* (Jean Dréville, 1960), but prior to this many other projects involving Soviet studios on one side, and French, Italian and American companies on the other side, had been suspended.[24]

From a Fairy Tale to a War: Co-productions inside the Soviet Bloc

Prior to 1960, Barrandov had made just seven movies in co-production with foreign partners: two with the USSR, two with Bulgaria and one each with the GDR, Poland, Yugoslavia and France.[25] The foreign policy of the participating countries and shifts in the Cold War atmosphere significantly influenced the conception, development and reception of each resulting film, starting with Barrandov's first two postwar co-productions: *Legenda o lásce/Legenda za ljubovstva* (A Legend about Love, Václav Krška, 1956) and *Labakan* (Václav Krška, 1956). While the latter of these fairy tales was devised as a side project to the first to maximize expenses for the stage setting, the former film was launched at the incentive of Bulgarian Prime Minister Valko Chervenkov and Czechoslovak Minister of Culture Ladislav Štoll.[26] As I discuss below in further detail, the co-production with the French company Le Trident, *V proudech*, was stimulated by political circles on both sides, yet the shaky political situation of the late 1950s led film critics and state officials to harshly criticize both this film and the comedy *Hvězda jede na jih/Zvijezda putuje na jug* (The Star Travels South, Oldřich Lipský, 1958), made together with the Yugoslav studio Lovčenfilm. After a scathing critique at the First Festival of Czechoslovak Cinema in February 1959, the distribution of this Yugoslav co-production was in fact suspended and the film was shelved. Although the official reason for this intervention was the film's 'political weakness and low quality', it was primarily the rising antagonism in Soviet-Yugoslav relations at the time that doomed *Hvězda jede na jih*.[27]

To understand the insecurity, risk and volatility of the field of co-productions in the second half of the 1950s, we must contrast the programmatic statements of both the officials and the film industry representatives with the actual fates of the individual projects, while also taking into account the impulses from the Soviet Union. Until early 1958, party officials still supported Czechoslovak State Film's enthusiasm for co-productions, and in that year the ČSF Central Administration proposed to the Ministry of Education and Culture a plan for thirty-two co-productions. Only one of these was actually realized: the children's film *Přátelé na moři/Poteryannaya fotografiya* (Friends Travelling at Sea, Lev A. Kulidzhanov and Stanislav Strnad, 1959), which was co-produced with the Soviet studio of Maxim Gorky in Moscow.[28] Of all the co-productions of the 1950s, only one managed to slip through without criticism: the ideologically bullet-proof Barrandov/Maxim Gorky Studio co-production *Májové hvězdy/Mayskie Zvyozdy* (May Stars, Stanislav Rostotsky, 1959), which relates four loosely connected stories of Red Army soldiers involved in the liberation of Czechoslovakia. The control mechanism over potential international projects was gradually tightening throughout 1958 and 1959. The Politburo of the Central Committee of the Communist Party of Czechoslovakia (Ústřední výbor Komunistické strany Československa, ÚV KSČ) decided in June 1958 to require the Ministry of Education and Culture to receive approval from the Ministry of Finance, Ministry of Foreign Affairs and ideological department of the ÚV KSČ before authorizing a co-production.[29] The fact that the newly appointed director of ČSF, Alois Poledňák, harshly criticized *Přátelé na moři* – a co-production with a Soviet studio – for violating this control system confirms that the entire practice of co-production had suddenly found itself in disfavour.

International Conferences: Spaces of (Dis)Harmony

These developments in co-production practice within the Soviet Bloc raise the question as to whether the abrupt shifts in attitude towards collaborative projects resulted from local officials' 'translation' of certain events possessing global political reverberation, or whether there was a significant transnational transmitter disseminating signals to encourage a 'proper' attitude towards co-productions. As demonstrated by the case of the Conference of Cinema Industry Workers of Socialist Countries, which took place in 1957, 1958 and 1960 – namely, in the attitudes towards co-productions presented there and the way in which the Soviets more or less conspiratorially organized this series of events – the authors of Soviet cultural policy strove to control and coordinate the ideological frameworks of the individual film industries. The first incentive to organize international conferences came from Soviet Minister of Culture Nikolai Mikhailov in September 1956, although the Soviets attempted to conceal their role as instigators behind what supposedly were the initiatives of Czech film officials.[30] The way the Soviets initiated and coordinated this first conference from behind the scenes supports the thesis that the Soviet Ministry of Culture saw the conference as a pragmatic tool for constructing a stage upon which rebellious satellite countries could be 'consensually' criticized by the whole socialist camp.

The conferences attempted to establish an institutionalized network for the dissemination of cultural values, ideological rules and aesthetic practices among the film industries. Although the values presented at the conferences typically came from the Soviet side, they were often distributed through other nodes of the network to give the impression that there was no centre to the web. Cultural agreements with individual governments, together with the work of bodies such as the various Societies of Soviet Friendship, were partially able to compensate for the lack of proper coordinating agencies on a bilateral level, but there was no overarching body to coordinate the cinema industries on the transnational level throughout the whole Soviet Bloc – a situation that the institutionalization of these conferences was intended to rectify.

The first of the three conferences was organized in Prague in December 1957. Yugoslavia feared that the resulting resolutions might be constraining and took part only as an observer, but delegates from eleven other countries came to Prague as official participants. In the following year, the Romanian mountain resort Sinaia hosted the event, which maintained its massive dimensions – close to 100 delegates from twelve countries participated, although the Soviets sent only four delegates due to a concurrent visit to Hollywood by several of their prominent filmmakers. The final conference took place in the Bulgarian capital Sofia in November 1960.[31]

The various activities discussed and planned at the first conference included thematic plans of production (aimed at avoiding overlap in the topics implemented by the national film industries), publication of a multilingual theoretical journal, exchanges of personnel and experiences among the national associations of film clubs and cinema workers, and last but not least, cultivation of the practice of co-productions. Alongside the concept of socialist realism and the critique of schematism, co-productions remained a consistent topic at the conferences. Although the discussion of socialist realism evolved from a re-confirmation of the conservative conception in 1957 to a mildly liberalized approach in 1960, the attitude towards co-productions did not follow this pattern – at least, not in the sense that a general support of co-productions developed in the wake of liberalization. The consideration of co-productions at the conferences began with strong support for films made within the Soviet Bloc as well as in cooperation with Western partners, and ended with a conditional ban on co-productions after the Soviets clearly signalled that it would be preferable to supplant the practice of co-productions with the exchange of individual filmmakers and actors.[32]

Some of the talks at the last conference in Sofia provide insight into the reasons for this shift in attitude: they sent a signal that film production should be more competitive within the international arena and should be inspired by Western art film production (e.g. Soviet director Sergei Gerasimov expressed his respect for the films of Federico Fellini, Alain Resnais and Stanley Kramer in the conference's main presentation).[33] This signal was recognized by creative personnel and in a secret report for the SED central committee where DEFA scriptwriter Wolfgang Kohlhaase enthusiastically summarized the conference's conclusions as moving towards a 'world language of cinema' (*die Weltfilmsprache*), which would make socialist art a part of 'world film art' (*die Weltfilmkunst*) and would help films from the Soviet Bloc achieve a 'world-class standard' (*das Weltniveau*).[34] In effect, at the end of the conservative interlude of the late 1950s, the practice of co-productions was nearly brought to a standstill and then supplanted by a supposedly more effective model that focused on the exchange of individual personnel (both filmmakers and actors). The original reasons for initiating the conferences were quickly vanishing due to processes of 'consolidation' within the Bloc (primarily in Poland and Hungary) and the stronger emphasis on competitiveness in the contest with Western cinema for both festival and regular audiences. The attempt to use conferences to rigidly institutionalize ideologically driven interaction between Soviet Bloc countries gave way to a more flexible and pragmatic mode of cooperation that was established on an ad hoc basis utilizing personal contacts. The Soviets' attempt to control the dissemination of values through co-productions, as practised from 1953 to 1959, was deferred in favour of the proposed exchange of individual practitioners.

Beyond the 1950s, in Colour and Widescreen

The role of co-productions as a tool for tightening and rationalizing relations between the film industries of the Soviet Bloc was finally doomed in November 1959, when the Soviet film industry, following the 'recommendation' of the Central Committee of the Communist Party of the Soviet Union to 'strongly reduce international co-productions', strove to halt as many co-productions as possible. Soviet studios suspended twelve features; only five others too far along in their development to shelve were kept on the plan.[35] In accordance with the hints emerging from the last conference and with the general tendency towards opening the cultural sphere to direct competitiveness, the practice of co-production gave way to a more practical, flexible strategy of individual ad hoc networking. After 1960, Soviet co-productions were perceived as inadequate to the goal of achieving accolades at competitive international film festivals.

However, the Czech film studio Barrandov did not entirely give up on co-productions at the start of the 1960s. The main incentives for a partnership with Western producers were essentially the same as before, though now acted upon with a much stronger sense of pragmatism and self-confidence. The 'fifties' lasted a little longer for Barrandov, in practice coming to an end in 1962, when it made four co-productions with partners from the Soviet Bloc and 'developing' countries.[36] The primary factors leading to the halt in co-production practice in Czechoslovakia were the critical attitude of the Central Committee of the KSČ towards weak export results and the fact that no co-productions had achieved significant laurels at international film festivals.[37] After only two years without co-productions, however, Barrandov resumed the practice with Western partners. The first such project was *31 ve stínu* (Ninety Degrees in the Shade, Jiří Weiss, 1965), made with British producer Raymond Stross. The directors of the New Wave generation made four films with Western partners,[38] which secured the otherwise unattainable assets of hard currency and, consequently, technical equipment, precious colour film stock, attractive exteriors, distribution access to Western markets and, not least, much higher pay for directors and scriptwriters. The partnership contributed to increased artistic recognition, more festival awards, and improved creative conditions for the young directors of the Czechoslovak New Wave involved in the productions (Vojtěch Jasný, Miloš Forman, Věra Chytilová and Jiří Menzel). One of the four co-productions directed by the young New Wave generation was shot in widescreen, and all were shot with precious Eastmancolor material instead of the notoriously unreliable East-German Agfa/Orwo film stock. Reflecting on *Hoří, má panenko!* (The Firemen's Ball, Miloš Forman, 1967), shot on Eastmancolor, Miloš Forman aptly remarked that 'only the oldest and the most prominent directors ... got the East-German colour stock Orwo.... Ponti's money gave us the chance to purchase high-quality film stock from the West'.[39]

Conclusion

Some of the above-mentioned instances of co-production emerged as a manifestation of the Soviet cultural policy's tendency to use international projects as a mechanism of control over the cultural sphere and ensure the proper representation of national myths (*Skanderbeg, Geroi Shipki*). The strongest, yet strictly negative, impulse on the part of the Soviets came in the late 1950s, when the Ministry of Culture conspired first to control and coordinate co-production, and ultimately to discontinue the practice. Before this, however, Barrandov had managed to shoot a film with a French company, which served as a means for technological improvement and aided the transition towards widescreen production. At the same time, at least one of the co-productions (*Ročník 21*) was clearly intended to send a political message of loyalty to the 'socialist camp' while also acting as an ideological curtain that was supposed to make cooperation with Western partners more acceptable.

As these examples from both the Soviet and Czech viewpoints suggest, the 'local' party and film industry functionaries did not depend on their own interpretations to determine whether an international co-production conformed to the current constellation of international policy: instead, the relevant Soviet officials found ways to signal the proper attitude. After the mid-1950s, though, the signals were not interpreted and executed with the same obedience as before, and film industry functionaries in particular attempted to pursue their own interests more closely. In effect, the Soviet Ministry of Culture attempted to use the Conference of Cinema Industry Workers of Socialist Countries as an institution for the transmission of clear, strong signals instructing the national film industries on how to behave. Yet despite local political and cultural functionaries' decisive support for the ultimate restriction of co-productions, their motives and incentives were mostly indigenous, though they also found agreement with the Soviet strategy.

As the analysis in this essay demonstrates, co-productions served a wide range of overlapping goals and purposes, and it is difficult to categorize them simply according to a conservative or a liberal tendency of cultural policy – in some cases, even individual projects themselves were labelled in a seemingly contradictory way. Furthermore, the expansion of the practice of co-production did not occur in parallel with a process of liberalization. Of course, cooperation with Western partners was inevitably related to a certain degree of liberalization in the cultural sphere, whereas the 'preferred' cooperation within the Bloc occasionally served the intentions of the Soviets. Nevertheless, the curbing of co-productions at the end of the 1950s by no means signified a final defeat of liberal tendencies,[40] nor did it mark a shift away from direct competition with the West and a return to isolationism. Starting in the early 1960s, co-productions were perceived as a less effective, more expensive, clumsier mode of production that did not conform to the USSR's offensive ambitions in the cultural sphere – ambitions that were manifested, for example, in the Soviet Ministry of Culture's move to force Czechoslovak State Film to organize the festival in Karlovy Vary on a biannual basis in order to 'make a space' for the Moscow International Film Festival in the alternating years.[41] How the individual national film industries of the Soviet Bloc coped with the situation is another question: Barrandov, for example, participated in an alternative strategy of exchange among film practitioners by providing experienced filmmakers for production at DEFA. In the second half of the 1960s, the Czech film studio resumed co-operation with Western partners on projects that served to supplement the efficiency of the talented representatives of the Czechoslovak New Wave.[42]

Pavel Skopal is an assistant professor at the Department of Film Studies and Audiovisual Culture, Masaryk University, Brno, Czech Republic. In 2010–2012 he was a visiting researcher at the Konrad Wolf Film and Television University in Potsdam, Germany (research project supported by the Alexander von Humboldt Foundation). He has edited anthologies devoted to local cinema history in Brno and to the Czech film industry in the 1950s, and published *The Cinema of the North Triangle* (in Czech, 2014), a book of comparative research on cinema distribution and exhibition in Czechoslovakia, Poland and the GDR in the period 1945–1970.

Notes

1. The 'Film Europe' project was the first extensive attempt to implement a vision of transnational film cooperation in Europe. See Andrew Higson and Richard Maltby (eds), *'Film Europe' and 'Film America': Cinema, Commerce, and Cultural Exchange 1920–1939* (Exeter: University of Exeter Press, 1999).
2. See Anne Jäckel, 'Dual Nationality Film Productions in Europe after 1945', *Historical Journal of Film, Radio and Television* 23(3) (2003), 213–243.
3. For an analysis of the communist project in Eastern Europe as 'the largest deliberately designed experiment in globalization in modern history', see György Péteri, 'Nylon Curtain: Transnational and Transsystemic Tendencies in the Cultural Life of State-Socialist Russia and East-Central Europe', *Slavonica* 10(2) (2004), 113–123; and for the specific case of the Soviet Film Monopoly's plan for global expansion, see Jindřiška Bláhová, 'A Tough Job for Donald Duck: Hollywood, Czechoslovakia, and Selling Films behind the Iron Curtain, 1944–1951' (Ph.D. thesis, University of East Anglia and Charles University-Prague, 2010), pp. 152–179.
4. Letter from Kalatozov to A. M. Jegolinov and L. S. Baranov, All-Union Communist Party (Bolsheviks) (Vsesoyuznaya Kommunisticheskaya Partiya /Bol'shevikov/, VKPb), 19 January 1948. Published in Valerij Fomin, 'Političeskij effekt filma ‚Russkyj vopros' propadajet... Iz opyta sovetizacii poslevoennogo kinoprokata i kinoproizvodstva v Centralnoj i Vostočnoj Evrope', *Kinovedčeskie zapiski* 71 (2005), 219.
5. D. Shepilov and L. Iljitschev to the secretaries of Central Committee of the All-Union Communist Party (Bolsheviks) (CK VKPb) Andrej A. Zhdanov and Michail A. Suslov, 7 February 1948, in Fomin, 'Političeskij effekt filma', pp. 229–230.
6. See Peter Kenez, *Cinema and Soviet Society: From the Revolution to the Death of Stalin* (London and New York: I.B. Tauris, 2001), p. 189. During the initial postwar years, the output of Soviet studios dropped from 18 films in 1945 to 12 in 1950.
7. Rossiiskii gosudarstvennyi arkhiv sotsial'no-politicheskoi istorii (RGASPI), Moscow, fond (f.) 17, opis (op.) 132, edinica khranenija (ed. khr.) 250, report from 4 April 1949; see also a decree by CK VKPb about a measure to aid the cinema industries of Czechoslovakia, Hungary, Rumania, Bulgaria, Albania and North Korea, ibid.
8. See Ivan T. Berend, *Central and Eastern Europe, 1944–1993: Detour from the Periphery to the Periphery* (Cambridge: Cambridge University Press, 1999), p. 58; Miroslav Tejchman, 'Jugoslávie. Jugoslávský stalinismus a roztržka se Stalinem (1944–1948)', in Miroslav Tejchman (ed.), *Sovětizace východní Evropy. Země střední a jihovýchodní Evropy v letech 1944–1948* (Prague: Historický ústav, 1995), pp. 136–137. In fact, the anti-Tito allegorical depiction of Skanderbeg was so obvious that even the Soviet reviewer of the script complained about it. Rossiiskii gosudarstvennyi arkhiv literatury i iskusstva (RGALI), Moscow, f. 2453 – Mosfilm, op. 3, ed. khr. 228.
9. For an analysis of the movie as an example of a Stalinist monumentalist epic infused with a tone of tragic lyricism, see Sergei Kapterev, 'Post-Stalinist Cinema and the Russian Intelligentsia, 1953–1960: Strategies of Self-Representation, De-Stalinization, and the National Cultural Tradition' (Ph.D. thesis, New York University, 2005), pp. 279–282. For the influence of the Soviet international policy regarding the Balkans on the indigenous Mosfilm project *Admiral Nakhimov*, see Sarah Davies, 'Soviet Cinema and the Early Cold War: Pudovkin's *Admiral Nakhimov* in Context', in Rana Mitter and Patrick Major (eds), *Across the Blocs: Cold War Cultural and Social History* (London: Routledge, 2004), pp. 39–55.

10. For more details on this partnership, see the chapter by Mariana Ivanova in this volume.
11. See Marc Silberman, 'Learning from the Enemy: DEFA-French Co-Productions of the 1950s', *Film History* 18(1) (2006), 21–45.
12. Quoted in a report from the Czechoslovak embassy in Berlin to the Ministry of Culture and the Ministry of Foreign Affairs, 12 May 1955. Archiv Ministerstva zahraničních věcí (AMZV), Prague, TO obyčejné, 1945–1959, NDR, karton (k.) 27 – osvěta.
13. A letter from 10 November 1955, ibid.
14. A report from the Czechoslovak embassy in the GDR, 17 March 1958, ibid.
15. Seven years later, DEFA's attitude toward Barrandov transformed into sincere interest: the Czech studio achieved such impressive results in genre production that the DEFA studio began to actively lure Czech filmmakers for cooperation (rather than pursuing problematic relations with Western partners). See Pavel Skopal, 'Reisende in Sachen Genre: von Barrandov nach Babelsberg und zurück. Zur Bedeutung von tschechischen Regisseuren für die Genrefilmproduktion der DEFA in den 1960er und 1970er Jahren', in Michael Wedel, Barton Byg, Andy Räder, Skyler Arndt-Briggs and Evan Torner (eds), *DEFA International: Grenzüberschreitende Filmbeziehungen vor und nach dem Mauerbau* (Wiesbaden: Springer, 2013), pp. 249–266.
16. According to György Péteri, offensive isolationism was particularly manifest in the Soviet attitude toward the United States and Western Europe in the late 1940s and early 1950s, when discourses of Soviet superiority were combined with attacks on foreign influences. Péteri links the strategy of defensive integrationism – manifested in the effort to import and domesticate Western knowledge – mainly with the 1960s. The case of co-productions discussed here implicates that this pattern had been pervasive in the film industry since the mid-1950s. See Péteri, 'Nylon Curtain', pp. 113–123.
17. Národní archiv (NA), Prague, f. 861 – Ministerstvo informací, inventární číslo 559, k. 233.
18. Initiated on the 'recommendation' of Soviet leadership during Czechoslovak President Zápotocký's visit to Moscow in July 1953.
19. NA, f. 867 – Ministerstvo kultury 1953–1956, k. 351, Státy – Francie – Film.
20. As we know from secret reports on their talks, officials from the U.S., French and British embassies welcomed any cooperation in the sphere of film production as an opportunity to support the liberalization of the sphere of artistic creativity. In 1958, the counter-intelligence police department wiretapped the embassies and compiled a report 'on the infiltration of hostile ideology into artistic and intellectual circles in Czechoslovakia, organized by the embassies of the U.S., England, France, and, in recent months, by Yugoslavia as well'. Archiv Ministerstva vnitra, Prague, odbor bezpečnostních složek MV, f. A 34 – II. správa SNB, 1948–1974, arch. j. 1779, p. 18.
21. See the analysis of Radio Free Europe's Office of the Political Advisor from August 1958, as quoted and interpreted within the context of Soviet-American co-productions in Marsha Siefert, 'Co-Producing Cold War Culture: East-West Filmmaking and Cultural Diplomacy', in Peter Romijn, Giles Scott-Smith and Joes Segal (eds), *Divided Dreamworlds? The Cultural Cold War East and West* (Amsterdam: Amsterdam University Press, 2012), p. 79; see also the report on the 'reorganization of the communist film industry: research for new appeal in communist films', Office of research and intelligence, United States Information Agency, p. 6. Open Society Archives, Budapest, Records of Radio Free Europe, subfond 7 – Soviet Union, Series 6, box 5.

22. See Ludvík Veselý, 'Kde nic není, ani smrt nebere', *Film a doba* 4(7) (1958), 486–487; Jiří Plachetka, 'V stojatých proudech', *Rudé právo* 38(134) (1958), 3; František Vrba, 'Široké plátno pro široké svědomí?', *Literární noviny* 22 (1958), 4.
23. For insight into the practice of co-productions as a tool of cultural diplomacy between the USSR and Western countries, see Marsha Siefert, 'Co-Producing Cold War Culture'; and Siefert, 'Russische Leben, Sowjetische Filme: Die Filmbiographie, Tchaikovsky und der Kalte Krieg', in Lars Karl (ed.), *Leinwand zwischen Tauwetter und Frost: Der osteuropäische Spiel- und Dokumentarfilm im Kalten Krieg* (Berlin: Metropol, 2007), pp. 133–170.
24. The first project with a French company was under consideration as early as March 1954, and various negotiations were underway after that. The main points of disagreement between the potential partners were the topics preferred by the respective sides: while the French and American potential partners were interested in an adaptation of classic Russian literature (e.g. Michael Todd proposed an adaptation of Tolstoy's *War and Peace*), the Soviets refused to entrust their national themes to foreigners and instead proposed adapting American novels or topics that would require shooting in the United States. See RGALI, f. 2329 – Ministerstvo kul'tury, op. 12, ed. khr. 4010; RGALI, f. 2329, op. 12, ed. khr. 4017; Rossiiskii Gosudarstvennyi arkhiv noveishei istorii, Moscow, f. 5 – Apparat CK KPSS, 1952–1984, op. 36, ed. khr. 30.
25. In addition, the Slovak studio Koliba produced two other features: *Dáždnik svätého Petra/Szent Péter esernyöje* (St. Peter's Umbrella, Vladislav Pavlovič, Frigyes Bán, 1958) with Hungary, and *Prerušená pieseň/Prervannaya pesnya* (Interrupted Song, Nikoloz Sanishvili and František Žáček, 1960) with the USSR.
26. Report on a discussion of the film's working group in Bulgaria. Barrandov Studio a. s., archiv, Prague, sbírka Scénáře a produkční dokumenty – *Labakan*; a report from the Central Administration of Czechoslovak Film for a session of the Ministry of Education and Culture, 15 May 1958. NA, f. 994 – Ministerstvo školství a kultury, kolegium ministra č. 9, 1958, p. 2.
27. See Ivan Klimeš (ed.), 'Banská Bystrica 1959. Dokumenty ke kontextům I. festivalu československého filmu', *Iluminace* 16(4) (2004), p. 152; and a report on the situation of the relations between Czechoslovakia and Yugoslavia, AMZV, TO tajné 1955–59, Jugoslávie, k. 2.
28. A report from ČSF to the committee meeting of the Minister of Education and Culture, 15 March 1958. NA, f. 994 – Ministerstvo školství a kultury, kolegium ministra č. 9, 1958.
29. NA, Archiv ÚV KSČ, f. 1261/0/11 – Politické byro 1954–1962, svazek (sv.) 181, archivní jednotka (a. j.) 247, bod (b.) 8, pp. 1–22.
30. After Minister Mikhailov's initial impulse to organize the conferences in September 1956, the Soviets almost immediately transferred the official 'initiative' for organizing the first conference to the Czechoslovak film industry and monitored the planning from behind the scenes. See the correspondence in RGALI, f. 2329, op. 12, ed. khr. 4021.
31. RGALI, f. 2329, op. 12, ed. khr. 4113; NA, f. 994 – Ministerstvo školství a kultury, kolegium ministra č. 4, 1958, č. 2, 1959, and č. 47, 1960.
32. Instructions for the conference in Sofia received by Sergei Gerasimov and Igor Ratchuk from the Ministry of Culture contain unequivocally formulated recommendations: instead of new co-productions, it was necessary to study the results of the already finished projects and to support the wishes of actors, directors or

cameramen to take part in movies shot in other countries of the 'socialist camp'. RGALI, f. 2329, op. 12, ed. khr. 4321.
33. See the texts of the conference papers at Filmarchiv Potsdam, f. Frank Beyer, 9/2003/ N024.
34. Ibid.
35. A report from the head of the Central Administration of the Soviet Cinema Igor Ratchuk to Minister of Culture Michailov from 17 November 1959. RGALI, f. 2329, op. 12, ed. khr. 4208.
36. *Praha nultá hodina/Koffer mit Dynamit* (Prague at Zero Hour, Václav Gajer, 1962), *Neděle ve všední den/Pirosbetüs hétköznapok* (A Work Day Which Is a Sunday, Félix Máriássy, 1962), *Komu tančí Havana/Para quién baila La Habana* (For Whom Havana Dances, Vladimír Čech, 1963), *Akce Kalimantan/Aksi Kalimantán* (Operation Kalimantan, Vladimír Sís, 1962).
37. NA, f. 02/4 – Sekretariát ÚV KSČ, a. j. 378, sv. 224, bod 4.
38. *Dýmky* (Pipes, Vojtěch Jasný, 1966), *Hoří, má panenko!* (Firemen's Ball, Miloš Forman, 1967); *Ovoce stromů rajských jíme* (Fruit of Paradise, Věra Chytilová, 1969), *Skřivánci na niti* (Larks on a String, Jiří Menzel, 1966).
39. Miloš Forman and Jan Novák, *Co já vím? Autobiografie Miloše Formana* (Brno: Atlantis, 1994), p. 210.
40. For background on the conflict between liberals and conservatives in the Soviet cultural policy of the late 1950s and early 1960s, see Josephine Woll, *Real Images: Soviet Cinema and the Thaw* (London and New York: I.B.Tauris, 2000), pp. 57–160.
41. For the history of the Karlovy Vary film festival from a transnational perspective, see Jindřiška Bláhová's essay in this volume. For the Moscow festival in the context of the Thaw, see Lars Karl, 'Zwischen politischem Ritual und kulturellem Dialog. Die Moskauer Internationalen Filmfestspiele im Kalten Krieg 1959–1971', in Lars Karl (ed.), *Leinwand zwischen Tauwetter und Frost. Der osteuropäische Spiel- ind Dokumentarfilm im Kalten Krieg* (Berlin: Metropol, 2007), pp. 279–298.
42. For Barrandov co-productions in the 1960s, see Skopal, 'Reisende in Sachen Genre' and Francesco Di Chiara and Pavel Skopal, 'Příliš kruté pro Američany. Carlo Ponti, česká nová vlna a barrandovské koprodukce se západní Evropou', in Anna Batistová (ed.), *Hoří, má panenko* (Prague: Národní filmový archiv, 2012), pp. 56–79.

Select Bibliography

Berend, Ivan T. *Central and Eastern Europe, 1944–1993: Detour from the Periphery to the Periphery*. Cambridge: Cambridge University Press, 1999.

Bláhová, Jindřiška. 'A Tough Job for Donald Duck: Hollywood, Czechoslovakia, and Selling Films behind the Iron Curtain, 1944–1951'. Ph.D. thesis, University of East Anglia and Charles University-Prague, 2010.

Davies, Sarah. 'Soviet Cinema and the Early Cold War: Pudovkin's *Admiral Nakhimov* in Context'. In Rana Mitter and Patrick Major (eds), *Across the Blocs: Cold War Cultural and Social History*. London: Routledge, 2004.

Higson, Andrew, and Richard Maltby (eds). *'Film Europe' and 'Film America': Cinema, Commerce, and Cultural Exchange 1920–1939*. Exeter: University of Exeter Press, 1999.

Jäckel, Anne. 'Dual Nationality Film Productions in Europe after 1945'. *Historical Journal of Film, Radio and Television* 23(3) (2003), 213–243.

Kapterev, Sergei. 'Post-Stalinist Cinema and the Russian Intelligentsia, 1953–1960: Strategies of Self-Representation, De-Stalinization, and the National Cultural Tradition'. Ph.D. thesis, New York University, 2005.

Karl, Lars (ed.). *Leinwand zwischen Tauwetter und Frost: Der osteuropäische Spiel- und Dokumentarfilm im Kalten Krieg*. Berlin: Metropol, 2007.

Kenez, Peter. *Cinema and Soviet Society: From the Revolution to the Death of Stalin*. London and New York: I.B. Tauris, 2001.

Siefert, Marsha. 'Co-Producing Cold War Culture: East-West Filmmaking and Cultural Diplomacy'. In Peter Romijn, Giles Scott-Smith and Joes Segal (eds), *Divided Dreamworlds? The Cultural Cold War East and West*. Amsterdam: Amsterdam University Press, 2012.

Silberman, Marc. 'Learning from the Enemy: DEFA-French Co-Productions of the 1950s'. *Film History* 18(1) (2006), 21–45.

Skopal, Pavel. 'Reisende in Sachen Genre: von Barrandov nach Babelsberg und zurück. Zur Bedeutung von tschechischen Regisseuren für die Genrefilmproduktion der DEFA in den 1960er und 1970er Jahren'. In Michael Wedel, Barton Byg, Andy Räder, Skyler Arndt-Briggs and Evan Torner (eds), *DEFA International: Grenzüberschreitende Filmbeziehungen vor und nach dem Mauerbau*. Wiesbaden: Springer, 2013.

Woll, Josephine. *Real Images: Soviet Cinema and the Thaw*. London and New York: I.B.Tauris, 2000.

Chapter 5

Co-productions (Un)Wanted

1950s East/West German Film Collaborations and the Impact of Sovietization on DEFA's Prestige Agenda

Mariana Ivanova

In the early 1950s, East German artists and political authorities attempted to consolidate the role of film in the recently founded socialist state. Following the division of Germany in 1949, the cinema of the German Democratic Republic (GDR) had to endorse a new cultural and historical self-definition envisioned by its government. To this end, politicians and filmmakers alike conceived of co-productions with West European partners as tools in the struggle for the GDR's recognition abroad and as manifestations of their claim on German cultural heritage. At the same time, contracting well-known Western directors, producers and actors became a strategy for combating the shortage of experienced personnel and films popular with audiences.[1] More importantly, by attracting these filmmakers, the East German studio DEFA (Deutsche Film-Aktiengesellschaft) hoped for easier access to West European screens – especially after 1951, when the official film exchange among the four occupation zones was suspended.[2]

DEFA's endeavours to work with internationally renowned filmmakers in order to improve the images of the studio and the state abroad comprise the first aspect of what we may call a 'prestige agenda'. Another aspect thereof is the reappropriation of formerly successful genres such as literary adaptations of classical works, or costume dramas in the tradition of Weimar cinema as developed by UFA (Universum Film AG). As early as the 1920s, UFA had entertained the idea of an all-European network for film co-productions and artistic collaborations, and sought to establish a sort of hegemony within this network.³ Similarly, DEFA's prestige agenda thrived on the development and maintenance of contacts with other film producers and studios in order to share sets, talent and production costs, or secure the release of DEFA films in the West. Cultural prestige as a concept thus refers to DEFA's effort to build a reputation as an equal partner in the circulation of films and services within Europe while also relying on transnational contacts among primarily East and West German filmmakers and producers.

By recontextualizing the East/West German co-productions during the period of political confrontation in the 1950s, this chapter seeks to illuminate forgotten collaborations and their significance for our understanding of both DEFA's motivation to pursue such projects and the impact Sovietization had on the studio's agenda for international acclaim. Drawing on archival research with film production files, I will demonstrate how DEFA's prestige agenda complemented the studio's political mandate, which legitimized its 1950s film co-productions in an effort to promote recognition of the GDR state in the West. To illustrate this argument, I will look closely at the co-production history of *Das Fräulein von Scuderi* (Mademoiselle de Scudéri, Eugen York, 1957) and comment on the ways in which both the film's representation and DEFA's negotiation with a celebrity, Henny Porten, can be read as allegories for the artist's entanglement with state policies. Elaborating on the gradual politicization of the agenda for international prestige during the 1950s, I move on to the case of *Die Schönste* (The Beauty, Ernesto Remani and Walter Beck, 1959). With its prolonged censorship history, two cinematic versions and a premiere four decades later, this last DEFA co-production with the western company Pandora attests to the inevitable demise that East/West German co-productions faced once DEFA initiated a new model of co-productions limited to socialist partners, thus endorsing a Soviet model of co-production. Consequently, by the end of the 1950s, the rapidly progressing Sovietization of the East German and other East European film industries, which had begun in the mid-1940s, ultimately suffocated collaboration between DEFA and Pandora.

By the mid-1950s, the West German government had taken measures against collaboration on cultural grounds and banned film imports from most socialist countries for fear of indoctrination. In 1953, an Interministerial Commission for East/West Questions was formed in the Federal Republic.⁴ This commission met the following year to explicitly address the question of co-productions with DEFA, and rejected the possibility of such projects in the future. In response, the East German Ministry of Culture attempted to coerce filmmakers based in West Berlin to relocate to the East by threatening to discontinue their contracts.[5] The pressure on film professionals in both German states became unbearable and threatened many long-existing interpersonal contacts.

In this precarious context, the Munich-based producer Erich Mehl created a new film company in Stockholm called Pandora. Subsequently, he and DEFA collaborated on four films labelled as East German/Swedish co-productions: *Leuchtfeuer* (Navigating Light, Wolfgang Staudte, 1954), *Das Fräulein von Scudéri*, *Spielbank-Affäre* (Casino Affair, Arthur Pohl, 1957) and *Die Schönste*. Several factors in Pandora's history point to its status as a private company founded abroad in order to circumvent legal restrictions on film co-production in the Federal Republic of Germany (FRG). Shot primarily in Babelsberg and only occasionally in Sweden, with German actors and exclusively in the German language, the four films were released solely in the GDR and the FRG (sometimes under different titles), and never in Sweden or other Scandinavian countries. Furthermore, although Mehl's company worked with an Austrian distributor, Austria Filmverleih, there is no record of cooperation or exchange of services and actors with the domestic Swedish film industry. It was Mehl's practice to make use of already existing contacts and acquaintances, primarily among former UFA employees or German émigrés. Pandora thus typically hired directors and scriptwriters who lived in West Berlin, had previously been involved in DEFA productions and had the approval of the studio and the East German officials.

UFA's Legacy

The transnational contacts that existed among filmmakers in Europe during the 1950s, along with the continuity between DEFA and UFA in terms of artistic talent, development of particular genres and technical equipment, proved crucial for both the initiation and the realization of co-productions for international prestige. In 1946, when DEFA moved to the film city Babelsberg, where some of the most innovative pictures of German and European cinema of the 1920s had been made, the studio inherited not only facilities, costumes, film stock and sets, but also highly trained film personnel (cinematographers, film editors, designers, technicians, sound specialists) and directors who had worked with French, Italian and British colleagues and were mainly experienced in making genre films like melodramas, musicals, revue films and costume dramas. Several of the filmmakers who later became involved in East/West German co-productions lived in West Berlin or the FRG and worked for film companies such as Artur Brauner's Central Cinema Company[6] or for people like the Munich-based tradesman and film producer Erich Mehl.[7] At the time, Soviet cultural officers familiar with the international successes of Weimar cinema encouraged DEFA to entice German intellectuals, returnees and filmmakers to the newly founded studio in Babelsberg.[8] In response, DEFA offered contracts to more than ten former UFA directors, among them Arthur Pohl, Erich Engel, Paul Verhoeven, Hans Deppe, Georg Wildhagen, Arthur Maria Rabenalt, Wolfgang Schleif, Hans Müller, Gerhard Lamprecht and Wolfgang Staudte.[9] In the late 1940s and early 1950s, these directors helped Babelsberg produce a remarkable number of popular and critically successful films that were released in both the East and the West. However, due to the intensifying division between the two German states, most of these directors had only short-lived appointments with DEFA, and very few managed to keep their contracts through the 1950s. Wolfgang Staudte, for instance, who is considered the most prolific of the former UFA directors, made seven films for DEFA between 1946 and 1955 compared to four for independent producers in the Federal Republic, as well as the first co-production by East and West German filmmakers, *Leuchtfeuer*. Similarly, other UFA directors such as Arthur Pohl, Hans Müller and Gerhard Lamprecht maintained contracts with DEFA parallel to working with the above-mentioned West German producers Artur Brauner and Erich Mehl, which also explains their subsequent involvement in co-productions with DEFA. In addition, one third of the scriptwriters at DEFA in the later 1940s and early 1950s came from the FRG and were able to work simultaneously for the East German film studio and Western film companies until the late 1950s, when their contracts with DEFA were suspended.[10] Finally, in order to attract Western distributors and audiences to these directors' films, DEFA competed for internationally acclaimed UFA stars, such as Henny Porten, Leny Marenbach and Zara Leander, as well as actors Theo Lingen and Hans Klering. The studio profited from a lasting and fruitful collaboration with Henny Porten, for instance, whose return to Babelsberg was widely publicized in both the East and West German presses.

The East German studio's initial endeavours to contract with former UFA employees or present them on screen during this transitional phase (1947–1955) reflect its desire to achieve present goals by building upon former successes. The existing production capacity of the largest studios in Europe, the socialist government's aspirations to achieve cultural hegemony by claiming Germany's cultural heritage, and competition with films from the West comprised essential conditions for the collaboration with Western directors and actors. More importantly, DEFA's ambition to achieve cultural prestige by employing West German filmmakers resonated with the prerogatives of the GDR government at the time, that is, its attempts to re-educate the Germans and legitimize the East German state, as one of DEFA's founders, Alfred Lindemann, suggested in 1947:

> We welcome everyone who wants to help the new and true democracy with creativity, directing, and acting, no matter in which zone one lives.... [It is] of great importance to produce as many German films as possible. Our priority lies not in economic concerns but in the great relevance of film as a means for the democratic re-education of the German people.... For this reason, we feel obliged to help in a comradely manner every German producer who needs our help for his project, under the condition that his film is artistically sound and serves the greater goal of democratization.[11]

Das Fräulein von Scuderi

In order to understand how political prerogatives intertwined with the project of transnational collaboration between DEFA and Pandora, we need to scrutinize the mechanisms of state control and the filmmakers' involvement in one of these projects: *Das Fräulein von Scuderi*. Most artists who participated in this film came from the FRG, yet they had in common either their past at UFA or their progressive political convictions. For example, former UFA chief Eugen York, who agreed to direct the co-production, had already shot his major feature film *Morituri* in Babelsberg, and the project had been sponsored by the West Berlin producer Artur Brauner, a Jewish émigré from Poland. Born in Moscow, Eugen York had moved to Berlin as a teenager and worked at UFA as an editor and assistant director. Under the guidance of UFA's prolific documentary filmmaker Walter Ruttmann, York received acclaim for his short and documentary films. What made the former UFA director attractive for the *Mademoiselle de Scudéri* project was his previous work on two West German film adaptations released in 1950, *Lockende Gefahr* (A Tempting Danger) and *Export in Blond*. During these projects York had collaborated with some of Germany's most respected authors, such as DEFA screenwriter Artur Kuhnert and the Luxembourg-born

West German author of the popular Mabuse films, Norbert Jacques. Similarly, *Mademoiselle de Scudéri*'s scriptwriters, Joachim Barckhausen and Alexander Stenbock-Fermor, were a successful DEFA screenwriting team living in West Berlin and specializing in film adaptations of literary works.[12] Since the inception of the East German studio, they had written eight scripts for DEFA, including several antifascist films.[13] Stenbock-Fermor, who like Eugen York had immigrated from tsarist Russia to Germany, met Barckhausen as a young communist in the early 1930s, and the two became close friends and collaborators. Their relationship to communist circles during the Weimar Republic made them attractive to DEFA, and the studio employed the screenwriting team until the construction of the Berlin Wall in 1961, when both authors insisted on making West Berlin their home.

E.T.A. Hoffmann's novella *Das Fräulein von Scudéri*, published between 1819 and 1821, focuses on the social role of an artist, Mademoiselle de Scudéri, who has two tasks as a public intellectual: to disclose the truth about crimes committed by a prominent public figure (René Cardillac), and to assert the victory of virtue over false accusations. The 1955 film by York, Stenbock-Fermor and Barckhausen differs from previous adaptations in its blending of genres such as musical, costume drama and period film.[14] More importantly, it instigates questions: What is the relationship between art and the artist? Can art be made for art's or the artist's sake and if so, what are the implications for society? What value do we assign to artefacts that serve to please those in power?[15] The co-production addresses these complex questions through the juxtaposition of two types of artists: the jeweller René Cardillac, who is consumed by his art and struggles to separate himself from it; and the elderly poetess Scudéri, who in her efforts to please the French King Louis XIV represents an artist compliant with power. At the time of the film's release, its sociopolitical dimensions resonated with the debates over the autonomy of art, art as means of education and state-sponsored art production that informed the GDR public sphere in the 1950s.[16]

The 1955 film adaptation introduces further thematic and structural alterations that underscore its agenda of addressing the contemporaneous question of the artist's entanglement with the state. First, Mademoiselle de Scudéri's relationship to the king is reinforced by her position as a theatre director who stages opera and ballet performances (whereas in the novella she is only a writer); hence, her public appearance and authority invite comparison with the role of the film director in a socialist society. Second, the exclusion of the daemonic aspects from Cardillac's character, the restraint from moral judgement exhibited in his criminal acts, and the deliberate focus on his artistic talent and the struggle to salvage his art from becoming a commodity raise questions about art production and reception, and the material versus aesthetic value of artefacts.

In this sense, the film endorses the reconsideration of Mademoiselle de Scudéri, an artist compliant with political power who restores the social status quo, and Cardillac, a proponent of *l'art pour l'art*, as two artist types that do not necessarily contradict but complement each other. While Cardillac's figure stands for the artist as a solitary creator of ideas, the poetess always negotiates with the king in public, which reinforces her status as a visibly recognized and respected adviser. Thus, she represents the kind of public figure that GDR politicians envisioned as cultivating the prestige of their state, that is, a mediator between the source of authority and the citizens.

In the context of the 1950s, when the GDR was actively pursuing political recognition, this mediation implied the reappropriation of past literary traditions to legitimize both the power of the state and the role it assigned to intellectuals as 'tutors of the nation', to borrow a phrase from historian Michael Geyer.[17] Furthermore, although artists were granted privileged status, this status had a dual nature, as David Bathrick emphasizes:

> Viewed from the perspective of the socialist public sphere, GDR writers were at once the creators of a new audience and a variant of the official voice. As spokespeople and representatives for a struggle to enlarge and enhance the freedoms of speech, their very existence was enabled by, indebted to, and an expression of power. The fact that some of them had been censored, hunted, questioned, and ridiculed does not belie the fact that they were also – and sometimes even simultaneously – privileged, nurtured, courted, and coddled.[18]

In other words, the interdependence of the state and artists in socialist society entailed numerous privileges for the artists that nonetheless came at a price. In the case of former UFA actors drawn to work in the GDR, the price was the loss of their careers in the West. At the same time, for actors like Henny Porten who had been long unemployed in the FRG, a DEFA contract represented the opportunity to return to the stage, if only for a short time, and perhaps even to relive their previous glamour.

In this sense, the parallel between Scudéri's and Porten's artistic personas is indicative of the important role that former UFA actors as public figures played in early DEFA co-productions. In 1955, Michael Lentz commented in the FRG newspaper *Westdeutsche Allgemeine* on Porten's illustrious comeback as Mademoiselle de Scudéri after a long break from her star career with UFA:

> This scene is almost creepy. It clearly shows Henny Porten 'in her element'; she appears in a world of illusions and glow, where neither problems in the East or the West, nor political facts exist. The scene shows that this lady needs the dream factory, the light of the projectors and the magic of opulent film premieres. She is neither a martyr nor émigré, I think. She is and will remain a film star as long as she has this opportunity.[19]

For Porten, as Lentz asserts, appearing in a DEFA production was a conscious (though self-delusive) attempt to reconnect to her own former successes as one of the most celebrated silent film stars of the dream factory UFA. At the same time, despite Lentz's critique of Porten's ignorance of Cold War rivalries, her agreement to film with the East German studio had much larger political implications than he anticipated.

The story of Henny Porten's attraction to this co-production illuminates the symbiotic relationship between the state-owned East German studio and a number of Western film stars who sought to reconnect to their own past prestige. Such film stars included Curt Bois, Hans Klering, Emil Stör, Gisela Uhlen and Walter Suessenguth, to name a few.[20] Porten was first cast in *Carola Lamberti – eine vom Zirkus* (Carola Lamberti from the Circus, Hans Müller, 1954), a project that she herself suggested to the DEFA studio managing director, Sepp Schwab. His enthusiasm for working with Porten is evident in a letter dated 27 July 1951.[21] In this document he offered the former UFA actress a work contract that included coverage of all relocation costs, a special exchange rate from West to East German marks, a travel visa, a luxurious villa in Potsdam, documents for the intelligence services, and even a leading position for her husband as a physician in a prestigious East Berlin hospital. By promising Porten privileges shared by few East German artists at the time, DEFA revealed its intention to showcase a star neglected in the West and rediscovered in the East. As Porten's biographer Helga Belach has suggested, by 1954 the actress had long waited in vain for a role in the West and faced serious financial challenges and depression.[22] Ironically, Porten's decision to allow her (past) prestige to enhance the studio's reputation recalls Scudéri's relationship to the French king. At the same time, the trajectories of this and other co-productions for prestige demonstrate the ways in which artistic exchange and personal agendas were intertwined with the political mandate that the socialist state assigned to artists, namely, to lobby for the recognition of the GDR state abroad. To understand how the ideological prerogatives led to the redefinition of DEFA's prestige agenda, we need to ask what changed in the years between the making of *Fräulein von Scuderi* and the last DEFA film project with Pandora, *Die Schönste*.

The Redefinition of DEFA's Prestige Agenda

Although collaboration with Pandora was initially profitable for both artists and politicians in the socialist state, East/West German co-productions had become unwanted by the late 1950s. This fact became evident in the making of *Die Schönste*, a film project first discussed in 1954, when DEFA's prestige agenda and collaboration with Erich Mehl's company were still welcome in the eyes of GDR politicians. It took two years for DEFA to find an author and a director for the project, so the film script was presented at the studio in the summer of 1956 during a short-lived period of liberalization in the wake of the Twentieth Congress of the Communist Party of the Soviet Union and de-Stalinization. However, the vagaries of the Cold War political discourse in the following years, given the encroaching stagnation after the Hungarian revolution of 1956, the '*große Fluchtwelle*' (great wave of flight) in 1957 and the subsequent building of the Berlin Wall in 1961, led this project to be banned from both East and West German screens. In addition, the DEFA project of co-production was fundamentally redefined in the years between 1957 and 1960, when the future development of socialist film art in terms of its ideological, thematic, and aesthetic orientation was debated at three international conferences of East European filmmakers. These debates led to the affirmation of film as a tool for propagating friendship and political unity, a concept that starkly resonated with GDR politicians' turn away from the desire to achieve a positive image in Western eyes to instead embrace the idea of strengthening ties to other countries in the Socialist Bloc.

Die Schönste

Taking DEFA's prestige agenda as a departure point for a comparison of York's and Remani's films, we can notice surprising similarities in the ways the studio enticed directors, screenwriters and actors for both projects. To begin with, DEFA found director Ernesto Remani (born in Austria as Ernst Rechenmacher) appealing because of his idea of re-editing UFA's successful film *Münchhausen* (Josef von Báky, 1943) for contemporary audiences. Even though this project ultimately failed due to the preferences of the American distributors, Remani received the offer to film *Die Schönste*, together with a generous budget and a luxurious villa in Potsdam.[23] DEFA's managing director, Albert Wilkening, was impressed by Remani's successes at home and abroad, including his former collaboration with Luis Trenker, his career in Italy making musicals and finally his special prize at Cannes in 1955.[24] At the same time, the East German press celebrated the choice of 'Italian director Ernesto Remani' and his acclaim at Western film festivals in France and Italy. What was not revealed at the time was that Ernesto Remani was none other than the former Bavaria-Filmkunst director Ernst Rechenmacher, who had collaborated with the Nazis as they established control over the Czech studio Barrandov, and then escaped to Italy and changed his name after the war. However, DEFA and GDR party functionaries saw Remani's expertise and international reputation as enough to 'erase' his past. In other words, as in the case with Eugen York, the not-yet recognized socialist state utilized Remani's reputation to its benefit.

DEFA and Mehl made a serious investment in this masterpiece. Not only did they raise a budget of 1.7 million marks, but they also brought together the best West German experts in entertainment and DEFA's most experienced architects and costume designers. For instance, screenwriter Artur Kuhnert, like his West German colleagues Joachim Barckhausen and Alexander Stenbock-Fermor, specialized in genre films, especially musicals and operettas. DEFA's best architect, Alfred Hirschmeyer, was also part of the promising filmmaking team. In addition, the relative liberalization that characterized art production in East Germany during 1956 permitted the DEFA studio management to give this project the green light without explicitly consulting the Ministry of Culture. By the time the first version of *Die Schönste* was finished in 1957, however, the ideological climate within the Socialist bloc had changed: joint projects between East and West European artists were now undesirable and even unthinkable. *Die Schönste*, therefore, marked the end of Pandora and all East/West German co-productions. But how could a comedy about two boys comparing their mothers contribute to the end of all East/West German co-productions and to the demise of Pandora?

Remani's version of the film opens with a scene depicting a fight that erupts between Thomas, the son of a wealthy West Berlin wholesaler, and his friend Hannes, the family driver's son, as they are flipping through a glossy women's magazine. 'My mom is the most beautiful woman!' exclaims the Thomas, pointing at an image of his mother, a made-up blonde wearing a brilliant, sparkling necklace. To the driver's son, however, it is only the necklace that makes this rich woman more beautiful than his own mom. Each boy dares the other to steal his mother's most valuable jewellery so that they can compare their genuine beauty.

This story of comparing rich and poor mothers mirrors the accelerating competition in divided post–World War II Germany. Furthermore, the plot evolves in quite a remarkable way. Having stolen their mothers' most valuable pieces of jewellery, the boys accidentally throw them into a car on the street. The next morning, the car leaves for Hamburg, so Thomas and Hannes embark on a journey in pursuit of the diamond necklaces. Some of the boys' adventures along the way raised the censors' eyebrows: for example, the young men illegally cross the existing border between the GDR and the FRG, escape from the police in Hamburg and become involved in dubious deals with port workers who successfully blackmail the rich Berlin family. On top of these social issues, which were quite precarious for the late 1950s, the film presented the glamour of upper-class society's lavish partying, expensive cars and fashionable clothes. In contrast to *Fräulein von Scuderi*, where both story and criticism were displaced into the past, *Die Schönste*'s visual references to wealthy West Germany appeared quite subversive of the ideals of a socialist-realist artwork.

To meet the demands of East German political officials, Remani shot several new scenes in the fall of 1957. Two different endings were proposed for East and West German audiences respectively, as was a black-and-white version for the GDR release.[25] Starting in January 1958, repeated viewings and negotiations at the film studio and the East German Ministry of Culture only resulted in the rejection of the film's release. After all, 1957 was the year of the 'great wave of flight', and presenting the allures of the West on-screen during this time of struggles and debates in the East was unthinkable.

In a desperate attempt to save the project in the fall of 1958, DEFA appointed a new director, Walter Beck, and a new author, Heinz Kahlau, both politically innocuous East Germans and enthusiastic filmmakers with little experience. They replaced the scene of the boys and their dare at the film's opening with one depicting two shabby workers involved in a discussion about 'Sein und Schein' – 'fact and fiction'. This step, along with the addition of twelve new scenes that injected the story with propaganda value, obliterated DEFA's prestige agenda, its co-production ambitions and the references to the tradition of UFA's vibrant visual aesthetics. Yet even Beck's edits did not satisfy the cultural functionaries. On 24 August 1961, eleven days after the beginning of the Berlin Wall's construction, *Die Schönste* – The Beauty – was ultimately banished to the shelves of the archives.

The New Model for Co-productions among Socialist States

The prolonged battle for the release of *Die Schönste* and its ultimate ban come at no surprise, considering the political developments that had led to the adoption of a Soviet model in all DEFA film projects, including the co-productions. By 1957, as Andreas Kötzing maintains in his contribution to this volume, the control of the Socialist Unity Party of Germany (Sozialistische Einheitspartei Deutschlands, SED)'s over artists and art distribution had begun to tighten, resulting in the revision and outright denunciation of East German artists' previous contacts with West German filmmakers and writers. This critique, which came to a head at the fifth SED conference in July 1958, targeted in particular the previously state-promoted concept of all-German culture (compare to Lindemann's 1947 statement, mentioned earlier in this chapter). Criticism was also directed at former GDR Minister of Culture Johannes R. Becher, who at the Fourth German Writers Congress in 1956 had presented his vision of a 'harmonious pan-German communion of art and people, to be developed on new social foundations and based on the German classics, which he valued above all'.[26] Two years later, in 1958, the SED rejected Becher's pan-German concept of culture as detrimental to the official cultural policy, and Alfred Kurella, the chair of the Committee for Culture at the SED Politburo, announced that GDR socialist art must henceforth denounce the (ideological) differences defining the West and East German societies and values.

With this in mind, it is not difficult to understand why Pandora's co-productions with DEFA and specifically *Die Schönste* and *Spielbank-Affäre* became scapegoats in the studio's attempts to comply with the ideological demands of the GDR state. At the 1958 international film conference in Sinaia, Romania, which had preceded the fifth SED conference by only a couple of days, DEFA leaders were already distancing themselves from the desire to cater to both East and West German audiences; instead they promoted their films – in the spirit of Soviet filmmaking – as educational rather than entertaining. This privileging of education versus entertainment was justified primarily by denouncing Erich Mehl's and DEFA's 'artistically immature', 'weak', 'petit bourgeois' co-productions *Die Schönste* and *Spielbank-Affäre*, and it went hand in hand with a new demand for adoption of Soviet-style co-productions.[27] The new priorities of DEFA's co-production agenda were summarized in the treatise 'On Socialist Art, Theses for the Hauptreferat, 2. Draft', which was intended for presentation at a DEFA internal meeting sometime after July 1958. Without even mentioning that the films were in fact East/West German co-productions, this document deprecates their failure to adequately critique capitalist conditions and claims that they only feign opposition but in fact 'water down, fail to name, diminish, even praise' capitalist deficiencies.[28]

Later on, the treatise endorses the proposed turn towards 'Soviet-style co-productions' by referring to the first international conference of East European filmmakers in Prague in 1957:

> This art [i.e. Soviet art] was always a paragon and teacher to us, it still is and will always be. We understand this in the sense of Jiri Marek's words at the Film Conference in Prague: 'Soviet art has become the teacher of our art.'[29]

The international film conferences of 1957 in Prague and 1958 in Sinaia, with their decisions to consolidate East European filmmakers' artistic and aesthetic agendas and encourage collaborations and exchange primarily within the Socialist bloc, greatly contributed to the discontinuation of East/West German co-production. Debates on the 'new' and 'effective' socialist realist model for filmmaking and praise of Soviet directors' achievements were repeatedly brought up during discussion of the feasibility of further DEFA co-productions with Erich Mehl and French or Italian partners. The final decision to discontinue such efforts was made at the fifth SED conference in 1958, when GDR Minister of Culture Alexander Abusch announced that only partners from socialist countries should be considered for future DEFA co-productions: 'The consequences must be drawn from the studio's previous co-productions and our concerted efforts must be oriented primarily towards co-productions with the Soviet Union and other countries in the socialist camp.'[30]

From the early 1960s and throughout the 1970s, DEFA co-production partners came exclusively from Central and Eastern Europe and the Soviet Union. These collaborations are characterized by a redefined, ideologically compliant agenda for cultural prestige. The DEFA annual report from 1970 announces that 'co-productions serve not only to increase the potential of our films to attract audiences, but they are first and foremost a significant tool for the stabilization and consolidation of socialist collaboration with our comrades from socialist film studios.'[31] With the encouragement of artistic exchange within Central and Eastern Europe, the task of film co-productions became primarily to showcase East German production facilities and artistic talent at international film festivals in Moscow, Karlovy Vary and Leipzig.

Conclusion

In 1999, film historian Ralf Schenk found 319 film reels from the last East/West German co-production, including various scenes, edits, screen tests and musical scores. Both the numerous versions of the script and the meticulously documented four-year long debates also survived; they can be found in the Federal Archive in Berlin. In 2002, *Die Schönste* was rereleased and publicly celebrated at the Babylon, a prominent movie theatre in the former East Berlin. The preservation of this project in its astonishing entirety attests above all to the importance of the East/West German co-productions, for instance, in providing a model for subsequent East German co-productions with French film companies, as well as with Yugoslavian, Polish and Czech partners.

The story of DEFA co-productions with West European partners, and specifically with Erich Mehl's private company Pandora, is largely one of experimentation with and negotiation of the imperatives imposed on socialist cinemas by the vagaries of Cold War politics and, ultimately, the Sovietization of East European cinemas. Joint film projects for cultural prestige, as the case of *Fräulein von Scuderi* demonstrates, disclose not only the artistic but also the political dimensions of filmmaking in the GDR. These co-productions appropriated the presocialist traditions of Weimar cinema, yet they also responded to a cultural policy that endorsed a political goal: the achievement of the socialist state's legitimacy. The growing discrepancy between the cinema's two state-imposed mandates, namely, entertainment and ideological instruction, eventually dampened DEFA's initial aspirations to collaborate with Western partners and achieve international acclaim as one of the largest studios in Europe. In addition, the encroaching process of Sovietization had the major implication of reducing DEFA's prestige agenda to a 'promotional' agenda. As a result, DEFA co-productions openly promoted solidarity among socialist nations and the project of education over entertainment from the late 1950s on. The redefinition of DEFA's prestige agenda in the 1950s, coupled with the Sovietization of the industry, was symptomatic of the loss of privileged status for artists in socialist societies and of the enduring intertwinement of political and aesthetic mandates in the cinemas of these societies.

Mariana Ivanova is an assistant professor of German at Miami University in Oxford, OH. She wrote her dissertation on film cooperation between DEFA and East and West European film studios, and is currently writing a book on DEFA co-productions between 1949 and 1989 and the legacy of Film Europe in East German cinema. Her research has received support from the DEFA Foundation in Berlin, the DEFA Library in Amherst, MA, and the German Academic Exchange Service, DAAD. She has published on the Berlin wall films of 1961 and the memory of the GDR in contemporary cinema, as well as on the continuities between UFA and DEFA. She is also the author of several short documentaries about former DEFA filmmakers.

Notes

1. See Thomas Heimann's discussion of the DEFA crisis of 1952–1953 in Thomas Heimann, *DEFA, Künstler und SED Politik* (Berlin: Vistas, 1994), pp. 130–134. Lack of experienced authors and well-developed scripts caused a rapid decline in domestic and international audiences' interest. According to Heimann, the East German studio shared this crisis with the cinemas of the Soviet Union and other East European countries.
2. Ralf Schenk (ed.), *Das zweite Leben der Filmstadt Babelsberg: DEFA-Spielfilme 1946–1992* (Berlin: Henschel, 1994).
3. For a detailed discussion of Film Europe and UFA's role in it, see Andrew Higson and Richard Maltby (eds), *'Film Europe' and 'Film America': Cinema, Commerce, and Cultural Exchange 1920–1939* (Exeter: University of Exeter Press, 1999).
4. For a detailed discussion on the topic, see Andreas Kötzing, 'Die Filmpolitik der Bundesregierung gegenüber der DDR und der Interministerielle Ausschuss für Ost-West-Filmfragen', in Andreas Kötzing, *Kultur und Filmpolitik: Die Filmfestivals von Leipzig und Oberhausen in gesamtdeutscher Perspektive* (Göttingen: Wallstein, 2013), pp. 36–43.

5. 'Programmerklärung des Ministeriums für Kultur der Deutschen Demokratischen Republik. Zur Verteidigung der Einheit der deutschen Kultur', *Sinn und Form* 2 (1954), 303.
6. Artur Brauner had escaped to the Soviet Union during WWII and returned in 1946. He was involved with DEFA on several film projects, including two with former UFA directors employed by DEFA: *Morituri* (1948), directed by Eugen York, and *Man spielt nicht mit der Liebe* (One Should not Play with Love, 1949), directed by Hans Deppe. For more information on Brauner, see Tim Bergfelder, *International Adventures: German Popular Cinema and European Co-Productions in the 1960s* (New York: Berghahn Books, 2006), pp. 105–135 and Schenk, *Das zweite Leben der Filmstadt Babelsberg*, p. 87.
7. Erich Mehl, who had rescued a Jewish friend during the Third Reich, had strongly antifascist and socially critical views. In an article about his film project *Großstadtgeheimnis* (Big City Secret, Leo de Laforgue, 1952), the West German magazine *Der Spiegel* describes him as a very active, well-connected, resourceful producer who travelled across the border in Berlin and worked equally well with East and West German film companies; see Gebrüder Sass, 'Wer ersetze den Ausfall?' *Der Spiegel* 52 (1951), 28–29.
8. See Christiane Mückenberger and Günther Jordan, *'Sie sehen selbst, Sie hören selbst...': Eine Geschichte der DEFA von ihren Anfängen bis 1949* (Marburg: Hitzeroth, 1994), pp. 9–32.
9. See Heinz Kersten, *Das Filmwesen in der sowjetischen Besatzungszone Deutschlands* (Bonn: Gesamtdeutsches Ministerium, 1963), p. 21.
10. Such examples include R. A. Stammle, Georg C. Klaren, Gerhard Menzel, Gerhard Grindel, Bobby Lüthge, Arthur Maria Rabenalt, Alf Teichs, Erich Ebermayer, Arthur A. Kuhnert, Joachim Barckhausen and Frank Clifford, see ibid., p. 22; see also Albert Wilkening, *Betriebsgeschichte des VEB DEFA Studio fur Spielfilme*, vol. 1 (Berlin: VEB DEFA Studio für Spielfilme, 1981), pp. 109–110.
11. Cited in Wilkening, *Betriebsgeschichte des VEB DEFA Studio fur Spielfilme*, pp. 76–78.
12. Such films include their adaptations of Honoré de Balzac, *Karriere in Paris* (Career in Paris, 1951), directed by Georg C. Klaren in the GDR, and of Hans Christian Andersen's fairy tale *Das Mädchen mit den Schwefelhölzern* (The Little Match Girl, 1953), directed by Fritz Genschow in West Germany.
13. Examples include *Grube Morgenrot* (The Morgenrot Mine, Erich Freund and Wolfgang Schleif, 1948) and *Familie Benthin* (The Benthin Family, Kurt Mätzig and Slatan Dudow, 1950).
14. By the mid-1950s, Hoffmann's novella had been adapted several times for German and European audiences: by the prolific Mario Caserini in the Italian production *Mademoiselle de Scudery* (1911, Italy), by Gottfried Hacker and Karl Frey in their silent film *Das Fräulein von Scudéri* (Mademoiselle de Scudéri, 1919, Germany), and by Austrian-born director Paul Martin in his West German picture *Die tödlichen Träume* (Deadly Nightmares, 1951), a fantastical drama loosely based on motifs from several works by E.T.A. Hoffmann.
15. The early nineteenth-century concept of *l'art pour l'art* (art for art's sake) proposed an intrinsic and genuine value of art as divorced from any propagandistic, didactic, moral or utilitarian functions. In the young GDR state, this view was denounced as bourgeois and ideologically problematic. Barton Byg provides an excellent discussion of the aversion to this notion in official GDR policy and the debates on stylized filmmaking. See Barton Byg, 'DEFA and the Traditions of International Cinema', in

Seán Allan and John Sandford (eds), *DEFA: East German Cinema, 1946–1992* (New York: Berghahn Books, 1999), pp. 22–41.
16. For a detailed discussion on artistic debates in the 1950s and the status of the artist in the socialist state in general, see David Bathrick, *The Powers of Speech: The Politics of Culture in the GDR* (Lincoln and London: University of Nebraska Press, 1995), pp. 1–26.
17. Michael Geyer (ed.), *The Power of Intellectuals in Contemporary Germany* (Chicago: Chicago University Press, 2001), p. 2.
18. David Bathrick, *The Powers of Speech*, p. 11.
19. Michael Lentz, 'Vergessen? Der Star hinter dem Eisernen Vorhang', *Westdeutsche Allgemeine* (Essen), 10 April 1955.
20. Like Henny Porten, former UFA actress Gisela Uhlen had by 1954 been long unemployed in the West and faced legal difficulties because of a recent divorce. DEFA not only gave Uhlen work, but also assisted her in relocating to the East together with her son, whom she feared losing in the trial with her former husband. Similarly, Curt Bois, one of UFA's best-known comic actors, received a contract from DEFA and a monthly salary as early as 1951 on condition that he move to East Berlin. Like Porten, Bois enjoyed numerous private and financial privileges. See Schenk, *Das zweite Leben der Filmstadt Babelsberg*, pp. 100–102.
21. Sepp Schwab, *Nachlass*, Bundesarchiv Berlin (BArch), VEB DEFA-Studio für Spielfilme DR 117/15964, p. 69.
22. Helga Belach, *Henny Porten: Die erste deutsche Filmstar 1890–1960* (Berlin: Haude & Spener, 1986), p. 146.
23. Sepp Schwab, *Nachlass*, DR 117/15964, p. 28.
24. Ralf Schenk, *Die Schönste – Rückblick und Restaurierung* (documentary), in *Die Schönste*, DVD, Icestorm Entertainment GmbH (Berlin, 2003).
25. BArch, DR 117/2825.
26. See Simone Barck, Martina Langermann and Siegfried Lokatis, 'The German Democratic Republic as a "Reading Nation": Utopia, Planning, Reality, and Ideology', in Michael Geyer (ed.), *The Power of Intellectuals in Contemporary Germany* (Chicago: University of Chicago Press, 2001), pp. 89–90.
27. BArch, Ministerium für Kultur DR 1/4667, p. 17.
28. BArch, DR 1/4667, pp. 20–21.
29. BArch, DR 1/4667, p. 23.
30. BArch, DR1/7904.
31. BArch, DR 117/19120, p. 23.

Select Bibliography

Barck, Simone, Martina Langermann and Siegfried Lokatis. 'The German Democratic Republic as a "Reading Nation": Utopia, Planning, Reality, and Ideology'. In Michael Geyer (ed.), *The Power of Intellectuals in Contemporary Germany*. Chicago: Chicago University Press, 2001.

Bathrick, David. *The Powers of Speech: The Politics of Culture in the GDR.* Lincoln: Nebraska University Press, 1995.

Belach, Helga. *Henny Porten: Die erste deutsche Filmstar 1890–1960.* Berlin: Haude & Spener, 1986.

Byg, Barton. 'DEFA and the Traditions of International Cinema'. In Seán Allan and John Sandford (eds), *DEFA: East German Cinema, 1946–1992*. New York: Berghahn Books, 1999.

Heimann, Thomas. *DEFA, Künstler und SED Politik*. Berlin: Vistas, 1994.

Higson, Andrew, and Richard Maltby (eds). *'Film Europe' and 'Film America': Cinema, Commerce, and Cultural Exchange 1920–1939*. Exeter: University of Exeter Press, 1999.

Kersten, Heinz. *Das Filmwesen in der sowjetischen Besatzungszone Deutschlands*. Bonn: Gesamtdeutsches Ministerium, 1963.

Kötzing, Andreas. *Kultur und Filmpolitik im Kalten Krieg: Die Filmfestivals von Leipzig und Oberhausen im gesamtdeutschen Perspektive 1954–1972*. Göttingen: Wallstein Verlag, 2013.

Mückenberger, Christiane, and Günther Jordan. *'Sie sehen selbst, Sie hören selbst...': Eine Geschichte der DEFA von ihren Anfängen bis 1949*. Marburg: Hitzeroth, 1994.

Schenk, Ralf (ed.). *Das zweite Leben der Filmstadt Babelsberg: DEFA-Spielfilme 1946–1992*. Berlin: Henschel, 1994.

Wilkening, Albert. *Betriebsgeschichte des VEB DEFA Studio fur Spielfilme*. Vol. 1. Berlin: VEB DEFA Studio für Spielfilme, 1981.

Chapter 6

No TV without Film

Production Relations between the *DEFA* Studios and *Deutscher Fernsehfunk*

Thomas Beutelschmidt

This article provides an outline of the production relations between film and television in the German Democratic Republic (GDR). The sheer number of (primarily fictional) TV programmes made in and with the assistance of the DEFA studios is already an indication of the institutional and artistic ties between the two. According to my investigations,[1] the two media outlets made more than 800 contract productions together, making up about 50% of DEFA (Deutsche Film-Aktiengesellschaft) output between 1959 and 1990. These figures point to a dependency that both institutions viewed with ambivalence. East German television, *Deutscher Fernsehfunk*, profited enormously from the film industry, as an 'extended workbench' so to speak, and indeed it could not have managed to rise to the status of a mass media without the professional assistance of DEFA given the limited production capacities within the planned economy. The increase in television viewers, the growing volume of daily broadcasts, and not least of all the medium's enhanced political significance increasingly demanded TV programming with cinematic form and more opulent visuals. Cinema, on the other hand, gradually lost its position as a defining audiovisual medium with the establishment of television – a development analogous to that seen in other industrial nations, on both sides of the East-West divide. In the long run, *Deutscher Fernsehfunk* competed with DEFA for market shares and viewers as well as for economic resources and narrative traditions. Ultimately, though, the expansion of the electronic medium did not supplant motion pictures, but instead contributed diversity to the range of available culture in East Germany.

The Introduction of Television and Its Positioning in the Media Ensemble of the GDR

In 1951, a commemorative publication in honour of the fifth anniversary of DEFA's founding celebrated cinema as 'the greatest mass art form'.² But the initial euphoria over the post-war films that are today considered classics soon gave way to a crisis of orientation in the context of the Cold War and the socialist experiment of the young GDR. This crisis was linked to interventions by the party and resulted in a drastic decline in output, from eight films in 1950 and eleven in 1951 to a mere five in 1952.³ The film studios certainly made every effort to fulfil their propaganda duties in the 1950s and, according to a tally by Klaus Finke,⁴ delivered about 40 productions focusing on the *socialist way of life*, the working world and the issue of peace. Yet, despite all its displays of submissiveness, DEFA was still regarded by the party as a potentially loose cannon – a suspicion grounded in the company's original mission as well as its staff structure. Even if the Socialist Unity Party of Germany (Sozialistische Einheitspartei Deutschlands, SED) party line was binding, the DEFA was in its early years nonetheless likewise indebted to the Allied strategy of *anti-Fascist democratic renewal*, which sought to harness bourgeois-liberal forces⁵ in the spirit of the anti-Nazi Popular Front. Moreover, its artistic concept was not yet unilaterally fixed on the construct of *socialist realism*, whose notorious stereotypes and sentimental pathos originated in the Stalinist cultural policy of the mid-1930s with Andrei Zhdanov as its mouthpiece.

This broad, basic consensus eventually led to conflicts when the party shifted emphasis to folksiness (*Volksverbundenheit*) and partisanship (*Parteilichkeit*). Party leaders accused filmmakers of not grasping 'deeply enough … such terms [as] perspective, balance of power, Socialist camp, taming German militarism or building Socialism in the GDR'.⁶ The experience of crisis in the early 1950s and the attendant mistrust of staff with a bourgeois background played a not inconsiderable role in the gradual shift in focus from film to television. It seems logical that, in introducing this new *instrument of the workers' and peasants' state*, functionaries were keen to obviate any 'birth defects' and assert their full influence from the very start: 'The television centre is a state and political institution […]. With the new possibilities of propaganda and agitation offered by television, [programming] has the task of convincing workers of the correctness of party and government policies, while inspiring and mobilizing them to solve the tasks of the new course'.[7]

The party and state leadership had allocated considerable investment resources Since late 1949 to build a television centre in Berlin-Adlershof.[8] By mid-1951 alone about 5.6 million East German marks had been budgeted for construction costs and studio equipment,[9] whereas the investment plan for the *film industry* in the following year amounted to only around 4.5 million.[10] The new 'collective organizer' television, in extension of Lenin's definition of the press,[11] was subordinated to the State Radio Committee (Staatliche Rundfunk Komitee), established in 1952.[12] An analogous State Committee for Film Affairs (Staatliches Komitee für Filmwesen) was set up by the Council of Ministers of the GDR.[13] But the new authority was not up to the task of planning, controlling and authorizing films, and by January 1954 its responsibilities had been transferred to the Central Film Administration (Hauptverwaltung Film, HV Film) in the newly formed Ministry of Culture.[14]

Political and administrative control of the media had thus been successfully centralized, fulfilling one of the objectives set by guidelines of the Second Party Conference of the SED from July 9-12, 1952: the systematic construction of the foundations of socialism. With the launching of a test programme in honour of Stalin's 70th birthday on December 21, 1952, the GDR joined the ranks of the Soviet Union, Czechoslovakia, and Poland as well as Great Britain, France, Italy, Switzerland and the Federal Republic of Germany in being among the first European states to have a regular broadcast service. With this development the East German state could stake its claim in the international allocation and authorization of television channel frequencies.[15]

Due to the lack of television sets and the limited broadcasting range of transmitters, the service met with little response well into the mid-1950s, however. What's more, the early test programmes were hardly impressive in technical and artistic terms, let alone a viable alternative to cinema. Television studios with their temperamental equipment were clearly still in the experimental phase. Its live broadcasts were limited at first to illustrated news, discussion groups and magazine programs, complemented by children's hours, non-fictional entertainment and brief, dialogue-laden sketches with the quality of chamber theatre.

Artistic and purely fictional productions were still more or less DEFA's domain. It was only later that the East German film academy[16] began to train its graduates for careers in the television industry and thus early TV directors endeavoured to recruit experienced staff from Babelsberg to collaborate on its test programmes. The executive board of DEFA was generally willing to offer its support and helped make the television pilot project a success.[17] In retrospect, however, it is clear how difficult it was for the few staff members with cinema experience to adjust to the new electronic medium: 'I remember one time being given the wonderful answer: "Herr Luderer, this is not DEFA here!" That was Arthur Nehmzow [the then head of production, T.B.], and I told him: "Right you are, I noticed that too, but we make movies on celluloid, and there are certain requirements you have to keep in mind or certain implications you can't just ignore". Trying to convey these things to people or getting your way [...], that was incredibly hard at the start'.[18]

Technicians, in particular, found promising career opportunities at the nascent television centre. Intellectuals and artists, on the other hand, were reluctant to get involved in a medium they considered profane, with a tendency to flatten and trivialize. Many directors even feared for their reputations and refused to work in the television despite lucrative offers, because in their view only cinema had a certain prestige attached to it and could generate a response at large festivals. The result was that '[g]ood directors went to Babelsberg', as director Horst E. Brandt, among others, observed.[19] Only later did prominent DEFA figures such as Egon Günther, Ralf Kirsten or Horst Seemann take the opportunity to explore more rational production methods by making the occasional foray into television or to develop their talent and deal with different subject matter in the form of a TV miniseries.

But cinema contributed in another way to establishing television as a mass medium. It was the availability of films that satisfied television's demand for fictional programmes in the first place and broadened television's meagre programming. Well aware of its own programming deficits and in an effort to make itself more attractive to viewers, television programmers reserved several prime-time slots per week for broadcasting documentary and feature films.

Since the newly founded television centre naturally did not have its own film archive, it had to cooperate with the State Film Archive as well as with DEFA's Division of Foreign Trade (DEFA-Außenhandel) and Progress Film Distribution (Progress Film-Vertrieb). Forty-six foreign pictures have been documented for 1953 alone, the centre's first year of operation.[20] But the airing of films on television would remain a bone of contention in the cinema faction of the state culture industry. Consequently, although the new medium was able to secure a regular flow of broadcast rights, it did not have general access to the newest productions. The central distributor, for its part, was troubled by the constant presence of feature films on television and the dwindling number of moviegoers as a result. Whereas cinemas had more than three million visitors annually between 1953 and 1957, by 1960 the number of filmgoers had dropped to just under 2.4 million.[21] Yet radical steps such as banning feature films from television altogether – a demand that was voiced in West Germany as well – were never undertaken.

By January 1956, the pilot project had progressed to the point that *Deutscher Fernsehfunk* (DFF) could begin its regular broadcasting service. The Politbüro and the relevant Agitation Department of the Central Committee seemed content with the development of their new means of communication. DEFA, however, was put to the ideological test at the Third Party Conference of the SED from March 24-30, 1956. Fearing a loss of power after the Twentieth Party Congress of the Communist Party of the Soviet Union (CPSU) and the de-Stalinization of Eastern Europe in the brief period of thaw that followed, East German leaders redoubled their pressure on the film studio. They called for an existential 'battle of the new with the old', warning against 'noncommittalism and liberalism' along with 'the false path of ideological coexistence' in reference to the reform movement in Hungary.[22]

The ever more popular medium of television, by contrast, was fulfilling its system-stabilizing function as organ of propaganda, transmitter of knowledge, and source of art and entertainment. The service even gained a boost in quality thanks to new transmission technology available since late 1955. Television was finally mobile and could cover events throughout the republic, whether politics, sports, shows or theatre, making good on its promise as a 'window to the world'.

DEFA as a Producer for East German Television

It was during the end-1950s that the conditions for producing TV films, or telefilms, were established. There were obvious advantages to This approach – for instance, TV would have its own high-quality film copies for showing reruns or subsequent use in cinemas, for international export and for participation at festivals and fairs. Furthermore, certain subjects such as those based on historical material, more demanding literary adaptations or realistic portrayals of the workplace and daily life called for atmospheric location shooting, greater action, and visual mise-en-scène instead of mere reproduction with the camera.

But studio and copying equipment beyond that required for news and reporting had not been taken into account when setting up the television centre. The GDR did not want and could not afford a second full-fledged film studio alongside Babelsberg. The creation of facilities comparable to the West German television subsidiaries of 'Bavaria', 'Taunus-Film' or 'Studio Hamburg' would have exceeded the financial and material means of the GDR. *Deutscher Fernsehfunk* had to therefore repeatedly rely on support from DEFA. So as not to create bottlenecks, in early 1953 the Film Committee stipulated that 'equipment [...] can only be lent to other institutions if the needs of the DEFA studios have been met'.[23] In the early years, film cameras were only used sporadically to document or rebroadcast teleplays, with camera angles and montage always proceeding in linear fashion. It was not until the mid-1950s that TV directors began trying to enrich their work with premade film sequences – lengthy exterior shooting or hand-held shots – that were impracticable with cable-bound electronic cameras. These sequences were then edited into live teleplays in order to diminish the theatrical stage effect, to offer a change of perspective, or to make the action more believable and the setting more realistic. This media-mixing method, however, with its less than compatible set pieces was an unsatisfactory compromise. For one thing, the transitions from electronic to celluloid shots were distracting because of varying contrast values and degrees of sharpness. For another, the differing characteristics of studio versus outdoor shots created stylistic incongruities that seriously impaired the overall aesthetic of such hybrid forms.

Film capacities had to be expanded to meet the rapidly growing expectations of both producers and viewing audience over the long term as well as enabling 'the entire channel to reach the international standard'.[24] DFF was provided with additional 16-mm and 35-mm cameras (Moskva, Arri, Cameflex, Arriflex, Bolex) for internal film productions from the start of its regular broadcasting service until the end of the 1950s. In addition, the party leadership exerted pressure to help television executives gain access to the studios of neighbouring Johannisthal in the early 1960s. These studios had formerly been operated by Johannisthaler Film-Anstalten GmbH (JOFA) and, later, by Ton-Bild-Syndikat AG (Tobis). After 1945 the Soviet joint-stock company LINSA overtook the site as part of reparation payments, but a U.S.S.R. government decision transferred it back to German ownership in 1950, at which point it became the legal property of DEFA-Studio für Spielfilme, the DEFA motion-picture studio.[25] Dramatic arts, entertainment and science departments were promptly set up there, alongside production teams. DFF was also allocated additional film production staff previously employed by DEFA.[26]

Although this broader foundation helped improve the quality of TV film productions,[27] the television drama department, for instance, could only meet the increasing demand for more sophisticated films through cooperation with tried and tested DEFA teams. Seven co-productions were scheduled, which the otherwise rival producers interpreted as 'jumping over boundaries previously thought impassable'.[28] An ambivalent start with *Damals in Paris* (Those Days in Paris, Carl Balhaus, 1956), which deals with the anti-Fascist, resistance was followed by elaborate literary adaptations such as *Tiefe Furchen* (Deep Furrows, Lutz Köhlert, 1965), *Jakob der Lügner* (Jacob the Liar, Frank Beyer, 1974), *Die Leiden des jungen Werthers* (The Sorrows of Young Werther, Egon Günther, 1976), *Die Verlobte* (The Fiancée, Günther Rücker/ Günter Reisch, 1980), the contemporary comedy *Hiev up* (Heave Up, Jo Hasler, 1978) and the short feature film *Weiberwirtschaft* (Petticoat Rule, Peter Kahane, 1984).

Contract productions were considerably more numerous. Such politically motivated cooperation can be understood as an economic optimization strategy in light of scarce resources. On the one hand, the income from contract productions helped cushion the excessive operating costs of the film studios and relieve the culture budget. On the other hand, technical and staff capacities at DEFA that were not absorbed by cinema productions could be fully utilized by making them available to DFF. More challenging subject matter was chosen for telefilms, geared to the quality standards of an international audience or – as in the case of popular miniseries – demanding considerable resources, all of which could only be done with an experienced, industrial studio at every stage of production.

Television determined the overall budget as well as the limits for each individual project in regular 'annual performance contracts', which were based on general cooperation agreements. According to available sources, more than two-thirds of all resources each year went to the motion-picture studio for contract productions. The figures range from 5.4 million marks in 1960,[29] the first year of cooperation, to 33.1 million in 1970[30] and 40.5 million in 1980.[31] But even after the *Wende*, the now democratized television industry stood by an economically endangered DEFA. According to its provisional director Hans Bentzien, DFF spent 'almost 67 million marks'[32] on what would be its final productions in 1990.

In general, the financial resources for contract films were higher on average than for in-house TV productions. These expenditures, occasionally twice as high, signalled not only higher artistic standards but also cultural-political significance, propagandistic goals or export requirements. In other words, the budgets were sizable and comprised a large part of television's overall expenditures. Hence, production managers were always trying to cut costs. A stricter time schedule was needed, but also more flexibility in the case of extended production, delays or cancellations. The latter could be caused unexpectedly by conceptual changes[33] or interruptions during shooting or post-production due to personnel shortages – especially unavailable actors – or even weather conditions. Both partners struggled time and again with (overly) long production periods on bigger projects spanning several business years or with the termination of individual projects whose budgets were suddenly freed up and had to be quickly reallocated. In practice, these modifications or disruptions of the production process meant that the budgets fixed in the plan requirements had to be constantly adjusted to the actual state of affairs – to the detriment or benefit of the respective contractual partner. It was the unchanging 'main task' that had to be fulfilled: 'Increasing the overall performance of the studio in the form of producing more broadcast minutes with the same finance volumes through a targeted reduction of costs per broadcast minute'.[34]

The 'general agreements' reached between DEFA and DFF in 1960 governed the individual working stages, the time schedule and practical issues in the production process. The latter was planned, directed and supervised on the part of DFF by the director of the film department in the production section. In addition, an employee of the Dramatic Arts Main Department of DFF was delegated to the motion picture studio to act as an on-site coordinator and ensure the smooth execution of projects and short decision-making processes.

The spheres of responsibility in handling contract productions were therefore firmly established:

- the television station was responsible for political-ideological content as well as for the basic artistic concept, whereas the studio and select creative staff had a say in their implementation;
- the film studios, for their part, were responsible for production and organization.

Television not only endeavoured to establish a clear division of responsibilities between itself and cinema in the area of film production. It also wanted to play the part of initiator and client, showing the outside world what telefilms could do compared to motion pictures from Babelsberg. In this respect, DEFA was not involved in the decisions about certain themes, authors and the scope of a project. As a contractor it generally steered clear of such delicate issues and only rarely intervened, such as in the extreme case of the rather overblown Thälmann project of the mid-1980s.[35]

According to the DEFA Foundation film database, between four (1959) and twenty-three (1980) short and feature-film-length TV productions were made per year, along with numerous documentary, journalistic and entertainment (short) films made by the other DEFA studios. The adjusted list is comprised of nearly 500 separate contract productions made by East German television.[36] Since many of these projects were two- to five-part series or serial films with as many as twelve episodes, the number of actual productions was even greater. We can therefore safely assume that a total of about 840 individual films of all lengths were made. This works out, in purely mathematical terms, to an average of 26 films per year between 1959 and 1990. We should also bear in mind that the motion-picture studio by no means produced only fictional teleplays or cinematic opera performances for the television drama section. Well into the 1970s, the studio turned out nearly 40 productions of between 10 and 75 minutes in length belonging to the categories of ballet and revue films, documentaries, cultural programs, (musical) entertainment and cinema advertising.

These were the figures for television productions. By way of comparison, about 550 DEFA feature films were made between 1959 and 1990, with production levels dropping to an average of fifteen titles per year by the late 1960s. All together, about 25 hours of feature films were produced each year as opposed to 31 hours of telefilms. Thus, with a few notable exceptions, the annual production of telefilms after 1963 was quantitatively higher than that of motion pictures.

The fruitful cooperation between DFF and DEFA began with the comedy thriller *Spuk in Villa Sonnenschein* (Spook in the Sunshine Villa, Gerhard Klingenberg, 1959), a production that was still characterized by the slow-moving, dialogue-centred tradition of the teleplay, which film crews were ill-prepared to deal with. Some departments had 'not [taken] the work with telefilms seriously enough' and 'thought instead [...] that the films were more or less a sideline, made with whatever people and equipment happened to be available, no matter if they were good or bad in terms of quality'.[37] Despite the sceptical attitude towards the unaccustomed approach, the pilot film did have an important learning effect. With its lower fees, larger amount of useful footage and shorter production times the project costs were well below those of a motion picture. Thus, the more economically effective production of telefilms became a favourite argument of DEFA producers for lowering studio norms and adapting motion-picture production to the more rational working methods of television. At first, artists such as director Kurt Maetzig viewed this development as a 'harmful tendency',[38] as it restricted creative freedom and even further lowered the quality of feature films. Given the limited resources available, this was a conflict that could never be resolved, which meant that every project was confronted with a discrepancy between ideal and reality.

Telefilms, by contrast, were growing ever more sophisticated as a genre and learned a lot from the cinema. Already in 1960, the range of more film-like contract productions was expanding. For example, the sensitively told tale of German-Soviet friendship in *Immer am Weg dein Gesicht* (Always Your Face Along the Way, Achim Hübner, 1960) appeared alongside adventure films such as *Flucht aus der Hölle* (Flight from Hell, Hans-Erich Korbschmitt, 1960). The latter multipart production was the prelude to epic 'telenovels' and noticeably stood out from the comparatively crude and linear kitchen-sink comedies of that period such as *Papas neue Freundin* (Daddy's New Girlfriend, Georg Leopold, 1960). These and other emancipatory attempts even earned the praise of film critics, who particularly emphasized the 'progressive departure from the schema and norm, in the choice and arrangement of the material, in the creation of the characters as well as in the language and dialogues.'[39]

In this manner, DEFA promoted the 'cinematization' of fictional TV productions, while gradually rendering the boundaries between television and cinema more fluid. Television productions now proved in many instances to be on par with comparable DEFA works, exhibiting not only solid workmanship, multifaceted images and complex montage techniques but also various temporal levels, flashbacks and parallel or contrasting storylines. The *dramatic arts* underwent a tremendous surge in artistic innovation, freeing themselves from the corset of internal studio performances and orienting themselves more and more to the standards of cinema. The gradual decline of the teleplay was bemoaned as a loss by some DFF pioneers, however. The artistic challenge of a live performance would be lost, they claimed, whereas the uneven production method of telefilms, operating from take to take as it were, unfortunately 'neglect[ed] the principles of focused dramatic action'.[40]

The consolidation and diversification of television in the GDR by the 1960s led to the converging of two audiovisual mass media.

Nevertheless, cinema and television continued to differ in their functional ascriptions, their areas of responsibility, content focus and artistic objectives. Thus, despite growing similarities, these structural differences meant that they still pursued divergent interests as well as serving different target groups. In this respect, *cinema* had not only found an equal partner but also a tough competitor that, much to its dismay, was able to attract an ever broader audience.[41] East German journalists, however, citing their Party Chairman Ulbricht, defended television as the new defining medium. They argued that television was unjustly 'decried as the "gravedigger" of theatre, cinema and the book', because after all it gave 'millions of people the incentive to "storm the heights of culture"'.[42]

If motion pictures were initially a major influence on telefilms, these later gave new impetus to cinematic productions. Television scholar Peter Hoff has even spoken of a 'decisive innovation process in the field of audiovisual media arts', which began in television drama and also caught on in other socialist countries.[43] A case in point was the internationally acclaimed five-part series *Gewissen in Aufruhr* (Conscience in Turmoil, Günter Reisch/Hans-Joachim Kasprzik, 1961), a biopic about a German Wehrmacht officer during the period of systemic conflict after 1945. Hoff repeatedly points out that, given the inherent competitive advantage of the ubiquitous television set, DEFA was forced to focus on young people as its prime viewing audience as well as tackling more contemporary topics – particularly successful examples, in his opinion, were *Sieben Sommersprossen* (Seven Freckles, Herrmann Zschoche, 1978), *Bis dass der Tod euch scheidet* (Till Death Do You Part, Heiner Carow, 1979) and *Solo Sunny* (Konrad Wolf, 1980).[44]

The cross-media experiences of DEFA directors who worked for Adlershof and experimented in TV-specific subject matter had a lasting effect on the film studios. Some directors such as Bernhard Stephan even switched from film to television.[45] To a certain extent this fulfilled the hope of an increase in competence through TV work: 'The artistic performance of motion-picture studio employees in telefilm productions has to be taken into consideration by studio heads in discussing the artistic standards and qualifications of individual artists'.[46] Yet, few DEFA employees, such as Heiner Carow, were willing to admit the influence that telefilm's overall aesthetic and its focus on daily life had on cinema, which for its part gradually lost its pioneering role and was subject to a latent pressure to conform: 'The influence of television, the influence of its possibilities with regard to narrative standpoint, the choice of subject matter and the type of film has been underestimated. Filmmakers themselves have often fiercely denied these influences.'[47]

There is also reason to assume that the form of light entertainment practiced by television was a source of inspiration and ideas for DEFA planners as well. Thus, for instance, the positive reception of a number of comedies initially broadcast on television and later screened in movie theatres led to a noticeable expansion of DEFA's entertainment offerings. Of similar interest was the historical adventure series *Hannes Scharf* (Karlheinz Carpentier/ Erich Böbel, 1967), an action-packed and humorous DEFA contract production with a surprising resemblance to the subsequent swashbuckling film *Hauptmann Florian von der Mühle* (Captain Florian of the Mill, Werner W. Wallroth, 1968).

In retrospect, given its orientation towards television we might ask to what extent DEFA distinguished itself at all as an independent art form in the last two decades of its existence and if its products were able to fulfil their intended public function. Cowboy and Indian stories, science fiction adventures or impressive stand-alone works such as Goya (Konrad Wolf 1971) still promised a powerful movie-going experience. The majority of later films, however, lacked the key elements of form and effect that set cinema apart from television and were demanded by cultural administrators: 'Ever since the existence of television, the demands on cinematic art have changed. The viewing audience demands qualitatively new productions both of a higher artistic quality and with more opulent scenery and costumes: [...] great themes, cinemascope, colour, popular actors, interesting locations, powerful and impressive images, greater visual appeal and projection on the big screen with a multichannel sound system'.[48]

Conclusion

The relations between DEFA and DFF, in structural and organizational terms as well as with regard to culture and media policy, reveal themselves to be quite contradictory, marked by attempts at cooperation as well as by competitive behaviour. On the one hand, alongside mutual creative impulses and concrete cooperation on co-productions, there was overlap and hence a certain convergence at the level of ideological requirements and staff. On the other hand, the two mass media were different in terms of their political functions and tasks, their content and artistic aims, as well as their target groups and effect, i.e., a private setting as opposed to a collective cinematic experience. Thus, despite all the appeals of state and party leaders to recognize their shared interests and strengthen cooperation, film and television pursued different aims and strategies, as seen in the competition to secure well-known writers, popular stories, qualified staff and, naturally, audience approval.

Nevertheless, neither medium can be viewed as an autonomous communicator; each can only be adequately described in the overall framework of the 'socialist media landscape'. For all the dissonance between the centrally steered but separately operating party apparatuses (Culture Department and HV Film versus Agitation Department and State Television Committee), film and television in the GDR were basically equal institutions subordinate to a *single* state authority, subject to a *single* cultural policy and dependent on a joint state budget. For this reason, the established doctrine always posited a 'partnership in competition' rather than a state of rivalry, 'as economic compulsion is lacking and the socialist system effectively guarantees a secure basis for productive developments'.[49]

Thomas Beutelschmidt studied German studies, art history and political science in Freiburg and Berlin. He is a media historian, author, and curator. He is currently conducting an interdisciplinary research project on the international exchange of TV programs among European broadcasters from the early 1950s to the end of the system conflict in 1990 (Centre for Contemporary History in Potsdam/ ZZF).

Notes

1. Thomas Beutelschmidt, *Kooperation oder Konkurrenz? Das Verhältnis zwischen Film und Fernsehen in der DDR* (Berlin: DEFA-Schriftenreihe, 2009).
2. Anton Ackermann, 'Zum 5-jährigen Bestehen der DEFA', in Deutsche Film-AG (ed.), *Auf neuen Wegen. 5 Jahre fortschrittlicher deutscher Film* (Berlin [DDR]: Deutscher Filmverlag, 1951), p. 11.
3. The figures refer to time of production and not the premiere dates. See Susanne Brömsel and Renate Biel, 'Die Spielfilme der DEFA', in Filmmuseum Potsdam, eds., *Das zweite Leben der Filmstadt Babelsberg* (Berlin: Henschel, 1994), pp. 356–541; there were thus ten premieres in 1950, eight in 1951 and six in 1952.
4. Klaus Finke, *Politik und Film in der DDR* (Oldenburger Beiträge zur DDR- und DEFA-Forschung, 2 vols. (Oldenburg: BIS-Verlag, 2007), vol. 2, p. 630.
5. See the 'film artist' profile in Heinz Kersten, *Das Filmwesen in der sowjetischen Besatzungszone Deutschlands.* (Bonn: Gesamtdeutsches Ministerium, 1963), pp. 21–25, as well as the information on staff structure in Dieter Wiedemann, 'Lebenswelten und Alltagswissen', in Christoph Führ and Carl-Ludwig Furck, *Handbuch der deutschen Bildungsgeschichte*, vol. VI, part 2 (Munich: Achims Verlag, 1998), pp. 69–100, here p. 74.

6. Anlage 1 zu TOP 4 'Verbesserung der DEFA-Spielfilmproduktion im Jahre 1961/62', in *Protokoll Nr. 52/61 der Sitzung des Politbüros des Zentralkomitees am Montag, dem 9.10.1961*, Stiftung Archiv der Parteien und Massenorganisationen der DDR im Bundesarchiv Berlin (SAPMO-BArch), SED, DY 30/J IV 2/2/794, 1, p. 5.
7. Arthur Nehmzow/Fernsehzentrum, *Die Aufgaben der Chefredaktion und der Sendeleitung des Fernsehzentrums Berlin*, Berlin, 11.3.1954, Bundesarchiv Berlin (BArch), Staatliches Komitee für Fernsehen, DR 8/2, p. 1.
8. Plans for television in the GDR began in late 1949, apparently – though not substantiated by archive material – by order of the German Economic Commission under the supervision of Ernst Augustin, chief engineer of the 'central laboratory' of the radio director's office; studio equipment was developed and tested as of early 1950; the foundation stone was laid in June of the same year, the topping-out ceremony for the first building at the television centre in Berlin-Adlershof was celebrated in July 1951, and June 1952 marked the begin of unofficial test broadcasts and the development of the first series.
9. 'Zusammenstellung der Investitionsnachplanung Adlershof für 1951' (5.9.1951), Anlage zu Ministerpräsident Grotewohl, *Schreiben an den Vorsitzenden der Staatlichen Plankommission Rau*, Berlin, 22.10.1951, BArch, Staatliches Komitee für Rundfunk DR 6/342.
10. Staatliches Komitee für Filmwesen, *Protokoll der 7. Kollegiumssitzung vom 12.11.1952*, Berlin, 24.11.1952, BArch, Ministerium für Kultur DR 1/4468, TOP 2, p. 2.
11. Wladimir I. Lenin, Womit beginnen? in *Ausgewählte Werke in zwei Bänden*, vol. 1 (Berlin [DDR] 1959), p. 309.
12. The State Radio Committee (with its first chairman Kurt Heiss) was constituted on September 9, 1952 by order of the Council of Ministers with a separate Television Director's Office whose tasks included 'directing the Berlin television centre and developing television in the GDR'; see §4e of the Decree on the Formation of the State Radio Committee of August 14, 1952.
13. The office began its activities on October 1, 1952 under its chairman Sepp Schwab according to the Decree on the Formation of the State Committee for Cinema in the Council of Ministers of the GDR of August 7, 1952.
14. The Ministry of Culture of the GDR under Johannes R. Becher was founded on January 7, 1954, including the creation of the HV Film under Anton Ackermann.
15. The available broadcast frequencies were allocated at the first European Frequency Conference of the Consultative Committee on International Radio (CCIR) in Stockholm in June 1952, allowing individual states the creation of their own national broadcast networks.
16. The German Film Academy (Deutsche Hochschule für Filmkunst) was founded on November 11, 1954 in accordance with a law passed on October 4, 1954 and was renamed the Academy of Film and Television of the GDR (Hochschule für Film und Fernsehen der DDR) in 1969.
17. Protokoll der 4. Sitzung des DEFA-Vorstandes am 7.2.1952 (Archivbestand Thomas Heimann), p. 10.
18. Wolfgang Luderer, in Hans Müncheberg, eds., *Experiment Fernsehen. Vom Laborversuch zur sozialistischen Massenkunst* (Podium und Werkstatt 15/16, Berlin [DDR], 1984), p. 99.
19. Conversation of the author with Horst E. Brandt in Berlin on May 5, 2005.

20. Bundesarchiv-Filmarchiv/DEFA-Stiftung, *Ausländische Spiel- und abendfüllende Dokumentarfilme in den Kinos der SBZ/DDR 1945-1966*. Filmografie (Berlin: Bundesarchiv-Filmarchiv/DEFA-Stiftung, 2001), pp. 54 und 35.
21. See the figures provided by the State Central Administration for Statistics of the GDR as well as Elizabeth Prommer, *Kinobesuch im Lebenslauf. Eine historische und medienbiographische Studie* (Konstanz: UVK Medien, 1999).
22. See e.g. Helmut Brandis, 'Mehr Filme, billigere Filme, bessere Filme', Berlin, 28.9.1957, BArch, DR 1/4479, pp. 7 and 2.
23. Staatliches Komitee für Filmwesen, *Protokoll der 14. Kollegiumssitzung vom 21.1.1953*, Berlin, 22.1.1953, BArch, DR 1/4468, TOP 5, p. 3.
24. Heinz Adameck, *Schreiben an Staatliches Rundfunkkomitee/Ley mit Anlage 'Perspektive der Programmentwicklung des Deutschen Fernsehfunks nach den bis jetzt vorliegenden Erfahrungen'*, Berlin, 13.11.1956, BArch, DR 6/279, pp. 1f.
25. Staatliches Komitee für Filmwesen, *Protokoll der 9. Kollegiumssitzung vom 3.12.1952*, Berlin, 8.12.1952, BArch, DR 1/4468, TOP 4, p. 3.
26. Deutscher Fernsehfunk/HA Produktion II, *Planung der Arbeitskräfte des DFF 1962*, Berlin, 23.1.1962, BArch, DR 8/25, p. 3.
27. See the first major production *Der Andere neben Dir* (The Other Beside You, Ulrich Thein, 1963) an attempt to shed light on and help understand the historically strained relations between Czechs and Germans.
28. Hans Müncheberg, *Blaues Wunder aus Adlershof. Der Deutsche Fernsehfunk. Erlebtes und Gesammeltes*. (Berlin: Das Neue Berlin, 2000), p. 95.
29. *Rahmenvertrag zwischen dem Staatlichen Rundfunkkomitee-Deutscher Fernsehfunk- und der VVB Film*, Berlin, [no year, =1960], BArch, DR 1/4363, p. 1.
30. See the overview for 1970 of September 9, 1975 provided as an appendix to HA Ökonomie/Abt. Kooperation, *Analyse der Kostenentwicklung der im DEFA-Studio für Spielfilme hergestellten Auftragsproduktionen im Zeitraum 1970-1974*, Berlin, 18.11.1975, DRA Schriftgut Fernsehen (SGFS)/DraKu/Planungsunterlagen DEFA-Analysen 1978-87.
31. HA Ökonomie/Abt. Planung, *Analyse über die ökonomische Effektivität der Auftragsproduktion im VEB DEFA-Studio für Spielfilme hergestellten im Jahr 1981*, Berlin, 25.2.1982/ DRA SGFS/DraKu/Planungsunterlagen DEFA-Analysen 1978-87, p. 7.
32. Ralph Kotsch/Volker Müller, 'Alle Kräfte, die für Erneuerung eintreten, haben gleiche Chancen.' Gespräch mit Hans Bentzien, *Neues Deutschland*, January 18, 1990.
33. See, for example, the change of directors during the production of *Rottenknechte* (Henchmen, Frank Beyer, start of production 1969/broadcast 1971) which apparently incurred extra costs of 890.000 marks – Ministerrat/Ministerium für Finanzen, *Revisionsprotokoll*, Berlin, 24.9.1969, BArch DR, 8/94, p. 9.
34. Fachdirektion Ökonomie/Abt. Planung, *Diskussionsvorschlag zur im Kampfprogramm der GO und im Plan der Hauptaufgaben der Fachdirektion genannten Aufgabe, die Eigenleistungen des DEFA Spielfilmstudios im Rahmen der Auftragsproduktion für das DDR-F künftig zur Hauptkennziffer für die Planerfüllung und Stimulierung zu machen*, Berlin, 8.4.1986, DRA SGFS/DraKu/DEFA Analysen 1978–87, p. 3.
35. The first and only telefilm made by decree of the Politbüro was a two-part, four-hour biopic in honour of the proletarian leader's 100th birthday, the 40th anniversary of the merger of the KPD and SPD as well as the Eleventh SED Party Congress (Georg Schiemann 1986). The project had a budget of 22.5 million marks.

36. See Thomas Beutelschmidt, *Die Auftragsproduktionen des DEFA-Spielfilmstudios für das DDR-Fernsehen von 1959 bis 1990* (Berlin, 2010), database version at the DEFA Foundation website http://defa-stiftung.de/cms/beutelschmidt.
37. *Schlussbericht Film NL 806 'Spuk in Villa Sonnenschein'*, Babelsberg, 30.9.1959, BArch, VEB DEFA-Studio für Spielfilme DR 117/25420, p. 3.
38. Kurt Maetzig in a 1959 letter to studio director Prof. Albert Wilkening, 'Bessere Planung', in Kurt Maetzig, *Filmarbeit. Gespräche – Reden – Schriften* (Berlin [DDR]: Henschelverlag, 1987), p. 279.
39. Erwin Reiche, 'Fernsehfilme – Fernsehspiele', in *Deutsche Filmkunst*, 6 (1961), p. 202.
40. Wolfgang Luderer and Wilhelm Gröhl, respectively, in their contributions to the working group 'History of the Art of Television' in the Association of Film and Television Workers (VFF), cited in Hans Müncheberg, 'Und wieder: Fernsehspiel', in *Film und Fernsehen* 9 (1982), p. 48.
41. The increasing role of television was a major factor in the successive decline of movie-theatre attendance in the GDR, from 316 million in its peak year of 1957 to only 65 million in 1989, see Elizabeth Prommer, *Kinobesuch im Lebenslauf*, p. 352.
42. Günter Raue, *Geschichte des Journalismus. 1945–1961* (Leipzig: Bibliographisches Institut Leipzig, 1986), p. 211.
43. Peter Hoff, 'Wettbewerbspartner oder Konkurrent? Zum Verhältnis von Film, Kino und Fernsehen in der DDR', in *Beiträge zur Film- und Fernsehwissenschaft* 4 (1985), p. 63.
44. Ibid., p. 64.
45. After the crime series Täter unbekannt (Offender Unknown) and the episode *Blutgruppe AB* (blood group AB) of series *Polizeiruf 110* (Police Call 110) in 1972, he made his DEFA debut with the youth drama *Für die Liebe noch zu mager* (Too Poor for Love, 1974).
46. DEFA Studio für Spielfilme/Studioleitung, *Bericht über die Erfüllung des Politbürobeschlusses über die 'Verbesserung der DEFA-Spielfilmproduktion im Jahre 1961/62' vom 9.10.1961*, Potsdam-Babelsberg, 18.9.1962, SAPMO-BArch, DY 30/IV 2/2.026/76, p. 3.
47. Heiner Carow, 'Zwischenbilanz', in *Film und Fernsehen* 4 (1977), pp. 5–9, here p. 9.
48. Anonymous [= HV Film], *Perspektivprogramm des Film- und Lichtspielwesens der DDR bis 1970*, BArch DR 1/4790, p. 2.
49. Peter Hoff, 'Wettbewerbspartner oder Konkurrent?', p. 74.

Select Bibliography

Beutelschmidt, Thomas and Franziska Widmer. *Zwischen den Stühlen. Die Geschichte der Literaturverfilmung „Ursula" von Egon Günther: eine Koproduktion des Fernsehens der DDR und der Schweiz.* Leipzig: Leipziger Universitätsverlag, 2005.

Filmmuseum Potsdam, eds. *Das zweite Leben der Filmstadt.* Babelsberg: Henschelverlag, 1994.

Geiss, Axel. *Repression und Freiheit. DEFA-Regisseure zwischen Fremd- und Selbstbestimmung.* Potsdam: Brandenburgische Landeszentrale für Politische Bildung, 1997.

Hochschule für Film und Fernsehen der DDR, eds. *Film- und Fernsehkunst der DDR. Traditionen – Beispiele – Tendenzen*, Berlin (DDR): Henschelverlag, 1979
Kaltofen, Günter, eds. *Das Bild, das deine Sprache spricht*. Berlin (DDR): Henschelverlag, 1962.
Mückenberger, Christiane. 'Internationale Arbeitstagung zum Thema:,Film im Fernsehen' in Berlin-Adlershof.' *Filmwissenschaftliche Mitteilungen* 1 (1965), p. 175–182.
Münz-Koenen, Ingeborg. *Fernsehdramatik. Experimente – Methoden – Tendenzen*. Berlin (DDR): Akademie Verlag, 1974.
Prümm, Karl. 'Film und Fernsehen. Ambivalenz und Identität.' In Wolfgang Jakobsen et al., eds., *Geschichte des deutschen Films*. Stuttgart – Weimar: J.B. Metzler Verlag, 2004.
Stiehler, Hansjörg. 'Spielfilmeinsatz im DDR-Fernsehen: Auswirkungen der Programmreform von 1982/83.' In Claudia Dittmar – Susanne Vollberg, eds., *Alternativen im DDR-Fernsehen? Die Programmentwicklung 1981 bis 1985*. Leipzig: Leipziger Universitätsverlag, 2004.

PART III

NONFICTIONAL CINEMA

Chapter 7

MILITARY FILM STUDIOS BEFORE 1970

Between Cinematic Avant-Garde and Films on Command

Václav Šmidrkal

One of the socialist army's most significant features was the endeavour to create an elaborate media system of its own that made it largely independent from the civilian media industry. Such a system forced the army into cooperation with state media monopolies – radio, television, film studios – that was beyond both the army's financial possibilities and its political self-assertion. The relationship between military and civilian media systems, on the other hand, was usually one of mutual cooperation, though cutthroat competition occasionally came into play. In the case of film, both the Czechoslovak and East German armies realized sooner or later that they could not rely solely on their respective state film industries and therefore must develop their own production capacities to cover the pressing internal need for documentary, training and news films. Such products were to be made 'on command', issued or approved by an authorized ministerial department to which the studios should be accountable.

In Czechoslovakia, this kind of military film studio was established under the name Czechoslovak Army Film (Československý armádní film, ČAF)[1] during the military training year 1950/51, whereas in the German Democratic Republic the Army Film Studio (Armeefilmstudio, AFS)[2] was not founded until 1960. Although one might expect many similarities due to their affiliation with the Warsaw Pact army and the general affinities between Czechoslovakia and East Germany, prior to 1970 these two studios were poles apart in terms of their production objectives. The Soviet practice did not provide a transferable model, since film production for the Soviet Army was accomplished through a more complex collaboration with the state film industry until the early 1960s. Therefore, the most important factors in creating these striking distinctions were their divergent chronological developments and different artistic conceptions of the studio's function.

In her published doctoral dissertation, Alice Lovejoy presents the argument that free spaces for avant-garde filmmaking within communist Czechoslovakia, especially during the second half of the 1960s, could be found in what initially seemed to be unexpected places, such as ČAF.[3] In another article, Lovejoy stresses the ČAF's artistic exclusivity when she claims that *certain* military films 'of this period were frequently more radical, in form and politics, than those of the contemporaneous Czechoslovak New Wave'.[4] These few films prove that the studio was an active participant in the innovative, progressive Czechoslovak film culture of the 1960s. When the ČAF is compared with its East German counterpart, the argument for the ČAF's exceptionality seems more than adequate. The thirty years of AFS's existence produced hardly any attempts there to foster a specific artistic language or means of expression, and little evidence of a desire to place artistic values and an auteur approach above utilitarian function as determined by the party apparatus or military command. This is one reason why Matthias Rogg, in his works[5] on the AFS, does not raise the issue of artistic freedom or avant-gardism – terms that are hardly relevant – but instead treats AFS documentary production as purely loyal party propaganda. He even calls into question the use of the term 'documentary' to describe the reality-distorting, ideologically charged *Dokumentarfilme*.[6]

Considering these two studios together can bring to light new facts that remain concealed in individual case studies.[7] Comparison of the ČAF and the AFS before 1970 draws attention to striking differences that are not clearly deducible from basic documents or evaluative reports but became evident in production outputs. Whereas some films are nearly interchangeable, some are distinctively unique in terms of their thematic originality, authorial independence and aesthetic progressiveness. Even though both studios were founded for the same reason – to serve military and political objectives and to produce 'films on command' – each studio achieved these goals in different environments and with different results.

The concept of 'films to order' (*účelový film*, *Gebrauchsfilm*), though not clearly defined, is sometimes used as a framework for works in which artistic ambition is subordinated to any kind of clearly expressed 'order', such as those stipulated in the statutes of military film studios and enforced by the 'ordering party'.[8] How can we thus explain the fact that the ČAF was able to overcome, at least with some films, the predetermined course of 'cinema on command' such that its directors were able to enjoy degrees of artistic freedom that were inconceivable with the AFS?

Interconnected with the aforementioned phenomenon of 'cinema on command', a comparison of the studio's histories shows that despite parallel yet asynchronous developments in the first two decades, both studios fell markedly in step with each other around 1970 and numerous ideological dissonances were replaced by almost harmonic conformity. The aim of this essay is to clarify the roots of the differences between the studios, as defined in part by the position of the military within state as well as contemporary cultural politics, and to identify the reasons why these discrepancies suddenly dissipated, thereby enabling the two studios to ultimately become loyal 'brothers in arms'. I argue that even though their production was to a certain degree identical with regard to the types of films they made, there were important differences in terms of priorities, personnel policy and managerial routines. After a brief discussion of these three issues, I chronologically outline the distinctly different paths taken by the ČAF and the AFS until they finally 'met' around 1970 and continued on the same wavelength.

Types of Films

Both military film studios produced four main types of films: training, documentary, news and feature films. They were also able to dub their own productions into foreign-language versions or foreign films into their languages. In addition, the AFS produced acoustic recordings for political agitation and the ČAF created slide series as a visual aid for military lecturing. In the first two decades, training films for the army consistently took up about one third of the ČAF's production capacities; the remaining two thirds were devoted to documentary, feature and news films for the Main Political Administration (Hlavní politická správa).[9] Overall production output doubled starting in the early 1970s, and this proportion changed as films made on commission according to the commercial demands of various institutions – predominantly Czechoslovak Television, which had launched its second channel in

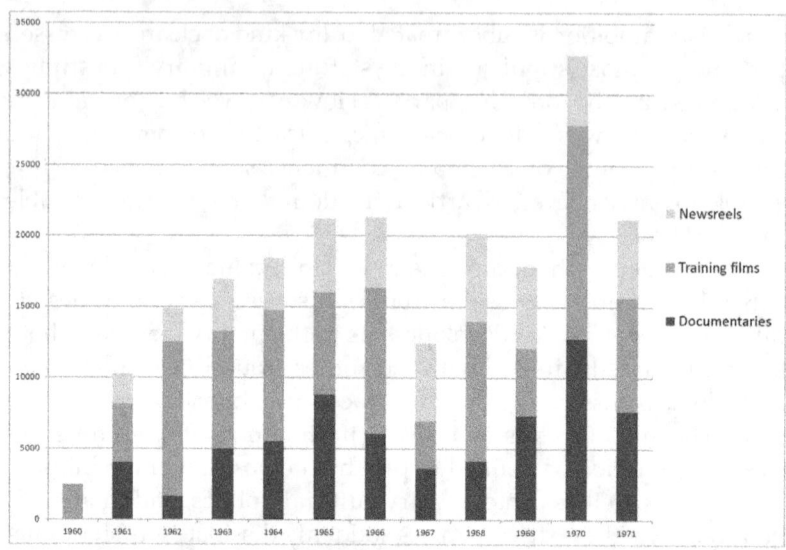

Figure 7.1 Yearly Production Volumes of the AFS (footage in metres, 35 mm film). [Produktionsübersicht 1961–76, BArch-MA, Filmstudio der Nationalen Volksarmee, DVP 3-3/12706]

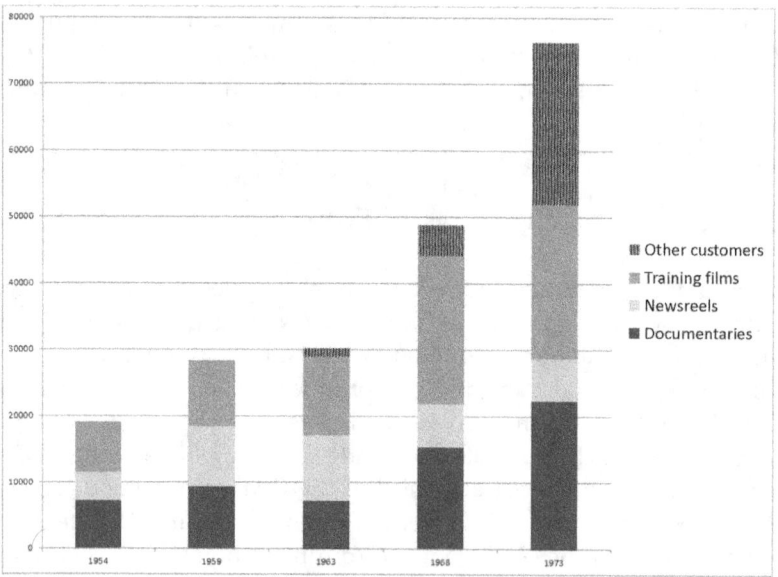

Figure 7.2 Yearly Production Volumes of the ČAF (footage in metres, 35 mm film) [Václav Šmidrkal, *Armáda a stříbrné plátno: Československý armádní film 1951–1999* [The Army and the Silver Screen: The Czechoslovak Army Film Studio 1951–1999] (Prague: Naše vojsko, 2009), p. 146]

1970, and the Federal Ministry of Interior, which did not have its own film studio – began to occupy up to one third of the production volume. At the AFS, the average yearly production volume was set at 20,000 metres of film, approximately half of what the Czechoslovak studio was producing during the 1960s (see Figures 1 and 2).

Training films were shot on demand as ordered by the military branches, which used them in educational programmes to prepare soldiers for their military specialization. These sometimes classified films were designated for internal military use only, which meant they could circulate only within the army's own distribution circuit. The two studios' training films were similar in terms of aesthetics and form, favouring pedagogical function and the illustrative aspect of cinema. Some Czechoslovak training films from the early 1950s, whose unexpectedly epic structures generously employed the methods of feature films, were exceptions to this general rule. In some cases, there was a further distinction between 'methodical' (*metodický*) and 'demonstrative' (*ukázkový*) training films. The former presented theoretical military knowledge in the context of practical exercises, while the latter were more like filmed instruction manuals.

Figure 7.3 Shooting for the Training Film *Seskok padákem* (Parachute Jump) [Photography courtesy of Miroslav Fojtík.]

The ČAF usually made documentary films for the Main Political Administration, which was equivalent to a department of the Central Committee of the Communist Party of Czechoslovakia. In accordance with communist media theory, the purpose of these documentary films was to propagate, inform and educate from the communist point of view. They were made in a variety of formats, from pure political propaganda to relatively unbiased documentary accounts to popular science films and many other documentary subgenres. These films best reflect the differences in development between the ČAF and the AFS.

Newsreels featured either general news on military issues or specialized news on military science and technology. The AFS produced the monthly *Armeefilmschau* (Army Film News) starting in 1961 and the quarterly *Militärtechniches Magazin* (Military Technical Magazine) after 1965. The situation in the ČAF was more complicated. At first it issued the monthly *Naše vojsko* (Our Military, 1951–1953), which later became the monthly *Armádní zpravodaj* (Army Newsletter, 1954–1965; biweekly from 1959–1962). For a while, the Army Newsletter was made parallel with the *Armádní filmový měsíčník* (Army Film Monthly, 1962–1965). In the second half of the 1960s, the monthly *Magazín ČAF* (ČAF Magazine, 1966–1972) featured general news while the quarterly *Armádní technický magazín* (Army Technical Magazine, 1965–1969) presented a summary of technical news.[10]

Each studio also shot a couple of feature films but abandoned such ambitions by 1970. The ČAF saw feature films as a primary means of realizing artistic self-assurance. The AFS experimented with feature films to discover whether it was capable of creating more artistically demanding films that could be used to fulfil the studio's mission.

Staff

One of the keys to understanding the difference between the ČAF and the AFS lies in their personnel policies. There were dissimilarities in both the overall number of staff working in these studios and the recruitment process for creative posts. The number of staff at the ČAF increased rapidly in the early 1950s but was cut back again by the end of the decade. Out of 190 persons working or serving in the studio in 1957, shortly before its 'post-Stalinist' reduction,[11] only 121 remained by 1960.[12] By contrast, the AFS steadily recruited more staff throughout the 1960s. In the beginning, it made do with 30 or 40 people, but by 1968 it had 84 posts planned and kept expanding.[13]

The Czechoslovak Ministry of National Defence decided from the outset to staff the cultural and artistic military institutions with young, promising personnel, particularly conscripts who were art school graduates and reservists with appropriate professional experience. Thus, every year a new cohort of conscripts joined the permanent employees and servicemen of the ČAF. The studio became a sought-after destination for most young male film professionals enlisted for two years of compulsory military service (graduates from military departments of universities were required to serve only one year), who saw it as a place where they could continue their work and further develop themselves professionally. The ČAF subsequently recruited its new staff from the ranks of those who had become familiar with the studio during their compulsory service. In this way many outstanding Czechoslovak filmmakers were influenced by the military environment, and the military environment was reciprocally influenced by their films.

The principal attitude of the East German National People's Army (Nationale Volksarmee, NVA) was to not make systematic exceptions for artists when enlisting new conscripts. The policy of noncompromise in this matter was clearly demonstrated to the public in the DEFA (Deutsche Film-Aktiengesellschaft) feature film *Der Reserveheld* (The Reserve Hero, Wolfgang Luderer, 1965), shot in cooperation with the NVA. The film depicts the well-known comic actor Rolf Herricht essentially playing himself, a character named Ralf Horricht, who is called up for reserve service in the NVA. All his 'petty bourgeois' attempts to escape compulsory service fail, and he has to fulfil his duties in exactly the same manner as every other soldier, despite his public popularity. Furthermore, since the AFS consistently sought stability, it would have been awkward for them to continuously incorporate strangers who could potentially disturb their internal routines.

Until 1956 most of the ČAF staff wore uniforms, even though not all of them were soldiers in the legal sense. Directors, cameramen, producers and others were accorded officer ranks to stress their social position within the military. After 1956, only the commander and a few officers in management positions remained professional soldiers; the rest became civilian employees of the military administration. In contrast to ČAF personnel, the AFS staff was always a mixture of officers, noncommissioned officers and civilian employees, and there were no well-known or acknowledged artistic personalities among them. Even though their annual reports and working plans stressed the need to improve the artistic aspects of their production, the filmmakers were more concerned about striving for technical perfection in their works and meeting the expectations of their superiors.

Managerial Routines

As stated above, personnel policy accounts for one of the key differences between the two studios. The integration of conscripts into the operation of the studio was not a panacea, though. The ČAF continued this practice even after 1970, but it no longer allowed the rank and file to interfere with the production plan as it had done in the 1950s and 1960s. Therefore, another crucial element to consider is the managerial routine.

The strict system of multilevel approvals in the AFS discouraged directors from any bold attempts in their work and forced them to adapt themselves to their superiors' expectations. Even when a film eventually made its way through the circle of approvals within the studio, it had also to be approved by the studio's supervisors in the Main Political Administration (or by representatives of the military branch that commissioned the training film), who typically knew little about film, being instead trained in ideology and party politics. This system founded on military hierarchy and 'democratic centralism' in the communist party operated consistently at the AFS until 1989. The boundaries were fixed by approved production plans, treatments and scripts of films. Long-term production plans were signed by the Minister of National Defence himself, while short-term plans were approved by the head of the Main Political Administration. Oversight of the various creative stages of individual films fell to the director of the studio and the editor-in-chief (*Chefredakteur*).[14] The focal point in the production process was the 'approval screening' (*Abnahme*), where the first version of the film (often still without a completed soundtrack) was presented to the 'customer', who could suggest modifications or in some cases even reject the whole film as unusable. For example, the fierce political documentary that 'unmasked' the true nature of the West German army, *So werden Söldner gemacht* (This Is How Mercenaries are Made, Karlheinz Pappe, 1968) was returned from the 'approval screening' seven times for re-editing to increase its 'impact'.[15] Although differing perspectives meant that conflicts between authors and 'censors' were unavoidable, they were often limited by the attitude of the military filmmakers, who did not wish to provoke their more powerful supervisors and thereby risk their own security.

The procedure of multilevel approvals with the 'approval screening' (*schvalovací projekce*) as its centrepiece was also a part of the managerial routines at the ČAF, especially in the 1950s and after 1970, when they became a part of the studio's new identity. Nevertheless, change in this practice was a crucial step in the easing of the political surveillance in the 1960s. In line with the liberalization process at this time, responsible political officers tended to hold back, interfering only in cases of 'serious, disputed and difficult material'.[16] The decision-making process was transferred from the upper levels of the Main Political Administration to the ČAF management itself, and since this management was headed by a relatively tolerant military commander (Lt. Col. Bedřich Benda), together with reformist communists and sensitive artists such as lead script editor Roman Hlaváč and lead director Pavel Háša, the way for more artistic freedom was open. The Ideological Artistic Council (Ideově-umělecká rada), an advisory body that included civilian film professionals, also played an important role. The self-confidence (or insolence) of the directors, who risked neither life nor professional existence, rose enormously; they were not even loath to mock the inherent peculiarities of military life in their films (e.g. *Vzpomínka na tři rána v českém lese* [The Memory of Three Mornings in the Czech Forest, Ivan Balaďa, 1966] or *Jejich uniformou budiž frak* [Let Tailcoat be Their Uniform, Pavel Mertl, 1968]). In the words of the writer Arnošt Lustig, the military filmmakers were also occasionally a 'dog that bites the hand giving him a sausage'.[17]

This period ended by autumn 1970 at the latest, when the ČAF got a new military commander (Lt. Col. Jiří Lelek) and a new main script editor (Lt. Col. František Říčka). More than half of the directors were dismissed in subsequent personnel purges, and a number of documentary films, mostly from the years 1968–1969, were 'expelled' from distribution. The ČAF consequently declared itself subordinate to the Main Political Administration as a component of the party media machinery within the military branch, which it remained until 1989.

Czechoslovak Army Film until 1970: Swinging from one Extreme to Another

In my book, which provides an overview of ČAF history, I divide the development of the studio in four distinctive periods: 1951–1962, 1963–1969, 1970–1989 and 1990–1999. To a certain extent, each of these periods negated the preceding one in matters of the studio's conception. This also applies to the studio's 'pre-history' from 1945 to 1950.[18]

When Czechoslovak postwar cinematography was nationalized, the state became the authority running the professional film business (Presidential Decree No. 50/1945 from 11 August 1945).[19] The only exemption from this provision applied to film activities within the Ministry of National Defence, which had a continuous tradition of its own film production dating to the Czechoslovak Legions in World War I. In different institutional settings and under various working conditions, the interwar Ministry of National Defence produced documentary, training and news films on military themes for its internal needs as well as for public enlightenment and propaganda. During World War II, these activities continued in Great Britain, which was the seat of the Czechoslovak government in exile. From 1945 to 1950, the restored military film studio repeatedly modified its organizational structure, name and premises; in this period its scarce production was negligible. Few primary sources are available for these years, with the exception of a lengthy situational report from August 1946 written by the head of the Film Department for the Ministry of National Defence, Jiří Jeníček (1895–1963). As an accomplished photographer and filmmaker, Jeníček had worked extensively for the Czechoslovak Army during the 1930s. His report fiercely criticized the overall situation in the Film Department, which lacked not only a clear vision but also modern technical equipment and a motivated, skilled staff. During its first year of operation the department managed to finish only one short documentary, *Pod praporem svobody* (Under the Banner of Freedom).[20]

Aiming to continue his prewar successes with military film productions, Jeníček set ambitious goals. He aimed to develop the department into an institution 'that the general public will recognise as a creator of cinematographically valuable and ideologically precious displays and as a collaborator on the realisation of the government programme'.[21] Furthermore, he thought, a military film should be respected not only as a 'military product' but also as an 'artistically, intellectually and politically weighty work'. Interestingly, his plan envisaged the wedding of political goals and artistic needs into the type of generally valuable work that matched his experience in the late 1930s, when he directed successful military propaganda films appealing for the defence of Czechoslovakia against Nazi Germany. His willingness to serve the motherland with artistic means, combined with his nature as a seasoned military filmmaker and photographer, found expression in his assessment of the footage of the expulsion of Germans from Czechoslovakia shot by the department in the years 1945–1946. The original intention to show 'how well and decently we treat the Germans' had failed, because the 'looks of the Germans express hatred towards us'. Therefore, Jeníček assumed, public exhibition of these images 'would play into our enemies' hands and would result in our political detriment'.[22] Jeníček did not remain as the head of the Film Department for long, though – having realized that his vision was not practical under the current circumstances, he left the Film Department before the end of 1946.

In contrast to the situation with civilian cinematography, the communist coup in February 1948 and forced communization of the cultural sphere did not signal a clean break in the tradition of military filmmaking. This did not come until much later, in April 1950, when Minister of National Defence Ludvík Svoboda, a war hero and army general, was replaced by Alexej Čepička, a communist careerist and son-in-law of Czechoslovak President Klement Gottwald. Čepička accelerated the 'Sovietization' of the Czechoslovak army and built up his own cult of personality from his powerful position within both the Communist Party and the state hierarchy. As a former avid theatre amateur, he supported the development of culturally enlightening work (*kulturně-osvětová práce*), and with a series of executive commands he established a network of professional cultural institutions subordinated to the military political apparatus with the Main Political Administration at the top. Ideas of this kind were not unique or new – they had been alive within certain parts of the ministry since 1945 – but it was Čepička's effort that made these plans come true.[23]

Czechoslovak Army Film was established on the foundation of its predecessor during the training year 1950/51, opening a new chapter in Czechoslovak military filmmaking. Čepička expected technically perfect, artistically strong, ideologically persuasive films from the ČAF. To these ends, the studio was provided with optimal conditions, despite the general economic constraints imposed by central economic planning and massive investment in heavy industry and arms production. Minister Čepička did not want the ČAF to limit its work to films for internal military use only. On the contrary, his aim was to build up a respectable military counterpart to the state film monopoly that would be capable of making any kind of film on broadly defined military themes, including highly demanding full-length feature films.[24] Pressing ahead with his plan, he managed to equip the studio with the necessary technologies and, more importantly, to acquire talented young filmmakers. Czechoslovak 'Stalinism' demanded spectacular, impassioned, colourful documentaries overflowing with big words, burning enthusiasm and optimism. Apart from short documentary films, the ČAF was assigned to shoot politically weighty, formally epic documentaries about important political events such as the annual military parades at Letná in May, or the increasing Czechoslovak-Chinese 'friendship', which resulted in several unique documentaries from China. Military filmmakers also travelled to North Korea to 'report' on the situation in the divided peninsula or on the work of Czechoslovak military doctors and their field hospital. The pinnacle of the ČAF's political documentaries during the 'cult of personality' period was the bombastic documentary *Rozloučení s Klementem Gottwaldem* (Farewell to Klement Gottwald, Ivo Toman, 1953), which depicted the funeral of the deceased president and communist leader in March 1953.

During Čepička's tenure, which lasted until spring 1956, the ČAF also shot three full-length feature films that were distributed in the civilian cinema network and were relatively popular with audiences.[25] Most of these were finished with substantial help from Czechoslovak State Film, which was not, however, credited for its contribution. Mounting tension between the two studios was resolved by a decision issued by the Central Committee of the Communist Party of Czechoslovakia in 1955 stating that the ČAF had breached both written und unwritten norms by producing full-length feature films. A military creative group (comprised of Bedřich Kubala, Lubomír Možný and Ladislav Novotný) assigned to ensure the presence of military themes in nationwide feature film production was transferred from the ČAF to Czechoslovak State Film – this was believed to be the first step in the dismantling the ČAF.[26] After Čepička's abrupt fall in spring 1956, the ČAF came to be seen as a remnant of 'wrong politics' and its future existence was called into question. There were even plans to integrate it into Czechoslovak State Film, but this idea was eventually dropped when the ČAF argued that it was needed to meet the military's internal need for training films.[27]

The year 1956 sparked off a crisis lasting several years, during which the ČAF lost most of its prominent directors and cameramen and sought another identity. The new creative period began at the start of the 1960s. The Twelfth Congress of the Communist Party of Czechoslovakia in December 1962, despite its contradictory conclusions, opened up a process of liberalization in culture.[28] After 1963 the ČAF began working with new styles of documentary filmmaking that critically evaluated reality and emphasized the opinions and feelings of individuals. In place of grandiose and colourful yet untruthful films, an aesthetics based on formal austerity and scepticism in judgement set in. In this period, a sizeable portion of films from the overall production stood out due to their artistic ambitions; many were screened at respected film festivals and received prizes. However, most of these films were barely known among the general public, who had difficulty gaining access to the civilian distribution network or to television. Directors such as Rudolf Adler, Ivan Balaďa, Vladimír Drha, Václav Hapl and Tomáš Škrdlant far exceeded the 'cinema on command' scheme and pushed the borders of the possible – some of their films undoubtedly qualify as avant-garde or auteur films. Other, rather routine directors and future mainstays of the 'normalized' ČAF, such as Stanislav Brožík, Miroslav Burger and Karel Forst, also benefited from the new liberal atmosphere and shot more open films.

The renewed self-confidence of the ČAF can be illustrated by the example of the Czechoslovak New Wave film *Konec srpna v hotelu Ozon* (The End of August at the Hotel Ozone, 1966).[29] This internationally acclaimed feature-length narrative film was directed by Jan Schmidt, at the time a private serving in the ČAF, who managed to gain approval to realize a screenplay written by his colleague, scriptwriter and director Pavel Juráček. The driving force here was not the ČAF's naked ambition to compete with other film studios as it had done in the early 1950s; in this case, the studio management simply wanted to take advantage of the situation to produce a film that otherwise might not have been realized at all. Despite its sci-fi, futuristic setting, the film had a strongly political-military message, since it depicted the Earth after a nuclear war in which both sides lost, leaving only a few scattered survivors. The Main Political Administration did not remain calm in this case and initially tried to stop the already ongoing production. At the same time, however, unwilling to waste the invested financial means or lose control over the film if its production were to be transferred to the state film studio, it eventually sought to alter the film's content. These attempts hindered the production but did not halt it, since the political officers could not fully assert themselves by issuing authoritative orders.[30] In the end, director Jan Schmidt employed the strategy of a 'porcelain doggy',[31] intentionally including a politically provocative yet artistically unimportant scene at the beginning of the film to divert the censors' attention from the main theme, and the film indeed obtained approval.

In 1968–1969 the progressive trend at the ČAF reached its peak when the studio produced Vladimír Drha's and Karel Hložek's short film tetralogy on the consequences of the Soviet occupation of

Czechoslovakia and completed work on Ivan Balaďa's documentary of Jan Palach's funeral, *Les* (Forest), in early 1969.[32]

The Army Film Studio until 1970: Steady Growth towards Stability

In the Soviet Occupation Zone in Germany, everyday cultural life was quickly re-established as one of the Soviets' priorities. The nationalized state film monopoly DEFA took up its work in early 1946.[33] However, German military structures were dismissed and not officially re-established until 1956, when the National People's Army was founded. This remilitarization had begun covertly back in 1948 under the auspices of the German People's Police. The Barracked People's Police (Kasernierte Volkspolizei), founded in 1952, were a direct forerunner of the NVA. These institutions had no remarkable ambitions to influence film production or produce films themselves; rather, they were mere consumers of civilian films.[34]

The NVA's starting position in 1956 was paradoxically worsened by the fact that the German Democratic Republic, including its cinematography, was considerably consolidated. Given its initial humble production requirements, the NVA decided to commission film projects from specialized DEFA studios. In 1956 and 1957, the DEFA studios produced three documentaries as well as one popular-scientific and one educational film for the NVA. The army's plans extended even further: through DEFA, it intended to commission a feature film about the navy called *The Commander*, based on a screenplay by Heino Brandes. In addition, writer Ludwig Turek submitted a proposal for a feature film; however, the Political Administration of the NVA ultimately rejected it. In assessing its cooperation with DEFA, the NVA was dissatisfied with both the studio's high level of influence over the choice of topics and its tendency to prefer impressive military settings such as the air force or the navy while neglecting the more typical environment of the ground forces. The Ministry of National Defence advocated the drafting and resolution of a comprehensive prospective plan for production of films according to a clear military-political conception.[35] In the years 1957–1959, the Ministry considered three institutional solutions for military film production: (1) establishment of a special working group for military films within the DEFA, (2) creation of its own military film studio independent from the DEFA, or (3) production and exchange of training films under the auspices of the Warsaw Pact Joint Command in Moscow.[36] It also discussed mixed plans like that submitted in 1957 by one of the DEFA studio directors, Günther Klein, which suggested setting up a small military studio with just 19 employees, who could produce six or seven short films (15–20 minutes of footage each) a year with the support of the DEFA's technical base.[37]

Finally, the East German ministry decided to follow the Czechoslovak and Polish examples (the Czołówka Military Film Studio was 're-opened' in Warsaw in 1958), and in mid-1960 it established the Army Film Studio as a military institution seated in Berlin-Treptow. The AFS's first documentary film was a collection of clips titled *Reportage 60* (Report 60).[38] In 1961 the AFS launched its monthly newsreel, *Armeefilmschau* (Army Film News), and produced several other documentaries as well as training films. The poor quality of the early production compelled Minister of National Defence Heinz Hoffmann to send a proposal to Minister of Culture Hans Bentzien in mid-1962 proposing that the AFS be integrated into the DEFA structures as the Artistic Creative Group Military Film (Künstlerische Arbeitsgruppe Militärfilm, comprised of six officers and twenty-two civilians), which would begin operation on 1 May 1963.[39]

The official reason for this proposal was the need to ensure the 'higher artistic quality and force of films' while also economizing on both human and material resources.[40] For example, the officials in the responsible department of the NVA's Main Political Administration had been annoyed by the 1961 documentary *Septembertage* (September Days), which depicted a joint manoeuvre of Soviet, Polish and East German troops on Polish territory. They complained that the film's 'artistic and technical deficiencies prevented it from presenting a really convincing picture about the strength and extent of the socialist armies and the brotherhood in arms of their soldiers'.[41] The Main Political Administration even considered commissioning the DEFA to make a documentary film about the 'October Storm' manoeuvre that was to take place in the GDR in autumn 1963, in order to avoid another such fiasco with the AFS.[42] However, the Ministry of Defence ultimately relinquished the idea of dissolving the young AFS when it recalculated the budget and realized that at the price DEFA was asking for the expected yearly volume of 20,000 meters, expenses would be approximately twice those of the AFS.[43] It took more than two years for the newly established AFS to overcome these initial troubles and to ensure its institutional existence. In 1963 the AFS was reorganized; it hired additional staff and was equipped with more up-to-date technical equipment. The studio continued this process of gradually increasing its capacities throughout the 1960s.

Production at the AFS was marked by subordination to superiors. Axioms such as 'ideological clarity and partisanship are the fundaments of a creative artistic work' throttled any tendencies towards artistic emancipation.[44] The pressure to economize and to be maximally politically useful resulted in a shift away from production of short satirical feature films (*satirische Kurzfilme*) in the late 1960s, since such films were costly and carried a high risk of failure. Using satire as a form of education, these films criticized bad habits in the NVA in a humorous way. Various misdemeanours were exposed in about a dozen instalments of the series *Die Rakete* (The Rocket), which featured performances by actors from the military cabaret *Die Kneifzange* (The Pliers). The AFS also made use of the then popular TV show format *Die Rumpelkammer* (The Junk Room), presented by Willi Schwabe, which East German Television began broadcasting in 1955. In cooperation with external authors, the AFS produced three episodes of *The Junk Room* devoted to the NVA (Hubert Hoelzke, 1965, 1966, 1968).

In terms of complexity, the history of the AFS was 'smoother' than that of its Czechoslovak counterpart, as the German studio did not encounter the strong turbulence and numerous paradoxes faced by the ČAF. Only during its initial stages in the early 1960s and the period of collapse in 1990–1991 did the AFS experience erratic conditions due to organizational factors. This does not mean, however, that the creative process at the AFS was entirely free of friction or that all members of the staff were committed communists. The factor that most differentiated the AFS from the ČAF was that no one expected anything more than 'films on command' from the AFS and thus the studio had no option but to fill the niche for the creation of military films, which it eventually managed to do in the 1970s by establishing itself as a producer of political-military documentaries.

However, further detailed research is needed to determine how far AFS staff were, under the given conditions, eventually able to pursue their own professional visions (or *Eigen-Sinn*) and where the demarcation line between conformity and confrontation can be drawn in the case of this studio. Thus far, the German tabloid *Bild* has reported that in 1982 some AFS staff set up an amateur film club where erotic films were shot using technical equipment and human resources from the AFS. This rather sensational titbit undoubtedly suggests that not everyone at the AFS in this period was a fully screened Marxist-Leninist diehard, although the official film production offers no evidence of such nonconformity.[45]

Conclusion

Despite a number of general and superficial similarities, the AFS and ČAF were clearly differentiated until 1970. The AFS's loyalty to the system was secured by strict subordination to the military-political apparatus that closely supervised its production. The continuity of East German history did not permit anything more than cosmetic changes in the studio's mission. Furthermore, AFS personnel lacked driving artistic ambitions, and the filmmakers were reconciled to their work being subordinated to the principle of 'cinema on command'. The studio pursued the goal of becoming a respectable producer of military training films and military political documentary films. The outside forces that questioned East German statehood increased ideological stubbornness on the inside and did not allow much space for 'ideological diversions'.

In contrast, the history of the ČAF is fragmented and marked by unprecedented swings. From an inferior ministerial film department (1945–1950), it boomed into a challenge to the state film monopoly (1950–1955). It was almost liquidated after losing this battle, but it resurged and painstakingly emancipated itself from political tutelage, a process that peaked with achieving the position of an avant-garde studio, paradoxically funded by the Main Political Administration. Ultimately, though, it became a victim of the political rape of morality and reason after 1968. Once the ČAF had undergone personnel purges, submitted to ideological reassessments of past productions that ultimately banned scores of films (including *The End of August at the Hotel Ozone*), and finally accepted a new production philosophy that stressed the 'cinema on command' claim, its institutional position moved much closer to that of the AFS. The East German studio had cut its teeth early on and ensured itself greater stability within a specific production segment, whereas the ČAF had to become politically faithful and economically efficient even as it buried its long-held illusion of artistic autonomy under state socialism.

Václav Šmidrkal earned his Ph.D. in Modern History from the Charles University in Prague. He is currently a project researcher at the Masaryk Institute and the Archive of the Czech Academy of Sciences and a lecturer at the Charles University in Prague. His publications include *Armáda stříbrné plátno. Československý armádní film 1951–1999* [The Army and the Silver Screen: Czechoslovak Military Film Studio, 1951–1999] (Prague, 2009).

Notes

1. Modifications to the studio's name relatively accurately signalize changes in its character. During the period of slight de-Stalinization and restructuring of the army after 1956, the original name 'Czechoslovak Army Film' was replaced by 'Czechoslovak Army Film Studio' (Československé armádní filmové studio), which was only inconsistently used for a few years. In the period 1965–1972 the name changed to 'Studio ČAF', in which use of an acronym obscured the studio's army affiliation. The period of 'normalization' after the Prague Spring saw a return to the original name – now, however, abbreviated as ČSAF to strengthen the Slovak element, which was typically underrepresented anyway. The name 'AF studio' was briefly used after 1989 before the final version, 'Czech Army Film' (Český armádní film) was instituted in the wake of Czechoslovakia's split.
2. The original official full name 'Army Film Studio of the National People's Army' was often shortened to 'Army Film Studio'. Later the name was changed to 'Film Studio of the National People's Army' (Filmstudio der Nationalen Volksarmee). In the transition period 1990–1991 it was renamed Projektfilm Berlin.
3. Alice Lovejoy, *Army film and the Avant Garde. Cinema and experiment in the Czechoslovak military*. Bloomington: Indiana University Press, 2015.
4. Alice Lovejoy, 'A Military Avant Garde: Experimentation in the Czechoslovak Army Film Studio', *Screen* 52(4) (2011), 428.
5. Matthias Rogg, 'Filme für die Armee – Filme über die Armee: Die Produktionen des Armeefilmstudios der NVA zwischen ideologischer Erziehung und militärpolitischen Öffentlichkeitsarbeit', in Heiner Timmermann (ed.), *Das war die DDR* (Münster: Lit.-Verlag, 2004), pp. 148–166; idem, 'Filme von der Fahne. Das Armeefilmstudio der Nationalen Volksarmee der DDR', in Bernhard Chiari (ed.), *Krieg und Militär im Film des 20. Jahrhunderts* (Munich: R. Oldenburg Verlag, 2004), pp. 611–634; idem, *Armee des Volkes? Militär und Gesellschaft in der DDR* (Berlin: Ch. Links, 2008), pp. 117–121.
6. Rogg, *Armee des Volkes?* p. 119.
7. Heinz-Gerhard Haupt, 'Comparative History', in *International Encyclopedia of the Social & Behavioral Sciences*, eds. Neil J. Smelser, Paul B. Baltes (Amsterdam: Elsevier, 2001), pp. 2400–2401.
8. Guy Gauthier, *Le Documentaire, un autre cinéma* (Paris: Armand Collin, 2005), pp. 106–107.
9. In the Czechoslovak Army, the Main Political Administration was created in 1950 from the Main Administration for Education and Enlightenment (Hlavní správa výchovy a osvěty). The analogous structure in the East German Army was called the Political Administration (Politische Verwaltung) from 1956–1960, which became known as the Main Political Administration (Politische Hauptverwaltung) after 1961.
10. Šmidrkal, *Armáda a stříbrné plátno*, pp. 148–149.
11. Zápis o revizi finančně-hospodářské činnosti Československého armádního filmového studia [Protocol on the review of financial and economic activities of the Czechoslovak Army Film Studio] (July 1957), Vojenský ústřední archiv-Vojenský historický archiv, Prague (VÚA-VHA), fond (f.) Ministerstvo národní obrany (MNO) 1957, karton (k.) 87, p. 12.
12. Zápis o předání a převzetí funkce náčelníka Československého armádního filmového studia [Protocol on transferring and assuming the function of Czechoslovak Army Film Studio commander], 26 October 1960, VÚA-VHA, f. MNO 1960, k. 54.

13. Stellenplanvorschlag für 1968, Blatt (Bl.) 99–100, Bundesarchiv-Militärarchiv Freiburg im Breisgau (BArch-MA), DVP 3-3/12614.
14. Produktionsablauf eines Dokumentar- oder Ausbildungsfilmes, Bl. 95, BArch-MA, DVP 3-3/6264.
15. „So werden Söldner gemacht", Bl. 46–47, BArch-MA, DVP 3-3/1541.
16. Zásady pro tvorbu filmů v ČAF [Rules for film production in ČAF], 13 February 1965, p. 2, VÚA-VHA, f. MNO 1965, k. č. 56.
17. Jan Lukeš,'"Byli jsme pes, který kouše ruku, jež mu dává buřta": Filmová tvorba 1965–1969,' ['We were the dog that bites the hand giving him a sausage': Films 1965–1969], in Helena Kupcová (ed.), *Pražské jaro 1968: Literatura, film, média* [Prague Spring 1968: Literature, Film, Media] (Prague: Literární akademie, 2009), p. 29.
18. Šmidrkal, *Armáda a stříbrné plátno*.
19. See the contribution by Jiří Knapík to this volume.
20. The modest production of one to three documentary films a year continued until 1950. Jiří Havelka, *Československé krátké filmy 1945–1970* (Prague: Československý filmový ústav, 1977), pp. 7–14.
21. Zpráva o filmovém oddělení [Report on the Film Department], 3 August 1946, p. 7, VÚA-VHA, f. MNO 1946, k. č. 87.
22. Ibid., p. 2.
23. Jiří Pernes, Jaroslav Pospíšil and Antonín Lukáš, *Alexej Čepička: šedá eminence rudého režimu* [Alexej Čepička: The Grey Eminence of a Red Regime] (Prague: Brána, 2008), pp. 20–22, 231–232.
24. Petr Bilík, *Ladislav Helge: Cesta za občanským filmem* [Ladislav Helge: The Way to a Civic Film] (Brno: Host, 2011), pp. 132–133.
25. *Dnes večer všechno skončí* (Everything Will End Tonight, Vojtěch Jasný and Karel Kachyňa, 1954), *Tanková brigáda* (The Tank Brigade, Ivo Toman, 1955), *Ztracená stopa* (The Lost Track, Karel Kachyňa, 1956).
26. Koncept zprávy náčelníka HPS genpor. Jána Zemana [Draft of the Main Political Administration Chief Lt Gen Ján Zeman's report], VÚA-VHA, f. MNO, r. 1956, k. č. 41.
27. Decentralizace řízení a organisování stranickopolitické a politickovýchovné práce v čs. lidové armádě [Decentralization of control and organisation of party political and political educational work in the Czechoslovak People's Army], p. 2, VÚA-VHA, f. MNO, r. 1956, k. č. 56.
28. Jan Mervart, 'Dvanáctý sjezd Komunistické strany Československa' [The Twelfth Congress of the Communist Party of Czechoslovakia], in Jiří Knapík and Martin Franz (eds), *Průvodce kulturním děním a životním stylem v českých zemích 1948–1967* (Prague: Academia, 2011), vol. 1, pp. 293–294.
29. Peter Hames, *The Czechoslovak New Wave* (Berkeley: University of California Press, 1985), pp. 166–167.
30. Author's interview with Jan Schmidt, Prague, March 2007; author's interview with Jiří Krob, Prague, February 2007.
31. Kamila Budrowska, *Literatura i pisarze wobec cenzury PRL 1948–1958* [Literature and writers facing censorship in People's Republic of Poland, 1948–1958] (Białystok: Wydawnictwo Uniwersytetu w Białymstoku, 2009), pp. 240–257.
32. For a close analysis of the aesthetics of these films see Lovejoy, 'A Military Avant Garde', pp. 434–440.
33. See the contribution by David Bathrick in this volume.

34. Lars Karl, '"Von Helden und Menschen...": Der Zweite Weltkrieg im sowjetischen Spielfilm und dessen Rezeption in der DDR, 1945–1965' (Ph.D. thesis, Eberhard Karls University, Tübingen, 2002), pp. 241–243, 250–255.
35. Herstellung von Filmen über die Nationale Volksarmee und der Filmaustauch zwischen dem Ministerium für Nationale Verteidigung der Deutschen Demokratischen Republik und den Verteidigungsministerien der Staaten des sozialistischen Lagers, 4 February 1958, Bl. 436, BArch-MA, Politischen Hauptverwaltung der NVA, VA-P-01/041, Band 2.
36. Ibid., Bl. 437.
37. Grünberg's letter to Stoph, 18 April 1957, Bl. 439, BArch-MA, VA-P-01/041, Band 2.
38. Streitkräfteamt – Abteilung I – Informations- und Medienzentrale der Bundeswehr (ed.), *Findbücher zu Beständen des Medienzentralarchivs, Band 2, Ausbildungs- und Dokumentationsfilme, Armeefilmschau der Nationalen Volksarmee (1955–1991)* (Sankt Augustin: Informations- und Medienzentrale der Bundeswehr, 1995), p. 89.
39. Hoffmann's letter to Bentzien, 8 November 1962, Bl. 4, BArch-MA, VA-P-01/211.
40. Ibid.
41. Goßens's memo to Verner, 23 January 1963, Bl. 79, BArch-MA, VA-P-01/208.
42. Ibid.
43. Lapacz's memo to Goßens, Bl. 17, BArch-MA, VA-P-01/211.
44. Bericht über Arbeitsergebnisse im Produktionsjahr 1971, Bl. 263, BArch-MA, DVP 3-3/11193.
45. 'Honeckers Sex-Armee', retrieved 29 February 2012 from http://www.bild.de/regional/berlin/armee/sex-armee-4107880.bild.html.

Select Bibliography

Bilík, Petr. *Ladislav Helge: Cesta za občanským filmem*. Brno: Host, 2011.
Budrowska, Kamila. *Literatura i pisarze wobec cenzury PRL 1948–1958*. Białystok: Wydawnictwo Uniwersytetu w Białymstoku, 2009.
Findbücher zu Beständen des Medienzentralarchivs / Bd. 2, Ausbildungs- und Dokumentationsfilme, Armeefilmschau der Nationalen Volksarmee (1955–1991). Sankt Augustin: Informations- und Medienzentrale der Bundeswehr, 1995.
Gauthier, Guy. *Le Documentaire, un autre cinéma*. Paris: Armand Collin, 2005.
Hames, Peter. *The Czechoslovak New Wave*. Berkeley: University of California Press, 1985.
Haupt, Heinz-Gerhard. 'Comparative History'. In *International Encyclopedia of the Social & Behavioral Sciences*, eds. Neil J. Smelser, Paul B. Baltes. Amsterdam: Elsevier, 2001.
Havelka, Jiří. *Československé krátké filmy 1945–1970*. Prague: Československý filmový ústav, 1977.
Karl, Lars. '"Von Helden und Menschen...": Der Zweite Weltkrieg im sowjetischen Spielfilm und dessen Rezeption in der DDR, 1945–1965'. Ph.D. thesis, Eberhard Karls University, Tübingen, 2002.
Lovejoy, Alice. 'A Military Avant Garde: Experimentation in the Czechoslovak Army Film Studio'. *Screen* 52(4) (2011): 427–441.
Lovejoy, Alice. *Army film and the Avant Garde. Cinema and experiment in the Czechoslovak military*. Bloomington: Indiana University Press, 2015.

Pernes, Jiří, Jaroslav Pospíšil and Antonín Lukáš. *Alexej Čepička: šedá eminence rudého režimu*. Prague: Brána, 2008.

Rogg, Matthias. 'Filme für die Armee – Filme über die Armee: Die Produktionen des Armeefilmstudios der NVA zwischen ideologischer Erziehung und militärpolitischen Öffentlichkeitsarbeit'. In Heiner Timmermann (ed.), *Das war die DDR*. Münster: Lit.-Verlag, 2004.

Rogg, Matthias. 'Filme von der Fahne. Das Armeefilmstudio der Nationalen Volksarmee der DDR'. In Bernhard Chiari (ed.), *Krieg und Militär im Film des 20. Jahrhunderts*. Munich: R. Oldenburg Verlag, 2004.

Rogg, Matthias. *Armee des Volkes? Militär und Gesellschaft in der DDR*. Berlin: Ch. Links, 2008.

Šmidrkal, Václav. *Armáda a stříbrné plátno: Československý armádní film, 1951–1999*. Prague: Naše vojsko, 2009.

Chapter 8

SOCIALISM FOR SALE

Czechoslovakia's Krátký film, Custom-Made Film Production and the Promotion of Consumer Culture in the 1950s

Lucie Česálková

Sometimes it is a matter of getting people to remember a new commercial brand, other times it is to save coal or to join a certain organization or to have their children vaccinated against diphtheria.[1]

At first sight, this quotation from a book about Short Film (Krátký film, KF)[2] issued in Czechoslovakia soon after the war may give the impression of generalization and a lack of conceptuality in defining of short film's functions. Nevertheless, the implied mixture of ideological and commercial objectives was a very characteristic feature of discussions about the importance of short film in a socialist state. This conception remained part of the discourse about the relationship between the state and short film for a long time, throughout the various historical, economical and sociocultural developments of the postwar period. The term 'short film' entered the discourse of Czech film magazines, filmmakers and state institutions in the mid-1930s as a general label for films that supplemented (and preceded) feature film programmes. To a considerable measure it was synonymous with the German *Kulturfilm* or cultural film, since it served mostly educational or uplifting purposes. Short films were defined by their length: they were not necessarily small-gauge; in fact, it was common to produce them in various format versions at the same time.

This article takes a more detailed look at the relationship between the state and short film by focusing on a specific group of custom-made films that governmental bodies and individual state institutions ordered as special projects from KF.[3] My analysis of KF's custom-made productions for state bodies offers a deeper understanding of the importance of film promotion and advertising within the socialist system. It also takes into account the internal structures of consumer culture and the official state bodies' attitudes towards consumerism in general. My approach combines the study of so-called 'useful film', custom-made film and film propaganda – including a consideration of the specifics of exhibition in a nontheatrical environment – with an examination of the role of state-promotional film within socialistic consumer culture more generally.

The films I deal with did not, in a practical sense, function as political propaganda in the form we are familiar with from studies of totalitarianism in Nazi Germany or the communist Soviet Union[4] or the war campaigns of World Wars I and II and the Cold War.[5] Politically tendentious films of postwar Czechoslovakia, especially from the time immediately following the communist putsch of 1948, were not custom-made but were realized as part of a state plan that involved different organizational practices and relied on various methods of funding. By contrast, custom-made films appeared in a range of contexts and ideological campaigns, addressing such concerns as workers' morale, methods of work, hygiene, safety, and so forth. Quite often, custom-made films also served a commercial function, promoting the tendencies of state business policy by depicting desired forms of shopping and consumption. Although a significant number of these productions were similar in form to industrial films, they were not produced for private customers – factories or companies – but at the insistence of the state apparatus, since the whole industry was state owned after 1945. The paradoxical situation whereby the state ordered the promotion of its services and goods in a market without competition provides a unique opportunity for a detailed examination of the nature of the relationship between the state, consumer culture and the promotional potential of the cinema.

Whereas industrial films are typically discussed in terms of utility[6] or usefulness[7] and analysed with regard to their persuasive potential as educational tools, films made in the context of state-run production tend to be viewed primarily as propaganda. What should not be overlooked, however, is how similar the aims of these two cinematic modes were, regardless of whether they served public or private interests. This study attempts to overcome this difference in perception, which is often only a terminological distinction, in order to regard custom-made films as a part of the broader state pedagogical discourse. Its analysis of films, whether they address work methods and the operation of machinery or deal with consumption, is primarily concerned with describing their civil-formative, social-educative aspects and their role within the symbolic discourse inherent to socialist Czechoslovakia.[8]

My approach is greatly informed by Zoë Druick's method for studying the films of the National Film Board of Canada.[9] Like Druick, I understand such films as a tool within the state policy of economic and social modernization, with the difference that my analysis takes into consideration the difficulties of such processes in the context of socialism. I address questions related to the exhibition of these films and the state's efforts to occupy a broad spectrum of nontheatrical venues only partially, as the accessible archival materials do not provide sufficient background for a more detailed analysis.

Much as in capitalist cultural-political conditions, under socialism the small-gauge format was used to help extend the reach of film production to various institutions. Equipping factories and collective farms as well as hospitals and advisory centres with technical facilities for 16mm projection did not proceed ideally, however, and the results did not meet the expectations. In this respect, Czechoslovakia's film infrastructure lagged behind that of Western countries, where educational institutions and private entertainment facilities, such as restaurants or department stores, had been equipped with TV sets since the 1950s.[10] By contrast, work to establish a nontheatrical network similar to those developed in other countries before World War II[11] ended unsuccessfully in Czechoslovakia.

My examination of the discourse of the period concerning state film orders also seeks to investigate the nature of socialist film advertising. In addition, I aim to link this study with work done on the consumer cultures of other socialist countries in Eastern Europe.[12] On the one hand, the establishment of advertising film in Czechoslovakia at the end of 1950s was viewed as necessary to confront the problems that the national economy encountered during the first half of the decade. On the other hand, such films presented a significant ideological problem with regard to the conceptualization of consumerism under socialism at that time. By looking at the points of connection between the dynamics of the country's economical development and the dynamics of custom-made film production, I aim to test the working hypothesis that key organizational and conceptual developments in state-promotional film were, to some extent, directly related to the country's current economic situation, that is, that changes in state-promotional film occurred in reaction to the state's economy. This conclusion implies that more general processes within the history of consumer culture under socialism can also be analysed according to the concepts of promotion and advertising, particularly film promotion and advertising, within the context of local cultural traditions.

In this study, I conceive of all films ordered from KF (from any of the studios after 1950) by any ministry, state company or state research institute as custom-made productions (see also note 4). I limit my study to the period from 1945 to 1961 in order to concentrate on the role that the momentous political events of 1948 and subsequent sociocultural and economic circumstances (five-year plans, economic crisis and monetary reform, the period of so-called thaw, etc.) played in the establishment and conceptualization of state-promotional films. I worked with the catalogues of short films published by Jiří Havelka[13] to identify the group of films for study and to compile the statistics that I use in the first section below. Since the lack of archival sources containing production data makes definitive identification of films and verification of their production circumstances difficult, it is certainly problematic to think about the data presented here in terms of absolute accuracy. However, my method presumes that this data is still relevant for the complex analysis at hand, even if specific points are only approximations. In the following, I interpret the results of serial film analysis[14] for the above-defined corpus of custom-made films in a more contextual fashion and introduce knowledge relating to the nature of individual film texts to support my arguments. In addressing the research questions I have defined, I combine the examination of this statistical production data with an analysis of the discourse relating to the contemporary conception of state film propaganda more generally in order to achieve a better understanding of this textually and thematically quite heterogeneous group of films.

The State as a Client of KF

Between 1945 and 1961, KF produced over 1,500 short films by order of the government, its subordinate state agencies and state research institutions.[15] As a part of KF's total production, this segment of the production is not substantial (making up only about 17 per cent), but these films are interesting because they were subject to a regime of planning, production and distribution differing greatly from that applied to the majority. As the practical result of thematic plans created according to the proposals of individual ministries, KF maintained a monopoly on the state production of short fiction and nonfiction films, as well as newsreels.

Each year, individual ministries put forward subjects for films that would fulfil their visions of how the public should be informed about current activities within the scope of the ministry's concern. For example, the Ministry of Health proposed topics related to basic health principles or raising public awareness of children's medical care issues, the Ministry of Agriculture requested films depicting new methods for growing crops or breeding animals, and the Ministry of Civil Engineering wanted to promote the development of new housing structures. The individual ministries' plans were usually short, indicating the name of the topic followed by a brief description and a comment on the preferred method of implementation – for example, whether the film should be animated or use puppets, whether the form should be instructional or documentary, and so on. The Ministry of Information oversaw all matters related to cinematography in Czechoslovakia after World War II (until 1953, when the Ministry of Culture replaced it in this function) and therefore processed the proposals of the other ministries and determined KF's budget according to the financial demands of each production. KF did not produce only films directly mandated by the state plan, though. Its activities were in fact much broader, in part because any company's good reputation in socialist Czechoslovakia was closely connected to exceeding the plan. In addition to making films based on topics proposed by filmmakers themselves and to those delimited by state plan, KF also produced films on the orders of individual state ministries or state institutions – that is, films that were not part of the primary plan. The main difference between planned films and films ordered beyond the plan was that these additional 'orders' were financed by individual ministries, state institutions or state companies – that is, not directly, with money assigned by the state to KF; but indirectly, with money assigned to individual ministries and state institutions. In addition, the intended distribution of these custom-made films was not primarily for ordinary cinemas like those made as part of the state plan, but for nontheatrical circuits in factories, agricultural collectives, professional and special-interest institutions, and the like.

Thematic plans primarily concerned with films of wide accessibility and reach, especially documentary, popular-scientific and animated films. By contrast, instructional and educational films were aimed at more narrow audiences. Thus they were understood as complementary projects to be created according to the requirements of the individual entities and their plans for raising public awareness. Consequently, the individual entities were also responsible for covering the production costs of such films. For example, the Ministry of Agriculture ordered the production of the 1952 instructional film *Včely a květy* (Bees and Flowers, 1952). According to an official declaration, this film directed by Miro Bernat was intended to 'serve mainly for the promotion of progressive beekeeping among country viewers: farmers' and was recommended for agricultural schools and courses of instruction as well as employees at agricultural cooperatives.[16] By contrast, the 1951 film *Včely budou žít!* (Bees Will Be Alive! Miro Bernat, 1951) by the same director was not created to a direct order and was therefore understood as a popular-scientific film with an agricultural theme that was 'interesting for laymen too'.[17]

The topic of KF's custom-made production within socialist Czechoslovakia is interesting in several respects. The production statistics unequivocally indicate which sectors and companies understood film as a key medium for promotion of their activities and what the trends were in their branch. We can deduce the primary ideological interests of individual clients based on the custom-made films they ordered, specifically by considering the form they desired for presenting themselves to the public. This insight about custom-made films also allows us to rethink the role of cinema within the cultural policy of socialist Czechoslovakia more generally. Moreover, the prevailing emphasis on business messages rather than ideological and educational messages in the orders made during the 1950s invites us to reconsider the importance of promotional films in the process of planting the idea of consumer society in a socialist system, and at the same time to reassess the relationship between promotional and advertising films within the socialist environment. Given that custom-made production created a body of films intended for nontheatrical patterns of distribution and exhibition, this study also suggests a 'spatial' expansion of the history of public film presentation outside of ordinary cinemas, namely, within the noncommercial educational sphere.

The number of custom-made productions during the postwar era in Czechoslovakia grew constantly in concert with the expansion of short film production more generally. Within this long-term trend we can identify several key turning points. Whereas KF produced only about 15 films a year on order prior to 1953, the total suddenly jumped to 57 in 1954 and then skyrocketed to 147 films in 1955. After 1958, average production exceeded 200 films per year.[18] These quantitative leaps resulted from the state's current political-economic situation as well as structural changes within the organization of KF. These two causes were in fact rather closely linked, because the production of KF was consistently connected with the state's ideological and economical priorities. All its departments called on KF to assist in the promotion of new scientific, technical or cultural segments, which was accomplished with both newsreels and films from the popular-scientific and instructional production branches. For this reason, the planning and production of KF were influenced by both the cultural policy of the state and economic factors (particularly industrial and agricultural production together with internal and foreign trade).

The first of the above-mentioned turning points, the year 1953, brought with it a critical revision of the state's existing economic orientation. Facing a drop in personal consumption along with rising prices and other factors, the state realized the need for a change that would increase the supply of food and consumer goods, raise living standards, decrease prices and improve the housing situation, among other things.[19] With regard to solving the state's economic problems, the first five-year plan, originally defined for the period 1949–1953, was not successful; consequently the decision was made to manage the economy according to one-year plans in 1953 and 1954. Although these changes only slightly impacted other areas of cultural production, if at all (e.g. the average feature film production remained the same, increasing only after 1958[20]), KF production increased slightly in 1953 and massively in 1954. This growth was also reflected in the production of custom-made films. New cultural-political and economic initiatives increased the overall demand for custom-made production, and the range of clients also became more varied.

The Ministries of Agriculture, Health, and Information were the primary clients of custom-made production in the initial postwar years in the liberated republic. The situation changed substantially under new state leadership after the Communist Party took power in February 1948. The transformation to the new economic model of five-year planning, together with a reorganization of KF's internal departments according to the studio system, led to a short-term decrease in production volume. Nevertheless, the above-mentioned ministries, newly joined by the Ministry of Education and Ministry of Labour, submitted most of the orders for custom-made films.

The fact that until 1953 almost all postwar custom-made production reflected the state's consistent ideological interests in certain fields (health policy, agricultural policy, etc.) suggests that the creation of custom-made films was not strictly determined by historical events but was also influenced by other developmental dynamics in the film industry. KF's passage through the critical year of 1948 without any significant change in the focus and volume of production, however, is a testament to the enduring, unchanging opinions that postwar socially engaged documentary filmmakers and state agencies held about the key tasks of short film production. According to their conception, the natural importance of short film in a socialist society was to unify informative and tendentious aspects to achieve the intended goals. We will return to this conception of film's joint civic-educational function later in this study.

The changes that occurred in custom-made film production after 1953 resulted from a shift in Czechoslovakia's trade policy. The quantitative increase in orders and qualitative shift in the range of ordering entities clearly reflect a strengthened commercial orientation on the foreign market. After 1954, more than a third of orders were placed by the Czechoslovak Chamber of Commerce or other agencies involved in foreign trade, such as Machine Export (Strojexport), Technology Export (Technoexport), or Commercial Enterprise (Reklamní podnik). In 1953, after two unsuccessful economic years, Czechoslovakia shifted its dependency on imports to positive figures and maintained this trend in the following years, with the exception of 1957.[21] State ministries also increased their demands for custom-made films in this period. Although the Ministry of Agriculture retained its primacy, new governmental sectors became increasingly interested in promoting their ideas with short films, particularly in the form of instructional films. These ministries hoped to use these films as a tool to communicate their ideas to the country's industrial sector in order to improve production practices.

The liberalizing trend during the period after 1956 and the transformation of KF into an independent economic organization with its own accounting department in 1957 precipitated a sudden increase in demand for custom-made films. Given the substandard production conditions at KF at the time, a special studio, Propagfilm, was established to meet this new demand. The studio's title itself was significant in many respects, reflecting a rhetorical turn from education or 'mass-political work' to propaganda and advertising. The range of entities ordering short films illustrates a tendency towards business interests. In addition to the Czechoslovak Chamber of Commerce, Commercial Enterprise and Machine Export, which had ordered films before 1957, other state agencies and organizations started to become involved. A significant portion of the orders came from organizations operating above the level of the state agencies, including entities coordinating more complex promotional campaigns, such as Print, Editing and Promoting Service of the Local Economy (Tisková, ediční a propagační služba místního hospodářství, Teps) or Business advertising (Reklama obchodu); the trade-promotional units of individual state agencies such as Filmexport, Motokov, Technoexport and Pragoexport; and to a lesser extent individual smaller companies such as Čedok (the state travel agency) and Jablonex (a glass production company). But although custom-made production numbers leapt to over two hundred, and eventually to over three hundred in 1960, the proportion of business messages within custom-made production on the whole did not increase. The more varied range of ordering bodies reflected a general decentralization process that occurred at all levels of the Czechoslovak economy after 1957. So even though more entities ordered the production of films for more varied purposes, the proportion of ideological themes compared to business campaigns remained more or less constant: commercial entities ordered less than 40 per cent of custom-made films.

This statistical overview of the structures of Czechoslovak custom-made film production of the late 1940s and 1950s serves two main points: on one hand, it illustrates how the developmental dynamics of short film production resonated primarily with economic developments in the state; and on the other, it establishes a foundation for understanding short film as a medium for the promotion of the state. These points will remain crucial in subsequent parts of the analysis. The next section looks at data related to custom-made film production with the goal of understanding how the above-mentioned aspects (i.e. clients of KF and their interests) influenced the division of work among KF employees and the formal structure of the films.

From Passing Down Ideas to Selling Goods and Services

Czechoslovak state authorities understood film as a tool for spreading their promotional intentions as early as the mid-1930s – this was not just a development of the postwar period.[22] Analysis of the state orders sent to KF in postwar socialist Czechoslovakia provides an opportunity to also examine sociocultural and economic processes of a more general nature. In what follows I look at advertising film as a cultural-commercial form, seeking primarily to uncover how the state understood its relation to goods and consumption. My analysis also complements existing (though rather rare) studies dealing with the nature of consumer culture of the late 1950s in socialist Czechoslovakia. Taking into consideration the demands of film production, which is more expensive and requires much more time to implement than, for example, designing and producing a poster or arranging a shop window, the following investigates which types of goods were promoted by film and attempts to determine why these products were preferred.

Operating within the structures of KF, the specialized unit Propagfilm was essential to achieving massive dissemination of the commercial film message in Czechoslovakia during the 1950s. Until 1957, KF realized all custom-made film orders in the Studio of Popular-Scientific Films (Studio populárně-vědeckých filmů). But the Studio of Popular-Scientific Films was relieved of some of its tasks upon the establishment of Propagfilm as a separate production department of KF that was intended to take on the production of all instructional, advertising and recruitment films.[23] This division of labour – together with the fact that, at least in the early years, not all recruitment, instructional and advertising films actually came under the purview of Propagfilm – accounts for the ambivalence in the official structures' (the state and its organs') approach to goods and consumption under socialist conditions. A closer examination of the process of removing these films' production from the Studio of Popular-Scientific Films and incorporating it within a new structure (Propagfilm) says more about the conception of commercial film messages in this period than might at first seem. As the following section will show in more detail, all these short films had very similar goals and uses within the socialist state. First, though, I will examine how the system of state-promotional task organization within KF according to its series model helped to shift the official discourse on instructional, advertising and recruitment film.

KF's most active clients usually did not order just one particular film with a specific focus. Instead, these entities typically requested the production of multiple films, usually in a sort of series format, to communicate their strategic interests. As methodological manuals issued by the ministries and their institutions illustrate, ideological campaigns were communicated through series of several films with a unifying topic.[24] Although such unified cycles were not the general rule, clients had a certain tendency to order custom-made films according to this model. These series were comprised of either multiple films that communicated the same topic in different forms, or several formally similar films that dealt with different sub-topics. A notable series that included work from various authors was made for the State Insurance Company (Státní pojišťovna) at the end of the 1950s. Each of the relatively short films in the series advertised the advantages of different types of insurance (for homes, weekend cottages, motor vehicles, etc.) by depicting some sort of negligence or accident that could be covered by an insurance plan.

Starting in 1957, KF began to promote Propagfilm as a production unit specializing in advertising films. At the same time, there was an increase in orders from entities whose concern was not ideological education but commercial trade. This did not mean, however, that Propagfilm had taken over the commercial sector completely, or that the custom-made films were losing their instructional rhetoric. With regard to the above-mentioned tendency of ordering bodies to request films as a series, KF applied various strategies to satisfy the demand – for instance, it tended to delegate multiple films from one client to the same individuals or small groups of authors who had worked for that client before, rather than to those who were not busy at the time. In addition, KF worked with the client to come up with more focused ideas for each film and negotiated issues of film length and order price with them. Most directors came to Propagfilm from the 'parent' Studio of Popular-Scientific Films. Several other factors determined the production of promotional films with an instructional, popular-scientific focus – for example, requirements for the promotion of goods depended upon the current priorities of internal and foreign business policy. Other factors included the intended target audience and the shifting contemporary opinions on which goods should be promoted by film, given its status as the most demanding and expensive advertising tool.[25]

Within the unstable conditions of the socialist market, the tool of film was considered unsuitable for promoting seasonal goods or goods that threatened to be in short supply on the domestic market.[26] For this reason, film was only rarely employed to promote small consumer goods such as clothing, fashion accessories or certain food products. Instead, most of the first films promoting goods were intended for foreign markets and aimed to support export. The first products promoted were larger household appliances, such as washing machines or food processors, and the films highlighted how these products would benefit housewives by saving them time and exertion in their daily work. Unsurprisingly, films about such mechanical products included voice-over commentary to explain the technical specifics and advantages of the product. Food products and consumer goods like nylons, however, had to be sold differently. The most commonly trusted technique was simply to display images of the products, for the main focus of promotion under socialism was not the brand but rather the basic product itself: butter biscuits, cheese, frozen products, fruit juices, and so forth.

The only occasions for more complex reflexions and reconsiderations of the problems of producing advertising films were the regular competitions at Czechoslovak advertising film festivals, organized by Commercial Enterprise as of 1957. Official press commentaries relating to the festivals appraise the advertising films of the late 1950s with regard to the following four aspects: the educational tasks of advertising; the relation of film to other modes of advertising in the campaign for specific goods; a film's 'beneficial effect' in relation to its production costs and the length of its feasible 'lifetime'; and the distribution of advertising films together with the related question of 'multi-purposefulness', which was understood as theoretically undesirable but practically necessary. Debates about advertising involved representatives of the Ministry of Commerce and of Advertising Production (Reklamní tvorba, the state specialists in advertising campaigns and their media: decorated shop windows, posters, brochures, etc.), as well as filmmakers and film journalists. These debates took place mostly in the pages of *Reklama* (the central trade journal for advertising issues) and in instructional advertising manuals published by Commercial Enterprise. A common feature of the period discourse on advertising was scepticism of the actual effectiveness of films with a commercial message on ordinary viewer-consumers.

Period studies on advertising show that many ordering parties considered radio programmes, newspapers or women's magazines to be the most effective modes of advertising and did not think of film as the key medium of their campaign. In these studies, film ranked among the most important tools in the hierarchy of advertising media, alongside flyers, handbills, posters, notice-boards, banners, slides and television,[27] yet its potential effectiveness was overshadowed by the large investment of time and money needed for its realization. For this reason, the filmic medium was chosen for topics with long-term potential, so that each film could be ideally used multiple times and for various purposes. In the late 1950s, however, advertising films helped to shape the conditions of local consumerism, which were quite ambiguously conceptualized within socialist cultural policy. Although recognized as essential to the economy, consumer culture was also ideologically too closely related to capitalism not to be potentially dangerous. As a result, Commercial Enterprise and KF created a specific theory for use in the official press discourse to explain the acceptance of advertising film within the socialist system. Contemporary advertising films were not understood as 'true' advertising in the capitalistic sense, but rather as a newly created form of promotional film that had arisen in the socialist environment to meet the needs of socialist society – in other words, this new form was not seen as sharing any continuity with the commercial film practices of the capitalist system that had been overcome.

Orienting Viewers' Sight: Points of Connection between Advertising and State Propaganda under Socialism

In the previous section I observed that in the late 1950s, advertising was discursively described as a new cultural political form, distinct from earlier commercial practices. According to this 'theory', the development of prewar capitalist advertising had had to be interrupted so that new, socialist advertising should arise. Like the trope of purification from capitalism, the trope of 'interrupted continuity' was paradoxically common and invoked to justify the use of similar, pre-existing (capitalist) methods for other, more generous (socialist) purposes. The trope of 'interrupted continuity' helped to enforce the theory that the true 'advertising film' had not previously existed in Czechoslovakia as such, other than in a prewar capitalist mutation, and was only able to assert itself after private enterprises' activities were briefly interrupted after the war. Precisely this idea of a 'cleansing phase' – a period devoid of advertising that allowed advertising to shed its capitalist residues and develop anew – helped to define the status of advertising film in Czechoslovakia in the late 1950s.

A general resistance to the word 'advertising' was evident in the rhetorical dodging around the mention of advertising films and advertising practices in general. This aversion became even clearer at the beginning of the 1960s, when the magazine *Reklama* (Advertising) was renamed *Propagace* (Promotion). The need for a new title is evidence that the word 'advertising' had been deemed incompatible with the socialist environment. In socialism, advertising was not just a simple matter of offering goods to consumers but incorporated more complex purposes. Consequently the label 'advertising' came to be seen as a degradation of other socialist means of promotion. In order to promote goods in an entertaining way without being accused of opposing the socialist ideology, the film discourse introduced this 'second stage of erasure': just as the memory of capitalist advertising had had to be erased in the second half of the 1950s, at the beginning of the 1960s the word 'advertising' had to be forgotten too.

To better understand the essence and ideological origin of this rhetoric, I now return to a discussion of the tradition of state-promotional film production in the postwar period. A closer examination of various debates from the 1940s and 1950s makes it evident that the word 'advertising' and the practice of film advertising production presented an enduring ideological problem for socialist Czechoslovakia. The two most significant points for consideration are the debate about other short film forms that surrounded advertising film when Propagfilm was separated from the Studio of Popular-Scientific Films in 1957, and the discussions related to the newly established KF's orientation towards promotional production in 1945 and 1946.

To openly declare that 'the main advantage of advertising film was that it gave us a chance to notify the customer of quality, benefits and advantages of a certain article in an entertaining way'[28] – as Josef Vilímek, the director of Pragofilm production company, did in 1940 – was not such an easy thing in postwar Czechoslovakia. In the early postwar period from 1945 to 1948, when Czechoslovakia was socialist but not yet communist, the state was concerned with rejuvenating industry more generally after the devastation of war. Consequently, it privileged collective support of such production over individual interests and sought to counterbalance the role of entertainment with labour. As František Gürtler wrote in 1945, 'in a socialist state, the private interest is subordinated to public interest. Thus, the limitation given by the dominance of public interest over private interest applies for advertising'.[29]

Postwar debates on the importance of short film involved much dispute about the medium's potential to fulfil aesthetic and other functions. These discussions, led by influential socially engaged filmmakers of the 1940s who had become important figures in directorial functions of KF after the war (Jiří Lehovec, Jan Kučera, Jiří Weiss, Elmar Klos and others), ultimately garnered support for short film production with an engaged, civic-educational focus. Some commentators in the early postwar years even talked about short film's 'obligation' to the state and its interests. In fact, these voices supported the concept asserted by the influential film theorist, critic, filmmaker and educator Jan Kučera. For Kučera, short film was a 'working film', that is, a medium essentially connected with the key task of a socialist citizen: work.[30] Kučera's interpretation corresponded to the leftist view of the postwar filmmaker elite, which had long promoted the nationalization of the cinema (a process finally realized via a presidential decree on 11 August 1945). In the tradition of left-wing avant-gardes, Kučera also spoke of the unification of art and function within the medium of short film, which he understood as capable of serving the state interest in a natural and beneficial way that did not exclude the author's artistic freedom.

Support for the civic-educational function of all kinds of short films (animated, feature, popular-scientific) also included the idea of 'multi-purposefulness' and was compatible with the state's initiative to expand the spectrum of exhibition environments. As a result, film distributors had to target specific non-cinema environments. In most cases, the films were used as supplemental materials in professional education – for example, as a part of lectures or public courses – but recommended venues also included advisory centres for women with children, embassies for foreign customers, and other such settings.

However, the ideal of a complex distribution network equipped with projecting equipment was far from realistic. The named institutions often did not own projectors for small-gauge films, and at the same time not all films were copied to 16mm format. Furthermore, the distribution of films promoting goods, that is, advertising films, was unsatisfactory. Only a few of the many films produced actually made it to cinemas, and the use of these films on television was discouraged because film was deemed an inappropriate medium for presenting socialist messages. The biggest problems of television were its small format and black-and-white picture, which both presented specific aesthetic challenges for filmmakers, namely in terms of graphics, colours and the use of close-ups. The few commercials presented on television met with strong criticism, for quite obvious reasons. For example, in a commercial for Kominík washing powder, the laundry looked dirty both before and after washing.[31] Therefore, most of the promotional films remained entirely unused. Evidence of the lack of conceptual planning in film distribution can be found in an official complaint filed by a village near Sušice, which reportedly got the same film, namely *Loupací radlička* (Peeling Little Ploughshare, Ladislav Rychman, 1951), every time it wanted to enrich an agricultural event with a film screening.[32]

The idea that a particular film held potential for multipurpose application – for example, it could both attract foreign customers to various glass products and inform pupils about the work of glass blowers –was foundational to the high degree of distribution specialization. There was much overlap between propaganda and advertising, not just in terms of meaning but also with regard to purpose. As František Gürtler starkly illustrated at the beginning of the period under consideration, despite the various debates about the distinction between propaganda and advertising, the common denominator between these two modes was their similarity to 'blinders that are used with horses in order to orient their sight in the required direction'.[33]

Conclusion

Even though the discussions about advertising were still quite undecided at the beginning of the 1960s, it was nevertheless deemed necessary to eliminate the term itself from the discourse. This was demonstrated by the magazine *Reklama*'s renaming as *Propagace*, and by the accompanying detailed editorial explanation of the ideological reasons behind the measure. It should also be added that in 1960 and 1961, many films promoting small consumable goods continued to feature in Propagfilm production, although they were shorter and shorter. These films usually used colour, were oriented around particular goods, and combined various cinematographic techniques (such as the polyecran effect, the combination of animated and acted film, etc.). Unfortunately, the scarcity of extant sources from the period makes it very difficult to reconstruct the actual application of these films, including how often and where they were projected. Though the scant information related to advertising films may often provide insight into the reception of specific titles, such data is statistically insufficient to provide a complete picture of short film exhibition practice.

The above analysis of the process of excluding advertising film from custom-made productions ordered by the state and its commercial agencies has identified particular phenomena in the development of consumer culture in socialist Czechoslovakia. One of the key propositions in Mark Landsman's study of consumer culture in the German Democratic Republic between 1945 and 1961[34] demonstrates how socialist planning emphasized performance and efficiency and strove to supply citizens with consumer goods in order to develop an enduring ideological connection with (or, to use Landsman's term, 'belief in') productivity to ensure the desired flow of consumer goods on the market. The case of Czechoslovakia is quite similar to the GDR in this respect. In addition, I have also shown how advertising films that were intended to support consumer culture presented a surprising challenge to socialism, one that cultural policy failed to address for quite some time. Because the medium demanded substantial production time and costs, film itself had the potential to expose imbalances between the ideals of socialism and consumer culture. For example, a film promoting nylons might reach cinemas at a time when nylons were in short supply, thus highlighting the consumer market's instability and sensitivity to variances in supply. Although the custom-made film production of the 1950s was highly disorganized in many regards, it should be seen as an important preparatory stage for later developments in which films advertising ordinary consumer goods intended for local markets were utilized in an attempt to revive the state's ailing economy.

Acknowledgement

This text is a part of a larger research project titled *The Establishment of Krátký film*, which was supported by the Czech Science Foundation (No. P409/10/P159).

Lucie Česálková is an assistant professor at the Department of Film Studies and AV Culture, Masaryk University Brno, Czech Republic. She works also as a research department head at the National Film Archive, Prague, and is editor-in-chief of the Czech peer-reviewed film journal *Iluminace*. Her research focuses on nonfiction and nontheatrical cinema, especially the concept of Czech short films and their utility functions (educational, promotional, instructional, etc.).

Notes

1. František Gürtler, 'Náborový film', in Artuš Černík (ed.), *Co je krátký film* (Prague: Knihovna Filmového kurýru, 1945), pp. 74–81.
2. KF was the production company established by the nationalization of the film industry in 1945 as a state-owned company for the production of short films. In this study, I use the Czech term to describe the production company and English terms for the works they produced.
3. In this study, I use the term 'custom-made' film instead of the more common expression 'sponsored' film to avoid misconceptions about the economic background of short film production in postwar Czechoslovakia, and to differentiate the conditions

of custom-made film production for the purposes of my argument. After 1945, when the whole film industry was state owned, all film production, including short films, was in a way 'state sponsored'. Custom-made films were not only sponsored by the state but also received financial backing from specific ministries beyond the official production plan.

4. Richard Taylor, *Film Propaganda: Soviet Russia and Nazi Germany* (London and New York: I.B. Tauris, 1998); David Welch *Propaganda and the German Cinema, 1933–1945* (London and New York: I.B. Tauris, 2001).
5. Karel Dibbets and Bert Hogenkamp (eds), *Film and the First World War* (Amsterdam: Amsterdam University Press, 1995); James Chapman, 'Cinema, Propaganda and National Identity: British Film and the Second World War', in Justine Ashby and Andrew Higson (eds), *British Cinema, Past and Present* (London and New York: Routledge, 2000), pp. 193–206; James Latham, '1918: Movies, Propaganda, and Entertainment', in Charlie Keil and Ben Singer (eds), *American Cinema of the 1910s: Themes and Variations* (New Brunswick, NJ: Rutgers University Press, 2009), pp. 204–224; Ronnie D. Lipschutz, *Cold War Fantasies: Film, Fiction, and Foreign Policy* (Lanham, MD: Rowman & Littlefield, 2001).
6. Yvonne Zimmermann, 'Jak zkoumat průmyslové filmy: Metodologická úvaha', *Iluminace* 16(4) (2004), 5–23.
7. Charles R. Acland and Haidee Wasson (eds), *Useful Cinema* (Durham, NC, and London: Duke University Press, 2011).
8. Vladimír Macura, *Šťastný věk (a jiné studie o socialistické kultuře)* (Prague: Academia, 2008).
9. Zoë Druick, *Projecting Canada: Government Policy and Documentary Film at the National Film Board* (Montreal, London and Ithaca: McGill-Queens University Press, 2007).
10. Anna McCarthy, *Ambient Television: Visual Culture and Public Space* (Durham, NC, and London: Duke University Press, 2001).
11. Anthony Slide, *Before Video: A History of the Non-Theatrical Film* (New York, Westport, CT, and London: Greenwood Press, 1998); Lee Grievson and H. Wasson (eds), *Inventing Film Studies* (Durham, NC, and London: Duke University Press, 2009).
12. Susan Reid and David Crowley (eds), *Style and Socialism: Modernity and Material Culture in Postwar Eastern Europe* (Oxford: Berg, 2000); David Crowley and Susan Reid (eds), *Pleasures in Socialism: Leisure and Luxury in the Eastern Block* (Evanston, IL: Northwestern University Press, 2010); Susan Strasser, Charles McGovern and Matthias Judt (eds), *Getting and Spending: European and American Consumer Societies in the Twentieth Century* (Washington, DC: The German Historical Institute and Cambridge: Cambridge University Press, 1998).
13. Jiří Havelka, *Čs. krátké filmy 1945–1970. Díl 1* (Prague: Československý filmový ústav, 1977); idem, *Čs. krátké filmy 1945–1970. Díl 2* (Prague: Československý filmový ústav, 1977); idem, *Čs. krátké filmy 1945–1970. Díl 3* (Prague: Československý filmový ústav, 1977).
14. Michele Lagny, 'Film History, or History Expropriated', *Film History* 6(1) (1994), 26–44.
15. Havelka, *Čs. krátké filmy 1945–1970. Díl 1*; idem, *Čs. krátké filmy 1945–1970. Díl 2*; idem, *Čs. krátké filmy 1945–1970. Díl 3*.
16. 'Včely a květy', *Filmová kartotéka* 5(21) (1953), 10.
17. 'Včely budou žít', *Filmová kartotéka* 3(33) (1951), 10.
18. Havelka, *Čs. krátké filmy 1945–1970. Díl 1*; idem, *Čs. krátké filmy 1945–1970. Díl 2*; idem, *Čs. krátké filmy 1945–1970. Díl 3*.

19. Jiří Knapík, *V zajetí moci: kulturní politika, její systém a aktéři 1948–1956* (Prague: Libri, 2006); Lenka Kalinová, *Společenské proměny v čase socialistického experimentu: k sociálním dějinám v letech 1945–1969* (Prague: Academia, 2007).
20. Pavol Bauma, *Ekonomika československého filmu* (Bratislava: Slovenské vydavatelstvo Technickej literatury and Filmový ústav, 1965), p. 200.
21. Jaroslav Nykryn, *Zahraniční obchod v ČSSR* (Prague: Nakladatelství Svoboda, 1988), pp. 48–49.
22. Lucie Česálková, 'Oběť ve státním zájmu. Kulturně-propagační dodatek a filmová politika 30. let', *Iluminace* 21(2) (2009), 135–155.
23. Návrh thematického plánu Studia populárně-vědeckých a naučných filmů Praha pro rok 1958. Národní filmový archiv, Prague, fond Krátký film (unprocessed).
24. Bohdan Ganický, *Seznam zdravotnických filmů* (Prague: SZdN, 1953).
25. Bohuš Häckl. *Propagační prostředky: Jak je vytvářet, posuzovat, používat* (Prague: Vydavatelství obchodu, 1962), pp. 80–81.
26. Ibid.
27. Bohuš Häckl, *Propagace* (Prague: Státní pedagogické nakladatelství, 1968), pp. 51–69.
28. Jiří Vilímek, 'Reklamní film', in Václav Poštolka (ed.), *Kniha o reklamě* (Prague: Reklamní klub, 1940), pp. 315–319.
29. Gürtler, 'Náborový film', p. 77.
30. Jan Kučera, 'Jde o krátký film', *Svět práce* 1(5) (1945), 13.
31. Jaroslav Pejčoch, 'Jak dál v televizní reklamě?' *Reklama* 6(5) (1960), 98–99.
32. Vlastimil Vávra, 'Nedostatky a chyby našich krátkých zemědělských filmů', *Film a doba* 3(6) (1954), 1077.
33. Gürtler, 'Náborový film', p. 79.
34. Mark Landsman, *Dictatorship and Demand: The Politics of Consumerism in East Germany* (Cambridge, MA: Harvard University Press, 2005).

Select Bibliography

Acland, Charles R., and Haidee Wasson (eds). *Useful Cinema*. Durham, NC, and London: Duke University Press, 2011.

Bauma, Pavol. *Ekonomika československého filmu*. Bratislava: Slovenské vydavatelstvo Technickej literatury and Filmový ústav, 1965.

Česálková, Lucie. 'Oběť ve státním zájmu. Kulturně-propagační dodatek a filmová politika 30. let'. *Iluminace* 21(2) (2009), 135–155.

Chapman, James. 'Cinema, Propaganda and National Identity: British Film and the Second World War'. In Justine Ashby and Andrew Higson (eds), *British Cinema, Past and Present*. London and New York: Routledge, 2000.

Crowley, David, and Susan Reid (eds). *Pleasures in Socialism: Leisure and Luxury in the Eastern Block*. Evanston, IL: Northwestern University Press, 2010.

Dibbets, Karel, and Bert Hogenkamp (eds). *Film and the First World War*. Amsterdam: Amsterdam University Press, 1995.

Druick, Zoë. *Projecting Canada: Government Policy and Documentary Film at the National Film Board*. Montreal, London and Ithaca: McGill-Queens University Press, 2007.

Grievson, Lee, and Haidee Wasson (eds). *Inventing Film Studies*. Durham, NC, and London: Duke University Press, 2008.

Havelka, Jiří. *Čs. krátké filmy 1945–1970. Díl 1*. Prague: Československý filmový ústav, 1977.
Havelka, Jiří. *Čs. krátké filmy 1945–1970. Díl 2*. Prague: Československý filmový ústav, 1977.
Havelka, Jiří. *Čs. krátké filmy 1945–1970. Díl 3*. Prague: Československý filmový ústav, 1977.
Kalinová, Lenka. *Společenské proměny v čase socialistického experimentu: k sociálním dějinám v letech 1945–1969*. Prague: Academia, 2007.
Knapík, Jiří. *V zajetí moci: kulturní politika, její systém a aktéři 1948–1956*. Prague: Libri, 2006.
Lagny, Michele. 'Film History, or History Expropriated'. *Film History* 6(1) (1994), 26–44.
Landsman, Mark. *Dictatorship and Demand: The Politics of Consumerism in East Germany*. Cambridge, MA: Harvard University Press, 2005.
Latham, James. '1918: Movies, Propaganda, and Entertainment'. In Charlie Keil and Ben Singer (eds), *American Cinema of the 1910s: Themes and Variations*. New Brunswick, NJ: Rutgers University Press, 2009.
Lipschutz, Ronnie D. *Cold War Fantasies: Film, Fiction, and Foreign Policy*. Lanham, MD: Rowman & Littlefield, 2001.
Macura, Vladimír. *Šťastný věk (a jiné studie o socialistické kultuře)*. Prague: Academia, 2008.
McCarthy, Anna. *Ambient Television: Visual Culture and Public Space*. Durham, NC, and London: Duke University Press, 2001.
Reid, Susan, and David Crowley (eds). *Style and Socialism: Modernity and Material Culture in Postwar Eastern Europe*. Oxford: Berg, 2000.
Slide, Anthony. *Before Video: A History of the Non-Theatrical Film*. New York, Westport, CT, and London: Greenwood Press, 1992.
Strasser, Susan, Charles McGovern and Matthias Judt (eds). *Getting and Spending: European and American Consumer Societies in the Twentieth Century*. Washington, DC: The German Historical Institute and Cambridge: Cambridge University Press, 1998.
Taylor, Richard. *Film Propaganda: Soviet Russia and Nazi Germany*. London and New York: I.B. Tauris, 1998.
Welch, David. *Propaganda and the German Cinema, 1933–1945*. London and New York: I.B. Tauris, 2001.
Zimmermann, Yvonne. 'Jak zkoumat průmyslové filmy: Metodologická úvaha.' *Iluminace* 16(4) (2004), 5–23.

PART IV

CHILDREN'S CINEMA

Chapter 9

BETWEEN MAGIC AND EDUCATION

The First Fairy Tale Films in the GDR

Christin Niemeyer

From 1945 onwards, the Soviet Military Administration encouraged the restoration of German cinema as part of the re-education programme for the German population after World War II. This film industry would of course be under Soviet control and unambiguously socialist in orientation. In his speech on the occasion of the licensing of DEFA (Deutsche Film-Aktiengesellschaft) in 1946, General Tiul'panov underlined the educational function of East German film production.[1] Soon, this educational approach also led to a particular interest in film production for children. In 1952 the *Verordnung über die Bildung des Staatlichen Komitees für Filmwesen* (Ordinance regarding the creation of a state-run committee for films) confirmed this particular concern by creating a studio dedicated to producing films exclusively for children. Quite quickly, one particular genre proved very important for this studio: the fairy tale film.

After World War II in the Soviet zone of occupation, the popular discourse about the values inherent in literary fairy tales – a genre that had been widely appreciated by National Socialist cultural policy – also influenced the orientation of the young East German cinema. At this time, this genre's success (in comparison to other types of films shot in the German Democratic Republic /GDR/) was far from foreseeable. The genre did not find immediate appreciation amongst the political leadership or East German ethnologists and literary scholars. On the contrary, as Katrin Pöge-Alden demonstrates in her study about fairy tale reception in Germany, there were many arguments against the ethnological study of fairy tale stories and the creation of a distinct branch of research on this topic. In 1952 Ilse Korn, an East German librarian, teller of fairy tales and employee of the GDR Ministry of Culture, outlined four principal arguments against reintroducing fairy tales into the East German cultural scene.[2] First of all, these stories – due to their origins in nonprogressive periods of history – would not positively influence the present socialist state and would even harm the development of democratic pacifism. Her second argument criticized fairy tales for their utopian and illusionist tendencies and lack of a firm anchor in reality. For this reason, she contended, they have the potential to distract the reader's attention from the needs, duties and responsibilities of reality. Furthermore, her third point argued, the moral value of fairy tales should be questioned due to the excessive violence in their storylines. In this context, the author reminds readers not to forget that precisely these kinds of stories contributed to the German chauvinism and militarism that ultimately led to the formation and implementation of fascist ideology. A fourth and final argument reinforced her first point by highlighting the archaic language of fairy tales, thereby suggesting that they could hardly be recommended for teaching the German language or even being learned in school.

In fact, it took some time to dissipate the widespread opinion that fairy tales were 'one of the sources of fascist "Ungeist"'.[3] While most arguments demonstrated a certain ignorance of the genre, they typically alluded to the Nazi regime's manipulation of fairy tales and their integration within National Socialist ideology as propagated by authors like Edmund Mudrak and Karl von Spieß.[4] 'The linking of folklore research and folklore tradition to volkisch [sic] ideology and the philosophical tenets of German Romanticism had a profound effect on the initial reception and coding of the folklore tradition in the GDR'[5] and the handling of Grimm's fairy tales in particular. From the 1950s on many ethnologists and other intellectuals started to fight against these prejudices. For example, the articles of Wolfgang Steinitz, who can be considered a pioneer of East German ethnology, represent a turning point in the common opinion about fairy tales. In a 1951 article in *Neues Deutschland* (16 and 17 November), which served as the mouthpiece of the Socialist Unity Party of Germany (Sozialistische Einheitspartei Deutschlands, SED), Steinitz argues for incorporating fairy tales into the 'national cultural heritage' (*nationales Kulturerbe*) and criticizes the widespread negative attitude towards fairy tales as a deficiency in the commitment to the labour movement (*Arbeiterbewegung*) and the result of insufficient knowledge about the history and structure of fairy tales.⁶ In this way, he succeeded in partly liberating Grimm's fairy tales from an ambiguous attitude about folklore in the GDR rooted in the discrepancy between folklore's function in developing a popular culture, and the 'potential threat to the self-proclaimed rationalist *Kulturpolitik*'⁷ posed by the mystical and romantic character of folklore in general and fairy tales with their dreamy and utopian content in particular.

Another factor influencing the reintegration of fairy tales into the 'national heritage' can be seen in the GDR's reception of the very active research on Russian folklore and fairy tales being done in the Soviet Union, most famously by Vladimir Propp.⁸ Furthermore, the great success of the Soviet fairy tale film *Kamenni tsvetok* (The Stone Flower, Aleksandr Ptushko, 1946), first shown in GDR cinemas in 1948, motivated discussion about the possibility of an East German fairy tale production of the same quality.⁹ As was all too often the case, the example of the 'big socialist brother' was the impetus for a paradigm shift in the GDR.

Between 1948 and 1970 the official attitude towards fairy tales was determined by the work of Steinitz, who demanded that these stories be considered part of the national heritage so that the working class of the GDR could know and appreciate them.¹⁰ And indeed, his efforts reaped benefits. At the Eighth Congress of the SED in 1971, Steinitz's assertions were even accentuated in a very socialist way: as literary creations, fairy tales were now seen as real testimonials of people's lives and struggles in past centuries, and could even give voice to people's social aspirations for a better world. As indicated in the following passage, written in 1979 by ethnologist and German studies specialist at the Humboldt University in Berlin Waltraud Woeller, the research and the propagation of fairy tales had become a priority for the study of the life and culture of the working class:

> The Marxist-Leninist study of fairy tales sees them as examples of the poetic formulations of the working people and as the expression of their social aspirations. It integrates the fairy tale into the broader examination of the way of life and culture of the working classes.¹¹

Once it was agreed that fairy tales very positively influenced a child's development in the socialist sense, they became an inherent part of the 'national cultural heritage'. In this context, it was all too natural that this new attitude would influence the development of the new East German cinema. In fact, two of the first DEFA films to enjoy a high level of success – *Das kalte Herz* (Heart of Stone, 1950) by Paul Verhoeven and *Die Geschichte vom kleinen Muck* (The Story of Little Mook, 1953) by Wolfgang Staudte[12] – were adaptations of literary fairy tales. As a consequence of these first successes, fairy tale films began to play a large part in East German film production at this time. Nevertheless, keeping the previous debates in mind, official political requirements obliged film crews to make sure that the script brought to light the historical context of the individual fairy tale in order to lend a 'progressive interpretation' to the cinematographic adaptation.[13] Indeed, the script of every fairy tale film shown in East German cinemas had been revised or rewritten in this sense. These interpreted versions served the socialistic identity and ideology because they 'transmitted the historical lessons of the present time to young people' and helped 'to educate [them] in becoming fully-fledged socialists'.[14] From then on, any fairy tale film production was scrutinized for its 'pedagogical and ideological content'.[15] The official policy now argued in favour of fairy tales' aesthetic qualities and their capacity to open children's eyes to a bright future in the form of socialism while also cherishing the common past narrated by these tales.

Some more or less precise directives concerning the realization of a valuable socialistic interpretation of fairy tales were set during the 1950s. In 1955, Werner Hortzschansky, then director of the GDR's Central Institute of Pedagogy (Zentralinstitut für Lehrmittel), outlined these directives in the official East German film journal *Deutsche Filmkunst*:

> In so far as it corresponds to the character of the fairy tale material, the social conflicts present in them should be realized as realistically as possible and the critical moments that reflect the attitudes of the common people to their oppressive conditions should be emphasized. Thus, the fairy tale film will make clear the resistance of the general masses against the ruling systems and the longing of oppressed peoples for a better and brighter future.[16]

Later in this text, Hortzschansky reaffirms that Soviet adaptations of fairy tales would continue to serve as models for any socialist fairy tale film, outlining and praising their 'profound humanism and their remarkable abundance of folklore'.[17] This was certainly not the only alignment with the Soviet model. For example, in a summary of a conference of the DEFA cartoon studios in November 1958, Ruth Herlinghaus points out that Soviet fairy tale films in particular proved that this genre accorded highly with the socialist party line, for whether the fairy tale reflected socialist reality or not depended on the individual artist.[18] So, as official critics never tired of repeating, Soviet fairy tale productions were meant to serve as models for the DEFA productions. However, the actual criteria for this modelling function of the Soviet films were barely more precisely articulated than in the Hortzschansky passage cited above. The actual influence of the Soviet take on fairy tale films in the development of DEFA fairy tale films is a fascinating topic for further investigation – one that would require further research in the DEFA archives, which unfortunately puts it beyond the scope of the present study.

Thus were the foundations of DEFA's rich fairy tale film production laid in the 1950s. During the forty years of the GDR's existence, the films in this genre figured amongst the most important in East German cinematography and are, even nowadays, often cited as some of the highest quality DEFA films. Moreover, they can be regarded as reflections of political development and social change over the course of the GDR's history. Their 'progressive interpretation' (with regard to character, style, obviousness of their socialist message, etc.) varied considerably over the years depending on the particular political and cultural situation. Therefore, the particularities of the initial fairy tale productions during the years of 'constructing socialism' (the general policy of the 1950s) are not directly transferrable to any other period of the GDR's history. In any analysis of films from the following decades, it is just as important to take into consideration the particular political and social context as it is for films of the previous and the upcoming period. From this perspective, the relatively small number of DEFA fairy tale films[19] enables us not only to analyse them extensively, but also to examine, via the example of this one genre, the various shifts and continuities in the close interrelations among the GDR's politics, history, society and art.

Large-Scale Realization in the 1950s and the Political Implications of These Productions

The first fairy tale films from the DEFA studios were *Das kalte Herz* by Paul Verhoeven and *Die Geschichte vom kleinen Muck* by Wolfgang Staudte. Though neither film was produced expressively for children, both were considered vanguard examples of the fairy tale genre due to their 'progressive interpretation' and 'artistic realization'.[20] In reality, the plot of the literary fairy tale of *Der kleine Muck* (*Little Mook* by Wilhelm Hauff, 1826) was subjected to a number of modifications to reinforce the social aspects and problems of this tale in the cinematic version.²¹ The frame narrative presents the problems that an individual – in this case, an old, disfigured man – can encounter when confronted by a collective. At the beginning of Staudte's film, this man is persecuted by a gang of children who mock and insult him precisely for his deformity. Ultimately, he manages to find a place where the children cannot approach him and starts to tell them the story of his life: the story of young Mook, who had once saved the country from harm. By sharing the memories of his past with the children, Mook gains their respect and manages at last to be accepted by the collective from which he was once excluded. The major part of the film is devoted to the account of young Mook's adventures, where the use of satire to critique the despotism of the sultan's court can be understood as a general social critique of monarchic or other elitist regimes.²²

Nevertheless, the slight traces of ideology in *Die Geschichte vom kleinen Muck* are barely noticeable and largely derive from the original storyline, which is not the case with all DEFA fairy tale films of this period.²³ In the quite different approach of *Das tapfere Schneiderlein* (The Valiant Little Tailor, Helmut Spieß, 1956), for instance, the film's images and patterns are awkwardly infused with socialistic messages. In this interpretation, the young tailor is so affected by the socialist *habitus* that, in the end, he chases away all the members of the royal court who tried to betray him. Correspondingly, he of course does not marry the princess but rather the maidservant who has helped him faithfully since his arrival at the court; then, wearing the typical headpieces of their profession instead of crowns, the tailor and maidservant assume the throne and found a new kingdom of the people. Even for Marxist critics, the particularly obvious socialist overtones in this film were carried too far – so far that one critic wondered ironically if the Brothers Grimm themselves had had a Marxist education.²⁴ An examination of the archival documents on this film in the Bundesarchiv in Berlin Lichterfelde reveals that these modifications to the plot of the literary fairy tale were the result of long pre-production discussions and that the initial screenplay underwent various modifications and extensive cuts due to official directives to emphasize a socialist message and a 'progressive interpretation'.²⁵

The opposite approach can be observed in Francesco Stefani's *Das singende klingende Bäumchen* (The Singing Ringing Tree, 1957), likely one of the most popular fairy tale films ever shown in East German cinemas and on GDR television. Creating a veritable fairy-tale atmosphere with its abundance of marvellous images, the film seems to correspond perfectly to a child's world of imagination. However, the GDR critics did not share this opinion and accused it of transmitting primarily a 'bourgeois idyll' and not providing enough points of reference for children, who – according to the official policy – had to be prepared for integration into the socialist community.[26] In 1985 Hellmuth Häntzsche summed up the crux of the issue with the film: 'The problem with *Das singende klingende Bäumchen* was that there was no clear socialist realist interpretation. One got lost in its idealistic conception.'[27] Yet, as previously mentioned, these critics failed to inhibit the film's national – and even international – success.[28]

A third example to illustrate the diversity of DEFA productions in the 1950s is *Die Geschichte vom armen Hassan* (The Story of Poor Hassan, Gerhard Klein, 1958). The conception of its screenplay represents an interesting experiment in applying Bertolt Brecht's theory of popular theatre to a fairy tale film. However, this attempt proved unsuccessful and had no influence on the further evolution of DEFA fairy tales. The Uyghur tale is realized as a parable.[29] At the beginning of the film, the poor servant Hassan is exploited by his master but remains completely compliant with his position at the bottom of the capitalist society into which he was born. However, after suffering increasing exploitation and cruelty he grows to discover that richness and poorness are *not* given by Allah and not, therefore, eternal and unalterable values. Some East German critics, especially those referring to it decades later, were very enthusiastic about this stylistic experiment accompanied by a veritable reflection on the class struggle. Still, other critics writing at the time of the film's release and a great part of the children's audience at the time did not appreciate the repletion of socialist morality and found the film lacking in the magical fairy-tale element. Therefore, this experiment remained the only one of its kind.[30]

In this context, it is worthwhile to take a closer look at the further development of DEFA's work on children's productions. As a first step, a group of DEFA filmmakers assembled in the autumn of 1952 to create a special working group for children's films.[31] Walter Beck, who would later become one of the most productive directors of children's films, would call this first initiative 'the germ cell of children's film' in the GDR.[32] Two years later, the Central Committee of the SED encouraged DEFA to set up a special dramaturgy group for children's film (Kinderfilm-Dramaturgengruppe).[33] The objective of this group was to research forms and criteria in order to increase the quality of children's films while at the same time assuring a high pedagogical level and – most important of all – monitoring the political value of the films to be shot. So the task was at least threefold: to shoot a high number of films that would be sure to instruct, indoctrinate and, not least, enchant the young audience. This first working group was dissolved in 1959.[34] From this point on, work on this genre was integrated within the studio in charge of general feature film production (Spielfilmstudio). A new working group specializing in films for children and teenagers (Kinder- und Jugendfilm) was created in 1964 but likewise dissolved shortly afterwards.[35]

In spite of all the tumult over the organization of the work on children's films, the genre itself, and in particular the fairy tale film, never lost its eminent role in DEFA production. In fact, these ups and downs in the formation of a veritable institution for children's film evoke some parallels with the development of the same genre in the USSR. As Steffen Wolf points out in his monograph on children's film in Europe, Soviet films not only served as models for production but also provided some institutional signals in the late 1950s. To cite just one example: the famous Gorki Studios, which opened in 1936 as the first studio in the world to produce exclusively children's films, were closed during World War II and did not reopen until 1963. In the meantime, specifically from 1958 to 1962, many official debates and discussions revolved around the need for a central organization to plan and realize children's film in the USSR. It was certainly not by accident that similar discussions took place in GDR at this same time.[36]

The importance that the political leaders in East Berlin accorded to children's film is evident in a number of official critiques on this subject. At the Conference on the Feature Film (Spielfilmkonferenz) in 1958, chief SED ideologist Anton Ackermann criticized recent children's productions for their 'distance from reality' (*Wirklichkeitsferne*) and their 'lack of partisanship' (*mangelnde Parteilichkeit*), decrying the fact that 'no DEFA children's film ever contributed to the socialist education of our children'.[37] Whereas Ackermann's statement shows the political importance of this genre by pointing out the shortcomings of recent children's film productions, other official statements underline their potential positive influence. For example, Hans-Joachim Laabs, minister for national education from 1950 to 1952, characterized children's films as

> an important instrument for the development of a socialist consciousness in the upcoming generation.... They affect the formation of the future to a greater degree than films for adults. Therefore, it is important that children's films deal with typical material, present typical characters, and profile and graphically formulate the propulsive element of progress. These films must be politically 'correct', they must not tolerate any ideological carelessness.[38]

After the late 1950s, many considered children's films in general and fairy tale films in particular to be stalwarts of film production and rather 'riskless' genres. This 'quality' of the marvellous genre was reinforced in the following decades. For example, after one of the female director Iris Gusner's films was banned for political reasons in the 1970s, Albert Wilkening, then DEFA's general director, strongly advised her to shoot a fairy tale film so that her former ideological faux pas would be forgotten: 'Make a fairy tale film. You can't offend anyone that way. This is your chance to redeem yourself and show that you are proficient in your profession.'[39] In the following years, the fairy tale seemed to become a perfect instrument for making one's mark at DEFA, or exculpating oneself from a mistake or a bad reputation, all the while working under conditions that were much more accommodating than those for feature films and productions for adults.

In any case, we can observe a tremendous variety of styles, representations and stage props during this first period of the DEFA fairy tale film. This large range can be explained by the enthusiasm and willingness that the first directors of this genre displayed towards trying new approaches and styles. The atmosphere of cinematic rejuvenation during these first years of DEFA allowed a certain degree and range of experimentation. At the same time, the fairy-tale film genre stood to benefit from its 'niche existence' within the larger genre of children's film, where working conditions were considered less rigorous than in other genres, and from the great importance that the political class accorded to this genre. In fact, it seemed perfectly suited for the moral indoctrination of future socialists, if for no other reason than its great success with young spectators.[40]

Conclusion
(Looking Ahead to Production in the 1960s)

After the popularization of television in the GDR at the beginning of the 1960s, attendance rates in East German cinemas dwindled considerably. This development also affected children's films because East German television proposed very interesting programmes for children from the outset. Accompanying the coexistence of the two institutions were newly created supervisory bodies. Starting in 1961, the National Centre for Children's Film in the GDR (Nationales Zentrum für Kinderfilm in der DDR) oversaw all production for children, be it for television or the cinema.[41] From then on, DEFA and the TV studios of the GDR joined forces and worked together on various projects. Naturally this new situation provoked new discussions, including some about the different aesthetic criteria for TV films versus those produced for the big screen. These debates remained for the most part theoretical, specifying technical details as to the length of scenes or the relation between picture and sound.

The ideological ground rules for fairy-tale film production were established by the end of the 1950s. After the dissolution of the Artistic Working Group for Children's and Youth Films (Künstlerische Arbeitsgruppe für Kinder- und Jugendfilm), the field was open to any director trying to produce films for a young audience. As mentioned above, the relatively liberal working conditions allowed a significant number of directors to experiment in this field, with varying levels of success and official recognition.[42] In the 1960s, however, the advent of a new generation of directors working in this genre prompted a noticeable shift in the character of DEFA fairy tale film production. During these years, some directors of children's films even became specialized in fairy tale productions and shot some of the best known and most shown productions of this genre. One of DEFA's most active fairy tale directors was Walter Beck (born in 1929), who began his career in the 1960s and continued to shoot fairy tale adaptations until the collapse of the GDR.[43]

One of the more notable films of the 1960s is *Die goldene Gans* (The Golden Goose, 1964), directed by Siegfried Hartmann (born in 1927). A veteran of children's and fairy tale films, Hartmann possessed a lengthy filmography including three of the most famous DEFA fairy tale productions: *Das Feuerzeug* (The Tinder-Box, 1958), *Die goldene Gans* and *Schneeweisschen und Rosenrot* (Snow-White and Rose-Red, 1979). All three depict quite classical settings without experimentation and are widely congruent with the literary model. The same diagnosis is valid for Gottfried Kolditz's first fairy tale film *Schneewittchen* (Snow White, 1961). It is Kolditz's third[44] fairy tale film *Frau Holle* (Mother Holle, 1963) that stands out from the others. This film was entirely shot in a studio and deliberately accentuates the artificial aspects of the setting. This approach, typically used in the GDR primarily in order to reduce the cost of production, turned out to be rather successful and found one of its most active imitators in Walter Beck, who used a very similar setting for his film *König Drosselbart*.

In a completely different context, two fairy tale films deserving of mention were made by Rainer Simon (born in 1941), who can be considered the *enfant terrible* of the DEFA fairy tale family. Both his first DEFA fairy tale, *Wie heiratet man einen König* (How to Marry a King, 1968), and his second, *Sechse kommen durch die Welt* (How Six Men Got On in the World, 1972) introduce a large number of new elements to the classical genre of the fairy tale, such as erotic allusions, intertextual references and a questioning of the traditional way of telling a tale by deliberately casting doubt on the conventional point of view and presenting itself as a story 'that could be a tale' (or not).

In these later years, DEFA fairy tale production certainly left behind any of the doubts as to its legitimacy that it had encountered in the beginning. The fairy tale film genre was now well established in the GDR; its ideological premises were laid. In the following decades, the ground rules that had been set down in the 1950s were applied and subverted to varying degrees, such that the historical value of the fairy tale films of the 1960s and 1970s often lies in the level of divergence from the required 'progressive interpretation'. From this perspective, fairy tale films can serve as a mirror reflecting the cultural life and cultural policy of the GDR. Although this is the case for any cultural production in any country, the limited number of DEFA fairy tales enables us to use this genre as a small but complete corpus of one special cultural domain. Since these adaptations are anchored in and extremely dependent on the political situation and the shooting conditions of the particular moment in which they were produced, they also help us trace the ups and downs of East German history from the Soviet occupation until the fall of the Wall. The nearly forty years of the GDR's existence correspond to forty years of DEFA fairy tale films. All these tales, innocent and inoffensive at first sight and barely known beyond the German border, marvellously illustrate one of the most interesting aspects of the history of the German Democratic Republic, including the image that it would have liked and the one it actually gave itself.

Christin Niemeyer has lived in France since 2002. She studied history and German literature at the Universities of Rostock (1997–2002) and Nantes (Master Research, 2005–2006). At present, she works as a lecturer/ATER (Attaché temporaire d'enseignement et derecherche) in the Department of German Studies at the University of Caen Basse-Normandie. She is an associated member of the local research group ERLIS and is working on her Ph.D. in German civilization at the Universities of Potsdam (Germany) and Metz (France) under the direction of Professors Stefanie Stockhorst (Potsdam) and Ulrich Pfeil (Metz). Her Ph.D. dissertation examines the ideological implications of the DEFA fairy tale film in the period between 1946 and 1990.

Notes

1. Cyril Buffet, *Défunte DEFA: Histoire de l'autre cinéma allemand'* (Paris: Edition du cerf, 2007), p. 20.
2. See Kathrin Pöge-Alder, *Märchen als mündlich tradierte Erzählungen des Volkes. Zur Wissenschaftsgeschichte der Entstehungs- und Verbreitungstheorien von Volksmärchen von den Brüdern Grimm bis zur Märchenforschung in der DDR* (Berlin and New York: Peter Lang, 1994), p. 195.
3. Friedel Wallesch, 'Sozialistische Kinder- und Jugendliteratur der DDR', *Schriftsteller der Gegenwart* 25 1977), p. 24.
4. Karl von Spieß and Edmund Mudrak, *Deutsche Märchen – deutsche Welt* (Berlin: Verlag Herbert Stubenrauch, 1939).
5. David Bathrick, *The Powers of Speech: The Politics of Culture in the GDR* (Lincoln and London: University of Nebraska Press, 1995), p. 173.
6. Wolfgang Steinitz, 'Die deutsche Volksdichtung – ein wichtiger Teil des nationalen Kulturerbes', *Neues Deutschland*, 16 and 17 November 1951.
7. Bathrick, *The Powers of Speech*, p. 169.
8. Pöge-Alder, *Märchen als mündlich tradierte Erzählungen des Volkes*, p. 197. See also Vladimir Propp, *Morphologie du conte* (Paris: Seuil, 1965).
9. Marc Silberman, 'The First DEFA Fairy Tales', in John Davidson and Sabine Hake (eds), *Framing the Fifties: Cinema in a Divided Germany* (New York and Oxford: Berghahn Books, 2009), p. 109.
10. Wolfgang Steinitz, *Deutsche Volkslieder demokratischen Charakters aus sechs Jahrhunderten*, 2 vols. (East Berlin: Akademie-Verlag, 1954 and 1962), as quoted in Pöge-Alder, *Märchen als mündlich tradierte Erzählungen des Volkes*, p. 199.
11. Waltraud Woeller, 'Märchen', in Ulrich Bentzien and Hermann Strobach (eds), *Deutsche Volksdichtung*, 2nd edition (Leipzig: reclam, 1987), p. 127.
12. *The Story of Little Mook* and *Heart of Stone* are generally cited amongst the first DEFA fairy tale films, yet they were produced and distributed without any specific target audience in mind and thus cannot be considered fairy tale films for children. They merit discussion in this very particular context of fairy tale films because of the impulse their immense success gave to this genre and their importance for the East German cinema in general. This importance is illustrated, for example, by the large number of reviews referring to their extraordinary quality and the fame of their directors (Wolfgang Staudte and Paul Verhoeven).
13. Anne Reimann, 'Märchenfilme in der DDR', *Informationen Jugendliteratur und Medien* 2 (1990), 50.
14. Ibid.
15. Dieter Wiedemann, "Es war einmal...' – Reise ins DEFA-Märchenland', in Ingelore König, Dieter Wiedemann and Lothar Wolf (eds), *DEFA-Märchen – Arbeiten mit Kinderfilmen* (Munich: KOPÄD, 1998), p. 12.
16. Werner Hortzschansky, 'Das Märchen im Film', *Deutsche Filmkunst Beilage* 5 (1955), 19.
17. Reimann, 'Märchenfilme in der DDR', 50. Nevertheless, comparison of Soviet and East German fairy tale films of this and of later periods reveals many differences in both setting and general approach. The Soviet productions accentuate Russian folklore (e.g. folkloric songs and famous fairy tale characters such as the witch Baba Yaga or Ded Moroz [Father Frost, a sort of Russian analogue to Santa Claus]). By contrast, East German fairy tale films – especially those of the 1960s

and 1970s – develop in the direction of a minimalistic setting and tend to remain rather classical in approach, with hardly any folkloric elements, songs or traditional costumes to be found in them.

18. Ruth Herlinghaus, 'Gedanken zu einer Konferenz', *Deutsche Filmkunst* 12 (1958), 379.
19. Depending on the system of counting and classification, between 39 and 130 fairy tale films were produced between 1950 and 1990. In his essay on the DEFA fairy tale studios, Walter Beck mentions '39 classical fairy tale films'; see Walter Beck, 'Zur Geschichte des DEFA-Märchenspielfilms für Kinder', in Regina Bendix and Ulrich Marzolph (eds), *Hören, Lesen, Sehen, Spüren. Märchenrezeption im europäischen Vergleich*, Schriftenreihe RINGVORLESUNGEN der Märchenstiftung Walter Kahn 8 (Baltmannsweiler: Schneider, 2008), p. 185. In another recent publication, Joachim Giera counts 130 DEFA fairy tales; see Joachim Giera, 'Vom Kohlenmunk-Peter, dem kleinen Muck und seinen Leuten. Märchenfilme aus den DEFA-Filmstudios', in Helge Gerndt and Kristin Wardetzki (eds), *Die Kunst des Erzählens. Festschrift für Walter Scherf* (Potsdam: Verlag für Berlin-Brandenbhurg, 2002), p. 293. It is likely that Walter Beck's tally is more accurate, especially if the count is limited to classical adaptations of fairy tales to the exclusion of modern fairy tale films.
20. Hellmuth Häntzsche, 'Die Entwicklung einer sozialistischen deutschen Kinderfilmproduktion – künstlerische Prinzipien und Tendenzen', in Hellmuth Häntzsche (ed.), *Und ich grüsse die Schwalben: der Kinderfilm in europäischen sozialistischen Ländern* (East Berlin: Henschelverlag, 1985), p. 253. Contemporary critics emphasized that the adaptation of *Die Geschichte vom Kleinen Muck* succeeded in 'bringing the fairy tale to life in a new way; it breathes the spirit of our present time yet still remains a whole and real fairy tale'. Furthermore, they ennobled this film as a model for the future production of literary adaptations. See H.U.E., *Berliner Zeitung*, 24 December 1953, quoted in F.B. Habel, *Das große Lexikon der DEFA-Spielfilme* (Berlin: Schwarzkopf & Schwarzkopf-Verlag, 2001), p. 205.
21. Reimann, 'Märchenfilme in der DDR', 51.
22. Ibid., 52.
23. In an article in the West German magazine *Der Spiegel*, one journalist – using language clearly marked by Cold War discourse – mentions precisely *Die Geschichte vom Kleinen Muck* and *Das kalte Herz* as two DEFA films that are certain to be 'guaranteed politically sterile' (*politisch garantiert keimfrei*); *Der Spiegel* 3 (1955), http://www.spiegel.de/spiegel/print/d-31968921.html (viewed 4/02/2014).
24. Horst Knietsch, 'Die seltsame Mär vom Schneiderlein', *Neues Deutschland* 3 October 1956.
25. See Bundesarchiv Berlin (BArch), VEB DEFA-Studio für Spielfilme DR 117/32349 and DR 117/26308 (T1 /4). Here is one example to illustrate this: in the first original screenplay (which was later abandoned), written by Peter Podehl, it was planned that the tailor should marry the princess at the end of the film – an ending that in fact corresponds to the plot of the literary tale. However, a report dated 26 April 1955 from the Produktionsgruppe Jugend- und Kinderfilm harshly criticized this ending because it 'obscures the clearness of the critique of the feudalistic social order' (*verwischend für die Eindeutigkeit der Kritik an der feudalistischen Gesellschaftsordnung*) that is clearly evident in the rest of the plot. Quoted in BArch DR 117 26308, 1/4. Later, a new character is introduced: Traute, a maidservant at the court and the tailor's faithful friend during his adventures. At the end of the final version, Traute marries the protagonist and creates a new kingdom of the people with him, while the mean princess and the entire court are banished.

26. Häntzsche, 'Die Entwicklung einer sozialistischen deutschen Kinderfilmproduktion', p. 253. This critique corresponds *ex post* to contemporary reviews of the film, which detest the fact that the film has 'intensified the shortcomings the of the book' (*hat die Mängel des Buches noch verstärkt*) and 'neglected the content in favour of the form' (*der inhaltlichen Aussage zugunsten der Form zu wenig Bedeutung geschenkt*), the latter critique being one of the most frequent and most negative reproaches in the context of the anti-formalism campaign of the 1950s. See Charlotte Czygan, *Deutsche Filmkunst*, 17 December 1957, quoted in F.B. Habel, 'Das große Lexikon der DEFA-Spielfilme' (Berlin: Schwarzkopf & Schwarzkopf-Verlag, 2001), p. 553.
27. Häntzsche, 'Die Entwicklung einer sozialistischen deutschen Kinderfilmproduktion', p. 253. One critic at *Deutsche Filmkunst* was even harsher, attacking this 'conception rife with pseudo fairy-tale-romanticism' as 'not suitable for forming the political will and the character of our children'. See Charlotte Ewald, 'Zwei neue Kinderfilme der DEFA', *Deutsche Filmkunst* (1) (1958), 2.
28. In the appendix of his monograph on the history of the DEFA studios, Cyril Buffet reproduces a table listing the most successful DEFA films between 1946 and 1989. *Das singende klingende Bäumchen* comes in at 26th place with 5.1 million spectators. See Cyril Buffet, *Défunte DEFA: Histoire de l'autre cinéma allemand* (Paris: Edition du cerf, 2007), p. 306 (Annexe IV).
29. Brecht particularly appreciated theatre plays presented as parables. He conceived these plays to make it easier for his audience to apply the plots to their own lives and experience as well as to the society they lived in (see e.g. *Der gute Mensch von Sezuan* [The Good Person of Szechwan, 1938–1940] or *Der aufhaltsame Aufstieg des Arturo Ui* [The Resistible Rise of Arturo Ui, 1941]). Works of this genre always contain a moral or a political message intended to guide and to improve the social attitude of the audience. The plot of *Die Geschichte vom armen Hassan* is clearly organized according to Brecht's model of parabolic narration.
30. See, e.g., Christoph Funke in *Der Morgen* (26 November 1958), quoted in F.B. Habel, *Das große Lexikon der DEFA-Spielfilme* (Berlin: Schwarzkopf & Schwarzkopf-Verlag, 2001), p. 204. General assessments of GDR fairy tale films written at a later date commonly hold positive appraisals of the interesting transposition of Brecht's theatre experience to a children's film and, at the same time, refer to the film's failure with child audiences (see Häntzsche, 'Die Entwicklung einer sozialistischen deutschen Kinderfilmproduktion', p. 255 and König, Wiedemann and Wolf, *DEFA-Märchen*, p. 14). No known sources indicate the precise data of this failure, but the following document is recommended for audience statistics on this DEFA production: E. Quett, *Filmografie der künstlerisch-technischen und ökonomischen Daten DEFA Kinospielfilmproduktionen*, vol. 1, *1946–1966*, in BArch, DR117, DEFA-Studio für Spielfilme.
31. Steffen Wolf, *Kinderfilm in Europa* (Munich-Pullach and Berlin: Verlag Dokumentation, 1969), p. 159.
32. Beck, 'Zur Geschichte des DEFA-Märchenspielfilms für Kinder', p. 187. Original quotation: 'Die Gruppe gilt als die "Keimzelle Kinderfilm", wie damals einmal protokolliert wurde'.
33. In a letter from Siegfried Wagner, the head of the Culture Department of the Secretary of the Central Committee of the SED, to Erich Wendt, vice-minister of culture in the GDR, dated 25 January 1958, p. 2. Stiftung Archiv der Parteien und Massenorganisationen der DDR im Bundesarchiv Berlin, DY 30/IV 2/906/204, Fiche 1.

34. Wolf, *Kinderfilm in Europa*, p. 159.
35. Günter Jordan has assembled dates, facts and figures on the history of DEFA: Günter Jordan, *Film in der DDR. Daten, Fakten, Strukturen*, edited by Filmmmuseum Potsdam (Potsdam: Filmmuseum, 2009), pp. 136–137.
36. Steffen Wolf, *Kinderfilm in Europa*, p. 167. Wolf cites the Tenth Party Conference of the Soviet Communist Party in February 1956, an article from January 1958 in *Komsomolskaya Pravda* and another in the same newspaper from January 1960, and an article in *Iswestij*. He also refers to discussions on the Seventh Komsomol Central Committee Plenum and to the Arts Council for Children's film at the Ministry of Culture in May 1960 (J. Gurevitch, *Iskusstwo kino* 5 (1962); Wolf quotes from *Film*, special issue [1962], 74–91).
37. Anton Ackermann, 'Zur Parteilichkeit in der Filmkunst', *Einheit* 4 (1958), quoted in Steffen Wolf, *Kinderfilm in Europa*, p. 161.
38. Steffen Wolf, *Kinderfilm in Europa*, p. 159, quoting Hans-Joachim Laabs, 'Pädagogische Bemerkungen zum Kinderfilm' *Deutsche Filmkunst* 5 (1954), 5.
39. Ingrid Poss and Peter Warnecke (eds), *Spur der Filme. Zeitzeugen über die DEFA* (Berlin: LINKS-Verlag, 2006), p. 314.
40. Ingelore König, Dieter Wiedemann, and Lothar Wolf (eds), *Zwischen Marx und Muck. DEFA-Filme für Kinder* (Berlin: Henschelverlag, 1995), p. 11. These authors show that the films of the first decade (1950s) achieved the greatest success with audiences. In spite of the excellent quality of some of them, the productions of the 1960s and 1970s did not reach the level of their predecessors. However, it is important to take social change into consideration, particularly the development of television, which had an enormous impact on attendance in East German cinemas. Another aspect to bear in mind is the contemporary political situation: a film shot at the time of the Eleventh Plenum of the SED in 1965 was certainly less likely to succeed than was a production of the early 1970s, when the calm period after Erich Honecker's rise to power increased many artists' hopes for greater freedom in GDR cultural life.
41. Hans-Dieter Kübler (ed.), *Kinderfernsehsendungen in der BRD und der DDR – Eine vergleichende Analyse*, Medien in Forschung und Unterricht 3 (Tübingen: Niemeyer, 1981), p. 230.
42. Steffen Wolf notes the key benefits of working for a children's production at the beginning of one's career: whereas a director who failed with a regular feature film provoked many problems for his studio and his colleagues, a failure with a fairy tale film had no dramatic consequences – the risk was minimal. On the other hand, a great success in the children's genre often saw the director shifted towards the production of 'real' films, which meant the loss of a gifted director for further children's productions. Thus, children's films were typically considered a 'testing ground' for young directors who left this first step behind as soon as they could aspire to greater projects. See Steffen Wolf, *Kinderfilm in Europa*, p. 164.
43. His filmography contains more than fourteen children's films and seven fairy tales, including *König Drosselbart* (King Thrushbeard, 1965), *Dornröschen* (Sleeping Beauty, 1971), *Der Prinz hinter den sieben Meeren* (Across the Seven Seas, 1982), *Der Bärenhäuter* (The Man in the Bear's Skin, 1985), and *Froschkönig* (Frog King, 1987). Beck often adopts and blends elements from different fairy tales and even introduces historical or literary allusions to his setting; this approach is particularly evident in *Dornröschen*, one of his most 'ideological' fairy tale films.
44. His second fairy tale film was *Die goldene Jurte* (The Golden Tent, 1961).

Select Bibliography

Bathrick, David. *The Powers of Speech*. Lincoln: University of Nebraska Press, 1995.

Beck, Walter. 'Zur Geschichte des DEFA-Märchenspielfilms für Kinder'. In Regina Bendix and Ulrich Marzolph (eds), *Hören, Lesen, Sehen, Spüren. Märchenrezeption im europäischen Vergleich*. Schriftenreihe Ringvorlesungen der Märchenstiftung Walter Kahn 8. Baltmannsweiler: Schneider, 2008.

Buffet, Cyril. *Défunte DEFA: Histoire de l'autre cinéma allemande*. Paris: Edition du cerf, 2007.

König, Ingelore, Dieter Wiedemann and Lothar Wolf (eds). *Zwischen Marx und Muck. DEFA-Filme für Kinder*. Berlin: Henschelverlag, 1995.

König, Ingelore, Dieter Wiedemann and Lothar Wolf (eds). *DEFA-Märchen – Arbeiten mit Kinderfilmen*. Munich: KOPÄD, 1998.

Pöge-Alder, Kathrin. *Märchen als mündlich tradierte Erzählungen des Volkes. Zur Wissenschaftsgeschichte der Entstehungs- und Verbreitungstheorien von Volksmärchen von den Brüdern Grimm bis zur Märchenforschung in der DDR*. Berlin and New York: Peter Lang, 1994.

Poss, Ingrid, and Peter Warnecke (eds). *Spur der Filme. Zeitzeugen über die DEFA*. Berlin: LINKS-Verlag, 2006.

Propp, Vladimir. *Morphologie du conte*. Paris: Seuil, 1965.

Reimann, Anne. 'Märchenfilme in der DDR'. *Informationen Jugendliteratur und Medien* 2 (1990), pp. 50-60.

Silberman, Marc. 'The First DEFA Fairy Tales'. In John Davidson and Sabine Hake (eds), *Framing the Fifties: Cinema in a Divided Germany*. New York and Oxford: Berghahn Books, 2009.

Chapter 10

Children's Films

Between Education, Art and Industry

Lukáš Skupa

The nationalization of Czechoslovak cinema after World War II brought, among other things, considerable debate about the possibilities for a systematic production of films for children. In those days probably no one would have anticipated that in a few years this genre,[1] which had almost no tradition in the Czech cinema, would become the 'showcase' of Czechoslovak State Film (Československý státní film, ČSF). The purpose of this study is not to describe the development of Czechoslovak children's film from its primitive beginnings to the 'golden age'. Rather, I will attempt to evaluate the institutional sources of early children's film and examine the period of genre standardization from 1945 to 1955. The study follows and investigates the genre as it took shape during two different historical eras, given that the development of Czechoslovak cinema prior to 1948 differed substantially from its development after the communist coup of 1948. Sociopolitical changes after 1948 influenced the character and organization of film production as well as the development of children's film as a genre. Prior to the mid-1950s, however, one can talk about only the beginnings of a genre. Its final standardization in 1955 followed the abolition of the Studio for Children's, Cartoon and Puppet Films (Studio dětského, kresleného a loutkového filmu), whose founding is considered the last effort to unite all types of children's film production within one institution. The genre's development had been influenced by a series of industrial, artistic and ideological interventions, including the imposition of requirements for high artistic standards or the educational impact of films for children. Conclusions about the formation and standardization of Czech children's film as a genre will thus be based on the interaction of these assumptions.

Education by Art: The Status of Children and Youth in Czechoslovakia after World War II

Postwar debates about film and other art forms aimed at children referred to the need for new educational approaches. The leading arguments for re-evaluation of the educational system pointed to the system's stagnation in the previous period.[2] Intensifying political impact and state control after World War II meant new approaches to organizing children's care and education were required. It was mainly the Ministry of Education, together with the Ministry of Social Care, that now pressed for changes in the institutions responsible for children's care and education. According to a so-called Two-Year State Plan, schools were supposed to educate children in a national democratic manner and to support socialist and 'builder' efforts.[3] The increasing politicization and state intervention in the educational and school system eventually culminated on 21 April 1948, when the conception of a 'Unified Czechoslovak School' was enacted as law and became the only admissible model, to the exclusion of any alternatives.[4] The extracurricular education system also went through a similar process. After 1948 various youth organizations were disbanded and replaced by an umbrella group called the Czechoslovak Youth Organization. The foundation of a pioneer organization inspired by the Soviet model led to the liquidation of all noncommunist youth organizations such as Junák, the Czech scout organization.[5]

All these changes in the educational system were intended to follow the conclusions of contemporary pedagogical analysis. Public and scientific research was conducted by the Pedagogic Research Institute (Výzkumný ústav pedagogický), which was founded in Prague in 1945.[6] Studies on the impact of the media on children and youth were centralized in the institute's special Education by Art division. In 1946 the Ministry of Education founded another institution interested in such research, the Film and Diapositive Institute (Ústav pro film a diapozitiv).[7] In 1949, without any specific explanation, this institute ceased to exist, probably as a consequence of the transformation of scientific research institutions that took place in 1948.

The communist 'educational' rhetoric grew even stronger after 1948. 'Education by art' – which implied the correction of taste and even society's re-education through cinema, literature, radio broadcasting and theatre – became a distinctive strategy in this period. The label was defined against the background of previous historical periods; therefore, 'education by art' was meant to differ terminologically from 'artistic education', an old concept that had been employed during the so-called First Republic and in the Protectorate (of Bohemia and Moravia), when art was considered a privilege for only a few chosen people.[8] The new concept of 'education by art' was meant to guarantee the elimination of kitsch from a child's immediate environment. Libraries and radio stations were supposed to get rid of 'trashy literature' and 'low taste romance' and replace them with 'quality' books, songs and artistic images.[9] This process was intended to affect children and youth through both the comprehensibility of artistic form and the high availability of production.

Artistic production for children was supposed to adhere to the rules of socialist realism, which sought to keep children from false, romantic illusions of the world in order to help them understand the true reality of the world as soon as possible.[10] The educational quality was thus already to be embedded in the media content. Nevertheless, the family, youth organizations and of course school, were to serve as the ultimate guarantees that nothing harmful would be spread among children.[11] 'Education by art' fit well into the new concept of a unified school system and its regulations. Teachers were supposed to educate children to be 'socialistically aware' citizens, guide them to the correct understanding of art and foster their artistic taste and abilities.[12]

Media Control from Book to Record

The entire media sphere was revised similarly to the educational system. Cinema, radio broadcasting, literature and theatre were no longer to act as mere intermediaries of undemanding entertainment and mechanisms for economic profit. On the contrary, they were to serve as tools for educating children and cultivating their personalities. After 1948, a series of consolidation interventions in the administration of different media branches helped to strengthen their role in a communist manner by such means as compulsory radio listening at school, foundation of a centralized publishing company for children's books or the removal of Western children's films from distribution.

Compulsory radio listening at school was not enforced until after the nationalization of radio broadcasting in 1948. The Czechoslovak State Radio broadcasting company (Československý státní rozhlas) then started producing special school and pioneer programmes that blended cultural news programmes and fiction genres. In addition, it was important to control the reception of the broadcasting and ensure its correct educational effect. To this end, teachers were supposed to first establish an appropriate mood in the class before the start of the programme. Then, after it ended, they would analyse the content with the class, expand on the information presented in the broadcast and integrate it into the lesson.[13] Schools were also advised to establish their own collections of gramophone records. The cultural service of the Gramophone Company in Prague compiled programmes of records and lent them to schools along with special texts and illustrative slides.[14]

Increasingly rigorous control of production and distribution was also apparent in the realm of literature. Commercial production of entertaining children's books and magazines – a dominant model of children's literature production until then – was explicitly rejected. Educational magazines published lists of books recommended for children. The favoured concept of literary education stabilized after the ratification of the unified school system. Meanwhile, the entire realm of literature moved towards a monopolization of publishing, which was centralized in the State Publisher for Children's Books as of 1950.[15] In addition, specialized theatres for children were founded under the influence of state cultural policy after 1948. The goals set for theatre and literature essentially resembled those in other media disciplines: close connections and mutual influence among teachers and artists, an emphasis on collective reception and a rejection of art as entertainment or an instrument of relaxation.[16]

Such strategies resulted from the assumption that children were passive recipients. The impact of a work on child viewers, whose age and mental predispositions made them more susceptible to accepting harmful messages, was attributed to the artistic mode of production.[17] It was therefore necessary to find methods of disrupting children's passive reception and stimulating their response activity in the proper way. Efforts to make these educational postulates work in a real world were concentrated mainly on schools and educational institutions. The first experimental conceptions of children's film as a genre based on sociological or psychological research were planned shortly after 1945 but never realized. The Pedagogic Research Institute's attempts to influence the production of films for children were quite isolated from the centres of film management and production, which soon began their own production of animated and feature films for children. The scientifically oriented conception of the genre model could not succeed in the new socialist era. After 1948, many scientific disciplines degenerated under the influence of Marxist-Leninist theories. At the same time, the Film and Diapositive Institute was abolished and the Pedagogic Research Institute was transformed.[18]

The Children's Film Genre within the Czech Studio System

Alongside the activities of The Ministry of Education, discussions about the production of children's films were under way within the film studios at this time. The children's film genre had almost no tradition in Czechoslovakia prior to 1945.[19] The nationalization of the Czechoslovak film industry introduced a different situation, yet the new system of production was initially not well suited to systematic production of children's films. The early stage of the nationalized cinema is defined by the collision of highly incompatible artistic, ideological and industrial factors. Although the official reasons for the nationalization were purely artistic, certain production methods showed the industrial essence of the push towards nationalization. Thus, the existing economical, technical and production requirements and restrictions affected both the quality and quantity of the children's films produced at the time.

Animated Films for Children

Immediately after World War II, the production of animated movies came under the auspices of the Czechoslovak Film Institute (Československý filmový ústav, ČSFÚ). Subsequently, three main centres were established under the administration of Short Film (Krátký film, KF). Many animators from the liquidated studio AFIT[20] began to work in the new Prague studio Brothers in T-Shirts (Bratři v triku),[21] founded on 12 May 1945. The production of puppet films, which had begun during the Protectorate, continued in the Zlín studio. Nationalization caused production of cartoon and puppet films to become more regular in Brno. Soon, animated film acquired exceptional status in the Czechoslovak film industry thanks to its success at international film festivals and in foreign export, and the studios and individual filmmakers producing these features consequently gained the official support of Czechoslovak politicians. Karel Zeman, Jiří Trnka and Hermína Týrlová – the three most prominent film animators at the time – became laureates of many state awards and honours. Their films were appreciated not only from the artistic point of view, but also for purely economic reasons.[22]

In this sense, animated production was shaping up to be the 'showcase' of the nationalized cinema. The print media exalted Czech animation's success in international markets and at film festivals as well as the artistic freedom of Czechoslovak filmmakers. The media accounts, however, forbore to reflect on the mechanical nature of production and obscured certain important facts. In 1946, Elmar Klos, the top executive at KF, pointed out that full-length feature films still occupied a prominent position in the minds of both cinema management and film audiences. Animated films, cultural films and newsreels, on the other hand, were inferior in status and unprofitable.[23] The lower reputation of animated film compelled management to seek out strategies that would guarantee profit. The leaders of the studios, well aware of the possibilities for export and trying also to think of other ways to make good use of their work, considered a new line of products focused on younger audiences.[24] This inspired the publication of children's books with drawings and pictures from the films *Zvířátka a Petrovští* (Animals and Bandits, Jiří Trnka, 1946), *Zasadil dědek řepu* (Grandfather Planted a Beet, Jiří Trnka, 1945) and *Vánoční sen* (A Christmas Dream, Karel Zeman, 1945). Czech animators were also to cooperate with foreign film studios, specifically the French film studio Les Gemeaux. A Czech delegation went to Paris in 1946 to discuss the joint film project *Pastýřka a kominíček* (Herdswoman and Chimney Sweep), but the intended coproduction ultimately was not realized.[25] The communist coup d'état in 1948 put an end to such plans for international cooperation for a long time.[26]

Another problem that undoubtedly influenced the struggle for self-sufficiency and profitability was ČSF's strict economic policy. To maximize production and minimize expenses, the management of the nationalized cinema promoted a policy of austerity. Thus, animated film footage was regulated with the aim of enhancing production and lowering costs. The Ministry of Information decided on an aliquot sum[27] for one metre of animated film and also participated in decisions about film budgets. Adherence to the prescribed quotas could be controlled in the pre- or postproduction phase, and even films that implemented the required norms were expected to achieve higher savings.[28] Studio employees, however, sought to avoid these norms and restrictions by submitting budgets for approval only after the start of shooting, or agreeing to a budget reduction for one planned film so that they could then exceed the norms of another selected film.[29] This regulation of expenses could have an important impact on the final appearance of the films, determining, for example, the use of colour versus black-and-white material, a particular artist's availability or the choice of animation technique.

The supremacy of industrial factors played a crucial role in the dissolution of the animation film group in Brno. The group's first duty after being integrated under the ČSFÚ was to finish the film *Pošťácká pohádka* (A Postman's Tale), which had been started before 1945 in Zlín. Overall expenses became too high, however, and the Prague management halted the work because of allegedly unsatisfactory economic results. The next project, *Švandova noc svatojánská* (Švanda's St. John's Night) should have secured the studio's future existence, but once again the Prague management was not satisfied with the economic results and stopped the shooting. The animation film group in Brno was to finish *Pošťácká pohádka* using black-and-white material instead of colour. The additional expenses would have covered laboratory processing, image and sound editing, production of a combined copy and the cost of electricity, but not the filmmakers' salaries. The fulfilment of these guidelines was the last chance to improve the unsatisfactory situation in Brno.[30] Neither *Pošťácká pohádka* nor *Švandova noc svatojánská* was finished, and Otakar Brenten, the chief of the Brno group at the time, was replaced by Jan Fuksa in 1947. Production of cartoon films in Brno came to an end in April 1949, and a new group of puppet film creators, founded under the direction of Václav Zykmund, specialized in the production of puppet films for children until its dissolution in 1952.[31]

Every story idea for an animated film had to be approved by the dramaturgical board. The process for gaining approval, however, was not particularly difficult, and objections were only rather sporadic and related to current affairs or certain ambiguous motives.[32] In general, the approval process for animated films was not as exhaustive and complicated as it was for feature films:

> Story ideas or scripts for animated films did not require eagle-eyed political supervision. Furthermore, if the boards were to discuss a script of a feature film, they would simply read the text on the right side of a page and express their opinions on it. In the case of animated film the scripts were

usually so complicated that nobody could understand the structure. There were occasionally efforts by the ČSF board to influence scripts, but actually almost nobody paid attention to them. The situation for a feature film was much more complicated.[33]

The relative lack of interest in animated films on the part of approval boards – namely State Dramaturgy (Státní dramaturgie) and the Film Council (Filmová rada, FR) – in comparison with feature films existed even beyond the year 1948. Nevertheless, at this time a noticeably stronger emphasis was placed on ideological argumentation during the approval process, such that some authors had to alter 'unsuitable' storylines.[34] Meanwhile, the production plans of animated film studios changed substantially under the influence of the higher authorities.

Complete centralization of film production for children was not achieved until the founding of the Studio for Children's, Cartoon and Puppet Films. However, signs of the move towards centralization became visible after 1948, when changes to film organization transformed production plans and compelled critics to revise their attitude towards the development of Czech animated film. As of January 1948, each division of KF had its own production plan, which was subordinated to the Central Board for the Production of KF. This board's main tasks were to coordinate all the divisions' production and production plans, to approve story ideas and scripts – which were then forwarded to the FR (the central board for film certification and censorship) – and to monitor the ideological and artistic quality of short film production.[35] As of November 1, 1949 animated and puppet films were incorporated with the production of art films. The Prague, Brno and Zlín sections were integrated together into one team under the direction of Jiří Trnka. The title Creative Team for Children's, Cartoon and Puppet Films suggested the future development of the entire animated sector.[36] In addition, previous developments in children's film production were increasingly criticized after 1948. Vladimír Václavík, the executive director of ČSF, declared at the organizational conference in 1948 that animated film – despite its high technical standards – had yet to find correct themes that would really touch and impress Czech audiences. Thus, the production plan was to focus primarily on fairy tales and films such as Karel Zeman's puppet agitprops featuring the character Mr. Prokouk.[37] The official report for the Central Committee of the Communist Party of Czechoslovakia (Ústřední výbor Komunistické strany Československa, ÚV KSČ), which was to evaluate the February events' consequences for ČSF, noted that the content of animated films was problematic and that animated films even displayed the negative traits of so-called formalism.[38]

At the same time, film critics were re-evaluating the state of animated films. Their initial praise was replaced by multiple analyses of the crisis in animated film after 1948. The absence of tradition and experience were perceived as the main reasons for the crisis. Critics complained that filmmakers focused on experimenting with technical and artistic aspects and creating mainly films for adult viewers.[39] Instead, animated film production should focus on the child audience from now on and strive to become a means of education. Even filmmakers themselves were very self-critical in this respect. For example, in 1950 the film magazine *Kino* published a statement by the working collective Brothers in T-Shirts about its future concentration on the 'ideological re-education of children'. According to the statement, the collective had previously paid almost no attention to young viewers but now saw that it was necessary to encourage the development of socialistic qualities from an early age. From now on, fairy tales 'purged of all idealistic connotations of the old society' would have preferred status in their production plans.[40] This implied a return to 'the educational function of art' in the realm of film production, which was now transformed by the momentous events of February 1948.

Thus, animated film studios were forced to produce children's films on the direct orders of the authorities, whose main argument was that children needed to be ideologically re-educated. In 1950, fairy tales became the key element of animated film production. The following table displays the overall Czech animated production of the period, including custom-made films. Children's films are singled out in the second line:

Table 10.1. Czech animated production in the period 1945-1955

	1945	1946	1947	1948	1949	1950	1951	1952	1953	1954	1955
Total Animated Films	2	5	21	18	18	10	16	6	8	11	16
No. of children's films (from this total)		2	2	4	3	5	5	9	4	6	5	7

Source: Data taken from the almanacs by Jiří Havelka: *Československé filmové hospodářství 1945–1950* (Prague: Československý filmový ústav, 1970) and *Československé filmové hospodářství 1951–1955* (Prague: Československý filmový ústav, 1972).

Prior to 1950, it is difficult to distinguish children's films from family films or films focused on adults. Up to that time, fairy tale films, together with comedies and satirical films, were only a small part of the overall production of the Prague and Zlín studios.

Although some films, such as *O makovém koláči* (The Poppy Cake, Zdeněk Miler, 1953), *Pohádka o drakovi* (Fairy Tale about a Dragon, Hermína Týrlová, 1953) or *Pohádka o stromech a větru* (Fairy Tale about the Trees and Wind, Václav Bedřich, 1951),[41] did display explicit ideological motives typical of that period, media reflections enhanced and sometimes even created the educational and ideological function of a film. For example, the explication of the fairy tale film *Hrnečku, vař!* (Cook, Mug, Cook! Václav Bedřich, 1953) in a period journal emphasizes that screenwriter Josef Alois Novotný updated the existing story by adding the figures of a greedy rich farmer and his wife, who steals the magic cup from their servant.[42]

The systematic production of animated and puppet children's film was also intended to satisfy the steady demand for children's programming in movie theatres. In 1947, for example, a critical shortage of films for children under twelve became evident upon the opening of Prague's first movie theatre for children. Film programmes for the youngest audience members had to be supplemented with narrated slide shows due to a lack of suitable motion pictures.[43] We can therefore conclude that the push to increase the production of animated children's films was motivated by both cultural-political and economic factors.

Feature Films for Children

The aforementioned examples from the sphere of animated film production illustrate how industrial, ideological and – to a certain extent – educational stimuli shaped the production and final form of individual short children's films. Feature film production was influenced by the same awkward combination of industrial-economic and artistic-ideological factors that often caused conflict between filmmakers and authorities. Compliance with the regulated ration of film material remained a major problem. Director Jaromír Pleskot recalls the order to extend the length of his film *Obušku, z pytle ven!* (Stick, Start Beating! 1955):

> The original plan was to shoot a medium-length feature film. But the studio had a given norm of shot-metres per year and our chief told us to make the film longer to avoid problems – one of the studio's projects had failed and we needed to get rid of the redundant film material. We were thinking how to make it longer and so the songs for the film were created.[44]

At the same time, filmmakers had to be careful not to exceed the given norms for film material consumption, as this could cause huge problems, particularly for the production of films involving child actors. For example, as the crew of the film *Malý partyzán* (Little Partisan, Pavel Blumenfeld, 1950) explained, their consumption of negative film material was increased because their young actors had almost no experience in movies; consequently, many scenes had to be interrupted and reshot.[45] Fixed average costs presented another distinctive limitation, as in the case of the film *Na dobré stopě* (On the Right Track, Josef Mach, 1948), which was approved only after the expenses for direction, music, sets, insurance and actors were reduced so that the final budget corresponded to the average film budget for the year 1948.[46] However, the budgets of children's films typically did not exceed the average costs for genre films, with the exception of fairy tales and certain spectacular costume features.[47]

The following table displays the total numbers of Czech children's feature films of full and medium length from 1945 to 1955:[48]

Table 10.2. The number of Czech children's feature films in the period 1945-1955

	1945	1946	1947	1948	1949	1950	1951	1952	1953	1954	1955
Children's Feature Films	–	–	–	3	2	1	1	1	2	5	3

Production of children's feature films was clearly sluggish until the Studio for Children's, Cartoon and Puppet Films was created in 1953. This initial stagnation was due primarily to the attitude of the approval boards, which frequently postponed or cancelled the production of children's films due to artistic or ideological concerns. *Zelená knížka* (The Green Notebook, Josef Mach, 1948) is considered the first Czech full-length children's film of the nationalized cinema. However, various story ideas for children's films already existed in production plans before 1948 – for example, the unrealized projects *Bylo nás pět* (There Were Five of Us), *Princezna pampeliška* (Princess Dandelion) or *Zlatý střapec* (The Gold Tassel). Objections to these projects usually cited their poor artistic treatment.[49]

It should be noted that artistic-ideological demands had a much greater impact on the final form of children's feature films than on animated films. Children's feature films were more flexible with regard to the precondition of 'education by art', even after the ideological shifts brought by the events of February 1948. The demand for new themes oriented to contemporary times was closely connected with the way the central cinema apparatus approached feature films, as the approval process differed substantially from that in the animated film sector. In general, much greater significance was attributed to feature films, so the scripts often had to be approved multiple times before the start of production. The case of the feature film *Konec strašidel* (The End of Ghosts, Jiří Slavíček, Jan Matějovský, 1952) illustrates the type of demands put forward by the FR. In the written assessment of the script about a group of young pioneers who help to catch saboteurs, we can find the following ideological objections:

> It is necessary to show more convincingly the educational significance of a pioneer organisation in the script. It should be absolutely clear that the primary obligation of a pioneer is to help his schoolmates and that the work of pioneers is not limited to just collecting scrap paper.... The screenwriter must create an exemplary type of an adult hero, who can serve as a model of proper behaviour and conduct for children.[50]

Scripts that successfully passed the approval process were often adaptations of accepted novels or narratives based on true stories or inspired by actual historical events. The plot had to correspond with a paradigm of realism, as only in this way could adventure or romantic motifs be justified. *Zelená knížka* was based on Václav Řezáč's novel *Poplach v Kovářské uličce* (Alarm at Blacksmith Alley), a fictional story about a group of children during the great economic depression of the 1930s. *Malý partyzán*, an adaptation of the eponymous novel by Václav Vaňátko, tells the story of a boy living in the Nazi-occupied borderlands who makes contact with local partisans. The acclaimed book *Děti velké lásky* (Children of a Great Love) by Alena Bernášková served as the source for *Olověný chléb* (Red Whitsuntide, Jiří Sequens, 1953), which was intended to present a portrait of the life of proletarian children during the First Republic. The executive director Josef Träger confirmed this orientation towards existing novels and present-day themes at a conference on children's and youth literature sponsored by the Union of Czechoslovak writers (Svaz československých spisovatelů) in 1955.[51]

Film critics also helped to shape the paradigm of realism for children's feature films. If a film's realistic motivations were not explicit, the critics sought to justify the presence of unrealistic elements and offer a desirable interpretation. We can notice a distinct effort to suppress fantasy motifs in critical reviews of fairy tale films. For example, one critic wrote that 'the colourful and formally diversified nature of setting and costumes in *Pyšná princezna* (The Proud Princess, Bořivoj Zeman, 1951) are not connected to any particular historical style. We can notice some period gothic elements, but they are intentionally exaggerated in order to create the hyperbolic visual spectacle that is employed to emphasize the decadency of the kingdom.'[52] Even though *Pyšná princezna* was regarded as a success, the film's visual style seemed problematic because the filmmakers had not successfully stressed the Czech nature of the fairy tale setting.[53] In an even more striking example of this kind of interpretation, the romantic, exotic and adventure motives in the film *Cesta do pravěku* (A Journey into the Primeval Times, Karel Zeman, 1955) were almost completely ignored, regarded as merely a means to a better presentation of the film's scientific content. The film, characteristically labelled 'popular science fantasy' or 'educational fantasy', was critically acclaimed for its alleged accuracy with regard to the findings of contemporary palaeontology.[54]

The unilaterally positive critical reception of *Pyšná princezna* and *Cesta do pravěku* was the exception rather than the rule. The unique discussion that appeared in the film magazine *Kino* after the premiere of *Malý partyzán* illustrates the typical attitude to children's feature film at the time: the pedagogue Marie Vaňorná's negative review of the film aroused massive reaction from readers.[55] Some of them defended *Malý partyzán* as a good example of an adventure film, whereas others pointed out its lack of educational function and realism, which was the leading standard for evaluation at the time.[56] Children's feature films generally were not much appreciated by either film critics or the authorities, which may be one of the reasons the genre stagnated during this period.

Children's Films in Theatrical Distribution

One of the main (though rarely openly expressed) reasons behind the interrupted production of many children's feature films was that they were perceived as unprofitable. Elmar Klos saw children's films' inadequate potential for economic exploitation as the main obstacle to their distribution. Young audiences could attend only special school screenings or afternoon screenings at a reduced price.[57] Data on box office grosses of 1957 indicate that full-length children's feature films were not very profitable, undoubtedly also because of the lowered entrance fee.[58] Yet at the same time, some of them achieved solid success as exports, even to capitalist countries.[59] Animated and short children's films were usually assembled into composed programmes or used as a supplement to the screening of a full-length film. Thus the net profit of these films often could not be determined at all, as the films were not separately accounted for when they were screened together with full-length films.[60] Consequently, a substantial lack of available information obscures the distributional profits of children's animated or short-length films. We can therefore only speculate about the extent to which audience attendance and profits (or lack thereof) might have influenced production.

Unlike their production, the distribution of children's films was standardized quite soon. The genre had many possibilities for exploitation within the nationalized networks of theatre distribution. Short and animated films had been a regular part of full-length feature film screenings since the first years of nationalized cinema.[61] The final programming strategy was defined by a regulation issued by the Ministry of Information on 1 January 1948. Each cinema programme had to consist of a newsreel, a short film and a full-length film with an overall length of at least 3,000 metres.[62] Different types of films were combined with varying intentions. The most preferred form for the distribution of children's films, the composed programme, usually consisted of available Czech and Soviet films or films from other socialist countries that could be deliberately interconnected.[63] Another opportunity for the screening of children's films was provided by the network of movie theatres called Time (Čas), which screened only short films.[64] Attendance of children's film programmes was also improved by many specialized film events with a cultural-political function. The increase in such events is particularly apparent after 1948, for example when the Film Festival for Children was incorporated into the Film Festival of Workers (Filmový festival pracujících). Special film events were also held at the beginning of the school year or on the occasion of various public holidays or anniversaries.[65]

The chain of Youth Cinemas (Kina mladých) could have provided the optimal distribution system for children's films, particularly in light of the preconditions of 'education by art'. The first of these cinemas opened in 1947 in Prague, and others soon followed in cities throughout the republic. A report on the reconstruction of cinemas and the planned technical outfitting provides evidence of the educational purpose of this project. In the list of equipment demands for 'the first Youth Cinemas in the history of Europe', we can find, for example, a 16mm projector, a slide projector, a commentator booth, a projecting table in the balcony for teachers, a conference room for teachers and school film offices.⁶⁶ This special outfitting for the Youth Cinema in Prague was an exception meant to present to the public a cinema with opulence. By contrast, the Studio movie theatre in Brno merely changed its name to Youth Cinema and began including children's films in its programme, continuing its screenings for adult audiences. Although the Youth Cinemas remained in operation after 1948, it is symptomatic that they gradually ceased to be mentioned as locations for scientific research and education.

The Studio for Children's, Cartoon and Puppet Films

For a long time, children's animation production and children's feature film production developed independently from each other, even though coordination of their plans would have allowed for a mutually advantageous collaboration of filmmakers and helped to resolve problems related to distribution or material-technical complications in the studios. Although a common platform for production of children's films had been announced in the early 1950s, the Central Administration for Children's, Cartoon and Puppet Films was not founded until 1 October 1953. The individual groups involved in the production of children's feature and animated film in Prague and the collectives of puppet film production in Prague and Zlín were united under this Central Administration, which functioned as a self-governing division of ČSF.⁶⁷ According to its director, Svetozar Vítek, the administration's founding was motivated by the need for a compact unit that could guarantee a material-technical foundation, coordinate production activities and manage film distribution. The Studio for Children's, Cartoon and Puppet Films was intended to produce primarily short and medium-length films that could then be brought together into composed programmes. This strategy seemed advantageous in terms of both distribution and economic efficiency, as the focus on short and medium-length films could minimize expenses and maximize production at the same time. The administration's most important task was to start regular production of children's feature films.⁶⁸

Svetozar Vítek refers to the group as 'a small, unique sanctuary of freedom in production' and remembers that the studio's ability to make decisions quite independently from the 'centre' was a primary factor in the comfortable working conditions.⁶⁹ Of course, all story ideas and scripts approved by the studio's board also had to receive the approval of the FR. Similarly, the studio was obliged to observe all the norms and regulations described in the previous sections. Nevertheless, self-governance had its advantages, one of them being that the studio had a great deal of freedom in selecting its collaborators. For example, one of the film directors employed by the studio was the theatre director Jaromír Pleskot, who had been barred from his profession for political reasons. The studio also supported the production of the film *Dědeček automobil* (Vintage Car, 1956) by Alfréd Radok, who had encountered a great deal of trouble in his previous work for the nationalized cinema. The studio's direction defended Radok's production by arguing that it enriched the genre of sport films.[70] *Dědeček automobil* was one of the last projects the studio realized in 1954.

Both the Studio and and the Central Administration for Children's, Cartoon and Puppet Films ended on 1 June 1955, before they were able to fully demonstrate organizational advantages. The particular reasons for the demise of these institutions are not exactly known. According to Jiří Havelka, the administration's work was not sufficiently effective.[71] Yet, as Svetozar Vítek remembers, Eduard Hofman, who replaced Vítek as studio director, did not maintain the initial course of production.[72] The administration was the last attempt to create a central unit to improve coordination of production plans and film distribution. With its collapse, the initial era of the children's genre also came to an end, at a point when its standardization was nearly accomplished.

After 1956 the production of children's films was centralized in a special production group at Barrandov, and the films were distributed within the network of movie theatres. Although only three children's films were produced in Czechoslovakia in 1956 and 1957, ten were released in 1959. The overall increase in full-length feature film production in the country also manifested itself in the children's genre – children's feature films were also produced in the Zlín film studio and in the film studio Koliba in Bratislava. The new trend of producing a relatively high number of children's films continued into the 1960s, when filmmakers like Ota Hofman, Věra Plívová-Šimková and Josef Pinkava began to concentrate on the genre.[73] Children's animated films represented a stable element in production plans for the animated and puppet film studios in Prague and Zlín. Standardization was further supported by the introduction of special events such as the Film Festival for Children and Youth in Zlín, which first took place in 1961.

Conclusion: The Standardization of the Children's Film Genre in Czechoslovak Cinema

The year 1948 was an important milestone in the standardization and systematic development of the genre of children's film. Its formation during two different historical eras reveals shifts in individual conceptions and competition between these conceptions before and after 1948. The key principle of 'education by art' brought film, radio, literature and the theatre together and revised the modes of their production, distribution and reception. The first postwar conception of the children's film genre was founded on this precondition, but its scientific inclination and economic naivety were incompatible with the situation after 1948, as arranged by the nationalized cinema management and linked with the apparatus of the ÚV KSČ. Up to 1948, we can also observe signs of 'market-oriented' genre formation, especially in the production of animation (which focused on export, utilized marketing synergy and made attempts at international co-production), in which educational aims were often secondary to industrial-economic interests. However, more systematic production of children's animated and feature films coincided with the cultural-political modifications that took place in ČSF after 1948.

The reconstruction of the process of genre formation within the Czechoslovak studio system also suggests several general facts. Most importantly, it reveals the difference between outward presentation and actual work in the studios. The media often stressed the educational potential of children's films or the artistic freedom of filmmakers, but the genre actually took shape under the influence of many internal forces – mostly industrial-economic interventions relating to budgets, regulations on film length and the ideological requirements of approval boards. However, the genre of children's film is quite unique within the context of the Czechoslovak studio system, in part because of the Ministry of Education's interest in these films. This genre's specialness is also due to its heterogeneous character, which incorporates multiple genres, makes use of both feature and animated forms, and has a quite specific distribution system. Nevertheless, the clash of industrial-economic and artistic-ideological factors seen here also significantly influenced the formation and development of other genres in Czechoslovakia.

Lukáš Skupa studied at the Department of Film Studies and Audiovisual Culture, Faculty of Arts, Masaryk University in Brno. In addition to the history of Czech films for children, he has also concerned himself with the conditions of Czech cinema and censorship in the 1960s. He has published in various Czech film journals and magazines including *Iluminace, Cinepur* and *Literární noviny*.

Notes

1. The term 'children's film' includes several different genres (e.g. fairy-tale, detective film or comedy), yet journalistic discourse and dramaturgical plans distinguished children's film as an autonomous generic category. Inspiration for my research on Czech children's film came from Rick Altman's *Film/Genre* (London: British Film Institute, 2000) and his semantic-syntactic-pragmatic approach to film genre as a complex phenomenon. Therefore, I concentrate on the role of spectators, production, distribution and media reflection in determining the emergence of the genre.
2. Ladislav Görlich, *S mládeží k lepší budoucnosti* (Prague: Cíl, 1947); František Stuchlý, *Mládež včera, dnes a zítra* (Prague: Universum, 1947).
3. B. Kujal, 'Dvouletý plán a škola', *Pedagogický průvodce* 2(11) (1946), 1.
4. *Výchova dětí předškolního a školního věku* (Prague: Ministerstvo práce a sociální péče, 1950), pp. 8–9.
5. Jiří Knapík, *Únor a kultura: sovětizace české kultury 1948–1950* (Prague: Libri, 2004), pp. 162–163.
6. 'Organizační statut Výzkumného ústavu pedagogického J. A. Komenského v Praze a jeho pobočky v Brně', *Věstník Ministerstva školství a osvěty* 3(10) (1947), 251–254.
7. 'Ústav pro film a diapozitiv ministerstva školství a osvěty. Vnitřní organizace', *Věstník Ministerstva školství a osvěty* 3(1) (1947), 3–4.
8. František Bulánek, *Výchova mládeže uměním* (Prague: Brázda, 1949), p. 6.
9. Václav Vodák, 'Umělecká výchova', in Anon. (ed.), *Mládež naše budoucnost* (Rokycany: Okresní pedagogický sbor, 1946), p. 33.
10. Milan Skalník, *O dramaturgických problémech divadla pro mládež* (Prague: Karlova univerzita, 1952), p. 26.
11. *Výchova dětí předškolního a školního věku*, p. 24.
12. Věra Brčáková, *Osvětová práce s dětmi: methodické rady, bibliografie článků s anotacemi a další informace* (Prague: Orbis, 1954), p. 6.
13. 'Školský rozhlas. Zavedení relativně povinného poslechu', *Věstník Ministerstva školství a osvěty* 4(17) (1948), 403–404.
14. Brčáková, *Osvětová práce s dětmi*, pp. 16–17.
15. Pavel Janoušek, *Dějiny české literatury 1945–1989*, vol. 2, 1948–1958 (Prague: Academia, 2007), p. 431.
16. Skalník, *O dramaturgických problémech divadla pro mládež*; Oldřich Kryštofek, 'Tři české premiéry Pražského městského divadla pro mládež', *Štěpnice* 4(5) (1951), 206–212.
17. 'Film a jeho nejmenší diváci', *Kino* 6(2) (1951), 38–39.
18. Schools, pioneer houses, children's homes and recreation centres became the only places where the Ministry of Education maintained an influence over the exploitation of film as well as the only sites of any actual coordination with Czechslovak

State Film. Distinctive parallels are evident between the exploitation of film and the strategies for using literature, theatre or radio broadcasting. Teachers were advised to watch the film in advance, prepare a film lecture (to be given before the screening) and think about possible uses for the film in a lesson. For approved films, the Ministry of Education published special lists that teachers could use as inspiration for their treatment of the films.

19. We have only fragmentary information about the production context of the first Czech films for children. They were often individual endeavours involving the director's own production investments. For example, Josef Kokeisl produced several feature fairy tales with educational subtexts at the end of the 1920s. *Kašpárek kouzelníkem* (The Clown Magician, Josef Kokeisl, 1927) promoted the drinking of milk, and *Kašpárek a Budulínek* (The Clown and Budulínek, Josef Kokeisl, 1927) demonstrated proper dental care. Feature films for children became even more marginalized with the transition to sound film. For example, Oldřich Kmínek directed two second-rate fairy tales, *Perníková chaloupka* (The Gingerbread House) and *Sněhurka a sedm trpaslíků* (Snow White and the Seven Dwarfs) in 1933. Animated films for children were shot more systematically under the Nazi Protectorate at studios in Zlín and Prague.

20. The Prague advertising agency AFIT (Ateliér filmových triků) became the Department of Animated Film Production under the management of Prag-Film during the Protectorate. Prag-Film managed to finish only a few animated films, including *Svatba v Korálovém moři* (A Wedding in the Coral Sea), which was released after World War II.

21. The studio's name 'Bratři v triku' is a play on words. On a literal level it translates into English as something like 'brothers in T-shirts'. However, the Czech word 'trik' also suggests animation or special effects, such that the name could also be understood as 'brothers in animation'. Both of these possible interpretations are inherent in the Czech name.

22. E.g. Karel Zeman and Hermína Týrlová received a large financial premium in 1947 for their convincing artistic work and economical results. The Board of Management appreciated that films made primarily for export, such as *Ukolébavka* (Lullaby, Hermína Týrlová, 1947) and *Co jim schází?* (What Is Missing? Hermína Týrlová, 1947), were also suitable for domestic distribution, and that the films of Karel Zeman were also successful abroad. K. Zeman – H. Týrlová – výkonnostní odměna, 7 April 1948, Národní archiv (NA), Prague, fond (f.) 861 – Ministerstvo informací (MI), karton (k.) 209.

23. Elmar Klos, 'Hospodářské a organisační otázky krátkého filmu', *Filmová práce* 2(39) (1946), 2.

24. At the meeting of delegates in July 1947 the director Jaroslav Jílovec spoke about the intention to produce and sell toys or books related to the animated films. Záznam o poradě zplnomocněnců a ředitelů na Barrandově, 4 July 1947, NA, f. MI, k. 206.

25. 'Československo-francouzský kreslený film', *Kino* 1(15) (1946), 238.

26. The first animated international co-production, the Czechoslovak-French film *Stvoření světa* (The Creation of the World, Eduard Hofman, 1957), was not realized until 1957.

27. The sum was set at Kčs 6,000–6,300 per one metre of colour film material in 1948. This coefficient was used in the production of animated films throughout the period. Rozpočty kreslených filmů, 27 July 1948, NA, f. MI, k. 170.

28. E.g. the production of *Atom na rozcestí* (Atom on the Crossroad, Čeněk Duba, 1947) was able to lower its budget by cutting expenses on artistic direction, creative

work and the amount of (both negative and positive) film material used. Rozpočet kresleného barevného filmu 'Atom na rozcestí', 16 April 1947. NA, f. MI, k. 170.

29. E.g. the increased budget and length of the film *Basa tvrdí muziku* (No Music without Bass, Karel Mann, 1948) was justified by its difficult script and the work needed to realize it, but this increase was counterbalanced by lowering budgets for the other planned films *O milionáři, který ukradl slunce* (About the Millionaire Who Stole the Sun, Zdeněk Miler, 1948) and *Vzducholoď a láska* (Airship and Love, Jiří Brdečka, 1948). Budget of the animated film *Basa tvrdí muziku*, 31 July 1947, NA, f. MI, k. 170.
30. Animated films produced by a Brno group *Pošťácká pohádka*, *Švandova noc svatojánská* and *Závodník*, 20 May 1948, NA, f. MI, k. 170.
31. Artuš Černík, *Výroční zpráva o čs. filmovnictví, rok 1949* (Prague: Československý státní film, 1954), pp. 87, 92.
32. Although the state board tasked with evaluating plots and themes from a cultural-political viewpoint approved the movie *Proč sedají ptáci na telegrafní dráty* (Why Do Birds Sit on Wires? Eduard Hofman, 1948) for realization in 1946, it also advised the author 'to avoid certain allegories that could be misinterpreted given the touchy nature of contemporary international diplomacy. We strongly recommend placing more emphasis on dialogues that make clear that the movie is only and purely a fable'. Norbert Frýd: Proč sedají ptáčci na telegrafní dráty. Návrh na filmovou úpravu pohádky, 2 December 1946. NA, f. MI, k. 170.
33. Břetislav Pojar interviewed by the author, March 2009.
34. The short story 'Jak se člověk naučil létat' (How a Man Learned to Fly) by Jiří Brdečka was not approved by Filmová rada because 'it does not explain the mechanics of flying, while focusing instead on strange oddities and mainly on Western inventions'. Usnesení 31. schůze předsednictva Filmové rady, 9 July 1951, NA, f. 19/7 – ÚV KSČ, archivní jednotka (a. j.) 670.
35. Černík, *Výroční zpráva o čs. filmovnictví, rok 1949*, pp. 85–86.
36. Ibid., p. 80.
37. *Zpráva o první celostátní podnikové konferenci Československého státního filmu* (Prague: Československý státní film, 1948), p. 25.
38. Československý státní film, 1949, NA, f. 19/7, a. j. 658.
39. 'Náš kreslený film', *Kino* 3(35) (1948), 651.
40. 'Bratři v triku odpovídají', *Kino* 5(7) (1950), 158.
41. The movies mentioned here deal with themes such as 'work' or 'man's domination of nature'.
42. 'Pohádka Hrnečku, vař! v kresleném filmu', *Filmové informace* 2(38) (1952), 17.
43. Record of the meeting of assistant directors, 8 July 1947, NA, f. MI, k. 205; Record of the meeting of assistant directors, 23 June 1947, NA, f. MI, k. 205.
44. Jaromír Pleskot interviewed by the author, August 2008.
45. Barrandov Studio a. s., archive (BSA), Prague, sbírka Scénáře a produkční dokumenty – *Malý Partyzán*, The final account of the film Malý Partyzán – no. 10009, undated.
46. Record of the meeting of assistant directors, 8 July 1947, NA, f. MI, k. 205; Record of the meeting of assistand director, 23 June 1947, NA, f. MI, k. 205.
47. Jiří Havelka, *Československé filmové hospodářství 1951–1955* (Prague: Československý filmový ústav, 1972), pp. 88–89.
48. Data taken from almanacs by Jiří Havelka: *Československé filmové hospodářství 1945–1950* (Prague: Československý filmový ústav, 1972) and *Československé filmové hospodářství 1951–1955* (Prague: Československý filmový ústav, 1972).

49. Zprávy výroby o nezpracovaných námětech, 5 December 1947, NA, f. MI, k. 208.
50. Usnesení 8. schůze pléna Filmové rady, 2 July 1951, NA, f. ÚV KSČ, a. j. 670.
51. Josef Träger, 'Spisovatelé pro naši mládež a dětský film', *Kino* 10(24) (1955), 382–383.
52. 'Rozsáhlé pohádkové stavby pro film O pyšné princezně', *Filmové informace* 2(51) (1951), 17.
53. Za vysokou ideovou a uměleckou úroveň československého filmu, April 1954, BSA, f. Barrandov – historie, k. 1954/2.
54. 'Nová forma popularisace vědy', *Filmové informace* 6(20) (1955), 7–8.
55. Marie Vaňorná, 'Malý partyzán', *Kino* 6(20) (1951), 482.
56. 'Stránka našich dopisovatelů – diskutujeme o filmu pro mládež', *Kino* 6(22) (1951), 534–535.
57. Elmar Klos, 'Byl jednou jeden dětský film', *Kino* 4(6) (1949), 67.
58. Zpráva o provedených a připravovaných opatřeních za účelem zhospodárnění a dalšího rozvoje československé kinematografie, 5 June 1958, NA, f. Ministerstvo školství a kultury, k. 1089a.
59. The most exportable children's feature films of the period were *Cesta do pravěku* (71 export markets), *Pyšná princezna* (36 export markets) and *Dobrodružství na Zlaté zátoce* (The Adventure in the Golden Bay, Břetislav Pojar, 1955; 27 export markets). No other feature films from the period 1945–1955 gained even ten export markets. Československý hraný film pro děti – údaje a čísla, 1980, Marcela Pittermannová's private archive.
60. Hospodářská data, týkající se filmů K. Zemana, 2 December 1948, NA, f. MI, k. 170.
61. Milan Noháč, 'Bilance kresleného filmu', *Filmová práce* 2(3) (1946), 3.
62. Hospodářský plán, 19 December 1947, NA, f. MI, k. 170.
63. According to the statistics, 60 Soviet, 29 Czech, 5 American and 2 British film programmes for children were presented in Czechoslovak movie theatres from 1945 to 1950. See Havelka, *Československé filmové hospodářství 1945–1950*, p. 202. From 1951 to 1955 there were 45 Soviet programmes, 30 Czech, 5 German, 3 Polish, 2 Chinese, 1 Korean, 1 Hungarian and 1 British programme. Havelka, *Československé filmové hospodářství 1951–1955*, p. 297.
64. Havelka, *Československé filmové hospodářství 1945–1950*, p. 224.
65. 'Dětské filmové festivaly', *Filmová práce* 1(8–9) (1954), 121.
66. Zpráva o průběhu prací, spojených s úpravou Komorního kina v Klimentské ulici na Kino mladých, undated, NA, f. MI, k. 198.
67. 'Prozatímní statut Správy studií dětského, kresleného a loutkového filmu', *Věstník Československého státního filmu* 7(9–10) (1953), 37–38.
68. Letter written by Svetozar Vítek to Marcela Pittermannová, undated, private archive of Marcela Pittermannová.
69. Letter written by Svetozar Vítek to Marcela Pittermannová, undated, Private archive of Marcela Pittermannová.
70. Letter written by Josefa Träger to the Ministry of Culture, 20 April 1955, NA, f. Ministerstvo kultury, k. 141.
71. Havelka, *Československé filmové hospodářství 1951–1955*, p. 108.
72. Eva Strusková, 'Knihu džunglí jsem nenapsal. Rozhovor se Svetozarem Vítkem', *Iluminace* 12(4) (2001), 121–133.
73. Československý hraný film pro děti – údaje a čísla, 1980, Marcela Pittermannová's private archive.

Select Bibliography

Altman, Rick. *Film/Genre*. London: British Film Institute, 2000.
Černík, Artuš. *Výroční zpráva o čs. filmovnictví, rok 1949*. Prague: Československý státní film, 1954.
Havelka, Jiří. *Československé filmové hospodářství 1945–1950*. Prague: Československý filmový ústav, 1970.
Havelka, Jiří. *Československé filmové hospodářství 1951–1955*. Prague: Československý filmový ústav, 1972.
Janoušek, Pavel. *Dějiny české literatury 1945–1989*, vol. 2, *1948–1958*. Prague: Academia, 2007.
Knapík, Jiří. *Únor a kultura: sovětizace české kultury 1948–1950*. Prague: Libri, 2004.

PART V

FILM FESTIVALS

Chapter 11

DECREED OPEN-MINDEDNESS

The Leipzig Documentary and Short Film Festival in the 1960s as an Example of the Self-Representation of the East German State

Andreas Kötzing

The cultural policy of the Socialist Unity Party of Germany (Sozialistische Einheitspartei Deutschlands, SED) was a primary factor in the history of East German film production from its very beginning. The entire film production process, from the first version of the screenplay to the approval of the finished film and its premiere in cinemas, was state-controlled. Throughout this process the SED pursued one basic goal: films should spread communist ideology and inspire the audience as much as possible to build a socialist society in East Germany. Beyond these propagandistic motives, though, several other important concerns influenced SED film policy. At times, the SED temporarily tolerated the production and screening of dissident films and granted more artistic freedom to filmmakers in order to present East German society in a maximally liberal light to Western audiences. With this 'decreed open-mindedness' the SED hoped to improve East Germany's reputation and secure international acceptance of the state. Often, these liberal episodes were cancelled after a few years. The rich example of the history of the International Leipzig Film Festival in the 1960s lends itself to analysis of the ambivalent tendencies of SED film policy.

The Origins of the Leipzig Festival

The International Leipzig Festival for Documentary and Animated Film is one of today's most important European film festivals. Founded in 1955 under the name Leipzig Cultural and Documentary Film Week (Leipziger Kultur- und Dokumentarfilmwoche), the festival was modelled on similar events in Mannheim and Oberhausen, where cultural film weeks had taken place on a regular basis since 1952 and 1954 respectively. However, compared to its West German counterparts, the Leipzig Festival, which had been founded by the East German Filmmakers' Club (Club der Filmschaffenden der DDR), started out with a different focus: it was designed exclusively for an all-German film exchange.[1] The all-German approach of the film week was reflected in several aspects. The jury, for example, was made up of East German and West German representatives in equal measure, and during the festival's programme, films produced by the East German state-owned film company DEFA (Deutsche Film-Aktiengesellschaft) were shown alongside West German productions.[2]

The film week enjoyed very a positive reception from all participating West and East German directors, since outside of events like this there was hardly any opportunity for exchange with colleagues from the respective other part of Germany. Discussions about artistic matters, possible co-productions or cooperation with the festivals in Mannheim or Oberhausen were at the centre of attention as often as debates about the political situation in Germany. The press assessed the artistic standard of the films shown in Leipzig rather critically, however. For example, the film journalist Ludwig Thomé described the first Leipzig film week as a bitter test of the audience's nerves and patience. Apart from Heinz Sielmann's nature documentary *Zimmerleute des Waldes* (Carpenters of the Forest, 1954) and some somewhat excellent, in his opinion, silhouette and puppet films from East Germany that he highlighted as exemplary, Thomé wrote that one would not wish upon one's worst enemy the torture of the all-German mediocre or even substandard offerings assembled in Leipzig.[3] The quality of the films decreased even further the following year, so much so that the jury opted not to award some of the designated prizes. Instead, a group of journalists presented 'awards' of their own called 'Gesamtdeutsche Gartenzwerge' (All-German Garden Gnomes) of the first, second and third degree for the worst films.[4]

In the following three years, no film festival was held in Leipzig. According to the records of the former festival organizers, there were several reasons for this, such as the low quality of the available films and the negative press response after the Second Leipzig Cultural and Documentary Film Week. Furthermore, a significant reorientation in the cultural policy of East Germany's leading SED party was a crucial factor in the Leipzig Festival's inability to continue in its original form. After a short, comparatively tolerant phase in which many artists and intellectuals were granted certain freedoms, the SED's regulation of those involved in culture and arts intensified once again in 1957.[5] In October of that year, a comprehensive *Kulturkonferenz* harshly condemned the allegedly 'decadent' and 'revisionist' developments in the cultural sector. During a separate feature film conference in July 1958, high-ranking SED politicians criticized various DEFA productions and demanded that principles of 'socialist realism' be the sole guidelines for future film production.[6] The denunciation of people involved in culture and the arts continued only a few days after the feature film conference when the SED, during its Fifth Party Conference (from 10 to 16 July 1958), distanced itself significantly from the previous 'all-German' approach in the cultural sphere. At the party conference, Alfred Kurella, leader of the Culture Committee in the SED Central Committee's Politburo since 1957, criticized the Ministry of Culture because, according to him, it had become dominated by the wrong perspective – a conservative (literally: a 'maintaining') concept of German culture and its future. Kurella specifically referred to events of an all-German nature during which representatives of the German Democratic Republic had supported an 'all-German culture' without sufficiently reflecting on the differences between East Germany and West Germany.[7] Against the backdrop of these political developments, the abandonment of the all-German concept of the Leipzig Festival comes as no surprise.

The New Conception in the Context of the Construction of the Berlin Wall

The third Leipzig Festival, held after a three-year break under the title Leipziger Dokumentar- und Kurzfilmwoche (Leipzig Documentary and Short Film Week), featured international participation for the first time. The festival's new name and the participation of foreign directors were not the only changes, however. In place of the former dialogue between East and West, there was a systematic dissociation with West Germany. This can be seen, for example, in the inclusion of films condemning the hand that West German politicians had had in Nazi crimes or generally characterizing West Germany as a fascist state, such as *Ein Tagebuch für Anne Frank* (A Diary for Anne Frank, Joachim Hellwig, 1958) and *Aktion J* (Action J, Walter Heynowski, 1960), which were awarded the festival's main prize in 1960 and 1961 respectively.

The polemical dissociation from West Germany was reflected not only in the film programme but also in various other events during the festival. In 1961, for example, the Culture Department of the SED Central Committee instructed festival director Wolfgang Kernicke to establish a panel of foreign delegates during the film week, on which the representatives of various states would discuss 'the East German government's opinion on the necessity of a peace treaty and the conversion of West Berlin into a demilitarised free city'.[8] This initiative was advanced against a background of recent demands by the Soviet government under Khrushchev that West Berlin be turned into a 'free city', which the Soviets hoped to negotiate at a new peace conference with the Western Allies.[9] This 'forum' discussion took place at the Ring-Café in Leipzig on 16 November 1961. Among the participants were Deputy Foreign Secretary of East Germany Paul Wandel and the mayor of Leipzig, Walter Kresse. Wandel took advantage of the podium to denounce West Germany as the 'Hauptkriegsherd in Europa' (the main point of origin of war in Europe) and to evoke the threat of war: 'the militarists and revanchists from Bonn have a fully developed base at their disposal as we speak, enabling them to initiate serious provocations that, following the adventurous and dangerous desires and declarations of aggressive forces in West Germany and West Berlin, include the ultimate risk, i.e. a nuclear world war'.[10]

This ideologically motivated dissociation from West Germany was closely linked to the objective of making political and social conditions in East Germany appear as positive as possible. As early as 1960, an official decree stated with regard to the Leipzig Festival that the film week should be used to offer foreign participants 'insight into the successful establishment of Socialism in East Germany',[11] in order to improve 'the international reputation of the first German workers' and farmers' state'.[12] This objective became even more significant after the construction of the Berlin Wall on 13 August 1961. The SED now increased its efforts to present East Germany as a peaceable, open-minded state so as to conceal the repressive and restrictive characteristics of its ruling system and force the state's international acceptance. A cultural event such as the Leipzig Film Festival, which at this point was attracting numerous foreign guests, seemed predestined to help achieve these goals. Accordingly, Deputy Minister of Culture Hans

Rodenberg, who also headed the Association of State-Owned Film Enterprises (Vereinigung Volkseigener Betriebe Film) at the Ministry of Culture, declared the international and national consolidation of the German Democratic Republic's sovereignty to be a central focus of the film week. For example, he recommended that the festival's organizational committee include 'an artistically convincing documentary film about the measures implemented by the party and the government since August 13th, 1961'[13] and speed up 'the completion of films that present the international community with a convincing image of Socialist development in East Germany'.[14] It remains unclear whether Rodenberg actually thought film projects like these could be realized in such a short period of time. In any case, his statement is indicative of the political expectations of the festival immediately after construction of the Wall.

The SED's instrumentalization of the Leipzig Film Festival in the context of cultural policy remained a distinctive feature in the film week's further development in the 1960s. In this regard the party leadership operated on the assumption that the festival could be utilized to influence the political views of the participants. A consideration of the political goals set for the festival at the time makes evident how far-reaching these notions were. These goals were put in writing for the first time in a comprehensive conceptual document submitted to the SED Central Committee in May 1964 and officially approved that July, after some minor additions. Among other things, the document tasked the festival's management with acquiring for competition as many films as possible that would communicate a complete image of the 'peaceful life of the world's people, about the development of the Socialist countries as well as their fight for peace, and social and political liberation, at a high artistic standard'.[15] Moreover, films from 'young national states' were to be a focus of the festival as long as they dealt with 'problems of overcoming the colonialist legacy and of developing a national economy and culture'.[16]

Most remarkably, the concept described in the document indicated that 'dogmatic limitations' were to be avoided in the selection of films. That is, showing films with different ideological views was explicitly allowed, as long as films based upon Marxist ideology predominated. The jury was to exercise similar 'openness' in awarding prizes. While the principle here was the predominance of socialist countries, it was also to be taken into consideration that films based on Marxist ideology were not the only ones worthy of awards. However, this pluralistic approach was in no way an expression of an essentially liberal festival policy. Rather, it was an integral part of a larger cultural policy concept that aimed to propagate East Germany's supposed 'open-mindedness'. In this context, the conceptual document stated, the focus of the festival was to be 'the aggressive representation of our politics.... The Festival must contribute to enhancing East Germany's international recognition and the effectiveness of its foreign policy'.[17] The presentation of films that were not limited to one-sided political propaganda was seen as a suitable means to achieve this, as it was the most effective way to show participants, particularly those from Western Europe, that East Germany was not a state that systematically suppressed freedom of thought.

An overview of the Leipzig festival's development during the first half of the 1960s makes it very apparent that even in the period immediately after construction of the Wall, international interest in the festival grew rapidly while the Documentary Film Week developed into a solid point of attraction for filmmakers from all continents. As early as 1963, Chris Marker caused a sensation at the festival with his essay-film *Le jolie Mai/Der schöne Mai* (The Lovely Month of May, 1963), a multi-faceted portrait of Paris consisting of images recorded spontaneously as well as snippets of conversation and narrated text (the French original was narrated by Simone Signoret). Marker, who appears in the film as an interviewer, presented the film for discussion at the Fourth Documentary and Short Film Week and in so doing brought *Cinéma Vérité* to Leipzig. This documentary film style, established in France in the 1960s, discouraged staged or re-enacted scenes as well as explanatory off-comments by the director. The aim was instead to capture the everyday life of the subjects as directly as possible, allowing the filmmakers to take advantage of a much easier technique that facilitated spontaneous shooting and simultaneous recording of image and sound.[18] Marker's film was awarded the Goldene Taube – the main prize of the festival – and impressed not only the participating young DEFA directors but also many East German journalists who were encountering this new form of documentary for the very first time.[19]

Two years later Mikhail Romm's famous film *Obyknovennyy fashizm/Der gewöhnliche Faschismus* (Triumph over Violence, 1965), a comprehensive documentary about National Socialism, achieved similar success. The Soviet film distinguished itself mainly through Romm's laconic commentary, which questioned the propagandistic images from the National Socialist era and pushed audiences to form their own opinion. This differentiated the film from other socialist countries' documentaries about the era of National Socialism, which typically just sought to create a visual document of a prefabricated interpretation. The openness of Romm's film, which received the special prize of the jury, prompted several unofficial discussions in Leipzig about whether the analysis of dictatorship, for which Romm used National Socialism as an example, could be applied to other dictatorships as well – for instance, the Soviet Union or even East Germany itself.[20]

These two film examples illustrate the special character of the Leipzig festivals during this period. This exceptionality, which contributed greatly to the international renown of the Documentary Film Week, attracted filmmakers from East and West equally – in 1964, Henry Storck, John Grierson, Ivor Montague, Joris Ivens, Dusan Vukotić, Santiago Alvarez, Basil Wright, Richard Leacock, Alberto Calvacanti, Paul Rotha and Bert Haanstra, among many others, came to Leipzig. The presence of these figures gave the Documentary Film Week a unique international flair. In 1963 the number of countries sending films to Leipzig increased to over fifty. According to official data, more than 65,000 people visited the festival in the mid-1960s, making it one of the largest annual cultural events in East Germany.[21]

Ideological Tightening in the Context of the 'Kahlschlag-Plenum'

Despite its party orientation, the political profile of the Leipzig Film Week was controversial at the time. For individual members of the festival staff and some responsible officials from the Ministry of Culture and the SED Central Committee, the propagation of socialist ideology did not go far enough. The opening of the festival to Western states, which had made showing films like *Le Jolie Mai* possible in the first place, caused some disagreement. Wolfgang Kernicke and other members of the East German Filmmakers' Club – among them Werner Rose, who maintained an abundance of contacts with Western states including West Germany – advocated an East German festival that continued to be as open as possible. The predominance of socialist ideology was to be maintained without exhausting itself in superficial propaganda. In contrast, another group that included Andrew Thorndike, Joachim Hellwig and Walter Heynowski, criticized festival policy and demanded that films not conforming to socialist ideology be turned down on principle.[22]

The dispute ended in a significant ideological tightening that started as early as 1964 and intensified continuously throughout the following years.[23] In 1965, for example, the 'Freie Forum', an open platform for discussion that had been accessible for participation by all Festival guests in the previous years, was replaced by a prepared panel discussion.[24] Parallel to this, a 'philosophical debate' took place by order of the Ministry of Culture in agreement with the SED Central Committee. Ultimately, it served as a pseudo-academic platform for propagation of the SED's cultural policy. In addition, 1965 was the first year that the Ministry of Culture acted as the official host of the Documentary and Short Film Week, along with the East German Filmmakers' Club and the East German TV broadcaster Deutscher Fernsehfunk. This added to the festival's outward appearance of close alignment with the government. Political regulation was not only noticeable in the structure of the festival programme but also affected the selection of films. From 1965 on, the work of the selection committee, an independent board responsible for viewing the films sent to Leipzig, was regulated by a separate statute that had to be confirmed by the hosts of the event.[25] In the following years, the criteria for film selection were increasingly oriented towards the SED's cultural policy.[26] Accordingly, in 1967 for example, the selection committee guidelines proclaimed prior to the Tenth Documentary and Short Film Festival that the selection of films must support the reputation and the attractiveness of the tenth-anniversary festival in Leipzig:

> It must strengthen Leipzig's standing in that it is *the* festival of documentary and short films as well as of TV journalism. Its films must be seen to promote peace, social progress, national independence, humanism and international solidarity. They must document the superiority of a socialist society convincingly, and reveal the inhumanity of imperialist aggressors and the various consequences of government-monopolistic capitalism in a fierce manner and with clear conviction.[27]

The ideologically overloaded criteria for film selection predetermined a one-sided political ideology to be promoted in the context of the Leipzig Festival. Films dealing critically with social and political problems in socialist states were not suitable for the programme; neither were films showing a differentiated image of Western states that did not reduce them to buzzwords such as 'imperialism', 'neo-Nazism', 'psychological warfare' and 'brutalization of the human being'. This became abundantly clear on the one hand in the strong concentration on the Vietnam War, which became a focus of the Leipzig festival, and on the other hand in the large number of films that were not admitted to the festival for political reasons. In 1966, for instance, numerous films from Western countries were disallowed because, it was claimed, their objectivistic point of view facilitated historical and social falsehoods.[28]

The political interventions that started in 1964 and resulted in the Leipzig festival becoming more and more ideologized must be viewed in direct relation to the new general orientation of the SED's cultural policy, as determined at the Eleventh Plenum of the SED Central Committee in December 1965. Because of its severe interventions, the plenum is often called the 'Kahlschlag-Plenum' (plenum of clearcutting).[29] The speeches and presentations of the Eleventh Plenum did not at first deal with cultural policy but rather with economic decisions regarding the establishment of a new system of planning and leadership that was to make the existing centrally planned economy more flexible by partially reducing centralized control.[30] Beyond this, however, the plenum also evoked the Western threat, deeming the cultural influence of West Germany and other capitalist states as particularly responsible for 'decadent' phenomena in East German culture. This criticism was simultaneously levelled against intellectuals and writers, specifically Wolf Biermann, Stefan Heym and Robert Havemann, and even more so against numerous filmmakers who were publicly rebuked because their films failed to toe the political line. Twelve feature films in total – nearly a whole year's production of DEFA films – were either banned or halted in mid-production in the wake of the plenum. DEFA never managed to recover fully from the *Kahlschlag*'s serious effects on the East German film industry.[31]

Example: DEFA Films

The specific effects of the *Kahlschlag* political interventions on East Germany's self-representation in the context of the festival become evident upon consideration of individual DEFA productions shown in Leipzig before and after the debate about the political orientation of the film week. Apart from the aforementioned propagandistic aspects reflected in numerous films opposing West German politics, the Leipzig festival became a platform for a new, younger generation of DEFA directors from the documentary studio in the years after construction of the Wall. In 1962, for example, two DEFA films in the festival programme – *Ofenbauer* (Stove Fitters, Jürgen Böttcher, 1962) and *Nach einem Jahr* (After a Year, Winfried Junge, 1962) – were both remarkable for their efforts to take a more differentiated look at everyday life in East Germany. Böttcher showed, reportage-style, how a 2,000-ton blast furnace was moved a few metres in a state-owned company in Eisenhüttenstadt. He used this procedure, which was itself purely technical, as a detailed study of the impact of hard labour on workers: close-ups of strained faces and worn hands visualized the energy-sapping labour of the furnace builders. Clearly inspired by the *Cinema Vérité* style, Böttcher managed to realize the film using only original sound recorded on-site.[32] Winfried Junge's *Nach einem Jahr* was impressive not so much because of its visual elements, but rather because of its authentic approach. Following *Wenn ich erst zur Schule geh* (When I Finally Go to School, Winfried Junge, 1961), this was the second part of a documentary about a group of children from the small town of Golzow in the Brandenburg region, whose journey in life was to be documented by a series of films. Originally planned as a report on a new generation growing up in a socialist state, the project developed into a long-term documentary unique in the international history of film. Winfried Junge continued the project with his wife Barbara even beyond the turning point of 1989/90.[33]

Both *Ofenbauer* and *Nach einem Jahr* were awarded the 'Silberne Taube' at the Fifth Documentary and Short Film Week in Leipzig. This success was noted both in East Germany and abroad, especially because the films differed significantly from the dogmatic commissioned productions. The situation changed the following years, however. Jürgen Böttcher had completed his new film *Barfuß und ohne Hut* (Barefoot and Hatless, 1964), which the DEFA documentary studio vigorously recommended for the Leipzig festival.[34] Nevertheless, this film about several young people revelling in their summer holiday on the Baltic coast was not approved for screening in East Germany and did not receive permission to be shown in Leipzig, either.[35] That same year, *Deutschland – Endstation Ost* (Germany – Terminus East, Frans Buyens, 1964), another DEFA documentary film that the documentary studio had recommended for the Leipzig film week – became a source of debate. Belgian director Frans Buyens had completed the film under the commission of DEFA.[36] The documentary studio recommended *Deutschland – Endstation Ost* based on the opinion that it presented an objective image of the republic without embellishment and without omitting criticism. The studio hoped the film would engage sympathy for the republic even among those who had previously opposed it due to a lack of knowledge. The film was supposed to be shown on the opening night of the Leipzig Festival, as it promised to be a good prelude 'not just because of the depth and openness of its content, but also from an artistic point of view'.[37]

The film was indeed extraordinarily unreserved: among other things, it permitted citizens of East Berlin to openly state their opinions about the Wall and the division of the city. For example, on being asked whose fault it was that the Wall had been built, one woman replied: 'Well, you know, it's never just one person's fault. I'm telling you as it is, but what else can I say. No need for further comment. I hope you don't cut what I've said here.' In addition, Buyens interviewed members of the East German border police about the official firing order and asked whether they would really shoot at people attempting to escape, if it came to that. The film also featured a number of discussions among workers and students about the development of East Germany. Buyens showed these discussions uncut, even when the interviewees expressed dissatisfaction or lamented the inability to travel freely outside their country. Despite these critical voices, the film was after all clearly a plea in favour of continued socialism in East Germany. The political system was not questioned and optimistic voices predominated, thus creating the image of a country still being constructed and still facing many problems, but also possessing citizens who continued to believe in a positive future for their state.[38]

Buyens' film had been made with the energetic support of Günter Witt, head of the main administration in the Film Department of the Ministry of Culture, as well as that of Werner Lamberz, head of the Department for Foreign Information in the SED Central Committee. In the end, though, its planned screening at the launch of the Leipzig Festival did not take place because the debate the film had spawned within the SED Central Committee resulted in *Deutschland – Endstation Ost* being removed from the opening night. At most, the film could still be part of the festival's framework programme, but ideally it should not be shown at all, if possible. Only when Buyens personally travelled to Leipzig, vigorously protested against the decision to abolish the film and further threatened to make the debate public was an ad hoc screening organized for the second-to-last day of the festival. The film was supposed to open in cinemas in May 1965 but was ultimately disallowed shortly after the festival. It was not screened again in East Germany after that, except at a few nonpublic events.

The handling of films such as *Barfuß und ohne Hut* and *Deutschland – Endstation Ost* illustrates an ideological tightening in the DEFA documentary department even prior to the 'Kahlschlag-Plenum'. The Leipzig festival's inability to evade this development becomes particularly apparent upon examination of the DEFA films shown in place of these productions in 1964. On the opening night, part of a comprehensive

East German retrospective – initially scheduled to be screened during the festival to commemorate the fifteenth anniversary of East Germany's founding – was brought forward on short notice. Also at the Seventh Documentary and Short Film Week, the DEFA production *Drei Tage im Mai* (Three Days in May, Heinz Müller et al., 1964), a commissioned ideological documentary about the Deutschlandtreffen der Jugend, a youth festival arranged by the youth organization Free German Youth (Freie Deutsche Jugend) that was to take place in Berlin, was put forward for the festival competition.[39] This film conformed fully to state propaganda and was hardly suited to improving the East German state's international reputation as the official conception of the festival had intended.

Conclusion

The Leipzig Documentary and Short Film Week was the largest and most important film festival in East Germany. Founded in 1955, it was styled as an all-German film week in its first two years. However, this original conception of the festival was dropped after the orientation of cultural policy shifted, turning away from any 'all-German' approaches. After a three-year break, the festival was again held in 1960, this time as an International Film Week under a new political-ideological orientation. Subsequently, the festival took the shape of an 'anti-imperialist' film week.

One of the most important tasks set for the Leipzig festival in the 1960s was to represent East Germany as positively as possible. Particularly when it came to international recognition of the East German state, the SED misappropriated the film week for political purposes. In the context of the construction of the Berlin Wall, which sparked numerous international protests, making East Germany appear to be a pluralistic and peaceful state became a central objective. The conceptual document approved by the SED Central Committee explicitly intended not only to present films that conformed to the SED ideology, but to also allow different opinions, as long as they did not fundamentally question the socialist view of the world. This instrumentalization of the festival in the context of cultural policy – a process here termed *decreed open-mindedness* – contributed to the festival's international success.

The new orientation of the SED's cultural policy in the context of the 'Kahlschlag-Plenum', however, led to an ideological tightening reflected in many areas of the festival, such as in the politically motivated interventions regarding film selection and in the propagandistic panel discussions that promoted official SED policy. The festival's increasing ideologization also affected East Germany's practice of self-representation through the festival: DEFA films that displayed new artistic approaches or critically questioned social developments in East Germany, such as *Barfuß und ohne Hut* or *Deutschland – Endstation Ost*, could not be shown at the festival at all or were 'hidden' within the programme, despite the original intention to present them prominently at the festival. At the time of the 'Kahlschlag-Plenum', there was no space for critical opinions about East Germany's development – even those uttered with purely constructive intentions.

Translation: Wiebke Düwel (Limerick, Ireland)

Andreas Kötzing studied history and cultural sciences at the University of Leipzig (1998–2004) and worked as a research fellow at the Federal Agency for Civic Education in Bonn (2005–2006). In the period 2007–2008, he served as a research fellow at the Hans-Böckler-Foundation in Düsseldorf. From 2008 to 2012 he received Ph.D. research funding from the German National Academic Foundation. Since 2013 he has worked as a research fellow at the Hannah Arendt Institute in Dresden.

Notes

1. See Caroline Moine, Cinéma et guerre froide: Histoire du festival de films documentaires de Leipzig (Paris: Publications de la Sorbonne, 2014); see also Christiane Mückenberger, 'Fenster zur Welt. Zur Geschichte der Leipziger Dokumentar- und Kurzfilmwoche', in Günter Jordan and Ralf Schenk (eds), *Schwarzweiß und Farbe. DEFA- Dokumentarfilme 1946–92* (Berlin: Jovis, 2000), pp. 364–381.
2. International films from countries such as France or Czechoslovakia were first presented in 1956. However, these ran outside of the official competition.
3. Ludwig Thomé, 'Gesamtdeutsches Kurzfilm-Einerlei. Zur 1. Kultur- und Dokumentarfilmwoche in Leipzig', *Frankfurter Rundschau*, 28 September 1955, p. 9.
4. See Ralf Schenk, 'Von Gartenzwergen und Schulversagern', in Ralf Schenk (ed.) *Bilder einer gespaltenen Welt. 50 Jahre Dokumentar- und Animationsfilmfestival Leipzig* (Berlin: Bertz + Fischer, 2007), pp. 12–15.
5. See Manfred Jäger, *Kultur und Politik in der DDR. 1945–1990* (Cologne: Edition Deutschland-Archiv, 1994), p. 82ff.
6. See Dagmar Schittly, *Zwischen Regie und Regime. Die Filmpolitik der SED im Spiegel der DEFA-Produktionen* (Berlin: Christoph Links, 2002), p. 85ff.
7. Kurella's speech is published in Elimar Schubbe (ed.), *Dokumente zur Kunst-, Literatur und Kulturpolitik der SED*, vol. 1, *1946–1970* (Stuttgart: Seewald, 1972), pp. 536–538.
8. Wolfgang Kernicke, 'Protokoll der 5. Sitzung des Organisationskomitees der IV. Internationalen Leipziger Dokumentar- und Kurzfilmwoche', Berlin, 16 September

1961, Stiftung Archiv der Parteien und Massenorganisationen der DDR im Bundesarchiv Berlin (SAPMO-BArch), SED, DY 30/IV 2/9.06/229, pp. 16–18, here p. 17.
9. Hermann Wentker, *Außenpolitik in engen Grenzen. Die DDR im internationalen System. 1949–1989* (Munich: Oldenbourg, 2007), p. 212ff.
10. N.N., 'Reges Internationales Forum', *Leipziger Volkszeitung*, 17 November 1961, p. 4.
11. 'Beschluss über die III. Leipziger Kurz- und Dokumentarfilmwoche', Bundesarchiv Berlin (BArch), Ministerium für Kultur, DR 1/4171.
12. Ibid.
13. Wolfgang Kernicke, 'Protokoll der 5. Sitzung des Organisationskomitees der IV. Internationalen Leipziger Dokumentar- und Kurzfilmwoche', Berlin, 16 September 1961, SAPMO-BArch, DY 30/IV 2/9.06/229, pp. 16–19, here p. 18.
14. Ibid.
15. 'Konzeption der Leipziger Dokumentar- und Kurzfilmwoche, Anlage Nr. 9 zum Protokoll der Sitzung des Sekretariats des ZK der SED', 22 July 1964, SAPMO-BArch, DY 30/J IV/2/3/995, pp. 40–50, here p. 41.
16. Ibid.
17. Ibid., pp. 42–43.
18. Wilhelm Roth, *Der Dokumentarfilm seit 1960* (Munich and Lucerne: Bucher, 1982), p. 8ff.
19. Fred Gehler, 'Viel zu viel *Le joli Mai*', in Schenk, *Bilder einer gespaltenen Welt*, pp. 31–35.
20. See Wilhelm Roth, 'Ein Meilenstein: Der gewöhnliche Faschismus', in Schenk, *Bilder einer gespaltenen Welt*, pp. 40–43. See also the documents and letters about the reception of the film in Leipzig published by Maja Turowskaja in Wolfgang Beilenhoff and Sabine Hänsgen (eds), *Der gewöhnliche Faschismus. Ein Werkbuch zum Film von Michail Romm* (Berlin: Vorwerk, 2009).
21. The mentioned numbers must be viewed critically, however. Several sources provide evidence that the number of participating countries was artificially inflated by counting individual foreign students or interns living in East Germany as representatives of their country of origin. See 'Erster Entwurf: Zu konzeptionellen Fragen der VII. Internationalen Leipziger Dokumentar- und Kurzfilmwoche', Berlin, November 1964, BArch, Komitee Internationale Leipziger Dokumentar- und Kurzfilmwoche, DR 139/6, p. 2.
22. Rüdiger Steinmetz, 'Zum vierzigsten Mal, aber mehr als 40 Jahre. Ein Blick zurück in das erste Jahrzehnt', in Rüdiger Steinmetz and Hans-Jörg Stiehler (eds), *Das Leipziger Dokfilm-Festival und sein Publikum* (Leipzig: Universitätsverlag, 1997), pp. 7–22.
23. Andreas Kötzing, *Kultur- und Filmpolitik im Kalten Krieg. Die Filmfestivals von Leipzig und Oberhausen in gesamtdeutscher Initiative* (Göttingen: Wallstein Verlag, 2013), pp. 189–195.
24. See 'Information', Leipzig, 24 November 1965, BArch, DR 139/7.
25. See 'Statut der Auswahlkommission', BArch, DR 139/9.
26. See Andreas Kötzing, *Die Internationale Leipziger Dokumentar- und Kurzfilmwoche in den 1970er Jahren. Eine Studie über das politische Profil des Festivals* (Leipzig: Universitätsverlag, 2004), p. 33ff.
27. 'Richtlinien für die Tätigkeit der Auswahlkommission zur Vorbereitung und Durchführung der X. Internationalen Leipziger Dokumentar- und Kurzfilmwoche 1967', BArch, DR 139/11, emphasis in the original.

28. See 'Bericht über die IX. Internationale Leipziger Dokumentar- und Kurzfilmwoche 1966. Vorlage für die Dienstbesprechung beim Leiter der HV Film am 19.12.1966', Berlin, 15 December 1966, BArch, DR 139/9, p. 5f.
29. Günter Agde (ed.), *Kahlschlag. Das 11. Plenum des ZK der SED 1965. Studien und Dokumente* (Berlin: Aufbau, 2000).
30. See Monika Kaiser, *Machtwechsel von Ulbricht zu Honecker. Funktionsmechanismen der SED-Diktatur in Konfliktsituationen 1962–1972* (Berlin: Akademie-Verlag, 1997), pp. 57–231.
31. Schittly, *Zwischen Regie und Regime*, pp. 127ff.
32. See Hans-Jörg Rother, 'Auftrag: Propaganda. 1960 bis 1970', in Günter Jordan and Ralf Schenk (eds), *Schwarzweiß und Farbe* (Berlin: Jovis, 2000), pp. 123f.
33. See Dieter Wolf (ed.), *Lebensläufe. Die Kinder von Golzow. Bilder, Dokumente, Erinnerungen* (Marburg: Schüren, 2004).
34. See 'Vorschlag für das Nationalprogramm der DDR zur VII. Internationalen Dokumentar- und Kurzfilmwoche Leipzig 1964: 'Barfuß und ohne Hut'. Anlage zum Schreiben von Inge Kleinert an Günter Witt', Berlin, 20 October 1964, BArch, DR 1/4272.
35. See Claus Löser, '"Wer ohne Sünde ist, der werfe den ersten Stein". Jürgen Böttcher und sein Film "Barfuß und ohne Hut"', in DOK-Filmwochen (ed.), *Seismogramme des Augenblicks. Texte zu Jürgen Böttcher* (Leipzig: Dok-Filmwochen GmbH, 2001), pp. 7–8.
36. Thomas Heimann, 'Wie ein Ausländer die DDR mit eigenen Augen sehen wollte. Frans Buyens bei der DEFA', in Ralf Schenk and Erika Richter (eds), *Apropos: Film 2001* (Berlin: Das Neue Berlin, 2001), pp. 105–132.
37. 'Vorschlag für das Eröffnungsprogramm der VII. Internationalen Dokumentar- und Kurzfilmwoche Leipzig 1964: 'Die DDR mit den Augen eines Ausländers gesehen', Anlage zum Schreiben von Inge Kleinert an Günter Witt', Berlin, 20 October 1964, BArch, DR 1/4272.
38. See Andreas Kötzing, 'Ein Hauch von Frühling', *Aus Politik und Zeitgeschichte* 31–34 (2011), 28–33.
39. See Rother, 'Auftrag: Propaganda. 1960 bis 1970', p. 125.

Select Bibliography

Agde, Günter (ed.). *Kahlschlag. Das 11. Plenum des ZK der SED 1965. Studien und Dokumente*. Berlin: Aufbau, 2000.

Heimann, Thomas. 'Wie ein Ausländer die DDR mit eigenen Augen sehen wollte. Frans Buyens bei der DEFA'. In Ralf Schenk and Erika Richter (eds), *Apropos: Film 2001*. Berlin: Das Neue Berlin, 2001.

Jäger, Manfred. *Kultur und Politik in der DDR. 1945–1990*. Cologne: Edition Deutschland-Archiv, 1994.

Jordan, Günter, and Ralf Schenk (eds). *Schwarzweiß und Farbe. DEFA-Dokumentarfilme 1946–92*. Berlin: Jovis, 2000.

Kaiser, Monika. *Machtwechsel von Ulbricht zu Honecker. Funktionsmechanismen der SED-Diktatur in Konfliktsituationen 1962–1972*. Berlin: Akademie-Verlag, 1997.

Kötzing, Andreas. *Die Internationale Leipziger Dokumentar- und Kurzfilmwoche in den 1970er Jahren. Eine Studie über das politische Profil des Festivals.* Leipzig: Universitätsverlag, 2004.

Kötzing, Andreas. 'Ein Hauch von Frühling'. *Aus Politik und Zeitgeschichte* 31–34 (2011), 28–33.

Kötzing, Andreas. *Kultur- und Filmpolitik im Kalten Krieg. Die Filmfestivals von Leipzig und Oberhausen in gesamtdeutscher Initiative.* Göttingen: Wallstein Verlag, 2013.

Moine, Caroline. *Cinéma et guerre froide: Histoire du festival de films documentaires de Leipzig.* Paris: Publications de la Sorbonne, 2014.

Roth, Wilhelm. *Der Dokumentarfilm seit 1960.* Munich and Lucerne: Bucher, 1982.

Schenk, Ralf (ed.). *Bilder einer gespaltenen Welt. 50 Jahre Dokumentar- und Animationsfilmfestival Leipzig.* Berlin: Bertz + Fischer, 2007.

Schittly, Dagmar. *Zwischen Regie und Regime. Die Filmpolitik der SED im Spiegel der DEFA-Produktionen.* Berlin: Christoph Links, 2002.

Steinmetz, Rüdiger. 'Zum vierzigsten Mal, aber mehr als 40 Jahre. Ein Blick zurück in das erste Jahrzehnt.' In Rüdiger Steinmetz and Hans-Jörg Stiehler (eds), *Das Leipziger Dokfilm-Festival und sein Publikum.* Leipzig: Universitätsverlag, 1997.

Wentker, Hermann. *Außenpolitik in engen Grenzen. Die DDR im internationalen System. 1949–1989.* Munich: Oldenbourg, 2007.

Wolf, Dieter (ed.). *Lebensläufe. Die Kinder von Golzow. Bilder, Dokumente, Erinnerungen.* Marburg: Schüren, 2004.

Chapter 12

NATIONAL, SOCIALIST, GLOBAL

The Changing Roles of the Karlovy
Vary Film Festival, 1946–1956

Jindřiška Bláhová

It took only six weeks in the spring of 1946 to establish the Karlovy Vary International Film Festival (Mezinárodní filmový festival Karlovy Vary, MFF KV) in the Czechoslovak towns of Mariánské Lázně and Karlovy Vary.[1] The swift execution of this operation reflects the festival's significance for its organizers: the communist-controlled Ministry of Information and the Czechoslovak State Film (Československý státní film, ČSF), a state-run, vertically integrated organization controlling film production, distribution and exhibition in the country.[2] Czechoslovak political and cultural elites deemed the festival important because it promised to play a key role in the development of the country's film industry and to contribute to articulations of national identity following the recent Nazi occupation of the country. Crucially, the festival was envisaged as an institution with an international presence based not only on regional projections of Czech national identity but on its capacity to assist in the Czechoslovak government's desire to see the national film industry become an internationally respected and prolific producer of films. As early as 1947, however, the emphasis on the festival's national dimensions had been superseded by the transnational and supranational interests of the Soviet Union.

Perhaps because of an insufficient understanding of relations between the USSR and her 'satellites', perhaps because the festival was seen as operating beyond the (Western) European festival circuit and limited to ideological battles, or perhaps because the economic and organizational aspects of state-controlled Eastern European film industries have only relatively recently come to the attention of scholars, the Karlovy Vary festival has remained largely peripheral to historical inquiry. The MFF KV's amorphous interests and scope during the early phases of the Cold War presented problems to the national approach, which saw scholars emphasize the national dimensions of festivals as well as festivals' relationships to national governmental policies,[3] and challenged the East/West dichotomy shaping histories of Cold War European cinema. Whereas scholars initially explored the roles festivals play with respect to national film industries, national film cultures and cultural diplomacy,[4] film historians began fairly recently to reveal the extent to which festivals function cumulatively as transnational networks supporting various economic interests, cultural hierarchies and aesthetic regimes,[5] and shape imagined communities.[6] As the case of the MFF KV shows, however, historical inquiry into the origin of film festivals, particularly those in Eastern Europe, and their role in film culture, film industry and (geo)politics is far from complete.

As a product of socialist transnational political and ideological frameworks, the MFF KV was unique among film festivals, embodying more than any other festival the oft-competing visions of the national and the transnational that characterized intra-Eastern Bloc dynamics while also serving the Soviet Union's global economic and ideological agenda. Moreover, on those rare occasions when the MFF KV's history has been touched upon, it has been argued that the festival was established to showcase socialistic film production. Such accounts oversimplify the reasons for the festival's founding, ignore shifts in the ways that different political and cultural bodies used the festival, and also stop short of offering satisfactory explanations as to why socialist production was being showcased (and for what purpose).

Considering national aspects of the festival alongside relevant transnational and supranational forces permits a deeper understanding of the festival's roles in disseminating communist ideology and building global socialism. This approach also sheds new light on its political and economic links to the Czechoslovak film industry, its relationships to other European film festivals and film cultures (even beyond the Iron Curtain), and relations between the Soviet and Czechoslovak film industries.[7] Focusing on the first decade of the festival's history and basing its conclusions on extensive research in Czechoslovak and Russian archives combined with analyses of the popular and trade press, this chapter therefore explores how the various political agents behind the MFF KV conceptualized the festival and sought to convey its changing cultural and political functions to the public, and argues that the festival became a signifier that shifted under the influence of competing national and supranational forces in the region.

The Czechoslovak Film Festival: A Symbolic Gesture of Greatness, 1946

Dances, garden parties and tennis tournaments accompanied the screenings of the thirteen films that comprised the programme of the inaugural, non-competitive MFF KV in 1946. As in Venice and later in Cannes, leisure activities were included to infuse the festival with a sense of glamour and cosmopolitan vibrancy, which together would make it attractive to an affluent international crowd. But whereas broader economic considerations were important, the issues of national identity and the national film industry were pivotal and cannot be underestimated. The first festival was primarily envisaged as a vehicle for the Czechoslovak government's domestic and foreign policies and as a public relations platform for the Czechoslovak film monopoly.

A key role of the festival was to enhance the morale of the Czechoslovak people and cultivate a sense of Czechoslovak national identity befitting what would be proclaimed a strong, independent and free nation. As a noteworthy public event, the festival lent itself ideally to an initiative, detailed by the Czechoslovak government in 1946, for a programme of political and economical renewal pertaining to foreign policy, the building of a fairer society and the quest to refashion Czechoslovak national identity. In the interwar years, festivals emphasized international aspects in order to offset the notion of nationalism, which was seen as petty and dangerous as it eventually led to militaristic conflicts.[8] However, nationalism was embraced with new vigour after World War II, particularly in the countries that had been occupied by the Nazi Germany. Envisaged in strictly national and nationalistic terms by the festival organizers and Czechoslovak film elites – including the festival director, leading film critic and future dean of the Film faculty of the Academy of Performing Arts (Filmová fakulta Akademie múzických umění, better known as FAMU), A.M. Brousil – the 1946 Czechoslovak festival was expected to support the state's agenda and promote cinematic output that was considered to express national specificity via articulations of what was deemed national identity.[9] In the words of prominent poet Vítězslav Nezval, who was in charge of the film division at the Ministry of Information, the once discredited 'national' was to be rehabilitated as a symbol of greatness.[10]

The location of the festival was chosen specifically for its capacity to enrich nationalistic sentiment by invoking painful recent memories of the wartime Nazi occupation of the country. Holding the festival close to the German border in the heart of the Sudetenland, where pro-Nazi sympathy and collaboration had been prevalent, was a politically significant act rich in nationalist symbolism.[11] Purging the country of a German presence and of any lasting influence such a presence may have exerted were pivotal aspects of Czechoslovak postwar domestic policy. In metaphoric terms, the festival emblematized the retaking of what was historically the most pro-German region of 'our beautiful homeland, which until recently has been ruled by our enemies', as the film magazine *Filmová práce* explained.[12] Anti-German sentiment was prominent in promotion of, and commentary on, the festival. Echoing domestic policy, the festival's organizers demanded and promised that with the festival would come the total de-Germanization and de-Nazification of the region, so that 'foreign visitors realized finally that they were entering Czech lands, not a German province'.[13]

The festival was conceived of as an opportunity to measure Czechoslovak cinema against foreign films. This notion was expressed in the festival's name, which emphasized that the festival was first and foremost a Czechoslovak event in which foreign films simply took part in order to enable comparison with Czechoslovak films.[14] Therefore, the Czechoslovak films – *V horách duní* (Thunder in the Hills, Václav Kubásek, 1946), *Hrdinové mlčí* (The Heroes Are Silent, Miroslav Cikán, 1946) and *Nezbedný bakalář* (The Whimsical Bachelor, Otakar Vávra, 1946) – were accompanied by a selection of U.S., British, Swiss and Soviet films such as *Sergeant York* (1941), *The Sullivans* (Lloyd Bacon, 1944), *Blithe Spirit* (David Lean, 1945), *Die letzte Chance* (The Last Chance, Friedrich Wilhelm Murnau, 1945), and *Nepokoryonnye* (Undefeated, Mark Donskoy, 1945).

State officials and film industry representatives saw the content and themes of domestically produced films as central to the articulation of the new Czechoslovak national identity. This project of a 'specifically Czechoslovak' cinema was repeatedly emphasized in festival promotional materials and official statements. Consequently, Czechoslovak film officials believed that films made within the nation state would be internationally recognized as 'Czechoslovak national cinema' only if they were based on existing cultural products associated with the nation, dramatized aspects of the life of the Czechoslovak people and were underpinned by and expressed 'national values'. A reoccurring theme at the festival thus concerned the specific features that should and therefore would characterize Czechoslovak national cinema, thereby distinguishing it from the cinema of other nations – in short, the quest for an 'essence' that could manifest fully and unequivocally only when Czechoslovak-made films were contrasted to those produced in other countries. The festival organizers elevated the conceptual frameworks they were working in and drawing upon by distinguishing between national and other organizing principles on the one hand, and between different forms the national took in terms of off-screen and on-screen manifestations on the other. Compared to the national, the blandness of internationalism and cosmopolitanism (both of which were presented as erasing colourful difference) and the insularity and parochiality of the provisional[15] were found wanting. Moreover, whereas German national cinema was criticized for its supposed formal excessive elaborateness and an otherwise unspecified 'impurity', American films were lambasted for their excessive violence, high production costs, onscreen depictions of lavishness and distortion of historical and contemporary realities.[16]

In 1946, nationalism was largely cast in terms of one's responsibility to assist in the building of the new Czechoslovak state. Filmmakers were expected to participate in this process,[17] particularly by exploring and depicting the working class and its involvement in industry and agriculture.[18] Accordingly, rather than handing out awards for individual films, the festival celebrated the 'hard work' and institutional undertakings of the ČSF.[19] The notion of hard work and the building of a new society with the help of cinema connected the festival directly to the Czechoslovak national economy.[20]

State officials envisaged the festival as part of the planned economy being introduced in Czechoslovakia. The long-term state-supervised planning of film production (across two- and later five-year periods) – unlike purely profit-driven private enterprises – was expected to generate sustainable economic growth that would take into account the needs of society as a whole. ČSF officials anticipated that the output of the Czechoslovak film industry would increase fivefold by 1953, resulting in the production of up to fifty-two films.[21] As a result, the Czechoslovak monopoly would supply sufficient Czechoslovak films to the festival to guarantee a solid contribution to the reshaping of the national character and to ensure that the festival itself was regarded as central to that process. However, by 1949 it had become apparent that the Czechoslovak film industry was unable to meet its production quota due to economic and organizational crises within the industry that culminated in the production of only eight feature films in 1951, even fewer than had been made in 1946.[22]

A second key function of the 1946 festival was to serve as a public relations exercise that would celebrate the state-controlled film industry and the principles upon which it was based.[23] The festival was therefore timed to mark the first anniversary of the founding of the ČSF in August 1945. The monopoly represented a new economic model that was not governed by free-market economics or controlled by profit-oriented private entrepreneurs. Instead, it was heralded as an institution that would respond to the cultural and political needs of the state and the people. Following this line of logic, it would produce films that were superior in quality – both artistically and in terms of content – to those produced by private film industries.[24] Czechoslovak state officials and cultural elites perceived the ČSF and its film production as crucial for building a new, socially just society, which, it was believed, would replace 'outdated' capitalist systems, the failure of which had allegedly been demonstrated by the outbreak of World War II. Presented by Czechoslovak film officials as a pioneering model, the ČSF was seen to offer potential inspiration to other governments, which would dismantle private enterprise in favour of a centralized state-controlled model.

This perception of the film industry originated from a belief, held by many Czechoslovak political and cultural elites, that Czechoslovakia was destined to blaze the trail for other countries because of what they saw as its projection of social and political systems that merged selected principles of capitalist democracy with a degree of social justice that capitalism otherwise prevented.[25] Because of its arguably politically and culturally highly developed citizens, Czechoslovakia was, according to one film journalist, poised to become 'an important cultural and political centre of the world'.[26] Accordingly, a central part of the festival was a series of lectures and debates in which Czechoslovak journalists, academics and filmmakers explored the principles and advantages of the state-controlled film industry, especially its social responsibility, political consciousness, economic frugality and educational value.[27] These lectures and debates were intended for the eyes of Czechoslovak and overseas visitors alike, particularly those members of the Czechoslovak elite who were still either sceptical about the state taking control of the film industry or directly opposed to it.[28] They were also aimed at foreign journalists who, it was hoped, would promote the ČSF overseas and in doing so alleviate the scepticism of Western political and business elites,[29] which would, it was feared, endanger the Czechoslovak government's and the ČSF's plans to build a strong, internationally respected national film industry.

The festival continued to serve as a public relations platform for the Czechoslovak film monopoly in 1947.[30] However, as the Soviet government's influence in the region grew, the festival began to be used as a tool to advocate the interests not only of the Czechoslovak film monopoly, but of all Eastern European film industries.

From National to Slavic Film Festival, 1947

The 1947 MFF KV represented a stage of evolution from a 'national' to a 'socialist' vision of the festival. It was shaped by the notion of Slavism, a cornerstone of which was cooperation between the East European Slavic countries Czechoslovakia, Poland, Yugoslavia and Bulgaria. Slavism reflected the opportunistic Kremlin's foreign policy at that point in time,[31] which saw Slavic cooperation as cementing Soviet dominance in the region and propagating Soviet leadership. Placing emphasis on supposedly intrinsic and long-standing discourses of Slavic belonging helped to mask and naturalize the Soviet government's expansionist agenda, which sought to impose a single political, social and economic model upon East European countries. Accordingly, the principal role of the 1947 festival was to advance cooperation between Slavic nations and their respective cinemas – under the guidance of the Soviet Union.[32]

The festival provided an ideal platform for demonstrating Slavic unity in such a way that it would likely resonate both regionally and beyond – particularly in Western Europe and the United States. In stark contrast to the 1946 festival, Polish, Bulgarian and Yugoslavian films were celebrated alongside Czechoslovak films.[33] The politicized nature of Slavic unity was presented as beneficial for individual film industries because, it was argued, this unity would make them stronger when competing outside the region. In doing so, it would facilitate the given film industry's development, both economically and ideologically.[34] The Czechoslovak film industry, which boasted the most advanced infrastructure, was to become a centre for the film industries of other Slavic nations, with Prague's Barrandov Film Studios envisioned as what the Czechoslovak film press dubbed the 'Slavic Hollywood'.[35] Together with the Soviet film industry, the ČSF was seen as capable of assisting the underdeveloped film industries in the region by providing them with the opportunity to learn from one another and offering them access to the Barrandov facilities. The importance of forming a coalition of Slavic nations was foregrounded in and by a series of meetings and conferences involving film industry officials from 'Slavic' countries, which were held in Prague after the festival.[36]

The valorization of Slavism has considerably influenced the ways in which both Czechoslovak cinema and the ČSF have been framed in Czechoslovak history, and has also affected the understanding of their contribution to the development of a new Czechoslovak society. The notion of Slavism was invoked to overshadow the nationalistic dimension of Czechoslovak cinema, which in rhetorical terms became a mere derivation of the more general and conceptually fitting concept of a 'supranational' cinema that linked East European countries. In other words, what had been deemed Czechoslovak national cinema was recast as a vision of cinema that conveniently transcended national borders, erased national specificity and supposedly represented the cultural and political specificity of the Slavic bloc. Such a concept of cinema was ideally suited to reflecting the Soviet Union's foreign policy objectives, which were underwritten by transregional forces involving Eastern-hemisphere countries, with Moscow very much serving as a centre of power and influence. This conceptual shift preceded the subsuming of 'Czechoslovak national cinema' within the broader category of 'socialist' cinema and anticipated the festival's subsequent role in Soviet cultural and foreign economic policies.

Underpinning the cooperation between Slavic nations was an implicit conflict between the cinemas of Slavic and non-Slavic nations, a conflict that telegraphed the looming clash between 'socialist' and 'capitalist' cinemas that would come to characterize the MFF KV in the late 1940s and early 1950s.[37] Although the idea of Slavism was abandoned in 1948 following a dispute between Stalin and Yugoslav leader Josip Broz Tito, the unity it fostered, at least rhetorically, laid something of a foundation upon which to build the new role the festival was assigned by the Czechoslovak Communist Party in the period following the 1948 communist coup in Czechoslovakia and the resulting increase in Soviet influence. After 1948, competition between Slavic and non-Slavic cinemas was radicalized and transformed into a revolutionary confrontation between two political systems – socialism and capitalism.

'For a New Man, For Better Humankind': On the Road to Socialism and Global Dominance (1948–1949)

The 1948 communist coup in Czechoslovakia ushered in a new era in the history of the MFF KV. The festival was increasingly used to spread socialism by advancing the goals of Czechoslovak Communist Party cultural policy and serving Moscow's political and economic interests.[38] The goals of Czechoslovak national cinema were jettisoned in favour of 'socialist' cinema, conceived of as a supranational cinematic form that would facilitate Soviet foreign policy and the Kremlin's plans for cinematic and economic expansion. Before focusing on the character and main functions of the 1948 and 1949 festivals, it is necessary to consider the significance of the establishment of a formal film competition at the 1948 festival.

Establishing a formal competition to bestow markers of quality upon certain films was not simply a cosmetic change to the MFF KV but carried practical, propagandistic and symbolic meanings for the ČSF and the Soviet government. For the ČSF it symbolized the Czechoslovak film industry's transformation into a full-fledged state-controlled institution (a transformation emblematized by the word "state" being added to the name of the monopoly). The competition was designed to increase the festival's prestige among foreign producers and distributors and to elevate the MFF KV to the level of Cannes and Venice, and was therefore considered an apposite celebration of the ČSF entering a new period in its history. The ČSF also had economic incentives to establish the competition, since it understood the festival's potential vis-à-vis distribution circuits and international trade. A surge in interest from producers and distributors was expected to bring about an increase in international trade, which in turn would solve one of the ČSF's most acute economic problems: its dependency on a supply of U.S. films and an outflow of hard currency. After 1947, film distribution in Czechoslovakia underwent a dramatic transformation wherein the film monopoly strove to limit its reliance on U.S. distributors and their expensive products by decreasing the number of American films in circulation.[39] Consequently, the festival provided an opportunity to develop relationships with new suppliers and thus fill the void that would be left after the levels of imported American films on Czech markets were reduced.[40]

The Soviet film monopoly also benefited from the change in the festival's status. From 1948 on, the Soviet government boycotted festivals in Western Europe because of the allegedly anti-Soviet sentiments of festival organizers and their supposed discrimination against Soviet films.[41] To challenge Cannes and Venice, as well as the Western film industries that the Soviet Ministry of Cinematography had concluded were dominating the two festivals, the Soviet government announced plans to establish a Soviet film festival in Leningrad called the International Festival of Progressive and Democratic Film Art, scheduled to take place in August 1948.[42] Soviet Minister of Cinematography Ivan G. Bolshakov expected the Leningrad festival to bring the Soviet film industry economic and political advantages by helping to sell Soviet films abroad and, by extension, to disseminate communist ideology overseas.[43] The communist coup in Czechoslovakia, however, presented Moscow with a more economically and strategically attractive solution – using the existing, conveniently located Karlovy Vary Film Festival.

Establishing a competition at the MFF KV was essential for the Soviet government. As tensions between the United States and USSR grew, it was concluded that some of the distributors and producers Moscow aimed to attract would likely boycott a festival held in the Soviet Union. Attending a festival in Czechoslovakia, on the other hand, was assumed to be less politically controversial on account of Czechoslovakia's democratic past and Prague's comparatively favourable views on contact with Western countries. Moreover, awards conferred by an international (i.e. non-Soviet) festival would give credit to Soviet films and Soviet cinema, thus somewhat substituting for the lack of awards at Cannes and Venice festivals, which the Soviet government continued to boycott.[44] Therefore, sixteen Soviet films were screened at the MFF KV in 1948 – a substantial increase – and four were awarded some of the many awards. For instance, *Skazanie o zemle sibirskoy* (Symphony of Life, Ivan Pyryev, 1947) took the International Work Prize, and *Russkiy vopros* (The Russian Question, Mikhail Romm, 1947) was awarded the International Peace Prize. Unsurprisingly, in 1949, when the Soviet Minister Bolshakov referred to the MFF KV as a 'new triumph of Soviet cinema',[45] he was referring not just to the generous number of the many awards yet again received by Soviet films but also to their prestige: *Stalingradskaya bitva* (The Battle of Stalingrad, Vladimir Petrov, 1949) won the Main Prize, *Vstrecha na Elbe* (The Encounter on the Elbe, Grigori Alexandrov, 1949) won the Peace Award, and the Colour Film Award was given to *Mičurin* (Michurin, Alexander Dovzhenko, 1948).

Reflecting Moscow's approach to European film festivals as cultural and political battlegrounds of the Cold War, the 1948 and 1949 MFF

KVs became arenas of politicized combat. Already envisaged as a challenge to Cannes and Venice by its Czechoslovak organizers, the MFF KV provided a stage upon which competition between socialism and capitalism could take place in the form of two competing concepts of cinema: 'socialist' (Eastern/Soviet) and 'capitalist' (Western/American). This confrontation was conveyed through a number of specific ideological 'fights': a fight for cinemas disadvantaged by small production volumes and weak state economies, a fight against Hollywood and a fight against film 'kitsch'. Socialist cinema, whose supposed contribution to the development of the human race fostered increased levels of compassion, social responsibility and social equality, was deemed superior to capitalist cinema, which by default was ideologically compromised. In short, by abandoning the profit motivation that underwrote cinema in capitalist states, socialist (i.e. state-controlled) cinema was free to serve progressive and educational roles in socialist societies.[46] The ideological inferiority of capitalist cinema was encapsulated in the concept of kitsch, a category of cultural artefact defined by its perceived low cultural status and supposed lack of social relevancy. Kitsch, in this use of the word, was associated particularly with American cinema, which – according to the Czechoslovak minister of information, Stalinist, and leading communist party ideologue Václav Kopecký – 'poisoned audiences'[47] because it lacked the educational, progressive and political qualities of socialist cinema.[48] To draw a clear line between socialist and capitalist cinemas, films were demonstratively selected for the festival competition 'strictly' on the basis of cultural and political criteria, both of which were intended to highlight a film's social function.[49]

Importantly, the notion of the revolutionary fight served to carve a distinct niche for the MFF KV as an alternative film festival model befitting a socialist society. The fight for a new kind of human race together with a new form of cinema distinguished the festival from Cannes and Venice, which Czechoslovak journalists denounced as amounting to little more than markets that stripped films of their social value, reduced them to their profit potential and used them to perpetuate elitism and classism based on economic capital rather than social value. The way Czechoslovak elites perceived Cannes and Venice was encapsulated in the label 'film stock exchanges', which was used in an article published in the leading film journal to describe the festivals' degenerate state, due to their emphasis on commerce.[50] Czechoslovak communists considered Cannes and Venice to be stagnating because their organizers evaluated films solely according to their technical and artistic value (which was seen as a bourgeois conception of art that emphasized aesthetics over social value, thus alienating the films from everyday life). The MFF KV organizers, however, positioned their festival as progressive because the jury assessed films' moral value based on their perceived contribution to the building of a new society and to the development of a human race[51] freed from what the Czechoslovak press described as the 'prejudices and superstitions' that exemplified 'old' capitalist orders.[52] In their eyes, this programme of politically and socially relevant cinema made the festival superior to its Western counterparts. Long before the notion of political cinema and political festivals became fashionable in the West during the 1960s and 1970s,[53] the MFF KV offered a new model of festival that saw films as political entities advancing a political agenda.

To accelerate the clash between the two opposing forms of cinema and, by extension, the opposing political systems with which they were associated, the Kremlin mobilized to its advantage a major issue that preoccupied European governments after World War II: the U.S. film industry's alleged dominance on the continent and the threat it posed to indigenous film cultures and film industries.[54] The European cultural and political representatives who perceived the presence of American films on European markets in negative terms believed that the economic power of the U.S. film industry was such that it could dictate conditions of film trade to European countries and thus flood European markets – and festivals – with what were considered inferior films. Helpless in the face of Hollywood's economic might and the backing it received from the U.S. government, festivals in Western Europe were reduced, in the words of the Czechoslovak Communist Party's official newspaper *Rudé právo*, to 'meaningless film fairs where capitalist producers of film trash try to cover up... the deep decay and decline of bourgeois film production'.[55] The economic might of the U.S. film industry allegedly influenced festival policy in Cannes and Venice by affecting what films were shown at festivals, which film producing industries were given preferential treatment and which industries, producers and distributors were overlooked, discriminated against or prevented from taking part. Those claims echoed the complaints of Soviet film officials, who repeatedly stated that Cannes was particularly guilty of discriminating against Soviet films because its organizers wanted to remain on good terms with U.S. producers and distributors – especially the Motion Picture Association of America (MPAA), which represented the major Hollywood companies overseas. Since West European governments were dependent on U.S. governmental aid, and since their national film markets relied heavily on Hollywood imports, the MPAA was seen as sufficiently powerful to both interfere with festival organizers' decisions as to which films would be included in competition and negotiate preferential treatment for American films.[56] Therefore, Hollywood's dominance supposedly prevented the presence of films from less powerful film industries (Albanian, Bulgarian, Chinese, Indonesian, etc.) at Western festivals.[57] The MFF KV intended to solve this inequality by providing a safe haven for film industries that were struggling as a consequence of the U.S. film industry's international reach.[58] It promised egalitarian systems of participation and film selection, both of which were intended to encapsulate the supposed classlessness of socialist society. This ideologically motivated decision was reflected in a selection process that stipulated that the output of each nation, irrespective of size, be represented by a single film, thereby preventing preferential treatment for productions from particular countries and discrimination against films from certain nations.

Film historians have shown that relations between Hollywood and European cinemas indeed shaped film festivals in Western Europe, arguing that even as festivals fought against Hollywood's dominance, they simultaneously helped to maintain that dominance through their dependence on Hollywood stars and films.[59] The case of the MFF KV somewhat qualifies the notion of the European festivals' capitulation to Hollywood. Its profile and policy were built on the very notion of opposition to Hollywood. By distancing the festival from Hollywood, the MFF KV organizers aimed to avoid dependency and instead to become the last refuge for what its organizers defined as 'cinemas of small nations'. In so doing, as the socialist youth newspaper *Mladá fronta* argued, the festival helped prevent the U.S. film industry from becoming a dominant power in Eastern Europe.[60] Part of this defence strategy was based on the assumption that the festival, by virtue of its valued recognition of selected films, could serve as a springboard for East European cinemas' expansion into capitalist markets – which, it was believed, would subsequently undermine Hollywood's position there.[61] Furthermore, and importantly, those films would also disseminate communist ideology to the West and the rest of the world by showing 'ideals of new life, new democracy, and new socialist order'.[62]

Despite the presumed and declared egalitarianism and equality between cinemas, a hierarchy still characterized the relative value of the various socialist cinemas (and consequently the interests of film industries in the socialist countries). The Soviet cinema was elevated above the cinemas of the other socialist states by Czechoslovak Communist

Party ideologues who considered it the most ideologically advanced, given that the USSR was the birthplace of the socialist revolution. Inevitably, it was Soviet cinema that the festival celebrated as setting an example for the cinemas of other socialist nations, including even Czechoslovakia. This situation initiated a change from the previously nationalistic rhetoric that the ČSF had employed in 1946 and to some extent in 1947. Czechoslovak national cinema, no longer seen as a product of historical and political developments in a democratic, independent Czechoslovakia, was now regarded as an offshoot of the supposedly pioneering Soviet cinema. Consequently, Czechoslovak cinema was indebted to developments that had unfolded in the Soviet Union.[63] Accordingly, and in contrast to previous years, it was the thirtieth anniversary of the Soviet film monopoly – and not the anniversary of its Czechoslovak counterpart – that was celebrated at the 1949 festival.[64] The situation at the festival was symptomatic of the situation as a whole in the Czechoslovak film industry. As Czechoslovak state sovereignty was gradually sacrificed in favour of the interests of the Soviet Union, so too did the ČSF come to more dutifully serve the needs of its Soviet counterpart, for example by making its resources available and increasing the number of Soviet films produced at Barrandov.[65]

An escalation in the rhetorical conflict between Hollywood and some European cultural and political elites was, crucially, fuelled by a major transnational economic factor: the Soviet Ministry of Cinematography's attempt to limit the presence of Hollywood and its products on East European markets in order to advance its own goals of global economic, ideological and cinematic expansion. This intention is clearly indicated in memorandums issued by the Soviet Ministry of Cinematography and in reports completed by Sovexportfilm (SEF) representatives stationed in both Czechoslovakia and Moscow (SEF was the Soviet Film Monopoly's organization for film export and import).[66] Existing business relations between East European countries and the U.S. film industry had hampered this intended expansion. To facilitate its operation, the Kremlin aimed to control the East European markets it considered to be potentially lucrative sources of capital, know-how and human resources. It was decided that Eastern Europe would serve as a base for the Soviet expansion first to Western Europe and then, in the first half of the 1950s, to Asia, Latin America and Africa (as the next section shows).[67] Highlighting the fight against Hollywood distracted attention from the fact that this policy did not benefit national film industries as was being claimed, but served primarily the global interests of another large film industry – that of the Soviet Union.

'Fighting For Peace': International Festival, Global Politics (1950–1952)

While the 1948 and 1949 festivals were shaped by the consequences of the communist party's seizure of power in Czechoslovakia, the festivals held in the period 1950–1952 were affected by geopolitical developments, in particular the Korean War, which had started a month before the 1950 festival began. In the light of these developments, the character and reach of the festival shifted towards the global.[68]

In 1950 the festival was transformed into a pacifistic global institution characterized by the participation of not only East European states but countries of Asia and beyond. China and Korea took part in the festival for the first time, and the word 'peace' was added to the festival's motto. The festival's global reach under the umbrella of peace was encapsulated neatly in its promotional poster, which depicted a globe with a filmstrip running across it and a hand releasing white doves (Fig. 1). Film was seen as an effective tool in the fight for global peace due to its status as a popular medium and its capacity to project political ideals and positions in a way that was easily accessible to audiences. More importantly, however, the MFF KV served as a site from which film culture elites (including filmmakers and journalists) could be recruited for the cause of global peace.[69] The festival became a venue where film workers 'fought' for world peace and against what the Czechoslovak Communist Party's flagship newspaper *Rudé právo* called 'the aggression of Wall Street descendants of Hitler's fascism' in Korea.[70]

Delegates from twenty-five countries – including Western nations such as France, Great Britain and the United States – discussed how best to stop the expansive politics of Wall Street.[71] They also condemned the House Committee on Un-American Activities and criticized U.S. foreign policy. Hollywood cinema was castigated for stupefying audiences worldwide, stimulating the onset of a potential World War III by being a part of the U.S. military-industrial complex, and spreading propaganda in the name of its Wall Street financiers.[72] As Czechoslovak newspapers reported, film workers used the festival to support the working class and to defend progress, democracy and freedom.[73] The notion of the festival as a political forum was taken one step further during the 1951 festival.

Under Soviet tutelage, the 1951 festival was styled as an open political forum in the vein of the 1950 World Peace Congress in Warsaw and the World Peace Council in Berlin.[74] Thus the MFF KV, though excluded

Figure 12.1. Global Peace as the Main Star

from what De Valck describes as the 'film festival network' – a system of interconnected, hierarchically structured events that are part of a global media economy[75] –was integrated into a global circuit of non-cinematic events that could be seen as evincing similarities with the festival network but were primarily a vehicle for spreading socialism globally. The Czechoslovak government put forward a proposal to build in Prague an institution responsible for coordinating progressive filmmakers across the world.[76] New awards were introduced, including the 'Fighting for Peace Award' and the 'Friendship among Nations Award'.[77] The festival concluded with a mass call for peace and was lauded as a 'humanistic fight for the preservation of peace'.[78]

As had been the case in 1947, when Slavism had been the organizing principle of the festival, and in 1948–1949, when the notion of socialist cinema had prevailed, Moscow yet again mobilized the festival to advance its own geopolitical agenda, this time under claims of a 'fight for global peace'. Film workers from around the world were radicalized politically under the banner of 'peace' and cooperation. The festival had fitted into the Soviet government's geopolitical plans by serving as a space in which the Kremlin could increase its economic and political power by cultivating relations with Third World countries. New countries were recruited to the socialist cause at the festival, and consequently the ideas and ideals of communism were disseminated further.[79] Symptomatic of Moscow's plans to extend its global reach were the increasing numbers of nations of Asia (e.g. China with *Zhong Hua nu er* [Daughters of China, Zifend Ling-Qiang Zhai, 1949] and *Kang-tchie chang* [The Steel Warrior, Cheng Yin, 1950]), Latin America (e.g. Mexico with *Pueblerina* [The Villager, Emilio Fernández, 1949] and Brazil with *Rio 40 Graus* [Rio 100 Degrees F, Nelson Pereira dos Santos, 1955]) and Africa with developing film industries that were invited to the festival so that their representatives could learn the creative and business sides of film from their Soviet colleagues.[80] To ensure such industries were represented at the festival, the export office of the Soviet film monopoly, SEF, supervised their film exportation practices and served as a middleman between Czechoslovakia and those national film industries looking to participate in the festival.[81]

Historians have shown that communist governments saw film as an ideal medium for spreading communist ideas.[82] Even more important in this respect, however, was cinema's assumed capacity to create unity among various members of film culture worldwide. This quality was held to facilitate and to *naturalize* the global expansion of the Soviet Union – an expansion aided by the MFF KV.

Attempted Emancipation: International Festival, National Interests (1954–1956)

With no festivals held in 1953 and 1955, the Czechoslovak government saw 1954 as the right time to transform the festival from an ideological arena benefiting the Soviet Union into an economic platform that once again would profit the Czechoslovak Film Monopoly. The opportunity presented itself in 1953 when, within a few short months, the Korean War ended, Joseph Stalin and Czechoslovak Communist Party leader Klement Gottwald both died, and the Soviet government began to loosen its control over the festival amid signs that the gradual waning of U.S.–USSR Cold War antagonisms after 1956 was inviting changes to Soviet foreign and cultural policy.

The Czechoslovak government recognized the festival's economic potential and cultural value. In 1953, the ČSF faced an economic crisis resulting from the implementation of economic models that Moscow had imposed on the Czechoslovak economy. These models were poorly suited to the dynamics of the Czechoslovakian industry had had led to a drastic decline in film production. Czechoslovak film officials, together with the Ministry of Culture, considered the festival to be part of a solution to the ČSF's problem – it would provide opportunities to re-establish business relations with foreign producers and distributors, and increase the trade in films[83] that was needed to energize Czechoslovakia's struggling distribution circuit.

To facilitate this transformation of the festival, the Czechoslovak government increased the MFF KV budget for 1954. Meanwhile, festival organizers invited a record number of forty-five countries to participate and emphasized the festival's new cosmopolitan character.[84] The festival was less overtly politicized than it had been in previous years (despite the obligatory inflammatory ideological rhetoric on the dangers of imperialism) and more relaxed in terms of its atmosphere and the rules governing its organization.[85] Instead of protesting and holding meetings, actors and directors signed autographs and courted attention from passers-by.[86] The festival's cosmopolitan and international ambitions were articulated in the pages of Czechoslovak film journals. *Kino*, for instance, in reference to the Iron Curtain, declared that no curtains should be maintained between West and East, and that instead the festival should cultivate international cultural exchange.[87] In an attempt to emphasize the notion that the festival's organizers favoured a world united economically, if not ideologically, the festival's main award was shared by the Soviet film *Vernye druz'ya* (True Friends, Mikhail Kalatozov, 1954) and the American film *Salt of the Earth* (Herbert J. Biberman, 1954). Change was also apparent in how the Czechoslovak press referred to the festival and its Western counterparts: in stark contrast to the isolationist rhetoric of previous years, Cannes was no longer deemed a meaningless affair governed by commerce but instead was heralded as an important cultural event in which Czechoslovakia participated proudly and successfully. Czechoslovak films were also submitted to Venice, and the positive reception they received signalled to the Czechoslovak government the (mainly economic) potential of the Czechoslovak film industry's return to participation in Western markets.[88]

Crucially, the Czechoslovak government and the ČSF sought the MFF KV's inclusion in prominent Western festivals, an objective catalysed by political developments unfolding in 1955, particularly those associated with the Geneva Conference, at which the governments of the United States, USSR, France and Great Britain meet for the first time since the onset of the Cold War, thereby increasing the chances of cultural cooperation between East and West.[89] The Czechoslovak government responded swiftly. After consulting with the Soviet minister of cinematography,[90] the ČSF applied in October of 1955 to the International Federation of Film Producers Associations (Fédération Internationale des Associations de Producteurs de Films, FIAPF)[91] for the festival to be considered for inclusion among internationally recognized competitions – the so-called 'A' festivals, which also included Cannes and Venice. The bestowal of 'A' status would increase the prestige of the MFF KV while attracting the participation of capitalist countries and increasing business opportunities more generally.[92] Of particular interest to the ČSF (and its export branch Filmexport) was the prospect of renewing relations with the U.S. film industry, which in 1951 had been suspended from participation in the Czechoslovak market.[93] The communist party ideologues declared that the primary aims of the 'only important festival in the East Bloc' were to create 'a respected counterbalance to Cannes and Venice' and establish 'an internationally recognized centre for progressive filmmakers from all around the world'.[94]

To be included among the prestigious festivals, the MFF KV had to be depoliticized.[95] Accordingly, its 'Social Progress' and 'Work' Awards were dropped, and the word 'peace' was removed from the festival's motto because it implied that Cannes and Venice did not support peace.[96] These steps led to FIAPF's acceptance of the Czechoslovak government's proposal, and in 1956 the festival screened films from thirty-three capitalist countries, including the American Palme d'Or winning-drama *Marty* (1955).[97] Filmmakers from capitalist states were invited to attend not just by the ČSF but also by the Czechoslovak government directly.[98] The MFF KV also adopted many of the rules and procedures used by its Western counterparts: press and guest services were professionalized, and an advanced wide-screen cinema was purpose-built to boost the profile of the event.[99] The success of the 1956 festival demonstrated that the MFF KV had the potential to become an integral part of the festival circuit in Europe, a high profile cultural event and a part of the transnational film economy, from which the Czechoslovak film industry and film culture would benefit.[100] The economic potential of the MFF KV was especially foregrounded in a report that the Political Bureau of the Communist Party issued on the watershed 1956 festival: 'Karlovy Vary became crucial for expanding economic cooperation between world film industries. A number of film export/import and coproduction contracts have been signed during the festival among various film producers. The ČSF also benefited considerably from this business activity.'[101] A special supplement to the report listed the ČSF's achievements, for example, selling a number of puppet films on the U.S. market, expanding cooperation with the British Rank Organisation, and reaching a distribution agreement for the Indian market.[102] The report clearly showed that the ČSF was expanding its reach beyond the Eastern Bloc countries that until then had been its main partners.[103]

The trend towards freeing the festival of Moscow's influence in favour of serving the needs of the ČSF continued into 1957 and 1958.[104] However, the ČSF's ambitions were stifled in 1959. As culture became the primary sphere of competition between the United States and the USSR, and Western governments ceased to view the Soviet Union as an off-limits country, the Kremlin established a festival in Moscow to facilitate its foreign and cultural policy.[105] Because the MFF KV represented unwanted competition, the Soviet government imposed a new rule: only one international festival could be held annually in Eastern Europe. This ruling resulted in the MFF KV and the Moscow festival taking place in alternating years for the next three decades. Representatives of the ČSF resented the Soviet decision greatly,[106] feeling it had ruined the MFF KV's chances of becoming one of the world's major film festivals on a par with Cannes and Venice.

Conclusion

Between 1946 and 1956, the MFF KV – the only film festival behind the Iron Curtain during that period – underwent a series of radical conceptual transformations from a national film festival to a Slavic festival, a socialist festival, a global festival and, finally, back to a national film festival representing the interests of the Czechoslovak film industry. Founded after World War II, the festival was a symbol of the political sovereignty that the Czechoslovak state had regained, a platform for the articulation of a newly recalibrated vision of Czechoslovak national identity, and a showcase for the superiority of the state-controlled film industrial model that reflected the nation's transition from capitalist state to socialist-democratic state. With the growing influence of the Soviet Union in Eastern Europe, however, the national character of the festival was overwhelmed by the interests of supranational state formations – first a 'Slavic bloc' based on a politicized vision of shared ethnicity, and then the Eastern Bloc, underpinned by a shared socialist ideology. In 1948 and 1949, the Soviet government used the festival to stage a confrontation between the United States and the USSR – that is, between Hollywood and the Soviet film industry and, by extension, between socialism and capitalism. Exploring how the discourses orbiting the MFF KV were related to the clash between cinematic modes and political-economic systems helps to deepen understanding of the history of Hollywood in postwar Europe. It also enriches knowledge of socialist cinema as a global concept, of the relations between Hollywood and the indigenous film industries of Eastern Europe, and of the role Hollywood played as a conceptual category in defining the profiles of Eastern European national cinemas and Eastern Bloc film cultures.[107] At the end of the 1940s and in the first half of the 1950s, the festival served primarily the global interests – both ideological and economic – of the Soviet Union.

By examining the tensions that erupted between national, transnational and global concepts characterizing the MFF KV, this chapter has begun to show that when transnational political, cultural and economic forces are in motion, festivals are ideally understood as institutions that are constantly in flux – as shifting categories that defy the application of a single geographically determined prism, be it the national, the transnational or the global. Importantly, the chapter has also shed new light on the still poorly understood dynamics characterizing the relations between the Soviet Union and what are understood to have been its satellites. It therefore invites further consideration of relations between the Czechoslovak and Soviet Film Monopolies, a prospect that promises to illuminate in precise terms how the Soviet Union, as a dominating supranational force, influenced culture internationally. In doing so, the scope, mechanisms and concrete manifestations of Moscow's global ambitions can be detailed and understood. The ways those forces shaped the festival during the decades leading up to the 1989 collapse of the Eastern Bloc and the interaction and competition between MFF KV and the Moscow Film Festival offer only two of many possible avenues for further research on the transnational history of film festivals.

Jindřiška Bláhová is an assistant professor at the Department of Film Studies, Charles University in Prague, and a film critic. As film historian, she specializes in the relationships between the American and East European film industries, film culture under communist regimes, and the film festivals. She holds Ph.D.s in film history from the University of East Anglia (U.K.) and Charles University in Prague. Having worked as a critic and industry analyst for the leading Czech economic daily *Hospodářské noviny*, she is currently editor-in-chief of the film culture magazine *Cinepur*. In addition to publishing widely in her native Czech and serving as guest editor for the Czech film journal *Iluminace* (issues on Post-feminism, Banned Films in Eastern Europe, and Film Festivals), she has published award-winning English-language articles on the relationships between distribution, reception and politics in the *Historical Journal of Film, Radio and Television*, *Post Script* and *Film History*.

Notes

1. In 1946 and 1949 the festival took place in both cities but was centred in Mariánské Lázně. From 1950 onwards it took place exclusively in Karlovy Vary.
2. From 1945 to 1948, the Czechoslovak film monopoly was called the Czech Film Company (Česká filmová společnost). From 1948 onwards it was renamed Czechoslovak State Film. For the purposes of this chapter, I consistently use the name Czechoslovak State Film or its abbreviation ČSF.
3. Heide Fehrenbach, 'Mass Culture and Cold War Politics: The Berlin Film Festival of the 1950s', in *Cinema in Democratizing Germany: Reconstructing National Identity after Hitler* (Chapel Hill: University of North Carolina Press, 1995), pp. 234–259.
4. Marla Susan Stone, *The Patron State: Culture and Politics in Fascist Italy* (Princeton, NJ: Princeton University Press, 1998), pp. 100–110; Fehrenbach, *Cinema in Democratizing Germany*, pp. 234–253.
5. Marijke De Valck, *Film Festivals: From European Geopolitics to Global Cinephilia* (Amsterdam: Amsterdam University Press, 2007); Thomas Elsaesser, 'Film Festival Networks: The New Topographies of Cinema in Europe', in *European Cinema: Face to Face with Hollywood* (Amsterdam: Amsterdam University Press, 2005); Dina Iordanova and Ragan Rhyne (eds), *Film Festival Yearbook 1: The Festival Circuit* (St Andrews Film Studies: St Andrews, 2009).
6. Dina Iordanova and Ruby Cheung (eds), *Film Festival Yearbook 2: Film Festivals and Imagined Communities* (St. Andrews: St. Andrews Film Studies, 2010).
7. Only a few studies thus far have applied a supranational perspective to 'national' histories of East European countries. Jindřiška Bláhová, 'A Tough Job for Donald Duck: Hollywood, Czechoslovakia, and Selling Films Behind the Iron Curtain, 1944–1951' (Ph.D. thesis, University of East Anglia and Charles University, 2010); Lars Karl, 'Zwischen politischem Ritual und kulturellem Dialog. Die Moskauer Internationalen Filmfestspiele im Kalten Krieg 1959–1971', in Lars Karl (ed.), *Leinwand zwischen Tauwetter und Frost* (Berlin: Metropol, 2007), pp. 277–298. For an analysis of the local-national-global dynamics of the Cannes film festival and its

influence on French 'national' cinema, see Lucy Mazdon, 'Transnational "French" Cinema: The Cannes Film Festival', *Modern & Contemporary France* 15(1) (2007), 9–20.
8. De Valck, *Film Festivals*, p. 24.
9. A.M. Brousil, 'Náš festival', in A.M. Brousil (ed.), *II. Filmový festival v ČSR s mezinárodní účastí* (Prague: Československé filmové nakladatelství, 1947), pp. 5–6.
10. Vítězslav Nezval, 'Základní kámen k naší festivalové tradici', *Filmová práce* 2(31) (1946), 1.
11. Josef Brož, 'Festivaly jinde a u nás', *Filmová práce* 2(26–27) (1946), 1.
12. Nezval, 'Základní kámen k naší festivalové tradici'.
13. Jan Ren, 'Epilog poněkud místopisný', in Jaroslav Brož (ed.), *Filmoví novináři o československém filmu, K I. festivalu filmů v Československu s mezinárodní účastí* (Prague: Československé filmové nakladatelství, 1946), pp. 27–28.
14. Konečná zpráva o organizačních a hospodářských výsledcích II. filmového festivalu v Československu s mezinárodní účastí, konaného ve dnech 2.–17. srpna 1947 v Mariánských Lázních, 6. 12. 1947. Národní archiv (NA), Prague, f. 861 – Ministerstvo informací, karton (k). 227, inventární číslo (inv. č.) 462.
15. Jaroslav Brož (ed.), *Filmoví novináři o československém filmu, K I. Festivalu filmů v Československu s mezinárodní účastí* (Prague: Československé filmové nakladatelství, 1946), pp. 5–6.
16. Jaroslav Kučera, 'Náš film ve světě', in A.M. Brousil (ed.), *II. Filmový festival v ČSR s mezinárodní účastí*, pp. 9–10.
17. Brož (ed.), *Filmoví novináři o československém filmu*, p. 5.
18. Nezval, 'Základní kámen k naší festivalové tradici'.
19. Josef Brož, 'Festival – tentokrát československý', *Filmová práce* 2(31) (1946), 1.
20. Bohumil Brejcha, 'Vytváříme tradici festivalu v Mar. Lázních', *Filmové noviny* 1(30) (1947), 1.
21. Pětiletý plán Československý státní film, 3. 6. 1948. NA, f. 19/7 – ÚV KSČ, archivní jednotka (a. j.) 662.
22. Jiří Havelka, *Čs. Filmové hospodářství 1951–1955* (Prague: Československý filmový ústav, 1972), p. 80.
23. Filmový festival od 1.–15. VIII. 1946 v Mariánských Lázních, 11. 6. 1946. NA, f. 861, inv. č. 462, k. 227.
24. Kučera, 'Náš film ve světě'.
25. Josef Štrych, 'Národy velké a malé', *Kulturní politika*, 25 July 1947, p. 5; Alexej Kusák, *Kultura a politika v Československu, 1945–1956* (Prague: Torst, 1998), p. 150.
26. Rudolf Patera, 'Poslání našeho filmu', *Filmové noviny* 1(31) (1947), 1.
27. Brož (ed.), *Filmoví novináři o československém filmu*, p. 5.
28. Although all the political parties comprising the post-1945 Czechoslovak government (democratic and communist alike) had agreed it was necessary to nationalize the film industry, cultural and economic elites were divided in their opinion on the matter. Celebrating the Czechoslovak Film Monopoly at the festival thus served as a public relations exercise directed at those who preferred the old privately run model of the film industry. See Petr Mareš, 'Politika a "pohyblivé obrázky": Spor o dovoz amerických filmů do Československa po II. Světové válce', *Iluminace* 6(1) (1994), 77–96.
29. 'Zahraniční novináři na festivalu', *Filmové noviny* 1(33) (1947), 1.
30. Dodatek k hospodářské a organisační zprávě II. Filmového festivalu v Československu s mezinárodní účastí. NA, f. 861, inv. č. 462, k. 227.

31. Kusák, *Kultura a politika v Československu*, pp. 147–153.
32. Brousil, 'Náš festival', p. 5.
33. Dodatek k hospodářské a organisační zprávě II. Filmového festivalu v Československu s mezinárodní účastí, Prague, 6. 12. 1947, s. 2. NA, f. 861, inv. č. 462, k. 227; Rudolf Patera, 'Smysl našeho filmu', in A.M. Brousil (ed.), *II. Filmový festival v ČSR s mezinárodní účastí*, p. 41; Rudolf Patera, 'Poučení z Mariánských Lázní', *Filmové noviny* 1(34) (1947), 1. The emphasis on Slavic unity was also manifested in a number of film export/import agreements signed in 1947 between Czechoslovakia, Poland, Bulgaria and Yugoslavia. 'Smlouva s Bulharskem', *Filmové noviny* 1(21) (1947), 1.
34. Patera, 'Poslání našeho filmu'.
35. Lubomír Linhart, '50 let Československého filmu', in Jaroslav Dvořáček (ed.), *III. Mezinárodní filmový festival v Československu* (Prague: Československý filmový ústav, 1948), p. 23–27; 'Pro slovanskou spolupráci', *Filmové noviny* 1(33) (1947), 1; 'Barrandov, Slovanský Hollywood', *Filmové noviny* 1(34) (1947), 3.
36. 'Porady v Praze o slovanské filmové spolupráci', *Filmové noviny* 1(46) (1947), 1.
37. 'Průzkum mínění o letošním festivalu', *Filmové noviny* 1(31) (1947), 6.
38. Another festival ran parallel to the MFF KV and facilitated the Czechoslovak Communist Party's ideological programme: the so-called Workers' Film Festival (Filmový festival pracujících) complemented the MFF KV by 'servicing' the broader Czechoslovak population with films. Its function was to educate workers politically and ideologically. See Luděk Havel, '"O nového člověka, o dokonalejší lidstvo, o nový festival". Filmový festival pracujících, 1948 až 1959', in Pavel Skopal (ed.), *Naplánovaná kinematografie: český filmový průmysl 1945–1960* (Prague: Academia, 2012), pp. 321–35.
39. Jindřiška Bláhová, 'Hollywood za železnou oponou: vyjednávání o nové smlouvě o dovozu hollywoodských filmů do Československa po II. Světové válce', *Iluminace* 20(4) (2008), 16–62.
40. Operations of Motion Picture Export Association in Czechoslovakia, Prague, 28 December 1948, National Archives and Records Administration, College Park II, Maryland, USA (NARA), Department of States Files (RG59), DF1945–1949, 860F.4061 MP/12-2848.
41. In 1946 and 1947, the Soviets participated in both the Venice and Cannes film festivals with the aim of advancing their economic and political agendas in Western Europe. By contrast, Soviet Minister of Cinematography Ivan Bolshakov declined an invitation to attend the 1947 MFF KV sent to Moscow by Czechoslovak Minister of Information Václav Kopecký. Similarly, film directors Vselovod Pudovkin and Sergei Eisenstein, who were also invited, could not attend, and the Soviet government made its preference for Western European festivals clear by sending the leading Soviet stars to Venice. Z Moskvy ministru Kopeckému, 19. 7. 1947. NA, f. 861, inv. č. 462, k. 227. On the issues of the Soviet presence at and in relation to the Venice film festival during the early Cold War years, see Stefano Pisu, *Stalin a Venezia: L'Urss alla Mostra del cinema fra diplomazia culturale e scontro ideologico (1932–1953)* (Soveria Mannelli: Rubbettino, 2013).
42. 21 February 1948. Rossiiskii gosudarstvennyi arkhiv sotsiaľno-politicheskoi istorii, fond 17, opis (op.) 125, edinica khranenija (ed. khr.). 639, l. 132.
43. Ibid.
44. Karel Vaněk, 'Sovětští filmoví umělci na festival v Mariánských Lázních', *Rudé právo*, 31 July 1949, p. 4.

45. 'V Moskvě odevzdány ceny z našeho filmového festivalu', *Zemědělské noviny*, 2 September 1949, p. 3.
46. On the notion of the superior qualities of socialist cinema and the inferior quality of capitalist cinema in the rhetoric of Czechoslovak communists during the early stages of the Cold War see Jindřiška Bláhová, 'No Place for Peace-Mongers: Charlie Chaplin, *Monsieur Verdoux* (1947), and Czechoslovak Communist Propaganda', *Historical Journal of Film, Radio and Television* 29(3) (2009), 321–342.
47. 'Ministr Kopecký o našich festivalech', *Filmové noviny* 2(32) (1948), 2.
48. Karel Vaněk, 'Film v boji o nového člověka', *Rudé právo*, 3 July 1949, p. 4.
49. A.M. Brousil, 'Náš přínos do mezinárodních filmových soutěží', in Jaroslav Dvořáček (ed.), *III. Mezinárodní filmový festival v Československu*, p. 31.
50. Josef Kořán, 'Festival po rubu', *Kino* 4(17) (1949), 260–261.
51. Brousil, 'Náš přínos do mezinárodních filmových soutěží', p. 29.
52. František Kout, 'Poslání našeho festivalu', *Filmové noviny* 2(15) (1948), 2.
53. De Valck, *Film Festivals*, p. 27.
54. David W. Elwood and Rob Kroes (eds), *Hollywood in Europe: Experiences of a Cultural Hegemony* (Amsterdam: VU University Press, 1994); Geoffrey Nowell-Smith and Steven Ricci (eds), *Hollywood and Europe: Economics, Culture, National Identity: 1945–95* (London: BFI, 1998).
55. Karel Vaněk, 'Film v boji za mír', *Rudé právo*, 15 July 1950, p. 4.
56. bž: [Brož, Jaroslav], 'Československo a filmové festivaly', *Filmové noviny* 2(1) (1948), 1.
57. Pfn, 'Filmový svět hleděl k Mariánským Lázním', *Haló noviny*, 14 August 1949.
58. bž, 'Československo a filmové festivaly'; Rudolf Patera, 'Poučení z Mariánských Lázní', *Filmové noviny* 1(34) (1947), 1.
59. De Valck, *Film Festivals*, p. 24. See also Vanessa R. Schwartz, *It's So French!: Hollywood, Paris and the Making of Cosmopolitan Film Culture* (Chicago and London: University of Chicago Press, 2007), pp. 57–99.
60. 'Výzva k Chaplinovi, Whylerovi, Wellesovi a dalším mlčícím umělcům', *Mladá fronta*, 27 July 1950.
61. Hodnocení VIII. Mezinárodního filmového festivalu v Karlových Varech, NA, MI, f. 861, k. 280, inv.č. 512.
62. 'Ministr Kopecký o našich festivalech'.
63. Oldřich Macháček, 'Československý film k třicetiletí sovětské kinematografie', *Kino* 4(17) (1949), 248.
64. V. Bor, 'Za filmovými festivaly', in *Kulturní politika* 4, 2 September 1949, p. 3.
65. Rozbor současného stavu práce celého podniku a zjištění současných nedostatků, 8. 11. 1949. NA, Archiv ÚV KSČ, f. 1261/0/26 – Politické byro 1951–1954, svazek (sv.) 2, archivní jednotka (a.j.) 11, p. 30. Uspořádání VII. Mezinárodního filmového festivalu v Karlových Varech, 30. 5. 1952, p. 25. NA, Archiv ÚV KSČ, f.1261/0/22, sv. 28, a. j. 99, bod (b.) 20g.
66. Zástupce SEF v ČSR Lebeděv Sakontikovi, Prague, 28. 7. 1949, pp. 51–52, Rossiskii gosudarstvennyi arkhiv noveishei istorii, f. 2456 – Ministerstvo kinematografii, op. 4, ed. khr. 210.
67. Uspořádání VII. Mezinárodního filmového festivalu v Karlových Varech, v Praze, 27. 5. 1952. NA, A ÚV KSČ, f. 1261/0/22, sv. 28, a. j. 99, b. 20g, p. 25.
68. K zahájení VI. Mezinárodního filmového festivalu v Československu, Václav Kopecký, ministr informací a osvěty. NA, A ÚV KSČ, f. 100/45 – Václav Kopecký, sv. 3, a. j. 114.
69. RP, 'Před V. Mezinárodním filmovým festivalem', *Rudé právo*, 12 July 1950, p. 5.

70. Vaněk, 'Film v boji za mír'.
71. J. Tichý, 'Mezinárodní porady pokrokových filmových pracovníků v Československu zahájeny', *Mladá fronta*, 20 August 1950.
72. 'Film v kapitalistických zemích', *Práce*, 25 July 1950; 'Slavnostní udělení cen na filmovém festivalu', *Lidová demokracie*, 1 August 1950, p. 5.
73. D. Tomášek, 'Pátý filmový festival končí', *Zemědělské noviny*, 30 July 1950.
74. Ibid.
75. De Valck, *Film Festivals*, p. 30.
76. VI. Mezinárodní filmový festival Karlovy Vary 1951, p. 3. NA, A ÚV KSČ, f. 19/7, a. j. 673.
77. Ibid.
78. Havelka, *Čs. filmové hospodářství 1951–1955*, p. 51.
79. Návrh na uspořádání XIII. Mezinárodního filmového festivalu v Karlových Varech v roce 1962. NA, A ÚV KSČ, f. 1261/0/11, sv. 328, a. j. 419, b. 6.
80. -s, 'Nejmilejší a nejvzácnější hosté', *Kino* 7(17) (1952), 328.
81. E.g. in 1954, the Soviets secured Chinese, Japanese and Indian films. Spol. T/12 – film – VIII. MFF v Karl. Varech Čínské a japonské filmy, 30. 6. 1954. NA, f. Ministerstvo kultury (MK), inv. č. 512, k. 280; 'Indonéský film na Mezinárodní filmový festival v Karlových Varech', *Kino* 7(14) (1952), 275.
82. A.J. Liehm and Mira Liehm, *The Most Important Art: Eastern European Film after 1945* (Los Angeles: University of California Press, 1977).
83. Mezinárodní filmový festival a filmové festivaly pracujících v roce 1953, 6. 1. 1953, s. 2. NA, A ÚV KSČ, f. 1261/0/22, sv. 50b, a. j. 135, b. 34.
84. Rozpočet VIII. MFF. NA, MK, inv.č. 512, k. 280.
85. Hodnocení VIII. Mezinárodního filmového festivalu v Karlových Varech. NA, MK, inv. č. 512, k. 280, sv. MFF KV 1954, 1956.
86. Jiří Hrbas, 'O hrdinech, prostředí a ději festivalových filmů', *Kino* 9(17) (1954), 268–270; V. Bor, 'Za filmovými festivaly', *Kulturní politika* 4 (1949), 3.
87. Jan Žalman, 'Oč jde v Karlových Varech', *Kino* 9(15) (1954), 228.
88. Jiří Hrbas, 'Československá kinematografie v mezinárodní soutěži', *Kino* 9(15) (1954), 232.
89. 'Dulles Favors Films for USSR', *Variety*, 2 November 1955, pp. 2 and 55.
90. Zpráva o konsultaci návrhu na IX. MFF v Karlových Varech s ministerstvem kultury Sovětského svazu. NA, A ÚV KSČ, f. 1261/0/11, sv. 79, a. j. 97, b. 2, p. 9.
91. FIAPF was established at the Venice film festival in 1949 to defend its members' interests on international markets. Members were Argentina, Austria, Belgium, Denmark, Egypt, Finland, France, Germany, India, Israel, Italy, Japan, Mexico, the Netherlands, Pakistan, Spain, Portugal, Sweden, Switzerland, Turkey, the United Kingdom and the United States. NA, A ÚV KSČ, f. 1261/0/11, sv. 79, a. j. 97, b. 2, p. 14.
92. Uspořádání IX. Mezinárodního filmového festivalu v Karlových Varech. NA, A ÚV KSČ, f. 1261/0/11, sv. 79, a. j. 97, b. 2.
93. Bláhová, 'Hollywood za železnou oponou'.
94. Připomínky V. oddělení, Politické byro ÚV KSČ. NA, A ÚV KSČ, f. 1261/0/11, sv. 117, a. j. 143, b. 15, p. 3.
95. Mezinárodní federace sdružení filmových producentů, Řím, 6. 12. 1955, p. 19. NA, A ÚV KSČ, f. 1261/0/11, sv. 117, a. j. 143, p. 15.
96. Návrh na uspořádání IX. mezinárodního filmového festivalu v Karlových Varech, NA, A ÚV KSČ, f. 1261/0/11, sv. 79, a. j. 97, b. 2, p. 5.

97. Zpráva o IX. Mezinárodním filmovém festivalu v Karlových Varech a návrh na každoroční uspořádání mezinárodních filmových festivalů v Karlových Varech, počínaje rokem 1957. NA, A ÚV KSČ, f. 1261/0/11, sv. 117, a. j. 143, b. 15, p. 5.
98. Kopecký ústřednímu tajemníkovi KSČ Rudolfu Slánskému, 12. 5. 1951. NA, f. 19/7, a. j. 673, sv. 6; Mezinárodní filmový festival. Dopis zahraničního oddělení ČSF Rank Organization, 5. 3. 1956. NA, f. MK, inv. č. 512, k. 280, sv. Zahr. film MFF K. Vary 1954, 1956.
99. Návrh na uspořádání IX. Mezinárodního filmového festivalu v Karlových Varech, 14. února 1956. NA, MK, inv. č. 512, k. 280.
100. Zpráva o IX. Mezinárodním filmovém festival, p. 6.
101. Ibid.
102. Přehled obchodních jednání na IX. MFF v Karlových Varech. NA, A ÚV KSČ, PB 1954–1962, f. 1261/0/11, sv. 117, a. j. 143, b. 15, p. 11–13.
103. E.g. a similar report from 1953 shows that socialist countries such as the USSR, China, Korea, Albania, Poland, Bulgaria and Hungary represented the majority of economic exchange. Komentář k přiložené zprávě k dovozu a vývozu., NA, A ÚV KSČ, f. 1261/0/26, sv. 50B, a. j. 134, b. 34.
104. Jiří Havelka, Čs. filmové hospodářství 1956–1960 (Prague: Československý filmový ústav, 1975), p. 49.
105. See Lars Karl, 'Zwischen politischem Ritual und kulturellem Dialog: Die Moskauer Internationalen Filmfestspiele im Kalten Krieg 1959–1971', in Lars Karl (ed.), Leinwand zwischen Tauwetter und Frost. Der osteuropäische Spiel- ind Dokumentarfilm im Kalten Krieg (Berlin: Metropol, 2007), pp. 279–298.
106. NARA, RG59, DF1955-59, 25. 2. 1959, 849.452/2-2559.
107. On the discursive role that Hollywood played in Czechoslovak communist rhetoric, see Bláhová, 'No Place for Peace-Mongers'.

Select Bibliography

Bláhová, Jindřiška. 'A Tough Job for Donald Duck: Czechoslovakia, Hollywood, and Selling Films behind the Iron Curtain, 1944–1951'. Ph.D. thesis, University of East Anglia and Charles University in Prague, 2010.

Cull, Nicholas. *The Cold War and the United States Information Agency: American Propaganda and Public Diplomacy, 1945–1989*. Cambridge: Cambridge University Press, 2008.

De Valck, Marijke. *Film Festivals: From European Geopolitics to Global Cinephilia*. Amsterdam: Amsterdam University Press, 2007.

Elsaesser, Thomas. 'Film Festival Networks: The New Topographies of Cinema in Europe'. In *European Cinema: Face to Face with Hollywood*. Amsterdam: Amsterdam University Press, 2005.

Elwood, David W., and Rob Kroes (eds). *Hollywood in Europe: Experiences of a Cultural Hegemony*. Amsterdam: VU University Press, 1994.

Fehrenbach, Heide. 'Mass Culture and Cold War Politics: The Berlin Film Festival of the 1950s'. In *Cinema in Democratizing Germany: Reconstructing National Identity after Hitler*. Chapel Hill: University of North Carolina Press, 1995.

Iordanova, Dina, and Ragan Rhyne (eds). *Film Festival Yearbook 1: The Festival Circuit*. St Andrews Film Studies: St Andrews, 2009.

Karl, Lars. 'Zwischen politischem Ritual und kulturellem Dialog. Die Moskauer Internationalen Filmfestspiele im Kalten Krieg 1959–1971'. In Lars Karl (ed.), *Leinwand zwischen Tauwetter und Frost*. Berlin: Metropol, 2007.

Stone, Marla Susan. *The Patron State: Culture and Politics in Fascist Italy*. Princeton, NJ: Princeton University Press, 1998.

PART VI

DISTRIBUTION AND RECEPTION

Chapter 13

CINEMA CULTURES OF INTEGRATION

Film Distribution and Exhibition in the GDR
and Czechoslovakia from the Perspective
of Two Local Cases, 1945–1960

Kyrill Kunakhovich and Pavel Skopal

On 11 July 1945, Leipzig cinemas reopened after a brief wartime hiatus. For the second-largest city in eastern (soon to be East) Germany, this was the first step towards a distinctive socialist film culture. State officials gradually took control of selecting, circulating and screening films. Under their supervision, Leipzig cinemas developed new repertoires and cultivated new audiences. What emerged was an East German film-distribution system that shared some significant parameters with other states in the Soviet zone of influence, but also maintained some distinctive features.[1] Meanwhile, 450 kilometres south-east of Leipzig in Brno, the second largest Czechoslovak city, thirty-one cinemas were gradually opening their doors to cinemagoers. This study presents a comparative examination of the ideological foundations of film policy, the mechanisms for importing and distributing films, and the specific practices used to attract viewers to the cinemas in these large cities in two neighbouring states.

To investigate how film policy functioned in practice, this text focuses on the cases of Leipzig and Brno in the years from 1945 to 1960. Comparing cinema exhibition practices in Brno with those in Leipzig improves our understanding of the similarities rooted in the state-socialist system of cinema distribution and exhibition, as well as the differences deriving from each city's distinct traditions and postwar situations. Despite the fact that Leipzig was significantly larger,[2] the cities shared important characteristics: both were 'metropolises of the second grade'[3] – important regional centres with major universities, significant industry, a strong cultural infrastructure including a large cinema network (Brno entered the postwar era with 31 and Leipzig with 34 cinemas) and a representative role as trade fair cities.

We will follow the argument that both state regimes utilized cinema culture as a tool for integrating the population into the new socialist societies and promoting the citizens' identification with the values of the society. We seek to move beyond the standard argument that emphasizes the conflict between the ideological and economic goals pursued simultaneously by the regimes, as well as the differentiation between the message provided by 'preferred' movies loaded with ideology, on the one hand, and the 'appeasement' of the citizens with a few genre movies on the other.[4] We argue that both modes of cinema production primarily served the same goal according to the mandates of cultural policy: to integrate cinemagoers into the society by providing a range of different cultural opportunities.

This article brings together some results from three other projects[5] to compare distribution and exhibition practices in the German Democratic Republic (GDR) and Czechoslovakia and their significance for the respective cultural policies of the two state regimes. The comparison of film culture and cultural policy in these two states, which also takes into consideration the Soviet effort to shape them to its own ends, illuminates significant characteristics of the cultural sphere in the Eastern Bloc. This essay will highlight various features, both indigenous and imposed by Soviet authorities, that were shared by both countries and overcame the significant differences in their ideological foundations. Other aspects will be shown to reveal a sense of national specificity that persisted despite significant parallels in the internal political processes of both countries and the role in Soviet politics that the two states were supposed to play in relation to the Western Bloc.[6] The analysis of the two cinema cultures is organized in four sections covering ideological foundations, film selection, distribution and exhibition. Each section begins with the German case, for hermeneutical[7] as well as analytical reasons: throughout the first postwar decade at least some aspects of cinema culture in the GDR (or in the Soviet Zone of Occupation, as it was called until 1949) were under *direct* Soviet control. This fact makes the GDR the paramount case for considering the shapes and parameters of the Sovietization of cinema culture that took place in the postwar Soviet Bloc. This analysis is followed by a discussion of the Czechoslovak case.[8] After that, each section except the last one (focused exclusively on local case studies in Brno and Leipzig) concludes with a subsection devoted explicitly to the Soviet influences in both states and to mutual relations or influences between the GDR and Czechoslovakia.

Ideological Foundations

The GDR

Socialist film policy was rooted in the idea that culture has great political significance. East German officials believed that cultural life was about more than just entertainment: all forms of culture carried implicit messages that could transform mentalities and promote a new world view. Art, in other words, never existed purely for art's sake. The socialist state took it upon itself to regulate art in the name of the public good. It sought to expose society to 'positive' culture and protect it from 'negative' influences. This was the rationale for monopolizing film distribution and exhibition: film had to be closely monitored because it mattered. Such an approach reflected Soviet attitudes towards film, which provided constant inspiration to East German communists.[9] At the same time, this conception of culture had deep indigenous roots. Throughout the Weimar era, both communists and socialists organized screenings of 'worthy' movies to educate and mobilize workers.[10] Nazi authorities also recognized cinema's motivational potential and even looked admiringly at Soviet productions.[11] By the end of World War II, the notion that film carried political meanings was already firmly entrenched. As East German communists saw it, they were not politicizing culture but assuring that it was politically correct.

Although concern with the political function of film remained a constant in East German cultural policy, the specific functions assigned to film changed over time in accordance with the evolution of the state's socialist project. As Soviet tanks rolled into eastern Germany in 1945, de-Nazification became priority number one. Speaking at the opening of the DEFA (Deutsche Film-Aktiengesellschaft) film studios, the propaganda head of the Soviet Military Administration in Germany (Sowjetische Militäradministration in Deutschland, SMAD) described the main tasks of film as 'eradicating the remnants of Nazism and militarism from the consciousness of every German, [and] educating the German people ... in the spirit of true democracy and humanity'.[12] After the formation of the East German state, the focus shifted from confronting the past to mastering the future. In July 1952, the Socialist Unity Party of Germany (Sozialistische Einheitspartei Deutschlands, SED)'s Central Committee prepared a programme 'For the Improvement of Progressive German Cinema', declaring: 'It is essential to develop the socialist consciousness of workers, to fill the population with the idea ... of hate against imperialist warmongers, militarists, and traitors, to educate [the people] to deploy all their abilities for the building of socialism and for the successful completion of our Five Year Plan'.[13] In the era of high Stalinism, cinema became a school for socialism, charged with forming the New Socialist Man.[14]

Even as they emphasized film's didactic qualities, however, East German officials still acknowledged its entertainment value. 'Lighter' crowd-pleasers always remained part of GDR repertoires, though less so during the political offensive of the early 1950s. This situation changed after the popular uprising on 17 June 1953, which accelerated the leadership's New Course. During a Central Committee meeting in September 1953, Walter Ulbricht distanced himself from the past and advocated a more populist approach. 'The population ... calls for more films and for interesting films', he argued, adding: 'It is necessary to satisfy people's need for entertainment.'[15] Cultural officials began to promote comedies and pay attention to viewer preferences. In so doing, they improved cinemas' profitability at a time of economic reform. Appealing films brought in far more money than formulaic ideological productions, helping to finance the developing GDR film industry. The new emphasis on entertainment allowed the Thaw-era SED to kill two birds with one stone: it accommodated popular tastes while simultaneously increasing state revenue.[16]

Within a few years, however, the New Course and its film policy had come under attack. In 1956, popular protests in Poland and Hungary sent shockwaves through the SED leadership. Ulbricht responded by bolstering his authority, tightening ideological controls and reasserting the political nature of art. In October 1957, soon-to-be Culture Minister Alexander Abusch boasted that all 'cultural forms will turn into spiritual weapons for our socialist construction'.[17] 'Cinema is a weapon!' film officials duly proclaimed.[18] Once again they stressed film's educational mission and pushed popularity and profitability into the background. Still, these concerns never disappeared from view. By the end of the decade, officials were again pleading for better quality and more entertaining movies.[19] These twists and turns reflected a search for balance between two contradictory imperatives. On the one hand, officials believed that films should transform their viewers by spreading a socialist worldview. On the other, they realized that films had to appeal to their viewers, both to satisfy demand and to make money. This was the challenge of building a new society out of old pieces: East German officials tried to alter tastes and appease them at the same time. GDR film policy shuttled between these two poles throughout the 1950s and beyond. It favoured education at times and entertainment at others, but cinemas always struggled to find a balance between the two.

Czechoslovakia

While Germany was undergoing the change from the Nazi regime to the protectorate administered by the Allies, Czechoslovakia was re-emerging from the Protectorate of Bohemia and Moravia into a system of democracy founded on the National Front as an association of all authorized political parties, a system that endured for only three years. In spite of the democratic conditions, the Communist Party of Czechoslovakia (Komunistická strana Československa, KSČ) already wielded significant influence over the film industry in the first postwar months through its contacts with the industry's creative personnel, as well as through the Ministry of Information and Enlightenment, headed by the communist Václav Kopecký since 1945. The KSČ explicitly presented itself as the creator of ideology for the new Czechoslovakia and the main promoter of the 'democratization of culture'.[20]

A statement by Kopecký at the Eighth Congress of the Czechoslovak Communist Party in March 1946 (two years before the communist putsch in February 1948) underlines how the party perceived cinema and what demands it was already imposing on film distribution under comparatively democratic conditions: 'We have nationalized not only film production ... [but] also ... film renting, which means that it is impossible for foreign film agencies to nose around here freely and sell all kinds of rubbish as they did in the past.'[21] As Minister Kopecký's speech implies, cinema played an important role in communist rhetoric: its nationalization was a symbol of the victory of the 'national and democratic revolution' over the old order, and the new distribution system was portrayed as a matter of public interest and as a democratic and educational tool not restricted by the demand for profitability.

In accordance with state cultural policy, various distribution practices were utilized in massive campaigns for (re)education and labour mobilization. Starting in 1946, obligatory cinema screenings for schoolchildren were organized by the Ministry of Education and Culture, which was controlled by the communist party. The ministry classified predominantly Soviet movies as 'especially valuable for youth education', and after the communist putsch in 1948 the few American movies that had been on this list – e.g. *Wilson* (Henry King, 1944) or *Young Tom Edison* (Norman Taurog, 1940) – were excluded.[22] Villagers were another specific target of education and mobilization through cinema screenings aimed at gathering support for the process of collectivization and bolstering labour performance and morale. At the same time that the process of 'cinefication' was establishing permanent cinemas in 'central villages', travelling cinemas were deployed to ensure that all citizens were within the reach of cinema indoctrination and entertainment. The seemingly elaborate but poorly functioning system of travelling cinema tours reached its peak in 1955 with 127 cinemas in service and 74,670 screenings.[23] This system of distribution of 16mm copies was a significant deviation from the regime's effort to counterbalance the educational function of cinema with a dose of entertainment. The few available Western movies did not circulate in this network of distribution, and domestic colour genre pictures (comedies, biopics or historical spectacles) were screened either not at all, or only as black and white copies. The only exceptions were festivals, which aimed to facilitate villagers' integration into the regime's system (e.g. Film Spring in the Village or the Festival of Colour Movies).[24] The same kind of 'village festival' was organized in the GDR (Frühling auf dem Lande - Film Spring in the Village); a paper given by a local SED functionary in April 1953 provides a good illustration of the ideological charge in these village screenings: 'We are aware of the fact that the cultural work for the masses, especially in the sphere of cinema, is very important for the building of our society in the villages.... Our peasants demand good progressive movies.... To raise people in the spirit of Socialism is possible only through progressive movies.'[25]

Any consideration of the role assigned to cinema culture by the regime demands recognition of the role played by the production limits imposed on the national film industries within the Soviet Bloc. Beyond any possible conjecture as to the actual ideological effects that film screenings had on their viewers, it must be stated that the most fundamental factor affecting both the ideological efficiency of cinema culture and the rhetorical demands imposed on it was the lack of movies that were ideologically suitable for domestic distribution.

In 1949, Czechoslovak officials reshaped film distribution in accordance with the new cultural policy, which deemphasized the sheer number of premieres.[26] The prescribed distribution demand was set at a scant 100 movies per year, and the head of the distribution branch of Czechoslovak State Film (Československý státní film, ČSF), Jaroslav Málek, announced a shift from 'extensive' to 'intensive' distribution – in other words, from a high number of premieres to repeated screenings of a few preferred movies. The number of new films screened in cinemas had fallen sharply from 199 in 1947 to 92 in 1949 and 74 in 1950. The distribution system was given the task of significantly changing viewers' motivation by educating them in a new 'attendance tradition' and teaching them, in the words of Jaroslav Málek, 'not only to attend the new films but to learn from progressive films again and again, and to change the current state of affairs, whereby a viewer always sees a film only once'.[27] The models for a new viewer and a new film culture were to be rooted in the activity of visiting cinemas as a political act of self-education. These radical models had to be altered for various reasons, the two most significant being the slowly rising productivity of the Czech film industry and the fact that, for external and internal reasons, certain liberal tendencies opened the gates to greater import.

The Soviet Influence

As was the case in Germany, the communist party and leftist intellectuals in Czechoslovakia had already utilized the cinema for purposes of agitation as early as the interwar period.[28] However, after World War II these groups in both countries engaged in cinematic practices that shared characteristics with the domestic mainstream distribution system, including the Nazi one. For example, the movie rating systems instituted in the GDR and Czechoslovakia in the postwar era (examined below) display clear signs of continuity with the nationalized, politicized system of Nazi Germany. The National Socialists described their system of evaluating and rating films as 'positive censorship' and divided all UFA productions into eight categories, including 'particularly valuable', 'nationally valuable', 'artistic', 'nationally educational', and 'culturally valuable'.[29] In 1943, this German system of 'ratings' (*Prädikate*) was also instituted within the Protectorate of Bohemia and Moravia.[30]

The centralized, hierarchically organized structure of the nationalized film industry in postwar Czechoslovakia can be more adequately explained as a product of experience with the system from the Protectorate era, which had been modelled on the Film Chamber of the Reich (Reichsfilmkammer), than as a result of Soviet inspiration.[31] Indeed, the Soviet film industry could have hardly served as a model of an effective production system.[32] Minister of Cinematography Ivan

G. Bolshakov's ambitious plans to make Mosfilm the biggest European film studio had collapsed, and no Soviet political advisers were involved in the restructuring of film industry in Czechoslovakia, a fact that complicated the opportunity to follow the Soviet model for even the most zealous communists.[33] This does not mean, however, that we can entirely dismiss the pervasive admiration of the Soviet example as rhetorical padding. Numerous cultural engagements with the USSR provided patterns, examples and guidelines for Czechoslovak filmmakers and apparatchiks, including cultural and distribution agreements between the two countries, international conferences, a lecture series featuring Soviet cinema practitioners as well as ideologists, the translation of books and manuals, and visits to Moscow by Czechoslovak delegations.[34] In the following sections, we present some detailed examples of the transference of practices and values from the Soviet Union to Czechoslovakia.

When Soviet production collapsed in the late 1940s and early 1950s, there were not enough foreign movies to allay the resultant domestic film shortage, and the distribution offering was consequently far below the projected saturation level for the Soviet market: in 1949, for example, the offering of 13 new Soviet movies and 61 imported features accounted for a mere 20 per cent of the projected demand. In 1953, the Soviet Ministry of Culture proposed that a Soviet citizen should have the opportunity to see two new movies a week. This would imply a distribution supply of 100 movies per year,[35] the same number that was intended to satisfy demand in both Czechoslovakia and the GDR during the early 1950s, which in fact proved to be a very difficult goal to achieve. Significantly, the Soviet ministry's proposal equated the number of movies (the 'opportunity to see') with audience demand – no choice or differentiation of taste was taken into account. While the productivity of the Soviet studios was extremely low in the late 1940s and early 1950s, Soviet audiences were provided with a comparatively high number of American and West European movies thanks to the stock of 'trophy films'.[36] In Czechoslovakia and the GDR, however, modifications to the distribution standards occurred much more abruptly, consequently increasing the potential for negative perceptions of the communist regimes among the population.[37] As the case of trophy movies indicates, Soviet cultural policy assumed a pragmatic approach towards addressing the discrepancy between demands for cinema's educational function and the economic requirements of the industry. As we discuss in the following sections, the Soviets immediately imposed the practice of double features in the GDR to try to overcome this discrepancy, while the Czechoslovak communists 'out-Heroded Herod' in their attitude towards nonsocialist cinema and until 1953 presented double features made up of a Western feature and a Soviet documentary.

Film Selection

The GDR

The first step in implementing the SED's ideological programme was selecting and obtaining the right films. Until the creation of the GDR, this task fell to the Soviet military authorities and their Information Administration.[38] SMAD relied primarily on Soviet films, imported by the Sovexportfilm company (SEF) – a branch of the Soviet Ministry of Cinematography.[39] From 1946, the Soviets also allowed a considerable number of German films from the Weimar and Nazi eras, albeit stripped of any political or problematic references. German communists often opposed this practice, but Soviet officers defended old German movies as necessary – and profitable – entertainment.[40] The first film made at the DEFA film studios in the Soviet Occupation Zone (Sowjetische Besatzungszone, SBZ) also premiered in 1946, and Western productions appeared in the SBZ a year later, as part of an interzonal exchange programme.[41] SMAD officials chose films from this source pool and censored them, and also dubbed foreign productions. German communists were gradually integrated into the process; starting in 1948, the Central Administration for People's Education collaborated with SMAD to approve films for release.[42]

In 1949 East German authorities assumed oversight of cinema matters while the Soviets retreated into an advisory role. Initially, film came under the state's Office for Information and the communist party's Agitation Department, and it remained disconnected from the cultural apparatus until August 1952 – a telling fact that reveals what the new regime thought of cinema.[43] Soviet officials also relinquished their stake in the DEFA studios and ceded control over imports.[44] While SEF continued to supply films from the USSR, DEFA's Division of Foreign Trade (DEFA-Außenhandel) became responsible for all other foreign productions.[45] Most of these were acquired through exchange, but Western movies often had to be bought with scarce hard currency reserves. All imports were approved by special certification boards made up of political functionaries and cinema officials. The boards usually ordered cuts or textual edits during the dubbing stage and assigned each film a quality rating that would determine the scale of its release.[46] Similar committees also reviewed DEFA productions, ensuring that every film screened in the GDR passed through a thorough official review.

The precise nature of this review changed slightly over time. In 1952, control over film shifted to the newly created State Committee for Film Affairs (Staatliches Komitee für Filmwesen). Two years later it was incorporated into a Ministry of Culture, which had a Central Administration devoted to film (Hauptverwaltung Film). In 1958, a new body, the Association of People's Own Film Enterprises (Vereinigung Volkseigener Betriebe Film), took charge of the administrative and economic side of the film industry, leaving censorship to the Ministry of Culture. Throughout the decade, though, it was the SED's Central Committee that made major decisions on film issues and set the course of cultural policy.[47] As a result, GDR film repertoires reflected the changing political line. Old German entertainment films predominated under the Soviet occupation but increasingly gave way to forward-looking socialist productions under the new East German state. The number of Western films, meanwhile, spiked after the June 1953 uprising, only to fall again during Ulbricht's ideological offensive in the late 1950s.[48] Policy shifts affected the work of import agencies and certification boards, which in turn influenced what films were approved for screening in East Germany. After this stage, a complex distribution network determined what films were actually screened at the local level.

Czechoslovakia

In contrast to the situation in the SBZ, the Soviets had no direct administrative control over film selection in postwar Czechoslovakia. The only exception to this general condition was Soviet-organized screenings in individual cities during the first few weeks after their liberation. Even though the first screenings were intended primarily for Red Army soldiers, local audiences were also admitted, and screenings for locals soon followed.[49] Until the communist putsch in February 1948, movies for distribution were picked up by the Approval Board (aprobační komise) till 1947 and by the Board for Import (dovozní komise) afterwards, which consisted of employees of the state film enterprise, film critics, writers and scriptwriters. In 1947, the distribution of 175 imported features from seven countries provided a comparatively wide and diversified offering. A censorship board under the Ministry of Information and Enlightenment assessed the ideological acceptability of the domestic production from the Protectorate era, which was essential during the first postwar years. In contrast to the situation with Nazi-era movies in the GDR, however, these older Czech movies were mostly withdrawn from distribution. In the 1950s, in order to satisfy audiences as well as the financial needs of the film industry, these movies were occasionally distributed in urban peripheries but not widely publicized.

Although the distribution included production from a broad range of nations, Soviet movies were significantly privileged due to the direct influence the communist party exercised upon the film industry as well as the general leftist slant in postwar Czechoslovak society, particularly among intellectuals and artists.[50] The contract with the Soviet film industry signed in July 1945 favoured Soviet productions, granting 60 per cent of screening time in cinemas to films from Soviet distributor Sojuzintorgkino and obliging the Czechoslovak film industry to purchase at least a hundred Soviet films in the first year of the contract, with that number increasing by 5 per cent each following year. Because this strongly preferential treatment created a situation quantitatively identical with the conditions in the SBZ, the Soviet film industry had to deal with same problem as in the SBZ, namely, how to meet such high production volumes. A significant difference from the SBZ was grounded in the fact that the pro-Soviet, yet self-sustaining Czechoslovakian Film Association held responsibility for the supply of movies. Instead of an 'exchange' of movies with Western allies and extensive use of older domestic production (as was the case in the SBZ), the shortage of movies for distribution in Czechoslovakia was solved by an agreement with the Motion Picture Export Association representing the Hollywood studios, which ensured 34 American films would be accepted for distribution in 1946, and 82 in 1947.[51] Consequently, in 1946 there were almost as many screenings of movies from the United States and Western Europe as screenings of Soviet films, and in 1947 Western movies dominated the screens with an almost 50 per cent share of all screenings and 55.6 per cent of all attendance.

The changes after the communist putsch were harsh, even if they were implemented gradually, since it was not possible to break the bilateral contracts with the Western film studios immediately. The members of the previous Approval Board were replaced with new ones, including representatives of the centralized trade unions and of the Ministry of Information and Enlightenment. The excessive orientation towards distributing Soviet movies in Soviet Bloc countries, combined with the lack of new Soviet productions, led to the aforementioned policy of 'intensive distribution', that is, repeated exhibition of the same movies. In other words, the number of movies on the market was neither the only nor even the most significant indicator of the actual presence of a national cinema in the indigenous film culture: as the subsequent sections on distribution and exhibition will indicate, the number of screenings and the practices of exhibition were also influential, even decisive factors.

The Soviets and Their Movies

The role of Soviet cinema and SEF's position in distribution differed between the SBZ and Czechoslovakia. In the case of the former, the Soviets maintained full control over film selection until 1949, whereas in the latter they exerted an indirect and rather masked influence upon the independent Czechoslovakian Film Association (Československá filmová společnost) before 1948. The difference in SEF's approach to these markets continued after the communist putsch. The comparison provided by Figures 13.1 and 13.2 below reveals the parallels and differences. To recognize the similarities, we need to put aside the first three postwar years, when Czechoslovakia had a strongly different position relative to the Soviet Bloc, as well as its first two years of becoming 'attuned' to the new system and ridding itself of contract obligations. After doing so, we can see the that the distribution profile shifted in accordance with the main political changes that influenced the whole Soviet Bloc (the distribution offering's response to the conservative turn at the end of the 1950s was obviously delayed for one year in Czechoslovakia). The most striking fact, however, is that for most of this period, the number of pictures the Soviets supplied for Czechoslovak distribution, which was not under their direct control, was significantly higher than the number supplied for the SBZ/GDR. There are at least two consistent and mutually supportive explanations: first, an increase in Soviet pictures in the SBZ/GDR would have further damaged the economic efficiency of the market, which SEF had a share in into the mid-1950s (SEF had full control over film selection until 1948 and remained involved in distribution until 1955); and second, the risk of damage caused by screening movies that SEF perceived as low in quality was much greater in the occupied country of the former war enemy (SBZ/GDR) than in the left-leaning country liberated by the Red Army (Czechoslovakia).

The preferential treatment of Soviet movies in Czechoslovakia after the war is evident in the fact that no Soviet movie approved by the selection committee was banned by the censorship board in the years before the communist putsch. At most, the censorship board demanded certain 'emendations', such as omitting 'remarks disparaging of Czechoslovakia' in the film *Vysokaya nagrada* (High Award, Yevgeni Shneider, 1939). The board's decision on Konstantin Judin's movie *Serdtsa chetyryokh* (Four Hearts, 1941) is a telling example of the uncritical approach to Soviet production: representatives of the Ministry of Foreign Affairs and the Ministry of Information and Enlightenment recommended 'more careful selection' and advised that 'only the best pieces of Soviet film art' be proposed for distribution; nevertheless, the board approved the movie.[52] The censorship board, playing its part in the process of 'cleansing' film distribution in 1950, banned almost all Western and pre-1945 Czechoslovak movies in the process. Yet that same year, the board (which was replaced by a specialized office for pre-emptive censorship in 1953) banned only one Soviet movie, *Shchit Dzhurgaja* (Dzhurgay's Shield, Siko Dolidze and David Rondeli, 1944), on the grounds of the poor technical quality of the image.[53] Negative decisions by the censors regarding film import diminished in the coming years, as the selection committee at ČSF was careful enough to pick up mostly movies that would meet no objection.

During the post-Stalinist era, the role of the selection committees changed significantly in both Czechoslovakia and the GDR: Soviet movies were no longer accepted without hesitation, and SEF more critically evaluated movies proposed for distribution in the Eastern Bloc countries. In 1955, the GDR accepted 16 of 25 movies offered by the Soviets.[54] At the same time, SEF was even more critical towards Soviet production and therefore understood this high level of acceptance as a proof of low standards on the part of the German bodies: 'We cannot hide the fact that many weak movies were made. Still, the contemporary selection board at the Ministry of Culture in the GDR approaches our movies with specific criteria. These criteria are not based on high demands, but on a scruple, or even a fear against denying a Soviet movie.'[55] In a report on exports to Czechoslovakia, SEF acknowledged that the low level of production had resulted in the export of movies with 'low artistic value', some of which were rejected for distribution.[56] In 1957, 41 Soviet movies were accepted and 16 rejected for distribution in GDR.[57]

The number of Western movies in both the GDR and Czechoslovakia serves as an indication of how cultural policy was influenced by the more general waves of 'liberalization' and conservative turns in the respective societies (see Figure 13.2).[58] Meanwhile, the reports on the number of Soviet movies that were *not* accepted for distribution provide a more complicated image. In 1959, the conservative turn culminated in both Czechoslovakia and the GDR falling under the slogan of 'cultural revolution'; accordingly, more Soviet features (38 movies) were distributed in the GDR that year. However, this cultural offensive was not characterized strictly by unconditional obedience to the Soviet cultural programme: of the 89 features the Soviets proposed to the East Germans, 38 were denied, mainly due to a 'low ideologically artistic level'. The Soviet ambassador and the Ministry of Foreign Trade did not blame this situation on the Germans, but rather on the low quality of the Soviet movies, and SEF itself evaluated this 43 per cent acceptance rate as rather high.[59]

The Czechoslovak authorities rarely shared the specific reasons for rejecting a movie from the USSR or from a 'people's democratic' country, thereby eliciting complaints from SEF, but some of the

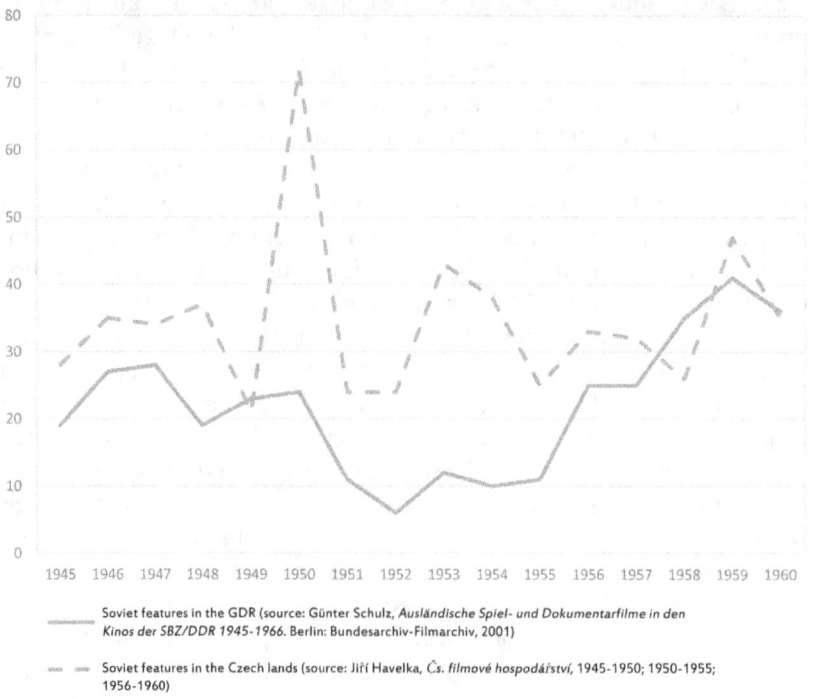

Figure 13.1 The number of Soviet movies distributed in the GDR and the Czech Lands.

available accounts are telling. In 1960, the five-member selection board in Czechoslovakia evaluated 26 Soviet movies or film series in Moscow; 10 of them were not 'recommended' for distribution[60] for various reasons, mostly for poor technical and aesthetic quality, weakly constructed characters, unnatural acting and, in one case, an unacceptable kind of humour (for a film from Tajikistan).[61] That same year, the East German selection committee at the Ministry of Culture explained that it had turned down the Soviet movie *Ivanna* (Viktor Ivchenko, 1959) because of a supposedly negative response from church leaders and their congregations.[62] This was not the first time that a movie attacking the church had become a source of a concern – the Czech comedy *Dobrý voják Švejk* (The Good Soldier Švejk, Karel Steklý, 1956) was not approved for distribution in the GDR until the initial decision was

American, French, Italian, British, and West German features in the GDR (source: Heinz Kersten, *Das Filmwesen in der Sowjetischen Besatzungszone Deutschlands*. Bonn: Bundesministerium für gesamtdeutsche Fragen, 1963. Children's movies excluded)

American, French, Italian, British, and West German features in the Czech Lands (source: Jiří Havelka, *Čs. filmové hospodářství*, 1945-50; 1951-55; 1956-60)

Figure 13.2 The number of West European and American movies distributed in the GDR and the Czech Lands.

reappraised the following year. The alleged reasons for the rejection were 'the complicated situation in the ecclesiastical sphere' and worries of a potentially negative influence on the members of the newly established People's Army.[63] According to a report from the Czechoslovak ambassador to the GDR, the negative attitude towards the movie came from 'political circles', not the selection committee.[64] However, the political elite's stance on the movie changed simultaneously with the 'successful completion' of building the People's Army and the 'exposure' of the church's 'hostile activities' to the citizens.[65] These examples offer a clear illustration of the differences between the GDR and Czechoslovakia with regard to distribution policy and the role of cinema in cultural policy. Certainly, the two shared some main goals: to support the state policy of social integration and to affirm the socialist regime.[66] However, the two countries contrasted with regard to their specific social structures, the historical experience of recent decades, and value systems, and were thus compelled to employ different strategies and practices in formulating cultural policy.

Film Distribution

The GDR

Bringing a film to Leipzig required collaboration between three different bodies: a distribution company supplied the reels, cinemas provided the space and equipment, and local government officials offered ideological guidance. All three had a say in Leipzig repertoire planning, though they all went through several incarnations and their specific competences varied. Confusion ran high in the immediate postwar period. Fourteen of Leipzig's forty-eight cinemas had been destroyed in the war, and nineteen others were owned by former Nazi party members. The new city authorities expropriated all nineteen, and even transferred some to the Soviets as reparation. The result was a patchwork of ownership: in 1947, thirteen of Leipzig's cinemas belonged to the city, fourteen were private, five were owned by SEF, one by the Red Army, and another by the provincial government of Saxony.[67] However, all these cinemas had a single supplier – SEF, which not only imported films but also distributed them throughout the Soviet Zone. Headquartered in Leipzig, SEF began to circulate film reels within days of the Red Army's arrival.[68] It sent lists of available movies to the cinemas and collected a percentage of the earnings – not just from Soviet films, but also from Nazi and DEFA productions.[69] Under this arrangement, individual cinemas retained a measure of autonomy. In 1947, for instance, private cinemas could choose to play more German movies than cinemas under city control.[70] Yet even they had to meet quotas for Soviet films. Starting in 1947, SEF mandated that Soviet films make up 40 per cent of the repertoire and run for at least a week.[71] Leipzig's Culture Department made sure that these rules were followed, but it had little influence over SEF and its film selection. Working under military occupation, German officials played only a subordinate role.

The Soviet monopoly over film distribution ended in October 1948, when DEFA began to circulate its own films. Two years later, DEFA merged with SEF to create the Progress Film-Vertrieb, a joint German-Soviet venture with a branch in Leipzig. Progress Film-Vertrieb was nationalized in 1955 and endured until the fall of the GDR. It provided reels and movie posters to all East German cinemas in exchange for 10 to 20 per cent of their profits.[72] By this time, cinema ownership had also stabilized. Leipzig's remaining private cinemas were taken over by the provincial administration of Saxony in 1948. In 1953, most city cinemas – 27 in all – were incorporated into a national cinema network; they were locally administered by the city government but ultimately subordinate to East Berlin. Only Leipzig's five SEF theatres remained independent until the Soviets ceded ownership in 1955.

Progress Film typically supplied Leipzig with two copies of each new release.[73] The larger SEF theatres often got to play these first, before passing them on to other city cinemas.[74] Starting in 1952, some productions were identified as 'emphasis films' for their ideological value and received a wider release. For instance, DEFA's two-part biopic of the German communist leader Ernst Thälmann was distributed in six reels for the city of Leipzig alone.[75] Such 'emphasis films' ran for at least two weeks at almost every cinema.[76] Progress retained final authority over programming but relied on local officials to coordinate distribution. Representatives of the Leipzig city government sat in on meetings to determine weekly cinema repertoires and at times took on a more active role.[77] In September 1953, local authorities negotiated an extension for the popular Western movie *La Putain Respectueuse* (The Respectful Prostitute, Charles Brabant, 1952). The film had enjoyed a successful run at Leipzig's largest cinema, but Progress planned to replace it with the socialist 'emphasis film' *The Revolutionary Year 1848* (*Revoluční Rok 1848*, Václav Krška, 1949). Leipzig officials appealed, arguing that in the aftermath of the 17 June uprising popular films were necessary 'on political grounds', and after four days of negotiation, Progress headquarters finally relented, so that *The Respectful Prostitute* played on.[78] As this episode shows, though, local intervention remained an exceptional event. Central authorities were prepared to listen in special circumstances but retained a firm grip on repertoire planning.

The situation changed in 1957 with the creation of Repertoire Committees at the district level. The committees consisted of local officials, ordinary residents and representatives of mass organizations. They mediated between Progress and city cinemas; each month, the committees put together repertoire plans and submitted them to the Leipzig District Council for approval. In practice, major decisions were still left to Progress, since it controlled the pool of films available for screening. At the same time, the new system did allow Leipzig party authorities to become increasingly proactive. In the late 1950s and early 1960s, the newly formed Repertoire Committee for Leipzig District began to review films locally before their release. On numerous occasions, it disagreed with central assessments and found certain movies 'unworthy to be shown in our district'.[79] Some Western films approved by Berlin were never released in Leipzig, and several others were pulled after the premiere. In at least one case, opposition from the Leipzig Party Committee forced central authorities to reconsider their position and withdraw a film from circulation.[80] Local officials thus preserved a degree of autonomy from the centre, but their power was purely negative. They could be more restrictive than Berlin but not more permissive.

Intervention by local officials was often a major headache for local cinemas, since it disrupted schedules and jeopardized plan fulfilment. Each time a problematic film was pulled, cinemas were forced to fill the gap with old reruns from the Weimar era.[81] All GDR cinemas had to meet revenue quotas, however, and also secure appropriate attendance at 'emphasis films'. Like any state-owned enterprise, a cinema worked according to a plan. Leipzig officials set annual targets for screenings, viewers and profits; often these numbers were completely unrealistic, and cinemas struggled to keep up.

Czechoslovakia

In certain respects, the efforts by the U.S. Department of State and the Hollywood film industry to achieve economic dominance and influence the system of values in Western Europe were analogous to the efforts of the Soviet Ministry of Cinematography and SEF to reach similar goals in their zone of influence.[82] In pursuing their political and economic goals, both Americans and Soviets had to cope with potential resistance to their cinema products and local audiences' preference for their own indigenous traditions of popular cinema.[83] Nevertheless, one striking difference resulted from the productivity of the film industries during and after the war. Hollywood studios had no access to the German and Czechoslovak markets after 1940 and 1942 respectively, and were ready to supply postwar markets with hundreds of movies they had produced during the war, most of which were of higher production quality then the pictures the Soviet studios produced during the same period. By contrast, the productivity of the Soviet film industry was faltering, despite Minister Bolshakov's megalomaniac vision of vast productivity.[84] The less the Soviets were able to supply the markets with new productions, the more the screen quotas for Soviet movies led to disappointment of the cinemagoers' preferences (due to the rerunning of older Soviet films) and the more important the concrete practices of distribution and exhibition became.

By February 1947 the general director of the Czechoslovak Film Association Lubomír Linhart was complaining at the meeting of regional cinema directors that American, not Soviet films were scheduled for the peak viewing times between Fridays and Mondays. This complaint points to an important clash between the centralized distribution system and the decision-making process at the level of exhibition. This fundamental discrepancy was never fully resolved, as the failure of the most radical attempt to avoid unpredictability at the level of exhibition confirms. A system of so-called 'circular distribution' was launched at the start of 1949 with the aim of guaranteeing rapid and firmly organized distribution of the 'most important movies' to selected cinemas.[85] This extremely rigid model was terminated in 1953, a few months after Stalin's death, and thereafter the tensions between the promoted distribution goals on the one hand, and the local implementation of diverse, even irreconcilable instructions and duties on the other, remained permanent features of the system until the end of the regime.

In fact, these tensions even intensified, in Czechoslovakia as well as in the GDR, during the changes instituted as part of the post-Stalinist wave of economic decentralization. As was also the case in the GDR, the distribution system in Czechoslovakia was extensively decentralized in 1957, creating economic interest in distribution for two new players in the system.[86] National Committees became cinema owners, with cinema revenues representing an important part of their budgets. At the same time, Regional Film Enterprises responsible for 'cost-accounting' (*khozraschet*) became the central link between the National Committees and ČSF. As part of the decentralization process, the Central Film Rental Office (Ústřední půjčovna filmů) was established on 1 January 1957. Three months later, the ownership of cinemas was transferred to municipal and local national committees.[87] The new system gave more authority to local organizations,[88] and an attempt to correct distribution practices in line with the criteria set by the communist party came soon after. In September 1957 a report for the Central Committee of the Communist Party of Czechoslovakia (Ústřední výbor Komunistické strany Československa, ÚV KSČ) blamed the rapid increase in attendance at Western films on weakened supervision by regional committees and party structures. 'Regional film corporations are trying to meet their difficult financial plans by increasing the number of screenings of Western films', the report commented. In effect, a resolution of the ÚV KSČ Secretariat instructed the Minister of Education and Culture to enforce the new rule of limiting Western movies to just 35% of all presentations.[89]

Figure 13.3 shows the numbers of screenings of Western movies in Czechoslovakia and superbly illustrates the trends in cinema distribution and their (relative) dependency on cultural policy. While the obvious yet not entirely unambiguous trends in the number of movies *acquired* for distribution reflect the cautious cultural policy, the marked trends in the number of Western movies *screened* (the steady and intensive increase from 1953 to 1957 and the decline after 1958) better represent pragmatic decisions and grass-roots tactics on the part of ČSF and local film organizations.

The urge to decentralize the bureaucratic system during the period of the Thaw was by no means limited to the sphere of cinema distribution, and was manifested in parallel developments in Czechoslovakia and the GDR. The process of decentralizing the cinema was, in fact, inspired by the example of Poland, where local authorities justified their measures by citing tendencies in Soviet distribution as described by a delegation of the Central Administration of Cinematography after a month-long stay in the USSR in January 1956.[90] These traces of mutual influences imply that the structural changes in film distribution during the second half of the 1950s were not a matter of orders handed down vertically from the power centre in Moscow, but rather of horizontal inspirations, justifications and rhetorical support. Across the Soviet Bloc, decentralization was the order of the day – a common reaction to the shared political pressure to overcome Stalin's cult of personality.

The Position of Soviet Cinema

As we have already mentioned, in 1945 the Soviets attained the extremely preferential quota of 60 per cent of screening time for their movies on the Czechoslovak market. However, the Czechoslovak film industry did not fulfil the agreement due to the small quantity of available Soviet movies. The pro-communist management at ČSF promoted Soviet cinema, but the extreme distortion of the distribution profile implied by endless repetition of a few Soviet movies was unacceptable to ČSF, at least in the period 1945–1948. In a letter to the Soviet foreign affairs minister, Minister of Cinematography Bolshakov complained that the Czechoslovaks were not maintaining their side of the agreement and that the screening time for Soviet movies had reached only 28 per cent in 1946 and 16 per cent in the first half of 1947. His proposal that this fact 'should be taken into account during negotiations for a business contract with Czechoslovakia'[91] reveals how differently Bolshakov dealt with cinema distribution in Czechoslovakia versus the SBZ: his indifference to the general economic performance of the Czechoslovak film market inspired him to propose the practice of economic blackmailing. However, his complaints were unjustified: the Czechoslovak film industry was strongly influenced by the communist party even before the communist putsch in February 1948, and despite strong criticism from the nonleftist press, its distribution practices were significantly bent to the advantage of Soviet production. It was mandated that Soviet movies be screened at preferred times from Friday to Monday.[92]

Another official initiative aimed at improving attendance for Soviet production was launched in 1953, namely, the above-mentioned coupling of Soviet documentaries with attractive genre movies. Dozens of features were shown as part of an 'extended programme' (i.e. coupled with a Soviet documentary),[93] among them *Fanfan la Tulipe* (Fan-Fan the Tulip, Christian-Jaque, 1952), *Where No Vultures Fly* (aka *Ivory Hunter*, Harry Watt, 1951) and *La Beauté du Diable* (Beauty and the Devil, René Clair, 1950). The practice of 'extended programmes' was an obvious attempt to resolve the incompatibility of ideological and economic demands through distribution rather than through production. The 'extended programme' addressed the contradiction by creating a hybrid composed of a Western-produced, entertaining piece like *Fan-Fan the Tulip* together with a propagandistic Soviet documentary presenting the alleged results of successful socialist modernization. Thus the entertainment qualities of popular pictures, both domestic and imported, were framed by emblematic images of modernized society presented in the documentaries: industrialization, science, education, transportation infrastructure and leisure time. A similar model of coupling an ideologically important Soviet movie with an entertainment genre picture had already been implemented by SEF in the SBZ. The Czechoslovak film industry found the required up-to-date support for a variation of the practice in the Soviet press[94] and utilised it for the more appealing possibility of supplementing features with popular-scientific movies. Intending to transform the screening of attractive genre/Western/colour movies into 'progressive' events, ČSF bent the model to its own goals.[95]

Apart from the screen quotas for movies from socialist countries, the most robust institutional support for Soviet movies in Czechoslovakia lay in the practice of dividing available movies into three categories. The majority of Soviet production fell into category 'A' – the 'ideologically and artistically most important movies' – which secured strongly preferential treatment in distribution and entitlement to the highest number of copies. This was essentially the same model as that applied in the GDR, with movies of 'average value' assigned to category 'B' and those deemed 'escapist productions' relegated to category 'C'.

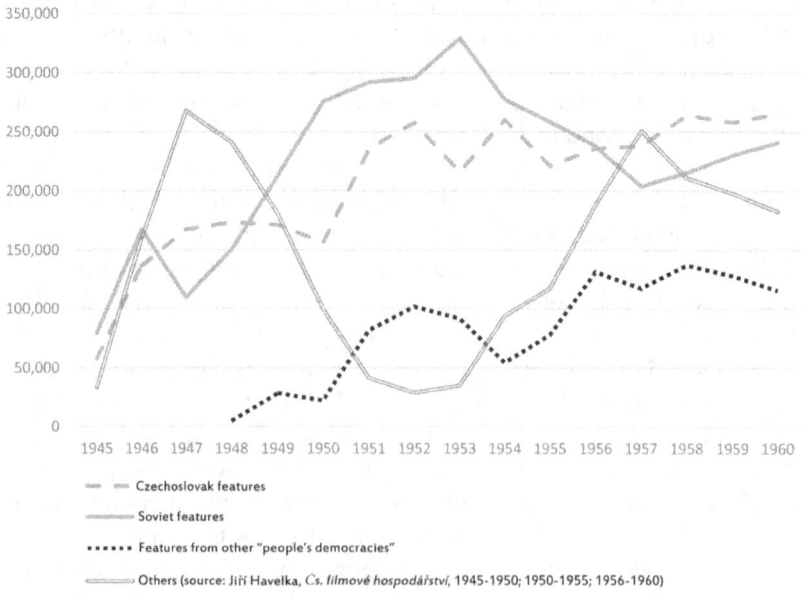

Figure 13.3 The number of screenings in Czech cinemas.

Film Exhibition

The GDR

Cinemas were by far the most successful and popular cultural institutions in Leipzig. While dramatic theatres and concert halls depended on state subsidies, cinemas turned a profit every year until the mid-1960s. They also attracted a large, steadily growing audience. In the early postwar years Leipzig cinemas struggled to supply heat and electricity but still brought in roughly eight million viewers a year. In 1948, the average Leipzig resident went to the movies once a month.[96] Attendance doubled over the course of the next decade, reaching an all-time high of twenty-four visits per person per year in 1957.[97] By this time, Leipzig cinemas drew more viewers each year than the city's dramatic theatres, concert halls, and opera houses did in an entire decade.[98] And although the number of cinemas stayed relatively constant from the mid-1940s to the mid-1960s, the number of film screenings exploded.[99] There were twice as many showings in 1958 as in 1948, and each one attracted close to 350 viewers.[100] Cinema, in short, was a booming business, as well as a flagship success story for GDR cultural officials.

The easiest way to attract viewers was to emphasize popular films. Leipzig cinemas could not control what they played, but they could usually determine how and when they played it. Blockbusters tended to appear at larger theatres in the centre, while 'worthier' socialist productions were relegated to the outskirts.[101] Many cinemas scheduled ideological films for early mornings or the middle of the day; throughout the 1950s, such screenings fulfilled official quotas without reducing prime-time profits.[102] Ideological shows also predominated during the summer, when many viewers were likely to be on vacation. At Leipzig's largest cinema in 1962, socialist films made up half the repertoire from January to April, but 70 per cent from May to August.[103] Above all, socialist movies played on special days in East Germany's symbolic calendar. Official celebrations like International Workers' Day and the Month of German-Soviet Friendship disrupted standard cinema repertoires and showcased ideological productions.[104] So too did election campaigns and occasional movie festivals, such as the annual Week of Cultural and Documentary Films that Leipzig authorities inaugurated in 1955. All these strategies allowed cinemas to limit the impact of socialist films and focus on more profitable Western blockbusters. To advertise the Leipzig premiere of *The Magnificent Seven* (John Sturges, 1960), cinema workers even hired a car with a megaphone and drove it around town.¹⁰⁵ They ended up selling so many tickets that three hundred viewers sat in the aisles on opening night. Such measures reveal just how desperate cinemas were to make a profit off the few Western films they received. A handful of movies had to bring in the bulk of all revenue, and cinemas treated them as cash cows. Ideological productions, meanwhile, were widely seen as a nuisance and often kept out of view.

Leipzig officials always condemned this approach. Separating ideology and profitability was like sitting between two chairs, they argued: cinemas neither educated their audience nor made enough money to fulfil the plan.¹⁰⁶ Instead, officials called on cinemas to make shows both attractive and beneficial. In the late 1940s, Leipzig's culture department advocated 'coupled' screenings of German and Soviet films.¹⁰⁷ Popular UFA productions were shown together with propaganda films.¹⁰⁸ This arrangement forced viewers to watch ideologically valuable films, but it also allowed cinemas to keep old German movies in the repertoire. Cinemas also displayed political posters, slides, and banners, especially around election time.¹⁰⁹ In this way, every trip to the movies became an educational experience – even if viewers had only come to see a Western blockbuster. To attract viewers to less popular films, meanwhile, cinemas sought to surround them with other forms of entertainment. As early as 1946, Sunday matinee shows occasionally included live music performances or small exhibits related to the film.¹¹⁰ From the late 1950s on, a series of 'film cafés' served viewers drinks and snacks during shows.¹¹¹ Cinemas, in short, were more than just rooms with projection screens. They were important public spaces offering both sociability and political education.

In the long run, though, the best option for cinemas was not to balance the ideological and the popular, but to make the ideological popular. By increasing attendance at socialist films, they could fulfil the plan and educate viewers at the same time. Leipzig theatres worked with city officials to draw cinemagoers to the appropriate movies. In the late 1940s, when commercial theatres still provided competition, city-owned cinemas sold discounted tickets to 'progressive' films.¹¹² They also set up 'film subscriptions' that offered viewers a set film programme at a low weekly price.¹¹³ Such subscriptions endured until the mid-1950s, but cinemagoers mostly stayed away, complaining that the programme included nothing but Soviet films and thus was not worth the savings.¹¹⁴ To get around the problem of popular choice, officials started to focus on a more captive audience – Leipzig's factory workers. By the mid-1950s, feature films were played directly in the workplace with the help of mobile projectors, so as to force workers to see the most valuable productions.[115]

Cinema workers and city officials saw sending workers to the cinemas in their free time as the ideal solution. Organized audiences first appeared in the early 1950s but did not become widespread until Ulbricht's cultural offensive at the end of the decade. They were made up of groups that were easy to mobilize: factory workers, schoolchildren, retirees. Honorary 'cultural functionaries' distributed cinema tickets in factories at a discount and gave some away as rewards for good performance. In the mid-1950s, Leipzig had more than five thousand such functionaries – one for every sixty workers.[116] Factory managers encouraged ticket sales by tying cultural participation to performance norms. Starting in 1958, for instance, workers stood to win financial bonuses by joining a Socialist Labour Brigade (Brigade der sozialistischen Arbeit) and fulfilling cultural tasks like going to the movies.[117]

Throughout the city, hundreds of 'film activist committees' helped coordinate viewers and send them to see the designated Film of the Month.[118] Officials staged competitions for the highest attendance at the most valuable productions between factories, cities or even GDR provinces. Such competitions put reputations on the line and could achieve impressive results. Nearly half of all Leipzig residents saw the second part of the Ernst Thälmann biopic, *Ernst Thälmann – Führer seiner Klasse* (Ernst Thälmann – Leader of the Working Class, Kurt Maetzig, 1955); roughly one in three saw the World War II movies *Du und mancher Kamerad* (You and Many a Comrade, Andrew Thorndike and Annelie Thorndike, 1956) and *Sud'ba cheloveka* (Fate of a Man, Sergei Bondarchuk, 1959).[119] These figures rivalled the most popular Western productions, demonstrating that socialist films could in fact be as profitable as capitalist ones. They required so much effort and organization, however, that Leipzig authorities could muster only one major film campaign a year.[120] Officials could make a few socialist productions more successful, but they could not make them more popular. East German film policy of the 1940s and 1950s capsized on the rock of popular taste.

Czechoslovakia

Cinemagoing in postwar Czechoslovakia was no less popular than in the GDR and in fact shows a similar pattern of development – the previous highest attendance levels in 1948 were overcome in 1957. In 1947 the average citizen of Brno visited the cinema twenty-two times per year (versus a 'scant' five visits to dance performances, three to dramatic theatres and two to sporting events).[121]

The competitions between cinema managers for the highest attendance and the massive energy invested in mobilizing cinemagoers, discussed above, well indicate both the possibilities and the limits of this prominent example of the GDR regime's efforts to present society as fully integrated under the banner of socialist values. Similar competitions were organized in Czechoslovak cities, and cinema employees were motivated by the prospect of a trip to the Soviet Union, as well as by financial reward.[122] The competition of competitions, however, was the one organized between the GDR and Czechoslovakia for the attendance of *Unternehmen Teutonenschwert – Archive sagen aus* (Operation Teutonic Sword, Andrew Thorndike and Annelie Thorndike, 1958).[123] The goal was not to prove which state had better *citizens*, but which one had the more effective machinery for bringing socialist citizens to cinemas and persuading them of the unquestionable value of the preferred movies.

The exhibition process is inevitably linked to a certain local level of decision-making – a fact that held true even in the excessively centralized system of distribution in the early 1950s. Local authorities and cinema managers partly influenced the concrete screenings, negotiated organized screenings for pupils and workers with schools and factories, and handled promotion.[124] In both Czechoslovakia and the GDR, local authorities and exhibitors held responsibility for implementing the tasks of cultural policy (since they had no influence on the quality and quantity of the distributed movies, they were constantly blamed or praised for their promotional activities and for educating cinemagoers). Inevitably, the success of the cultural policy's impact was measured quantitatively by the number of cinemagoers. Cinema managers in Brno strove to escape the trap of quotas that were contradictory to audience demand through practices similar to those of their colleagues in Leipzig: the ideologically most problematic movies, which received no promotional support, were screened in cinemas on the outskirts (e.g. Laurence Olivier's *Hamlet* [1948]). However, since it was unacceptable for any movie from a capitalist country to remain on the programme for long and the screen quota for Soviet movies had to be maintained, the inverse strategy was also employed: the most attractive spectacles (e.g. French movies with Gérard Philipe) were shown at the biggest central cinemas, as it was officially acceptable to pursue maximum receipts during the limited running time of such movies.[125]

As in the above-described situation in Leipzig, the rhythm of film exhibition in Brno was determined to a certain extent by the calendar of festivals, state holidays and anniversaries. The most pervasive interference in the 'standard' exhibition practice was the extra-preferential treatment of Soviet movies during the Month of Czechoslovak-Soviet Friendship in November, but other occasions influenced the programme as well, such as Soviet Aviation Day (when movies about the heroism of Soviet pilots were shown), International Women's Day (when the selected Soviet movies featured 'fighting and constructing women' in a major roles), and, inevitably, the dates of Lenin's and Stalin's birth and death.[126]

Another parallel between the cultural policies in the two countries was grounded in the coincident differentiation of the cinema culture. Film cafés, as a kind of 'hedonistic' consumption, were not acceptable until the second half of 1950s but finally opened in 1959 in both the GDR and Czechoslovakia.[127] In addition, film clubs introduced a qualitatively new distribution model first launched in Leipzig and Brno in 1956 and 1958 respectively.[128] As in the aforementioned case of the GDR, two cinemas in Czechoslovakia also offered variety shows with programmes composed of both movies and live performers; however, this was the only strictly entertainment-oriented variation of the cinema programme in use in Czechoslovakia before 1953, peculiarly justified by Minister of Information and Enlightenment Kopecký as modelled on the Soviet example.[129]

Most screenings that were related to anniversaries and festivities, which were often supported by organized attendance from enterprises and schools, could also be viewed as a way for the regime to discipline its citizens. Such rituals were devoted to exhibiting massive support for the regime's cultural policy – a support that was illusory in meaning but real in the sense that it (like the Leipzig sports festival) demanded the citizens' physical presence. In between the official rituals a 'normal' cinema culture was maintained; however, the rituals were so omnipresent that this 'normality' cannot be properly understood without taking its relation to these rituals into account. As German historian Malte Rolf has pointed out, festivals can serve regimes as important moments of integration, forging a link between the public on one side and the official order of the day on the other, and also as a tool for the colonization of time.[130]

Conclusion: Cinema as a Site of Integration

In Czechoslovakia as in the GDR, state authorities set out to create a distinctive socialist film culture. Going to the movies was meant to be more than a form of entertainment: officials sought to shape viewers' hearts and minds by selecting, distributing and screening particular kinds of films. As Leipzig's Culture Department explained in 1946: 'Our task is not just to show the film and earn money from it, but to educate our public bit by bit.'[131] To this end, state officials engaged in many practices of exclusion. They banned or censored countless films, especially those from the capitalist West. They imposed strict limits on cinematic production, dictating the topics that films could address as well as the people who could make them. Throughout the 1950s, many Czechoslovak and East German films explicitly identified certain classes or ideologies as 'enemies'. The bourgeoisie, the kulaks and members of former parties and organizations were often shown as dying out in the context of socialist societies.[132]

Though exclusion remained a constant of socialist film culture, we argue that cinemagoing also produced the opposite effect. Above all, state authorities viewed cinemas as a tool of social inclusion, capable of spreading shared values and emotions. Mass screenings in schools and factories were meant to promote a sense of collective identity. Special showings during holidays or festivals aimed to foster citizens' identification with official values. At a more basic level, cinemas helped integrate national communities in the aftermath of World War II – a process that centred on de-Nazification in the GDR and ethnic cleansing in Czechoslovakia.[133] Especially in the early 1950s, both regimes approached their respective audiences as *one* public with *one* taste.

Film offerings grew increasingly differentiated over the course of the decade, and cinemagoers gained more choice. This apparent unravelling of the state's integrative project pointed to rising tensions between ideological and financial objectives. Some scholars have highlighted the limits of social integration by exploring the notion of viewers' *Eigen-Sinn*[134] or oppositional readings of ideologically preferred movies.[135] While recognizing that socialist states failed to create a homogeneous audience, we argue that integration remained a key aspect of socialist film culture in the late 1950s and beyond. Screenings of Western productions or popular prewar movies served to establish a kind of social contract between state and society. They were meant to garner loyalty from the intelligentsia, to revive solidarity in moments of crisis and to ensure political participation in elections. Cinemas did in fact achieve considerable success on these counts – throughout the period under study, they were by far the most popular cultural form in Leipzig and Brno. By looking at the operation of cinemas at the city level, we have tried to identify essential commonalities between their roles in two socialist states. Foremost among these commonalities, we argue, was that cinemas served as sites of social integration.

Kyrill Kunakhovich is a Mellon Faculty Fellow in European Studies at the College of William & Mary. He defended his dissertation in history at Princeton University in 2013. His research has been supported by the German Academic Exchange Service, the Polish Ministry of Culture and the American Council of Learned Societies. His book manuscript, entitled *Culture for the People: Art and Politics in Communist Poland and East Germany*, examines the role that culture played in Soviet Bloc politics and the impact that socialism made on East European cultures.

Pavel Skopal is an assistant professor at the Department of Film Studies and Audiovisual Culture, Masaryk University, Brno, Czech Republic. In 2010–2012 he was a visiting researcher at the Konrad Wolf Film and Television University in Potsdam, Germany (research project supported by the Alexander von Humboldt Foundation). He has edited anthologies devoted to local cinema history in Brno and to the Czech film industry in the 1950s, and has published *The Cinema of the North Triangle* (in Czech, 2014), a book of comparative research on cinema distribution and exhibition in Czechoslovakia, Poland and the GDR in the period 1945–1970.

Notes

1. Many historians have examined aspects of the system, but none have traced it in its entirety. The best account of the distribution network in the GDR is still Heinz Kersten's *Das Filmwesen in der Sowjetischen Besatzungszone Deutschlands*, revised edition, vol. 1 (Bonn: Bundesministerium für gesamtdeutsche Fragen, 1963). More recent works include Thomas Heimann, *DEFA, Künstler und SED-Kulturpolitik: Zum Verhältnis von Kulturpolitik und Filmproduktion in der SBZ/DDR 1945 bis 1989* (Berlin: Vistas, 1994); Daniela Berghahn, *Hollywood behind the Wall: The Cinema of East Germany* (Manchester: Manchester University Press, 2005), chapter 1; and Hans-Rainer Otto, 'Kinoalltag und Kinokultur in der DDR', in *Der Geteilte Himmel: Höhepunkte des DEFA-Kinos 1946–1992*, Raimund Fritz (ed.), (Vienna: Filmarchiv Austria, 2001, volume 2).
2. In 1947, after displacement of the German minority, Brno had just 273,000 inhabitants; see Karel Kuča, *Brno. Vývoj města, předměstí a připojených vesnic* (Prague and

Brno: Baset, 2000), p. 184. After most of the soldiers returned home, Leipzig reached 627,000 inhabitants at the end of 1946; see Lieselotte Borusiak and Gertrud Höhnel (eds), *Chronik der Stadt Leipzig I. Teil, 1945–46* (Leipzig: Stadtarchiv Leipzig, 1971).
3. For a comparison between Leipzig and the French city of Lyons on the basis of these characteristics see Thomas Höpel, *Von der Kunst- zur Kulturpolitik: Städtische Kulturpolitik in Deutschland und Frankreich 1918–1939* (Stuttgart: Franz Steiner Verlag, 2007), p. 13.
4. See e.g. Ewa Gębicka. 'Sieć kin i rozpowszechnianie filmów', in Edward Zajiček (ed.), *Encyklopedia kultury polskiej XX wieku: Film i kinematografia* (Warsaw: Instytut Kultury and Komitet Kinematografii, 1994), pp. 415–451; Pavel Skopal, 'Za vysokou ideovou úroveň, a/nebo za vyšší tržby? Filmová distribuce v českých zemích z hlediska konfliktu ideologických a hospodářských cílů (1945–1968)', *Soudobé dějiny* 17(4) (2010), 641–666.
5. For Kyrill Kunakhovich's comparative research on the construction of 'socialist culture' in Leipzig and Kraków, see Kyrill Kunakhovich, 'In Search of Socialist Culture: Art and Politics in Krakow and Leipzig, 1918–1989' (Ph.D. thesis, Princeton, 2013); for Pavel Skopal's projects on cinema exhibition and reception in Brno see http://www.phil.muni.cz/dedur/?&lang=1; for those in Leipzig see http://www.phil.muni.cz/leipzigcinema/.
6. Together with Poland, Czechoslovakia and the GDR were conceived of as the 'Northern Triangle' (*nördliche Dreieck*), more firmly constructed after the conferences of the respective blocs in Moscow and Paris in 1954. See Beate Ihme-Tuchel, *Das „nördliche Dreieck". Die Beziehungen zwischen der DDR, der Tschechoslowakei und Polen in den Jahren 1954 bis 1962* (Cologne: Wissenschaft und Politik, 1994).
7. Both co-authors of this study deal with GDR cinema history (not to mention that other researchers have invested much more effort in scrutinizing the GDR's cinema culture compared to Czechoslovakia's), which provides them with more complex background material for the intended comparison.
8. While the basic patterns were the same for the Czech and the Slovak parts of the state, significant differences still stemmed from organizational specificities as well as the comparatively underdeveloped infrastructure of the film industry and cinemas in Slovakia. We will occasionally use the national state label to avoid such awkward phrasing as 'the Czech part of Czechoslovakia'. General patterns of distribution hold true for the whole country, but the statistics presented in the three charts below are based on data for the Czech Lands and would produce significantly different results for Slovakia. This telling problem is to be expected in the context of a transnational approach, as the national framework tends to suppress differences within the state borders. However, considering intrastate differences would make the structure of the essay too complicated.
9. On Soviet film policy, see Kristin Roth-Ey, *Moscow Prime Time: How the Soviet Union Built the Media Empire That Lost the Cultural Cold War* (Ithaca: Cornell University Press, 2011), chapters 1–2; Louis Cohen, *The Cultural–Political Traditions and Developments of the Soviet Cinema, 1917–1972* (New York: Arno Press, 1974); and Peter Kenez, *Cinema and Soviet Society, 1917–1953* (Cambridge: Cambridge University Press, 1992).
10. On Weimar film culture in Leipzig, see Höpel, *Von der Kunst- zur Kulturpolitik*, pp. 430–437. For the German Communist Party's attitude to cinema culture in the 1920s and 1930s in the spheres of film production (Prometheus Film) and film criticism (e.g. the party's press organ, *Die Rote Fahne*, or the attempts at

'workers–correspondents'), see Sabine Hake, *The Cinema's Third Machine: Writing on Film in Germany, 1907–1933* (Lincoln: University of Nebraska Press, 1993).
11. See e.g. Dagmar Schittly, *Zwischen Regie und Regime: Die Filmpolitik der SED im Spiegel der DEFA-Produktionen* (Berlin: Ch. Links, 2002), pp. 11–12.
12. Sergei Tiul'panov, quoted in Heimann, *DEFA*, p. 51.
13. Quoted in Kersten, *Das Filmwesen*, p. 15.
14. For the concept of the 'New Man', see e.g. Peter Fritzsche and Jochen Hellbeck: 'The New Man in Stalinist Russia and Nazi Germany', in Michael Geyer and Sheila Fitzpatrick (eds), *Beyond Totalitarianism: Stalinism and Nazism Compared* (Cambridge and New York: Cambridge University Press, 2009), pp. 302–341; and for its historical context see Irina Gutkin, *The Cultural Origin of the Socialist Realist Aesthetic 1890–1934* (Evanston: Northwestern University Press, 1999), especially pp. 113–130.
15. Quoted in Kersten, *Das Filmwesen*, p. 22; and also in Heimann, *DEFA*, p. 170.
16. For the shifts in the GDR's cultural policy, see the essay by David Bathrick in this volume.
17. Alexander Abusch, *Im ideologischen Kampf für eine sozialistische Kultur: Die Entwicklung der sozialistischen Kultur in der Zeit des zweiten Fünfjahrplanes. Rede auf der Kulturkonferenz der SED am 23.10.57 in Berlin* (East Berlin: Dietz, 1957), p. 13.
18. Quoted in Heidi Martini, *Dokumentarfilm-Festival Leipzig: Filme und Politik in Blick und Gegenblick* (Berlin: DEFA, 2007), p. 109.
19. See e.g. reports of the Leipzig District Council's Culture Department from 1960, in the Sächsisches Staatsarchiv (StA-L) Leipzig, Bestand 20237 – Rat des Bezirkes (RdB), Nummer (Nr.) 2978.
20. See the essay by Jiří Knapík in this volume for more details about the postwar political arrangement.
21. 'Ideová výchova a kulturní politika strany. Z referátu Václava Kopeckého na VIII. sjezdu KSČ' (March 1946), in Zdeněk Štábla and Pavel Taussig (eds), *KSČ a československá kinematografie (výbor dokumentů z let 1945–1980)* (Prague: Československý filmový ústav, 1981), p. 28.
22. See the ministry's bulletin, *Věstník ministerstva školství a osvěty*, for the years 1945–1949. For details on the stance of cultural policy in the GDR and Czechoslovakia towards film production for children, see the essays by Lukáš Skupa and Christin Niemeyer in this volume.
23. Michal Čarnický, '"Zítra se bude promítat všude". Dějiny putovních kin v československé zestátněné distribuční síti', in Pavel Skopal (ed.), *Naplánovaná kinematografie. Český filmový průmysl 1945 až 1960* (Prague: Academia, 2012), pp. 359–390.
24. With our thesis about festivals as tools of integration, we allude to the work of Malte Rolf (we return to this argument below). For history of the Film Spring festival, see Hana Květová, 'Filmové jaro na vesnici 1951 až 1956. Historie kulturně osvětové akce na českém venkově v 50. letech', in Pavel Skopal (ed.), *Naplánovaná kinematografie* (Prague: Academia, 2012), pp. 391–426.
25. StA-L, RdB, Nr. 2985, blatt (Bl.) 71. See also Heinz Kersten, *Das Filmwesen*, p. 288.
26. During the 1930s, the number of distributed movies dropped from 543 in 1930 to 318 in 1938 but never fell below 200 pictures. It is true that the highest attendance numbers were reached in 1944, a year when only 87 movies were in the distribution offering – this was, however, under the extreme conditions of war shortages, and at a time when the competing enterprises of dramatic theatres had been closed since summer 1944. Movie premieres numbered 210 in 1933, 336 in 1935 and 174

in 1940. The number dropped to under 100 movies in the years 1943–1945. See Jiří Havelka, *Filmové hospodářství v zemích českých a na Slovensku 1939 až 1945* (Prague: Čs. filmové nakladatelství, 1946), p. 39. When cinema industry practitioners planned the nationalization of the cinema industry during the war, they counted on about 200–250 imported movies per year. See Jindřich Elbl, 'Jak byl znárodněn československý film. Patnáct let filmové politiky 1933–1948', *Film a doba* 11(8) (1965), 399.

27. Národní archiv (NA), Prague, fond (f.) 19/7 Ústřední kulturně propagační komise a kulturně propagační oddělení ÚV KSČ 1945–1955, archivní jednotka (a. j.) 666.
28. For an overview of the attitudes of communist intellectuals and activities of the Left Front in the 1920s and 1930s, see Jaroslav Anděl and Petr Szczepanik (eds), *Cinema All the Time: An Anthology of Czech Film Theory and Criticism, 1908–1939* (Prague: National Film Archive, 2008).
29. See Klaus Kreimeier, *The UFA Story: A History of Germany's Greatest Film Company 1919–1945* (Berkeley, Los Angeles and London: University of California Press, 1999), p. 257.
30. This ratings system was related to tax allowances. In Czechoslovakia, there was only one category of this type: 'culturally educational movies'. Applied after 1928, this rating represented the only – and rather scarcely used – state intervention in evaluating a movie's quality. Starting in May 1943, however, five rating categories were used in the Protectorate: 'state-politically valuable', 'artistically valuable', 'culturally valuable', 'folkish valuable', 'respectable', and 'folkish educational'. See Havelka, *Filmové hospodářství v zemích českých*, pp. 42, 54, and Ivan Klimeš, 'Stát a filmová kultura', *Iluminace* 11(2) (1999), 125–137.
31. See Ivan Klimeš, 'Zrození centralizované kinematografie v Československu', unpublished paper presented at the international conference *Doświadczenie i dziedzictwo totalitaryzmu na obszarze kultur środkowoeuropejskich*, Warsaw, 21–22 October 2010.
32. In fact, the Soviets themselves most admired the vertically integrated Hollywood system. See Jamie Miller, *Soviet Cinema: Politics and Persuasion under Stalin* (London and New York: I.B. Tauris, 2010), pp. 35–37.
33. John Connelly has convincingly shown that one of the main barriers to rapid Sovietization of the higher educational system in Czechoslovakia was a lack of clear instructions from the Soviets. Connelly, *Captive University: The Sovietization of East German, Czech, and Polish Higher Education, 1945–1956* (Chapel Hill: University of North Carolina Press, 2000).
34. To provide a few examples: the Soviets initiated series of international conferences for cinema workers, as well as conferences for the Eastern Bloc countries' distribution organizations, in the late 1950s; textbooks and lectures by Soviet authors were translated as internal material for ČSF (e.g. 'Organization of the Distribution Network in the USSR' by A. Kopytov and 'On the Distribution of Seats in Movie Theatres' by E.M. Goldovskij); and delegations from ČSF travelled to Moscow to discuss questions of technical development, the purchase of movies, etc.
35. See Maria Belodubrovskaya, 'Politically Incorrect: Filmmaking under Stalin and the Failure of Power' (Ph.D. thesis, University of Wisconsin-Madison, 2011), pp. 4–5.
36. This term is used to describe movies confiscated during the war and never officially purchased. E.g. in 1949, only 13 new domestically produced films were screened in the Soviet Union, but this shortage was somehow balanced by 61 foreign releases.

See Sergei Kapterev, 'Illusionary Spoils: Soviet Attitudes toward American Cinema during the Early Cold War', *Kritika: Explorations in Russian and Eurasian History* 10(4) (2009), 790–791; and Peter Kenez, *Cinema and Soviet Society*, p. 192.
37. In Czechoslovakia, the number of new features in distribution dropped from its highest point of 199 in 1947 to 67 in 1951. In the Soviet Zone of Occupation and subsequently in the GDR, this number did not exceed 60 movies until 1952. See Jiří Havelka, Čs. *filmové hospodářství, 1945–1950* (Prague: Český filmový ústav, 1970), p. 202; idem, Čs. *filmové hospodářství 1951–55, I. díl* (Prague: Čs. filmový ústav, 1972), p. 296; Kersten, *Das Filmwesen*, pp. 360–361.
38. The Information Administration was headed by Marshall Sergei Tiul'panov and subordinated to SMAD's Political Department. Its original name was the Administration for Information and Censorship. Heimann, *DEFA*, 42; see also Norman Naimark, *The Russians in Germany: A History of the Soviet Zone of Occupation, 1945–1949* (Cambridge: Belknap Press, 1995), especially chapters 6 and 8.
39. Until 1945, Sovexportfilm was known as Sojuzintorgkino. Curiously, the company was headquartered in Leipzig.
40. Heimann, *DEFA*, pp. 64–65. For the postwar distribution of Soviet movies see also Lars Karl, 'Screening the Occupier as Liberator: Soviet War Films in the SBZ and the GDR, 1945–1965,' in this volume.
41. Heimann, *DEFA*, p. 64.
42. Heimann, *DEFA*, 46. Local approval committees had existed from the start of the occupation. See Thomas Höpel, *Die Kunst dem Volke: Städtische Kulturpolitik in Leipzig und Lyon 1945–1989* (Leipzig: Leipziger Universitätsverlag, 2011), p. 96.
43. Martini, *Dokumetarfilm-Festival*, p. 115; Schittly, *Zwischen Regie*, p. 48; Günther Schulz, 'Die DEFA, 1946–1990: Fakten und Daten', in Raimund Fritz (ed.), *Der Geteilte Himmel: Höhepunkte des DEFA-Kinos 1946–1992* (Vienna: Filmarchiv Austria, 2001), vol. 2, p. 88.
44. DEFA had been a German-Soviet joint stock company since November 1947; it was nationalized on 1 January 1953. See Berghahn, *Hollywood*, p. 18.
45. DEFA's Division of Foreign Trade was created in October 1950; with DEFA's nationalization in 1953, it was renamed the Film Acquisition and Foreign Trade Agency (DEFA-Filmübernahme- und Außenhandelsbetrieb). Heimann, *DEFA*, p. 223.
46. Berghahn, *Hollywood*, p. 27; Kersten, *Das Filmwesen*, pp. 33 and 273.
47. The Central Committee's Culture Department had a Film Sector that was responsible for cinema matters. Berghahn, *Hollywood*, p. 25.
48. For a full breakdown of feature films screened in East Germany, see Kersten, *Das Filmwesen*, pp. 360–361.
49. In the case of Brno, regular cinema screenings were cancelled on 15 April and re-established on 2 June. Starting on 6 May, however, the Red Army organized screenings in three of Brno's largest cinemas.
50. See the chapter by Jiří Knapík in this volume.
51. See Petr Mareš, 'Politika a "Pohyblivé obrázky." Spor o dovoz amerických filmů do Československa po druhé světové válce', *Iluminace* 6(1) (1994): 77–96; Jindřiška Bláhová, 'Hollywood za železnou oponou. Jednání o nové smlouvě o dovozu hollywoodských filmů mezi MPEA a ČSR (1946–1951)', *Iluminace* 20(4) (2008).
52. NA, f. 861 – Ministerstvo informací, karton (k.) 79. Three Soviet pictures (two war movies and one comedy) were withdrawn from distribution in 1948, probably at the request of SEF (Havelka, Čs. *filmové hospodářství, 1945–1950*, pp. 447–448). One of these was *V gorakh Yugoslavii* (In the Mountains of Yugoslavia, Abram Room and

Eduard Tisse, 1946), which was highly unacceptable both for the Soviets and the new Czechoslovak communist regime at the time of the Stalin-Tito split.
53. Rossiiskii gosudarstvennyi arkhiv literatury i iskusstva (RGALI), Moscow, f. 2918 – Sovexportfilm, op. 1, d. 128.
54. RGALI, f. 2918, op. 1, d. 111.
55. Ibid.
56. RGALI, f. 2918, op. 1, d. 128.
57. RGALI, f. 2918, op. 1, d. 113.
58. See the essays by Jiří Knapík and David Bathrick in this volume.
59. RGALI, f. 2918, op. 5, d. 26.
60. The final decision was made by the director of ČSF – however, he usually followed the recommendation of the selection board.
61. 'Travel report on the journey of a Czechoslovak delegation to the USSR', 27 December 1960, NA, f. ministerstvo školství a kultury (unprocessed files).
62. RGALI, f. 2918, op. 5, d. 134.
63. See 'Letter from the Czechoslovak embassy in Berlin to the Ministry of Education and Culture, Ministry of Foreign Affairs, and Czechoslovak Filmexport', 29 November 1957; and 'Letter from the embassy to the Ministry of Education and Culture and Ministry of Foreign Affairs', 27 January 1958, both in Archiv Ministerstva zahraničních věcí (AMZV), Prague, TO obyčejné, 1945–59, NDR, k. 27.
64. Ibid.
65. Ibid.
66. See Höpel, *Die Kunst dem Volke*, pp. 135–228.
67. Stadtarchiv Leipzig (StadtAL), Bestand Stadtverordnetenversammlung und Rat der Stadt (StVuR)(1), Nr. 7973, Bl. 8.
68. Ralf Nünthel, *UT Connewitz & Co. Geschichten aus Leipzig-Süd* (Beucha: Sax-Verlag, 2004), p. 62.
69. SEF typically collected around 40 per cent of the profits. See Kurt Enz, *Entwicklung der Filmwiedergabetechnik und des Filmtheaternetzes in der DDR von 1945 bis zur Gegenwart* (Berlin: Schriftenreihe der DEFA Zentralstelle für Filmtechnik, 1982), p. 128.
70. In April 1947, city cinemas screened Soviet films 533 times and German (or coupled) films 246 times. In private cinemas, the corresponding figures were 343 and 543. StAL, StVuR(1) Nr. 1980, Bl. 22.
71. These terms were part of standard cinema contracts, which usually ran for five years. Heimann, *DEFA*, p. 42.
72. Progress took 20 per cent of the profits until July 1955, and 10 per cent after that. Kersten, *Das Filmwesen*, p. 267. Cinema payments to Progress ended in 1974. Otto, 'Kinoalltag', p. 180.
73. StA-L, RdB, Nr. 4851.
74. Otto, 'Kinoalltag', pp. 176–177.
75. StA-L, RdB, Nr. 2241, Bl. 14.
76. Heimann, *DEFA*, p. 251.
77. StadtAL, StVuR(1), Nr. 2138, Bl. 64.
78. StA-L, RdB, Nr. 2235, Bl. 48.
79. StA-L, RdB, Nr. 2955, Bl. 131.
80. This was the case of the West German crime film *Treibjagd auf ein Leben* (Hunt for a Life, Ralph Lothar, 1961). StA-L, SED-Bezirksleitung, IV/A/2/9/2/363/7.

81. E.g., *Treibjagd auf ein Leben* was replaced with the classic German film *Der blaue Engel* (The Blue Angel, Josef von Sternberg, 1930). StA-L, RdB, Nr. 2267, Bl. 37.
82. For the practices of the U.S. Department of State and Hollywood studios in the western zones of Germany, see Heide Fehrenbach, *Cinema in Democratizing Germany: Reconstructing National Identity after Hitler* (Chapel Hill and London: University of North Carolina Press, 1995), and Jennifer Fay, *Theaters of Occupation: Hollywood and the Reeducation of Postwar Germany* (Minneapolis and London: University of Minnesota Press, 2008).
83. This was particularly true in Germany. For more on the misgivings or even aversion of German audiences in all occupation zones towards Soviet and/or American cinema, see Fehrenbach, *Cinema in Democratizing Germany*, p. 51–91; Naimark, *The Russians in Germany*, p. 419–423; and Pavel Skopal, '"It is not enough we have lost the war – now we have to watch it!" Cinemagoers' attitudes in the Soviet occupation zone of Germany (a case study from Leipzig)', in *Participations. Journal of Audience and Reception Studies* 8(2) (2011), 497–521. (http://www.participations.org/Volume%208/Issue%202/3j%20Skopal.pdf).
84. In 1945 Bolshakov proclaimed that Soviet film studios would produce 80–100 movies a year. Peter Kenez, *Cinema and Soviet Society*, 189. The actual production was between 9 and 24 movies a year in the period 1945–1952 and did not exceed 100 movies until 1956. See Ginette Vincendeau, *Encyclopedia of European Cinema* (New York: Files on File, 1995), p. 464.
85. For every quarter of the year, 13 Czechoslovak and Soviet movies were picked up, ordered into 'sequences', and circulated in a strictly organized manner throughout the cinemas. See Jiří Havelka, *Výroční zpráva Čs. státního filmu za rok 1952* (Prague: Ústřední ředitelství ČSF – Filmový ústav, 1964), p. 115.
86. Governmental decree, 16 January 1957 (4/1957) on the organization of the film industry: all property of cinemas, including real estate, was transferred to the National Committees. At the same time, regional film enterprises were established.
87. Jiří Havelka, *Čs. filmové hospodářství 1956–1960* (Prague: Československý filmový ústav, 1973), p. 184.
88. The programme was put together by the respective Regional Film Enterprises. In addition, the decision of the clerks about programming individual movies was influenced by many local and un-systemic elements – the traditional programme profile of individual cinemas, the number of copies available for the region, and, more importantly, by personal contacts, favouritism or animosities. See, for example, the recollections of a former cinema manager in Brno: http://www.phil.muni.cz/dedur/?id=4513.
89. A report, from the fourth department of the ÚV KSČ Secretariat to the ÚV KSČ Secretariat, on the contemporary cultural political difficulties of film distribution. NA, f. 1261 – KSČ - Ústřední výbor 1945-1989, svazek 130, a. j. 192, bod 3.
90. Filmoteka narodowa, Warsaw, f. A 208 – Naczelny zarząd kinematografii 1952–1971, k. 169, poz. 6, pp. 154–161.
91. Bolshakov's letter to the Ministry of Foreign Affairs, 19 July 1947. RGALI, f. 2456 – Ministerstvo kinematografii, d. 116.
92. The nationalized film industry stuck to the long tradition of programming in two periods: from Tuesday to Thursday and from Friday to Monday. Obviously, the weekend period was much more prized.
93. NA, f. 867 – Ministerstvo kultury 1953-1956, inv. č. 196, k. 141.

94. The bulletin of Czechoslovak State Film, *Filmové informace*, published an article about the new 'double-programme' model of exhibition and quoted from an article in the Soviet journal *Literaturnaya gazeta*. See *Filmové informace* 4(34) (1953), 16–17.
95. In the second half of the 1950s the practice changed, and the ideological element was suppressed: instead of Soviet documentaries, the second part of the programme was filled in with profiles of popular Czech actors.
96. StadtAL, StVuR(1), Nr. 8354, Bl. 88.
97. *Statistisches Jahrbuch der Stadt Leipzig*, vol. 11–12 (1957–1958).
98. Theatre attendance statistics are available in StA-L, RdB, 2955, Bl. 25, and also in *Statistisches Jahrbuch der Stadt Leipzig*, vol. 11–15 (1957–1963). Concert hall attendance (for the Leipzig Gewandhaus) can be found in StadtAL, StVuR(1) Nr. 8516.
99. Ralf Nünthel has traced the history of each Leipzig cinema. See Nünthel, *Johannes Nitzsche Kinematographen & Films: die Geschichte des Leipziger Kinopioniers, seiner Unternehmen und seiner Technik* (Beucha: Sax-Verlag, 1999), appendix.
100. StadtAL, StVuR(1) Nr. 8354, Bl. 88; *Statistisches Jahrbuch der Stadt Leipzig*, vol. 13.
101. See e.g. StA-L, RdB, Nr. 2208, Bl. 27.
102. StA-L, SED-Stadtleitung IV/A/5/1/232.
103. StA-L, RdB, Nr. 3243, Bl. 6.
104. For examples of festival schedules, see StA-L, RdB, Nr. 2238, Bl. 30; RdB, Nr. 2958, Bl. 38; see also a few examples of the programme at http://www.phil.muni.cz/leipzigcinema.
105. StA-L, SED-Bezirksleitung IV/A/5/1/232.
106. See e.g. StA-L, SED-Bezirksleitung IV/A/2/9/2/363.
107. Coupled films were introduced in June 1946. StadtAL, StVuR(1), Nr. 8354, Bl. 262.
108. Ibid., 12.
109. See e.g. StadtAL, StVuR(1), Nr. 7972, Bl. 16.
110. StadtAL, StVuR(1), Nr. 8354, Bl. 265.
111. The first 'film café' opened in November 1959. Enz, *Entwicklung*, p. 21. See also Kersten, *Das Filmwesen*, p. 286.
112. Discounted tickets were also provided by the Volksbühne, the 'people's stage' organization. See StadtAL, StVuR(1), Nr. 2134, Bl. 165–166.
113. StadtAL, StVuR(1), Nr. 8354, Bl. 148.
114. Ibid., 182.
115. StA-L, RdB, Nr. 2961, Bl. 39.
116. StA-L, SED-Bezirksleitung IV/2/09/02/536/114.
117. On the Socialist Labour Brigades, see Annette Schuhmann, *Kulturarbeit im sozialistischen Betrieb: Gewerkschaftliche Erziehungspraxis in der SBZ-DDR 1946 bis 1970* (Cologne: Böhlau, 2006); and Christoph Klessmann, *Arbeiter im 'Arbeiterstaat' DDR: Deutsche Traditionen, sowjetisches Modell, westdeutsches Magnetfeld (1945 bis 1971)* (Bonn: Dietz, 2007).
118. In 1957, Leipzig District had nearly 300 *Filmaktivs*. StA-L, RdB, Nr. 2955, Bl. 28.
119. StA-L, RdB, Nr. 2955, Bl. 28; StA-L, SED-Bezirksleitung IV/2/9/02/536/348.
120. StA-L, RdB, Nr. 2267, Bl. 48.
121. *Jak žilo Brno kulturně a jak se bavilo v roce 1947*, Osvětová rada zemského hlavního města Brna, Archiv města Brna (AMB), f. B 1/30 – Národní výbor města Brna – odbor školství a kultury (unprocessed file).
122. Memo of the District Film Enterprise Olomouc 1958–1960. Zemský archiv v Opavě, pobočka Olomouc, k. 1, číslo 2.

123. Czechoslovakia won in a tight contest, with 3,481,000 sold tickets in six months in the years 1959 and 1960. Supposing that each sold ticket correlated with an actual viewer, this would mean that over a quarter of all citizens saw the propagandistic documentary. See AMZV, TO obyčejné 1945–59, k. 27, GDR.
124. Promotional materials were centrally prepared, but the administration of a promotional campaign was delegated to Regional Directorates. Cinema journals regularly acknowledged cinema managers' activity and creativity as a tool in the fight against declining attendance.
125. See the database http://www.phil.muni.cz/dedur.
126. NA, f. 861/0/1 – Ministerstvo informací – dodatky 1945–1953, k. 134, inv. č. 471, Kulturně-politický plán distribuce filmů na r. 1952; NA, f. 994 - Ministerstvo školství a kultury, zasedání kolegia ministra 1956–66, kolegium 48, 10 December 1959, návrh plánu kulturně-politické činnosti a zvláštních akcí ÚPF na rok 1960.
127. The previous projects of alternative venues for cinema screenings, such as trains, were focused more on education and promotion of socialist values than on entertainment. For a discussion of unimplemented plans for such trains in 1948 in Czechoslovakia, see Lucie Česálková, 'Film v místech nevyužitého času', Iluminace 23(1) (2011), 115. For "Kinoabteile" (cinema sections) on commuter trains in the industrial regions of Saxony and Saxony-Anhalt, see picture no. 183-13499-0005, Bundesarchiv, Digitales Bildarchiv.
128. For details on the Leipzig film club, see the essay by Fernando Ramos Arenas in this volume.
129. See Kopecký's speech at a session of the minister's advisory assembly, 10 January 1952, NA, f. 861/0/1 – Ministerstvo informací – dodatky, 1945–53, k. 134.
130. Malte Rolf, 'Constructing a Soviet Time: Bolshevik Festivals and Their Rivals during the First Five-Year Plan. A Study of the Central Black Earth Region', Kritika. Explorations in Russian and Eurasian History 1(3) (2000), 470–473.
131. StAL, StVuR(1), Nr. 8354, Bl. 227.
132. The most obvious embodiment of this practice of exclusion is the category of 'former people'. The term, which originated in the post-revolutionary Soviet Union, was used by the Czechoslovak State Police as a label for 'enemies of the state'. See Christopher R. Browning and Lewis H. Siegelbaum, 'Frameworks for Social Engineering: Stalinist Schema of Identification and the Nazi Volksgemeinschaft', in Michael Geyer and Sheila Fitzpatrick (eds), Beyond Totalitarianism: Stalinism and Nazism Compared (Cambridge and New York: Cambridge University Press, 2009), pp. 231–265, and Jiří Knapík and Martin Franc et al., Průvodce kulturním děním a životním stylem v českých zemích 1948–1967, vol. 1 (Prague: Academia, 2011), pp. 167–169.
133. For the strategy of negative integration and its use for construction of a nation, see Hans-Ulrich Wehler, Das Deutsche Kaiserreich 1871–1918 (Göttingen: Vandenhoeck & Ruprecht, 1988), pp. 96–100. For building up a homogeneous society in postwar Czechoslovakia, in part through the expulsion of Germans and integration of other national minorities, see Matěj Spurný, Nejsou jako my. Česká společnost a menšiny v pohraničí (1945–1960) (Prague: Antikomplex, 2011).
134. For this use of Alf Lüdtke's term Eigen-Sinn, see Esther von Richthofen, Bringing Culture to the Masses: Control, Compromise and Participation in the GDR (New York and Oxford: Berghahn Books, 2009), pp. 10–12.
135. For a few examples of oppositional reading of Czech propaganda movies present in the testimonies of emigrants, see Pavel Skopal, 'Muži v sedle, v cirku a na

létajících strojích. Dějiny filmové recepce v českých zemích, 1945–1953', in Kristian Feigelson and Petr Kopal (eds), *Film a dějiny 3. Politická kamera – film a stalinismus* (Prague: Casablanca and ÚSTR, 2012), pp. 321–347.

Select Bibliography

Abusch, Alexander. *Im ideologischen Kampf für eine sozialistische Kultur: Die Entwicklung der sozialistischen Kultur in der Zeit des zweiten Fünfjahrplanes. Rede auf der Kulturkonferenz der SED am 23.10.57 in Berlin.* East Berlin: Dietz, 1957.

Belodubrovskaya, Maria. 'Politically Incorrect: Filmmaking under Stalin and the Failure of Power'. Ph.D. thesis, University of Wisconsin-Madison, 2011.

Berghahn, Daniela. *Hollywood behind the Wall: The Cinema of East Germany.* Manchester: Manchester University Press, 2005.

Browning, Christopher, and Lewis Siegelbaum. 'Frameworks for Social Engineering: Stalinist Schema of Identification and the Nazi *Volksgemeinschaft*'. In Michael Geyer and Sheila Fitzpatrick (eds), *Beyond Totalitarianism: Stalinism and Nazism Compared.* Cambridge and New York: Cambridge University Press, 2009.

Čarnický, Michal. '"Zítra se bude promítat všude". Dějiny putovních kin v československé zestátněné distribuční síti'. In Pavel Skopal (ed.), *Naplánovaná kinematografie. Český filmový průmysl 1945 až 1960.* Prague: Academia, 2012.

Cohen, Louis. *The Cultural-Political Traditions and Developments of the Soviet Cinema, 1917–1972.* New York: Arno Press, 1974.

Connelly, John. *Captive University: The Sovietization of East German, Czech, and Polish Higher Education, 1945–1956.* Chapel Hill: University of North Carolina Press, 2000.

Enz, Kurt. *Entwicklung der Filmwiedergabetechnik und des Filmtheaternetzes in der DDR von 1945 bis zur Gegenwart.* Berlin: Schriftenreihe der DEFA Zentralstelle für Filmtechnik, 1982.

Fay, Jennifer. *Theaters of Occupation: Hollywood and the Reeducation of Postwar Germany.* Minneapolis and London: University of Minnesota Press, 2008.

Fehrenbach, Heide. *Cinema in Democratizing Germany: Reconstructing National Identity after Hitler.* Chapel Hill and London: University of North Carolina Press, 1995.

Fritzsche, Peter, and Jochen Hellbeck. 'The New Man in Stalinist Russia and Nazi Germany'. In Michael Geyer and Sheila Fitzpatrick (eds), *Beyond Totalitarianism: Stalinism and Nazism Compared.* Cambridge and New York: Cambridge University Press, 2009.

Gębicka, Ewa. 'Sieć kin i rozpowszechnianie filmów'. In Edward Zajiček (ed.), *Encyklopedia kultury polskiej XX wieku: Film i kinematografia.* Warsaw: Instytut Kultury and Komitet Kinematografii, 1994.

Gutkin, Irina. *The Cultural Origin of the Socialist Realist Aesthetic 1890–1934.* Evanston: Northwestern University Press, 1999.

Hake, Sabine. *The Cinema's Third Machine: Writing on Film in Germany, 1907–1933.* Lincoln: University of Nebraska Press, 1993.

Heimann, Thomas. *DEFA, Künstler und SED-Kulturpolitik: Zum Verhältnis von Kulturpolitik und Filmproduktion in der SBZ/DDR 1945 bis 1989.* Berlin: Vistas, 1994.

Höpel, Thomas. *Von der Kunst- zur Kulturpolitik: Städtische Kulturpolitik in Deutschland und Frankreich 1918–1939.* Stuttgart: Franz Steiner Verlag, 2007.

Höpel, Thomas. *Die Kunst dem Volke: Städtische Kulturpolitik in Leipzig und Lyon 1945–1989.* Leipzig: Leipziger Universitätsverlag, 2011.

Ihme-Tuchel, Beate. *Das „nördliche Dreieck". Die Beziehungen zwischen der DDR, der Tschechoslowakei und Polen in den Jahren 1954 bis 1962.* Cologne: Wissenschaft und Politik, 1994.

Kapterev, Sergei. 'Illusionary Spoils: Soviet Attitudes towards American Cinema during the Early Cold War.' *Kritika: Explorations in Russian and Eurasian History* 10(4) (2009): 779–807.

Kenez, Peter. *Cinema and Soviet Society, 1917–1953.* Cambridge: Cambridge University Press, 1992.

Kersten, Heinz. *Das Filmwesen in der Sowjetischen Besatzungszone Deutschlands.* Bonn: Bundesministerium für gesamtdeutsche Fragen, 1963.

Klessmann, Christoph. *Arbeiter im 'Arbeiterstaat' DDR: Deutsche Traditionen, sowjetisches Modell, westdeutsches Magnetfeld (1945 bis 1971).* Bonn: Dietz, 2007.

Klimeš, Ivan. 'Stát a filmová kultura.' *Iluminace* 11(2) (1999): 125–137.

Kreimeier, Klaus. *The UFA Story: A History of Germany's Greatest Film Company 1919–1945.* Berkeley, Los Angeles and London: University of California Press, 1999.

Kunakhovich, Kyrill. 'In Search of Socialist Culture: Art and Politics in Krakow and Leipzig, 1918–1989'. Ph.D. thesis, Princeton University, 2013.

Květová, Hana. 'Filmové jaro na vesnici 1951 až 1956. Historie kulturně osvětové akce na českém venkově v 50. letech'. In Pavel Skopal (ed.), *Naplánovaná kinematografie. Český filmový průmysl 1945 až 1960.* Prague: Academia, 2012.

Mareš, Petr. 'Politika a "Pohyblivé obrázky." Spor o dovoz amerických filmů do Československa po druhé světové válce', *Iluminace* 6(1) (1994), 77–96.

Martini, Heidi. *Dokumentarfilm-Festival Leipzig: Filme und Politik in Blick und Gegenblick.* Berlin: DEFA, 2007.

Miller, Jamie. *Soviet Cinema: Politics and Persuasion under Stalin.* London and New York: I.B. Tauris, 2010.

Naimark, Norman. *The Russians in Germany: A History of the Soviet Zone of Occupation, 1945–1949.* Cambridge: Belknap Press, 1995.

Nünthel, Ralf. *Johannes Nitzsche Kinematographen & Films: die Geschichte des Leipziger Kinopioniers, seiner Unternehmen und seiner Technik.* Beucha: Sax-Verlag, 1999.

Nünthel, Ralf. *UT Connewitz & Co. Geschichten aus Leipzig-Süd.* Beucha: Sax-Verlag, 2004.

Otto, Hans-Rainer. 'Kinoalltag und Kinokultur in der DDR'. In Raimund Fritz (ed.), *Der Geteilte Himmel: Höhepunkte des DEFA-Kinos 1946–1992,* vol. 2. Vienna: Filmarchiv Austria, 2001.

Rolf, Malte. 'Constructing a Soviet Time: Bolshevik Festivals and their Rivals during the First Five-Year Plan. A Study of the Central Black Earth Region'. *Kritika. Explorations in Russian and Eurasian History* 1(3) (2000), 447–473.

Roth-Ey, Kristin. *Moscow Prime Time: How the Soviet Union Built the Media Empire that Lost the Cultural Cold War*. Ithaca: Cornell University Press, 2011.

Schittly, Dagmar. *Zwischen Regie und Regime: Die Filmpolitik der SED im Spiegel der DEFA-Produktionen*. Berlin: Ch. Links, 2002.

Schuhmann, Annette. *Kulturarbeit im sozialistischen Betrieb: Gewerkschaftliche Erziehungspraxis in der SBZ-DDR 1946 bis 1970*. Cologne: Böhlau, 2006.

Schulz, Günther. 'Die DEFA, 1946–1990: Fakten und Daten'. In Raimund Fritz (ed.), *Der Geteilte Himmel: Höhepunkte des DEFA-Kinos 1946–1992*, vol. 2. Vienna: Filmarchiv Austria, 2001.

Skopal, Pavel. 'Za vysokou ideovou úroveň, a/nebo za vyšší tržby? Filmová distribuce v českých zemích z hlediska konfliktu ideologických a hospodářských cílů (1945–1968)'. *Soudobé dějiny* 17(4) (2010), 641–666.

Skopal, Pavel. '"It is not enough we have lost the war – now we have to watch it!" Cinemagoers' attitudes in the Soviet occupation zone of Germany (a case study from Leipzig)'. *Participations. Journal of Audience and Reception Studies* 8(2) (2011), 497–521 (http://www.participations.org/Volume%208/Issue%202/3j%20Skopal.pdf).

Skopal, Pavel. 'Muži v sedle, v cirku a na létajících strojích. Dějiny filmové recepce v českých zemích, 1945–1953'. In Kristian Feigelson and Petr Kopal (eds), *Film a dějiny 3. Politická kamera – film a stalinismus*. Prague: Casablanca and ÚSTR, 2012.

Spurný, Matěj. *Nejsou jako my. Česká společnost a menšiny v pohraničí (1945–1960)*. Prague: Antikomplex, 2011.

Vincendeau, Ginette. *Encyclopedia of European Cinema*. New York: Files on File, 1995.

von Richthofen, Esther. *Bringing Culture to the Masses: Control, Compromise and Participation in the GDR*. New York and Oxford: Berghahn Books, 2009.

Wehler, Hans-Ulrich. *Das Deutsche Kaiserreich 1871–1918*. Göttingen: Vandenhoeck & Ruprecht, 1988.

Chapter 14

A Decade between Resistance and Adaptation

The Leipzig University Film Club (1956–1966)

Fernando Ramos Arenas

Introduction

When a group of students of Karl Marx University screened the film *Der Student von Prag* (*The Student of Prague*, Hanns Heinz Ewers and Stellan Rye, 1913) in the Pavilion of the Nationale Front in Leipzig on 9 October 1956 at 8:00 p.m., they were laying the foundation stone for one of the German Democratic Republic (GDR)'s most peculiar and lasting cultural organizations. Following several weeks of hasty preparations, this first screening marked the birth of the Leipzig University Film Club (Leipziger Universitätsfilmklub, LUF), an institution that, after undergoing several name changes and structural modifications and overcoming all manner of physical shortages over more than thirty-five years, would even outlive the Socialist Unity Party of Germany (Sozialistische Einheitspartei Deutschlands, SED) state before eventually ending in 1992. As one of the most important film clubs in East Germany, the LUF was a good example of a quite unorthodox formation: a democratic organization that managed to develop its activities despite the limitations the Soviet Union imposed on distribution and exhibition practices and the GDR's later adoption of such constraints in the 1950s.

Drawing on archival materials documenting the work of the LUF, secondary literature, interviews with one of its main representatives – the director of the LUF during the early 1960s and later film journalist

Fred Gehler – and reports of the mass state youth organization Free German Youth (Freie Deutsche Jugend, FDJ) preserved in the University Archive Leipzig, my research in this essay focuses on the LUF's first decade of existence, a period characterized by the Sovietization of distribution and exhibition practices, de-Stalinization (from the late 1950s onwards) and the period of growing cultural openness between the erection of the Berlin Wall in August 1961 and the Eleventh Plenum of the SED in December 1965. My analysis ends with 1966, when the LUF established itself independently from the university and FDJ, receiving the new designation Leipzig Film Club (Leipziger Filmklub).

The implications of the cultural policies implemented by the SED state are central to understanding the emergence of film clubs, their position as institutions tolerated by the state (but also in constant conflict with its representatives) and their development into a stable organization at the national level. I would also like to point out some characteristics of LUF's history that help to situate the evolution of this institution and of many of its East German peers within a broader, trans-European understanding of film culture. French film historian Antoine de Baecque has described *cinephilian* culture as a new way 'of watching films, talking about them and spreading these discourses'[1] that appeared in France during the post–World War II period and then dispersed across French borders during the 1950s to influence the national film cultures of the U.K., Italy, Spain and the Federal Republic of Germany. The spread of cinephilian discourses also accompanied the emergence of the various European New Waves, provoking a renaissance of the film club movement and the institutionalization of local film cultures (through the founding of film museums, national film archives, film departments at universities, etc.), which until this time had been condemned to a shadowy existence. Despite the SED's strict control of film cultural activities, which included monitoring the reception of foreign films and the circulation of foreign magazines, the cultural exchange necessary for the evolution of cinephilian discourse also occurred in East Germany. The LUF provides a very good example for analysing some of these developments, an example in which the official cultural policies were challenged by the activities of a group of enthusiasts trying to live out their passion for motion pictures.

In the introductory part of this essay, I will briefly lay out the evolution of the film club movement from the early 1920s to the 1950s. As I understand it, this was a trans-European process, which is important to comprehending the emergence, activities and self-conception of the LUF in adequate context. In the second part, I describe early examples of film-club-like events in the GDR and discuss the formation of these clubs within the context of East German cultural policy. The main part of this essay will then treat the history of the LUF's activities from 1956 until 1966: its founding in 1956, its evolution until 1960 and its institutional renaissance and programmatic changes after 1962. The examination of a heated discussion following the film club's screening of the Czechoslovak film *Snadný život* (An Easy Life, Miloš Makovec, 1957) in November 1958 supplements my analysis of the everyday undertakings and ideological debates in the institution.

Watching Films and Talking about Them: Film Clubs

The names may differ but their function remains: film societies, film clubs or *ciné-clubs* were born as associations to promote film culture through the screening of works (usually obscure films falling outside the distribution mainstream) and their public discussion, occasionally producing published output in the form of brochures or magazines in the process. Their story can be traced back to the 1920s and is usually linked to avant-garde circles and alternative cinema circuits.[2] In 1920, the Italian film theoretician Ricciotto Canudo founded in Paris what is today considered to be the first film club in history: the Circle of Friends of the Seventh Art (Club des amis du septieme art). Louis Delluc's Cinéclub, founded in the same city just two years later, gave these seminal groups their definitive name. Parallel to the emergence of these first French examples, British film culture began to organize around film societies from 1925 onwards. In contrast to the artistic interests of their French film clubs, the British societies maintained a more educational profile by actively promoting local as well as foreign films otherwise banned from British screens for political reasons (especially German and Soviet films) in opposition to American productions. Compared to their French or Spanish counterparts, which developed a culture of discussion around film projection, the British film societies relied more on introductory speeches and projection; discussions involving the active participation of the audience were quite rare.[3]

Although left-wing groups supported many of these institutions in various European countries like England, Belgium or the Netherlands, organized film reception during these early years was most highly politicized in Germany. The German-based Workers International Relief (Internationale Arbeiter-Hilfe), an organization ancillary to the Communist International, became active in screening films for proletarian circles in the early 1920s. The film association Volksfilmverband and the production and distribution company Prometheus, both closely tied to the Communist Party, were also part of this increasingly important German left-wing film culture, which disappeared when the Nazis came to power in 1933.[4]

Following a period of general decline during World War II, film clubs underwent a tremendous expansion in the postwar era, especially in France. Also in this period, the first international film club association, the Fédération Internationale des Ciné-Clubs, was founded on 16 September 1947 in Cannes. Originally brought to life by French and British film club members, its leadership was expressly oriented towards internationalization and left-wing positions: its first directors were the French communist film historian Georges Sadoul and the Italian communist film theorist and scriptwriter Cesare Zavattini. This organization was intended as a forum for promoting cultural exchange in film art, particularly through cooperation between film archives and other cultural organizations. Its founding can also be seen as a protest against the proliferation of American commercial films in Europe in the years after World War II.[5]

At this time, France, the birthplace of *cinephilia*, had become the most significant European stronghold of the film club movement. By the mid-1950s there were 180 institutions of this kind with around sixty thousand members.[6] Although less strongly represented in other West European nations, the film club movement also made essential contributions to local film cultures there. In Eastern Europe, Polish and Czechoslovak film audiences also caught up with these developments, organizing themselves in independent associations during these years (1956 in Poland) or in the next decade (1964 in Czechoslovakia).

Film Clubs in the GDR

Although some early attempts to promote film cultural initiatives in the new East German state can be traced back to the late 1940s (e.g. the Film-Club Berlin, founded in the British sector of the German capital), the first wave of film clubs did not emerge until around 1956. These clubs grew out of, among other factors, the previous film cultural activities that had been taking place in well-established organizations and institutions like the Society for German-Soviet Friendship (Gesellschaft für Deutsch-Sowjetische Freundschaft), the FDJ or the East German army (Nationale Volksarmee), established in 1956. In this regard, the cultural mass organization known as the Kulturbund, in which – at least during its early years – different political tendencies were represented, also played a pivotal role not just by organizing cultural activities, but by doing so *parallel* to the official line in many cases.[7]

The founding of the State Film Archive (Staatliches Filmarchiv, SFA) in 1955 was extremely relevant to the work of all these institutions. It was established as a centre for the collection and scientific study of film historical documents and films, but also functioned de facto as a non-commercial institution for film distribution, providing the early film clubs with necessary yet scarce film copies. In contrast to the official distribution company Progress Film-Vertrieb, the SFA could supply films that were not part of the mainstream – such as old German productions from the 1920s or Soviet films from the 1920s and 1930s – at extremely low prices.

Another important pillar of the film cultural work in this period was the Filmaktiv movement, which the state authorities officially promoted between 1951 and 1960. Within the broader context, this movement can be seen as part of the transformation of East German political and social structures along Soviet lines, an ongoing process that had shaped production and distribution in the East German film industry since the late 1940s. Originally recruited by the state distribution company Progress Film-Vertrieb, the approximately 3,000 members of Filmaktiv received obligatory training and were then charged with steering the reception of films according to the official ideological line. Although its distance from the more 'independent' activities of the film clubs is obvious, Filmaktiv prefigured some of the characteristics of the film club work, especially its self-understanding as connection point between producers and audiences.[8]

Up to this point, authorities in the SED state had regarded the tradition of independent but also organized film audiences with distrust: the film clubs, unlike the Filmaktiv initiative, were not easily manageable; they were the result of a movement 'from below', and merely an extension of the previous work done by film enthusiasts. Moreover, independent federations like those that existed in other socialist countries like Poland were not allowed in the GDR. Therefore the film clubs' organizational structures were rapidly integrated into the official framework provided by the SED and other state organizations. As I will illustrate with the case of the LUF, the supporting organizations (universities, the FDJ, the Society for German-Soviet Friendship, the Kulturbund) provided not only representation in organs of political power and financial support, but also ideological control. At the local level, film clubs wishing to secure facilities for film screenings were also forced to work together with institutions like theatres or cinemas.

Apart from the problems of their institutional affiliation, the film clubs posed other challenges to the official culture political line. Their most basic definition as institutions that sought to bring 'artistically valuable' films to the masses pointed indirectly to a deficiency in film cultural education that was typically not acknowledged by the officials. At the same time, the interest in art film caused a lot of friction with state authorities: film clubs were seen in this logic as elitist institutions that organized private screenings and were unwilling to engage with the 'proletarian' aesthetics of the new state (such as socialist realism) due to a preference for traditional, 'bourgeois' cultural forms. Just a few months before the founding of the LUF, Eberhard Richter, a press aide with the Ministry of Culture at the time, published an article in *Forum* (1956/12), the official print organ of the FDJ, that summarized the official SED line on the existence of film clubs:

> We consider that a student film club, as an independent organization, is not necessary. The task of the film clubs in the western countries is to make artistically valuable films accessible to the public. In the German Democratic Republic there are no barriers to prevent the screening of artistically valuable films.[9]

What, then, led in the second half of the 1950s to the aforementioned wave of film club formations, including the LUF's, in spite of these official impediments? Developments abroad, particularly the founding of the Polish Film Club Organization in 1956, were indeed seen as encouraging examples of active film cultural work operating 'from below'.[10] In the cultural-political climate following discussions of the Central Committee of the SED between 21 and 27 October 1955, the FDJ had already voiced criticism of the bureaucratic structures of the party, citing its distance from the real problems and needs of young people. It also campaigned for building special interest groups and associations that would re-establish a strong sense of boundaries.[11] Several months later, at the Twelfth Conference of the Central Committee of the FDJ in February 1956, the organization opted for increased cooperation with cultural and sport groups in order to secure its proximity to the masses. The founding of six film clubs during the subsequent months – including the LUF in October – can therefore be interpreted as part of the state authorities' efforts to promote a closer relationship to youth in general and college students in particular.

In 1956, the self-critical positions expressed at the Twentieth Congress of the Communist Party of the Soviet Union in February and that year's protests in Hungary and Poland also had consequences for Karl Marx University in the next months.[12] During the last months of 1956 and early 1957, the initial sense of cultural openness gave way to a wave of repression against intellectuals (e.g. the so-called Harich Platform organized around the SED functionaries Wolfgang Harich, Bernhard Steinberger and Manfred Hertwig, who argued for a different, uniquely 'German way' towards socialism, or the campaigns against the philosopher Ernst Bloch and the Germanist Hans Mayer at Karl Marx University). The goal was to eliminate any traces of a cultural thaw in the GDR. The Thirtieth Conference of the Central Committee of the SED from 30 January to 1 February 1957 made these dispositions official.

In 1957, SED Central Committee member Alexander Abusch proclaimed at a cultural conference that one of the state's fundamental goals was to saturate the entire realm of entertainment and amusement with the socialist spirit.[13] Following this notion, at the Fifth Party Congress (from 10 to 16 July 1958), the SED introduced the idea of a 'Socialist Cultural Revolution' as one of the main objectives of state politics. The work of the film clubs re-entered the spotlight, and they were allowed to form once again, often as an *ensemble*, a typical denomination for emerging cultural groups before the Fifth and between the Fifth and Sixth Party Congresses. A good dozen film clubs appeared in the next three years. The direct impact of these political discussions about the work of cultural institutions in general and the everyday activities of the film clubs in particular is clear in a fifteen-page document prepared shortly after the Fifth Party Congress by the Progress Film-Vertrieb distribution company and distributed to various film organizations. The document included a list of film suggestions that would help illustrate the '10 Commandments for the New Socialist Man' proclaimed by Walter Ulbricht during the congress.[14]

The Leipziger Universitätsfilmklub

Although the founding of the LUF can be seen primarily as a result of the confluence of the spontaneous initiative of a group of students interested in cinema with favourable culture political circumstances, its existence was made possible only within the boundaries of already existing structures, in this case the FDJ and the university group (*Hochschulgruppe*) of the Kulturbund. The FDJ was expected to handle the 'problems of the students' while the Kulturbund would provide cultural-political assistance,[15] but in fact the FDJ assumed a commanding role. It controlled the ideological line, received reports of the club's activities at its headquarters in Berlin and also paid the bills for the films or for visiting lecturers, who were intermittently invited to comment on a particular exhibition or explain a broader film-historical or film-political subject. From December 1957 onwards, and in parallel with the official name change from *Filmklub* to *Arbeitsgemeinschaft* (AG) or a 'film working team' at the Student Club of Karl Marx University, the club was exclusively subordinated to the FDJ.

What were the purposes and responsibilities of the LUF? According to a concept paper[16] from April 1957, these included the screening of films and their public discussion. In this document, LUF members also explained their approach to interpreting a film work as 'ideological appraisal of the content and of its social implications' and 'engagement with the artistic-aesthetic problems and means of expression in film, whereby the unity of both factors must be emphasized' with a set of goals in line with the guiding premises of socialist realism. Given the great social pressure to conform that pervaded East German universities during this period, it is not surprising that the members of the LUF (all of whom were students) acted so in step with the official ideological precepts on film reception. Reflecting on the first two and a half years of activity in a report of winter 1959, the film club's administration commented that a great portion of those attending the initial screenings were 'only interested in film historical and film aesthetic questions'. Yet, as the club leadership remarked with a certain pride, when the club started to 'discuss ideological questions, many of the original spectators simply left.[17] The work of the LUF was also integrated with local cultural policies in Leipzig: ever since a Filmaktiv conference in 1953, the city had tried to promote discussion of progressive film and the political indoctrination of audiences. Therefore, parallel to the activities of the film club, the People's Film College (Filmvolkshochschule, founded in 1958) began offering documentary film cycles in the facilities of the Filmeck movie theatre.[18]

The club was originally structured around a small group of seven students that functioned as the organ of government and managed day-to-day business, selecting films, organizing screenings and lectures, contacting lecturers, managing finances, and so on. The directors of the LUF, as in other film clubs in the GDR, were autodidacts who worked without remuneration. Facilities were provided by the university as well as by other state organizations like the National Front (Nationale Front) or the university's Sport Institute.

The screenings were originally set up as private events for a maximum of 230 members, a number that was rapidly achieved. Most of these students were members of the Institute for Journalism or studied German philology, but the Graphic Arts Institute and the Section of Performing Arts were also significantly represented. The films were initially screened exclusively for the members of the club; in this way, the LUF leadership hoped to be allowed to show films otherwise banned for regular audiences[19] – a request that ultimately could not be fulfilled. The private character of the screenings was modified in October 1957, presumably according to official directive: from this point onwards, the film club was accessible to anyone interested in cinema.

Though the film club's activities were controlled by the FDJ, the LUF directors also had to work together with the university on a regular basis. A four-man scientific committee composed of members of the university was set up to provide the activities of the Film Club with the necessary 'professional guidance'; however, it was not involved in routine decisions about the selection of films to be screened in the club. Still, its interference reached beyond these 'professional' questions: for example, in January 1957 Dr Erhard John, a member of this committee and of the Department for Aesthetics in the Institute for Philosophy at Karl Marx University used his privileged position to provide fifteen of his students access to the club, which by that point had already reached its limit and was not admitting any new members.[20]

Films were screened twice a month on average in sessions (sometimes a session included more than one film); the prints were obtained primarily from the State Film Archive in Berlin for a price of 30 East German mark per picture. This cooperation with the SFA was also instrumental for ensuring the screening of certain titles belonging to the tradition officially embraced by the SED, including:

- German films of the 1920s like *Das Kabinet des Dr. Caligari* (The Cabinet of Dr. Caligari, Robert Wiene, 1920), *Berlin – Symphonie einer Großstadt* (Berlin, Symphony of a Great City, Walter Ruttman, 1927), Friedrich W. Murnau's *Der letzte Mann* (The Last Laugh, 1924) and *Faust* (1926) or Fritz Lang's *Die Frau im Mond* (Rocket to the Moon, 1929). A kind of sub-category among the German films consisted of works of the so-called Proletarian Cinema like *Mutter Krausens Fahrt ins Glück* (Mother Krause's Journey to Happiness, Phil Jutzi, Germany, 1929) and *Kuhle Wampe oder: Wem gehört die Welt?* (Kuhle Wampe or to Whom Does the World Belong?

Slatan Dudow, Germany, 1932), which had been produced in the late 1920s and 1930s.
- A series of international films by directors who enjoyed ideological appeal in the socialist state, such as Charlie Chaplin (*The Great Dictator*, 1940) or Joris Ivens (*De Brug*, 1928, and *Misère au Borinage*, 1933) to whom the LUF dedicated a screening cycle in October and November 1957. During this period the defence of Charlie Chaplin as an anticapitalist artist could already be observed in *Deutsche Filmkunst*, the most important film magazine in the GDR.
- And, of course, classic Soviet films such as *Oktyabr': Desyat' dney kotorye potryasli mir* (October: Ten Days That Shook the World, Sergei M. Eisenstein, 1927), *Aleksandr Nevskiy* (Alexander Nevski, Sergei M. Eisenstein, 1938), *Putyovka v zhizn* (Road to Life, Nikolai Ekk, 1931) or *Dezertir* (Deserter, Vsevolod Pudovkin, 1933).

In order to reaffirm the political aspect of the screenings, some of these films were presented in cycles, such as a 'Sergei Eisenstein' series, 'Masterpieces of Soviet Cinema' (which included film screenings and conferences) and 'The Image of the German Worker in Film', all of which were presented in 1957 and 1958.

Notably absent from this list of films screened by the LUF are contemporary East German DEFA (Deutsche Film-Aktiengesellschaft) productions. Some exceptions were Georg C. Klaren's *Karriere in Paris* (Career in Paris, 1951) or *Der Richter von Zalamea* (The Judge of Zalamea, Martin Hellberg, 1956), which was shown in the LUF only two years after its premiere in Berlin. In this respect, this film club acted like many other institutions of its kind in Western Europe, stressing the distance between art-house cinema production (in this particular case, in the form of 'artistically valuable progressive cinema') and the 'official' films offered by the state tradition of quality. On the one hand, this mode of action conforms to the club's original goals as formulated in its concept paper. On the other hand, contemporary films were also exhibited in regular movie theatres, so the film club's screening of these works would present traditional, commercial exhibition practices with undesirable competition and thus be unwelcome.

The range of films available to the clubs was strictly limited, which meant that many titles were screened multiple times. The selection of films and elaboration of a coherent programme presented consistent problems for the LUF. After only its first year of operation the club informed the central office of the FDJ[21] that its activities were being complicated by the impossibility of receiving the appropriate films from the archives (SFA) or planning their rental in advance. Material shortages influenced not only the pictures shown but also the activities that accompanied the screenings, such as the printing of brochures and the organization of discussions about the films with scholars or directors in attendance from the German Academy of Cinema Art in Babelsberg.

The Student Film in 1958: Untruthful, Negative and Atypical

As an illustration of the type of discussions held in the LUF, I would like now to analyse the debate that followed the screening of the Czechoslovak film *Snadný život*, by Miloš Makovec, on 28 November 1958. Members of the film club recorded the debate in a discussion protocol. The film tells the story of a group of students at a Czechoslovak university in the 1950s, and the members of the film club expected it to be a faithful portrait of contemporary youth in a communist country. The picture had been playing in some regular GDR cinemas since the previous summer when the LUF picked it up because of its theme, which they expected would touch on experiences they could relate to. The screening of the film was also intended to provide a basis for a broader discussion about the possibility of such student films in the GDR – inexistent up to this point – which could illustrate the reality of life at East German universities.

After lamenting the previous month's shrinking audiences[22] and identifying the cause of this problem to be the club's lack of activities besides film screenings, the LUF members prepared a special event for *Snadný život*: director Heinz Thiel and two other members of the Dramaturgy Section at the DEFA studio, Dieter Scharfenberg and Wolfgang Pieper, were invited to take part in a discussion to be held after the screening.

The protocol of this discussion shows no sign of deviance from the official line dictated by the party by either the members of the DEFA studio or the students. All the members present at the discussion lambasted the film: 'The film is untruthful. It is not only negative, but also atypical', exclaimed one participant. One medical student furiously remarked right at the beginning of the discussion, 'We don't want to see such a film again!' adding that the things depicted in the film 'could not even happen in a capitalist country, not to mention in a socialist one'.[23] As already noted, the members of the DEFA studio supported this line of argument and also offered self-criticism as filmmakers: when questioned about the nonexistence of realistic depictions of the student world, they explained that no scripts dealing with this topic were available. According to Scharfenberg, though, the absence of such texts was not a problem of craftsmanship but a political one: 'The reason why there are no good scripts is that most of the authors lack the correct ideology.'[24]

To support their opinions, the participants drew on contemporary official discourses, for example, Walter Ulbricht's speech at the Fifth Party Congress,[25] in which he proclaimed that the first goal of socialist national culture was to bring the people and culture together.[26] The discussion also consistently mentioned the consequences of the Twentieth Congress of the Communist Party of the Soviet Union for internal GDR politics and the subsequent waves of liberalization and revolts in Hungary and other East European countries. For instance, Thiel condemned the film in the following way: 'The pernicious message is in alignment with a false interpretation of the 20th Congress, intending to deviate from the formula. The result is dull revisionism.'[27] Handel, an LUF member also present at the discussion, interpreted the film in broader (and in his view more alarming) cultural-political terms: he argued that the film encouraged tendencies that 'soften' (*aufweichen*) the socialist countries, as had been already observed in the Polish and Hungarian revolutions of 1956. Therefore, the film was deemed bad not only because of its intrinsic qualities but also because of its critical assessment of the principles of socialist realism. The resolution formulated after the discussion noted that 'film should recount the serious scientific, social and practical work of students'[28] and, in so doing, should also cast the students in a positive light.

Building on this resolution, the LUF also prepared a letter of protest to DEFA. On 16 December Blumenthal, the director of the film club at the time, wrote to the export department of the film studios demanding an explanation for the exhibition of such a 'harmful work'.[29] The campaign against the film culminated with an article titled 'Not Real Student Problems', which was published in *Forum*,[30] the fortnightly journal of the Central Council of the FDJ in Berlin. The article attacked DEFA as responsible for purchasing a film 'which could have been produced in any capitalist land'.

Though the discussions of this film and its consequences are abundantly documented in the archives, the lack of more material of this kind makes it impossible to determine whether such a virulent reaction was a common 'natural' response to films that called some principles of socialist realism into question, or whether this event was to some extent 'staged' to achieve greater political resonance for the club's activities (further aided by the letters promptly sent to DEFA and *Forum*).

When discussing the FDJ's role during the early 1960s, LUF director Fred Gehler recounted how members of the youth organization tried to steer discussions against his work as the club's new leader, accusing him of lacking political commitment, a situation that provoked significant tensions between Gehler and the FDJ (Gehler, personal communication, 22 November 2011). We can therefore assume that, by the late 1950s – a period in which there were still no relevant discrepancies between the club's leadership and the youth organization – the FDJ representatives played a central role in both generating the political overzealousness observed in this discussion and influencing how events like these were politically utilized to work towards the party's dispositions (even if DEFA's activities were thereby criticized).

1962: A Renaissance

By 1960 the LUF had for all practical purposes disappeared. According to the official line, 'manpower shortage' was the cause. As the former SFA employee Rudolf Freund explained, however, the real reason seems to have been the competition this institution posed for the state distribution company Progress Film-Vertrieb and its monopoly.[31] Film distribution at the SFA had already been suspended for this reason between 1960 and the beginning of 1962. In any case, by 1959 the film club had reached the point where it was no longer functioning as active institution. Delays in payments to the SFA, a constant problem for the film club since its early days that dominated much of the institution's mail correspondence in 1957 and 1958, had increased in the past months. Unanswered letters and invitations collected in the archives in 1959 and from 1960 until the first months of 1962, when new activities, such as screenings in cooperation with the House of Polish Culture in Leipzig, were being planned.

The reactivation of LUF was a response to cultural-political developments in the country. Following the building of the Berlin Wall in August 1961, First Secretary of the SED Walter Ulbricht embarked on a policy of cultural liberalization. Cultural institutions were encouraged to offer activities that would secure closeness between youth and the party. Two years later, the Sixth Party Congress of the SED directly addressed the cultural education of the masses as a central goal.

For the film club, this new period after 1962 was also a phase of growing ideological friction. In late 1962, the new FDJ-appointed leadership had worked out a new concept paper for the institution.³² The club also acquired a new name: the FDJ Film Club of Karl Marx University (FDJ-Filmklub der Karl Marx Universität). In addition to the usual description of goals and subjects, the concept paper also included among its objectives an analysis of the work of a series of 'bourgeois filmmakers', a subject usually condemned by the cultural authorities. As the FDJ members in charge of editing the paper noted in its margins, the document did not directly discuss the party principles regarding art and literature either. The text was rejected and substituted some months later, in summer 1963, with a new version that presented the film club's work as a direct execution of the dispositions discussed at the Seventeenth Plenum of the SED.³³

Charged with taking control of a de facto nonexistent organization by the FDJ, the new members of the LUF leadership very soon demonstrated a clear distance from the official ideological line in their practices. On the one hand, the screenings showed an increasing interest in films of the 'New Cinemas' of other socialist countries like Poland, Czechoslovakia and Hungary – František Vláčil's *Holubice* (White Dove, Czechoslovakia, 1960) and Roman Polanski's *Nóż w wodzie* (Knife in the Water, Poland, 1963) were shown in Leipzig as early as 1962 and 1963 (the former had even been originally banned by the SED authorities). At the same time, the screenings neglected the productions of the East German DEFA. By virtue of its contacts with the House of Czechoslovak Culture, and motivated by film club member Hans-Burckhard Schnaß's personal interest in Czechoslovak film, the LUF was able to screen some examples of the young, flourishing cinema of this neighbouring country, such as *Ostře sledované vlaky* (Closely Watched Trains, Jiří Menzel, 1966) until shortly before the Prague Spring in 1968. This openness, however, did not extend to West European productions – in most cases, their arrival on GDR screens was delayed for several years (e.g. the first work of the French New Wave to be shown in East Germany, Truffaut's *Les quatre cents coups* [The 400 Blows, 1959], did not premiere until 1968).

The discussions surrounding the reception of these films revealed the influence of other theoretical and ideological traditions that posed a challenge to the socialist realist line still defended by the authorities. During a conference on 22 January 1963, the FDJ administration in Leipzig discussed how some of these, in their view, 'dangerous' attitudes influenced the LUF's activities. Regarding the work of the new club director, Fred Gehler, the FDJ noted:

In a political-ideological sense, his work needs to be more effective for the purposes of the party. He lets himself be pushed from the right and the left and he is very inconsistent. He does not possess a clear political conception.[34]

Apparently, however, Gehler was not to be the only one whose attitude caused headaches for the FDJ:

Some members of the Film Club are not free from arrogance towards the films of the DEFA and contemporary socialist art. Especially the friends [Hans-Burkhard] Schnaß and Schkerl tend towards an exaggerated adoration of form and ignore content. In this, the influence of Prof. Mayer (Institute for History of German Literature) is also evident.[35]

During these years, the discussion of content versus form, which had been at the root of most debates on art and literature in the GDR since the early 1950s, converged with the challenges posed by the film production and developments in film theory and criticism in other European countries. When confronted with this 'official' evaluation of his work by the FDJ in this period, Gehler admitted to having been influenced by writings in contemporary leading European film journals such as the French *Cahiers du Cinéma* or the West German *Filmkritik*. His work for the leading East German film magazine at the time, *Deutsche Filmkunst*,[36] from summer 1961 until its suspension in December 1962, provided him access to ideas and intellectual currents that were prohibited for most regular East German cinemagoers (Gehler, personal communication, 17 January 2012). His connection to *Deutsche Filmkunst* had also been a major factor in his selection as LUF director in 1962: Gehler – who was no longer a student at Karl Marx University but an assistant at its Institute for Journalism – was offered the job at the film club precisely because of his experience with film publications. In the following years, Gehler's influence also enabled the LUF to develop its own screening programme, which was increasingly in conflict with the SED ideological line, in spite of its official subordination to the FDJ.

The growing distance between the LUF and the FDJ also manifested itself physically, namely in the screening facilities. Since the early 1960s, many film clubs that had emerged as attachments to universities in the 1950s were now establishing formal relationships with cinemas. For several months, LUF screenings took place in the film hall of the Grassi Museum, and thereafter the club took up residence in a much bigger venue in the Leipzig city centre: the Casino Theatre, an institution without any formal connection to the state youth organization.

The scarcity of film copies that had restricted the film club's activities in the 1950s also posed a problem in this second period. Therefore, the club's members sought to gain access to films through personal connections with foreign institutions such as the Polish and Czechoslovak Cultural Centres in Berlin. These unofficial networks are central to understanding the club's relationship with the International Leipzig Documentary and Short Film Week.[37] As the most important East German film festival after its revival in 1960, this event provided LUF members with access to international filmmakers, representatives of West German film clubs,[38] publications and, of course, films.

The new personnel constellation, together with these relationships with the Film Week, the Casino Theatre and the film publications, show that despite a certain institutional continuity, the period around 1960 marked a turning point in the history of the LUF. Its evolution during the following years can only be understood within these parameters, which usually promoted screening and discussion practices that ran contrary to the official line.

Not all members who attended screenings, however, unconditionally accepted the film club's shift towards the contemporary film critical discourses already spreading in other European countries.[39] As already noted, Roman Polanski's *Nóz w wodzie* was shown in Leipzig in May 1963, two years before its official premiere in regular East German cinemas, and the response of certain audience members illustrates the gap between the goals of the LUF leadership and the mass of spectators that still accepted the official party line on film aesthetics. On 13 June 1963, the university newspaper published one infuriated viewer's reaction as an article titled 'Whom do you serve, Film Club?' Member Rolf Rothke used the combined screening of Roman Polanski's first feature-length film and *Grausige Nächte* (Nights of Terror, Lupu Pick, Germany, 1921) on 31 May 1963 as a platform to attack the film club's activity on ideological grounds. 'Did the latest discussions on partisanship, popularity and artistic mastery not penetrate the brains of our friends in the Film Club?' Rothke asked. Although Rothke admitted he had not seen Polanski's film, he attacked both pictures, which, according to him, could have been 'dug out by a decadent snob of a West German existentialist club'. The article ends with an ironic remark addressed to the film club: 'comrades Khrushchev, Lenin, Kurt Hager and Walter Ulbricht would not be angry if you first study their discourses on the problems of art and literature'.[40]

The publication of this criticism of the Film Club triggered a fast reaction from the FDJ: ideological overseers contacted the club directors

Fred Gehler and Hans-Burckhard Schnaß for explanation. Gehler and Schnaß formulated a response in which they defended the club's decision to screen the films. To support their opinions, they did not defend the intrinsic qualities of the films but reasoned entirely along official party lines, asserting that 'our principal ideological goal was to work, using the means and methods specific to our effort, towards realizing our main cultural-political task'.[41]

The LUF's new leaders also found themselves engaged in a battle that is key to understanding East German film clubs since their early days in the mid-1950s: the attempt to have various clubs represented at the national level within one unified organization. The founding of the Film Club Association (AG Filmclubs) in December 1963 was the culmination of this long and theretofore fruitless struggle. Back in autumn 1956, members of LUF had been contacted by their colleagues from the Film Club of the Martin Luther University in Halle to exchange some ideas and experiences. After explaining their intentions and suggesting the film cycles they had in mind, they frankly asserted their disagreement with the authorities' lack of support for the creation of film clubs and declared their intention to establish a platform from which to express their demands.[42] Several months later, in the summer of 1957, Stephan Heinig, writing on behalf of the LUF, submitted a report to the central headquarters of the FDJ demanding the formation of an organization that would unify the East German film clubs.[43] Further attempts to establish such an institution were to be made at a conference of the University Film Clubs of the GDR organized by the University Section (Hochschulgruppenleitung) of the FDJ, which was scheduled for 22 and 23 April 1960, in Berlin, during the aforementioned period of LUF inactivity. Nevertheless, these early efforts did not bear fruit until the AG Filmclubs was created three years later.

After its revival in 1962, the LUF made significant, though informal, contacts with other film clubs, particularly the one at Martin Luther University in Halle, which provided a basis for future association. In 1963 the two clubs even jointly published two issues of a magazine called *Filmklubmitteilungen* (Film Club Reports). The project of a national organization, however, could not be realized without state intervention: in the end, it was the GDR State Film Archives that invited 120 representatives of East German film clubs and of the Club of Filmmakers (Club der Filmschaffenden) – an organization that had been created in 1953 to promote the study of the progressive cinema – to Berlin on 6 and 7 December 1963 to proclaim the establishment of the Provisional Committee of Film Clubs at the Club of Filmmakers (Provisorische

Arbeitsgemeinschaft Filmclubs beim Club der Filmschaffenden).[44] The national film club association was subordinated to the Club der Filmschaffenden, which provided the budget for the meetings and for the publication of a magazine (*Film*, printed between 1963 and 1968, when it was shut down due to ideological conflicts with the official party line) and assumed responsibility for the international representation of East German film culture. Fred Gehler, already known for his work at the LUF and his film publications, was elected president of the AG Filmclubs.

The founding of the AG Filmclubs marked an important shift in the dynamics of the film clubs within the power structures of the SED State. First, it gave them institutional representation. In this respect, some members saw it as a chance to promote exchange among the various film clubs, which up to this point had been difficult to maintain, as well as an opportunity to increase their presence and power in dealing with the authorities. Second, because this institutionalization also provided the authorities with more direct control, the AG Filmclubs became a battlefield for competing conceptions of film club activities. The most notable examples of the AG Filmklubs' agitated existence are the tension surrounding the organization of two pivotal workshops in 1966 and 1967 in the city of Meißen (a third, which had originally been planned for 1968, was never realized due to ideological issues) and the publication of the magazine *Film* (likewise dissolved in 1968).[45]

Many film club members saw this newly won representation at the national level as a chance to build contacts with other foreign film clubs and obtain privileged access to a number of international films, which, they hoped, they would be permitted to screen within the restrictive circles of the clubs despite the ban for general audiences. The first wave of film clubs from 1956 and 1957 had already addressed the matter of international integration. In April 1957, the members of the LUF announced their intentions to establish contact with other film clubs 'in West Germany and abroad'.[46] Integration with international structures, particularly the Fédération Internationale des Ciné-Clubs,[47] was therefore understood as one of the goals behind the formation of the AG Filmclubs.[48] This was seen as a first step towards gaining access to the modern films of the European New Waves, which the LUF had heard or read about but rarely seen. However, contacts with this institution, which finally admitted the GDR in 1965, were principally maintained by the Club der Filmschaffenden, so the East German film clubs and their foreign counterparts never arrived at a fruitful and direct collaboration.

In spite of the autonomy the LUF enjoyed during this period in the early 1960s, its structural dependence on the FDJ and the control the youth organization exercised quite often led to open conflict. After screenings, which now took place on Thursdays at 7:00 p.m. in the large Casino Theatre, the club members moved on to the Club House of the FDJ Kalinin at the university, where lectures and discussions took place in a more familiar atmosphere. In these facilities, debates were often steered by affiliates of the FDJ sitting in the audience, who would call into question the selection of the films shown or criticize the films' lack of ideological commitment, especially when they could not be found in 'normal' cinemas (Gehler, personal communication, 22 November 2011).

The collateral damage from the attacks on LUF director Fred Gehler also influenced the film club's development during these years. In 1965 Gehler had been expelled from the university after an article published in the May 1965 issue of the political and cultural magazine *Sonntag* severely denounced his film critical texts and seriously questioned his political commitment. For several years in his journalistic work for *Deutsche Filmkunst* and *Sonntag*, Gehler himself had criticized many DEFA productions in a manner that was not acceptable to the authorities. After his public denunciation in 1965, he was forced to leave both his job as assistant at Karl Marx University and his position as president of the AG Filmclubs.[49]

When Gehler left his post, the close cooperation between the film club and the FDJ went with him. The lack of formal attachment between the main club members and the university, where they were no longer students or scholars, together with growing tensions with the FDJ on the one hand and the structural security provided by long-standing cooperation with the Casino Theatre on the other, compelled the film club's leadership to register a change of name and affiliation without informing the FDJ beforehand. In 1966 the FDJ-Filmklub der Karl Marx Universität became the Leipziger Filmklub. To avoid conflicts with the officials, many of the film club's activities in the coming years would be presented as extraterritorial events of the Houses of the Polish and Czechoslovak Culture in cooperation with the Casino Theatre (Gehler, personal communication, 17 January 2012). Surprisingly enough, neither the FDJ nor the university seemed to take notice of this shift – in any case, neither of them demanded an explanation. Liberated from the direct control of these organizations, the LUF was able to continue functioning for many years, until 1992.

Conclusions and Outlook

During the twenty years following the end of World War II, the film club movement experienced an extraordinary evolution in most European countries. From 1956 onwards this trans-European development also exerted an influence on East German film culture, which until then had been officially steered according to the party line in terms of production and distribution as well as reception. The mere existence of film clubs posed a challenge to this status quo.

The development of the LUF during the late 1950s can be understood as typical of the experiences of a larger group of sixteen film clubs, all of which emerged within a four-year period.[50] The LUF arose as a democratic organization 'from below' and represented an important alternative to the centralized politics that had been developing in East German society and cultural life since the late 1940s. The GDR's general embrace of the Stalinist social and cultural model, which was adopted as a central tenet of state discourse after the second party conference in summer 1952, had been preceded in the field of film production by the establishment in 1950 of a commission to politically monitor every film made by DEFA. The head of this commission, Hermann Axen, had previously been director of the Central Committee of the SED's Department of Agitation.

In keeping with the movement to intensify political control in every social realm, the intent to exercise centralist guidance of cinema also started to cover the area of film reception in this period, primarily through the activities of the Filmaktiv. The rapid, forced integration of film clubs into already existing mass organizations like the FDJ or the Kulturbund some years later can be seen as further evidence of this tendency. The early obstacles to the national organization of the clubs and the problems of film distribution reflect the tension between two different conceptions of the work of the film clubs: the democratic approach of their founders on the one hand, and the Stalinist-oriented SED cultural policy on the other. These contradictory notions often pushed the clubs to a marginal existence: they were officially accepted but not actively promoted. In the eyes of the authorities, they represented an elitist, undercontrolled approach to film reception.

Still, the example of the LUF also shows that film clubs' activities during their early phase in the late 1950s were far from achieving the sort of subversive effects on official cultural policy that the authorities feared. Its proceedings and discourses from the late 1950s display no signs of ideological sedition. In a film cultural panorama dominated by material and intellectual scarcity, the work of the students who constituted the LUF was oriented towards extending official film cultural activities, not questioning them. Although at the beginning of its existence there was a desire to propose alternatives to the state line on the politics and aesthetics of film reception, the integration of LUF with the FDJ soon resulted in homogeneous conformity, as observed in the concept paper from April 1957 and in the protocol of the discussion of December 1958.

When the FDJ contacted Fred Gehler and Hans-Burkhard Schnaß in 1962, it was hoping to resuscitate the film club with support from a group of cinema enthusiasts who could offer expertise and contacts with other institutions as well as a loose attachment to the university. The new members embraced a programme to open the LUF up to contemporary cinema developments in other East European countries, establish a more critical approach to East German productions and promote a set of aesthetic views not compliant with the official line. The tensions emerging in this period between the film club and the FDJ culminated in 1966 with a change of names (eliminating the word 'University') and disengagement from the FDJ.

Although the LUF's structure in this period remained essentially similar to that of its first incarnation in 1956, the new personnel made efforts to connect it to other European developments. The foundation of the AG Filmclubs in 1963 increased the institutional presence of film clubs and produced a magazine (*Film*), which allowed for the dissemination of ideas that had previously only been discussed in small groups. This organization also rapidly became an ideological battlefield for competing notions of film reception.

In this regard, the way discourses of modern cinema were received in East Germany and the way they influenced the activities of the film club point to interesting aspects of the cultural policies of the country and also of the ideas themselves. The discourses of modern cinephilia, which were disseminated throughout Europe from the early 1960s onward, were characterized by a mixture of aesthetic modernism and left-wing politics.[51] As these conceptions of modern cinema fought for positions in various European film cultures, they drew on intellectual traditions with subversive potential in each country. Film publications offer good demonstrations of this process, for example in the undeniable influence of the Spanish Communist Party on *Nuestro Cine* or of the Italian Communist Party on *Cinema Nuovo*. Likewise, left-wing political positions played important roles in France in the evolution of the magazines *Positif* and *Cahiers du Cinéma* (which would culminate in the latter magazine's Maoist phase around 1968). The intellectual tradition of the Frankfurt School was a key force behind the West German journal *Filmkritik*. In the case of East Germany, modern cinephilia drew less on the left-wing tradition, which would have situated it in a position closer to the official cultural policies, than on a type of aesthetic modernism – often discredited as formalism by the SED authorities – that helped them to interpret and praise new cinema developments.

The conflicts that arose within the LUF in the early 1960s, after some of its members had established contact with international debates and films related to (or actively constituting) the cinematic New Waves, illustrate a clear evolution away from the first phase of the film club movement, which had developed within the boundaries of state cultural directives. They also demonstrate how important the international transfer of ideas about film criticism and theory within non-official networks is for understanding this complex film culture, which offered its own unique response to the birth of modern cinema.

Acknowledgement

This essay is part of the research project 'Cinéphilie unter der Diktatur. Europäische Filmkultur zwischen 1955 und 1975 am Beispiel Spaniens und der DDR' (Cinephilia under the Dictatorship: European Film Culture between 1955 and 1975 in Spain and the GDR) carried out at the Institute for Communication and Media Studies, University of Leipzig, Germany, and financed by the German Research Foundation (DFG)..

Fernando Ramos Arenas is an assistant professor of film and media studies at the University of Leipzig, Germany, where he earned his Ph.D. in 2010 with a doctoral thesis on the history of authorship discourses in cinema. He is currently working on a project that examines film reception practices and discourses in Europe during the 1950s and 1960s with a comparative focus on the film cultures in the dictatorial systems of the GDR and Spain. Other fields of research include contemporary media and cultural theories, film criticism and cinema historiography.

Notes

1. Antoine de Baecque, *La cinéphilie. Invention d'un regard, histoire d'une culture 1944–1968* (Paris: Fayard, 2003), p. 11.
2. Malte Hagener, *Moving Forward, Looking Back: The European Avant-Garde and the Invention of Film Culture, 1919–1939* (Amsterdam: Amsterdam University Press, 2007), p. 119.
3. Thorold Dickinson, 'Film Societies', in *Film, New Media, and Aesthetic Education*, Special Issue, *Journal of Aesthetic Education* 3(3) (July 1969), 89.
4. See Bruce Murray, *Film and the German Left in the Weimar Republic: From Caligari to Kuhle Wampe* (Austin: University of Texas Press, 1990) pp. 139ff. and Günter Agde, 'Mit dem Blick nach Westen', in Günter Agde and Alexander Schwarz (eds), *Die rote Traumfabrik. Meschrabpom-Film und Prometheus 1921–1936* (Berlin: Bertz+Fischer, 2012), pp. 140–147.
5. Wieland Becker and Volker Petzold, *Tarkowski trifft King Kong. Geschichte der Filmklubbewegung der DDR* (Berlin: Vistas Verlag, 2001), p. 83.
6. See Richard Neupert, *A History of the French New Wave Cinema* (Madison: University of Wisconsin Press, 2002), p. 34.
7. Becker and Petzold, *Tarkowski trifft King Kong*, p. 32.
8. Ibid., pp. 46–62.
9. Eberhard Richter, 'Immer noch zum Problem. Studentenfilmklub', *Forum* 12 (1956) p. 9.
10. See the letter from Volkmar Clausnitzer (Filmklub der Martin-Luther-Universität Halle/Saale) to the LUF, 7 November 1956. Universitätsarchiv Leipzig (UAL), FDJ, 245, pp. 71–72, here p. 71.
11. Ulrich Mählert and Gerd-Rüdiger Stephan (eds), *Blaue Hemden – Rote Fahnen. Die Geschichte der Freien Deutschen Jugend* (Opladen: Leske und Budrich, 1996), p. 110.
12. Günther Heydemann, 'Sozialistische Transformation. Die Universität Leipzig vom Ende des Zweiten Weltkrieges bis zum Mauerbau 1945–1961', in Ulrich von Hehl, Günther Heydemann, Klaus Fitschen and Fritz König (eds), *Geschichte der Universität Leipzig 1409–2009: Band 3* (Leipzig: Leipziger Universitätsverlag, 2010), pp. 517ff.
13. See Esther von Richthofen, *Bringing Culture to the Masses: Control, Compromise and Participation in the GDR* (New York and Oxford: Berghahn Books, 2009), p. 154.
14. See the letter from Tinnenberg to the Bezirks- und Stadtleitungen der SED. UAL, FDJ, 245, pp. 7–21.
15. See Klubleitung, Arbeitsprogramm des Filmklubs für Studenten, Leipzig, 23 April 1957. UAL, FDJ, 245, pp. 96–97.
16. Ibid.
17. See AG Film, Arbeitsprogramm (Entwurf), Leipzig, 25 January 1958. UAL, FDJ, 245, pp. 138–144, here p. 140.
18. Thomas Höpel, *Die Kunst dem Volke. Städtische Kulturpolitik in Leipzig und Lyon 1945–1989* (Leipzig: Leipziger Universitätsverlag, 2011), p. 190.
19. See Stefan Heinig, Eingangs einige Bemerkung über Notwendigkeit und Zielsetzung einer Film – Arbeitsgemeinschaft, Leipzig, 10 August 1957. UAL, FDJ, 245, pp. 105–113, here p. 106.
20. See the letter from Erhard John to the Leitung des Filmklubs der Karl-Marx-Universität, Leipzig, 13 January 1957. UAL, FDJ, 245, pp. 83–84, here p. 83.
21. See Stefan Heinig, Eingangs einige Bemerkung über Notwendigkeit und Zielsetzung einer Film – Arbeitsgemeinschaft, Leipzig, 10 August 1957. UAL, FDJ, 245, pp. 105–113, here p. 108.

22. Letter from Blumenthal to the Zentralvorstand der Gesellschaft für Deutsch-Sowjetische-Freundschaft, Leipzig, 23 September 1958. UAL, FDJ, 245, p. 166.
23. Protokoll über die Diskussion um den Studentenfilm "Seine Karriere" am 28. November, 18 Uhr, in der Aula der ABF. Döllnitzer Str., Leipzig. UAL, FDJ, 245, pp. 206–211, here p. 206.
24. Ibid., p. 208.
25. Ibid., p. 210.
26. Höpel, *Die Kunst dem Volke*, p. 143.
27. Protokoll über die Diskussion um den Studentenfilm "Seine Karriere" am 28. November, 18 Uhr, in der Aula der ABF. Döllnitzer Str., Leipzig. UAL, FDJ, 245, pp. 206–211, here p. 207.
28. Dreht die DEFA den Studentenfilm? UAL, FDJ, 245, pp. 55–56, here p. 55.
29. See letter from Blumenthal (Leiter der AG Film) to the DEFA-Außenhandel, Leipzig, 16 December 1958. UAL, FDJ, 245, p. 190.
30. FDJ-Organisation der Karl-Marx-Universität Leipzig, Arbeitsgemeinschaft Film: 'Keine echten Studentenprobleme. Eine Frage an die Film-Abnahmekommision', *Forum* 2 (1959).
31. A letter written to the Progress Film-Vertrieb headquarters in Berlin (dated 17 October 1958) illustrates the film club's problems with the distribution company: 'As part of this cycle ['The Image of the German Worker in Film'] we wanted also to screen the film *Kuhle Wampe* and therefore contacted the regional head office of Progress Film-Vertrieb. The response we received astonished us: We were informed that the film was only distributed to commercial theatres. We cannot understand such a regulation, which contradicts the principles of a socialist cultural policy. It is beyond our comprehension, that such a significant film like *Kuhle Wampe* can be shown only in a situation whereby it also yields a certain financial profit but not when there is a political-ideological reason behind its screening. Hence, we would like you to reassess this regulation, so that the film will be made available to us. Your early response is appreciated.' UAL, FDJ, 245, p. 173.
32. Wer wir sind und was wir wollen. Aus der konzeption des fdj-filmclubs (1). UAL, FDJ, 242, p. 154.
33. Konzeption in UAL, FDJ, 60, pp. 5–7, here p. 5.
34. FDJ-Kreisleitung der Karl-Marx-Universität, Vorlage zur Sekretariatssitzung am 22.1.1963, Leipzig, 21 January 1963. UAL, FDJ, 242, pp. 117–130, here p. 123.
35. Ibid., p. 124. In the late 1950s and early 1960s, Professor Hans Mayer was an element of tension at the university because of his ideas on politics and aesthetics. An unorthodox Marxist, Meyer was also a celebrity within intellectual circles. Especially after the publication of his ideas on (and critiques of) contemporary East German literature in an article titled 'Zur Gegenwartslage unserer Literatur' in the 2 December 1956 edition of *Sonntag*, he became a target of persecution by the East German authorities. In 1963, he paid a visit to his editor in West Germany and did not return to the GDR. The LUF, however, did not establish any kind of contact with Professor Mayer.
36. See Günter Agde, 'Mehr Laboratorium als Katechismus. Die Deutsche Filmkunst (1953 bis 1962)', in Simone Barck, Martina Langermann and Siegfried Lokatis (eds), *Zwischen 'Mosaik' und 'Einheit'. Zeitschriften in der DDR* (Berlin: Christoph Links Verlag, 1999), pp. 402–411.
37. Becker and Petzold, *Tarkowski trifft King Kong*, p. 144.

38. In a conversation with the author, Fred Gehler mentioned being in contact with five or six representatives of the film club *Film Studio* at the Goethe University in Frankfurt, who were in Leipzig in autumn 1964. This contact gave Gehler the opportunity to exchange experiences with his West German colleagues as well as acquaint himself with their publication, *Filmstudio*. Thanks to these informal networks, LUF members also received an invitation to take part in the 1965 Congress of West German Film Clubs in Bad Eims. Rudolf Freund was sent there as the representative of East German film clubs.
39. Jim Hillier (ed.), *Cahiers du Cinéma: The 1960s* (London: Routledge and Kegan Paul, 1986); de Baecque, *La cinéphili*; Peter Kessen, '"Ästhetische Linke" und "Politische Linke" der Zeitschrift "Filmkritik" in den 60er Jahren unter besonderer Berücksichtigung Jean-Luc Godards' (Ph.D. thesis, Ludwig-Maximilians-Universität Munich, 1996); Fernando Ramos Arenas, 'Writing about a Common Love for Cinema: Discourses of Modern Cinephilia as Trans-European Phenomenon,' *Trespassing Journal* (2012), http://trespassingjournal.com/Issue1/TPJ_I1_Arenas_Article.pdf; Ivan Tubau, *Crítica cinematográfica española. Bazin contra Aristarco: La gran controversia de los 60* (Barcelona: Publications Editions Universitat de Barcelona, 1983).
40. Rolf Rothke, 'Wem dienst Du, Filmklub?' Leipzig, 13 June 1963. UAL, FDJ, 60, p. 1.
41. FDJ-Filmklub der KMU, Lassen wir Tatsachen sprechen, Leipzig, July 1963. UAL, FDJ, 60, pp. 8–12, here p.10.
42. See the letter from Volkmar Clausnitzer (Filmklub der Martin-Luther-Universität Halle/Saale) to the LUF, 7 November 1956. UAL, FDJ, 245, pp. 71–72, here p. 71.
43. See Stefan Heinig, Eingangs einige Bemerkung über Notwendigkeit und Zielsetzung einer Film – Arbeitsgemeinschaft, Leipzig, 10 August 1957. UAL, FDJ, 245, pp. 105–113, here p. 110.
44. Becker and Petzold, *Tarkowski trifft King Kong*, p. 127.
45. Ibid., p. 148; Fred Gehler, 'Cui Bono – Film 68? Montagestücke einer vergessenen Zeitschrift', in Barck, Langermann and Lokatis, *Zwischen 'Mosaik' und 'Einheit*, pp. 214–220.
46. See Klubleitung, Arbeitsprogramm des Filmklubs für Studenten, Leipzig, 23 April 1957. UAL, FDJ, 245, pp. 96–97, here p. 96.
47. Initial attempts to become part of this federation had been made as early as 1958, but East German film clubs were not granted full membership until 1965.
48. Becker and Petzold, *Tarkowski trifft King Kong*, p. 129 and 145.
49. See Fred Gehler, 'Ich war nie subversiv. Ein Gespräch mit Fred Gehler über Filmkritik in der DDR und die Auf- und Einbrüche in den sechziger Jahren', in *Apropos: film 2001. Das Jahrbuch der DEFA-Stiftung* (Berlin: Bertz+Fischer, 2001), pp. 87–97.
50. Becker and Petzold, *Tarkowski trifft King Kong*, p. 396.
51. Hillier, *Cahiers du Cinéma*; de Baecque, *La cinéphilie*; Kessen, '"Ästhetische Linke" und "Politische Linke"'; Ramos Arenas, 'Writing about a Common Love for Cinema.'

Select Bibliography

Agde, Günter. 'Mehr Laboratorium als Katechismus. Die Deutsche Filmkunst (1953 bis 1962)'. In Simone Barck, Martina Langermann and

Siegfried Lokatis (eds), *Zwischen 'Mosaik' und 'Einheit'. Zeitschriften in der DDR*. Berlin: Christoph Links Verlag, 1999.

Agde, Günter. 'Mit dem Blick nach Westen'. In Günter Agde and Alexander Schwarz (eds), *Die rote Traumfabrik. Meschrabpom-Film und Prometheus 1921–1936*. Berlin: Bertz+Fischer, 2012.

Becker, Wieland, and Volker Petzold. *Tarkowski trifft King Kong. Geschichte der Filmklubbewegung der DDR*. Berlin: Vistas Verlag, 2001.

De Baecque, Antoine. *La cinéphilie. Invention d'un regard, histoire d'une culture 1944–1968*. Paris: Fayard, 2003.

Dickinson, Thorold. 'Film Societies'. *Journal of Aesthetic Education* 3(3) (1969), 85–95.

Gehler, Fred. 'Cui Bono – Film 68? Montagestücke einer vergessenen Zeitschrift'. In Simone Barck, Martina Langermann and Siegfried Lokatis (eds), *Zwischen 'Mosaik' und 'Einheit'. Zeitschriften in der DDR*. Berlin: Christoph Links Verlag, 1999.

Gehler, Fred. 'Ich war nie subversiv. Ein Gespräch mit Fred Gehler über Filmkritik in der DDR und die Auf- und Einbrüche in den sechziger Jahren'. In *Apropos: film 2001. Das Jahrbuch der DEFA-Stiftung*. Berlin: Bertz+Fischer, 2001.

Hagener, Malte. *Moving Forward, Looking Back: The European Avant-Garde and the Invention of Film Culture, 1919–1939*. Amsterdam: Amsterdam University Press, 2007.

Heydemann, Günther. 'Sozialistische Transformation. Die Universität Leipzig vom Ende des Zweiten Weltkrieges bis zum Mauerbau 1945–1961'. In Ulrich von Hehl, Günther Heydemann, Klaus Fitschen and Fritz König (eds), *Geschichte der Universität Leipzig 1409–2009: Band 3*. Leipzig: Leipziger Universitätsverlag, 2010.

Hillier, John (ed.). *Cahiers du Cinéma: The 1960s*. London: Routledge and Kegan Paul, 1986.

Höpel, Thomas. *Die Kunst dem Volke. Städtische Kulturpolitik in Leipzig und Lyon 1945–1989*. Leipzig: Leipziger Universitätsverlag, 2011.

Kessen, Peter. '"Ästhetische Linke" und "Politische Linke" der Zeitschrift "Filmkritik" in den 60er Jahren unter besonderer Berücksichtigung Jean-Luc Godards.' Ph.D. thesis, Munich, 1996.

Mählert, Ulrich, and Gerd-Rüdiger Stephan (eds). *Blaue Hemden – Rote Fahnen. Die Geschichte der Freien Deutschen Jugend*. Opladen: Leske und Budrich, 1996.

Murray, Bruce. *Film and the German Left in the Weimar Republic: From Caligari to Kuhle Wampe*. Austin: University of Texas Press, 1990.

Neupert, Richard. *A History of the French New Wave Cinema*. Madison: University of Wisconsin Press, 2002.

Ramos Arenas, Fernando. 'Writing About a Common Love for Cinema: Discourses of Modern Cinephilia as Trans-European Phenomenon'. *Trespassing Journal* (2012). http://trespassingjournal.com/

Tubau, Ivan. *Crítica cinematográfica española. Bazin contra Aristarco: La gran controversia de los 60*. Barcelona: Publications Editions Universitat de Barcelona, 1983.

von Richthofen, Esther. *Bringing Culture to the Masses: Control, Compromise and Participation in the GDR*. New York and Oxford: Berghahn Books, 2009.

Chapter 15

SCREENING THE OCCUPIER AS LIBERATOR

Soviet War Films in the SBZ and the GDR, 1945–1965

Lars Karl

The following anecdote is taken from the memoirs of German writer and director Boleslaw Barlog. In it, he describes his encounter with postwar Soviet film production:

> On one of those evenings, they first showed a film about Stakhanov. A miner spent 36 hours digging coal non-stop and was given a jubilant reception when he returned to the surface. I found it silly and just said: 'My colleagues in Germany would have poured scorn on something like that.' This elicited furrowed brows from the Russians.
> Then there was a film about Stalin, with Papa Stalin in all manner of roles: as a general poring over maps, a farmer riding a tractor, as kisser of children, comforter of a little old lady, and so on. The film officer asked us for our opinion. Out of pure fright, most of them said: 'Very good.' I was furious and uttered a few harsh words of criticism, concluding with the statement: 'Hitler and Mussolini would be turning in their graves because such a degree of Byzantinism never occurred to them.' This time the Russians got angry. The double doors to the laden tables remained firmly shut and the meeting broke up to swearing.[1]

This episode from 1948 illustrates the difficulties inherent in the task of making propaganda films about the Soviet victory in World War II more appealing to the East German population, whose attitudes were directly shaped by their experience of military defeat.[2] All Soviet war films were primarily created for the Soviet public and attuned to the official cultural and political guidelines at the time and to the mental predispositions of this public.³ In this case, however, we see the attempt to 'plant' these films in an environment quite foreign to the Soviet context and present them to the target audience as an authoritative expression of a new world view. In this respect, the Soviet films of the 'Thaw' period are of particular interest. Having been made in a climate of de-Stalinization, the films were sent to the German Democratic Republic (GDR), where they encountered a political and cultural environment that had also experienced Soviet Stalinism and its social consequences, albeit in a significantly weaker form.⁴ However, the East German population also possessed its own distinct relationship on a personal level with the war-torn past. Therefore, lest Soviet films that aimed to rework the Stalinist past against the backdrop of the events of World War II 'miss their target' in the GDR, it was necessary to position them within a different interpretative framework on the official level and to present them to the population in a manner different from that employed for Soviet audiences.

Soviet films about the 'Great Patriotic War' also provided cultural bureaucrats in the GDR with a propaganda opportunity to underscore the superiority of socialism and legitimize the leadership of the Socialist Unity Party of Germany (Sozialistische Einheitspartei Deutschlands, SED) in East Germany within the context of the Cold War inter-German ideological rivalry. 'History' thus became one of the most important resources for mobilization and legitimization in the ideological conflict. In this regard, these films were particularly important for the GDR due to its position on the 'Western Front'.⁵

Building on these premises, the following essay examines how selected feature films from the Soviet Union were received officially in the GDR and made accessible to the East German public in the context of official film agitation and propaganda. For documentation on official reception strategies, my research draws on the pertinent censorship records of the Central Film Administration (Hauptverwaltung Film – HV Film) in the Ministry of Culture and published sources such as newspapers and magazines. How were Soviet War films to be made more accessible to the population of the GDR? What criteria were used to judge the films as 'important', 'sensational', and so forth? How were the films integrated into the contemporary political context? How was the relationship with the 'fraternal socialist nations' (especially the Soviet Union) and the 'enemy' nations of NATO (especially the Federal Republic of Germany, FRG) interpreted against the backdrop of these films? And how were World War II and the events associated with it reappraised (or not) in the area of official film reception?

SMAD Becomes Active

From the outset, the postwar Soviet military government placed great value on the revitalization of cultural life. According to one American inspection officer working in Berlin in July 1945, Soviet cultural officers often displayed 'an almost fanatical reverence for art and artists, paired with the belief that artistic activity was by itself a good thing and in times of uncertainty and suffering an urgent necessity'.[6] In fact, the Soviet Military Administration in Germany (Sowjetische Militäradministration in Deutschland, SMAD) had tried to reach the population through cultural offerings as early as 1945 and 1946, albeit to a modest degree. The cultural approach was a clever choice, as there was strong disinterest in politics among the population in the immediate postwar years. Instead, people desired entertainment that could distract them from the bleakness of their everyday lives.

Norman Naimark explained that the propaganda of the immediate postwar years was intended to communicate with the German population in two ways:

> First, Germans would learn about the ways in which the peoples of the Soviet Union overcame 'unbelievable difficulties', making Germany's problems of postwar construction seem less daunting and overwhelming. Second, lecturers were instructed to demonstrate that the Soviets had overcome all of their inherent problems of development, indeed had reached the pinnacle of modern civilization by the first half of 1941, when the Germans attacked. In other words, any problems with Soviet soldiers in the Zone or deficiencies in the organization of the military government were to be attributed not to some weaknesses in the Soviet system itself but to the devastation caused by the German-incited war.[7]

This approach was consistent with the occupying power's propagandistic way of dealing with the German population's negative attitudes towards the USSR, in which musical offerings and the screening of Soviet films were also intended to serve a purpose.[8]

Even before the founding of the GDR in October 1949 there was an organization in the Soviet Occupation Zone (Sowjetische Besatzungszone, SBZ) responsible for promoting Soviet society and Soviet culture among the German population. The Society for the Study of the Culture of the Soviet Union (Gesellschaft zum Studium der Kultur der Sowjetunion) was founded in the SBZ in 1947 and renamed the Society for German-Soviet Friendship (Gesellschaft für Deutsch-Sowjetische Freundschaft, GDSF) in the summer of 1949. Pro-Soviet propaganda emerged from the shared interests of the Soviet occupiers and the SED. Accordingly, Soviet and German authorities were both involved in the conception and implementation of propaganda. For a long time, the GDSF was a German-Soviet joint project, but during the 1950s Soviet input decreased as the SED gained in influence.[9]

With the goal of utilizing Soviet films to acquaint the broadest possible segments of the East German population with life in the Soviet Union, the company Sovexportfilm (SEF) delivered eighteen full-length feature films, twenty-five documentaries and several short cultural films (*Kulturfilme*) to the GDSF in October 1949 for showing at the organization's events. This delivery was comprised exclusively of Soviet productions.[10]

Film Screenings and Public Reaction

In general, the implementation of Soviet films accorded with SMAD's objective to dispel 'anti-Soviet' sentiment within the German population and familiarize the people with the 'achievements of Soviet art'. This goal, of course, was at odds with the Soviets' concurrent distribution of old UFA films, but all the occupying powers made such pragmatic concessions to German viewers.[11] During 1945 and 1946, the cinema programmes of East German cities, including the Soviet sector of Berlin, were comprised of 30 per cent German and 70 per cent Soviet films, while in most smaller towns this proportion was inverted to 70 per cent German and 30 per cent Soviet films.[12] The additional use of pre-censored 'old German' films (i.e. films made prior to 1945) enabled all operational cinemas in the SBZ to be fully supplied with films within a relatively short period. German communists had many reservations about this procedure, though.[13] The high number of UFA productions found in cinema programmes in the SBZ contradicted the political objectives of the SED and DEFA. However, as long as DEFA was unable to produce a sufficient number of films, the demand had to be met by other means. This was one reason prompting the heavy increase in the number of Soviet films in the overall cinema programme.

In the cases of films focused on the topic of the Great Patriotic War, these policies led to conflicts between SMAD and German authorities. For example, institutions within the German Administration for People's Education (Deutsche Volksbildungsverwaltung) responsible for youth support frequently refused to approve Soviet war films for distribution, invoking the spirit of the Potsdam Agreement, which called for German youth to be educated in 'antimilitarism' and 'peaceful coexistence'.[14] In March 1947 an employee at the Ministry for People's Education (Ministerium für Volksbildung) in Saxony justified this approach by arguing that youngsters did not understand films of this genre, which could lead to inappropriate reactions. For example, the depiction of war-related atrocities was met with laughter, Soviet tanks were equated with the tanks of the German Wehrmacht and therefore the overall message of these films was generally misunderstood. Furthermore, he claimed, such reactions among the youth distracted adult viewers in the cinema, thereby diminishing the desired educational effect on them as well. In this ministerial employee's estimation, young people were utterly unable to cope with such depictions: 'Beyond the fact that any positive artistic effect is disrupted by the children's behaviour, it is irresponsible to show such films to children.'[15]

It was not only among German youth that Soviet war films of the immediate postwar years encountered a lack of understanding. Based on their antifascist convictions and the consequences they experienced for these views during the Nazi period, German intellectuals also frequently opposed the ideas put forth by these films. In the eyes of these viewers, the parallels with the films of other totalitarian states were all too obvious. The above-cited episode related by Barlog is an example of this standpoint and his reaction can be seen as characteristic. Of course, such comments could not be casually tolerated by the Soviet occupying powers and thus provoked the occasional public 'counterstatement' in the daily press of the SBZ:

> Naturally, no Soviet films with militaristic tendencies have been shown in Germany since the end of the war – for the simple reason that such films do not exist. If certain movies contained battle scenes, it was either due to the historical nature of the work or because they depicted the events of the Russian October Revolution and were therefore clearly recognized as having not militaristic but distinctly antiwar intentions.[16]

The public dealt with the intense overload of Soviet films in widely varying ways. Viewers tended to reject pure propaganda movies from the Soviet Union, but they often welcomed productions that lacked overbearing political messages and operated within the generic modes of comedy, fairy tale or thriller. For these and other reasons, no 'Stalinist' war films were screened in the SBZ or early GDR except in a few rare cases. The only examples of such films being made available to audiences in the SBZ/GDR in 1949 and 1950 were the Stalinist epic *Padenie Berlina* (The Fall of Berlin, 1949/50) by Georgian director Mikheil Chiaureli and *Stalingradskaya bitva* (The Battle of Stalingrad, 1949), Vladimir Petrov's mythologizing portrayal of this decisive wartime incident.[17]

The Cult of Stalin in the GDR

Initially, the SBZ had no cult of Stalin comparable to that seen in the official culture of the Soviet Union. Concurrent with the founding of the GDR in October 1949, though, there were official efforts to institute a new political culture in eastern Germany that venerated Stalin in a mode similar to what had been the norm in the Soviet Union for nearly twenty years. This campaign reached its zenith on the occasion of Stalin's seventieth birthday on 21 December 1949. This gave rise to a situation that paralleled, albeit rather coincidentally, that in the Soviet Union, where the cult of Stalin had been enforced since his fiftieth birthday celebrations.[18] At the same time, 21 December 1949 was a pinnacle of the cult of Stalin on a much wider scale: Stalin's 'seventieth birthday mushroomed into an orgy of international homage that overshadowed all else – a true cacophony comprised of millions of voices offering up "great songs" to the distinguished leader of the moment in the form of recitatives and arias.'[19]

The German population required a plausible explanation for why they should take interest in venerating the state and party leader of the Soviet occupying power. It was therefore not just a matter of importing the specifics of the cult as developed in the Soviet Union; rather, the propaganda needed to establish a link between the concepts 'Stalin' and 'Germany' in order to make the cult of Stalin compatible with the SED leadership's nationally focused programme. Consequently, the GDR press consistently identified Stalin as 'the best friend of the German people'. The GDR needed to create its own tradition of Stalin worship. Enlisting the participation of the broadest possible levels of the German population would enable the SED to demonstrate how far it had advanced the process of integrating the GDR into the Soviet system.[20] As part of this campaign, the party instructed the country's mass organizations 'to exhibit films in which Stalin's role and personality come to the fore.'[21]

An Ode to the General: *The Fall of Berlin* (1950)

With regard to the cult of personality surrounding Stalin, one film stood out from the rest: *The Fall of Berlin* by Georgian director Mikheil Chiaureli. It premiered in 1950 to tremendous success, achieving an audience of 38 million.[22] Director and Stalin filmographer Chiaureli, who was more successful than any other in canonizing the 'Almighty Creator' Stalin, reached the pinnacle of excess with *The Fall of Berlin*.[23] The film's costs for materials and military equipment alone far outstripped the accumulated resource demands of Petrov's *The Battle of Stalingrad*: 5 artillery and infantry divisions, 4 tank battalions, 193 aircraft of various types, and 45 German 'trophy tanks' were mobilized for the battle scenes while the total volume of fuel required for shooting exceeded 1.5 million litres.[24]

Filmed in two parts at great expense, the war epic *The Fall of Berlin* depicts the late Stalinist interpretation of the events of 1941 to 1945. The lead protagonists are the steelworker Alexei, nicknamed Alyosha, and the schoolteacher Natasha from a small town in the western Soviet Union. They become acquainted and fall in love in 1941, on the eve of the German invasion of their homeland. Natasha is taken off to Germany, while Alyosha joins the battle. He fights in defence of Moscow and Stalingrad before marching westward with the Red Army and ultimately storms the Berlin Reichstag together with his comrades. During the resulting celebration, he is reunited with Natasha, who has just been liberated from a concentration camp.

The film was made in 1949, the year of the Berlin Blockade and the founding of the two German states, at a time when the Cold War had just started in the wake of Stalinist expansion in Eastern Europe in 1948. The film's presentation of the relationship between the Soviet Union and the Western Allies and the portrayal of the Germans during the Nazi period must be understood within this context. Roosevelt and Churchill appear as paper tigers in terms of their war leadership and as elements of diplomatic uncertainty. The film also repeatedly implies that they sympathized with Hitler almost more than they did with Stalin. The great leader is aware of these problems and realizes that the Soviet Union can rely only on itself in the march to Berlin.

'The Germans' as such are hardly present in the film. There are no counterparts to Alyosha and Natasha. We only see anonymous marching columns of soldiers in the initial stages and mostly Hitler and other members of the Nazi state's political and military leadership in the later parts. These figures are predominantly introduced and identified using cinematic techniques that symbolically emphasize Nazism and militarism, such as swastika flags, officers' caps with eagles and marching music. There is also an imbalance in the war sequences between dynamic images of Soviet cannons firing or triumphantly advancing Red Army units and the relatively few depictions of actual battle situations such as the storming of trenches and the like. No Germans appear to be killed in these battles except for the occasional underhanded and cowardly officer. In the final sequences of the film, average Germans are presented as victims of Hitler: in the ruins of Berlin a soldier's mother curses Hitler while mourning over the body of her son, and Hitler's secretary joins the rebellion when she hears of the plans to flood the subway tunnels.

The actual main protagonist of this monumental battle epic is, of course, Stalin. He is godlike, affectionate, wise and all-knowing. In lengthy sequences, he deliberates the state of the nation with the heads of the Politburo. After cursory glances at the battle map, he competently surmises the situation of his own forces and the tactics of the enemy and steers the Soviet army to victory with a confident hand.

The film ends with a celebration of victory in which cheers of joy, wild dancing and celebratory gunshots intermingle with the victorious shouts of soldiers from various regions of the Soviet Union. Suddenly a formation of aircraft appears over Berlin. The masses make their way to the airfield to greet the freshly arrived Stalin, who first congratulates his marshals and then informs the assembled regiments of the glorious future that lies ahead of them.[25] In the crowd, Alyosha and Natasha are reunited and fall exuberantly into each other's arms. Natasha asks Stalin if she may be allowed to kiss him as a demonstration of her gratitude. Her wish is granted while liberated concentration camp prisoners and people from all corners of the world shout their praises to Stalin.

The film was released in 1950, and its easily identifiable intentions were reflected in the marketing materials used in the GDR, which was undergoing its own process of Stalinization. One film programme from SEF displayed photographs of jubilant Red Army soldiers together with uplifting quotes about 'German-Soviet friendship' and the following text:

> When Berlin fell in May 1945, the people were filled with jubilation. The defenders of life, Stalin's soldiers, had stormed the fortress of death. The flag flying atop the devastated cupola of the Reichstag was not the striped one of General Motors, Northern Steel, or Standard Oil, which had accumulated $52 billion in profits from the genocide of World War II; atop the

Reichstag was not the red crisscrossed flag of Churchill, who had promised Stalin in 1942 that he would open a second front, but only did so on 6 June 1944 in order to ensure that the defeat of fascism would not also lead to a people's victory in Western Europe; the flag over Berlin was not the tricolour that had been stolen from the heroic French people by Vichy-fascist collaborators and Gaullist dollar-marionettes. The flag that waved over Germany's capital was the banner of Lenin and Stalin, the banner of the people's liberation.[26]

The film's East Berlin premiere in June 1950 was an event of such vital social significance that prime minister Otto Grotewohl was in attendance together with scriptwriter Pyotr Pavlenko, an official guest of the state. A GDR correspondent spoke of long lines in front of the cinema and frequent outbursts of applause, whereas a West Berlin colleague reported that the prominent leaders present at the screening conceded the film's inadequacies.[27] Even the western press, however, could not hide a certain admiration for the monumental scale of the Soviet screen spectacle.[28] It is notable that many GDR journalists maintained a sense of realism that apparently prevented them from accepting Stalin's arrival immediately following the capture of the Reichstag as a simple matter of artistic liberty within the context of socialist realism. In the eyes of Ferdinand Anders from *National-Zeitung*, for example, the airfield scene depicted Stalin's arrival at the Potsdam Conference.[29]

Even though the contemporary GDR press reviewed the film as a documentary (!), praising it in the Stalinist phraseology of the time, *The Fall of Berlin* did not achieve the desired effect among the East German population.[30] Viewers met it with such indifference that many cinemas removed it from their programme ahead of schedule. The director of the distribution company Progress Film-Vertrieb, Siegfried Silbermann, wrote on the matter: 'As a result of the fascist inflammatory propaganda against the Soviet Union ... a segment of the population maintains a certain degree of prejudice against Soviet cinema. Tremendous persuasive efforts are expended trying to acquaint these people bit by bit with Soviet cinema, which has a great heritage.'[31] Later, in March 1959, the GDR film studies journal *Deutsche Filmkunst* published the following on the situation of Soviet feature films in postwar Germany:

> The bias held by many people against serious cinema is most strongly and precisely reflected in the low attendance numbers for Soviet films, since Soviet cinema offers the public by far the highest ideals and political goals. At the same time, many viewers attempted to gild their prejudice against new Soviet films with exuberant praise for Soviet silent cinema.[32]

Viewers' failure to attend Soviet feature films, however, cannot be explained simply as a consequence of fascist inflammatory propaganda or prejudice against serious cinema. The German public's aversion was also precipitated by the questionable artistic quality of nearly all Soviet films made during the late Stalinist period, which bore no traces of the celebrated works of Soviet silent cinema. Despite the certainly undeniable bias against Soviet films, artistic quality was the decisive factor in the public's dismissive stance towards postwar films, as evidenced by the clear shift in attitude that came about when films such as *Letyat zhuravli* (The Cranes are Flying) and *Sud'ba Cheloveka* (Fate of a Man) reached new standards of artistic quality.[33]

The Fall of Berlin in the Barracked People's Police

Without a doubt, many areas of the GDR remained fertile ground for Nazi-promoted stereotypical 'anti-Bolshevik' images for several years after the war ended. The SED's attempt to confront this problem by promoting an equally one-sided yet positive image of the Soviets achieved only partial success, even in the armed forces. It was particularly important to clearly educate the members of the military on this issue in order to ensure that the soldiers of this 'new army' sustained their political motivation to fight on the side of their Soviet 'brothers in arms':

> In accordance with the glorious model set by the Soviet Army, the education of the national armed forces must aim to infuse the enlisted men, non-commissioned officers, and officers with the spirit of proletarian internationalism. They must be impassioned by their firm friendship with the Soviet Union, by their solidarity with the other people's democracies, by the national wars of liberation fought by suppressed peoples in the colonies and colonial territories, and by love and adoration for the great leader of all peace-loving people – comrade Stalin![34]

The love of peace, strength and invincibility were invoked here to posit the communist world power and its armed forces as the compulsory role model and brothers in arms of the Barracked People's Police (Kasernierte Volkspolizei, KVP).[35] These fixed dogmas were integral components of ideological indoctrination in the military. Consequently, the SED monitored each KVP member's attitude towards the Soviet Union as a general indicator of his political reliability.[36]

The authorities sought to instil belief in the 'exclusive truth' about the Soviet Union through political lessons that relied on the Soviet textbook *Geschichte des KPdSU(B). Kurzer Lehrgang* (The History of the CPSU[B]: A Brief Course) and articles from the daily press and magazines of the GDR. Contemporary Soviet cinema was a welcome medium in this context because of its vivid and presumably documentary qualities. These films were shown in the KVP to consolidate what had been 'learned' in the political lessons. *The Fall of Berlin* was thus a permanent fixture in the KVP film repertoire after its premiere in the summer of 1950, and was screened with the following political objectives:

1. To promote the leading role of the Soviet Union in the struggle to maintain and ensure world peace…;
2. To broadly propagate and illustrate the Soviet Union's friendship with the German people;
3. To further develop and reinforce the willingness to actively fight alongside the Soviet Union to restore peace in the event of imperialist aggression.[37]

We can only speculate about soldiers' reactions to the late-Stalinist battle epic. However, a memo from March 1951 titled 'Über den Verlauf von Filmvorführungen in den Objekten' (Regarding Film Screenings at Bases) makes reference to alcohol abuse before and during film shows and mentions the complaint of one projectionist who reported a group of soldiers 'in a drunken state causing a commotion during *The Fall of Berlin*'.[38]

Nevertheless, we should not underestimate the overall effect of films like *The Fall of Berlin* in the context of the exuberantly celebrated cult of Stalin that existed in the GDR in the early 1950s. Stalin's death in March 1953 provoked panic and helplessness in the KVP bases among both Soviet advisers and German officers. The authorities sought to combat a potential loss of direction in the bases with special pledges and assemblies:

> On 7 March 1953 all the affiliated members of the post … were required to pack into the so-called clubroom, the former riding hall. The post commander, Colonel L., announced in an emotional voice: 'The great leader of the Soviet Union, Generalissimus Stalin, is dead.' We rose from our seats in shock. No one was ashamed to show their tears. We were at a loss. How were things to progress now? The glorification of Stalin's personality in films, on the radio, in the press, in the required reading, and in the political lessons had also brought me to view Stalin as the 'greatest man in world history'….

There were no lessons on this day. In the assemblies and advisory sessions new pledges were made by the collective and by each individual to study and strive in Stalin's spirit in order to achieve the appointed goals.[39]

The explicit mention of film propaganda here (even before radio and the press) attests that the image of Stalin propagated in the contemporary Soviet films utilized for the general indoctrination of the troops had indeed made an impression on some soldiers.

Film Politics within the 'New Course' (1953–1955)

The earliest impulse of de-Stalinization can be read in a July 1953 directive from the Soviet distribution company SEF that provided the GDSF with a list of Soviet films to be removed from distribution 'immediately'. The Soviets gave no reason for the withdrawal of these films, many of which had been part of the standard repertoire for GDSF events in previous years. Notably, however, the list contained several films – including the monumental war epic *The Fall of Berlin* – that had contributed excessively to the cult of Stalin during the last years of the dictator's life. In addition, SEF ordered the return of all documentaries and films about agriculture. Clearly, Moscow had decided to fundamentally reform the international image of the USSR in cinema. To this end, some of the costliest projects of recent years disappeared from GDR cinemas (e.g. *Stalingradskaya bitva* [The Battle of Stalingrad] and *Nezabyvaemyy god 1919* [The Unforgettable Year 1919, Mikheil Chiaureli, 1951]). It was the Soviet authorities, therefore, that were the source of the first impulse in this internal, partial revocation of the cult of Stalin. The GDSF was merely required to comply with this directive.[40]

Several regional chapters of the SED fiercely criticized these measures. Many SED functionaries, seeing numerous heavyweights simply displaced by easily digestible entertainments such as *Das doppelte Lottchen* (Lottie and Lisa, Josef von Báky, 1950) and *Die Frau meiner Träume* (The Woman of My Dreams, Georg Jacoby, 1944), completely disagreed with this new emphasis in the film programme.[41] In subsequent years, the State Committee for Film Affairs (Staatliche Komitee für Filmwesen) and HV Film had to contend continually with requests for special permission to rent these Soviet 'focus films'. For example, on 27 November 1953 the district council in Erfurt enquired 'if and when the Soviet films about the Great Patriotic War will be reinstated to the film programme, or if there is some possibility to acquire them to be screened as part of the curriculum of party schools and schools of mass organizations'.[42] HV Film responded by categorically denying this request, citing the regulations instituted by the Soviet distributor: 'Sovexport does not authorize the release of these films, not even for special screenings such as those within the curriculum of party schools and schools of mass organizations.'[43] Even so, after consulting with the Department of Culture in the Central Committee of the SED in late October 1953, the State Committee for Film Affairs did grant approval for public screenings of several 'scrapped' films once all traces of the cult of Stalin had been 'purged', i.e., edited from them.[44]

The Ice Breaks: *The Cranes Are Flying* (1957)

Mikhail Kalatozov's film *Letyat zhuravli* (*The Cranes Are Flying*, 1957) centres on the contradictory 18-year-old Veronika (Tatyana Samoilova) and her love for her fiancé Boris (Aleksey Batalov). Boris goes to war while Veronika stays home, where she loses her house and parents in an air raid. When she does not receive any letters from her betrothed, she abandons herself to loneliness and despair, finally agreeing to marry Boris's cousin Mark, whose military service has been deferred. The marriage crumbles, however, due to Veronika's self-reproach and the baseness of her husband. When the war ends and the cranes are passing over Moscow, the abandoned girl sits at the train station waiting in vain for her beloved.

Viktor Rozov had originally worked with this story material in a successful stage play he wrote during the war called *Vechno zhiviye* (The Eternally Alive), which premiered in 1956 at Moscow's Sovremennik theatre. Yet the story's explosive potential was only fully realized when it was made into a film, despite certain concessions on the part of the dramaturgist and director: Mark is branded a scoundrel, and the child that the female protagonist rescues from suicide completely disappears once it has fulfilled its dramatic function. Samoilova's performance, together with the film's powerful visual language, confounds the expectations of a typical story of guilt and regret: Veronika lives her own life without conforming to expected norms – she makes her own decision, and the director does not condemn her for this but poeticizes her.[45]

In terms of the Soviet tradition, Kalatozov's film represents a highly idiosyncratic, unconventional treatment of the Great Patriotic War. The ambivalent depiction of Veronika contradicted the customary reliance on standard character types. Her mysteriousness and individuality stood in stark contrast to the canonical image of the war bride seen in Soviet cinema prior to this. For a long time Soviet critics, though thrilled with the film, did not know how to interpret the female protagonist. The journal *Iskusstvo kino* recognized the film as a work 'about love and loyalty to the people' and hoped it would foster a 'sense of civic heroism'.[46] At the same time, the scriptwriter Rozov was reproached for dramatic flaws, since the behaviour of the protagonist was illogical. One reviewer would have preferred the unfaithful girl to have found her way 'into the great life of the collective'.[47]

In fact, one can only search in vain for an explicit political message or stance in this film. As much as the condition of war dictates the fate of the female protagonist, the actual events of the war remain far removed – even the bullet that kills Boris comes from an undetermined location, as if out of nowhere. In addition, 'the Germans' do not appear in the film as personified enemies. Seen within the historical context of Soviet film production in the 1940s and 1950s, Kalatozov's film liberates war films from the predetermined paradigm of antifascist rhetoric and patriotic heroization of the defensive struggle that was characteristic of the 'Stalinist' war epics – i.e., when they were not concerned exclusively with depicting Stalin's greatness in the proper light. Veronika bears resemblance to neither the 'canonized' martyr figure Zoya Kosmodemyanskaya nor the exemplary loyal war bride in the film based on Konstantin Simonov's poem *Zhdi menya* (Wait for Me).[48]

As in the Soviet Union, *The Cranes Are Flying* appears to have somewhat confounded film bureaucrats in the GDR. A certain number of reviews published in the East German press and film journals attempted to interpret Kalatozov's film according to the familiar paradigm of socialist realism, as had become customary.[49] For example, the East Berlin newspaper *Sonntag* wrote in July 1958: 'The Soviet people's Great Patriotic War provides the social background for the film *The Cranes Are Flying*: the great Soviet morality is reflected in the high number of memorably vivid Soviet characters, most notably in the inner struggle of the errant heroine Veronika.'[50] In many discussions about the film, however, this analytical pattern gives way to a simple paraphrased retelling of the plot. Any fundamental assessment of the movie is lost among adoring paeans to Kalatozov, Samoilova and Batalov, and in the stereotypical reiteration of international reports about the film's success in the Soviet Union and the West.[51]

Remarkably, according to reports by East German correspondents, it was precisely the inhabitants of the 'frontline city' West Berlin who seemed particularly receptive to this cinematic appeal for peace from the East:

> This film will help alter the way that West Berlin intellectuals, members of the middle class, and youth view the thoughts and actions of the Soviet people.
> We spoke to high school students, who had viewed *The Cranes* together. They stated that it was the first time they had attended a Soviet film. They were amazed how honestly and convincingly the actors rendered their feelings and experiences in opposition to fascism. Most of all, they appreciated how nothing was sugar-coated – the war was depicted in all of its severity without any of the lowbrow antics that films from the West use to gloss over war events. The Soviet film's final scene gave the students a sense of the Soviet Union's commitment to uphold peace in the world.[52]

Despite the dubiousness of certain individual statements, SED cultural planners sought from the very beginning to exploit the films of the Soviet Thaw as a weapon in the 'struggle for peace' against the Western alliance. In this process, they also perpetually endeavoured to harness the sympathies that contemporary Soviet cinema aroused in 'progressive' segments of the West German population as assets in the struggle.

Interestingly, many GDR reviewers either imperfectly interpreted or completely misinterpreted one piece of original Russian symbolism from the film *The Cranes are Flying*: the flight of the cranes itself. In many discussions it is understood as a 'symbol of restless, unfulfilled desire' that is consistently found 'in Russian folklore'.[53] In Soviet scholarship, however, this interpretation occasioned extensive, heated debate.[54]

With an official audience of 2,836,058 in the GDR, *The Cranes Are Flying* was unquestionably one of the biggest hits of 1958. The only films that proved more successful were *Meine Frau macht Musik* (My Wife Wants to Sing, Hans Heinrich, 1958), *Unternehmen Teutonenschwert* (Operation Teutonic Sword, Andrew and Annelie Thorndike, 1958), *Tikhiy Don* (And Quiet Flows the Don, Sergey Gerasimov, 1957/58) and *Ich denke oft an Piroschka* (I Often Think of Piroschka, Kurt Hoffinann, 1955).[55] Moreover, once it had been imported to the GDR, *The Cranes Are Flying* played an important role in the regular training courses for GDSF activists involved with 'film agitation'. For example, we find that the film was included together with the DEFA feature *Betrogen bis zum jüngsten Tag* (Duped Till Doomsday, Kurt Jung-Alsen, 1957) in a 1958 instruction unit entitled 'The Socialist Film as a Weapon in the Struggle for Peace'.[56] Additionally, in the years after 1958 *The Cranes Are Flying* belonged to a group of films that were increasingly screened within the programme of 'cultural-political education' in SED schools to present the 'Soviet army's historic battle of liberation'.[57]

The Individual as Plaything of History: *Fate of a Man* (1959)

The 1959 film *Fate of a Man* took up and further advanced the theme of the individualized war experience. Based on the novella of the same name by Mikhail Sholokhov, director and lead actor Sergey Bondarchuk's film depicts the fate of a Soviet soldier who becomes a German prisoner of war.[58] The viewer follows the forlorn Andrei Sokholov on his march westward with the columns of other miserable, brown-clad prisoners. We witness an unsuccessful escape attempt and accompany him through various German detainment and concentration camps. Sokholov endures these horrors for several years with almost superhuman strength until he finally manages to escape through the German lines. He returns to military service and on the day of the German capitulation is informed of the death of his son, his last remaining relative.

The expressions and gestures of the protagonist in *Fate of a Man* are free of the Stalinist clichés of 'heroism'. Instead of a victorious hero, the film presents a man who, though characterized by fear, suffering and despair, nevertheless remains resilient in the face of adversity in an inhuman war. When he is taken prisoner, Andrei chooses to continue living, whereas earlier the code of honour dictated death in such a situation. When he strangles a fellow prisoner who is threatening to expose another comrade as an officer, Bondarchuk does not play the role of a hero, but rather brings out the character's revulsion at his own act of murder. His courage is put to the test when camp commandant Müller decides to enact a 'little Stalingrad' and humiliate his Russian 'Ivan'. Since Müller believes that all Russians are drinkers, he offers Sokholov a large glass of vodka with bread and bacon fat before his execution. The exhausted and starved Russian soldier proceeds to empty three glasses of vodka but refuses the food. Contrary to expectation, he remains on his feet and shows no signs of fear or drunkenness. Andrei's heroic behaviour wins the admiration of the German, who grants him his life, thereby ending this absurd trial. This scene was aimed primarily at domestic viewers, who were meant to identify the hero of this remarkable test of courage as a 'true Russian', far removed from the lofty, contrived characters of the Stalinist period.

Sholokhov wrote this story in 1946 but was unable to have it published until the beginning of the Thaw. The soldier Sokholov did not fight for Stalin, the party or the Soviets, but for his family and his Russian homeland. Although these motivations may have been credible, they were unacceptable to the censors. Also, a film about the fate of a Red Army soldier as a German prisoner of war would have potentially been quite volatile prior to 1956, as such men were often seen as traitors and sentenced to many years in the Gulag.[59] Only after the Twentieth Congress of the Communist Party of the Soviet Union had rehabilitated these former soldiers did it become feasible to film *Fate of a Man*.

The agitational-promotional campaign for *Fate of a Man* in the GDR did everything it could to minimize attention to those scenes that served as national concessions to Russian audiences. Actually, of all the Soviet war films that reached the GDR during the Thaw, the authorities showed the highest regard for *Fate of a Man*, and as a result it was the most intensively promoted of these films. In the acceptance report from 2 May 1959, the HV Film characterized the film as follows: 'This is an exceptional work of Soviet cinema that contains profound truth and a socialist-humanist message. The film content addresses important problems, which are rendered in a brilliant visual form.'[60] A few weeks later, the Ministry of Culture issued a directive ordering an 'action plan' for the intensive popularization of the film: 'This Soviet film needs to be extensively prepared for and supported in the appropriate way. Therefore, the party, the state apparatus, and the mass organizations should employ all possible means in support of this film.'[61] At a meeting of the Central Collective of Production Managers on 4 November 1959, its members were called upon to initiate a special competition in connection with *Fate of a Man*. The members signified their basic agreement with organizing such a campaign, but complained that the demand came on short notice and that the advertising materials provided by the distributor Progress Film-Vertrieb were not up to a satisfactory standard of quality. In addition, several members protested that insufficient film prints were available at that point to permit the screening of *Fate of a Man* in all available venues within a six-month period.[62]

'Action plans for intensive popularization' of films were a standardized phenomenon in the GDR by the 1950s, and the resulting press campaigns almost always occurred according to the same pattern. Across the nation, the press would publish reports on the film's grand premiere in Berlin and in the regional capitals. The press styled the first screenings in local districts as social extravaganzas, allotting a particularly central role to the publication of viewers' reactions.[63]

With the active support of the press department of the GDSF together with the Artists' Union (Gewerkschaft Kunst), the districts of the GDR entered into a competition to achieve the highest attendance numbers for *Fate of a Man*. Such competitions had been organized for several other films as well. The press unit's overall goal with these competitions was to prolong the screening of the films for as long as possible. Part of the plan would be regular reports about local workers' collectives, school groups and units of the National People's Army (Nationale Volksarmee) and People's Police (Volkspolizei) attending the film, combined with encouragement for readers to also see the film, even more than once, if possible. When necessary, arrangements were made to broadcast advertising campaigns on the radio and on television.[64] In the case of *Fate of a Man*, a short film depicting the friendly relationship between the GDR and the Soviet Union was created for screening prior to the start of the advertising campaign proper. This film contained footage of the Soviet state and party leader Nikita Khrushchev's visit to the GDR edited together with sequences from *Fate of a Man*. Employing the slogan '…and don't forget' ('…und nicht vergessen') the film aimed to effectively demonstrate the progression from 'then' to 'now'.[65]

The contents of this relatively widespread agitational-promotional campaign are multilayered and complex. What is striking, however, is that in addition to the stereotypical promotion of 'German-Soviet friendship', the bulk of the published materials and press reports contain clear propagandistic attacks on the other German state. On 7 November 1959, *Leipziger Volkszeitung* wrote:

> When watching this film, one thought occurs most prominently and refuses to leave one's mind for a long while: the instigators of these events that caused terror, distress, and the deaths of millions have more or less returned to their positions of power in the Western zone. They clothe themselves as ministers or some other state functionaries and breed all new manners of mischief. Our greatest common duty is to defend against this. The magnificent experience of Soviet art provides renewed strength and confidence in this struggle.[66]

Such writing redirects the film's negative portrayal of German soldiers in World War II to take aim at the contemporary Western Allies and the FRG in particular. In this context, the West German Army (Bundeswehr) is understood as a direct descendant of the Nazi Wehrmacht. To a certain extent, the SED leadership exploited Bondarchuk's film to bolster their arguments against the rearmament of West Germany and the development of the Bundeswehr.[67]

By contrast, the Soviet soldier Sokholov is a representative of the universal suffering man. As *Berliner Zeitung* wrote on 10 November 1959:

> Men such as Sokholov did exist and they continue to exist: simple people, who performed their heroic deeds without any grandiosity and out of a self-evident sense of duty, wherever people remained stronger than the sacrifices they were forced to make, even in Germany. The film *Fate of a Man* stands as a dignified, enduring monument to all of these men.[68]

Following this logic, the GDR press 'cleansed' the Red Army soldier Sokholov of everything that identified him as 'truly Russian' – that is, precisely those characteristics that established him as a potential figure of identification for the Russian viewer. The film stills printed in the press almost never showed Sokholov in his Red Army uniform, and none of the film reports mentioned the 'vodka scene' discussed above.

Very often, the reviews of *Fate of a Man* operated with the contemporary and conventional rhetoric of antifascism. As many reviewers saw it, the film depicts an extraordinarily authentic image of fascism without any level of exaggeration and presents brutally honest facts about the true nature of the National Socialist dictatorship. One reviewer wrote, for example, that 'the film expresses the dreadful reality of racist madness particularly well in the allegorical scene depicting lines of people entering the crematorium and the cruelty of the pan-Germanic master race in the quarry scene. The nature of fascism and its wars acquire an admonishing form.'[69] Readers were consistently reminded that judging by appearances, the hero was not a party member, and therefore his life is characteristic of 'millions of Soviet citizens'. This fact made Sokholov a particularly attractive figure of identification for German viewers.[70]

Understood in this context, the following viewer reaction printed in the GDR press reflects the SED cultural planners' efforts to emphasize the film's historical accuracy and ascribe a (quasi-)documentary quality to Bondarchuk's work:

> Tschekorke, foreman: 'The film is so memorably different from most antiwar films because it does not depict the war as a grand event with all of its factors and effects, but instead shows its impact on an individual. That's what made it seem so authentic to me – like a documentary. I was most moved by the scene in which a German soldier who is shaving himself

taunts the newly arrived prisoners of war as "Ivans". It was terrifyingly evident that the Soviet man behind the wire fence was superior in his thoughts and actions to the frivolous mercenary who had been bred to die on "this side" of the barbed wire. Another scene that made a strong impression on me was the defence of the communist in the church. Sokholov, who was not a communist, takes sides with his endangered comrade. That was a powerful moment.'[71]

Even though the soldier Sokholov is postulated as the model 'everyman' and portrayed as the innocent victim of a barbaric regime, only very rarely do the published viewer reactions contain comments about the viewer's own past that reveal the individual's process of coming to terms with National Socialist crimes. Instead, Germans tended to emphasize a shared victimhood as the 'bridge' between themselves and their former enemies.[72] Similarly compatible with this mode of interpretation are the isolated, always guarded complaints that the film contains too few 'good Germans' who oppose the Nazi dictatorship and thereby also end up as victims of the regime. For example: 'Karl Wächter, Brigadier: "I spent three years in Russia during the war and I know that terrible crimes occurred. But perhaps the film didn't have to depict only the bad Germans."'[73]

In general, official interpretations of the film were formulated according to the Marxist definition of fascism, which was, within contemporary discourse, directed against the West German state:

'The film raises a powerful accusation against the crimes of the Third Reich. For the younger generation it is simply unimaginable that anyone could conceive of and carry out such atrocities. Yet the film does not generally condemn the whole German nation or former soldiers, but passes irreproachable judgment on those criminals such as Oberländer, Speidel, and all the rest who move around freely in West Germany, hold ministerial posts, and either deny or try to trivialize what happened in Lviv, Lidice, the Warsaw ghetto, and concentration camps both inside and outside Germany.' Dieter Remone, Birkwenwerder.[74]

Quite commonly, published viewer comments praised the film with standardized expressions from the phraseology of the GDSF, thus promoting membership in the organization:

'But I am proud to have been a member of the Gesellschaft für Deutsch-Sowjetische Freundschaft [GDSF] for many years. Never again should Germans and Soviets face each other as enemies. Together, bound in brotherhood, we must confront every act of aggression and see to it that

German-Soviet friendship continues to grow ever firmer. Each one of us should see this rousing film work.' Gretel Vögtel, Stollberg/Erzgeb[irge].⁷⁵

In addition, the press sought to present contemporary experiences of individual viewers as evidence of the presumed authentic nature of the film. Reports on discussions with people from the Soviet Union and perpetual reiteration of the love of peace maintained by Soviet 'friends' were meant to demonstrate the concrete 'bridge' between the former enemies:

> 'Sokholov's story is not fictitious and it is not an individual fate. Here's another example: this year I travelled with a tourist group to the Soviet Union. When I was there a worker from Rostov told me: "The fascists killed my wife and children. My mother tried to save them and was beaten to death. I am remarried now, with kids, but can one forget?" Then he smiled, "The GDR is good. Our minds are open."' Erna Gazert.⁷⁶

Interestingly, published viewer statements were frequently supported with quotes from the Russian classics together with instructions to not just view the film but also read the original literary text by Mikhail Sholokhov:

> 'The Russian author Korolenko once wrote: "Man is born for happiness as a bird is born for flight." Seldom has such a tragic film made such an overall optimistic impression on me as Bondarchuk's *Fate of a Man*.' Alexander Z., Potsdam.

> 'After watching the film, I experienced the same shock when I once more read Sholokhov's story, which was published in German by Verlag Kultur und Fortschritt.' Beate W., Brandenburg.⁷⁷

Last but not least, in this context mothers were frequently encouraged to take their children to the film and then read the original literary text of *Fate of a Man* together with them:

> 'Through this double experience, you and your children will acquire an inspiringly deeper appreciation for one of the most mature achievements of Soviet art.'⁷⁸

The War as Everyday Experience: *The Ballad of a Soldier* (1959)

The series of 'men's destinies' continued in 1959 with Grigori Chukhrai's *Ballada o soldate* (Ballad of a Soldier). On the Eastern Front, the young soldier Alyosha (V. Ivashov) suddenly finds himself under attack by two German tanks. In the film's lone battle scene, Alyosha initially tries to flee, but then his survival instinct compels him to attack and destroy the two tanks. Declining a military decoration, he asks if he can instead receive a few days' leave to visit his mother and help fix her roof. He behaves less as a patriot and defender of the state than as a private citizen more concerned with his family's well-being than a medal for heroism.[79]

The nineteen-year-old's journey home becomes an odyssey through the chaos of war. He encounters a disabled soldier who is afraid to go home, Ukrainian refugees who have narrowly escaped massacre in a bomb attack, a corrupt sentry, an unfaithful wife and finally the young girl Shura (Z. Prokhorenko), with whom he falls in love. When he ultimately arrives in his hometown, he has only enough time to exchange a few words with his mother before a lorry transports him back to the front. As the viewer learns in the opening credits, the young soldier does not survive the war.

Ballad of a Soldier ought to have been released concurrently with Bondarchuk's film, since shooting for both began at the same time. However, Chukhrai suffered an accident that left him bedridden with severe injuries for half a year before he could start filming again, this time with all new actors. He did not fill the main roles with romantic leading man Oleg Strizhenov and mature actress Izolda Izvitskaya as had been originally planned, but instead with two seventeen-year-old students of the Moscow Film School, Vladimir Ivashov and Zhanna Prokhorenko. The studio demanded many corrections to Valentin Yezhov's screenplay for this 'ballad'. The author was criticized for dramatizing events that were too small and inconsequential. For example, they would have preferred to see the hero be a general rather than an inexperienced young soldier. They also wanted the girl Shura to be responsible for some 'heroic act' that would be equivalent to Alyosha's destruction of the German tanks.[80] However, Chukhrai insisted on his view of things. Initially, *Ballad of a Soldier* received merely a lukewarm reaction from viewers in the Soviet Union. Only after the film's international success, including winning the Special Jury Prize at Cannes in 1960, was it awarded the Lenin State Prize.[81]

In the acceptance report from 18 December 1959, the HV Film characterized the film as follows:

> The outstanding quality of this film rests in the fact that its form and content perfectly coincide. The characters are typified, as is necessary for a ballad, meaning that they embody fundamental, universal types that can be found in the literature of all peoples. This ballad-like typification is not carried out in cookie-cutter fashion, however. All the figures, their emotions and actions, are distilled from real life; in other words they directly touch the hearts of the viewers.[82]

In this vein, the authorities intended to present *Ballad of a Soldier* to the GDR public in the summer of 1960 as a sort of timeless parable.[83] Plot summaries use clichés to describe the soldier, who is above all upstanding, trustworthy and cooperative; the young girl he meets along the way; and the mother, who must send her son back to the war after she has barely had time to hug him.[84] At the same time, just as with *Fate of a Man*, the press presents the film to the public as another artistic portrait of the Soviet love of peace. A visit to the cinema is proposed as a chance to 'get to know and love the people of the great Soviet nation, whose heritage and history, both ancient and recent, are still very unfamiliar to many of us. The surest way to become acquainted with our friends in this neighbouring country is to see depictions of them as they truly are.'[85]

The War as Nightmare: *Ivan's Childhood* (1962)

For all their emphasis on images, the films of Kalatozov, Bondarchuk and Chukhrai communicate their message within the confines of narrative cinema, far removed from the reflexive language of the medium. By contrast, Andrei Tarkovsky's debut film, *Ivanovo detstvo* (Ivan's Childhood) forges a unique film language that offers new ways to reflect the individual's relationship with the world.[86]

With *Ivan's Childhood*, Tarkovsky broke with the Soviet war film tradition, in which children are depicted as brave little tin soldiers that are in no way inferior to adults, and war and revolution serve as rich material for creating a children's film atmosphere. Tarkovsky does not tell the 'adventures of a young scout', but the story of a character who was born of the war and ultimately devoured by it. Nikolai (Kolya) Burlyayev plays the eleven-year-old Ivan as a little monster with a shattered psyche, creating this impression with the angular movements of his gaunt body as well as his stuttering, nervousness and severity. Even more important in creating this impression was the film's expressive visual style, the counterpoint between sound and image, and the nullification of the opposition between dream and reality. There is no distinction between the boy's nightmares and the dream-like images of reality – a swampy landscape, an ominously dead forest, human figures that appear to be shadows, eerie silence, the disfigured bodies of hanged partisans, a burned village, dark military dugouts – a mood somewhere between night and day, reality and fantasy, life and death. The core of the film is not the plot but the images that linger on in the memory, images that 'literally shred the layers of time and reality'.[87]

The director, the son of idiosyncratic poet Arseny Tarkovsky, was a student of filmmaker Mikhail Romm. His debut film *Ivan's Childhood*, which is astonishing for its controlled and mature understanding of the medium, was actually the result of several chance events. The recent film school graduate was offered a minimal budget to save the failing production of a war-themed children's film.[88] Tarkovsky was expected to produce a new shooting script within two weeks, which he did in collaboration with fellow film school graduate Andrei Mikhalkov-Konchalovsky, although neither of their names appeared in the film credits. Despite adverse circumstances, including rain and the sickness of the lead actor, shooting was completed relatively quickly.

Soviet critics did not shower *Ivan's Childhood* with great praise. They found the film too unrealistic and criticized it as an extravagant 'formalist' game. In addition, they complained that the main characters were trapped by the tragedy of the story and thus operated in a fatalistic manner – a claim that, in the party's eyes, put the film in conflict with the official Soviet concept of progress.[89] Perhaps the greatest point of contention was Tarkovsky's poetic logic, which would become even more pronounced in his later films. The studio directors demanded that films be rationally comprehensible to the viewers. As a result, only a few of Tarkovsky's later projects were approved, and he had to continually defend each of them from the authorities' demands for changes to the completed film.

The functionaries in the GDR bureaucracy were also fully aware of the unclear nature of the film's message. For example, in the internal minutes from the 8 February 1963 meeting to approve the film, we read: 'There are various attitudes towards the original version. While some evaluated it very positively, others are of the opinion that it is too intellectual. Still others find it too macabre. The regional directors thought that it would not be publicly viable.'[90] It is therefore no wonder that, in comparison to previous Soviet films about World War II, *Ivan's Childhood* received little attention in official discourse and was rather neglected in terms of promotion.

In addition, relatively harsh criticism was levelled against the film in the GDR press, which was quite uncommon for Soviet films made during this period. On 28 March 1963, National-Zeitung, the official organ of the National Democratic Party of Germany (National-Demokratische Partei Deutschlands), wrote: '[The film] attempts to truthfully reflect the spiritual life of Soviet citizens in all of its richness and complexity, yet ends up being too complex itself: this is due in part to the nature of the subject matter, but also to the film's underdeveloped, excessive composition.'[91] More precisely, the GDR press strongly disapproved of Tarkovsky's compositional methods: 'Here are some of the problems: insufficient attention to the young hero, subplots that are too loosely connected to the main plot. Sometimes the border between dream and daytime is so blurred that important details and connections are not clearly evident.'[92]

The published discussions of the film obviously sought to prepare the viewer for an intellectual experience and apologize in advance for difficulties in comprehending the film:

> Nowadays, in order for great film traditions to constructively, experimentally, and innovatively advance, they require a number of film works that demand greater intellectual exertion than we are accustomed to. *Ivan's Childhood* is one of these works. One should not see this film on a day when one is seeking to relax and be distracted. The film demands exactly the opposite: great concentration, intellectual participation, capacity to absorb, the will to closely analyse each image. Unless the viewer is prepared to make this effort, I do not think that the viewing experience will be very profitable.[93]

As it had done for previous Soviet 'Thaw productions' dealing with World War II, the press styled the young main character of *Ivan's Childhood* as a 'true hero'. Furthermore, Tarkovsky's surrealistic dream worlds were interpreted as 'realities' worth defending in accordance with the tenets of socialist realism:

> The lanky, blond-haired Ivan serves his fatherland like a true hero. He overcomes ordeals that could only be mastered by the most extremely focused will. He also masters himself with a discipline derived from a highly distinctive character. At the same time, he is just a child, who discovers his reality in dreams, even in his waking hours if need be. But the waking

hours mean war, danger, and death. Little Ivan knows what he is defending when he fights against the unnatural nature of war: he is defending the reality of his dreams, the inviolable, natural rights of man.[94]

The press styled the figure of young Ivan as a hero, as an 'active character, which gives him the strength of a man, making him a moral compass in the battle for many men.'[95]

In their reviews, critics completely avoided any reference to their own – that is, the German – past, as they also did in reviews of previous war films. Only within this interpretive paradigm was it possible to use *Ivan's Childhood* to invoke the Soviet Union's love of peace and deploy the film as a powerful weapon in the 'peaceful struggle' against the reputedly aggressive Western Alliance:

> *Ivan's Childhood* represents the passionate protest of Soviet artists against the senselessness of war and against everyone who now flirts once again with the idea of war. No less importantly, it is also a great affirmation of life, peace, and happiness. This protest and this affirmation are written in one language, a language that excites due to its uncultivated nature, a language that captivates and invites interest.[96]

Although the GDR press paid unusually little attention to the film compared to other Soviet movies in this period, *Ivan's Childhood* was treated to an opening night ceremony that was reserved for only a few select films, such as *The Cranes Are Flying*, *Fate of a Man*, and *Ballad of a Soldier*. By the beginning of the 1960s, the structure of such premieres was highly ritualized. The first screening was often combined with a social event. The main actors were invited and summoned to meet with selected 'workers' in a local branch of the GDSF after the screening:

> On Sunday, visitors to the International Trade Fair experienced the first great cultural event of this year's spring fair: the GDR premiere of the multiple award-winning Soviet film *Ivan's Childhood*.... Valentina Malyavina and Valentin Subkov – who play the film's touching lovers, Lieutenant Masha and Captain Kholin – were enthusiastically welcomed by the citizens of Leipzig and their guests from around the world. After the premiere, the actors met with workers from VEB Verlade- und Transportanlagenbau [the nationally owned enterprise for the construction of loading and transportation equipment] in the House of German-Soviet Friendship for a stimulating discussion.
> With the magnificent work of cinema still fresh in their minds, the German workers thanked the Soviet artists for the unforgettable experience.[97]

The 1955 cultural agreement between the Soviet Union and the GDR provided for the exchange of delegations in the realm of film production. A delegation of two or three filmmakers from one country would visit the other country for about seven days to attend the premieres of three films, i.e., three Soviet films in the GDR or three DEFA films in the Soviet Union. In the opinion of Minister of Culture Alexander Abusch, the Soviet filmmakers' visits to the GDR had a consistently positive effect on the corresponding films' distribution in the country. In a letter to Deputy Minister of Culture of the Soviet Union Kaftanov on 19 March 1958, Abusch suggested inviting even more Soviet delegations in the future, which would 'contribute to the popularization of Soviet films in the GDR and foster a bond between the artists from the Soviet Union and the workers of the GDR.'[98]

The War of the Georgian Wine Grower: *Father of a Soldier* (1964)

The beginning of the 1960s also saw film production stimulated in the non-Russian Soviet republics, a phenomenon that would later be described in film studies as the 'emancipation of the national cinemas'.[99] In particular, Georgian film, which since the beginning had been developing its own character largely independent of Russian cinema, experienced a vibrant renaissance during the Thaw years.[100] Georgian studios in the capital Tbilisi were particularly successful in developing a new film language firmly rooted in the Georgian film tradition. A distinguishing characteristic of Georgian cinema is the frequent flight into a symbolic, metaphorically distancing language of poetry and humour – most impressively evident in the works of Otar Iosseliani (e.g. *Giorgobistve* [Falling Leaves, 1966], *Iko shashvi mgalobeli* [Once Upon a Time There Was a Singing Blackbird, 1970]) or in the masterpieces of Mikheil Kobakhidze (e.g. *Qortsili* [The Wedding, 1964]) and other short films of the Georgian School (e.g. Irakli Kvirikadze's *Kvevri* [The Jar, 1971]). Many Georgian films dealt with the uncertain future of a society that does not want to break with its traditions; this thematic material made several productions from Tbilisi famous around the world.[101] With a visual idiom that blended naturalism with the lyrical style of the nineteenth-century Georgian poet Vazha-Pshavela, director Tengiz Abuladze employed history to thematize fundamental moral questions.[102]

Director Rezo Chkheidze began his career as a 'Georgian neo-realist' together with the later world-famous Abuladze. Their co-directed debut, the 1955 film *Magdanas lurja* (Magdana's Donkey), won the award for 'best fiction short' at Cannes. After going their separate ways, each director made a film about the tragedy of the war. Abuladze's *Me, bebia, Iliko da Ilarioni* (Me, Grandma, Iliko and Ilarion, 1963) tells the story of a boy who experiences the war as an invasion by a foreign, hostile, technologically advanced civilization into the patriarchal world of the old ones left behind in the village. Chkheidze's 1964 film *Jariskatsis mama* (*Father of a Soldier*) depicts an old farmer who leaves his village in search of his son, who has been wounded at the front. Aided by the compelling performance of his lead actor, Sergo Zaqariadze, Chkheidze presents a Soviet 'road movie' about a clash of two worlds: one of Georgian wine growers and one of combat soldiers. The unpretentious old man, whose behaviour patterns are formed by village life, completely ignores the realities of the war. Even in the trenches, he continues to act according to his own rules, which provides the film with much of its drama and humour. Zaqariadze's performance in this film made him a favourite of the Soviet public.[103]

Audiences in the GDR learned next to nothing about the specifics of Georgian cinema from the press and advertising campaigns. The SED made efforts to showcase *Father of a Soldier* as an outstanding cultural contribution to the forty-eighth anniversary of the Great Socialist October Revolution, and as a documentation of 'human greatness' and 'true bravery'.[104] According to a pattern that had become common, *Neues Deutschland* styled the main character as an 'unheroic hero' and *Märkische Volksstimme* interpreted the old Georgian man as an ideal figure of identification for German viewers:

> There is complete accord between the Soviet hero and his German audience. For everything that Giorgi Makharashvili, this simple Georgian wine grower, this father of a soldier, who himself eventually becomes a soldier in order to find his son in the struggle against war, everything that this humane human feels, discovers, and does earns our sympathy, our appreciation, and our respect.[105]

Sergo Zaqariadze's intention that the audience strongly identify with the main character was so successfully realized that he won the award for best actor at the 1965 Moscow Film Festival, shortly before the film's premiere in the GDR.[106] Consequently, in addition to reviews of the film itself, the GDR press published interviews and brief portraits of Zaqariadze that styled the actor as an ideal example of artistic and human greatness. For example, *Norddeutsche Neueste Nachrichten* published an article with the subtitle 'Der alte Mann und der Krieg' (The Old Man and the War), which, among other things, claimed that:

> [Zaqariadze] maintains modesty and generates an abundance of creative thought. He never curries favour by catering to popular tastes – he is truly unassuming. He avoids the ordinary and the primitive – he is extraordinary and imaginative, like his brother in the fields and in the factory. His wit does not derive from foolish buffoonery, but from his intelligent naturalness.[107]

As with previous Soviet war films, the film reviews published in the GDR press operated within a framework of exonerative, politically functional strategies. Reviews of this film combined the well-known appeal for peace with a call for defence readiness, a condition that the 'unheroic' Georgian hero ought to instil in every viewer. This preparation for battle was seen as completely compatible with the film's inherent pacifist tendencies:

> The film does not have a convoluted, skilfully woven plot. Lacking in any external pathos, it tells the story of a farmer who sets out from his remote, isolated Georgian village in order to visit his son in a military hospital. Sergo Zaqariadze plays this straightforward person with unparalleled poignancy. He makes it completely understandable to the viewer why this utterly unwarlike man, who views the horrors and violence of the war with a sense of naivety, fear, and rejection, feels ultimately compelled to join the ranks of the fighting troops at all costs.[108]

Though they never called the ideological content into question, reviewers occasionally criticized the film's conventional style. Regardless of such criticisms, *Father of a Soldier* was considered the most outstanding Soviet film of 1965. It was seen as a 'war film against war' and a work that 'defends the values of humanism against the brutalities and brutalizing effects of war'.[109]

Conclusion

The Thaw that resulted from the Twentieth Congress of the Communist Party of the Soviet Union marked a turning point in Soviet film production. One of the consequences was a shift in the way that films dealt with the Great Patriotic War. Stereotypical heroes, schematic plot structures and the towering presence of Stalin in earlier films gave way to psychological portrayals of individuals encountering 'war' as an extreme condition. The sterile and sacrosanct hero of the Stalin era, who always operated as part of a collective, was replaced by the 'everyday man', the straightforward '*Homo sovieticus*', who bears his bitter fate on his own and thus achieves true human greatness. This strict, vibrantly nuanced concentration on the fate of an individual during a period of life marked by crisis spoke to an entire nation that had endured similar experiences of war, distress, occupation, sacrifice, the glories and miseries of victory, and the difficult times afterwards. History provided a space for the projection of certain polemics and appeals as well as sympathy and generalizations that were long overdue in the Soviet Union and welcomed by the climactic political changes of the day.[110]

The Soviet occupying power in the SBZ structurally combined pragmatic film policy with the intention to politically educate the populace. In the immediate postwar years, it did not always succeed in reconciling financial interests, reparation demands, educational ambitions and tactical comportment with the population's viewing expectations. These initial years were marked by conflicts of interest between public education authorities, Soviet film distributors and the newly created company DEFA, even though they shared the same fundamental goals. Disagreements arose between the Soviet administration and German educational authorities when the interests of the Soviet occupying power came into direct conflict with the German communists' cultural-political programme. Soviet films were not very effective with regard to the desired propaganda influence on the East German populace – much less so than American films were in the Western zones. The few surviving archival sources report extensive resistance among the public. The films faced decisive obstacles such as widespread bias against everything 'Russian' and a 'cultural gap' between the two nations.

When Soviet films about the war arrived in the GDR, the cultural bureaucracy of the SED received them with modified readings and reinterpretations. While the GDR was undergoing Stalinization, its newspapers and journals paraphrased the clearly evident intentions of Soviet productions of the immediate post-war years, which nevertheless received scant attention from the general public. The ongoing crisis of Soviet film production in the mid-1950s and the widespread unpopularity of contemporary Soviet films contributed to a situation in the GDR whereby Great Patriotic War films from the early 1950s appeared only sporadically and were for the most part completely removed from distribution.

By contrast, the surviving archival sources suggest that diverse segments of the GDR population showed a more favourable interest in films made during the Thaw than they had for those of the Stalin era due to a number of motivating factors.[111] The Thaw films were beloved by the public – even, occasionally, without the need for official promotional measures. This relative popularity provided the authorities with welcome opportunities to promote 'German-Soviet Friendship' on a grand scale, address current events and communicate corresponding propaganda messages. Discourse about the films was accompanied by a national rhetoric directed against the integration of the western zones into the Federal Republic of Germany. In addition, the discourse included praise for the 'humanist cultural tradition' cultivated in the 'socialist camp' and references to the pioneering actions of the SED as the 'Party of Peace'.

At the same time, these films presented an officially acceptable portrayal of the events of World War II, in which the very phenomenon of the war itself was interpreted according to Marxist-Leninist terminology within the agitational-promotional campaigns. Additionally, the films that impressively emphasized simple people and individual suffering served a sort of 'bridging function' in the process of reconciliation between former war enemies. These films offered each East German viewer the chance to identify with Soviet screen heroes and vicariously experience their fate on an emotional level.

Translation: Kevin Bradley Johnson (Appleton, Wisconsin, USA)

Lars Karl is an assistant professor of Eastern European history at the Leipzig Centre for the History and Culture of East Central Europe (GWZO). He earned his Ph.D. in 2003 with a doctoral thesis on the perception of Soviet WWII Films in East Germany from 1945 to 1965. He has published widely on the history of film in Eastern Europe during the Cold War. Other fields of research include remembrance culture and the politics of history in the Soviet Union and its successor states in the Caucasus, and the history of Pan-Slavism. He has published *'O geroyakh i lyudyakh…' Sovetskoe kino o voyne: vzgljad iz GDR* (2008) in Russian, edited *Leinwand zwischen Tauwetter und Frost: Der osteuropäische Spiel- und Dokumentarfilm im Kalten Krieg* (2007) and co-edited the volumes *Der lange Weg nach Hause. Die Konstruktion von Heimat im europäischen Spielfilm* (2014) with Dietmar Müller and Katharina Seibert, and *Post-Panslavismus. Slavizität, Slavische Idee und Antislavismus im 20. und 21. Jahrhundert* (2014) with Agnieszka Gasior and Stefan Troebst.

Notes

1. Boleslaw Barlog, *Theater lebenslänglich* (Munich: Universitas, 1981), p. 81.
2. The current text is a translation of an article previously published in German: Lars Karl, 'Das Bild des Siegers im Land der Besiegten: Der sowjetische Kriegsfilm in SBZ und DDR, 1945–1965', in Thomas Lindenberger (ed.), *Massenmedien im Kalten Krieg. Akteure, Bilder, Resonanzen* (Cologne: Böhlau 2006), pp. 77–110.
3. The examination of cinematic treatments of World War II in the Soviet Union has assumed a firm position in academic historical research. In recent years, Anglo-American historiography in particular has dedicated itself to pursuing historical questions in addition to addressing film studies concerns in its consideration of this material. See for example Richard Taylor and Ian Christie (eds), *Inside the Film Factory: New Approaches to Russian and Soviet Cinema* (London: Routledge, 1991); Richard Taylor and Derek Spring (eds), *Stalinism and Soviet Cinema* (London and New York: Routledge, 1993); Peter Kenez, *Cinema and Soviet Society, 1917–1953* (Cambridge: Cambridge University Press, 1992), 186–208; Anna Lawton, *The Red Screen: Politics, Society, Art in Soviet Cinema* (London and New York: Routledge, 1992); Josephine Woll, *Real Images: Soviet Cinema and the Thaw* (London and New York: I.B. Tauris, 2000). For research dealing with the Soviet-endorsed culture of memory about World War II, see Nina Tumarkin, *The Living and the Dead: The Rise and Fall of the Cult of World War II in Russia* (New York: Basic Books, 1994), pp. 77–78, 112ff.
4. See Michael Lemke (ed.), *Sowjetisierung und Eigenständigkeit in der SBZ/DDR (1945–1953)* (Cologne: Böhlau, 1999).
5. Thomas Heimann, 'Erinnerung als Wandlung: Kriegsbilder im frühen DDR-Film', in Martin Sabrow (ed.), *Geschichte als Herrschaftsdiskurs: der Umgang mit der Vergangenheit in der DDR* (Cologne: Böhlau, 2000), pp. 37–86.
6. Henry Alter in a report from 14 July 1945. Quoted in Thomas Heimann, *DEFA, Künstler und SED-Kulturpolitik: Zum Verhältnis von Kulturpolitik und Filmproduktion in der SBZ/DDR 1945 bis 1959* (Berlin: Vistas, 1994), p. 63.
7. Norman M. Naimark, *The Russians in Germany: A History of the Soviet Zone of Occupation, 1945–1949* (Cambridge, MA, and London: Harvard University Press, 1995), p. 410.
8. See Sergej Tjupanow, *Erinnerungen an deutsche Freunde und Genossen* (Berlin: Aufbau-Verlag, 1984), pp. 191f.
9. On the dissolution of the concept of German-Soviet friendship, see Jan C. Behrends, 'Sowjetische 'Freunde' und fremde 'Russen'. Deutsch-Sowjetische Freundschaft zwischen Ideologie und Alltag. (1949–1989)', in Jan C. Behrends, Thomas Lindenberger and Patrice G. Poutrus (eds), *Fremde und Fremd-Sein in der DDR: Zu historischen Ursachen der Fremdenfeindlichkeit in Ostdeutschland* (Berlin: Metropol, 2003), pp. 75–100.
10. Vereinbarung zwischen der Gesellschaft für DSF und Sovexportfilm, Oktober 1949, Stiftung Archiv der Parteien und Massenorganisationen der DDR im Bundesarchiv Berlin (SAPMO-BArch), Gesellschaft für Deutsch-Sowjetische Freundschaft, DY 32/1/1282, unpag.
11. Of the 1,300 UFA feature films and full-length documentaries, a total of 454 productions were approved for screening in the Western zones of occupation prior to August 1948. After the establishment of the FRG, the number fell to only 270 films, many of which were so-called *Durchhaltefilme* (films to encourage endurance through the difficult war years).

12. Data according to Heimann, *DEFA, Künstler und SED-Kulturpolitik*, p. 64.
13. Ibid.
14. In accordance with an agreement between the Administration for People's Education and SEF, every film was rated either 'jugendfrei' (suitable for children) or 'jugendverboten' (forbidden for children).
15. Quoted in Heimann, *DEFA, Künstler und SED-Kulturpolitik*, p. 65.
16. *Tägliche Rundschau*, 24 January 1947.
17. See Herbert Holba, *Filmprogramme in der DDR 1945–1975* (Vienna: Verlag des Dokumentationszentrums ACTION, 1977); Herbert Janssen and Reinhold Jacobi, *Filme in der DDR 1945–1986. Kritische Notizen aus 42 Kinojahren* (Cologne: Katholisches Institut für Medieninformation, 1987).
18. See Reinhard Löhmann, *Der Stalinmythos. Studien zur Sozialgeschichte des Personenkultes in der Sowjetunion (1929–1935)* (Münster: Lit Verlag, 1990), pp. 27–33.
19. See Gerd Koenen, *Utopie der Säuberung: was war der Kommunismus?* (Berlin: Alexander Fest Verlag, 1998), p. 357. German authors such as Erich Weinert, Stephan Hermlin and Johannes R. Becher also took part in this political circus. Together with Jean Kurt Forest, Kurt Barthel (aka Kuba) composed a 'Stalin cantata' that was first performed at a state event in the Friedrichstadtpalast on 20 December 1949. On the role of the FDJ in the cult of Stalin, see Ulrich Mählert and Gerd-Rüdiger Stephan (eds), *Blaue Hemden – Rote Fahnen. Die Geschichte der Freien Deutschen Jugend* (Opladen: Leske + Budrich, 1996), pp. 78ff.
20. On the implementation of the cult of Stalin in the GDR, see Jan. C. Behrends, *Die erfundene Freundschaft. Propaganda für die Sowjetunion in Polen und in der DDR* (Cologne: Böhlau, 2006), pp. 172–225.
21. See *Richtlinien zur Durchführung der Stalin-Kampagne in den Massenorganisationen* in SAPMO-BArch, DY 32/10126, unpag.
22. Maya Turovskaya, 'Das Kino der totalitären Epoche', in Oksana Bulgakova (ed.), *Die ungewöhnlichen Abenteuer des Dr. Mabuse im Land der Bolschewiki. Das Buch zur Filmreihe Moskau-Berlin* (Berlin: Freunde der Deutschen Kinemathek, 1995), p. 239.
23. See Mikheil Chiaureli, 'Voploshchenie obraza velikogo vozhdia', *Iskusstvo kino* 8 (1947), 18ff.
24. Gosudarstvennyi arkhiv Rossiiskoi Federatsii, Moscow, fond Sovet Narodnykh Komissarov SSSR – 5446, opis 51 a, d. 5659, listy 37–34,18. The term 'trophy tanks' describes German military equipment confiscated by the Red Army during World War II.
25. There are notable cinematic parallels between this sequence and the opening of Leni Riefenstahl's *Triumph des Willens* (*Triumph of the Will*, 1934), in which Hitler arrives for the Reichsparteitag in Nuremberg by plane and greets the assembled masses on the airfield.
26. *Der Fall von Berlin*, Filmprogramm der Sovexportfilm GmbH, Berlin 1950.
27. See the press overview for *Der Fall von Berlin* in Oksana Bulgakova and Dietmar Hochmuth, *Der Krieg gegen die Sowjetunion im Spiegel von 36 Filmen. Eine Dokumentation* (Berlin: Freunde der Deutschen Kinemathek, 1992), pp. 56ff.
28. Ibid.
29. Ibid, pp. 57–58.
30. See e.g. 'Eine ernste Mahnung. Der sowjetische Dokumentarfilm *Der Fall von Berlin* uraufgeführt', *Neue Zeit*, 25 June 1950; H. Ihering, 'Der Fall von Berlin', *Berliner Zeitung*, 25 June 1950; '*Fall von Berlin* – ein Friedensruf. Meisterwerk russischer Farbfilmkunst', *Die Union*, 28 June 1950; 'Der Fall von Berlin', *Leipziger Volkszeitung*,

2 July 1950; H. Lüdecke, 'Ein Film, der neue Maßstäbe gibt', *Neues Deutschland*, 9 July 1950; 'Lehren aus dem Film *Der Fall von Berlin*', *Sonntag*, 16 July 1950.
31. Siegfried Silbermann, 'Unser Filmprogramm muß noch vielseitiger werden', *Deutsche Filmkunst* 10 (1959), 312.
32. D. Wolf, 'Unser Film braucht ein kunstsinniges Publikum!' *Deutsche Filmkunst*, 3 (1959), 68.
33. See Lars Karl, '"Von Helden und Menschen...": Der Zweite Weltkrieg im sowjetischen Spielfilm dessen Rezeption in der DDR, 1945–1965' (Ph.D. thesis, Tübingen, 2002), http://tobias-lib.uni-tuebingen.de/dbt/volltexte/2003/790/; idem, *"O geroyakh i lyudyakh..." Sovetskoe kino o voyne: vzgljad iz GDR* (Moskva: Pamyatniki Istoricheskoi Mysli, 2008; 2nd ed. 2011).
34. *Brief des ZK der SED an die Mitglieder und Kandidaten der SED in den bewaffneten Kräften/Januar 1953*, Bundesarchiv-Militärarchiv Freiburg im Breisgau (BArch-MA), Politische Hauptverwaltung der NVA, VA-P-01/7535, p. 20.
35. For contemporary reflections on this relationship, see V. Müller, "An der Seite der Sowjetunion und ihrer Armee für die Einheit Deutschlands und den Weltfrieden," *Der Politarbeiter* 1 (1953), 1–2; H. Hoffmann, 'Es lebe die Waffenbrüderschaft mit der Sowjetarmee', *Der Kämpfer*, 8 May 1955, p. 1; 'Festigt die Waffenbrüderschaft mit den Armeen des sozialistischen Lagers', *Der Politarbeiter*, 2 (1955), 33–36.
36. Anyone who questioned, doubted or openly criticized the official view of the USSR could quickly be exposed as an 'enemy of the Soviet Union' and land in the anti-communist camp. Taboo areas included the role of the Red Army and its advancement campaign of 1944/45, doubts about the quality of Soviet technology or criticism of the activities of Soviet advisers in political organizations. For example, one KVP lieutenant, when relating his personal experiences in the period between 1943 and 1945 to his comrades, mentioned that his wife had been repeatedly raped by Russian soldiers. Upon hearing this, his superior officer filed to have him dismissed from the KVP for purportedly harbouring an anti-Soviet attitude. See Torsten Diedrich and Rüdiger Wenzke, *Die getarnte Armee: Geschichte der Kasernierten Volkspolizei der DDR 1952 bis 1956* (Berlin: Ch. Links Verlag, 2001), pp. 448–449.
37. *Arbeitsrichtlinie zur Durchführung des Monats der deutsch-sowjetischen Freundschaft vom 2.2.1950*, BArch-MA, Hauptverwaltung Ausbildung, DVH 1/681, p. 16.
38. BArch-MA, DVH 3/3430, 81.38.
39. H. Rost, *Der lange Weg ... I. Flugzeugführerlehrgang der DDR-Militärflieger. Episoden – Glanz und Gloria junger Männer* (Offenburg: Samira Verlag, 1998), pp. 23f.
40. *Betr. Sovexportfilm, Sekretariat Grünberg an Ebert, 14.7.1953*, SAPMO-BArch, DY 32/10805, unpag.
41. See SAPMO-BArch IV 2/906/247.
42. *Anfrage des Rats des Bezirkes Erfurt am 27.11.1953*, Bundesarchiv Berlin (BArch), Ministerium für Kultur, DR 1/4015, unpag. The district SED party school in Greifswald submitted a similar request on 5 June 1953: BArch, DR 1/4015, unpag.
43. *Antwortschreiben der HV Film an den Rat des Bezirks Erfurt, 3.12.1953*, BArch DR 1/14199, unpag.
44. See SAPMO-BArch IV 2/906/242.
45. See Gosfilmfond SSSR: *Letyat zhuravli*, Moscow 1972 (screenplay by Viktor Rozov). Fellow director Boris Barnet had previously dealt with this theme of a girlish woman with expressive facial gestures against the backdrop of towering ruins in his film *Odnazhdy nochyu* (*Dark is the Night*, 1945), which focuses on a young girl who hides a wounded Soviet paratrooper in the attic of a bombed-out building.

46. *Iskusstvo kino* 2 (1957), quoted in Christine Engel (ed.), *Geschichte des sowjetischen und russischen Films* (Stuttgart and Weimar: J.B. Metzler, 1999), p. 120.
47. Maya Turovskaya, "Da i nyet," *Iskusstvo kino* 12 (1957), 15–18, here 18.
48. Richard Stites assesses *Zhdi menya* as 'an elegiac if inelegant love poem that millions recited as if it were a prayer; that women repeated as tears streamed down their faces; that men adopted as their own expression of the mystical power of a woman's love.' Stites, *Russian Popular Culture: Entertainment and Society since 1900* (Cambridge: Cambridge University Press, 1992), p. 101.
49. See e.g. R. Harnisch, 'Ein mitreißendes Filmwerk! *Die Kraniche ziehen'*, *Deutsche Filmkunst* 4 (1958), 120–122; L. Kosmatov, 'Eine vollendete filmische Form', *Deutsche Filmkunst* 5 (1958) 139–140, 159.
50. "*Die Kraniche ziehen* – ein Beispiel", *Sonntag*, 28 July 1958.
51. See e.g. '"Goldene Palme" in Cannes für: *Die Kraniche ziehen*,' *Neues Deutschland*, 19 May 1958; A. Günter, '*Die Kraniche ziehen*', *Berliner Zeitung*, 4 June 1958; 'Seit sechs Wochen ausverkauft', *Neues Deutschland*, 3 September 1958; '*Kraniche* – triumphaler Erfolg', *Neues Deutschland*, 29 September 1958.
52. '*Kraniche* – ein triumphaler Erfolg', *Neues Deutschland, Montags-Ausgabe 'Vorwärts'*, 29 September 1958.
53. See e.g. R. Harnisch, 'Ein mitreißendes Filmwerk! *Die Kraniche ziehen'*, *Deutsche Filmkunst* 4 (1958), 120–122, here 120.
54. See Aleksandr V. Gura, *Simbolika zhivotnykh v slavyanskoy narodnoy traditsii*, Moscow: Indrik, 1977, pp. 646–667.
55. Data according to *Titel der 1958 zum Einsatz gelangten Filme und die Filmmiete*, DR 1/7827, unpag.
56. "Plan für die Lektionen des Filmlehrgangs in Dresden vom 30. Oktober bis 12. November 1958," SAPMO-BArch, DY 32/11142, unpag.
57. "Film-Vorschläge für die kultur-politische Erziehungsarbeit der SED und der sozialistischen Massenorganisationen 1958," BArch, DR 1/4496, unpag.
58. For a contemporary account of Bondarchuk as a person see Nina Ignatjewa, *Sergei Bondartschuk* (East Berlin: Henschelverlag Kunst und Gesellschaft, 1967); for an autobiographical account see Sergei Bondarchuk, *Zhelanie chuda* (Moscow: Molodaya gvardiya, 1981).
59. See Sabine R. Arnold, *Stalingrad im sowjetischen Gedächtnis: Kriegserinnerungs und Geschichtsbild im totalitären Staat* (Dortmund: Projekt-Verlag, 1999), pp. 68ff.
60. BArch-Film, DR 1, Ein Menschenschicksal, Protokoll Nr. 191/59, unpag.
61. *Entwurf eines Maßnahmeplanes für die Abteilung Kultur beim ZK der SED als Arbeitsgrundlage zur Ausarbeitung einer Beschlussvorlage für das Sekretariat des ZK zur Förderung und Auswertung des sowjetischen Filmes 'Ein Menschenschicksal' vom 30.6.1959*, BArch, DR 1/7721, unpag.
62. *Protokoll des zentralen Betriebsleiterkollektivs gemeinsam mit dem zentralen Arbeitskreis der Hauptbuchhalter am 3. und 4.11.1959*, BArch, DR 1/7721, unpag.
63. See e.g. '*Ein Menschenschicksal* – bald bei uns', *Schweriner Volkszeitung*, 1 November 1959; '*Ein Menschenschicksal* – Zur Aufführung dieses neuen sowjetischen Meisterwerkes der Filmkunst in unserem Bezirk', *Freiheit*, 6 November 1959; H. Gehler, 'Dem einfachen Menschen ein Denkmal', *Das Freie Wort*, 7 November 1959; '*Ein Menschenschicksal* – Der Film des Jahres', *Sächsische Zeitung*, 7 November 1959; '*Ein Menschenschicksal* aufgeführt', *Thüringer Tageblatt*, 7 November 1959; 'Triumph des Lebenswillens', *Ostsee-Zeitung*, 7 November 1959; F. Hentschel, '*Ein Menschenschicksal'*, *Volkswacht*, 7 November 1959; H. Knietzsch, 'Ein Lied

vom Helden unserer Zeit. Bondartschuks *Menschenschicksal*, ein Meisterwerk sozialistischer Filmkunst', *Neues Deutschland*, 8 November 1959; 'Poem vom neuen Menschen. Sergej Bondartschuks *Ein Menschenschicksal* – der Film des Jahres', *Wochenpost* (Berlin), 14 November 1959.

64. See e.g. '*Ein Menschenschicksal*: Im tiefsten Leid bewährt', *Berliner Zeitung am Abend*, 9 December 1959; '*Ein Menschenschicksal* – Den müßte jeder zweimal sehen. Erfurter Arbeiter sprechen über das Filmereignis des vergangenen Jahres', *Neues Deutschland*, 1 February 1960; 'Tief bewegt von dem sowjetischen Film *Ein Menschenschicksal*', *Volksstimme*, 5 February 1960; '*Ein Menschenschicksal*', *Wochenpost*, 12 March 1960; 'Keiner sollte den Film versäumen. *Ein Menschenschicksal* in Sondervorstellungen', *Ostsee-Zeitung*, 18 March 1960.
65. See e.g. *Einsatzplan 11159 der HV Film vom November 1959*, BArch, DR 1/4452, unpag.
66. V. M. Kaiser, 'Ich sah *Ein Menschenschicksal*', *Leipziger Volkszeitung*, 7 November 1959; see also '*Ein Menschenschicksal*', *Sächsisches Tageblatt*, 7 November 1959; 'Mahnende Flamme', *National-Zeitung*, 8 December 1959.
67. The SED leadership was certainly able to recognize that neither the Bundeswehr nor any other NATO forces were in a position to be a military threat or mount a surprise strategic attack on the countries of the Warsaw Pact. Nevertheless, the GDR leadership conducted a permanent campaign of disinformation that portrayed the West German and NATO armed forces as aggressive and poised to attack at any moment. See Rüdiger Wenzke, Die Nationale Volksarmee (1956-1990), in Thorsten Dietrich, Hans Ehlert and Rüdiger Wenzke (eds), *Im Dienste der Partei. Handbuch der bewaffneten Organe der DDR* (Berlin: Ch. Links Verlag 1998), pp. 448f.
68. 'Ein Menschenschicksal, das alle angeht', *Berliner Zeitung*, 10 November 1959; see also P. Ede, '*Ein Menschenschicksal* – Gedanken zu dem mit dem Großen Preis ausgezeichneten sowjetischen Film', *Berliner Zeitung am Abend*, 11 November 1959; 'Plauderei am Wochenende', *Thüringer Neueste Nachrichten*, 7 November 1959; for a report from the GDR press on the film's broad international impact, see 'In aller Welt erfolgreich', *Leipziger Volkszeitung*, 17 November 1959.
69. H. Albrecht, 'Poem des singenden Lebens. Der große sowjetische Film *Ein Menschenschicksal*', *National-Zeitung*, 7 November 1959.
70. See '*Ein Menschenschicksal*. Der Film des Jahres', *Sächsische Zeitung*, 7 November 1959.
71. 'Den müßte jeder zweimal sehen – Erfurter Arbeiter sprechen über das Filmereignis des vergangenen Jahres', *Neues Deutschland*, 1 February 1960.
72. Ibid.
73. Ibid.
74. 'Jeder sollte diesen Film kennen – Meinungen unserer Leser zum Filmereignis des Jahres', *Neues Deutschland*, 1 February 1960.
75. Ibid.
76. '*Ein Menschenschicksal*: Im tiefsten Leid bewährt', *Berliner Zeitung am Abend*, 9 December 1959.
77. 'Zum Glück geschaffen – wie der Vogel zum Flug. Das Gespräch der Woche: Der Film *Ein Menschenschicksal*', *Brandenburgische Neueste Nachrichten*, 15 November 1959.
78. M. Jahn, 'Mit dem Großen Goldenen Preis ausgezeichnet: *Ein Menschenschicksal*', *Die Frau von Heute*, 20 November 1959.
79. See Dmitry Shlapentokh and Vladimir Shlapentokh, *Soviet Cinematography 1918– 1991: Ideological Conflict and Social Reality* (New York: Aldrine Transaction, 1993), pp. 138f.

80. 'Varshavskii, Ja, 'Potrebnost molodoi dushi', *Iskusstvo kino* 1 (1960), 31. For contemporary reactions in the Soviet Union, see S. Agranenko, S Iyubovyu k geroyu-rovesniku, *Iskusstvo kino* 1 (1960), 68-69; N. Ignatieva, Eto nuzhno lyudyam, *Iskusstvo kino* 1 (1960), 74-76; S. Rostotskij, Ot imeni pokoleniya, *Iskusstvo kino* 1 (1960), 65-67; E. Vorobiev, 'Ja vam zhit' zaveshchayu', *Iskusstvo kino* 1 (1960), 69-71. See also Woll, *Real Images*, pp. 96–99.
81. See Engel, *Geschichte des sowjetischen und russischen Films*, pp. 124–126, 340; I. Sneiderman, 'Ballada o soldate', in N. Mervol'f (ed.), *Molodye rezhissery sovetskogo kino: sbornik statei* (Leningrad and Moscow: Iskusstvo, 1962), pp. 108–109.
82. BArch, DR 1, Ballade vom Soldaten, Protokoll Nr. 595/59, unpag.
83. See Hans Dieter Mäde, 'Der Mensch im Mittelpunkt. *Die Ballade vom Soldaten* und einige Überlegungen', *Deutsche Filmkunst*, 6 (1960), 206–208.
84. See e.g. '*Die Ballade vom Soldaten*. Ein neuer Höhepunkt der sowjetischen Filmkunst', *Freiheit*, 11 June 1960; '*Die Ballade vom Soldaten*. Ein meisterhafter Film des Regisseurs Grigori Tschuchrai', *Neues Deutschland*, 12 June 1960; '*Die Ballade vom Soldaten*', *Berliner Zeitung*, 14 June 1960; 'Ein Film des reinen Herzens. *Ballade vom Soldaten*, ein neues sowjetisches Meisterwerk', *Der Morgen*, 17 June 1960; 'Ein ergreifendes Filmgedicht', *Die Union*, 18 June 1960.
85. '*Die Ballade vom Soldaten*. Der neue Film des sowjetischen Regisseurs Grigori Tschuchrai', *Sonntag*, 22 May 1960; see also '*Die Ballade vom Soldaten*. Ein poetischer Film von tiefer Menschlichkeit', *Schweriner Volkszeitung*, 10 June 1960; 'Die Schönheit des Friedens. *Die Ballade vom Soldaten* – Meisterwerk sowjetischer Filmkunst', *National-Zeitung*, 12 June 1960.
86. See Andrej Tarkovskij, *Die versiegelte Zeit. Gedanken zur Kunst, zur Ästethik und Poetik des Films* (Berlin and Frankfurt am Main: Ullstein, 1985); for more on Tarkovsky's general work in film, see Peter W. Jansen and Wolfram Schütte (eds), *Andrej Tarkowskij* (Munich and Vienna: Carl Hanser Verlag, 1987); Vida T. Johnson and G. Petrie, *The Films of Andrei Tarkovsky: A Visual Fugue* (Bloomington: Indiana University Press, 1994); Mark Le Fanu, *The Cinema of Andrei Tarkovsky* (London: British Film Institute, 1987); Maja Turovskaja and Felicitas Allardt-Nostitz, *Andrej Tarkowskij, Film als Poesie – Poesie als Film* (Bonn: Keil, 1981).
87. Klaus Kreimeier, ‚Iwans Kindheit', in Jansen and Schütte, *Andrej Tarkowskij*, p. 88.
88. For strategic reasons, studio administrators in the 1960s often looked to children's films as debut projects for young directors. Often, two inexperienced graduates were paired as a team on these projects, whose small budgets minimized financial losses in the case of a flop. Hence, almost all young directors during this period made their debuts 'in the nursery'. In the case of *Ivan's Childhood*, though, the outcome was a high-quality film product. Other Russian debuts from this period include *Seryozha* (*Splendid Days*, Georgiy Daneliya and Igor Talankin, 1960) and *Drug moy, Kolka* (*My Friend, Kolka!*, Aleksandr Mitta and Aleksei Saltykov, 1961). In Georgia, Tengiz Abuladze and Rezo Chkheidze debuted with *Magdanas lurja* (*Magdana's Donkey*, 1955); in Kyrgyzstan, Larisa Shepitko with *Znoy* (*Heat*, 1963); in Tajikistan, Valdimir Motyl with *Deti Pamira* (Children of Pamir, 1963); and in Lithuania, Vytautas Žalakevičius as co-director of the anthology film *Gyvieji didvyriai* (Living Heroes, 1960). See Engel, *Geschichte des sowjetischen und russischen Films*, p. 151.
89. See e.g. L. Anninski, 'Iwans Kindheit von Tarkowski. Eine gesprengte Idylle', *Sowjetfilm* 6 (1972), 18–20; and Antoine de Baecque, *Andrei Tarkovski* (Paris: Cahiers du Cinéma, 1988), pp. 51–54.

90. BArch, DR 1, Iwans Kindheit, Protokoll Nr. 25/63, unpag.
91. 'Iwans Kindheit', *Nationalzeitung*, 28 March 1963.
92. *Berliner Zeitung*, 30 April 1963. See also the critique of the film's form and content in M. Haedler, 'Geträumtes Kinderglück. Zu dem preisgekrönten sowjetischen Film *Iwans Kindheit*', *Der Morgen*, 4 May 1963.
93. U. Hafranke, 'Vom Krieg geboren – vom Krieg verschlungen. *Iwans Kindheit* – eine poetische Filmtragödie aus der Sowjetunion', *Volksstimme*, 20 April 1963.
94. H. Hofmann, 'Bewegendes Filmgedicht: *Iwans Kindheit*', *Märkische Volksstimme*, 29 March 1963.
95. Ibid.; see also H. Knietzsch, 'Begegnung mit Filmkunst. Der sowjetische Film *Iwans Kindheit* in Leipzig, Dresden und Berlin uraufgeführt', *Neues Deutschland*, 8 March 1963; J. Domeyer, '*Iwans Kindheit* und der Krieg', *Brandenburgische Neueste Nachrichten*, 16 March 1963; '*Iwans Kindheit*', *Volkswacht*, 7 June 1963.
96. H. Knietzsch, 'Begegnung mit Filmkunst. Der sowjetische Film *Iwans Kindheit* in Leipzig, Dresden und Berlin uraufgeführt', *Neues Deutschland*, 8 March 1963.
97. 'Humanistisches Meisterwerk', *Märkische Volksstimme*, 7 March 1963.
98. Brief Abusch an Kaftanov, 19 March 1958, BArch, DR 1/4608, unpag.
99. See Engel, *Geschichte des sowjetischen und russischen Films*, pp. 116ff. Regarding Soviet 'multinational cinema', see V. Busin, 'Nasledniki velikana. O razvitii natsionalnogo kinoiskusstva soyuznykh respublik', *Druzhba narodov* 1 (1968), 219–234; Grigorii P. Chakhiryan, *Mnogonatsionalnoe sovyetskoe kinoiskusstvo* (Moscow: Iskusstvo, 1961); 'Edinoe, mnogonatsionalnoe. O razvitii sovyetskogo kinoiskusstva,' *Druzhba narodov* 12 (1962), 239–246; Liliya Ch. Mamatova, *Mnogonatsionalnoe sovyetskoe kinoiskusstvo* (Moscow: Znanie, 1982); idem, 'Prislo zreloe vremya ... O natsionalnom kharaktere sovyetskogo kinoiskusstva', *Druzhba narodov* 10 (1970), 223–236; D. Pisarevskiy, 'Mnogonatsionalnoe sovyetskoe kino', *Iskusstvo kino* 4 (1962), 100–111; Ilya. V. Vaysfeld, *Nashe mnogonatsionalnoe kino i mirovoy ekran* (Moscow: Znanie, 1975); idem, *Zavtra i segodnya. O nekotorykh tendentsiakh sovremennogo filma i o tom, chemu nas uchit opyt mnogonatsionalnogo sovyetskogo kinoiskusstva* (Moscow: Iskusstvo, 1968).
100. See D. Kandelaki, *Kino i iskusstvo* (Tbilisi, 1957).
101. E.g. Merab Kokochashvili's *Didi mtsavane veli* (Big Green Valley, 1967) and Lana Gogoberidze's *Peristvaleba* (Frontiers, 1968).
102. E.g. in *Vedreba* (The Plea, 1967) and *Natvris khe* (The Wishing Tree, 1976). See also his most famous film worldwide, *Monanieba* (Repentance 1984/87).
103. See M. Papava, 'Otets soldata', *Iskusstvo kino* 6 (1965); L.N. Kogan (ed.), *Kino i zritel': Opyt sotsiologicheskogo issledovaniya* (Moscow: Iskusstvo, 1968), p. 111.
104. B. Almstedt, 'Unheldischer Held. *Vater des Soldaten* – ein aufsehenerregender sowjetischer Spielfilm', *Freiheit*, 9 November 1965; see also F. Salow, 'Ein nicht alltäglicher Held. Zur deutschen Erstaufführung des sowjetischen Films *Der Vater des Soldaten*', *Neues Deutschland*, 27 October 1965; G. Sobe, '*Vater des Soldaten*. Ein grusinischer Film', *Berliner Zeitung*, 28 October 1965; B. Almstedt, '*Der Vater des Soldaten*. Ein Film, der auf die Weltrangliste der sowjetischen Filmkunst gehört', *Lausitzer Rundschau*, 2 November 1960; '*Der Vater des Soldaten*', *Sächsische Zeitung*, 6 November 1965; E. Gustmann, 'Ein meisterhafter Film ab heute in Schwerin – *Der Vater des Soldaten*', *Schweriner Volkszeitung*, 12 November 1965.
105. H. Hofmann, 'Ein wunderbares Menschenantlitz. Begegnung mit dem *Vater des Soldaten*', *Märkische Volksstimme*, 3 November 1965.
106. See M. Papava, 'Otets soldata'.

107. 'Sergo Sakariadse als *Vater des Soldaten*. Der alte Mann und der Krieg', *Norddeutsche Neueste Nachrichten*, 30 October 1965; 'Der Vater des Soldaten. Eine ausgezeichnete Leistung Sergo Sakariadses', *Die Union*, 4 November 1965; 'Der Vater des Soldaten. Großartiger Volksschauspieler in einem Film aus Grusinien', *Der Neue Weg*, 5 November 1965; H.D. Tok, 'Der Weinbauer aus Grusinien. Ein preisgekrönter Film: Der Vater des Soldaten', *Leipziger Volkszeitung*, 9 November 1965.
108. B. Almstedt, 'Unheldischer Held. Der Vater des Soldaten – ein aufsehenerregender sowjetischer Spielfilm', *Freiheit*, 9 November 1965.
109. G. Sobe, 'Vater des Soldaten. Ein grusinischer Film', *Berliner Zeitung*, 28 October 1965.
110. See also Lars Karl, 'Von Helden und Menschen. Der Zweite Weltkrieg im sowjetischen Spielfilm (1941–1965)', *Osteuropa* 1 (2002), 67–82.
111. See also 'Briefpost', *Der Fernsehzuschauer* 6 (March 1965), 35; 9 (October 1965), 26. *Der Fernsehzuschauer* was an internal periodical produced by state television broadcaster Deutscher Fernsehfunk in which representative letters from viewers were compiled to aid television programming.

Select Bibliography

Behrends, Jan C. *Die erfundene Freundschaft. Propaganda für die Sowjetunion in Polen und in der DDR*. Cologne: Böhlau, 2006.

Engel, Christine (ed.). *Geschichte des sowjetischen und russischen Films*. Stuttgart and Weimar: J.B. Metzler, 1999.

Heimann, Thomas. *DEFA, Künstler und SED-Kulturpolitik: Zum Verhältnis von Kulturpolitik und Filmproduktion in der SBZ/DDR 1945 bis 1959*. Berlin: Vistas, 1994.

Heimann, Thomas. 'Erinnerung als Wandlung: Kriegsbilder im frühen DDR-Film'. In Martin Sabrow (ed.), *Geschichte als Herrschaftsdiskurs: der Umgang mit der Vergangenheit in der DDR*. Cologne: Böhlau, 2000.

Karl, Lars. '"Von Helden und Menschen...": Der Zweite Weltkrieg im sowjetischen Spielfilm und dessen Rezeption in der DDR, 1945–1965'. Ph.D. thesis, Tübingen, 2002.

Karl, Lars. *'O geroyakh i lyudyakh...' Sovetskoe kino o voyne: vzgljad iz GDR*. Moscow: Pamyatniki istoricheskoy mysli, 2008 (2nd ed. 2011).

Kenez, Peter. *Cinema and Soviet Society, 1917–1953*. Cambridge: Cambridge University Press, 1992.

Lawton, Anna. *The Red Screen: Politics, Society, Art in Soviet Cinema*. London: Routledge, 1992.

Lindenberger, Thomas (ed.). *Massenmedien im Kalten Krieg. Akteure, Bilder, Resonanzen*. Cologne: Böhlau, 2006.

Naimark, Norman M. *The Russians in Germany: A History of the Soviet Zone of Occupation, 1945–1949*. Cambridge, MA, and London: Harvard University Press, 1995.

Shlapentokh, Dmitry, and Vladimir Shlapentokh. *Soviet Cinematography 1918–1991: Ideological Conflict and Social Reality*. New York: Aldine Transaction, 1993.

Taylor, Richard, and Ian Christie (eds). *Inside the Film Factory: New Approaches to Russian and Soviet Cinema*. London: Routledge, 1991.

Taylor, Richard, and Derek Spring (eds). *Stalinism and Soviet Cinema*. London: Routledge, 1993.

Tumarkin, Nina. *The Living and the Dead: The Rise and Fall of the Cult of World War II in Russia*. New York: Basic Books, 1994.

Woll, Josephine. *Real Images. Soviet Cinema and the Thaw*. London and New York: I.B. Tauris, 2000.

Filmography

...reitet für Deutschland Arthur Maria Rabenalt (Ride for Germany, Germany, 1941)
31 ve stínu Jiří Weiss (Ninety Degrees in the Shade, Czechoslovakia, 1965)
Akce B Josef Mach (Operation B, Czechoslovakia, 1951)
Akce Kalimantan/Aksi Kalimantán Vladimír Sís (Operation Kalimantan, Czechoslovakia/Indonesia, 1962)
Akrobat schö-ö-ön Wolfgang Staudte (Germany, 1943)
Aktion J Walter Heynowski (Action J, GDR, 1960)
Aleksandr Nevskiy Sergei M. Eisenstein (USSR, 1938)
Anděl na horách Bořivoj Zeman (Angel in the Mountains, Czechoslovakia, 1955)
Andere neben Dir, Der Ulrich Thein (The Other Beside You, GDR-TV, 1963)
Atom na rozcestí Čeněk Duba (Atom on the Crossroad, Czechoslovakia, 1947)
Auftrag Höglers, Der Gustav von Wangenheim (Hoegler's Mission, GDR, 1949)
Ballada o soldate Grigori Chukhrai (Ballad of a Soldier, USSR, 1959)
Bärenhäuter, Der Walter Beck (The Man in the Bear's Skin, GDR, 1985)
Barfuß und ohne Hut Jürgen Böttcher (Barefoot and without a Hat, GDR, 1964)
Basa tvrdí muziku Karel Mann (No Music without Bass, Czechoslovakia, 1948)
Beauté du Diable, La René Clair (Beauty and the Devil, France/Italy, 1950)
Berlin – Ecke Schönhauser Gerhard Klein and Wolfgang Kohlhaase (Berlin – Schoenhauser Corner, GDR, 1957)
Berlin – Symphonie einer Großstadt Walter Ruttman (Berlin – Symphony of a Great City, Germany, 1927)
Berliner Romanze, Eine Gerhard Klein and Wolfgang Kohlhaase (A Berlin Romance, GDR, 1956)
Betrogen bis zum jüngsten Tag Kurt Jung-Alsen (Duped Till Doomsday, GDR, 1957)
Bis dass der Tod euch scheidet Heiner Carow (Till Death Do You Part, GDR, 1979)
Blackboard Jungle Richard Brooks (USA, 1955)
blaue Engel, Der Josef von Sternberg (The Blue Angel, Germany, 1930)
Blithe Spirit David Lean (Great Britain, 1945)
Bronenosets Potyomkin Sergei Eisenstein (Battleship Potemkin, USSR, 1925)
Brug, De Joris Ivens (Netherlands, 1928)

Cabinet des Dr. Caligari, Das Robert Wiene (The Cabinet of Dr. Caligari, Germany, 1919)
Carola Lamberti – eine vom Zirkus Hans Müller (Carola Lamberti from the Circus, GDR, 1954)
Cesta do pravěku Karel Zeman (A Journey into the Primeval Times, Czechoslovakia, 1955)
Chemie und Liebe Arthur Maria Rabenalt (Chemistry and Love, SMAD, 1948)
Císařův pekař Martin Frič (The Emperor's Baker, Czechoslovakia, 1951)
Co jim schází? Hermína Týrlová (What Is Missing? Czechoslovakia, 1947)
Damals in Paris Carl Balhaus (Those Days in Paris, GDR-TV, 1956)
Dáždnik svätého Petra/Szent Péter esernyöje Vladislav Pavlovič and Frigyes Bán (St. Peter's Umbrella, Czechoslovakia/Hungary, 1958)
Dědeček automobil Alfréd Radok (Vintage Car, Czechoslovakia, 1956)
Deti Pamira Vladimir Motyl (Children of Pamir, USSR, 1963)
Deutschland – Endstation Ost/Die DDR mit den Augen eines Ausländers gesehen Frans Buyens (Germany: Terminus East, GDR, 1964)
Dezertir Vsevolod Pudovkin (Deserter, USSR, 1933)
Didi mtsavane veli Merab Kokochashvili (Big Green Valley, USSR 1967)
Dnes večer všechno skončí Karel Kachyňa and Vojtěch Jasný (Everything Will End Tonight, Czechoslovakia, 1954).
Dobrodružství na Zlaté zátoce Břetislav Pojar (The Adventure in the Golden Bay, Czechoslovakia, 1955)
Dobrý voják Švejk Karel Steklý (The Good Soldier Švejk, 1956)
doppelte Lottchen, Das Josef von Báky (Lottie and Lisa, West Germany, 1950)
Dornröschen Walter Beck (Sleeping Beauty, GDR, 1970)
Drei Tage im Mai Heinz Müller et al. (Three Days in May, GDR, 1964)
Drug moy, Kolka Aleksandr Mitta and Aleksei Saltykov (My Friend, Kolka! USSR, 1961)
Du und mancher Kamerad Andrew Thorndike and Annelie Thorndike (You and Many a Comrade, GDR, 1956)
Dvaasedmdesátka Jiří Slavíček (The Number Seventy-Two, Czechoslovakia, 1948)
Dýmky Vojtěch Jasný (Pipes, Austria/Czechoslovakia, 1966)
Ehe im Schatten Kurt Maetzig (Marriage in the Shadows, SMAD, 1947)
Ernst Thälmann – Führer seiner Klasse Kurt Maetzig (Ernst Thälmann – Leader of the Working Class, GDR, 1955)
Ernst Thälmann – Sohn seiner Klasse Kurt Maetzig (Ernst Thälmann – Son of the Working Class, GDR, 1954)
Export in Blond Eugen York (West Germany, 1950)
Familie Benthin Kurt Mätzig and Slatan Dudow (The Benthin Family, GDR, 1950)
Fanfan la Tulipe Christian-Jaque (Fan-Fan the Tulip, Italy/France, 1952)
Faust – eine deutsche Volkssage Friedrich Wilhelm Murnau (Faust, Germany, 1926)
Feuerzeug, Das Siegfried Hartmann (The Lighter, GDR, 1959)
Flucht aus der Hölle Hans-Erich Korbschmitt (Flight from Hell, miniseries GDR-TV, 1960)
Frau Holle Gottfried Kolditz (Mother Holle, GDR, 1963)

Frau im Mond, Die Fritz Lang (Rocket to the Moon, Germany, 1929)
Frau meiner Träume, Die Georg Jacoby (The Woman of My Dreams, Germany, 1944)
Fräulein von Scuderi, Das Eugen York (Mademoiselle de Scudéri, GDR/Sweden, 1957)
Fräulein von Scudéri, Das Gottfried Hacker and Karl Frey (Mademoiselle de Scudéri, Germany, 1919)
Fräulein von Scuderi, Das Mario Caserini (Mademoiselle de Scudéri, Italy, 1911)
Freies Land Milo Harbig (Free Land, SMAD, 1946)
Froschkönig Walter Beck (Frog King, GDR, 1987)
Für die Liebe noch zu mager Bernhard Stephan (Too Poor for Love, GDR, 1974)
Germania, Anno Zero Roberto Rosselini (Germany, Year Zero, Italy/France/West Germany, 1948)
Geroi Shipki/Geroite na Shipka Sergei Vasilyev (The Heroes of Shipka, USSR/Bulgaria, 1954)
Geschichte vom armen Hassan, Die Gerhard Klein (The Story of Poor Hassan, GDR, 1958)
Geschichte vom Kleinen Muck, Die Wolfgang Staudte (The Story of Little Mook, GDR, 1953)
Gewissen in Aufruhr Günter Reisch et al. (Conscience in Turmoil, miniseries GDR-TV, 1961)
Giorgobistve Otar Iosseliani (Falling Leaves, USSR, 1966)
goldene Gans, Die Siegfried Hartmann (The Golden Goose, GDR, 1964)
Goya Konrad Wolf (GDR, 1971)
Grausige Nächte Lupu Pick (Nights of Terror, Germany, 1921)
Great Dictator, The Charlie Chaplin (USA, 1940)
Großstadtgeheimnis Leo de Laforgue (Big City Secret, West Germany, 1952)
Grube Morgenrot Walter Schleif and Erich Freund (The Morgenrot Mine, SMAD, 1948)
Grün ist die Heide Hans Deppe (Green Is the Heath, West Germany, 1951)
Gyvieji didvyriai Vytautas Žalakevičius (Living Heroes, USSR, 1960)
Halbstarken, Die Georg Tressler (West Germany, 1956)
Hamlet Laurence Olivier (GB, 1948)
Hannes Scharf Karlheinz Carpentier and Erich Böbel (series GDR-TV, 1967)
Hauptmann Florian von der Mühle Werner W. Wallroth (Captain Florian of the Mill, DEFA GDR, 1968)
Hiev up Jo Hasler (Heave Up, GDR-TV, 1978)
Holubice František Vláčil (White Dove, Czechoslovakia, 1960)
Hoří, má panenko! Miloš Forman (Firemen's Ball, Italy/Czechoslovakia, 1967)
Hrdinové mlčí Miroslav Cikán (The Heroes are Silent, Czechoslovakia, 1946)
Hrnečku, vař! Václav Bedřich (Cook, Mug, Cook! Czechoslovakia, 1953)
Hvězda jede na jih/Zvijezda putuje na jug Oldřich Lipský (The Star Travels South, Czechoslovakia/Yugoslavia, 1958)
Ich denke oft an Piroschka Kurt Hoffmann (I Often Think of Piroschka, West Germany, 1955)
Iko shashvi mgalobeli Otar Iosseliani (Once Upon a Time There Was a Singing Blackbird, USSR, 1970)

Immer am Weg dein Gesicht Achim Hübner (Always Your Face along the Way, GDR-TV, 1960)
Irgendwo in Berlin Gerhard Lamprecht (Somewhere in Berlin, SMAD, 1946)
Ivanna Viktor Ivchenko (USSR, 1959)
Ivanovo detstvo Andrei Tarkovsky (Ivan's Childhood, USSR, 1962)
Jakob der Lügner Frank Beyer (Jacob the Liar, GDR-TV, 1974)
Jan Roháč z Dubé Vladimír Borský (Warriors of Faith, Czechoslovakia, 1947)
Jariskatsis mama Rezo Chkheidze (Father of a Soldier, USSR, 1964)
Jeden ze štafety Jaroslav Mach (The One of the Relay, Czechoslovakia, 1951)
Jejich uniformou budiž frak Pavel Mertl (Let Tailcoat Be Their Uniform, Czechoslovakia, 1968).
jolie Mai, Le Chris Marker (The Lovely Month of May, France, 1963)
Jud Süss (Veit Harlan, Germany, 1940)
Kabinet des Dr. Caligari, Das Robert Wiene (The Cabinet of Dr. Caligari, Germany, 1920)
kalte Herz, Das Paul Verhoeven (Heart of Stone, GDR, 1950)
Kameni tsvetok Aleksandr Ptushko (The Stone Flower, 1946)
Kang-tchie chang Cheng Yin (The Steel Warrior, China, 1950)
Karhanova parta Václav Wasserman, Zdeněk Hofbauer (Karhan's Team, Czechoslovakia, 1950)
Karriere in Paris Georg C. Klaren (Career in Paris, GDR, 1951)
Kašpárek a Budulínek Josef Kokeisl (The Clown and Budulínek, Czechoslovakia, 1927)
Kašpárek kouzelníkem Josef Kokeisl (The Clown Magician, Czechoslovakia, 1927)
Kein Platz für Liebe Hans Deppe (No Room for Love, SMAD, 1947)
Komu tančí Havana/Para quién baila La Habana Vladimír Čech (For Whom Havana Dances, Czechoslovakia/Cuba, 1963)
Konec srpna v hotelu Ozon Jan Schmidt (The End of August at the Hotel Ozone, Czechoslovakia, 1966)
Konec strašidel Jiří Slavíček and Jan Matějovský (The End of Ghosts, Czechoslovakia, 1952)
König Drosselbart Walter Beck (King Thrushbeard, GDR, 1965)
Kuckucks, Die Hans Deppe (The Cuckoo Family, SBZ, 1949)
Kuhle Wampe oder Wem gehört die Welt? Slatan Dudow (Kuhle Wampe or to Whom Does the World Belong? Germany, 1932)
Kvevri Irakli Kvirikadze (The Jar, USSR, 1971)
Labakan Václav Krška (Czechoslovakia, 1956)
Legenda o lásce/Legenda za ljubovstva Václav Krška (A Legend about Love, Czechoslovakia, 1956)
Leiden des jungen Werthers, Die Egon Günther (The Sorrows of young Werther, GDR-TV/DEFA, 1976)
Les Ivan Balaďa (Forest, Czechoslovakia, 1969)
Letjat zhuravli Mikhail Kalatozov (The Cranes are Flying, USSR, 1957)
letzte Chance, Die Leopold Lindtberg (The Last Chance, Switzerland, 1945)
letzte Mann, Der Friedrich Wilhelm Murnau (The Last Laugh, Germany, 1924)
Leuchtfeuer Wolfgang Staudte (Navigating Light, GDR/Sweden, 1954)
Lockende Gefahr Eugen York (A Tempting Danger, West Germany, 1950)

Loupací radlička Ladislav Rychman (Peeling Little Ploughshare, Czechoslovakia, 1951)
Mädchen mit den Schwefelhölzern, Das Fritz Genschow (The Little Match Girl, West Germany, 1953)
Magdanas lurja Tengiz Abuladze, Rezo Chkheidze (Magdana's Donkey, USSR, 1955)
Magnificent Seven, The John Sturges (USA, 1960)
Májové hvězdy/Mayskie Zvyozdy Stanislav Rostotsky (May Stars, Czechoslovakia/USSR, 1959)
Malý partyzán Pavel Blumenfeld (Little Partisan, Czechoslovakia, 1950)
Man spielt nicht mit der Liebe Hans Deppe (One Should not Play with Love, 1949)
Marty Herbert Mann (USA, 1955)
Me, bebia, Iliko da Ilarioni Tengiz Abuladze (Me, Grandma, Iliko and Ilarion, USSR, 1963)
Meine Frau macht Musik Hans Heinrich (My Wife Wants to Sing, GDR, 1958)
Mičurin Alexander Dovzhenko (Michurin, USSR, 1948)
Mikoláš Aleš Václav Krška (Czechoslovakia, 1951)
Milujeme Václav Kubásek and Jaroslav Novotný (We Love, Czechoslovakia, 1951)
Misère au Borinage Joris Ivens (Belgium, 1933)
Monanieba Tengiz Abuladze (Repentance, USSR, 1984/87)
Mörder sind unter uns, Die Wolfgang Staudte (The Murderers Are among Us, SBZ, 1946)
Morituri Eugen York (West Germany, 1948)
Münchhausen Josef von Báky (Germany, 1943)
Mutter Krausens Fahrt ins Glück Phil Jutzi (Mother Krause's Journey to Happiness, Germany, 1929)
Na dobré stopě Josef Mach (On the Right Track, Czechoslovakia, 1948)
Nach einem Jahr Winfried Junge (After a Year, GDR, 1962)
Nad námi svítá Jiří Krejčík (The Sun Is Rising above Us, Czechoslovakia, 1952)
Natvris khe Tengiz Abuladze (The Wishing Tree, USSR, 1976)
Neděle ve všední den/Pirosbetüs hétköznapok Félix Máriássy (A Work Day Which Is a Sunday, Czechoslovakia/Hungary, 1962)
Němá barikáda Otakar Vávra (Silent Barricade, Czechoslovakia, 1949)
Nepokoryonnye Mark Donskoy (Undefeated, USSR, 1945)
Nezabyvaemyy god 1919 Mikheil Chiaureli (The Unforgettable Year 1919, USSR, 1951)
Nezbedný bakalář Otakar Vávra (The Whimsical Bachelor, Czechoslovakia, 1946)
Normandie-Niémen Jean Dréville (USSR/France, 1960)
Nóż w wodzie Roman Polanski (Knife in the Water, Poland, 1963)
O makovém koláči Zdeněk Miler (The Poppy Cake, Czechoslovakia, 1953)
O milionáři, který ukradl slunce Zdeněk Miler (About the Millionaire Who Stole the Sun, Czechoslovakia, 1948)
Obušku, z pytle ven! Jaromír Pleskot (Stick, Stick, Start Beating! Czechoslovakia, 1955)

Obyknovennyy fashizm/Der gewöhnliche Faschismus Michail Romm (Triumph over Violence, USSR, 1965)
Odnazhdy nochyu Boris Barnet (Dark Is the Night, USSR, 1945)
Ofenbauer Jürgen Böttcher (Stove Fitters, GDR, 1962)
Oktyabr': Desyat' dney kotorye potryasli mir Sergei Eisenstein (October: Ten Days that Shook the World, USSR, 1927)
Olověný chléb Jiří Sequens (Red Whitsuntide, Czechoslovakia, 1953)
Ostře sledované vlaky Jiří Menzel (Closely Watched Trains, Czechoslovakia, 1966)
Ovoce stromů rajských jíme Věra Chytilová (Fruit of Paradise, Belgium/Czechoslovakia, 1969)
Padeniye Berlina Mikheil Chiaureli (The Fall of Berlin, USSR, 1950)
Pan Novák Bořivoj Zeman (Mr Novak, Czechoslovakia, 1949)
Papas neue Freundin Georg Leopold (Daddy's New Girlfriend, GDR-TV, 1960)
Peristsvaleba Lana Gogoberidze (Frontiers, USSR, 1968)
Perníková chaloupka Oldřich Kmínek (The Gingerbread House, Czechoslovakia, 1933)
Pětistovka Martin Frič (Motorbike, Czechoslovakia, 1949)
Pod praporem svobody (Under the Banner of Freedom, Czechoslovakia, 1945).
Pohádka o drakovi Hermína Týrlová (Fairy Tale about a Dragon, Czechoslovakia, 1953)
Pohádka o stromech a větru Václav Bedřich (Fairy Tale about the Trees and Wind, Czechoslovakia, 1951)
Polizeiruf 110 (Police Call 110, series GDR-TV, 1971-1990)
Praha nultá hodina/Koffer mit Dynamit Václav Gajer (Prague at Zero Hour, Czechoslovakia/GDR, 1962)
Přátelé na moři/Poteryannaya fotografiya Lev A. Kulidzhanov and Stanislav Strnad (Friends Travelling on Sea, Czechoslovakia/USSR, 1959)
Prerušená pieseň/Prervannaya pesnya Nikoloz Sanishvili and František Žáček (Interrupted Song, Czechoslovakia/USSR, 1960)
Prinz hinter den sieben Meeren, Der Walter Beck (Across the Seven Seas, GDR, 1982)
Proč sedají ptáci na telegrafní dráty Eduard Hofman (Why Do Birds Sit on Wires? Czechoslovakia, 1948)
Pueblerina Emilio Fernández (The Villager, Mexico, 1949)
Putain Respectueuse, La Charles Brabant (The Respectful Prostitute, France, 1952)
Putyovka v zhizn Nikolai Ekk (Road to Life, USSR, 1931)
Pyšná princezna Bořivoj Zeman (The Proud Princess, Czechoslovakia, 1951)
Qortsili Mikheil Kobakhidze (The Wedding, USSR, 1964)
quatre cents coups, Les François Truffaut (The 400 Blows, France, 1959)
Rat der Götter Kurt Maetzig (The Council of the Gods, GDR, 1949)
Rebel without a Cause (Nicholas Ray, USA, 1956)
Reportage 60 (Report 60, GDR, 1960).
Reserveheld, Der Wolfgang Luderer (The Reserve Hero, GDR, 1965)
Revoluční rok 1848 Václav Krška (The Revolutionary Year 1848, Czechoslovakia, 1949)
Richter von Zalamea, Der Martin Hellberg (GDR, 1956)

Rio 40 Graus Nelson Pereira dos Santos (Rio 100 Degrees F, Brazil, 1955)
Ročník 21/Jahrgang 21 Václav Gajer (Those Born in 1921, Czechoslovakia/ GDR, 1957)
Rottenknechte Frank Beyer (Henchmen, miniseries GDR-TV, 1971)
Rozloučení s Klementem Gottwaldem Ivo Toman (Farewell to Klement Gottwald, Czechoslovakia, 1953)
Russkiy vopros Mikhail Romm (The Russian Question, USSR, 1947)
Salt of the Earth Herbert J. Biberman (USA, 1954)
Sechse kommen durch die Welt Rainer Simon (How Six Men Got On in the World, GDR, 1972)
Septembertage (September Days, GDR, 1961).
Serdtsa chetyryokh Konstantin Judin (Four Hearts, USSR, 1941)
Sergeant York Howard Hawks (USA, 1941)
Seryozha Georgiy Daneliya and Igor Talankin (Splendid Days, USSR, 1960)
Schneeweisschen und Rosenrot Siegfried Hartmann (Snow-White and Rose-Red, GDR, 1978)
Schneewittchen Gottfried Kolditz (SnowWhite, GDR, 1961)
Schönste, Die Ernesto Remani and Walter Beck (The Beauty, GDR/Sweden, 1959/2002)
Schwarzwaldmädel Hans Deppe (Black Forest Girl, West Germany, 1950)
Shchit Dzurgaja Siko Dolidze and David Rondeli (Dzhurgay's Shield, USSR, 1944)
Sheriff Teddy Heiner Carow (GDR, 1957)
Sieben Sommersprossen Herrmann Zschoche (Seven Freckles, GDR, 1978)
singende klingende Bäumchen, Das Francesco Stefani (The Singing Ringing Tree, GDR, 1957)
Siréna Karel Steklý (The Strike, Czechoslovakia, 1947)
Skazanie o zemle sibirskoy Ivan Pyryev (Symphony of Life, USSR, 1947)
Skřivánci na niti Jiří Menzel (Larks on a String, West Germany/ Czechoslovakia, 1966)
Snadný život Miloš Makovec (An Easy Life, Czechoslovakia, 1957)
Sněhurka a sedm trpaslíků Oldřich Kmínek (Snow White and the Seven Dwarfs, Czechoslovakia, 1933)
So werden Söldner gemacht Karlheinz Pappe (This Is How Mercenaries are Made, GDR, 1968).
Solo Sunny Konrad Wolf (GDR, 1980)
Sonnensucher Konrad Wolf (Sun Seekers, GDR, 1958)
Spielbank-Affäre Arthur Pohl (Casino Affair, GDR/Sweden, 1956/1957)
Spuk in Villa Sonnenschein Gerhard Klingenberg (Spook in the Sunshine Villa, GDR-TV, 1959)
Stachka Sergei Eisenstein (Strike, 1925)
Stalingradskaya bitva Vladimir Petrov (The Battle of Stalingrad, USSR, 1949)
Štika v rybníce Vladimír Čech (The Pike in a Fish Pond, Czechoslovakia, 1951)
Student von Prag, Der Hanns Heinz Ewers and Stellan Rye (The Student of Prague, Germany, 1913)
Stvoření světa Eduard Hofman (The Creation of the World, Czechoslovakia, 1957)

Sud'ba cheloveka Sergei Bondarchuk (Fate of a Man, USSR, 1959)
Sullivans, The Lloyd Bacon (USA, 1944)
Svatba v Korálovém moři Horst von Möllendorff (A Wedding in the Coral Sea, Czechoslovakia, 1945)
Tagebuch für Anne Frank, Ein Joachim Hellwig (A Diary for Anne Frank, GDR, 1958)
Tanková brigáda Ivo Toman (The Tank Brigade, Czechoslovakia, 1955)
tapfere Schneiderlein, Das Helmut Spieß (The Brave Little Tailor, GDR, 1956)
Täter unbekannt Bernhard Stephan (episode of the series *Polizeiruf*/Police Call, GDR-TV, 1972)
Tatort Berlin Joachim Kunert (Place of Crime: Berlin, GDR, 1957)
Thälmann Georg Schiemann (GDR-TV, 1986)
Tiefe Furchen Lutz Köhlert (Deep Furrows, GDR-TV/DEFA, 1965)
Tikhiy Don Sergey Gerasimov (And Quiet Flows the Don, USSR, 1957/58)
tödlichen Träume, Die Paul Martin (Deadly Nightmares, West Germany, 1951)
Treibjagd auf ein Leben Ralph Lothar (Hunt for a Life, West Germany, 1961)
Triumph des Willens Leni Riefenstahl (Triumph of the Will, Germany, 1935)
Tři přání Elmar Klos, Ján Kadár (Three Wishes, Czechoslovakia, 1959)
Ukolébavka Hermína Týrlová (Lullaby, Czechoslovakia, 1947)
Unser täglich Brot Slatan Dudow (Our Daily Bread, GDR, 1949)
Unternehmen Teutonenschwert – Archive sagen aus (Operation Teutonic Sword, Andrew Thorndike and Annelie Thorndike, GDR, 1958)
Usměvavá zem Václav Gajer (The Smiling Country, Czechoslovakia, 1951)
V gorakh Yugoslavii Abram Room and Eduard Tisse (In the Mountains of Yugoslavia, USSR, 1946)
V horách duní Václav Kubásek (Thunder in the Hills, Czechoslovakia, 1946)
V proudech/La Liberté surveillée Vladimír Vlček (Twisting Currents, Czechoslovakia and France, 1957)
Vánoční sen Karel Zeman (A Christmas Dream, Czechoslovakia, 1945)
Včely a květy Miro Bernat (Bees and Flowers, Czechoslovakia, 1952)
Včely budou žít! Miro Bernat (Bees will be alive! Czechoslovakia, 1951)
Vedreba Tengiz Abuladze (The Plea, USSR, 1967)
Vergeßt mir meine Traudel nicht Kurt Maetzig (Don't Forget my Little Traudel, GDR, 1957)
Verlobte, Die Günther Rücker and Günter Reisch (The Fiancée, GDR-TV/DEFA, 1980)
Vernye druz'ya Mikhail Kalatozov (True Friends, USSR, 1954)
Vstrecha na Elbe Grigori Alexandrov (The Encounter on the Elbe, USSR, 1949)
Vysokaya nagrada Yevgeni Shneider (USSR, 1939)
Vzbouření na vsi Josef Mach (The Village Revolt, Czechoslovakia, 1951)
Vzducholoď a láska Jiří Brdečka (Airship and Love, Czechoslovakia, 1948)
Vzpomínka na tři rána v českém lese Ivan Balaďa (The Memory of Three Mornings in the Czech Forest, Czechoslovakia, 1966).
Weiberwirtschaft Peter Kahane (Petticoat Rule, GDR-TV/DEFA,1984)
Wenn ich erst zur Schule geh Winfried Junge (When I Finally Go to School, GDR, 1961)
Where No Vultures Fly Harry Watt (aka Ivory Hunter, GB, 1951)

Wie heiratet man einen König Rainer Simon (How to Marry a King, GDR, 1968)
Wild One, The (Laslo Benedek, USA, 1953)
Wilson Henry King (USA, 1944)
Young Tom Edison Norman Taurog (USA, 1940)
Zasadil dědek řepu Jiří Trnka (Grandfather Planted a Beet, Czechoslovakia, 1945)
Zde jsou lvi Václav Krška (Scars of the Past, Czechoslovakia, 1958)
Zelená knížka Josef Mach (The Green Notebook, 1948)
Zhong Hua nu er Zifend Ling-Qiang Zhai (Daughters of China, China, 1949)
Zimmerleute des Waldes Heinz Sielmann (Carpenters of the Forest, West Germany, 1954)
Znoy Larisa Shepitko (Heat, USSR, 1963)
Ztracená stopa Karel Kachyňa (The Lost Track, Czechoslovakia, 1956)
Zvířátka a Petrovští Jiří Trnka (Animals and Bandits, Czechoslovakia, 1946)

Index

Abuladze, Tengiz, 367–68
Abusch, Alexander, 34, 119, 278, 321, 367
Ackermann, Anton, 24, 33–34, 92–93, 138, 196
Adler, Rudolf, 157
Alvarez, Santiago, 235
Anders, Ferdinand, 349
Augustin, Ernst, 138
Axen, Hermann, 334
Baarová, Lída, 41
Balaďa, Ivan, 157–58
Barckhausen, Joachim, 112
Bareš, Gustav, 51, 80
Barlog, Boleslaw, 341, 345
Barthel, Kurt (also known as Kuba), 30
Batalov, Aleksey, 353–54
Bathrick, David, 113
Becher, Johannes R., 18, 29, 118, 138
Beck, Walter, 117–18, 195, 198–99
Behn-Grund, Friedl, 22, 36
Belach, Helga, 114
Benda, Bedřich, 153
Beneš, Edvard, 42
Bentzien, Hans, 131, 159
Beria, Lavrentiy, 28
Bernášková, Alena, 216
Bernat, Miro, 171
Bieler, Manfred, 29
Biermann, Wolf, 237
Bloch, Ernst, 321
Bois, Curt, 114, 123
Bolshakov, Ivan G., 90–91, 254, 268, 282, 293, 295

Bondarchuk, Sergey, 356, 359, 361–63
Borský Vladimír, 46, 78–79
Böttcher, Jürgen, 237–38
Brandes, Heino, 158
Brando, Marlon, 33
Brandt, Horst E., 128
Brauner, Artur, 110–11
Brecht, Bertold, 18, 25, 195, 202
Bredel, Willi, 28–29
Brenten, Otakar, 211
Brousil, A.M., 247
Brožík, Stanislav, 157
Buchholz, Horst, 33
Burger, Miroslav, 157
Burian, Vlasta, 41
Burlyayev, Nikolai, 363
Bussieres, Raymond, 94
Buyens, Frans, 238–39
Calvacanti, Alberto, 235
Canudo, Ricciotto, 317
Čáp, František, 50
Čapek, Karel, 94
Carow, Heiner, 37, 135
Čepička, Alexej, 155–56
Chaplin, Charlie, 324
Chervenkov, Valko, 95
Chiaureli, Mikheil, 346–47
Chkheidze, Rezo, 368
Chukhrai, Grigori, 362–63
Churchill, Winston, 347, 349
Chytilová, Věra, 99
Claudius, Eduard, 29
Claus, Horst, 31
Connelly, John, 4, 306
De Baecque, Antoine, 316

De Valck, Marijke, 260
Dean, James, 33
Delluc, Louis, 317
Deppe, Hans, 16–17, 110
Dessau, Paul, 25
Drda, Jan, 45
Drha, Vladimír, 157
Druick, Zöe, 168
Dudow, Slatan, 18, 26
Dymshits, Alexander, 21, 23
Eisenstein, Sergei M., 18, 268, 324
Elbl, Jindřich, 42
Engel, Erich, 110
Feix, Karel, 79
Fellini, Federico, 98
Finke, Klaus, 126
Forman, Miloš, 99–100
Forst, Karel, 157
Freund, Erich, 20
Freund, Rudolf, 327
Frič, Martin, 45, 79, 81
Fuksa, Jan, 211
Gall, Vladimir, 19
Galuška, Miroslav, 80
Gehler, Fred, 316, 327, 329, 331–33, 335, 338
Gerasimov, Sergei, 98
Gerlach, Jens, 29
Geyer, Michale, 113
Goebbels, Joseph, 35, 72
Gomułka, Władysław, 3, 9, 30
Gottschalk, Joachim, 26
Gottwald, Klement, 43, 53, 155, 261
Grierson, John, 235
Grimm, Jacob and Wilhelm, 190–91, 194
Grotewohl, Otto, 27, 349
Günther, Egon, 128
Gürtler, František, 179, 181
Gusner, Iris, 197
Haanstra, Bert, 235
Hager, Kurt, 330
Hájek, Jiří, 80
Halas, František, 44
Häntzsche, Hellmuth, 195
Hapl, Václav, 157

Harbig, Milo, 20
Harich, Wolfgang, 321
Harlan, Veit, 17
Hartmann, Siegfried, 198
Háša, Pavel, 153
Havel, Miloš, 41
Havemann, Robert, 237
Heimann, Thomas, 26, 121
Heinig, Stephan, 331
Hellwig, Joachim, 235
Herlinghaus, Ruth, 192
Herricht, Rolf, 151
Hertwig, Manfred, 321
Heym, Stefan, 29, 237
Heynowski, Walter, 235
Hirschmeyer, Alfred, 116
Hitler, Adolf, 259, 341, 347–48
Hlaváč, Roman, 153
Hložek, Karel, 157
Hoff, Peter, 135
Hoffmann, E.T.A., 112
Hoffmann, Heinz, 159
Hoffmeister, Adolf, 44
Hofman, Eduard, 220
Hofman, Ota, 220
Hortzschansky, Werner, 192–93
Hossein, Robert, 94
Iosseliani, Otar, 367
Ivashov, Vladimir, 362
Ivens, Joris, 235, 324
Izvitskaya, Izolda, 362
Jacques, Norbert, 112
Jasný, Vojtěch, 99
Jeníček, Jiří, 154–55
John, Erhard, 323
Judin, Konstantin, 287
Junge, Barbara, 238
Junge, Winfried, 238
Juráček, Pavel, 157
Kabelík, Vladimír, 79
Kádár, Jan, 61, 74
Kafka, Franz, 94
Kahlau, Heinz, 29, 117
Kahuda, František, 61
Kalatozov, Mikhail, 90–91, 353–54, 363

Kernicke, Wolfgang, 232, 235
Khachaturian, Aram, 24
Khrushchev, Nikita, 2, 28, 58, 232, 330, 358
Kirsten, Ralf, 128
Klaren, Georg C., 324
Klein, Gerhard, 31–32, 37
Klein, Günther, 159
Klering, Hans, 110
Kloboučník, Jan, 80
Klos, Elmar, 42, 61, 74, 80, 179, 210, 217
Kmínek, Oldřich, 223
Knef, Hildegard, 22
Kobakhidze, Mikheil, 367
Kohlhaase, Wolfgang, 31–32, 37, 98
Kokeisl, Josef, 223
Kolda, Ladislav, 79
Kolditz, Gottfried, 198
Kopecký, Václav, 44–45, 51, 54–55, 57, 80, 255, 268, 279, 301
Korn, Ilse, 190
Kosmodemyanskaya, Zoya, 354
Kott, Jan, 29
Kötzing, Andreas, 118
Kramer, Stanley, 98
Krejčík, Jiří, 76
Kresse, Walter, 232
Krška, Václav, 61
Kuba, see Barthel, Kurt
Kubala, Bedřich, 156
Kučera, Jan, 179, 180
Kuhnert, Artur, 111, 116
Kunert, Joachim, 37
Kurella, Alfred, 118, 231
Kvirikadze, Irakli, 367
Laabs, Hans-Joachim, 196
Lamberz, Werner, 239
Lamprecht, Gerhard, 16–17, 110
Landsman, Mark, 181
Leacock, Richard, 235
Leander, Zara, 110
Lehovec, Jiří, 179
Lelek, Jiří, 153
Lenin, Vladimir Ilyich, 127, 301, 330, 349

Lentz, Michael, 114
Liehm, Antonín J., 78
Lindemann, Alfred, 111, 118
Lingen, Theo, 110
Linhart, Lubomír, 42, 44, 293
Lipský, Oldřich, 61
Lovejoy, Alice, 146
Luderer, Wolfgang, 128
Lukács, Georg, 30
Mach, Josef, 50
Macháček, Oldřich, 47, 55, 74
Maetzig, Kurt, 19, 26–28, 37, 134, 299
Majerová, Marie, 45–46
Makovec, Miloš, 325
Málek, Jaroslav, 281
Malenkov, Georgy, 91
Mandlová, Adina, 41
Mařánek, Jiří, 45
Marek, Jiří, 55, 57, 62, 119
Marenbach, Leny, 110
Marker, Chris, 36, 234
Mayer, Hans, 29, 321, 329, 338
Mehl, Erich, 109–10, 115–16, 119–20
Menzel, Jiří, 99
Míka, Zdeněk, 75
Mikhailov, Nikolai, 97, 104
Mikhalkov-Konchalovsky, Andrei, 364
Montague, Ivor, 235
Možný, Lubomír, 156
Mudrak, Edmund, 190
Müller, Hans, 110
Naimark, Norman, 343
Nehmzow, Arthur, 128
Nejedlý, Zdeněk, 44, 54
Neuberg, Josef, 79
Nezval, Vítězslav, 44, 51, 247
Novotný, Josef Alois, 214
Novotný, Ladislav, 156
Olbracht, Ivan, 44
Olivier, Laurence, 300
Palach, Jan, 158
Papava, Mikhail, 92
Papoušek, František, 42
Pavlenko, Pyotr, 349
Péteri, György, 103

Petrov, Vladimir, 346–47
Philipe, Gérard, 300
Pieper, Wolfgang, 325
Pilát, František, 42
Pinkava, Josef, 220
Pleskot, Jaromír, 214, 220
Plívová-Šimková, Věra, 220
Pöge-Alden, Katrin, 189
Pohl, Arthur, 110
Polanski, Roman, 328, 330
Poledňák, Alois, 62, 96
Porten, Henny, 108, 110, 113–14, 123
Prokhorenko, Zhanna, 362
Prokofiev, Sergei, 24
Propp, Vladimir, 191
Ptáčník, Karel, 93
Pudovkin, Vsevolod, 18, 268
Pujmanová, Marie, 45
Rabenalt, Arthur Maria, 17, 20, 110
Radok, Alfréd, 94, 220
Rechenmacher, Ernst, see Remani, Ernesto
Reichl, Lavoslav, 79
Reimann, Zdeněk, 79
Remani, Ernesto (also known as Ernst Rechenmacher), 115–17
Resnais, Alain, 98
Řezáč, Václav, 45, 216
Říčka, František, 153
Rodenberg, Hans, 27, 232–33
Rogg, Matthias, 146
Rolf, Malte, 301
Romm, Mikhail, 234–35, 364
Roosevelt, Franklin Delano, 347
Rose, Werner, 235
Rosselini, Roberto, 32
Rotha, Paul, 235
Rothke, Rolf, 330
Rozov, Viktor, 353–54
Ruttmann, Walter, 111
Sadoul, Georges, 318
Samoilova, Tatyana, 353–54
Schall, Ekkehard, 31
Scharfenberg, Dieter, 325–26
Schenk, Ralf, 22, 120
Schleif, Walter, 20

Schleif, Wolfgang, 110
Schmidt, Jan, 157
Schnaß, Hans-Burckhard, 328–29, 331, 335
Schwab, Sepp, 114, 138
Schwabe, Willi, 160
Seemann, Horst, 128
Seghers, Anna, 18, 29
Sholokhov, Mikhail, 356–57, 361
Shostakovich, Dmitri, 24
Sica, Vittorio de, 32
Sielmann, Heinz, 230
Signoret, Simone, 234
Silbermann, Siegfried, 349
Simon, Rainer, 199
Simonov, Konstantin, 354
Škrdlant, Tomáš, 157
Škvorecký, Josef, 60
Slánský, Rudolf, 52–53, 80
Slavíček, Jiří, 50
Smrž, Karel, 79
Spieß, Karl von, 190
Staiger, Janet, 72, 85
Stakhanov, Alexey, 341
Stalin, Joseph, 24, 28–29, 46, 49, 53, 56, 83, 92, 127, 252, 261, 293–94, 301, 341, 346–54, 357, 369 346, 351–353, 374
Stallich, Jan, 79
Staudte, Wolfgang, 16, 19, 20–21, 35–36, 110, 192–94
Stefani, Francesco, 194
Steinberger, Bernhard, 321
Steinitz, Wolfgang, 190–91
Steklý, Karel, 46
Stenbock-Fermor, Alexander, 112, 116
Stephan, Bernhard, 135
Štoll, Ladislav, 95
Stör, Emil, 114
Storck, Henry, 235
Streubel, Manfred, 29
Strizhenov, Oleg, 362
Stross, Raymond, 99
Suessenguth, Walter, 114
Svoboda, Ludvík, 155
Tarkovsky, Andrei, 363–65

Tarkovsky, Arseny, 364
Thälmann, Ernst, 28, 291
Thiel, Heinz, 325–26
Thomé, Ludwig, 230
Thorndike, Andrew, 235
Tito, Josip Broz, 92, 252
Tiuľpanov, Sergei, 19–20, 189
Träger, Josef, 216
Trenker, Luis, 116
Trnka, Jiří, 46, 210, 212
Trotsky, Leon, 30
Truffaut, François, 328
Turek, Ludwig, 158
Týrlová, Hermína, 46, 210
Uhlen, Gisela, 114, 123
Uhse, Bodo, 18, 29
Ulbricht, Walter, 23, 30, 93, 135, 278, 284, 299, 321, 326–27, 330
Václavík, Vladimír, 212
Vaňátko, Václav, 216
Vančura, Vladislav, 41
Vaňorná, Marie, 217
Vávra, Otakar, 45, 50, 79–81, 248
Vazha-Pshavela, 367
Verhoeven, Paul, 110, 192–93
Vertov, Dziga, 18
Vilímek, Josef, 179
Vítek, Svetozar, 219–20
Vláčil, František, 328
Vlady, Marina, 94
Vlček, Vladimír, 94
Vukotić, Dusan, 235
Wandel, Paul, 15, 232
Wangenheim, Gustav von, 26
Werich, Jan, 76
Weisenborn, Günter, 16
Weiss, Jiří, 80, 179
Wildhagen, Georg, 110
Wilkening, Albert, 116, 197
Witt, Günter, 239
Woeller, Waltraud, 191
Wolf, Friedrich, 16, 18
Wolf, Konrad, 34
Wolf, Steffen, 196
Wright, Basil, 235
Yezhov, Valentin, 362
York, Eugen, 111–12, 115–16
Zaqariadze, Sergo, 368–69
Zápotocký, Antonín, 94
Zavattini, Cesare, 318
Zelenka, Antonín, 79
Zeman, Karel, 210, 212
Zhdanov, Andrei, 24–25, 44, 49, 80, 91, 126
Zykmund, Václav, 211
Zwerenz, Gerhard, 29

www.ingramcontent.com/pod-product-compliance
Lightning Source LLC
Chambersburg PA
CBHW072141100526
44589CB00015B/2036